Rural Entrepreneurship and Innovation in the Digital Era

Sachithra Lokuge
RMIT University, Australia

Darshana Sedera
Southern Cross University, Australia

IGI Global
PUBLISHER of TIMELY KNOWLEDGE

A volume in the Advances in E-Business Research (AEBR) Book Series

Published in the United States of America by
IGI Global
Business Science Reference (an imprint of IGI Global)
701 E. Chocolate Avenue
Hershey PA, USA 17033
Tel: 717-533-8845
Fax: 717-533-8661
E-mail: cust@igi-global.com
Web site: http://www.igi-global.com

Library of Congress Cataloging-in-Publication Data

Names: Lokuge, Sachithra, 1987- editor. | Sedera, Darshana, editor.
Title: Rural entrepreneurship and innovation in the digital era / Sachithra Lokuge and Darshana Sedera, editors.
Description: Hershey, PA : Business Science Reference, 2021. | Includes bibliographical references and index. | Summary: "This book explores the impact, trends, opportunities, and challenges of rural entrepreneurship and innovation in the digital era"-- Provided by publisher.
Identifiers: LCCN 2020013989 (print) | LCCN 2020013990 (ebook) | ISBN 9781799849421 (hardcover) | ISBN 9781799857235 (paperback) | ISBN 9781799849438 (ebook)
Subjects: LCSH: New business enterprises--Developing countries. | Rural industries--Developing countries. | Rural development--Developing countries. | Entrepreneurship--Developing countries.
Classification: LCC HD2346.5 .R87 2021 (print) | LCC HD2346.5 (ebook) | DDC 338/.04091734--dc23
LC record available at https://lccn.loc.gov/2020013989
LC ebook record available at https://lccn.loc.gov/2020013990

This book is published in the IGI Global book series Advances in E-Business Research (AEBR) (ISSN: 1935-2700; eISSN: 1935-2719)

British Cataloguing in Publication Data
A Cataloguing in Publication record for this book is available from the British Library.

Advances in E-Business Research (AEBR) Book Series

In Lee
Western Illinois University, USA

ISSN:1935-2700
EISSN:1935-2719

Mission

Technology has played a vital role in the emergence of e-business and its applications incorporate strategies. These processes have aided in the use of electronic transactions via telecommunications networks for collaborating with business partners, buying and selling of goods and services, and customer service. Research in this field continues to develop into a wide range of topics, including marketing, psychology, information systems, accounting, economics, and computer science.

The **Advances in E-Business Research (AEBR) Book Series** provides multidisciplinary references for researchers and practitioners in this area. Instructors, researchers, and professionals interested in the most up-to-date research on the concepts, issues, applications, and trends in the e-business field will find this collection, or individual books, extremely useful. This collection contains the highest quality academic books that advance understanding of e-business and addresses the challenges faced by researchers and practitioners.

Coverage

- Telework and Telecommuting
- E-Services
- Collaborative commerce
- Electronic communications
- Global e-business
- E-CRM
- Mobile Business Models
- Web Service-Based Business Systems
- Interorganizational information systems
- Evaluation methodologies for e-business systems

IGI Global is currently accepting manuscripts for publication within this series. To submit a proposal for a volume in this series, please contact our Acquisition Editors at Acquisitions@igi-global.com or visit: http://www.igi-global.com/publish/.

The Advances in E-Business Research (AEBR) Book Series (ISSN 1935-2700) is published by IGI Global, 701 E. Chocolate Avenue, Hershey, PA 17033-1240, USA, www.igi-global.com. This series is composed of titles available for purchase individually; each title is edited to be contextually exclusive from any other title within the series. For pricing and ordering information please visit http://www.igi-global.com/book-series/advances-business-research/37144. Postmaster: Send all address changes to above address.

Titles in this Series

For a list of additional titles in this series, please visit: http://www.igi-global.com/book-series/advances-business-research/37144

Multidisciplinary Approaches to Crowdfunding Platforms
Carla Sofia Vicente Negrão (University of Coimbra, Portugal) and João António Furtado Brito (UNICV, Cape Verde)
Business Science Reference • © 2021 • 300pp • H/C (ISBN: 9781799832263) • US $205.00

Management and Strategies for Digital Enterprise Transformation
Kamaljeet Sandhu (University of New England, Australia)
Business Science Reference • © 2021 • 335pp • H/C (ISBN: 9781799850151) • US $215.00

Advanced Digital Architectures for Model-Driven Adaptive Enterprises
Vinay Kulkarni (TCS Research, Tata Consultancy Services, India) Sreedhar Reddy (TCS Research, Tata Consultancy Services, India) Tony Clark (Aston University, Birmingham, UK) and Balbir S. Barn (Middlesex University, London, UK)
Business Science Reference • © 2020 • 364pp • H/C (ISBN: 9781799801085) • US $205.00

Interdisciplinary Approaches to Digital Transformation and Innovation
Rocci Luppicini (University of Ottawa, Canada)
Business Science Reference • © 2020 • 368pp • H/C (ISBN: 9781799818793) • US $215.00

Implications and Impacts of eSports on Business and Society Emerging Research and Opportunities
David J. Finch (Mount Royal University, Canada) Norm O'Reilly (University of Guelph, Canada) Gashaw Abeza (Towson University, USA) Brad Clark (Mount Royal University, Canada) and David Legg (Mount Royal University, Canada)
Business Science Reference • © 2020 • 185pp • H/C (ISBN: 9781799815389) • US $165.00

Tools and Techniques for Implementing International E-Trading Tactics for Competitive Advantage
Yurdagül Meral (İstanbul Medipol University, Turkey)
Business Science Reference • © 2020 • 395pp • H/C (ISBN: 9781799800354) • US $225.00

Handbook of Research on Strategic Fit and Design in Business Ecosystems
Umit Hacioglu (Istanbul Medipol University, Turkey)
Business Science Reference • © 2020 • 775pp • H/C (ISBN: 9781799811251) • US $295.00

IGI Global
PUBLISHER of TIMELY KNOWLEDGE

701 East Chocolate Avenue, Hershey, PA 17033, USA
Tel: 717-533-8845 x100 • Fax: 717-533-8661
E-Mail: cust@igi-global.com • www.igi-global.com

Table of Contents

Detailed Table of Contents

Innovation and entrepreneurship are intertwined as entrepreneurs seek opportunities and innovations are the instruments that make them successful. Entrepreneurship and innovation are not constricted to the initial stages of a new venture alone and these are invincible processes that can lead to growth and sustainability of business in the dynamic environment. Rural entrepreneurship can be regarded as risk-taking behavior appropriate to opportunity, as well as to mobilize human, material, and financial resources in order to fulfill innovative projects in rural areas. There are multifaceted issues associated with the growth of rural entrepreneurs which need intervention by various political, economic, and social organizations. This chapter attempts to highlight specific contextual factors for rural entrepreneurship and innovation.

Unless there are systemic investments in digitization of rural economies, rural entrepreneurs will suffer, and digital innovation activity will remain modest. Nonetheless, the authors do find examples of digital innovation practiced by firms in rural economies. These firms successfully fostered growth and revitalization due to co-evolution of business and digital strategies, investments in technology, and digitization of business processes. In this chapter, using three such small, rural firms in Ontario, Canada, the co-evolution of business and digital technology strategies and related performance impacts are described by using the lens of "digital ecodynamics," which is defined as the holistic confluence among environmental factors, capabilities, and digital technologies—and their fused dynamic interactions unfolding as an ecosystem. The focus on the development of resources and capabilities that are critical for the survival of the firms and the local ecosystem centered around a business incubator that supports and sustains them.

This study explores the benefits, disadvantages, and barriers for the internationalization of regional small and medium-sized enterprises (SMEs) through the adoption of electronic commerce (e-commerce). Interviews were conducted with directors of ten Australian regional SMEs for exploring their use of e-commerce in the internationalization process. This led to the identification and validation of benefits, disadvantages, and barriers for the internationalization of regional SMEs with the use of e-commerce. A better understanding of these benefits, disadvantages, and barriers would help e-commerce stakeholders develop appropriate strategies and policies for driving the adoption of e-commerce for the internationalization of regional SMEs.

This chapter attempts to explain the main strategies adopted by the hosts of manor houses when they engage in lodging activities. The present research draws on 53 non-structured interviews made to owners/hosts of housing tourism facilities (HT). The methodological approach used is classic grounded theory (CGT). CGT encompasses a set of strict research procedures leading to concepts which explain what is going on in the HT substantive area. Within this context, the authors reveal a theoretical code, designated as 'amplifying casual looping', which the authors believe has the merit of effectively conceptualizing the substantive codes generated by us. This causal model broadens in both directions: positive (virtuous circle) and negative (vicious circle).

The purpose of this chapter is to analyze some positive life changes happened through micro-finance-driven entrepreneurship development among a sample of marginalized women in Bangladesh. The chapter is based on both primary and secondary data collected from two villages in Rajshahi district in Bangladesh. The author argues that when poverty is reduced, women are better able to meet their practical gender needs; however, they are not empowered unless they are also able to meet their strategic gender needs. The author also argues in this chapter that although entrepreneurship development empowers women, it cannot bring empowerment to all women equally at all levels. In the concluding remarks, the author contends that although many women are empowered at the household level, very few are empowered at the community level.

The adoption of information communication technologies (ICT) in rural regions of Gujarat by the Gujarat Cooperative Milk Marketing Federation Limited (GCMMFL) can be considered as an iconic practice in the dairy industry in India. It is typically assumed that the efforts associated with the investment of ICT in rural area are not as effective as expected, though in the case of Amul, it was proved otherwise. Amul is a dairy farming company that produces a variety of milk products and GCMMF takes responsibility of distributing and marketing of the products of it. Amul has been a forerunner of rural India's adoption of ICT in dairy industry. This chapter shares the success story of Amul and how they utilized ICT in the dairy industry. The application of IT enabled Amul to get better control for the accumulated milk from scattered suppliers. The Amul case is a prime example for the enabling role of the technology for innovation.

Rural Vietnam can be defined in three settings that include agriculture, rural development, and rural livelihoods, in which the agriculture has played a critical role in Vietnam's economy, contributing 20% to the GDP and 40% to the working population. This chapter attempts to identify the facilitators and potential barriers to rural entrepreneurship in Vietnam by following a qualitative research design examining the literature. Further, the chapter particularly attempts to identify the facilitators and potential barriers to develop rural entrepreneurship in the high-tech context. The analysis of the study illustrates the two most critical facilitators for rural entrepreneurship in Vietnam as "enterprise capitals" and "innovation including technology." Further, the study also highlighted barriers such as "limited access to distribution channels" and "limited access to business support and technology."

The penetration of digital technologies has opened new avenues to integrate rural farmers into a new digitally driven agri-food system. Digitalization is fundamentally changing the way of the agricultural technologies and such new technologies help farmers, manufacturers, retailers, and customers in their daily activities. The development of digital technologies with the presence of information systems is essential in altering the mode of business processes. However, on the other hand, the differences between rural and urban technological facilities broadens due to a lack of information access. To bridge the rural and urban divide, technologies can play an important role among rural entrepreneurs. This chapter is an attempt to investigate the agricultural entrepreneurs or agripreneurs use of agricultural information systems to implement innovative approaches in dynamic market conditions.

Compared to the supply chain management of other business domains, agricultural supply chain management is affected with issues such as diversity of production and demand, the bulkiness of produce, perishability, seasonality, harvest uncertainty, and climate complexity. These issues are more prominent in rural agricultural sector. Availability of mature supply chain management processes and systems can enhance the productivity of rural agricultural communities. This chapter proposes a five-stage capability maturity model for the implementation and maintenance of supply chain management processes in farm management information systems. The capability maturity model is a valuable aid to determine the digitized supply chain process' ability to consistently and continuously achieve improvement and organizational objectives. The model is proposed based on the findings of the analysis of 121 supply chain

Foreword

The migration from rural to urban areas will continue, and as per United Nation's estimate, over 60% of the world's population will be urban in the next 10 years. The main reason for the migration is economic disillusionment with the agricultural sector or high unemployment, in some places (like the US) due to the shutdown of manufacturing plants. While there are definite patterns correlating urbanization with the GDP of a country, the growth comes at a cost of asymmetrical welfare of all citizens. It is therefore imperative to foster economic development in rural areas. Promoting rural entrepreneurship as an important component of that.

The simplest conceptualization of rural entrepreneurship is to foster a greater risk-taking posture. This could come from highly entrepreneurial people – but the sustainability of individuals to succeed requires the cultivation of a broader ecosystem, including infrastructure, capital support, education. Such an ecosystem can stimulate a virtuous cycle that spawns opportunities and jobs, which in turn enhance foundational elements like capital and education. The challenge is to foster this in rural areas that are underdeveloped, remote, have communities strongly tied to natural resources (agriculture) and may be seeing high unemployment and economic malaise. This seems difficult, but there are now enough substantive initiatives (many of which are discussed in this book) that illustrate how "digital" foundations can be the platform for such transformation.

So, what is digital – and why is it different from the more prevalent information technology (IT) term that has been common parlance for years? The "traditional" IT world is largely a world of boxes of hardware and software, that allow humans to understand and leverage their properties ex ante. So, a box for decision support, or a reservation system or ERP can be adopted in organizations with purpose. Digital extends IT boxes by "liquifying" them. This simply means that the fundamental digital objects (bitstrings) can be combined and reconfigured into innovative outcomes in ways that are unpredictable. The digital infrastructure offers a level of standardization and openness that allows such configuration. This leads to unlimited combinations of digital objects such as software, data, movies, special representations, symbols. This property of generativity is what makes digital different, with low entry barriers and high potential for innovation. Further, in the digital world, the agency is now increasingly not the human, but with big data and machine learning there is machine agency (e.g., the automated car).

Rural entrepreneurship as described above offers a problem, and digital innovation offers solutions. These solutions are particularly viable for rural areas where there are dependencies on physical resources because of the embeddedness of digital with the physical. This allows innovation to be propelled by engineering, medicine, science – in areas where characteristics of the physical (e.g., soil in agriculture) can be sensed and analyzed to facilitate increase in productivity or new value.

To make these solutions work, setting up a high-speed digital infrastructure in rural areas is critical. Government or private-public partnerships are facilitating this in various regions around the world. Other foundational components include capital support, possibly through microfinancing initiatives. With these elements, the key stimulus is to create incentives for urban entrepreneurs to move to rural area – and many might be inclined to get away from urban sprawl to less congested areas with open spaces, cheap land and office spaces. Local training programs to build technical competencies could also be fruitful, once a digital infrastructure is in place. However, all this will not lead to a sustainable rural industrialization, unless there is a virtuous cycle that reinforces entrepreneurship, through reinvestment, education, skills, and opportunities, where rural digital innovations are created that can both benefit from and contribute to the digital infrastructure itself. This requires clear success stories of local entrepreneurs that gained access to international markets through their digital reach, collaborated with local universities to create new apps, became an integral part of a food supply blockchain, empowered families and women to set up family businesses, among many others. These can serve as exemplars to motivate and change stagnant mindsets and establish a positive culture of possibilities.

Rural entrepreneurship (and innovation) is an exciting emerging area in the digital space. The chapters in this book offers several insights that can facilitate economic development by bringing the remote world closer.

Varun Grover
University of Arkansas, USA

Preface

Globalization and the advancements in the technology landscape have provided myriad opportunities for developing countries and rural regions. Due to the advent and the massive proliferation of digital technologies such as social media, mobile, analytics, cloud computing and internet of things, organizations in both developing and developed countries, and the rural communities have seen the potential of utilizing them for introducing new ventures, entrepreneurial opportunities, resolving societal problems and empowering needy and rural communities. Unlike traditional information technology (IT) solutions, these digital technologies epitomize flexible, easy-to-deploy, easy-to-adopt and cost-effective IT solutions. The innate characteristics of these digital technologies have enabled entrepreneurs to launch new business ideas and models, introduce new ventures, enhance and sustain the existing businesses, reach new communities, extend businesses to new consumers and most importantly empower rural communities and needy individuals. The digital technologies have transformed the nature of uncertainty inherent in entrepreneurial processes and such characteristics of digital technologies minimize the traditional barriers for entrepreneurs and innovators. As such, start-up firms and entrepreneurs with low capital intensities are provided with an equal opportunity to innovate in a similar fashion as their resourceful counterparts. As a result, rural entrepreneurship and innovation is said to have been augmented by the substantial growth in digital technologies.

Therefore, studying rural innovation and entrepreneurship will not only be valuable to academia, but it will also add value to the rural communities, governments, small business holders and not-for-profit organizations. However, less attention has been paid for this important topic. This book is an attempt to commence the much-required discussion of rural entrepreneurship and innovation in the digital era. As such, the book initiates the conversation on contextual factors, process, impact, trends, opportunities and challenges of rural entrepreneurship and innovation that will be beneficial for future researchers as well as practitioners.

This edited book is expected to provide guidelines for researchers and entrepreneurs for initiating and conducting research on rural entrepreneurship and innovation. As such, the content of this book is suitable for academics, researchers, graduate students, PhD students and entrepreneurs and practitioners who are involved in developing and implementing innovations in rural context. Below, a brief description of the content of the book is provided.

Chapter 1: Do Technological Factors Impact Differently on Rural and Urban New Venture Performance? Empirical Evidence From the Portuguese Case

This book chapter investigates the impact of technological-related factors on the performance of new ventures located in rural and urban areas. The authors use a sample of 408 newly created ventures located in Portuguese which includes business incubators and science parks. The findings highlight the importance of research and development (R&D) collaborations with universities, and other institutes.

Chapter 2: The Role of Digital Technology in Rural Entrepreneurship and Innovations

The advancement of the digital technologies, technological platforms and digital artefacts provide solutions for initiating entrepreneurial ventures and to minimize issues faced by the rural entrepreneurs. This book chapter explains how digital technologies could assist rural entrepreneurs in overcoming the problems they face. Further, the book chapter proposes a conceptual framework depicting the drivers of rural digital entrepreneurship.

Chapter 3: Contextual Factors for Rural Entrepreneurship and Innovation

While innovation and entrepreneurship have been studied for decades, rural innovation and entrepreneurship has been received less attention. Even though there are common characteristics among rural context and normal context, there are multifaceted issues associated with the growth of rural entrepreneurs which need intervention by various political, economic and social organizations. This book chapter investigates specific contextual factors for rural entrepreneurship and innovation.

Chapter 4: Digital Innovation in Small Firms of Rural Canada

In this chapter, by showcasing three small, rural firms in Ontario, Canada, the authors highlight the co-evolution of business and digital technology strategies and related performance impacts. It is considered that unless there are systemic investments in digitization of rural economies, rural entrepreneurs will suffer, and digital innovation activity will remain modest. Nonetheless, these cases are epitomes of firm that practiced digital innovation in rural economies. These firms successfully fostered growth and revitalization due to co-evolution of business and digital strategies, investments in technology, and digitization of business processes. The book chapter focuses on the development of resources and capabilities that are critical for the survival of the firms and the local ecosystem centered around a business incubator that supports and sustains them.

Chapter 5: SMEs Internationalization Through Electronic Commerce – Benefits, Disadvantages, and Barriers

This book chapter explores the benefits, disadvantages and barriers for the internationalization of regional small and medium-sized enterprises (SMEs) through the adoption of electronic commerce. By conducting interviews with directors of ten Australian regional SMEs, the book chapter provides a better understanding of the benefits, disadvantages, and barriers that would help e-commerce stakeholders to develop appropriate strategies and policies for driving internationalization of regional SMEs

Chapter 6: An Application of the "Amplifying Casual Looping" Model to Manor House Management

This book chapter provides an explanation of the main strategies adopted by the hosts of manor houses when they engage in lodging activities. The book chapter draws on 53 non-structured interviews made to owners/hosts of Housing Tourism facilities (HT) and utilize Classic Grounded Theory to analyze the data. Within this context, the authors reveal a theoretical code, designated as 'amplifying casual looping', which they believe has the merit of effectively conceptualizing the substantive codes generated by them. This causal model broadens in both directions: positive (virtuous circle) and negative (vicious circle).

Chapter 7: Empowering Marginalized Women Through Entrepreneurship: Breaking the Barrier

This book chapter investigates some positive life changes happened through micro-finance driven entrepreneurship development among marginalized women in Bangladesh. The book chapter is based on both primary and secondary data collected from two villages in Rajshahi district in Bangladesh. The book chapter highlights that when poverty is reduced, women are better able to meet their practical gender needs; however, they are not empowered unless they are also able to meet their strategic gender needs. The author also highlights that although entrepreneurship development empowers women, it cannot bring empowerment to all women equally at all levels and many women are empowered at the household level, very few are empowered at the community level.

Chapter 8: The ICT Adoption in AMUL: An Easy, Innovative, Self-Sustainable Approach for Rural Regions

The adoption of Information Communication Technologies (ICT) in rural regions of Gujarat by the Gujarat Cooperative Milk Marketing Federation Limited (GCMMFL) can be considered as an iconic practice in the dairy industry in India. It is considered that the efforts associated with the investment of ICT in rural area are not as effective as expected, though in the case of Amul, it was proved otherwise. Amul is a dairy farming company that produces a variety of milk products and GCMMF and is a forerunner of rural India's adoption of ICT in dairy industry. This book chapter shares the success story of Amul and how they utilized ICT in the dairy industry. The application of IT enabled Amul to get better control for the accumulated milk from scattered suppliers. The Amul case is a prime example for the enabling role of the technology for innovation.

Chapter 9: Rural Entrepreneurship in Vietnam: Identification of Facilitators and Barriers

In this book chapter, the authors attempt to identify the facilitators and potential barriers to rural entrepreneurship in Vietnam by following a qualitative research design examining the literature. Further, the book chapter particularly attempts to identify the facilitators and potential barriers to develop rural entrepreneurship in the high-tech context. The analysis of the study illustrates the two most critical facilitators for rural entrepreneurship in Vietnam as "Enterprise Capitals" and "Innovation including Technology." Further, the study also highlighted barriers such as "Limited access to distribution channels" and "Limited access to business support & technology."

Chapter 10: Strategic Use of Agriculture Information System by Agripreneurs in Rural Economies: Current Role and Future Prospects

The penetration of digital technologies has opened new avenues to integrate rural farmers into a new digitally driven agri-food system (USAID, 2018). Digitalization is fundamentally changing the way of the agricultural technologies and such new technologies help farmers, manufacturers, retailers and customers in their daily activities. The development of digital technologies with the presence of information systems is essential in altering the mode of business processes. However, on the other hand the differences between rural and urban technological facilities broadens due to a lack of information access. To bridge the rural and urban divide, technologies can play an important role among rural entrepreneurs. This book chapter investigates the agricultural entrepreneurs' use of agricultural information systems to implement innovative approaches in dynamic market conditions.

Chapter 11: Capability Maturity Model for Agricultural Supply Chain Management Software

Compared to the supply chain management of other business domains, agricultural supply chain management is affected with myriad issues. Availability of mature supply chain management processes and systems can enhance the productivity of rural agricultural communities. This book chapter proposes a five-stage capability maturity model for the implementation and maintenance of supply chain management processes in farm management information systems. The capability maturity model is a valuable aid to determine the digitized supply chain process' ability to consistently and continuously achieve improvement and organizational objectives. The model is proposed based on the findings of the analysis of 121 supply chain management software in the farming sector, the Capability Maturity Model by the Software Engineering Institute and the Supply Chain Process Management Maturity Model.

Chapter 12: From Lean Towards Frugal Product Development

Frugal innovation is considered as a disruptive growth strategy for businesses that focuses on the utilization of limited resources of rural areas. Similarly, lean management targets to develop new products in accordance with the customer requirements while managing the wastage. The purpose of this book chapter is to highlight a pathway to frugal product development through lean management experiences. This is particularly of interest to developing territories and rural areas due to their innate characteristics.

The analysis highlighted that innovation ideas have high diffusion rates if the product configuration is properly conducted. Despite the common objectives of lean and frugal development, this book chapter investigates distinguishing features and conducts a comparison of both methodologies in order to provide specific guidance for companies that follow lean management to capture the benefits of frugal product development.

Chapter 13: An Advancement to the Grameen Bank Model

This chapter highlights important facts about the Grameen Bank initiated by Muhammad Yunus, as a prototype for promoting rural entrepreneurship within the under-developed rural community governed by the digital portal. The Grameen model is considered as an advanced empathetic financial service that is appropriate for the needy poor women located in rural locations. By analyzing prior literature on Grameen model, in this book chapter, an advancement to the existing Grameen model is proposed.

Chapter 14: Engaging With Stakeholders for Developing an Effective Entrepreneurial Ecosystem in Universities based in Rural Setup

In this book chapter a new model that promotes and develops an entrepreneurial ecosystem with the collaboration of universities based in rural setup is proposed. As per the book chapter, the universities in rural areas can introduce business training, college business hatcheries, and college endeavor government-common society cooperation that enabled entrepreneurial behaviors. The target of a business college filling in as a pioneering entrepreneurial eco-system development center, is to animate financial advancement, produce work, and make imaginative innovation-based endeavors or acting as an administration organizations. While these services can be provided through a university, a university in a rural set up has an opportunity to act as a center for the economic development in rural areas.

Chapter 15: Theoretical Opportunities for Rural Innovation and Entrepreneurship Research

The advent of digital technologies has provided new opportunities for rural entrepreneurship and rural innovation discipline. Such opportunities provided through the digital technologies, challenge the orthodox view of IT use and innovation and challenge the existing theoretical understanding. This book chapter is an attempt to understand the existing literature on rural innovation and entrepreneurship in information systems discipline and to provide a conceptual model for studying future research areas in rural entrepreneurship and innovation in the digital era.

Sachithra Lokuge
RMIT University, Australia

Darshana Sedera
Southern Cross University, Australia

Chapter 1
Do Technological Factors Impact Differently on Rural and Urban New Venture Performance?
Empirical Evidence From the Portuguese Case

Lúcia Pato
https://orcid.org/0000-0002-2286-4155
CERNAS IPV-Research Centre, Polytechnic Institute of Viseu, Portugal

Aurora Amélia Castro Teixeira
https://orcid.org/0000-0002-3191-5217
CEF.UP Faculdade de Economia, Universidade do Porto, Portugal

ABSTRACT

Research on the relationship between entrepreneurship and context has gained considerable attention in recent years. However, this stream of literature has yet to adequately address the topic of entrepreneurship in rural areas. This chapter intends to fill this gap by investigating the extent to which technological-related factors affect the performance of new ventures located in rural and urban areas. Based on a sample of 408 newly created ventures located in Portuguese business incubators (BIs) and science parks (SPs), and employing logistic estimations, two main conclusions were derived. They are 1) support from BIs/SPs matters the most to the export and global innovation performance of new ventures located in rural areas and 2) support from universities and other higher education institutions, and the regularity of research and development (R&D) collaborations between new ventures and R&D institutions are more relevant to the turnover and innovation performance of new ventures located in urban areas than those in rural areas.

DOI: 10.4018/978-1-7998-4942-1.ch001

INTRODUCTION

In the last few decades, the study of entrepreneurship has drawn greater attention from governments, policy-makers and individuals, as it is considered a fundamental tool for the economic development of countries and regions (Escandón-Barbosa, Urbano, Hurtado-Ayala, Salas paramo, & Dominguez, 2019). It is therefore not surprising that entrepreneurship is considered as a key component of the European union's (EU) Europe 2020 strategy for smart, sustainable and inclusive growth (Strano et al., 2012).

Given that the institutional context in which the enterprises are located is a highly relevant factor, a vast amount of literature has explored the influence of institutional contexts on new venture creation and development (Welter, 2011; Welter & Smallbone, 2011; Zahra, Wright, & Abdelgawad, 2014). In fact, entrepreneurship is a socio-spatial activity, in which entrepreneurs take advantage of local resources and conditions (Trettin & Welter, 2011). As such, entrepreneurship can be regarded as a predominantly local/ regional event (Baumgartner, Pütz, & Seidl, 2013; Müller, 2016).

Research on the relationship between entrepreneurship and context has been dominated by theoretical approaches, such as agglomeration theory (Candau & Dienesch, 2015; Glaeser, Ponzetto, & Tobio, 2014), economic geography (Parrino, 2015), and institutional theory (Adomakoa, Opokub, & Frimpongc, 2018). Based on this conceptual diversity, scholars have developed relevant knowledge about critical contextual factors, processes and models (Ács, Autio, & Szerb, 2014) that foster creative, novel analyses and explanations by situating phenomena, theories and findings in their natural setting (Zahra et al., 2014).

However (and perhaps surprisingly), this stream of literature is profoundly problematic when applied to entrepreneurship in rural areas (Muñoz & Kimmitt, 2019). The focus on metropolitan and urban areas (Baumgartner, Schulz, & Seidl, 2013), and the assumption that entrepreneurship follows similar patterns in rural areas seems to imply the absence of efficient support mechanisms for entrepreneurship in rural contexts (Muñoz & Kimmitt, 2019).

In fact, the emphasis on general frameworks and institutional factors does not explain the factors that affect rural entrepreneurship and, thus, cannot inform policies at the regional or national levels. This signals a considerable weakness in the extant literature, restricting the understanding of entrepreneurial enablers and dynamics in rural contexts. This is all the more so if we consider that in the EU, rural areas are home to more than half of the population and cover more than three quarters of the territory (EU, 2016). Moreover, rural areas have distinctive qualities (Ring, Peredo, & Chrisman, 2010) and several opportunities emerge including increased demand for recreation and amenities, as well as quality products from the food and light manufacturing sectors (Stathopoulou, Psaltopoulos, & Skuras, 2004).

A recent study by Pato and Teixeira (2020) investigates the extent to which institutional factors impact distinctively on the performance of rural and urban new ventures. Technological-related infrastructures have proliferated in rural areas (Bruneel, Ratinho, Clarysse, & Groen, 2012; Ratinho & Henriques, 2010), namely business incubators (BIs) and science parks (SPs), universities and other higher education institutions, as well as research and development (R&D) centers. This study thus aims to complement Pato and Teixeira's (2020) research by focusing on the influence of technological-related factors on new venture performance and by investigating whether this influence varies in the case of new ventures located in rural versus urban areas.

Methodologically, logistic estimations have been used based on a sample of 408 new ventures located in BIs and SPs across Portuguese rural and urban areas, in this case, municipalities. We have opted specifically new ventures located in these infrastructures, not only because this approach serves to compare businesses that share a certain common profile, that is, technology-based and knowledge-intensive, but also because, at the European level and specifically in Portugal, regional development policies are progressively related with the promotion of the above-mentioned ventures (EC, 2013).

The chapter is structured as follows. The next section briefly overviews the relevant literature and puts forward the main hypotheses to be tested. Then, next section details the methodological underpinnings. The findings section presents and discusses the empirical findings of this research and finally the conclusion section the chapter summarizes the research and provide future research areas.

THEORETICAL BACKGROUND AND HYPOTHESES

Entrepreneurship as a Socio-Institutional Activity

Since the 1980s, entrepreneurship research has come to focus on the socio-spatial dimension of the phenomenon (Nijkamp, 2009), although it only gained greater momentum in more recent years (Muñoz & Kimmitt, 2019). Nowadays, a substantial amount of literature recognizes and explains how entrepreneurs are molded by their milieu (Trettin & Welter, 2011) and the effects their actions may have on their environments (Korsgaard, Müller, & Tanvig, 2015). In fact, according to Müller (2016), (1) there are spatial-structural conditions that influence entrepreneurial activities; and (2) entrepreneurial activities influence regional structures in terms of regional development.

The environment and the institutional context surrounding the (new) venture are important since they provide the incentives for different types of business activity (Adomakoa et al., 2018). Recently, particularly in the last ten years, the entrepreneurial ecosystem approach has gained considerable attention (Stam, 2015). Entrepreneurial ecosystems "are combinations of social, political, economic, and cultural elements within a region that support the development and growth of innovative start-ups and encourage nascent entrepreneurs and other actors to take the risks of starting, funding, and otherwise assisting high-risk ventures" (Spigel, 2017, p. 50).

While public sector institutions make laws, regulations and policies related to government assistance for the promotion of entrepreneurship, private sector establishments define the culture, norms, philosophies, and expectations of the activity (Saeed, Yousafzai, Yani-De-Soriano, & Muffatto, 2015). Thus, support for entrepreneurs can enhance creativity and efficiency, whereas less available support heightens the danger of chaos, which is detrimental to entrepreneurs (Adomako et al., 2019). The literature review by Trettin and Welter (2011) provides a rich overview of spatially oriented entrepreneurship research in the disciplines of geography and entrepreneurship. These authors identified a growing focus on the underlying socio-spatial processes that influence the type and the extent of entrepreneurial activities, i.e., the association between entrepreneurship and location. Taking these findings into account, Pato and Teixeira (2020) investigated the extent to which institutional factors – political, economic, socio-cultural and technological – have impacted on the performance of rural and urban new ventures. They concluded, as others before them ((Henry & McElwee, 2014; McElwee & Smith, 2014; Pato & Teixeira, 2018; Stathopoulou et al., 2004), that what really distinguishes ventures located in rural areas from those located in urban ones are environmental factors, which influence their start-up, growth and/ or failure rates.

There is a consistent argument across the literature concerning the strong influence of start-ups on job creation, prosperity, and economic and regional development (Fritsch, 2008, 2011; Müller, 2013; Muñoz & Kimmitt, 2019; Pfeilstetter, 2013). Joseph Schumpeter was one of the first contributors to this vision through his seminal book 'The Theory of Economic Development' (published originally in 1934), in which entrepreneurship is regarded as the primary engine of economic development with innovation at its core (Pato & Teixeira, 2016). More recently, a vast amount of information and knowledge driven by developments in the information and communication technology industries have contributed to the recognition of entrepreneurship as a driver of economic and regional development (Stough, 2016).

Research on entrepreneurship and regional development in rural areas has also flourished (see for instance Baumgartner, Pütz, et al., 2013; Baumgartner, Schulz, et al., 2013; Müller, 2013). In fact, the dramatic downturn in many countries and regions in recent times has led to the promotion of entrepreneurship as one of the most important tools to address the economic problems of rural communities, attracting renewed attention, particularly from public authorities and policy-makers (McElwee & Smith, 2014; Pato & Teixeira, 2016). For instance, Baumgartner et al. (2013) suggest a generally positive relationship between entrepreneurship and local development: rural municipalities with higher entrepreneurial potential generally show higher business tax revenues per capita and a lower share of social welfare cases among the population.

The Role of Technological-Related Factors in Entrepreneurship Across Rural and Urban Municipalities

Investment in innovation and technology is frequently seen as a key to the success of an enterprise (Nacu & Avasilcai, 2014). Based on an extensive literature review (e.g., Dobbs & Hamilton, 2007; Lampadarios, Kyriakidou, & Smith, 2017), Pato and Teixeira (2020) examined the role of universities and higher education institutions, as well as BIs and SPs and other companies or institutions located in the region, in bolstering research and development (R&D) and their impact on start-up performance.

The raison d'être or the mission of universities and other higher education institutions is typically rooted in the development of knowledge that can be translated into skills that advance the practice of professionals (Ven & Johnson, 2006). A number of universities are currently in a state of transition because they are expected to develop a wide range of relationships with stakeholders in order to enhance innovation and entrepreneurship (Guerrero, Urbano, Fayolle, Klofsten, & Mian, 2016). In fact, as universities are responsible for creating and transferring knowledge through both education and collaboration with businesses, they are critical in developing the innovation capabilities of new ventures (Roig-Tierno, Alcázar, & Ribeiro-Navarrete, 2016), giving rise furthermore to the concept of entrepreneurial universities (Mian, 2011; Pugh, Lamine, Jack, & Hamilton, 2018). In addition to teaching and research, these universities also support and promote the entrepreneurial activities of researchers and graduates, with strong connections to R&D centers, firms, BIs and governments, and other institutions (Fuster, Padilla-Meléndez, Lockett, & del-Águila-Obra, 2019). Therefore, generally speaking, entrepreneurial universities are oriented to the community as regional actors (Etzkowitz, 2017), providing a supportive ecosystem to entrepreneurs and their milieu (Guerrero et al., 2016).

However, the remoteness of many rural areas, their isolation from important business support networks and technological institutions continues to be a major obstacle (Moreira, 2015). The most prominent, older and entrepreneurial universities and related institutions tend to be located in urban areas and near cities (Pato & Teixeira, 2019a). For instance, in the Portuguese case, they are located predominantly on the coastal seaboard and near the two major urban centers, Lisbon and Porto (QS, 2020).

Based on the above, we conjecture that:

H1: Institutional support from universities and other higher education institutions in the region are likely to have a **less positive impact** on the performance of new ventures located **in rural areas** than those located in urban ones.

Many universities, namely the more entrepreneurial ones, have created and/or established close links with BIs and SPs. The core strength of both BIs and SPs lies in knowledge transfer from universities and R&D institutions as well as the creation of new and innovative ventures (Barbosa, 2013; Ratinho & Henriques, 2010). The many definitions for BIs and SPs have in common themes such as regional development, technology focus, prosperity, and job and wealth creation (Ratinho & Henriques, 2010). These technological infrastructures can be defined as property-based organizations with identifiable administrative centers focused on the mission of business acceleration through knowledge agglomeration and resource sharing (Phan, Siegel, & Wright, 2005).

Even though there are some differences between BIS and SPs (see Unesco, 2017), they share several goals and features (Mian, 2016; Ratinho & Henriques, 2010). These infrastructures provide not only the physical space for enterprises (offices, labs), but also supply a number of services, namely consultancy, networking, and access to venture capital, which are fundamental for the performance of new technology-based firms (Grimaldi & Grandi, 2005; Teixeira, 2017). Therefore, one of their key roles is to assist potential entrepreneurs, while also acting as catalysts for innovation, entrepreneurship and regional development (Mas-Verdú, Ortiz-Miranda, & García-Álvarez-Coque, 2016).

Harpa (2017) also mentions that rural areas do not have the infrastructure to support innovative start-ups, and certain initiatives, such as BIs, lack continuity because of poor planning and management. In fact, like universities and other higher education institutions, the most well-known BIs and SPs are located in urban areas or near large cities (Ratinho & Henriques, 2010).

Thus, we hypothesize that:

H2: Institutional support from BIs/SPs are likely to have a **less positive impact** on the performance of new ventures located **in rural areas** than those located in urban ones.

According to the Global Entrepreneurship Monitor (GEM) project, another factor affecting the performance of Small and Medium Enterprises (SME) is access to relevant R&D resources (Amorós, Bosma, & Levie, 2013); in other words, the extent to which R&D is available to newly founded ventures (Lampadarios et al., 2017). Many R&D centers refer to innovative activities undertaken by institutions located, for instance, in universities and other higher education institutions (Hormiga, de Saá-Pérez, Díaz-Díaz, Ballesteros-Rodríguez, & Aguiar-Diaz, 2017) or government labs/ public R&D institutions which develop new services or products (Investopedia, 2019). Because innovation is far from being an isolated procedure within ventures (Malerba & McKelvey, 2020), it is assumed that firms with better R&D strategies and links to R&D institutions develop better levels of experience, skills and knowledge, and come to be regarded as 'hotbeds' for entrepreneurial spawns (Andersson, Baltzopoulos, & Lööf, 2012).

Scientific research and R&D collaboration in rural areas has suffered from the constantly declining level of investments from both the public and private sectors, and is characterized by a limited number of highly trained specialists and R&D centers of excellence (Harpa, 2017).

Thus, we hypothesize that:

H3: Institutional **support derived from regular collaborations** with R&D centers and other companies **for R&D activities** are likely to have a **less positive impact** on the performance of new ventures located **in rural areas** than those located in urban ones.

DATA COLLECTION AND ECONOMETRIC MODEL SPECIFICATION

Data Collection Process

The main phases of the data collection procedures are illustrated in Figure 1. First, using the Portuguese parishes classification from the *Ministério da Agricultura, do Mar, do Ambiente e do Ordenamento do Território* (MAMAOT, 2012), similar to the OECD classification of regions, the Portuguese municipalities were classified into three main groups: 1) predominantly urban, when the share of population living in rural parishes is below 15%; 2) intermediate, when the share of population living in rural parishes is between 15% and 50%; and 3) rural, when the share of population living in rural parishes is higher than 50%.

Following the above typologies, mainland Portugal has 278 municipalities, 194 of which are considered 'predominantly rural', 17 'intermediate', and 67 'predominantly urban'. With the exception of two municipalities with a higher population density, all the intermediate municipalities have been classified as rural, that is, 75% (209 municipalities) of mainland Portugal is rural.

In the second phase, a database of new venture support infrastructures was built, including specifically BIs/SPs, which numbered approximately 100 in total, 39% of which located in rural municipalities.

The third stage involved the observation of new ventures headquartered in these BIs/SPS. At the end of this stage, we had identified 1400 new ventures in these infrastructures, 43% of which in rural municipalities.

A questionnaire was developed and implemented in the fourth phase, between April and May 2016, following a pilot test involving five new ventures. Apart from information about the context/environment, particularly the support provided for technological factors, the questionnaire included: 1) questions about the entrepreneur/human capital; 2) questions about generic characteristics of the new venture; 3) questions about innovation strategies, and 4) questions about venture performance. The questions concerning technological-related factors involved Likert scale measures (1. Not important…5. Very important).

At the end of the process, we obtained 408 completed questionnaires, 142 from rural municipalities. This represents a response rate of about 30%, a reasonable rate for a non-compulsory questionnaire, administered on-line (Nulty, 2008), which compares favorably with other similar studies (e.g., Eschker, Gold, & Lane, 2017).

Figure 1. Phases of the data gathering process (Source: Authors' elaboration)

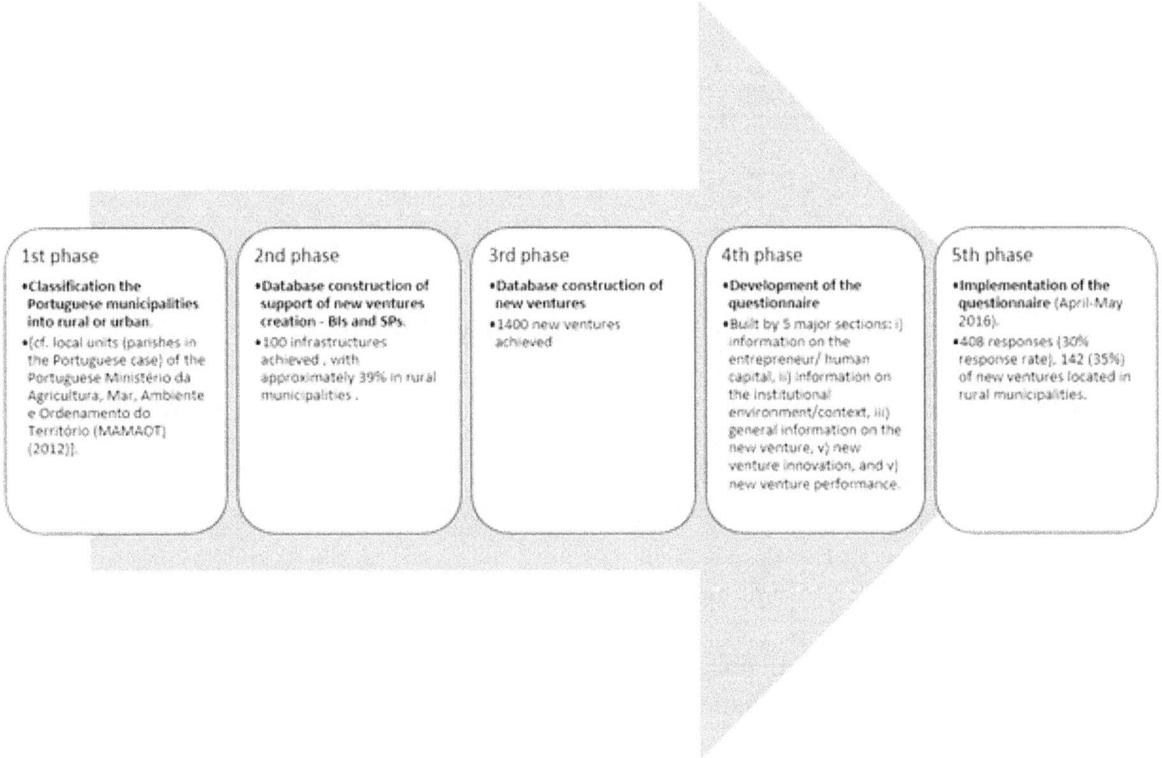

Econometric Model Specification

In order to test this study's main hypotheses,

H1: Institutional support from **universities and other higher education institutions** in the region are likely to have a **less positive impact** on the performance of new ventures located **in rural areas** than those located in urban ones

H2: Institutional **support from BIs/SPs** are likely to have a **less positive impact** on the performance of new ventures located **in rural areas** than those located in urban ones

H3: Institutional **support derived from regular collaborations** with R&D centers and other companies **for R&D activities** are likely to have a **less positive impact** on the performance of new ventures located **in rural areas** than those located in urban ones,

an econometric/ empirical specification was built which included new venture performance as a dependent variable and two sets of explanatory variables, related to institutional support from knowledge and technology infrastructures, that is, the technological-related factors, and business features (the independent control variables).

Algebraically, the specification is written as follows:

$$y_i = \beta_1 + \underbrace{\beta_2 Univ_i + \beta_3 BI\_SP_i + \beta_4 R\&D\_Collab_i}_{Technological-related\ factors} +$$

$$+ \underbrace{\beta_5 HC_i + \beta_6 Innovator_i + \beta_7 Exporter_i + \beta_8 Age_i + \beta_9 Micro\_sized_i + \beta_{10} Industry_i}_{Business\ features} + \varepsilon_i \tag{1}$$

Where,

y_i: the performance of new venture *i*;
Univ/ BI_SP: the importance new venture *i* attributed to Universities/ BIs & SPs;
R&D_Collab: the regularity of R&D collaborations by new venture *i*;
HC: human capital endowments of new venture *i;*
Innovator: whether new venture *i* innovated in global terms in the past three years*;*
Exporter: whether new venture *i* exports*;*
Age: number of years in operation of new venture *i;*
Micro_sized: size category of new venture *i;*
Industry: sector (primary, manufacturing; services) where new venture *i* operates*;*

We considered three metrics to proxy new venture performance, including sales turnover, exports and (global and technological) innovation.

Sales turnover is one of the most commonly used indicators to measure financial success in terms of profitability (Teirlinck, 2017), and export performance has been identified as an important characteristic of firms experiencing high growth (Lee, Kelley, Lee, & Lee, 2012). Furthermore, based on prior research, the link between innovation and firm performance is unquestionable (Dziallas & Blind, 2019; Storey, Cankurtaran, Papastathopoulou, & Hultink, 2016).

Given that the information on performance is sensitive and is often paved with non-responses (Pato & Teixeira, 2020), we decided to ask new ventures about turnover and exports using intervals instead of continuous scales, and about innovation using dichotomous questions. As such, the performance variable assumed the value 1 when the new venture presented a turnover above 50 thousand Euros, when the firm exported more than 30% of its products or services, and when it presented 6 or more (out of 11) distinct types of innovation or, alternatively, presented 3 or more (out of 4) distinct types of product or process innovation (i.e., technological innovators).

Given the binary nature of the dependent (performance) variable, the econometric estimation model chosen is the binary logit regression (Freedman, 2009), which serves to estimate the parameters of the odds of performance (Equation 1).

$$\ln\left(\frac{p_i}{1-p_i}\right) = \beta_1 + \underbrace{\beta_2 Univ_i + \beta_3 BI\_SP_i + \beta_4 R\&D\_Collab_i}_{Technological-related\ factors} +$$

$$+ \underbrace{\beta_5 HC_i + \beta_6 Innovator_i + \beta_7 Exporter_i + \beta_8 Age_i + \beta_9 Micro\_sized_i + \beta_{10} Industry_i}_{Business\ features} + \varepsilon_i \tag{2}$$

where

p_i is the probability of new venture *i* being a top performer. This variable is coded as 1 when the new venture had a sales turnover/gross value added above 50000 €/ when it exported above 30% of its turnover/ was a top (technological) innovator.

The proxies for the variables included in each of the five group of variables listed in Eq. (2) are described in Table 1.

EMPIRICAL RESULTS

Characteristics of the Sample

Newly founded ventures located in BIs/ SPs are very small in terms of sales. In 2015, slightly more than half (56%) had a sales turnover of more than 50,000 €. In terms of exports, only about a quarter of new ventures (25%) had exported more than 30% of their products or services. The fragility of new ventures is also evident in terms of innovation – slightly more than 59% of ventures were considered top global innovators (product/service, process, organizational or marketing), a percentage that dropped to 43% in the case of top technological (product or process) innovators (see Table 1).

In relation to institutional support from knowledge and technology infrastructures, specifically support from universities, professional business structures and R&D collaborations, the perceived importance of the support provided and regular R&D collaboration with R&D institutions and other companies was low. Only 21% and slight over 26% of the new ventures perceived the impact of universities and BIs/SPs as very important, respectively, while only 25% of the new ventures stated they were regularly involved in collaboration for R&D activities.

In relation to business features, on average, new ventures were small in 2015. The percentage of new micro ventures (less than 10 employees) in the sample was 72%. A minority of newly created ventures operated in the primary sector (5.8%), whereas 23% operated in the manufacturing industry. Finally, slightly more than 20% of the employees had a higher education degree.

Table 1. Proxies for the relevant variables and descriptive statistics

Variables/ Hypotheses			Description	Mean	Min	Max
Dependent variables	Performance	Top turnover	Dummy=1 when the firm presents a turnover above 50 thousand euros	0.563	0	1
		Top exporters	Dummy=1 when the firm exports 30% or more of its products	0.253	0	1
		Top global innovators	Dummy=1 when the firm presents 6 or more (out of 11) distinct types of innovation	0.593	0	1
		Top technological innovators	Dummy=1 when the firm presents 3 or more (out of 4) distinct types of product or process innovation	0.434	0	1
Technological related factors	Institutional support from knowledge and technology infrastructures	Universities **[H1]**	Universities and other higher education institutions (dummy=1 when very important)	0.210	0	1
		Incubators and Science Parks **[H2]**	Incubators and Science and Technological Parks (dummy=1 when very important)	0.268	0	1
		Collaboration in R&D **[H3]**	with other companies and institutions in the region (dummy=1 when regular)	0.250	0	1
Control variables	Business' characteristics	Human capital	Percentage of individuals employed with bachelors, graduation or more (category 1=0%... category 12= 100%) (in ln)	1.175	0	2.480
			Percentage of individuals employed with 9-12 years of schooling (category 1=0%... category 12= 100%) (in ln)	0.834	0	2.480
		Innovation	Top global innovator (dummy)	0.593	0	1
		Exports	Exports (dummy=1 when exports)	0.520	0	1
		Age	Years in business (in ln)	1.092	0	1.790
		Size (default: small and medium)	Micro (dummy)	0.720	0	1
		Sector (default: services)	Primary (dummy)	0.058	0	1
			Manufacturing (dummy)	0.230	0	1

Note: Total number of firms: 396.

Empirical Results: Testing the Main Hypotheses

We estimated four sets of models (see Table 2), according to the proxies for performance: Models 1R and 1U, for top performers in terms of turnover located in Rural (R) and Urban (U) areas, respectively; Models 2R and 2U for top performers in terms of exports; Models 3R and 3U for top performers in terms of global innovation; and Models 4R and 4U for top performers in terms of technological (product and process) innovation.

The models presented a reasonable goodness of fit with the percentage of correctly predicted observations ranging from 66% (Model 1R) to 76% (Model 1U), and the Hosmer-Lemeshow test presenting p-values above 10% (excluding the case of Model 3R), which means that the estimated models represent reality well.

Variance inflation factors did not show problems regarding multicollinearity among the selected independent variables.

Table 2. Determinants of new venture performance (logit estimates and robust standard errors)

Variables/ Hypotheses			Description	Turnover		Exports 30% over		Top global innovator		Top technological innovator	
				Model 1R	**Model 1U**	**Model 2R**	**Model 2U**	**Model 3R**	**Model 3U**	**Model 4R**	**Model 4U**
Technological related factors	Institutional s support from knowledge and technology infrastructures	Universities **[H1]**	Universities and other higher education institutions (dummy=1 when very important)	0.231 (0.591	**0.712*** **(0.444)**	-0.027 (0.594)	-0.675 (0.431)	**-1.256**** **(0.596)**	0.626 (0.400)	-0.475 (0.548)	**0.650*** **(0.374)**
		Incubators and Science Parks **[H2]**	Incubators and Science and Technological Parks (dummy=1 when very important)	-0.520 (0.523)	-0.375 (0.426)	**1.048**** **(0.535)**	0.579 (0.388)	**0.988*** **(0.530)**	-0.051 (0.375)	0.663 (0.474)	-0.434 (0.363)
		Collaboration in R&D **[H3]**	with other companies and institutions in the region (dummy=1 when regular)	0.228 (0.469)	0.339 (0.401)	0.377 (0.518)	0.538 (0.366)	**1.468***** **(0.523)**	**1.340***** **(0.378)**	0.653 (0.431)	**1.298***** **(0.334)**
Control variables	Business' characteristics	Human capital (default: less than 9 years of schooling)	Percentage of individuals employed with bachelors, graduation or more (dummy)	-0.028 (0.232)	-0.275 (0.171)	**0.402*** **(0.250)**	-0.086 (0.169)	0.017 (0.236)	-0.170 (0.153)	-0.016 (0.217)	-0.049 (0.152)
			Percentage of individuals employed with 9-12 years of schooling (dummy)	**0.626**** **(0.266)**	**0.545***** **(0.188)**	**0.681**** **(0.278)**	0.053 (0.168)	**0.545*** **(0.286)**	**0.258*** **(0.156)**	0.072 (0.247)	-0.064 (0.153)
		Innovation	Top global innovator (dummy)	0.399 (0.431)	0.456 (0.320)	**-1.017**** **(0.473)**	0.218 (0.313)				
		Exports	Exports (dummy=1 when exports)	-0.042 (0.402)	**0.768**** **(0.308)**			0.284 (0.401)	**0.869***** **(0.273)**	**0.769**** **(0.374)**	0.363 (0.270)
		Age	Years in business (in ln)	0.763 (0.616)	**2.541***** **(0.598)**	-0.265 (0.664)	0.148 (0.508)	0.104 (0.584)	**0.858*** **(0.466)**	-0.171 (0.551)	**0.864*** **(0.449)**
		Size (default: small and medium)	Micro (dummy)	0.023 (0.644)	**-0.965*** **(0.583)**	0.802 (0.748)	0.522 (0.553)	0.340 (0.644)	-0.617 (0.492)	0.619((0.601)	**-0.996**** **(0.480)**
		Sector (default: services)	Primary (dummy)	-0.088 (0.638)	-1.247 (0.809)	-0.540 (0.752)	0.493 (0.778)	0.710 (0.765)	-0.561 (0.830)	-0.419 (0.594)	-0.008 (0.776)
			Manufacturing (dummy)	**1.004**** **(0.465)**	**0.780*** **(0.403)**	0.072 (0.500)	0.475 (0.339)	-0.541 (0.452)	**-0.755**** **(0.326)**	-0.272 (0.433)	0.050 (0.319)
Number of observations				138	258	142	266	142	266	142	266
Top performer new ventures				64	159	35	67	87	153	68	110
Others				75	99	107	199	55	113	74	156
Goodness of fit			Nagelkerke R2	0.222	0.338	0.152	0.065	0.237	0.191	0.126	0.144
			Hosmer-Lemeshow chi2 (p-value)	10.562 (0.228)	10.466 (0.235)	10.565 (0.228)	3.789 (0.876)	22.428 (0.004)	3.525 (0.897)	7.291 (0.506)	4.197 (0.839)
			Correctly classified (%)	63.0	76.4	77.5	74.4	68.3	66.2	64.1	68.0

Note: R – Rural; U – Urban; ***(**)[*] statistically significant at 1% (5%) [10%]. **Bold text** denotes statistically significant estimates.

When performance was measured by turnover or technological innovation, the estimates showed that new ventures located in an urban setting that attributed higher importance to universities and other higher education institutions were, on average, more likely to be top performers, all other factors remaining constant. In the case of new ventures located in rural areas, no significant differences emerged between those that attributed higher or lower importance to such institutions.

When performance was measured by exports, the estimates suggested that support from universities and other higher education institutions did not impact on new venture performance, regardless of their location in rural or urban areas. Additionally, and quite unexpectedly, new ventures located in rural areas that attributed lower importance to support from universities and other higher education institutions tended to be top performers in terms of global innovation.

Summing up, H1 (*Institutional support from* ***universities and other higher education institutions*** *in the region are likely to have a* ***less positive impact*** *on the performance of new ventures located* ***in rural areas*** *than those located in urban ones*) is only partially supported by our data.

Institutional support from BIs/SPs did not seem to matter for the performance of both rural and urban new ventures, when performance was measured by total turnover of technological innovation. Notwithstanding, when performance was proxied by exports or global innovation, the estimations showed that, on average, new ventures located in rural area that attributed higher importance to support from BIs/SPs were more likely to outperform those for which such support was not relevant.

Thus, H2 (*Institutional* ***support from BIs/SPs*** *is likely to have a* ***less positive impact*** *on the performance of new ventures located* ***in rural areas*** *than those located in urban ones*) is not validated by our data.

Regarding the institutional support derived from regular collaborations with R&D centers and other companies for R&D activities, the estimates indicated that regular collaboration mattered for new venture performance in terms of global and technological innovation but not in terms of turnover or export intensity. Specifically, new ventures located in rural and urban areas that were involved in regular collaborations for R&D activities tended to be top performers in global innovation, whose impact was larger for new ventures located in rural settings. In the case of technological innovation, this is true only for new ventures located in urban areas.

In short, H3 (*Institutional* ***support derived from regular collaborations*** *with R&D centers and other companies* ***for R&D activities*** *are likely to have a* ***less positive impact*** *on the performance of new ventures located* ***in rural areas*** *than those located in urban ones*) is, in general, not validated.

CONCLUSION

The entrepreneurship literature tends to underline the importance of the context of new ventures, suggesting the embeddedness of entrepreneurial activities (Pato & Teixeira, 2019b; Trettin & Welter, 2011). However, due to differences in rural areas in comparison to urban ones (Smallbone, 2009) this literature is deeply problematic when it is applied to entrepreneurship in rural areas (Fortunato, 2014; Muñoz & Kimmitt, 2019). Moreover, although the importance of technological-related factors in the success of the ventures is widely acknowledged (Lampadarios et al., 2017; Nacu & Avasilcai, 2014), research focusing on rural and urban entrepreneurship has so far overlooked the conditions in which different technological contexts can affect firm performance.

Three main conclusions from the present study can be highlighted: 1) support from BIs/ SPs tends to improve the export and global innovation performance of new ventures in rural areas; 2) support from universities and other higher education institutions tends to improve the turnover and technological performance of new ventures located in urban areas; and 3) support derived from regular collaborations with R&D centers and other companies for R&D activities tends to improve global and technological innovation performance in urban areas and global innovation performance in rural areas.

Therefore, this study has important policy, academic and managerial implications, in addition to adding knowledge to the literature in the area. From a political point of view, rural and urban public authorities must follow specific strategies, including the establishment of a distinct entrepreneurial culture and a position of innovation, based on the specific particularities of each area (Fink, Loidl, & Lang, 2012; Pato & Teixeira, 2019a). In terms of academic and managerial implications, the connection between new ventures in rural areas and BIs/ SPs should be improved, since they seem to be an important enhancer of new venture performance. Moreover, R&D collaboration between new ventures located in rural areas and R&D centers and other companies should also be bolstered. This can be done by building innovation capacity and implementing innovative solutions, through which rural communities may overcome their intrinsic challenges and remain viable business locations (Fhlatharta & Farrell, 2017).

Despite the above-mentioned contributions, this study has some limitations, which nevertheless are likely to constitute interesting avenues for future research. First, it provides only a quantitative analysis of specific rural and urban new ventures. Thus, a qualitative analysis would be extremely useful especially when dealing with the impact of technological-related factors on firm performance. Second, the specific focus of this study's sample – new technology-based and knowledge-intensive firms located in BIs and SPs – limits the generalization of the findings to other types of new ventures (Pato & Teixeira, 2019b). Therefore, an interesting path for future research is to broaden the scope of the study to a wider set of companies located outside BIs and SPs.

REFERENCES

Ács, Z. J., Autio, E., & Szerb, L. (2014). National Systems of Entrepreneurship: Measurement issues and policy implications. *Research Policy*, *43*(3), 476–494. doi:10.1016/j.respol.2013.08.016

Adomakoa, S., Opokub, R. A., & Frimpongc, K. (2018). Entrepreneurs' improvisational behavior and new venture performance: Firm-level and institutional contingencies. *Journal of Business Research*, *83*, 10–18. doi:10.1016/j.jbusres.2017.10.006

Amorós, J. E., Bosma, N., & Levie, J. (2013). Ten years of Global Entrepreneurship Monitor: Accomplishments and prospects. *International Journal of Entrepreneurial Venturing*, *5*(2), 120–152. doi:10.1504/IJEV.2013.053591

Andersson, M., Baltzopoulos, A., & Lööf, H. (2012). R&D strategies and entrepreneurial spawning. *Research Policy*, *41*(1), 54–68. doi:10.1016/j.respol.2011.08.005

Barbosa, L. G. F. (2013). Incubadora de empresas de base tecnológica: Perceção dos empresários quanto aos apoios recebidos. *Revista de Administração e Gestão*, *10*(3), 208–229.

Baumgartner, D., Pütz, M., & Seidl, I. (2013). What Kind of Entrepreneurship Drives Regional Development in European? A Literature Review on Empirical Entrepreneurship Research. *European Planning Studies*, *21*(8), 1095–1127. doi:10.1080/09654313.2012.722937

Baumgartner, D., Schulz, T., & Seidl, I. (2013). Quantifying entrepreneurship and its impact on local economic performance: A spatial assessment in rural Switzerland. *Entrepreneurship and Regional Development*, *25*(3-4), 222–250. doi:10.1080/08985626.2012.710266

Bruneel, J., Ratinho, T., Clarysse, B., & Groen, A. (2012). The Evolution of Business Incubators: Comparing demand and supply of business incubation services across different incubator generations. *Technovation, 32*(2), 110–121. doi:10.1016/j.technovation.2011.11.003

Candau, F., & Dienesch, E. (2015). Spatial distribution of skills and regional trade integration. *The Annals of Regional Science, 54*(2), 451–488. doi:10.100700168-015-0662-4

Dobbs, M., & Hamilton, R. T. (2007). Small business growth: Recent evidence and new directions. *International Journal of Entrepreneurial Behaviour & Research, 13*(5), 296–322. doi:10.1108/13552550710780885

Dziallas, M., & Blind, K. (2019). Innovation indicators throughout the innovation process: An extensive literature analysis. *Technovation, 80-81*, 3–29. doi:10.1016/j.technovation.2018.05.005

EC. (2013). *REDI: The Regional Entrepreneurship and Development Index – Measuring regional entrepreneurship Final report*. Brussels: EC.

Escandón-Barbosa, D. M., Urbano, D., Hurtado-Ayala, A., Salas paramo, J., & Dominguez, A. Z. (2019). Formal institutions, informal institutions and entrepreneurial activity: A comparative relationship between rural and urban areas in Colombia. *Journal of Urban Management*. doi:10.1016/j.jum.2019.06.002

Eschker, E., Gold, G., & Lane, M. D. (2017). Rural entrepreneurs: What are the best indicators of their success? *Journal of Small Business and Enterprise Development, 24*(2), 278–296. doi:10.1108/JSBED-07-2016-0112

Etzkowitz, H. (2017). Innovation Lodestar: The entrepreneurial university in a stellar knowledge firmament. *Technological Forecasting and Social Change, 123*, 122–129. doi:10.1016/j.techfore.2016.04.026

EU. (2016). *CORK 2.0 DECLARATION "A Better Life in Rural Areas"*. Retrieved from https://enrd.ec.europa.eu/sites/enrd/files/cork-declaration_en.pdf

Fhlatharta, A. M. N., & Farrell, M. (2017). Unravelling the strands of 'patriarchy' in rural innovation: A study of female innovators and their contribution to rural Connemara. *Journal of Rural Studies, 54*, 15–27. doi:10.1016/j.jrurstud.2017.05.002

Fink, M., Loidl, S., & Lang, R. (2012). *Community-based entrepreneurship and rural development Creating favourable conditions for small businesses in central Europe*. Routledge Taylor & Francis Group. doi:10.4324/9780203108116

Fortunato, M. W.-P. (2014). Supporting rural entrepreneurship: A review of conceptual developments from research to practice. *Community Development (Columbus, Ohio), 45*(4), 387–408. doi:10.1080/15575330.2014.935795

Freedman, D. A. (2009). *Statistical Models: Theory and Practise*. Cambridge University Press. doi:10.1017/CBO9780511815867

Fritsch, M. (2008). How does new business formation affect regional development? Introduction to the special issue. *Small Business Economics, 30*(1), 1–14. doi:10.100711187-007-9057-y

Fritsch, M. (2011). The role of new business in regional development: introduction and overview. In M. Fritsch (Ed.), *Handbook of research on entrepreneurship and regional development* (pp. 1–10). Edward Elgar Publishing Limited. doi:10.4337/9780857936493.00005

Fuster, E., Padilla-Meléndez, A., Lockett, N., & del-Águila-Obra, A. R. (2019). The emerging role of university spin-off companies in developing regional entrepreneurial university ecosystems: The case of Andalusia. *Technological Forecasting and Social Change, 141*, 219–231. doi:10.1016/j.techfore.2018.10.020

Glaeser, E. L., Ponzetto, G. A. M., & Tobio, K. (2014). Cities, Skills and Regional Change. *Regional Studies, 48*(1), 7–43. doi:10.1080/00343404.2012.674637

Grimaldi, R., & Grandi, A. (2005). Business incubators and new venture creation: An assessment of incubating models. *Technovation, 25*(2), 111–121. doi:10.1016/S0166-4972(03)00076-2

Guerrero, M., Urbano, D., Fayolle, A., Klofsten, M., & Mian, S. (2016). Entrepreneurial universities: Emerging models in the new social and economic landscape. *Small Business Economics, 47*(3), 551–563. doi:10.100711187-016-9755-4

Harpa, E. (2017). Macroeconomic Analysis of the Competitive Factors which Influence Innovation in Rural Entrepreneurship. *Procedia Engineering, 181*, 965–968. doi:10.1016/j.proeng.2017.02.494

Henry, C., & McElwee, G. (2014). Defining and Conceptualising Rural Enterprise. In C. Henry & G. McElwee (Eds.), *Exploring Rural Enterprise: New Perspectives on Research, Policy and Practice* (pp. 1–8). Emerald Group Publishing Limited. doi:10.1108/S2040-724620140000004001

Hormiga, E., de Saá-Pérez, P., Díaz-Díaz, N. L., Ballesteros-Rodríguez, J. L., & Aguiar-Diaz, I. (2017). The influence of entrepreneurial orientation on the performance of academic research groups: The mediating role of knowledge sharing. *The Journal of Technology Transfer, 42*(1), 10–32. doi:10.100710961-015-9463-2

Investopedia. (2019). *Research and Development (R&D).* Retrieved from https://www.investopedia.com/terms/r/randd.asp

Korsgaard, S., Müller, S., & Tanvig, H. W. (2015). Rural entrepreneurship or entrepreneurship in the rural - between place and space. *International Journal of Entrepreneurial Behaviour & Research, 21*(1), 5–26. doi:10.1108/IJEBR-11-2013-0205

Lampadarios, E., Kyriakidou, N., & Smith, G. (2017). Towards a new framework for SMEs success: A literature review. *International Journal of Business and Globalisation, 18*(2), 194–232. doi:10.1504/IJBG.2017.081954

Lee, H., Kelley, D., Lee, J., & Lee, S. (2012). SME survival: The impact of internationalization, technology resources, and alliances. *Journal of Small Business Management, 50*(1), 1–19. doi:10.1111/j.1540-627X.2011.00341.x

Malerba, F., & McKelvey, M. (2020). Knowledge-intensive innovative entrepreneurship integrating Schumpeter, evolutionary economics, and innovation systems. *Small Business Economics, 54*(2), 503–522. doi:10.100711187-018-0060-2

MAMAOT. (2012). *Programa Rede Rural Nacional*. MAMAOT.

Mas-Verdú, F., Ortiz-Miranda, D., & García-Álvarez-Coque, J. M. (2016). Examining organizational innovations in different regional settings. *Journal of Business Research*, *69*(11), 5324–5329. doi:10.1016/j.jbusres.2016.04.132

McElwee, G., & Smith, R. (2014). Researching rural enterprise. In A. Fayolle (Ed.), *Handbook of Research on Entrepreneurship* (pp. 307–334). Edward Elgar.

Mian, S. (2011). University's involvement in technology business incubation: what theory and practice tell us? *International Journal of Entrepreneurship and Innovation Management, 13*(2), 113-121.

Mian, S. (2016). Business Incubations and Incubator Mechanisms. In P. Phan, S. Mian, & L. Wadid (Eds.), *Technology Entrepreneurship And Business Incubation: Theory, Practice, Lessons learned* (pp. 1–34). Imperal College Press. doi:10.1142/9781783269778_0001

Moreira, A. C. (2015). Entrepreneurial Tourism: The cration of business opportunities in the Adrimag Region, Portugal. In L. Carvalho (Ed.), *Handobook of Research on Entrepreneurial Sucess and its impact on Regional Development* (pp. 376–404). IGI Global.

Müller, S. (2013). *Entrepreneurship and Regional Development: On the interplay between agency and context* (PhD thesis). Department of Business Administration, Aarhus University, Aarhus.

Müller, S. (2016). A progress review of entrepreneurship and regional development: What are the remaining gaps? *European Planning Studies*, *24*(6), 1133–1158. doi:10.1080/09654313.2016.1154506

Muñoz, P., & Kimmitt, J. (2019). Rural entrepreneurship in place: An integrated framework. *Entrepreneurship and Regional Development*, 1–32. doi:10.1080/08985626.2019.1609593

Nacu, C. M., & Avasilcai, S. (2014). Technological Ecopreneurship: Conceptual Approaches. *Procedia: Social and Behavioral Sciences*, *124*, 229–235. doi:10.1016/j.sbspro.2014.02.481

Nijkamp, P. (2009). *Entrepreneurship, development, and the spatial context*. Retrieved from Helsinki: Nulty, D. D. (2008). The adequacy of response rates to online and paper surveys: what can be done? *Assessment & Evaluation in Higher Education*, *33*(3), 301–314.

Parrino, L. (2015). Coworking: Assessing the role of proximity in knowledge exchange. *Knowledge Management Research and Practice*, *13*(3), 261–271. doi:10.1057/kmrp.2013.47

Pato, L., & Teixeira, A. A. C. (2016). Twenty years of rural entrepreneurship: A bibliometric survey. *Sociologia Ruralis*, *56*(1), 3–28. doi:10.1111oru.12058

Pato, L., & Teixeira, A. A. C. (2018). Rural Entrepreneurship: the Tale of a Rare Event. *Journal os Place Management and Development, 11*(1), 46-59.

Pato, L., & Teixeira, A. A. C. (2019a). Are New Rural Ventures Different from New Urban Ones? *Journal of Entrepreneurship and Public Policy*.

Pato, L., & Teixeira, A. A. C. (2019b). Determinants of performance of new ventures located in portuguese incubators and science parks with a focus on institutional factors. Do rural and urban new ventures differ? *European Planning Studies*.

Pfeilstetter, R. (2013). Entrepreneurship and regional development in Europe: A comparative, socio-anthropological case study in Germany and Spain. *Anthropological Notebooks*, *19*(1), 45–57.

Phan, P. H., Siegel, D. S., & Wright, M. (2005). Science parks and incubators: Observations, synthesis and future research. *Journal of Business Venturing*, *20*(2), 165–182. doi:10.1016/j.jbusvent.2003.12.001

Pugh, R., Lamine, W., Jack, S., & Hamilton, E. (2018). The entrepreneurial university and the region: What role for entrepreneurship departments? *European Planning Studies*, *26*(9), 1835–1855. doi:10.1080/09654313.2018.1447551

QS. (2020). *Universities in Portugal*. Retrieved from https://www.topuniversities.com/where-to-study/europe/portugal/guide

Ratinho, T., & Henriques, E. (2010). The role of science parks and business incubators in converging countries: Evidence from Portugal. *Technovation*, *30*(4), 278–290. doi:10.1016/j.technovation.2009.09.002

Ring, J. K., Peredo, A. M., & Chrisman, J. J. (2010). Business Networks and Economic Development in Rural Communities in the United States. *Entrepreneurship Theory and Practice*, *34*(1), 171–195. doi:10.1111/j.1540-6520.2009.00307.x

Roig-Tierno, N., Alcázar, J., & Ribeiro-Navarrete, S. (2016). Use of infrastructures to support innovative entrepreneurship and business growth. *Journal of Business Research*, *68*(11), 2290–2294. doi:10.1016/j.jbusres.2015.06.013

Saeed, S., Yousafzai, S. Y., Yani-De-Soriano, M., & Muffatto, M. (2015). The Role of Perceived University Support in the Formation of Students' Entrepreneurial Intention. *Small Business Management*, *53*(4), 1127–1145. doi:10.1111/jsbm.12090

Smallbone, D. (2009). Fostering entrepreneurship in rural areas. In J. Potter & A. Hofer (Eds.), *Strengthening entrepreneurship development in East Germany: lessons from local approaches* (pp. 161–187). OECD.

Spigel, B. (2017). The Relational Organization of Entrepreneurial Ecosystems. *Entrepreneurship Theory and Practice*, *41*(1), 49–72. doi:10.1111/etap.12167

Stam, E. (2015). Entrepreneurial Ecosystems and Regional Policy: A Sympathetic Critique. *European Planning Studies*, *23*(9), 1759–1769. doi:10.1080/09654313.2015.1061484

Stathopoulou, S., Psaltopoulos, D., & Skuras, D. (2004). Rural entrepreneurship in Europe. A research framework and agenda. *International Journal of Entrepreneurial Behaviour & Research*, *10*(6), 404–425. doi:10.1108/13552550410564725

Storey, C., Cankurtaran, P., Papastathopoulou, P., & Hultink, E. J. (2016). Success factors for service innovation: A meta-analysis. *Journal of Product Innovation Management*, *33*(5), 527–548. doi:10.1111/jpim.12307

Stough, R. R. (2016). Entrepreneurship and Regional Economic Development: Some reflections. *Investigaciones Regionales – Journal of Regional Research, 36*, 129-150.

Strano, A., Hudson, T., Redman, M., Hegarty, M., O'Hara, E., Buffet, C., ... Gardner, S. (2012). EU Rural Review Rural Entrepreneurship. *European Union.*

Teirlinck, P. (2017). Configurations of strategic R&D decisions and financial performance in small-sized and medium-sized firms. *Journal of Business Research*, *74*, 55–65. doi:10.1016/j.jbusres.2017.01.008

Teixeira, A. A. C. (2017). The economic performance of Portuguese Academic Spin-offs: do Science & Technology infrastructures and support matter? In R. Fini & R. Grimaldi (Eds.), Process Approach to Academic Entrepreneurship: Evidence from the Globe (Vol. 11.1). World Scientific Reference on Entrepreneurship. doi:10.1142/9789813220621_0011

Trettin, L., & Welter, F. (2011). Challenges for spatially oriented entrepreneurship research. *Entrepreneurship and Regional Development*, *23*(7-8), 575–602. doi:10.1080/08985621003792988

UNESCO. (2017). *Science Policy and Capacity-Building*. Retrieved from http://www.unesco.org/new/en/natural-sciences/science-technology/university-industry-partnerships/science-and-technology-park-governance/concept-and-definition/

Ven, A. H. V., & Johnson, P. E. (2006). Knowledge for theory and practise. *Academy of Management Review*, *31*(4), 802–821. doi:10.5465/amr.2006.22527385

Welter, F. (2011). Contextualizing Entrepreneurship—Conceptual Challenges and Ways Forward. *Entrepreneurship Theory and Practice*, *35*(1), 165–184. doi:10.1111/j.1540-6520.2010.00427.x

Welter, F., & Smallbone, D. (2011). Institutional Perspectives on Entrepreneurial Behavior in Challenging Environments. *Journal of Small Business Management*, *49*(1), 107–125. doi:10.1111/j.1540-627X.2010.00317.x

Zahra, S. A., Wright, M., & Abdelgawad, S. G. (2014). Contextualization and the advancement of entrepreneurship research. *International Small Business Journal*, *32*(5), 479–500. doi:10.1177/0266242613519807

ADDITIONAL READING

Fortunato, M. W.-P. (2014). Supporting rural entrepreneurship: A review of conceptual developments from research to practice. *Community Development (Columbus, Ohio)*, *45*(4), 387–408. doi:10.1080/15575330.2014.935795

Harpa, E. (2017). Macroeconomic Analysis of the Competitive Factors which Influence Innovation in Rural Entrepreneurship. *Procedia Engineering*, *181*, 965–968. doi:10.1016/j.proeng.2017.02.494

Muñoz, P., & Kimmitt, J. (2019). Rural entrepreneurship in place: An integrated framework. *Entrepreneurship and Regional Development*, 1–32. doi:10.1080/08985626.2019.1609593

Pato, L., & Teixeira, A. A. C. (2016). Twenty years of rural entrepreneurship: A bibliometric survey. *Sociologia Ruralis*, *56*(1), 3–28. doi:10.1111oru.12058

Pato, L., & Teixeira, A. A. C. (2019). Are New Rural Ventures Different from New Urban Ones? An Exploratory Analysis of Businesses Located in Portuguese Incubators and Science Parks. *Journal of Entrepreneurship and Public Policy*, *8*(4), 470–482. doi:10.1108/JEPP-08-2019-113

Pato, L., & Teixeira, A. A. C. (2020). Determinants of performance of new ventures located in portuguese incubators and science parks with a focus on institutional factors. Do rural and urban new ventures differ? *European Planning Studies*, *28*(8), 1619–1638. doi:10.1080/09654313.2019.1694866

Ratinho, T., & Henriques, E. (2010). The role of science parks and business incubators in converging countries: Evidence from Portugal. *Technovation*, *30*(4), 278–290. doi:10.1016/j.technovation.2009.09.002

Teixeira, A. A. C. (2017). The economic performance of Portuguese Academic Spin-offs: do Science & Technology infrastructures and support matter? In R. Fini & R. Grimaldi (Eds.), Process Approach to Academic Entrepreneurship: Evidence from the Globe (Vol. 11.1): Series: World Scientific Reference on Entrepreneurship. doi:10.1142/9789813220621_0011

KEY TERMS AND DEFINITIONS

Business Incubators: Is a corporation that helps start-up companies to develop by providing services such as training or office space.

Entrepreneurship: New venture creation.

Performance: Measure by turnover and exports in this study, it is an indicator of success of ventures.

Rural: A municipality is considered rural if the share of population living in rural parishes (with less of 150 inhabitants per square kilometer) is higher than 50% or between 15 and 50%.

Science Parks: Is a corporation more supported on regional development by supporting young technology-based ventures as well as attracting anchor ventures to a given location.

Technological-Related Factors Support: Include the support of universities, business incubators/ science parks and collaboration and research and development.

Urban: A municipality is considered urban if the share of population living in rural parishes (with more of 150 inhabitants per square kilometer) is below 15%.

Chapter 2
The Role of Digital Technology in Rural Entrepreneurship and Innovations

Dinithi U. Abeysinghe
Swinburne University of Technology, Australia

Mohsin Malik
Swinburne University of Technology, Australia

ABSTRACT

Rural entrepreneurship paves the way to solve issues faced by rural population by spurring economic development in the rural areas. However, the entrepreneurial ventures within the rural areas also face a number of issues in initiating new ventures. The advancement of the digital technologies, technological platforms, and digital artifacts may provide a solution for such issues faced by the rural entrepreneurs. This chapter aims to explain how digital technologies assist rural entrepreneurs in overcoming the problems they face. In addressing this problem, the chapter will provide a broader understanding of the rural entrepreneurship and the issues it faces. The solutions for these issues are then discussed by highlighting the role of digital technology in supporting entrepreneurial ventures. Finally, a conceptual framework depicting the drivers of rural digital entrepreneurship is presented.

INTRODUCTION

The variations in the entrepreneurial activity across urban and rural economies have been observed by the entrepreneurship scholars over a period of time. This has provided the premise for understanding the entrepreneurial processes based on the various context it operates in (Lang, Fink, & Kibler, 2014). Additionally, the governments of developing countries have come to the realization that no development will be meaningful if the rural communities are not carried along (Nwankwo & Okeke, 2017). Rural entrepreneurship and rural innovation have assumed greater importance because of these factors.

DOI: 10.4018/978-1-7998-4942-1.ch002

The term rural usually reflects sparsely populated land and the rural communities generally face significant challenges in carrying out their day to day activities. According to the United States Census Bureau (2017), rural areas are 'areas with low population densities situated away from the urban areas.' The challenges faced by the rural communities include low income, low productivity, high degree of unemployment, low population rate, poor technological growth, low infrastructures, high illiteracy rate, malnutrition etc. (Nwankwo & Okeke, 2017). These challenges maybe overcome by rural entrepreneurship which is likely to spur the economic growth in rural communities (Sathya, 2019).

The process of entrepreneurship is supported by a number of underlying factors such as change management, innovation, technological and environmental turbulence, new product development, small business management, individualism and industry evolution (Murray & MacMillan, 1988). Entrepreneurship is defined as the process of innovating, risk taking, integrating resources in a unique way to satisfy an identified opportunity by taking the risks attached to it through the introduction of a new phenomenon or changing the existing nature or a phenomenon (Schumpeter, 1934; Hisrich, Langan-Fox, & Grant, 2007; Newman, Obschonka, Schwarz, Michael, & Nielsen, 2019). Rural entrepreneurship denotes the entrepreneurial activity that takes place in large open spaces and small population settlements (Korsgaard, Muller, & Tanvig, 2015). Rural entrepreneurship is formally defined as the entrepreneurial activity that is emerging at village level, taking place in a number of industries such as agriculture, tourism etc. and acts as a potential factor for overall economic development (Sathya, 2019). The increasing entrepreneurial capacity and capability of the rural areas has been identified as a way of addressing the economic development constraints and the underperformance in rural areas (Jordaan, Alderson, Warren-Smith, & Lehmann, 2003; Atherton, 2004; McElwee & Atherton, 2011).

Rural entrepreneurship faces a number of barriers such as inadequate resources (human, financial, knowledge), unavailability of infrastructure facilities, low access to markets etc. in conducting its operations. Digitalization or the use of technologies has provided opportunities for growth to entrepreneurs in general (Lekhanya, 2018; Raisanen & Tuovinen, 2020). Such technological capabilities may also allow the rural entrepreneurial ventures to innovate making them more competitive (Madrid-Guijarro *et al.*, 2009 cited in Kotey & Sorensen, 2014). The diffusion of technology in today's world and the ability of the rural population to access this technology has opened new avenues for rural entrepreneurship. For example, the rural entrepreneurs now can access new markets through e-commerce platforms, use technology to enhance communication between the suppliers and the customers, leverage financial technologies and gain new skills through educational services applications. All these allow the rural enterprises to act as large as the urban enterprises etc. at low costs, low experimental processes and low risks. Despite the potential, the rural entrepreneurship phenomenon has not fully exploited the opportunities provided by digital technologies. This chapter aims to explicate how rural entrepreneurship can effectively harness digital technologies to create social and economic value. Following are the three specific objectives of this chapter:

1. To provide a broader understanding of the concept of rural entrepreneurship and how the theories of entrepreneurship explain the concept of rural entrepreneurship.
2. To identify the issues being faced by entrepreneurs in rural environments.
3. To understand how technology may provide opportunities for rural entrepreneurs to resolve entrepreneurial challenges associated with a rural context.

To achieve the above three objectives, this chapter first provides the background of the study by defining the concept of rural entrepreneurship. The theoretical frameworks that can help explain the process of rural entrepreneurship are also reviewed in the background section. The background section also describes the issues faced by the rural entrepreneurs and aims to provide solutions by adopting technology as a means of overcoming the identified barriers. Finally, this study develops a conceptual framework to explain what factors drive rural digital entrepreneurship.

This study uses literature review as the research methodology. Scholarly works such as journal articles, book chapters and conference proceeding on various aspects of rural and rural entrepreneurship have been used to achieve the research objective of this chapter.

BACKGROUND

Defining Rural, Rural Entrepreneurship and Innovations in the Rural

The rural context implies large areas of land which are occupied by low population and situated far from urban centers. The rural economy is dominated largely by farming and farming related activities because of the high availability of the land resource. Looking at the definitions from the literature, rural areas are looked upon as open swath of lands with fewer buildings and homes with low population density (Rutledge, et al., 2011). These are areas which are sparsely populated, have low housing density and are situated far from urban centers (United States Census Bureau, 2017). In the United States, rural areas account for 97% of land mass with only 19.3% of population living in these lands (United States Census Bureau, 2017). In other words, what is left after excluding urban areas are called as rural areas (Ratcliffe, Burd, Holder, & Fields, 2016). In Europe, areas are classified as rural if the population densities are as low as 150 inhabitants per square kilometer and if that area does not contain a major urban center (OECD, 2011). Apart from the low population densities and availability of open swaths of lands, there are other characteristics of rural areas such as high unemployment rates, less developed infrastructures, malnutrition, low income etc. (Nwankwo & Okeke, 2017; Sathya, 2019). Rural areas, however, also display significant strengths both socially and economically through expansive housing, good labor relations, lower wages, lower rental and premises costs and greater space for business expansion (McElwee & Atherton, 2011) which would attract entrepreneurial opportunities within the rural.

Entrepreneurs are identified as innovators who bring about change within the markets through integrating new combinations in several forms such as introducing new methods, new production techniques, initiating new markets, conquest of new sources of supply of new materials and parts and setting up new businesses in any industry (Schumpeter, 1934). The concept of economic entrepreneurship has evolved to include newness or novelty, creating, organizing, risk taking and wealth generation (Hisrich, Langan-Fox, & Grant, 2007). The literature formally defines entrepreneurship as the process of discovery, evaluation and exploitation of opportunities to produce goods and services (Newman, Obschonka, Schwarz, Michael, & Nielsen, 2019).

Entrepreneurship plays a major role in solving the problems of poverty, unemployment and backwardness in rural economies by supporting the rural economic development (Sathya, 2019). The literature identifies entrepreneurial capacity and capability within rural as a solution to the economic development constraints and under-performance in rural areas (McElwee & Atherton, 2011). The rural entrepreneurial space, however, may have limited opportunities and resources to innovate may be a question. The plausible reasons for this may include the turbulent business economies (McElwee & Atherton, 2011).

The term rural entrepreneurship is defined as all forms of entrepreneurship that take place in areas characterized by large open spaces and small population settlements relative to the national context (Kalantaridis & Bika, 2006 cited in Korsgaard, Muller, & Tanvig, 2015). The place and the entrepreneurial activity display an intimate relationship in the discussion of rural entrepreneurship (Korsgaard, Muller, & Tanvig, 2015). Furthermore, rural entrepreneurship is regarded as the emergence or establishment of entrepreneurial activities in rural areas (Lekhanya, 2018). The term rural entrepreneur, is defined as an individual who uses the resources of the regional economy in order to gain a competitive advantage by trading the goods and services which generate social and economic capital for the rural environment in which the entrepreneur is located (McElwee & Atherton, 2011). The rural businesses are defined as those that conduct a series of activities which are primarily dependent of the natural and physical resources of the rural environment, occupied on a part time or full-time basis as a main source of income and/or utilizes the local labor in achieving the business objectives (McElwee & Atherton, 2011).

Innovation can be regarded as a tool in addressing the structural problem of poverty in the rural communities (Habiyaremye, Kruss, & Booyens, 2019). Innovation is often used in studies as a substitute for the term's creativity, knowledge or change (Crossan & Apaydin, 2010). According to Crossan & Apaydin (2010) "innovation is the renewal and expansion of products, services and markets; development of new methods of production and creation of new management systems through production or adoption, integration and exploitation of a value-added novelty in economic and social spheres". An important relationship can be identified between the rural natural resources and innovations (Habiyaremye, Kruss, & Booyens, 2019). Many innovations in health, housing and transport has emerged as a response to the growing demand in the primary rural sectors for transporting goods to ports and cities (Mahroum, 2007). The innovations taking place in the rural indicates that the rural areas no longer tend to be dominated in the agricultural or farming production (Lekhanya, 2018; Habiyaremye, Kruss, & Booyens, 2019). The rural economic landscape increasingly mirrors urban economic activities (Lekhanya, 2018; Habiyaremye, Kruss, & Booyens, 2019).

The above discussion of rural entrepreneurship provides the understanding that despite an increase in rural entrepreneurial activities, the process of rural entrepreneurship is different to the perspective of entrepreneurship described in literature. Therefore, it is important to understand first the theoretical underpinnings of entrepreneurship which can then help explain the rural entrepreneurship. To derive this understanding, the rural entrepreneurial aspects will be evaluated by examining the key theories of entrepreneurship in the next subsection.

Theories of Entrepreneurship from a Viewpoint of Rural Entrepreneurship

Entrepreneurship in the rural areas faces several issues such as unstable economies, lack of resources, low access to markets and opportunities, less knowledge and skills in managing ventures etc. In assessing the concept of rural entrepreneurship, it is important to understand whether the theories that explain the entrepreneurship in general, also justify the constructs of rural entrepreneurship. An evaluation of rural entrepreneurship with the key theories of entrepreneurship will generate insights, regarding the constitute mechanism of rural entrepreneurship. There exists a number of theories which explain the characteristics of entrepreneurship. Following key theories are considered below to explain the rural entrepreneurship:

1. Innovation theory
2. Resource based theory
3. Opportunity based theory
4. Psychological entrepreneurship theory
5. Anthropological entrepreneurship theory

Innovation Theory

The theory of innovations, introduced by Joseph Schumpeter, states that an entrepreneur is basically an innovator who introduces new combinations (Sledzik, 2013). These new combinations are of five types; 1) Introduction of new goods 2) New methods of production 3) New markets 4) New source of supply of raw materials and 5) New organization if an industry (Sledzik, 2013). Further he argued that anyone seeking profits must innovate as it motivates the employment of the existing supplies of an economic system productively (Sledzik, 2013). Furthermore, he stated that innovation is a crucial driver for competitiveness and economic dynamics (Sledzik, 2013).

Rural entrepreneurship is a means of survival for poorer households, development of the locality and job creation for the unemployed (Lekhanya, 2018). Innovations support in utilizing the untapped resources within the rural and the benefits of it would encourage the rural entrepreneurs for innovation rather than catering to solve the problems within the locality. In innovation, a network of rural enterprises could be helpful in knowledge acquisition and rural development (Ring, Peredo, & Chrisman, 2010). Digital networking may be the answer in connecting the rural entrepreneurs for knowledge and information acquisition given the remoteness in rural areas. (Raisanen & Tuovinen, 2020). This would aid the rural entrepreneurs in identifying the gaps and untapped resources to create innovations. Also, innovations will support the rural enterprises in attracting investments for business expansions and increase the competitiveness.

Resource Based Theory

Availability of a unique set of resources is understood to be important in satisfying the identified opportunities (Nothnagel, 2008). In the rural context, it can be seen that the human resources and land exists in large numbers compared to the other resources such as financial resources, infrastructure etc.

The resource-based theory of entrepreneurship argues that an entrepreneur's access to resources is important in terms of capturing opportunities and the growth of new ventures (Nothnagel, 2008; Alvarez & Busenitz, 2001). A unique bundle of resources different from the competitors are potentially valuable and contributes to an enterprises' competitive advantage (Alvarez & Busenitz, 2001; Sedera et al. 2016). It stresses on the importance of financial, social and human resources which would enhance an individual's ability to detect and react on an identified opportunity (Davidson & Honing, 2003 cited in Simpeh, 2011). This theory is further elaborated using the three theories; financial capital/ liquidity theory, social capital/ social network theory and human capital entrepreneurship theory.

Conferring to the financial capital/ liquidity theory, the entrepreneurs with adequate financial capital could acquire resources for effective exploitation of the identified entrepreneurial opportunities and create ventures in catering to these opportunities (Clausen, 2006 cited in Simpeh, 2011). The social capital or social network theory explains that a larger social network structure enables the entrepreneurs to transform an opportunity into a business start-up (Shane & Eckhardt, 2003 cited in Simpeh, 2011). Furthermore, the stronger the social ties with the resource facilitators, the easier the acquiring of resources become, enabling the entrepreneurs to exploit the opportunities (Aldrich & Zimmers, 1986 cited in Simpeh, 2011). The human capital entrepreneurship theory focuses on the two factors, education and experience (Becker, 1975 cited in Simpeh, 2011). The knowledge gained from education and experience is considered to be a resource that helps identify the opportunities and exploit them (Simpeh, 2011).

The rural entrepreneurs face several resource deficiencies. In terms of finance, the ability to get external funds through credit and tangible security is a barrier and thereby the rural entrepreneurs have very less risk bearing capacity (Lokuge and Sedera 2017; Sathya, 2019). The lack of infrastructure facilities despite the government effort to facilitate rural development, the marketing difficulties in coping with high competition due to the middlemen exploiting the rural entrepreneurs are problems to social networking. Thereby the entrepreneurs rely on internal linkages which encourages the flow of services, goods, ideas and information (Sathya, 2019). In terms of human capital, lack of knowledge on IT, low skills of the available human resources and the negative attitude towards entrepreneurship in the rural (Sathya, 2019; Sedera et al. 2001) shows the lack of experience and knowledge on the entrepreneurial process within the rural community.

Opportunity Based Entrepreneurship Theory

The opportunity-based theory is one of the main discussions done by Peter Drucker and Howard Stevenson (Simpeh, 2011). According to Drucker's opportunity concept, the entrepreneurs have an eye for more possibilities created by change than the problems (Simpeh, 2011). According to Stevenson, the entrepreneurial management hub is the "pursuit of opportunity without regard to resources currently controlled" (Simpeh, 2011).

Farming being a main component in the rural environments, it is identified that in 2002, 58% of the farmers surveyed were involved in some form of diversified activity such as tourism, retail business etc. (Atterton & Ward, 2007). In 2003/4, the total taxable income of farmers came from non-agricultural activities which gives the idea that the farmers are no more solely food producers, but they are increasingly expected to innovate in response to the wider policy and economic change (Atterton & Ward, 2007). This example shows that the rural entrepreneurs too have seen opportunities outside the resources (agricultural lands) they hold and has been able to satisfy the identified opportunities. Furthermore, the adoption of digital innovations brings around several opportunities due to the low costs and the reduced risks attached with it (Raisanen & Tuovinen, 2020). This will create several openings either be to the agriculture or non-agricultural enterprises.

Psychological Entrepreneurship Theory

The psychological entrepreneurship theory emphasises on the personal characteristics of an entrepreneur (Simpeh, 2011). This theory is further discussed by extending on three other theories; personality traits theory, locus of control and need for achievement theory.

The personality traits theory discusses on the inborn qualities or potentials of an individual that naturally makes him an entrepreneur (Simpeh, 2011). Locus of control refers to an individual's perception about the underlying reasons for the events in his/her life (Simpeh, 2011). The entrepreneur's success originates from his/her own abilities and support from outside where the former is referred to as the internal locus of control and the latter is referred to as the external locus of control (Simpeh, 2011). The theory of need for achievement introduced by McClelland, explains the need of humans to succeed, accomplish, excel or achieve (Simpeh, 2011; Dontigney, 2018). Entrepreneurs are driven by the need to achieve and excel (Simpeh, 2011). The achievement motivation may be the only convincing psychological factor related to new venture creation (Dontigney, 2018).

Rural entrepreneurs face several challenges in conducting their entrepreneurial ventures. Still they form ventures and create innovations with the prevailing resources. This shows the motivation of these individuals to achieve, which is mainly due to the benefits derived from these rural enterprises. As entrepreneurship is regarded as a way of overcoming the issues in the rural environments such as poverty, unemployment etc. (Lekhanya, 2018; Sathya, 2019) the rural entrepreneurs strive hard to utilize all possible skills and resources to gain the benefits derived from entrepreneurship which ultimately support in rural economic development.

Anthropological Theory

This theory focuses on the origin, development, customs and beliefs of a community. This theory further state that a venture is created based on one's own culture (Simpeh, 2011). The cultural practices are believed to lead to entrepreneurial attitudes such as innovation that also lead to venture creation behaviour (Baskerville, 2003).

The rural areas tend to be agricultural hubs due to the wide availability of land and a number of ventures were created basing the agricultural sector. However, looking at the present rural venture creations, agriculture which was 25% of primary income source in the 1970s now only represents 10% of the rural population (Ring, Peredo, & Chrisman, 2010). Even with the number of disadvantages within the rural, a high growth of ventures in the retail sector can be observed (Ring, Peredo, & Chrisman, 2010). Even though the anthropological theory states that venture creation is based on the cultural factors, it has proven to be otherwise in rural entrepreneurship.

The above evaluation of rural entrepreneurship in light of the theories of entrepreneurship, establish rural entrepreneurship as a distinct type of entrepreneurship. Furthermore, it has also been established that the rural entrepreneurs face several issues in creating their enterprises to exploit the identified opportunities. The inability to access the markets, lack of skills within the employees, inadequate infrastructure facilities, lack of resources; especially financial resources, which make them risk averse etc. are some of the issues faced by these entrepreneurs in conducting their enterprises (Kotey & Sorensen, 2014; Sathya, 2019). The new developments in the digital technologies, such as e-commerce platforms, cloud computing, 3D technologies, communication technologies, smart devices etc. it can be understood that these digital technologies may pave way in overcoming these issues risen within the rural entrepreneurial ventures.

BARRIERS TO RURAL ENTREPRENEURSHIP

When compared to the urban enterprises, the rural entrepreneurs face a number of issues such as lack of infrastructure, skill deficiency and low access to markets. This is due to the lack of facilities (infrastructure and the resources etc.) available in these areas for venture creations. Some of the issues faced by the rural entrepreneurs are listed below (Table 1):

Table 1. Barriers in rural environments

Barriers	References
Access to resources	(Kotey & Sorensen, 2014; Sathya, 2019)
Lack of infrastructure facilities	(Kotey & Sorensen, 2014; Sathya, 2019)
Low risk bearing capacity	(Kotey & Sorensen, 2014; Sathya, 2019)
Technical competency and managerial skills	(McElwee & Atherton, 2011; Kotey & Sorensen, 2014; Sathya, 2019)
Access to markets	(McElwee & Atherton, 2011; Kotey & Sorensen, 2014; Sathya, 2019)
Outmigration of skilled to the urban centers	(Movahedi & Yaghoubi-Farani, 2012; Sathya, 2019)
Economic and political conditions	(Kotey & Sorensen, 2014)
Low technology literacy	(Kotey & Sorensen, 2014)
Low social networks	(Kotey & Sorensen, 2014; Sathya, 2019)
Lack of government support	(Kotey & Sorensen, 2014)

Access to Resources

Compared to the urban entrepreneurs, the rural entrepreneurs face several issues in accessing resources that are required to innovate. Financial resources, and the required knowledge is seen to be lacking in the rural areas (Sathya, 2019; Kotey & Sorensen, 2014). Due to the unavailability of collaterals for financing and credit in the market, many rural entrepreneurs fail in receiving external funding (Sathya, 2019). The time taken in obtaining the loan facility from banks often disappoints the rural entrepreneurs (Sathya, 2019). The lack of educational facilities within the rural also limit the knowledge and awareness of individuals to engage in the entrepreneurial activities.

Lack of Infrastructure Facilities

The rural areas lack the basic infrastructure facilities such as proper roads, knowledge centers, technological facilities etc. Despite of the efforts made by the governments, the lack of adequate infrastructure facilities within the rural hinders the growth of the rural entrepreneurs (Sathya, 2019). This restricts the competitive ability of entrepreneurs and the long-term growth of the entrepreneurial ventures.

Low Risk Bearing Capacity

Even though an entrepreneur is regarded as a risk bearing individual, it is often seen that the rural entrepreneurs do not have the same risk bearing capacity as the urban entrepreneurs. This is mainly duc to the financial status of the rural entrepreneurs (Sathya, 2019). Low financial capabilities discourage the rural entrepreneurs in experimenting with innovations and adopting new techniques because of the fear of failure and the ensuing costs. This hampers their ability to innovate and compete among the emerging competitors of the markets.

Technical Competency and Managerial Skills

The low educational opportunities and the lack of exposure within the rural communities has limited the development of rural entrepreneurs when compared to the urban areas. The inability of rural entrepreneurs to implement entrepreneurial concepts within organizations has restricted the performance and the growth of these firms. Similarly, the deficiency of training facilities and other extensive services, creates a barrier in the development of rural entrepreneurship (Sathya, 2019).

Access to Markets

The remoteness to urban centers creates the issue of market access. Local rural markets are usually small and access to larger urban markets is required to scale up innovations (Kotey & Sorensen, 2014). Furthermore, low financial capitals of the rural entrepreneurs make it difficult to access remote urban markets. The inability to access markets restricts the information on the emerging trends and new market developments, resulting in less knowledge for innovations.

Outmigration of Skilled to The Urban

The people in the rural migrate to the urban areas for economic reasons (Movahedi & Yaghoubi-Farani, 2012). A number of skilled people migrate and settle in the urban areas leaving the low skilled older people behind. Due to this situation, the entrepreneurs in the rural are unable to employ workers with necessary skills. Consequently, extensive trainings need to be conducted for the available workers to adequately complete the job requirements, resulting in high costs and longer time in training (Sathya, 2019).

Economic and Political Conditions

The economic stability and the support of the government policies are important in conducting entrepreneurial processes. High interest rates on lending, need of securities for external financing and tough rules or policies in setting up a venture may discourage rural entrepreneurs. Absence of supportive economic and political policies for rural entrepreneurship discourage the rural entrepreneurs to innovate and adopt new methods for their enterprises.

Low Technology Literacy

Technology plays a vital role in the entrepreneurial process but the rural communities in general have low technology literacy. Information technology penetration is low within the rural areas (Sathya, 2019). Rural entrepreneurs' also face difficulties in adopting to digital technologies. For example, the rural entrepreneurs are unable to recruit tech savvy employees and find training resources for their existing force (Ismail, 2017). This restricts the rural entrepreneurs in making full use of technology in developing their entrepreneurial idea further.

Low Social Networks_

The rural entrepreneurs mainly depend on the facilities and connections within the locality. The lack of exposure to the outside world restricts access to information on new trends, markets, pricing strategies, technologies. Such information is critical to identify new business opportunities for the rural entrepreneurs. The disadvantage of using middlemen to access outside markets is that the rural entrepreneurs may become vulnerable to the 'middlemen'. The rural entrepreneurs have less knowledge on the pricing which allows the middlemen to make more profit (Sathya, 2019). The middleman channel restricts the profit margins which reduces the economic incentives for rural entrepreneurs.

Lack of Government Support

The rural businesses are the backbone for national economies (Lekhanya, 2018). Therefore, it is important to have institutional support and government policies in favor of rural entrepreneurial ventures to achieve economic development of a country. This would enable the rural ventures to operate efficiently and reduce their administrative costs (Lekhanya, 2018). In developing countries, the government's focus is more on the urban ventures than the rural ventures to formulate policies and resource allocation (Sechele, 2016). The developed countries seemed to have identified the importance of rural enterprises and its support to the economy (Nwankwo & Okeke, 2017).

The above factors give an understanding on the number of issues faced by the rural entrepreneurs. It is important to understand what mechanism would help the rural entrepreneurs overcome these barriers. It is suggested that businesses could take advantage of the available technological capabilities to innovate in order to survive, become competitive and grow (Madrid-Guijarro *et al.*, 2009 cited in Kotey & Sorensen, 2014).

SOLUTIONS AND RECOMMENDATIONS

Digital Technologies as a Panacea in Rural Entrepreneurship and Innovation

In this digital era, technology has provided new opportunities in driving innovation, improving productivity, stimulating economic growth as well as enhancing individual well-being and quality of life (OECD/European Union, 2019). Rural communities are usually remote and digital technologies may be an answer to the remoteness, as the internet services provide services and information that might not be otherwise possible to get in rural areas (Raisanen & Tuovinen, 2020). In terms of entrepreneurship, technology has given a substantial boost in entrepreneurship behaviours by the reduced costs of entry, resource availability and the low-cost experimentation (Nambisan, 2017; Satalkina & Steiner, 2020).

The introduction of new technologies, such as mobile computing, cloud computing, social media, 3D printing and data analytics has improved the ability of the entrepreneurs to resolve the uncertainty inherent in the entrepreneurial processes (Lokuge et al. 2019; Nambisan, 2017). The use of information technology has benefited the rural businesses by the creation of new jobs, increase in productivity and sales through access to new markets and administrative efficiencies (Qureshi, Kamal, & Good, 2008). These benefits will reduce the outmigration of young skilled workers as the jobs within the rural locality would match their expertise. Technology enables access to new markets outside the current locality providing opportunities to the rural entrepreneurs to scale up their innovations to bigger markets outside the locality. This would encourage them to innovate and identify potential opportunities within the new markets. E-business has been another driver for the rural entrepreneurs or small businesses to access new markets at reduced costs through administration efficiencies (Qureshi, Kamal, & Good, 2008).

The new technological developments have enabled the rural entrepreneurs to identify and adopt technological initiatives for their businesses. A consultation for over 800 businesses by Rural England and Scotland's Rural College (SRUC) found that four of five rural business owners believed digital tools and services were important to their future growth potential (Ismail, 2017). Rural business owners who export, plays an important role in adopting to technology as the export process chain mostly requires digital tools and services to trade goods and services with the global markets (Ismail, 2017). In Europe, the infrastructure improvements outside the large cities, including broadband access have facilitated higher growth for smaller businesses in rural areas (Dijkstra, Garcilazo, & McCann, 2013). It can be understood that borrowing size is not just limited to physical proximity between areas but on principal networks within regions through corporate relations, market pervasion and ICT networks (Vos, Lindgren, Ham, & Meijers, 2020).

Cloud computing has been recognised as a major driver, closely followed by 5G mobile networks, Internet of Things and machine learning/artificial intelligence (Ismail, 2017). Cloud computing provides compute power, storage, analytics, content delivery and other functionality to help rural entrepreneurs move faster, access lower IT costs and scale globally in minutes giving rise to innovations in businesses (Firdhous, Ghazali, & Hassan, 2013; Lokuge et al. 2016). This shows that the ability of rural businesses to quickly adapt to new technologies would determine their competitiveness.

The communication technology makes the entrepreneurial communication process more efficient. It enables the entrepreneurs to build connections with their suppliers, customer and all related parties in real time which enable them to make more informed decisions. The smartphone revolution which enabled easy access to several facilities has also helped the rural entrepreneurial process. In China, there were 829 million internet users by 2018 and out of which 27% accounted for internet users in the rural China (Nie, Ma, & Sousa-Poza, 2020). Apart from the advancement in mobile communication networks and smartphones, the commercial mobile applications too have contributed to the rural economic development (Nie, Ma, & Sousa-Poza, 2020). The smartphone applications have supported the rural entrepreneurship by facilitating financial, agricultural, health and educational services, enhancing agricultural production and marketing, stimulating job market participation, expanding social networks and reducing household exposure to risks (Okonkwo, Huisman, & Taylor, 2019). The potential of smartphone usage in facilitating the rural economic development shows that technology can help overcome the traditional challenges faced by the rural entrepreneurs.

The discussion so far shows that the technology provides opportunities for rural entrepreneurs to be more effective. It would allow the rural enterprises to act as large as the urban enterprises, enabling the rural enterprises to borrow size through the technological tools and services. However, the issues in adopting to digital tools and services goes beyond the availability and quality of supporting infrastructure (Ismail, 2017). The attitude towards IT adoption, computer self-efficacy and the individual innovativeness also determines the ability of rural entrepreneurs to utilize the technology infrastructure to their advantage. (Qureshi, Kamal, & Good, 2008; Raisanen & Tuovinen, 2020; Sedera and Lokuge 2017). The next section will elaborate the factors that gives rise to digital entrepreneurship within the rural areas.

Drivers of Rural Digital Entrepreneurship

The review of the relevant literature shows that the technology enables the rural entrepreneurs to overcome a number of issues that have traditionally restricted the growth of rural enterprises. The conceptual framework presented in Figure 1 brings together all relevant factors that facilitate the digital entrepreneurship in the rural.

Figure 1. Drivers of rural digital entrepreneurship

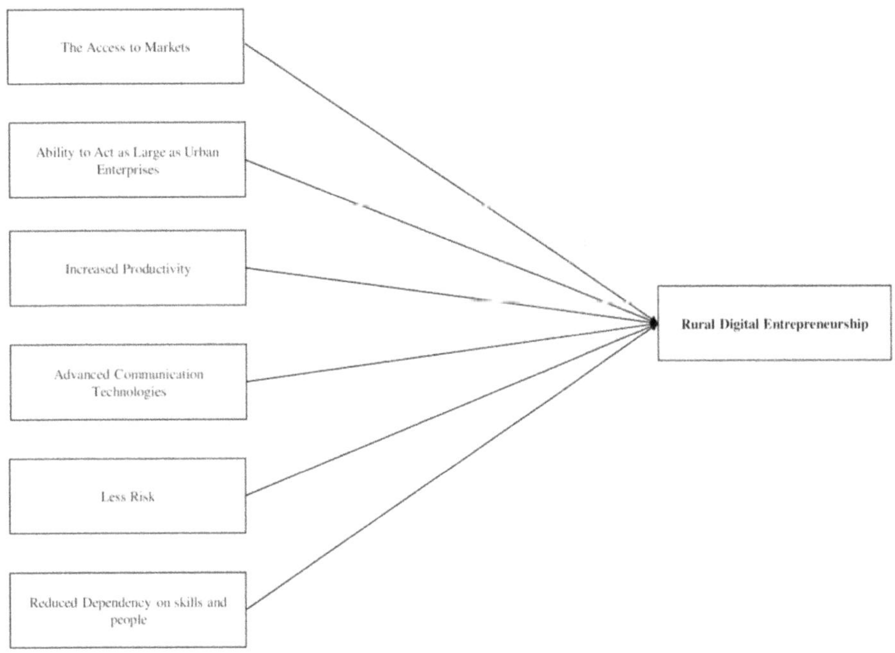

The Access to Markets

Technology provides the rural entrepreneurs with the ability to reach markets beyond the local area. The platforms such as e-commerce, enable the entrepreneurs to find suitable markets away from their business base. This provides opportunity to scale up their innovative products and services generating more economic benefits. The direct contacts with suppliers and customer through e-commerce platforms diminishes or eliminates the involvement of the middleman, therefore, improving the profit margins.

Ability to Act as Large as Urban Industries

The adoption of technologies by the rural enterprises enable the entrepreneurs to borrow size from the urban industries to reach markets, obtain financial support and manage the business processes in real time. This allows the rural enterprises to compete with the urban enterprises who tends to have access to bigger markets and a more skillful workforce.

Increased Productivity

Technological processes, applications, platforms and tools enable the entrepreneurs to be more productive. The various instant messaging apps and communication software enable the effective flow of information within the enterprises allowing the entrepreneurs to take informed decisions. The collaboration tools and software support the businesses to outsource the secondary business processes and conduct the core processes efficiently. Thus, enabling the entrepreneurs to gain more profits while achieving high productivity levels and reliability.

Advanced Communication Technologies

Being connected to one another and keeping up relationships can be done in real time with the current improvements in digital media and the introduction of smartphones. The smartphone has enabled the rural to reach out of the locality through the social media and other networking platforms which gives rise to more marketing options. The advanced communication technologies allow the entrepreneurs to get their tasks done while being in one location. The virtual platforms enable the entrepreneurs to keep track of their suppliers and customers, thus, increasing their social capital. The increased use of applications which aid in financing, health, education etc. provides the rural entrepreneurs with the ability to attract external investments and provide the training needed for employees at a reduced or zero cost.

Less Risk

The low investments needed and the free availability of technological platforms, facilitate the creation of innovations at low risks and costs. The assurance given by the wide use of technological platforms helps entrepreneurs to derive the risks and avoid them. The less need for experimentation, as these technologies are already tested, reduce the possible failures on the innovations. This enable the entrepreneurs to gain confidence in innovating through technological platforms and thus help in competing with the urban enterprises.

Reduced Dependency on Skills and People

With the development of technology, access to a wide range of learning materials have been made available through the internet. These learning materials can be in the form of courses, assessments/ exams, videos, e-books, podcasts or even in the form of quizzes. Users are able to expand their knowledge and skills by enrolling themselves for these e-learning materials completely free of charge or by paying a small amount as a subscription. With these developments, the dependency or the need for companies to allocate time and human resources for training and development has reduced.

Furthermore, with the evolution of technology, the business processes have become less people dependent since most of the processes are handled through systems like Enterprise Resource Planning. Although technical knowledge in handling these systems is very high, there are a wide variety of learning techniques available; often offered by the software companies itself.

FUTURE RESEARCH DIRECTIONS

This chapter is aimed at understanding rural entrepreneurship, the issues it faces and how digital technologies can help solve these issues. In this chapter, it was noted that the literature does not fully appreciate the distinctive characteristics of rural entrepreneurship. This provided the premise for this study that an in-depth and extensive analysis of rural entrepreneurship is needed. The future research on rural entrepreneurship should try to understand the cognitive underpinnings of the rural entrepreneurship and how the cognitions of rural entrepreneurs influence the adoption of technologies to support the rural enterprises. Furthermore, an investigation of how the rural entrepreneurs respond to unusual circumstances such as natural disasters would generate insights on what strategies entrepreneurs employ to survive challenging times.

The literature identifies entrepreneurs as individuals who adapt to the dynamic environment. The availability of resources and infrastructure facilitates the entrepreneurial ventures in the urban settings. How the scarcity of resources and poor infrastructure support in the rural areas affect rural entrepreneur's ability to respond to dynamic environment is not known. Therefore, a study to understand this shall inform both the literature and the practice.

CONCLUSION

Rural areas are open swaths of land with less population densities. These rural environments face a number of challenges such as unemployment, lack of infrastructure, poor living conditions etc. Rural entrepreneurship may provide opportunities to resolve these issues. However, being part of the rural economies, rural entrepreneurship also faces a number of similar issues. The findings outlined in the chapter illustrated the concept of rural entrepreneurship and how technology acts as a solution in overcoming the issues within rural environments.

In this chapter, rural entrepreneurship is discussed as entrepreneurial activities that are taking place in the rural areas. The theories of traditional entrepreneurship were applied to rural entrepreneurship to understand the challenges faced by the rural entrepreneurs. The improved understanding of the rural entrepreneurship enabled in identifying the solution to the barriers faced by the rural entrepreneurship. The issues faced by the rural entrepreneurs were also discussed in detail. Lack of access to resources, lack of infrastructure facilities, low risk bearing capacities, inadequate skills, less access to markets, outmigration of the skilled to the urban, lack of support from the economic and political environments, low technology literacy, low social networks, lack of government support were identified through the literature analysis. This study suggests that the adoption of digital technologies can help resolve these challenges. The benefits of accessing new markets, ability of networking, create innovations at lower costs, job creation and the ability to develop one's skills through the use of digital technologies can support the entrepreneurial activities within the rural areas. Furthermore, it would provide a new scope in creating innovations in the rural areas.

This study culminated in a conceptual framework to illustrate the drivers of rural digital entrepreneurship. In constructing the framework, the benefits of digital technologies on the rural entrepreneurial process were considered. The access to markets, ability to act as large as the urban enterprises, increased productivity, advanced communication technologies, less risk, reduced dependency on skills and people were conceptualized as the drivers of rural entrepreneurship. It was suggested that these factors would motivate the rural entrepreneurs in adopting digital technologies to develop and implement their entrepreneurial ideas.

REFERENCES

Alvarez, S. A., & Busenitz, L. W. (2001). The Entrepreneurship of Resource-Based Theory. *Journal of Management*, *27*(6), 755–775. doi:10.1177/014920630102700609

Atherton, A. (2004). Unbundling Enterprise and Entrepreneurship: From Perceptions and Preconceptions to Concept and Practice. *The International Journal of Entrepreneurship and Innovation*, *5*(2), 121–127. doi:10.5367/000000004773863273

Atterton, J., & Ward, N. (2007). Diversification and Innovation in Traditional Land-Based Industries. In S. Mahroum, J. Atterton, N. Ward, A. M. Williams, R. Naylor, R. Hindle, & F. Rowe (Eds.), Rural Innovation (pp. 12-23). NESTA.

Baskerville, R. F. (2003). Hofstede Never Studied Culture. *Accounting, Organizations and Society*, *28*(1), 1–14. doi:10.1016/S0361-3682(01)00048-4

Crossan, M. M., & Apaydin, M. (2010). A Multi-Dimensional Framework of Organizational Innovation: A systematic Review of the Literature. *Journal of Management Studies*, *47*(6), 1154–1191. doi:10.1111/j.1467-6486.2009.00880.x

Dijkstra, L., Garcilazo, E., & McCann, P. (2013). The economic Performance of European Cities and City Regions: Myths and Realities. *European Planning Studies*, *21*(3), 334–354. doi:10.1080/09654313.2012.716245

Dontigney, E. (2018, April 13). *What are the Theories of Entrepreneurship?* Retrieved August 1, 2020, from azcentral.: https://yourbusiness.azcentral.com/theories-entrepreneurship-23795.html

Firdhous, M., Ghazali, O., & Hassan, S. (2013). Cloud Computing for Rural ICT Development: Opportunities and Challenges. In *International Conference on Computing, Electrical and Electronic Engineering* (pp. 680-685). Khartoum: IEEE. 10.1109/ICCEEE.2013.6634022

Habiyaremye, A., Kruss, G., & Booyens, I. (2019). Innovation for Inclusive Rural Transformaton: The Role of the State. *Innovation and Development*, 1-14.

Henderson, J., Low, S. A., & Weiler, S. (2009). Drivers of Regional Entrepreneurship in Rural and Metro Areas. In N. Walzer (Ed.), *Entrepreneurship and Local Economic Development* (pp. 81–102). Rowman & Littlefield Publishers, Inc.

Hisrich, R., Langan-Fox, J., & Grant, S. (2007). Entrepreneurship Research and Practice: A call to Action for Psychology. *The American Psychologist*, *62*(6), 575–589. doi:10.1037/0003-066X.62.6.575 PMID:17874898

Ismail, N. (2017, December 11). *Rural Businesses See Digital Technology as Key to Growth but Face Skills and Training Barriers*. Retrieved August 9, 2020, from Information Age: https://www.information-age.com/rural-businesses-digital-technology-key-growth-123469962/

Jordaan, J., Alderson, M., Warren-Smith, I., & Lehmann, M. (2003). Enterprise Development in Rural Communities: Experiences and Preliminary Results on the Use of an Integrated Demonstration and Training Business. *13th Global Conference on Internationalizing Entrepreneurship Education and Training.*

Korsgaard, S., Muller, S., & Tanvig, H. W. (2015). Rural Entrepreneurship or Entrepreneurship in the Rural - Between Place and Space. *International Journal of Entrepreneurial Behaviour & Research, 21*(1), 5–26. doi:10.1108/IJEBR-11-2013-0205

Kotey, B., & Sorensen, A. (2014). Barriers to Small Business Innovation in Rural Australia. *Australian Journal of Regional Studies, 2*(3), 405–429.

Lang, R., Fink, M., & Kibler, E. (2014). Understanding Place-based Entrepreneurship in Rural Central Europe: A Comparative Institutional Analysis. *International Small Business Journal, 32*(2), 204–227. doi:10.1177/0266242613488614

Lekhanya, L. M. (2018). The digitalisation of Rural Entrepreneurship. In S. M. Brito (Ed.), Entrepreneurship - Trends and Challenges (pp. 36-63). Intech. doi:10.5772/intechopen.75925

Lokuge, S., & Sedera, D. (2017). Turning Dust to Gold: How to Increase Inimitability of Enterprise System. In *Pacific Asia Conference on Information Systems.* Langkawi, Malaysia: AIS.

Lokuge, S., Sedera, D., Atapattu, M., & Samaranayaka, D. (2016). Exploring the Role of IS in Agriculture: Creating an Agenda Towards Agri-Informatics. In *Pacific Asia Conference on Information Systems.* Chiyai, Taiwan: AIS.

Lokuge, S., Sedera, D., Grover, V., & Xu, D. (2019). Organizational Readiness for Digital Innovation: Development and Empirical Calibration of a Construct. *Information & Management, 56*(3), 445-461.

Mahroum, S. (2007). Overview: Rural Innovation. In S. Mahroum, J. Atterton, N. Ward, A. M. Williams, R. Naylor, R. Hindle, & F. Rowe (Eds.), *Rural Innovation* (pp. 4–11). NESTA.

McElwee, G., & Atherton, A. (2011). Rural Entrepreneurship. In L. P. Dana & L.-P. Dana (Eds.), *World Encyclopedia of Entrepreneurship* (pp. 377–384). Edward Elgar Publishing. doi:10.4337/9781849808453.00048

Meijers, E. J., & Burger, M. J. (2017). Stretching the Concept of 'Borrowed Size'. *Urban Studies (Edinburgh, Scotland), 54*(1), 269–291. doi:10.1177/0042098015597642

Movahedi, R., & Yaghoubi Farani, A. (2012). Analysis of the Barriers and Limitations for the Development of Rural Women's Entrepreneurship. *International Journal of Entrepreneurship and Small Business, 15*(4), 469–487. doi:10.1504/IJESB.2012.046476

Murray, L. B., & MacMillan, I. C. (1988). Entrepreneurship: Past Research and Future Challenges. *Journal of Management, 14*(2), 139–161. doi:10.1177/014920638801400202

Nambisan, S. (2017). Digital Entrepreneurship: Toward a Digital Technology Perspective of entrepreneurship. *Entrepreneurship Theory and Practice, 41*(6), 1029–1055. doi:10.1111/etap.12254

Newman, A., Obschonka, M., Schwarz, S., Michael, C., & Nielsen, I. (2019). Entrepreneurial Self-efficacy: A systematic Review of teh Literature on its Theoritical foundations, measurmenet, antecedents and outcomes and an agenda for future research. *Journal of Vocational Behavior, 110*, 403–419. doi:10.1016/j.jvb.2018.05.012

Nie, P., Ma, W., & Sousa-Poza, A. (2020). The Relationship between Smatrphone use and Subjective Well-being in Rural China. *Electronic Commerce Research*. Advance online publication. doi:10.100710660-020-09397-1

Nothnagel, K. (2008). The Central Proposition of Resource-based Theory. In K. Nothnagel (Ed.), Empirical Research within Resource-Based Theory (pp. 11-49). Gabler.

Nwankwo, F. O., & Okeke, C. S. (2017). Rural Entrepreneurship and Rural Development in Nigeria. *Africa's Public Service Delivery and Performance Review, 5*(1).

OECD. (2011, January 25). *OECD Rural Policy Reviews: England, United Kingdom 2011*. Paris: OECD Publishing.

OECD/European Union. (2019). What Potential Does Digital Entrepreneurship have for Being Inclusive. In *The Missing Entrepreneurs 2019: Policies for Inclusive Entrepreneurship* (pp. 177–218). OECD Publishing.

Okonkwo, C. W., Huisman, M., & Taylor, E. (2019). Socio-Economic Contributions of Mobile Applications in Africa: Impact of Local Mobile Applications. In *International Multidisciplinary Information Technology and Engineering Conference* (pp. 1-8). Vanderbijlpark, South Africa: IEEE. 10.1109/IMITEC45504.2019.9015912

Phelps, N. A., Fallon, R. J., & Williams, C. L. (2001). Small Firms, Borrowed Size and the Urban-Rural Shift. *Regional Studies, 35*(7), 613–624. doi:10.1080/00343400120075885

Qureshi, S., Kamal, M., & Good, T. (2008). *Adoption of Information by Micro-enterprises: Insights from a Rural Community*. AMCIS.

Raisanen, J., & Tuovinen, T. (2020). Digital Innovations in Rural Micro-Enterprises. *Journal of Rural Studies, 73*, 56–67. doi:10.1016/j.jrurstud.2019.09.010

Ratcliffe, M., Burd, C., Holder, K., & Fields, A. (2016, December 11). *Defining Rural at the US Census Bureau*. Retrieved July 12, 2020, from United States Census Bureau: https://www.census.gov/content/dam/Census/library/publications/2016/acs/acsgeo-1.pdf

Ring, J. K., Peredo, A. M., & Chrisman, J. J. (2010). Business Networks and Economic Development in Rural Communities in the United States. *Entrepreneurship Theory and Practice, 34*(1), 171–195. doi:10.1111/j.1540-6520.2009.00307.x

Rutledge, K., Ramroop, T., Boudreau, D., McDaniel, M., Teng, S., Sprout, E., . . . Hunt, J. (2011, August 6). *Resource Library*. Retrieved July 12, 2020, from National Geographic: https://www.nationalgeographic.org/encyclopedia/rural-area/

Satalkina, L., & Steiner, G. (2020). Digital Entrepreneurship and its Role in Innovation Systems: A Systematic Literature Review as a Basis for Future Research Avenues for Sustainable Transitions. *Sustainability, 12*(7), 27–64. doi:10.3390u12072764

Sathya, I. (2019). Rural Entrepreneurship in India. *Research & Exploration*, *5*(22), 7–12.

Schumpeter, J. A. (1934). *The Theory of Economic Development an Inquiry into Profits, Capital, Credit, Interest, and the Business cycle*. Transaction Publishers.

Sechele, L. (2016). Urban Bias, Economic Resource Allocation and National Development Planning in Botswana. *International Journal of Social Science Research*, 44-60.

Sedera, D., & Lokuge, S. (2017). The Role of Enterprise Systems in Innovation in the Contemporary Organization. In R. G. Galliers & M.-K. Stein (Eds.), *The Routledge Companion to Management Information Systems* (p. 608). The Routledge. doi:10.4324/9781315619361-21

Sedera, D., Lokuge, S., Grover, V., Sarker, S., & Sarker, S. (2016). Innovating with Enterprise Systems and Digital Platforms: A Contingent Resource-Based Theory View. *Information & Management, 53*(3), 366–379.

Sedera, D., Rosemann, M., & Gable, G. (2001). Using Performance Measurement Models for Benefit Realization with Enterprise Systems - the Queensland Government Approach. In *European Conference on Information Systems*. Bled, Slovenia: AIS.

Simpeh, K. N. (2011). Entrepreneurship Theories and Empirical Research: A summary Review of the Literature. *European Journal of Business and Management*, *3*(6), 1–8.

Sledzik, K. (2013). Schumpeter's View on Innovation and Entrepreneurship. In S. Hittmar (Ed.), Management Trends in Theory and Practice (pp. 89-95). Faculty of Management Science and Informatics, University of Zilina. doi:10.2139srn.2257783

United States Census Bureau. (2017, August 11). *What is Rural America?* Retrieved July 12, 2020, from United States Census Bureau: https://www.census.gov/library/stories/2017/08/rural-america.html

Vos, D. D., Lindgren, U., Ham, M. V., & Meijers, E. (2020). Does Broadband Internet Allows Cities to 'Borrow Size'? Evidence from the Swedish Labour Market. *Regional Studies*, *54*(9), 1175–1186. doi:10.1080/00343404.2019.1699238

ADDITIONAL READING

Cetindamar, D., Lammers, T., & Sick, N. (2018). Establishing Entrepreneurship Ecosystems Based on Digital Technologies: A Policy Roadmap Approach at the City Level. *Portland International Conference on Management of Engineering and Technology* (pp. 1-5). Honolulu: IEEE. 10.23919/PICMET.2018.8481849

Chen, P.-C., Chan, W.-C., Hung, S.-W., & Lin, D.-Z. (2019). How Entrepreneurs Recognise Entrepreneurial Opportunity and its Gaps: A Cognitive Theory Perspective. *Technology Analysis and Strategic Management*, 223–238.

Hisrich, R., Langan-Fox, J., & Grant, S. (2007). Entrepreneurship Research and Practice. *The American Psychologist*, *62*(6), 575–589. doi:10.1037/0003-066X.62.6.575 PMID:17874898

Livonen, S., Kyro, P., Mynttinen, S., Sarkka-Tirkkonen, M., & Kahiluoto, H. (2011). Social Capital and Entrepreneurial Behaviour Advancing Innovativeness in Interaction between Small Rural Entrepreneurs and Researchers: A Phenomenographic Study. *Journal of Agricultural Education and Extension*, *17*(1), 37–51. doi:10.1080/1389224X.2011.536348

Muller, S., & Korsgaard, S. (2018). Resources and Bridging: The Role of Spatial Context in Rural Entrepreneurship. *Entrepreneurship and Rural Development*, 224-255.

Nastase, C., & Lucaci, A. (2018). Rural Entrepreneurship in the Nordic Countries. USV Annals of Economic and Public Administration, 7-17.

Sanchez, M. S.-O., & Sanchez, M. R. (2017). Digital Technologies and Rural Women's Entrepreneurship. *Prisma Social*, 259–277.

Wamuyu, P. K. (2015). The Impact of Information and Communication Technology Adoption and Diffusion on Technology Entrepreneurship in Developing Countries: The Case of Kenya. *Information Technology for Development*, *21*(2), 253–280. doi:10.1080/02681102.2014.948372

KEY TERMS AND DEFINITIONS

Digital Technologies: Electronic artifacts, platforms, infrastructure that enable the storing and processing of data.

Entrepreneurship: The process of satisfying an opportunity identified by creating an innovative product or service by undertaking all risks attached with it.

Innovation: New concepts for existing or completely new products, services and ideas which are generated to satisfy an identified market need.

Rural: Areas with open swaths of land with less population and more issues in conducting one's lifestyles.

Rural Entrepreneurship: Entrepreneurial activities that take place in the rural areas which are conducted by individuals residing in the rural areas.

Rural Innovations: Novel concepts for existing or completely new products, services and ideas which are generated to satisfy an identified market need arising from the rural areas.

Rural Issues: Problems arising within the rural environmental context which disrupts the daily functioning of individuals.

Chapter 3
Contextual Factors for Rural Entrepreneurship and Innovation

Ruchi Khandelwal
https://orcid.org/0000-0002-5826-4573
Amity University, Noida, India

Ruchi Jain
Amity University, Noida, India

Deepa Kapoor
Amity University, Noida, India

ABSTRACT

Innovation and entrepreneurship are intertwined as entrepreneurs seek opportunities and innovations are the instruments that make them successful. Entrepreneurship and innovation are not constricted to the initial stages of a new venture alone and these are invincible processes that can lead to growth and sustainability of business in the dynamic environment. Rural entrepreneurship can be regarded as risk-taking behavior appropriate to opportunity, as well as to mobilize human, material, and financial resources in order to fulfill innovative projects in rural areas. There are multifaceted issues associated with the growth of rural entrepreneurs which need intervention by various political, economic, and social organizations. This chapter attempts to highlight specific contextual factors for rural entrepreneurship and innovation.

INTRODUCTION

Entrepreneurship has acquired a wide variety of meanings, with due credit to entrepreneurial researchers and the contexts in which research has been carried out (Nanni, 2019). The world around us is neither new to the word entrepreneurship nor unknown of the various areas to which this label has been ascribed.

DOI: 10.4018/978-1-7998-4942-1.ch003

Before addressing other pertinent issues, it's important to briefly examine the sense of the word entrepreneurship. 'Entrepreneurship' has its origins in German and French where it connotes, 'to undertake'. The earlier theorists on entrepreneurship namely Say (1800) and Mill (1848), defined the concept from economic sense as the entrepreneur identifies opportunity, take risks and uses resources for superior productivity and more yield (Nanni, 2019). However, entrepreneurship was leveraged into capitalist societies thorough the works of Schumpeter, 1934 (Shane and Venkatraman, 2000).

More recent researches have added more weight to the term as well as to its application. Several perspectives on entrepreneurship have been identified namely creation of wealth, forming of enterprise, design of innovation, conception of change, generation of employment, creation of value, and foundation of growth (Drucker, 1985; Gartner, 1990; Morris et al., 1994; Amit and Zott, 2001, George and Zahra, 2002). A lot of research finds overlap in these identified perspectives of entrepreneurship and these are innovation, creation of organizations/employment, creation of value, and foundation of growth (Nanni, 2019). However, Slevin and Kovin (1990) posited entrepreneurship as organizational behavior that is related to change and innovation having an appropriate culture and structure to breed and support innovation.

Entrepreneurship is increasingly recognized as an important driver of economic growth, productivity, innovation, and job creation, and as a key aspect of economic dynamism (Karimi, 2015). Over the years the studies of entrepreneurship have been confined to large scale businesses and industry, and to small scale industrial sector. Of late, this phenomenon percolated to artisans and farmers, the two major forces of rural transformation (Sharma, Vandana, Rajni, & Ranchan, 2013).

Entrepreneurship is considered as a strategic development intervention that could speed up the process of rural development. Increase in entrepreneurship in rural areas will lead to balanced regional growth, increase in overall per capita income, equitable distribution of power, reduce the migration of rural population to urban areas, improve literacy rate of rural population and lead to overall improvement in the standard of living.

Rural areas are disadvantaged in some ways compared to the urban areas; there is a huge difference in the economic performance between these regions (Smallbone, 2009). The challenges faced by rural entrepreneurs are paucity of funds, lack of adequate infrastructure facilities in terms of transportation, warehousing and electricity; unavailability of information and communication technologies, skilled human resources and technology (Desai, 2007; Larson & Shaw, 2001; Stathopoulou et al., 2004). According to Sundar and Srinivasa (2009) managerial inadequacies is one of the crucial reasons for the failures in decentralized industrial sector in rural scenario. It is observed that entrepreneurship in rural areas is hindered by access to finance, technology, information and marketing. The development of rural entrepreneurs is a complex problem which can be tackled by the social, political and economic institutions. The sooner various stakeholders realize this fact and considers entrepreneurship as a development strategy the better will be rural development.

One of key solution for bringing change in the lives of people in rural areas is useful inventions. This study primarily focuses on the conceptual foundations of innovation as an essence for entrepreneurship. It further establishes the factors which are anticipated to be present in the entrepreneurs to transform the innovative approach or idea in form of products and commercial solutions with perseverance. While doing so, the macrosystem of rural setup may pose various challenges due to inherent structure and various other factors deeply rooted in the Indian ecosystem. Thus, study also highlights those challenges and further concludes with live examples of rural innovations offering solutions to recurring problems posed by these impediments in rural India.

IMPEDIMENTS OF RURAL ENTREPRENEURSHIP IN INDIA

Rural entrepreneurship can be regarded as an attempt to create the management for risk-taking appropriate to enact on the opportunities, as well as to mobilize human, material and financial resources to fulfil the project in rural areas (Saxena, 2012). Various authors have identified entrepreneurship as a process helpful in eradicating poverty particularly in rural areas or at Bottom of Pyramid (BOP) where the underprivileged socio - economic groups had experienced social exclusion for long (Behrman et al., 2003). Barriers to undertake entrepreneurship in the rural areas has been categorized in eight points, i.e. Social, Financial, Legal, Human resource, technological, marketing, infrastructure and governance. (Chaturvedi and Goyal, 2012). In rural areas of Zimbabwe, the challenges in undertaking entrepreneurship by youth has been Lack of capital, technology, logistics, availability of skilled labor and corruption by local authorities as it affects further access to resources (Chimucheka, 2012). According to Agbenyegah (2018), it is important to study effect of Social capital elements on growth of entrepreneurship in rural areas, the Social capital elements has been categorized as Personal and Business (PB) and, Business and Operational (BOPs). Personal and business caters to risk aversion, absence of family support, absence of confidence among individuals and shortage of marketing opportunities. On the other hand, Business and operational issues includes lack of resources, no assistance and support from authorities, poor infrastructure and unavailability of skilled manpower.

There are multifaceted issues imposed as specific challenges by the rural environment resulting in the variable outcomes of entrepreneurial efforts. Rural areas are disadvantaged in some ways compared to the urban areas; there is a huge difference in the economic performance between the regions (Smallbone, 2009).

1. **Demographic/Infrastructure Impediments:** Rural India is sparingly populated thus causing difficulty in distribution and logistics along with uneven demand patterns. This results into smaller markets and poor accessibility to the channel members (Stathopoulou et al.,2004). Moreover, the population is having less per capita income and erratic income cycle due to heavy dependence on seasonal harvesting.
2. **Financial Impediments:** Despite regular efforts by government, infrastructural facilities in rural area in India are not at par with urban. For instance- majority of the rural population is unbanked thus causing paramount challenge in financial transactions. Also, the flow of credits in rural area are inadequate due to apprehensions faced by the financers while venturing at high risk geographical areas (Jaydatta, 2017). It declines the risk bearing capacity of entrepreneurs thus making them averse of implementing new ideas in rural setup. The cost of manufacturing also increases in rural area as there are low levels of skilled labor available thus increasing the cost of transportation and logistics.
3. **Technological Impediments:** Inadequate infrastructural facilities lead to availability of obsolete technology and machinery in rural area. It results into low productivity and poor-quality standards of finished products. Also, non-access to technology causes more dependence of entrepreneurs and customers on middleman. It makes them vulnerable to be exploited by channel members due to less awareness.
4. **Social Impediments:** Rural entrepreneurs lack exposure and adequate financial resources which also has a detrimental effect on their propensity to take risk. The rural youth are under tremendous

pressure to prove themselves and earn a livelihood. The financial inadequacy increases the burden and takes away the family support from most struggling entrepreneurs.

5. **Policy Impediments:** According to Sundar and Srinivasa (2009) managerial inadequacies is also one of the crucial reasons for the failures in decentralized industrial sector in rural scenario. Poor self-image of the rural youth and insufficient motivation are the primary contributors in it. In India, the development of rural entrepreneurs is a complex problem which can be tackled by the synchronized efforts of social, political and economic institutions. Various stakeholders need to realize this condition and work upon the entrepreneurship as a developmental strategy for enhanced rural growth.

Figure 1. Impediments to rural entrepreneurship
Source: Compiled by Authors based on literature review

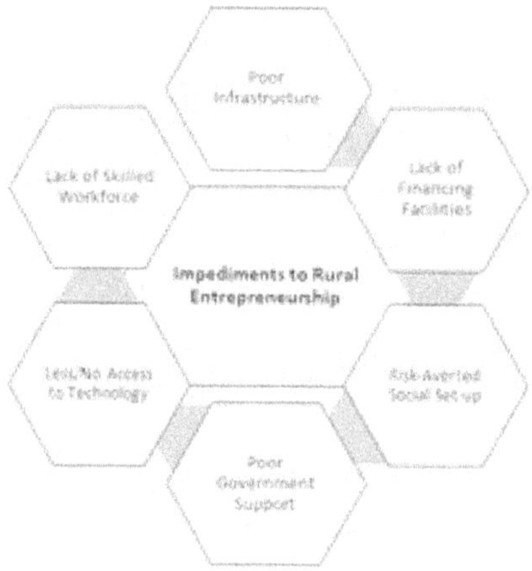

Figure 1 shows the factors which act as barriers to entrepreneurship in rural areas. Entrepreneurial ecosystem is combination of people, technology and markets, which provides opportunities that keep on changing with environmental conditions. However, the challenges in rural areas are mostly high due to geographical distances as it further leads to problems of gap in cultural knowledge, raising of capital, access to technology, literate and skilled labor and marketing of products (Sharma et. al, 2013). Lower literacy levels, poor technical and management skills, poverty are factors which effect the Entrepreneurial intentions in rural areas (Mwatsika, 2015). Different studies have further confirmed that lack of infrastructure (Taomina & Lao, 2007; Asabi 2017; Nwankwo & Okeke, 2017), poor entrepreneurial skills, absence of financing facilities (Das, 2012; Young & Flores, 2011) and not so favorable government policies (Ahmad and Xavier, 2012) hinders entrepreneurship development in rural areas. Few other factors influencing people in rural areas to opt for entrepreneurial activities includes communal and religious issues, migration of labor from rural to urban areas, lack of communication facilities as well as insecurity of lives among rural people (Asabi, 2017)

ESSENCE FOR GROWTH OF ENTREPRENEURSHIP

It is important to understand the factors affecting individuals to undertake entrepreneurial activity as it will help to further stimulate the entrepreneurship culture in rural areas by formulating relevant policies. The main indicators leading to entrepreneurship can be categorized as individual personality traits, External Business Environment factors and Socio-cultural factors. (Audretsch et al., 2008; Noseleit, 2013)

Entrepreneurial Traits

Some personality traits and psychological attributes owned by individuals are considered as predictor of intention to undertake Entrepreneurship. The following characteristics has been researched upon to predict the Entrepreneurial intention of the individuals:

Locus of Control

The locus of control indicates the level to which people believe that their accomplishments are result of their personal behavior. Everyone varies in their perception and acceptance about personal responsibility for their behavior. Locus of control can be categorized as internal LoC and external LoC. Individuals believing more on luck and blaming others for the happenings and their performance are the ones categorized with External Locus of control, they do not take charge of their lives. (Koh, 1996). On the other hand, people with an internal Locus of control trust themselves and are certain about controlling various events of their lives. (Hansemark, 1998)

Research suggests the existence of a positive correlation between entrepreneurial success and locus of control, it differentiates between successful and unsuccessful entrepreneurs. People who tend to have Internal LoC are motivated to select entrepreneurship as career choice. (Birdthistle, 2008; Othman & Ishak, 2009). Positive entrepreneurial attitude helps in developing a higher level of self-efficiency and control among individuals. (Robinson et al. 1991).

Need for Achievement

Need for achievement theory given by McClelland (1961) is widely applied to study the entrepreneurial intention of the individuals. Desire for achievement motivates individual to work hard for gaining perfection in their initiatives. There is positive and significant correlation between need for achievement and inclination towards entrepreneurship; it pushes individual to look for higher achievements in their lives. (Suan et al., 2011). This trait in individuals motivates entrepreneurs to overcome obstacles and strive for their goals. People with motive for achievement displays behaviors like undertaking variety of challenging tasks, are ready to face uncertainty and are accountable for their work. (Sagie & Elizur, 1999). Comparative researches among non-entrepreneurs and entrepreneurs shows that there is highly significant and positive correlation between need for achievement among individuals and their entrepreneurial intent. (Scott, 1998; Littunen, 2000).

Risk-Taking Propensity

According to Koh, (1996), an individual's orientation towards taking risks in uncertain decision-making situations defines his or her risk-taking propensity. In an uncertain environment an individual with entrepreneurial inclination is ready to take risks associated to family relations, economic well-being, career development, psychological and emotional. (Erdem, 2001; Littunen, 2000). One the crucial factor differentiating employed individual from entrepreneur is the uncertainty and the risk taken by the latter. (Entrialgo et al., 2000). Entrepreneurs are willing to take risks but based on calculation and expect high rewards for bearing the uncertain risks. (Lowe & Marriott, 2006).

Innovativeness

Innovation is a regular quest for the changes and finding opportunities for fresh ideas, new products, developing new production methods and getting into an untapped market. (Cromie, 2000; Utsch & Rauch, 2000). Innovativeness is considered as one of the important entrepreneurial trait and focal point of entrepreneurship. (Baden-Fuller 1995; Thomas & Mueller 2000). Budding entrepreneurs are consistently looking for new opportunities, have risk-taking behavior and are willing to accept the change. (Blake et al. 2005; Wood & Swait 2002; Yang 2005).

Socio-Cultural Environment

Social system elements and culture which affect and influence entrepreneurial behavior comprises the social-cultural environment of entrepreneurship. Socio-cultural environment includes principles, values, attitudes and person lifestyles which are formed over a period from educational, cultural and social setting of the individual. (Adeleke et. al, 2003) Entrepreneurship is not just an economic activity but also a social phenomenon and thus, entrepreneurial variations can be understood by social environment in which company is formed. (Steyaert, 2007).

Hofstede (2001) provided that there four measurable dimensions which reflects cultural differences among societies i.e. individualism, power distance, uncertainty avoidance and masculinity. As per Hayton et al. (2002), Cultures that are on the one hand low in uncertainty avoidance and power-distance and on the other hand high in masculinity and individualism generally facilitate entrepreneurship. Innovation value, failure embarrassment, work importance and status of entrepreneurship represent factors of socio-cultural environment influencing interest in taking entrepreneurial journey by individuals (Begley & Tan, 2001).

Socio-cultural background of the people determines the entrepreneurial traits of individuals as they undergo the process of socialization and develops suitable values promoting entrepreneurship. (Shivani et al., 2006). As per Gupta et al. (2014), Some culture may be more conducive to entrepreneurship than others, and individualistic culture focusing on wealth and materialistic achievement is more supportive of entrepreneurial activities.

External Factors

The individual's intent for entrepreneurship is affected by availability of supportive business environment including both qualitative and quantitative factors. Quantitative or Extrinsic variables of business performance include economic and financial results of the company (Zolin et al. 2013; Weber & Geneste, 2014). Intrinsic variables are more subjective in nature and also known as Qualitative variables are represented as effects on the entrepreneur, success perception of positive consequences, or development platform ascent (Baron and Henry, 2011; Dalborg et al., 2012; Fisher et. al, 2014).

Urbano & Turro (2013) specifies that business environment influence entrepreneurship, External factors like Unemployment and availability of few alternate opportunities leads to entrepreneurial growth. In addition, presence of better research facilities, innovation systems and market conditions provide platform to entrepreneurs. (Minniti & Naude, 2010).

Entrepreneurial prospects increase with presence of three factors in the ecosystem, i.e. technologies, people and markets. In order to succeed as a rural entrepreneur individual must take into consideration institutional barriers, availability of resources in market, influence of technology and capital accumulation.

In rural areas there are issue with appropriate infrastructure facilities which is very crucial for development of rural entrepreneurs. Local networks are very important for the formation and growth of rural entrepreneurs. Networking for business can be easier and efficient as residents are closely related in rural areas. The proximity among people in rural areas create networks which has more chances to reach bigger markets, provide more flexibility and ability to take more risks. (Young, 2010).

Since rural areas has challenges of vast distances, poor connectivity, high transportation costs and small market size, it is crucial to have presence of Information and communication technologies for growth of entrepreneurship in rural areas. Strong communication technologies will improve reachability, managing resources, connectivity and help broaden the market. (Stathopoulou et al., 2004).

INNOVATION - THE SILVER LINING

Innovation can be most narrowly associated with invention (Zhao, 2005); however, in actuality, it is multidimensional and can be expressed as any proposed theory or design that blends existing knowledge, practices, procedures, systems and skills to do something new (Sundbo, 1998). Innovations are further identified as radical or incremental, process-based or product based and administrative or technological (Cooper, 1998). The literature is replete with theories discussing the conceptual relationship between entrepreneurship and innovation (Zhao, 2005).

In the era of globalization there has been transition the way innovation is done, given the technological advancements and competition in agricultural markets. Emerging economies like India, Brazil and China have been in forefront in conducting innovation. (Chandy, & Eisengerich, 2013; Ramani & Szirmai, 2014). Innovation and entrepreneurship activities are closely linked to each other; entrepreneurs are creating value for themselves by exploring new opportunities and providing relevant products and services to the society.

There are numerous definitions of innovation ranging from narrow view of innovation being linked to initial commercial exploitation to broader views which considers not only the initial adoption but encompasses the invention and distribution of new ideas or products. (Brockhoff 1994, Hauschildt 1997). Innovation has been defined as invention of a new product or radically changed product or services or it can be a unique business process and practice, or a marketing technique. It can be considered as new to the world or new to the market or new to the company. One of the comprehensive ways of defining the "enterprise innovation" is identification and implementation of opportunities stimulating the fresh ideas and processes of conducting business, launching products and services or entering new markets, which further leads to long-term prosperity for individuals and society at large.

In most of the literature innovation has been examined more from product innovation perspective and not ideological like innovative management practices (Hausman 2005; Rogers 1995). Innovation is not only restricted to new establishments, it can take place in any size or phase of the organization, although it is generally believed that there is positive relationship between innovation and firm size. (Eggink, 2012). For the success of micro and small enterprises innovation has been usually perceived as a key for development and success. (Mahemba and De Bruijn 2003, Rogers 2004; Hausman 2005)

Irrespective of the area, innovation process must consider consumers' needs and demands as they help in transferring knowledge to the companies. Customers' have ability to influence innovation in three ways, firstly their awareness about their needs leads to generation of ideas, secondly customers' interaction assists in seeking solutions for the new product development and thirdly, adoption and response of customers to new products and services affect the motivation and need to innovate. (Earl & Gault, 2006, Bloch, 2007)

Researches shows that innovations done specifically in rural India are different from the traditional structured approach to innovation in three ways, firstly, in terms of Planning- large organization adopt highly planned approach through their R&D departments, their approach is more rigid and sequential. On the other hand, Indian innovators are generally flexible in their approach to innovation, the reason of the same can be response to the uncertain and changing Indian business environment (Jain & Sharma,2013). Secondly in terms of Cost, innovators in rural India are proficient in conducting innovation process from idea generation to the development of products to its commercialization at least cost. (Prahalad, 2012)

Thirdly, innovators in India believes in inclusive approach to innovation. There focus is generally on developing solutions for strata of society which have been underserved. Since large number of populations in India still lives in informal economy having limited access to infrastructure, products and services one of the main reasons behind inclusive innovation. (George, Nicholson, & Corbishley, 2015).

Innovative solutions can help people below poverty line transform their lives. Rural innovations have been inspiring people living in urban areas to innovate and improve their standard of living. Numerous rural innovations have been based on ideas of designing and delivering products at affordable prices. There are many examples that show real innovation has indeed happened in absence of required resources like funds, skilled labor or advanced technology.

It has been observed that people staying in rural regions have come out with innovations that have improved their standard of life. These innovations are driven by their basic need or by solution of a problem faced by them. This is backed by their inability to meet their needs through existing options in society. In the presence of many constraints such as lack of education and severe cash crunch – many have successfully shown new ways of improving products or even made a new product. They have also come with ways of reducing cost and time of making a product and even helped in conserving environment.

Rural innovators may not have any formal degree or training but their familiarity with local issues and environment assist them to innovate solutions for the problems. Lujthe et al. (2005) It is rightly said that Necessity is the mother of invention and aptly applies to the rural innovators. they realize the needs of the local communities and convert that crucial information in providing products and services through innovations. Lujthe and von Hippel (2006). That is, innovators from rural communities are ingeniously using available technologies and resources, they are combining creativity with logic for helping rural population (Ahlstrom, 2010).

Product or service innovations in the rural areas typically are initiated funds and resources using informal innovation networks. Due to financial constraints and lack of formal education it is extremely difficult for innovators in rural areas to arrange formal networks. However, in order to grow beyond their villages and market products and services for commercialization there is need for institutional support from educational institutes and government or private organization.

INNOVATION AS FORTITUDE OF ENTREPRENEURSHIP

There have been disparate viewpoints in defining the term "entrepreneur". The earlier theorists Say (1800) and Mill (1848), defined the concept from economic sense as the entrepreneur identifies opportunity, take risks and uses resources for superior productivity and more yield (Nanni, 2019). Also, entrepreneurship is defined as value creation process which uses medley of resources to sense and utilize the opportunity (Stevenson & Jarillo- Mossi,1986). These opportunities when redeemed through entrepreneurial functions results into emergence of new economic outlets (Reynolds,2005). In addition to these outcomes, the entrepreneurship is also identified as the act of incorporating innovation, creation of organizations/ employment, creation of value, and foundation of growth (Nanni, 2019). Innovation being one of the primary traits of an entrepreneur, was firstly mentioned by Schumpeter (1934: 74). Various roles in innovation were identified by Schumpeter like the inventor, the capitalist or the commercialization of new idea by an entrepreneur. He propagated innovation and its resultant as the drivers of economic prosperity instead of traditional thought of building up wealth.

With the advent of time various researchers have appended several perspectives on entrepreneurship apart from innovation like creation of wealth, forming of enterprise, design of innovation, conception of change, generation of employment, creation of value, and foundation of growth (Drucker, 1985; Gartner, 1990; Morris et al., 1994; Amit and Zott, 2001, George and Zahra, 2002). The 'innovative entrepreneurs" were matched with the "productive entrepreneurs" by Baumol (1990). While they were differentiated from the "alert entrepreneurs" by virtue of noticing opportunities of profit making by utilizing their existing knowledge (Kirzner, 1978) Such alert entrepreneurs play crucial role in rural settings where weak institutional settings and low education standards posit significant challenge while exploring the opportunities (Shane, 2003).

With more emphasis on social inclusion, the studies of entrepreneurship had percolated to artisans and farmers, the two major forces of rural transformation (Sharma, Vandana, Rajni, & Ranchan, 2013). The remote and rural areas can be nurtured by fortifying the entrepreneurship and related opportunities in the region (Beneworth,2004). The limited resources of the area can be best utilized by innovative ideas of new age entrepreneurs. As the financial goals of rural entrepreneurs are projected towards the development of rural area (Paul & Sharma, 2013). Galvanising entrepreneurship in rural areas will lead to balanced regional growth, increase in overall per capita income, equitable distribution of power, reduce the migration of rural population to urban areas, improve literacy rate of rural population and lead to overall improvement in the standard of living. It will help in curbing the migration of youngsters from the rural areas, it will also aspire them to be entrepreneur (Parida & Sahney, 2018). The women will also be benefitted by entrepreneurship in terms of creating more job opportunities in rural areas (Hopkinson & Aman, 2017).

Elena Harpa et al. (2014) proposed a model that could determine the innovation in the context of rural entrepreneurship. As per the model, the innovation is composite of factors namely, types of innovation, level of entrepreneurial innovation, degree of novelty of the innovation strategy and process of innovation generation. These factors are evidently dependent upon entrepreneur features, internal features of the company, external features of the company and location.

MILESTONES OF INDIAN RURAL ENTREPRENEURS ON THE PATH OF INNOVATION

Rural innovators may not have any formal degree or training but their familiarity with local issues and environment assist them to innovate solutions for the problems. Lujthe et al. (2005) It is rightly said that Necessity is the mother of invention and aptly applies to the rural innovators. They realize the needs of the local communities and convert that crucial information in providing products and services through innovations. Lujthe and von Hippel (2006). That is, innovators from rural communities are ingeniously using available technologies and resources, they are combining creativity with logic for helping rural population (Ahlstrom, 2010).

Based on the discussion of rural ecosystem in India, the following section encompasses the listing of innovative approaches of rural entrepreneurs despite all the odds. These entrepreneurial solutions are meant to offer the valid problem-solving approach to the impediments faced in various situations.

ENTREPRENEURIAL SOLUTIONS TO AGRICULTURE BASED PROBLEMS

Solar powered Desalination

Most of the Indian villages face the dearth of clean water. All the agricultural practices are dependent upon the groundwater which is deteriorating fast in terms of its saline content. An innovation which has turned the table is solar powered desalination which has made the fresh water available for farming in rural India. When challenged by Mr. Ratan Tata to solve the water crisis in Indian villages, UNSW's Global Water Institute (GWI) has fostered an innovative, version of desalination technology called Capacitive Deionization (CDI) which is solar driven.

The Cotton Harvester

In the dry lands of Gujarat, Cotton is grown as a common commercial crop. Many livelihoods in rural areas of Gujarat are dependent on the harvesting of cotton. But picking of cotton is a tedious and labor-intensive task which has always challenged the farmers. Also, as the task is seasonal pushing the small-scale farmers to hire the laborers at high wages otherwise the crop may get wasted. In pursue of a sustainable innovative solution to this problem, Natubhai Vader from Erwada, Gujarat came up with movable cotton ball picking machine which is also designed to separate cotton fiber from the seed balls. Hence, this grassroot innovation now has provided a permanent solution to one of the prevalent problems of the region.

The Milking Machine

Unlike western countries where motorized pumping machines are used for milking the cattle, rural India still practices it manually. Dependence of uninterrupted power supply is also required for using such imported technology. Moreover, the task can be performed manually one by one at a time by a skilled person. To work upon these ordeals of rural India, Raghav Gowda from Karnataka innovated the indigenous milking machine to ensure affordable, hygienic and quick. This milking machine solved many agonies of rural people and is adopted eagerly by population.

ENTREPRENEURIAL SOLUTIONS TO PRODUCTION BASED PROBLEMS

Fresh Farm Produce for Long

Poor storage facilities and perishable nature of food products make them prone to get wasted in rural India. The farm produce needs to be stored with big warehouses and cold storages by the farmers, thus making a dent in their earnings. To overcome this challenge, innovation has taken the shape of Ecofrost by, Devendra Gupta, Prateek Singhal, and Vivek Pandey. It is a solar-powered cold storage unit in which the temperature can be easily controlled by phone and fresh produce like vegetables can be stored up to 21 days. The device not only enhances the shelf life of produce, but it also keeps the freshness intact.

The Modified Machines for Weavers

Weavers community in rural India uses handloom and related techniques to make the region-specific clothes like munga silk (Assam) or Pochampalli Silk saree (Andhra Pradesh). They must use intensive hand movements for a considerable period of time to bring out desired patterns. Chintakindi Mallesham from Andhra bring the social and financial revolution by modifying the Asu machine to weave a tie & dye Pochampalli sari. Whereas, Deepak Bharali from Assam invented a machine to make the production of Munga silk sari faster by 60% and thus increasing the production of the community. These rural innovations have induced the new life in the productivity and earnings of rural India.

Designing Low-Cost Tractors

The tractor market is dominated by big brands and their high-power vehicles are underutilized in farming of groundnut and orchards in regions of Gujarat. Most of the farmers are not able to purchase them due to lack of resources. To provide solution to this condition, Bhanjibhai Mathukiya from Junagarh, Gujarat invented a low horsepower tractor with the help of structure of a jeep and Diesel engine. This contraption is available at less than half of the price of tractor with approximately 10 Horsepower- just right for groundnut farmers. This innovation has increased the productivity and profit margins of farmers in rural India.

ENTREPRENEURIAL SOLUTIONS TO SOCIAL CHALLENGES

An online Platform for Artisans

Dependency on middleman and absence of market connect are few of the reasons taking away the glamour from the localized art of rural India like Pattachitra (palm leaf etching) of Odisha. These factors are also responsible for less interest of youth in traditional art forms and involving in commercialization at a larger level. The geographical distance also creates problems of distribution and logistics. To mitigate it, art enthusiast entrepreneurs are working upon the possibilities of e-commerce platforms for providing a wider exposure to such art forms. One of such examples is Gina Joseph the entrepreneur behind Zola India. In an ordeal to empower female rural artisans, Gina is working cohesively with the Dhokra and Pattachitra artists and bringing their work in limelight without the hassles of any middlemen.

The Women-Friendly Kitchen Gadgets

Females in rural India spend most of their time and efforts in kitchen and household chores. Their health also suffers due to high smoke emission from the biomass (cow dung cakes) used as fuel in Indian villages. Many innovations in rural setup been designed to improve their situation. The prominent example is high efficiency stove made up of steel and cast iron by V Jayaprakash of Kerala. These stoves have innovative two-tier system of burning biomass with more energy and less pollution. The community stoves are also conceptualized by Jayaprakash. On the same lines to lessen the manual efforts required to roll the Indian bread (Roti/chapati), Mr. Bommai from Karnataka devised a machine which can roll efficiently 180 chapatis in an hour with very less efforts.

Low-Cost Incinerator to Dispose Used Sanitary Napkins

Swati Bedekar was initially looked down upon by rural women when she broached upon the topic of menstrual hygiene and waste but her ardent efforts paid good dividends and she along with her husband was successful in creating 'Ashudhinashak', a clay incinerator which could burn the used sanitary pads. Bedekars had initially started their entrepreneurial journey with low cost sanitary napkins for rural females, which could improve their menstrual hygiene. They soon realized the pathetic state of menstrual waste disposition in the rural areas where they were familiarizing the rural women with the use of sanitary pads. They then shifted their focus on creating a solution that could both be viable and cost effective. Thus came 'Ashidhinashak'.

Swati Bedekar had realized that a lot of girls were not sent to school during their monthly period cycle as they did not have a proper mechanism to dispose of the used pads. Their innovation in the form of a terracotta or cement pot, which could be used to burn the sanitary pads without littering the environment, was well accepted by the state governments of Rajasthan, Maharashtra and Gujarat. The residue ash produced by burning could be used for increasing fertility of the agricultural land. Many incinerators are installed in health centers, hospitals, schools and universities making the life easier for girls and women and keeping the environment clean.

ENTREPRENEURIAL SOLUTIONS IMPROVING LIFE AND LIVELIHOODS

Low-Cost Efficient Devices

Many innovations are done by rural entrepreneurs to raise the standards of life in rural area. One of such innovations is to cure the mosquito menace in area of Kerala by Mathews K. Mathews. He used sunlight and biogas to trap mosquitos for their destruction. Similarly, Charu Monga from IIT invented a solar backpack for those area where no electric connections are available. Young entrepreneurs Goutham Sharma and Jervis Anthony Saldanha from Bengaluru have equipped the drone with medical emergency supplies meant for rural areas. Such drone ambulance can reach the remote areas quickly for providing timely medical aid.

Electrification Using Rice Husk

In a developing country like India, the access to uninterrupted power is a big challenge especially in rural areas. Manoj Sinha, Ratnesh Yadav and Gyanesh Pandey innovated a miracle in the form of Husk Power Systems (HPS) in 2007, which has electrified more than 12000 households across 350 villages in India. Husk Power Systems make use of rice husks to generate electricity for rural households and small businesses. It is the world's first company that uses 100 percent biomass gasification and provides uninterrupted power through its completely reliable, hybrid-powered mini-grid system. HPS's Business model is direct-to customer which is not only operationally more efficient but also more cost-effective. HPS practices a process of gasification as opposed to burning for heating rice husk to generate electricity, and thus has minimal carbon footprint. Using energy supply provided by HPS, the local community has also seen an economic upturn in terms of new business opportunities of selling purified water to ice-creams, having easy access to power for charging mobile phones, being able to read and study without hindrance and above all seamless employment prospects in the power plants. The by-product of the power plants could be sold to concrete manufacturers providing alternative revenue stream. Additionally, HPS also uses charred rice husk to produce incense sticks through their incense stick making unit thereby engaging local rural women.

Skilling up Rural Youth to Provide Employment

A confluence of business and technology with rural workforce gave rise to Saloni Malhotra's venture of DESI CREW, a BPO that provides IT-based jobs in rural regions of India. With a social mission, Desi Crew was incubated out of the portals of IIT Madras and grew as a successful firm, which trained the capable, educated, but unemployed men and women of the rural areas.

Desi Crew competes with the likes of MNREGA (Mahatma Gandhi National Rural Employment Guarantee Act) creating on an average 4 million rural jobs with an average wage of over Rs.5000 per month for the entire year and impacting about 20 million rural people directly. Majority of Indian population lies in rural regions, Tier II and Tier III cities. Desi Crew's founder, Saloni Malhotra, an engineering graduate of Pune is much admired for performing the mountainous task of setting up a IT-enabled service firm in rural regions and hiring and training the amateurish people from these regions. Though it was an arduous assignment to train the rural team members and to bring them at par with their urban counterparts, the inadvertent fruits were considerable cost savings, reduced attrition rates and positive image building by being responsible corporate citizen.

Most of the other entrepreneurs may not have chosen the hardship-ridden path of setting up the rural BPO but to the management team of Desi Crew, challenges seemed motivating. So, whether it was replicating the sophisticated business infrastructure of their clients from metropolitan cities and molding the client's ideology about the quality of work; or making the rural workforce comprehend the challenge of delivering the global benchmark quality to maintain clientele. To ensure the success of the BPO in the rural sector and to facilitate its acceptance by the mainstream, the Desi Crew team emphasizes on building the human resource competence, which includes equipping the rural work team with computer operations, basic office management, HR practices, data entry and Internet usage. The delivery model of Desi Crew is an arrangement of micro-centers strategically located in several rural and semi-urban locations, where each center having a 25-seat facility is competently managed in 2 shifts to provide back-end services to global clients. The sites for setting up of micro-centers are deliberately identified in regions with a population strength ranging from 10 to 100 thousand. The most critical advantage that Desi Crew can deliver to its clients is lower costs, as the overheads at these micro-centres are far cheaper.

Table -1 represents synthesis of above-mentioned case studies of innovation in rural areas. Based on factors identified for impediments to rural entrepreneurship; and characteristics of innovation, the case studies have been summarised in the Table- 1.

Table 1. Synthesis of Case Studies

Case Study	Type of Impediment highlighted	Innovation basis
Solar powered desalination	Technological	Process based, Universality, High Impact on rural society, High cost Innovation, Institutional support
The Cotton Harvester	Financial Technological	Process based, Localization, Low impact on society, Low cost Innovation
The Milking Machine	Financial and Technological	Process based, Universality, High Impact on Society, Low cost Innovation, Institutional Support
Fresh farm Produce for long	Infrastructure	Product Based, Universality, High Impact on Society, High cost innovation, Institutional Support
The modified Machines for Weavers	Social and Financial	Product Based Universality High Impact on Society Low cost innovation
Designing low cost tractors	Demographic and Financial	Product Based, Localization, High Impact on Society, Low Cost Innovation
An online platform for artisans	Social and Financial	Process Based, Universality, High Impact on Society, Low cost Innovation
The women-friendly kitchen gadgets	Demographic and Social	Product Based, Universality, High impact, Low cost innovation
Low-cost incinerator to dispose used sanitary napkins	Demographic and Social	Product Based, Universality, High impact, Low cost innovation, Institutional support
Low-cost efficient devices	Infrastructure, Demographic and Financial	Product Based, Universality, High impact, Low cost innovation, Institutional support
Electrification using rice husk	Infrastructure	Process Based, Localization, High Impact, High Cost Innovation, Institutional Support
Skilling up rural youth to provide employment	Policy	Process Based, Universality, High Impact, Low cost Innovation, Institutional Support

Source: Compiled by Authors based on literature review

CONCLUSION

The rural entrepreneurship is the most appropriate medium to mobilise the much needed resources in terms of human resources, finances and materials, in order to create opportune business models that can aid in job creation, productivity and economic growth. The phenomenon is not limited to large scale business firms only; rather the small and medium size firms can more flexibly create strategic interventions through support of government, and other agencies which can lead to business models that can aid in fulfilling the national agenda of achieving balanced regional growth, increase in overall per capita income, equitable distribution of power, improved literacy rate of rural population and overall improvement in their standard of living.

REFERENCES

Adeleke, A., Oyenuga, O. O., & Ogundele, O. J. K. (2003). *Business Policy and Strategy. Mushin.* Concept Publications Limited.

Agbenyagah, A. T. (2018). Determining the risk & effect of selected social capital elements on rural entrepreneurship: Empirical study of two rural district municipalities. *Risk Government and Control: Financial Markets & Institutions*, *8*(1), 36–48.

Ahmad, Z. S., & Xavier, R. S. (2012). Entrepreneurial Environments and Growth: Evidence from Malaysia GEM data. *Journal of Chinese Entrepreneurship*, *4*(1), 50–64. doi:10.1108/17561391211200939

Asabi, M. O. (2017). Entrepreneurship Development: A Panacea for Rural Development in Nigeria. *African Journal of Management*, *2*(3), 135–147.

Audretsch, D. B., Bönte, W., & Keilbach, M. (2008). Entrepreneurship capital and its impact on knowledge diffusion and economic performance. *Journal of Business Venturing*, *23*(6), 687–698. doi:10.1016/j.jbusvent.2008.01.006

Baden-Fuller, C. (1995). Strategic Innovation, Corporate Entrepreneurship and Matching Outside-in to Inside-out Approaches to Strategy Research 1. *British Journal of Management*, *6*(s1), S3–S16. doi:10.1111/j.1467-8551.1995.tb00134.x

Baron, R. A., & Henry, R. A. (2011). Entrepreneurship: The genesis of organizations. In APA handbook of industrial and organizational psychology, Vol 1: Building and developing the organization (pp. 241-273). American Psychological Association.

Begley, T. M., & Tan, W. L. (2001). The socio-cultural environment for entrepreneurship: A comparison between East Asian and Anglo-Saxon countries. *Journal of International Business Studies*, *32*(3), 537–553. doi:10.1057/palgrave.jibs.8490983

Birdthistle, N. (2008). An Examination of Tertiary Students' Desire to Found an Enterprise. *Education + Training*, *50*(7), 552–567. doi:10.1108/00400910810909027

Blake, B. F., Neuendorf, K. A., & Valdiserri, C. M. (2005). Tailoring new websites to appeal to those most likely to shop online. *Technovation*, *25*(10), 1205–1214. doi:10.1016/j.technovation.2004.03.009

Chaturvedi, A., & Goyal, S. (2012). Changing severity of impediments for entrepreneurs in India: An empirical analysis. *International Journal of Entrepreneurship and Small Business*, *16*(1), 1–32. doi:10.1504/IJESB.2012.046914

Chimucheka, T. (2012). Impediments to youth entrepreneurship in rural areas of Zimbabwe. *African Journal of Business Management*, *6*(38), 10389–10395.

Cromie, S. (2000). Assessing entrepreneurial inclinations: Some approaches and empirical evidence. *European Journal of Work and Organizational Psychology*, *9*(1), 7–30. doi:10.1080/135943200398030

Dalborg, C., Friedrichs, Y. V., & Wincent, J. (2012). Beyond the numbers: Qualitative growth in women's businesses. *International Journal of Gender and Entrepreneurship*, *4*(3), 289–315. doi:10.1108/17566261211264163

Das, S. (2012). Entrepreneurship through Micro Finance in Northeast India: A Comprehensive Review of Existing Literature. *Information Management and Business Review*, *4*(4), 168–184. doi:10.22610/imbr.v4i4.978

DC Anusha. (n.d.). *DesiCrew Solutions.* Retrieved from ChangeMakers: https://www.changemakers.com/socialbusiness/entries/desicrew-solutions

Desai, V. (2007). *Small Scale Industries and Entrepreneurship*. Himalaya Publishing House.

DesiCrew's Saloni Malhotra's story…. (2015, April 21). Retrieved from Social EntrepreneurshipRevisited: https://socialentrepreneurshiprevisited.wordpress.com/2015/04/21/desicrews-saloni-malhotras-story/

Entrialgo, M., Fernández, E., & Vázquez, C. J. (2000). Characteristics of managers as determinants of entrepreneurial orientation: some Spanish evidence. *Enterprise and Innovation Management Studies, 1*(2), 187-205.

Erdem, F. (2001). A cultural approach toward risk taking propensity and tolerance for ambiguity of entrepreneurs. *Akdeniz IIBF Dergisi*, *2*, 43–61.

Fisher, R., Maritz, A., & Lobo, A. (2014). Evaluating entrepreneurs' perception of success. *International Journal of Entrepreneurial Behaviour & Research*, *20*(5), 478–492. doi:10.1108/IJEBR-10-2013-0157

Gupta, V. K., Guo, C., Canever, M., Yim, H. R., Sraw, G. K., & Liu, M. (2014). Institutional environment for entrepreneurship in rapidly emerging major economies: The case of Brazil, China, India, and Korea. *The International Entrepreneurship and Management Journal*, *10*(2), 367–384. doi:10.100711365-012-0221-8

Hansemark, O. C. (1998). The effects of an entrepreneurship programme on need for achievement and locus of control of reinforcement. *International Journal of Entrepreneurial Behaviour & Research*, *4*(1), 28–50. doi:10.1108/13552559810203957

Hayton, J. C., George, G., & Zahra, S. A. (2002). National culture and entrepreneurship: A review of behavioral research. *Entrepreneurship Theory and Practice*, *26*(4), 33–52. doi:10.1177/104225870202600403

Hofstede, G. (2001). *Culture's consequences: Comparing values, behaviors, institutions, and organizations across nations*. Sage.

Karimi, S. (2015). Rural entrepreneurship: Challenges and opportunities. *Journal of Entrepreneurship in Agriculture*, *1*(3), 101–119.

Koh, H. C. (1996). Testing hypotheses of entrepreneurial characteristics: A study of Hong Kong MBA students. *Journal of Managerial Psychology*, *11*(3), 12–25. doi:10.1108/02683949610113566

Larsson, E., Hedelin, L., & Garling, T. (2003). Influence of export advice on expansion goals of small businesses in rural Sweden (Global perspective). *Journal of Small Business Management*, *41*(2), 205–212. doi:10.1111/1540-627X.00076

Littunen, H. (2000). Entrepreneurship and the characteristics of the entrepreneurial personality. *International Journal of Entrepreneurial Behaviour & Research*, *6*(6), 295–310. doi:10.1108/13552550010362741

Lowe, R., & Marriott, S. (2006). *Enterprise: Entrepreneurship and Innovation Concepts, Contexts and Commercialization* (1st ed.). Elsevier Ltd.

McClelland, D. C. (1961). *The Achieving Society, D.* Van Norstrand Co Inc. doi:10.1037/14359-000

Minniti, M., & Naudé, W. (2010). Introduction: What Do We Know About the Patterns and Determinants of Female Entrepreneurship Across Countries? *European Journal of Development Research, 22*(3), 277–293. doi:10.1057/ejdr.2010.17

Mwatsika, C. (2015). Entrepreneurship development and entrepreneurial orientation in rural areas in Malawi. *African Journal of Business Management, 9*(9), 425–436. doi:10.5897/AJBM2014.7552

Noseleit, F. (2013). Entrepreneurship, structural change, and economic growth. *Journal of Evolutionary Economics, 23*(4), 735–766. doi:10.100700191-012-0291-3

Nwankwo, F. O., & Okeke, C. S. (2017). Rural Entrepreneurship and Rural Development in Nigeria. *Africa's Public Service Delivery and Performance Review, 5*(1), 1–7.

Othman, N., & Ishak, S. B. (2009). Attitude towards choosing a career in entrepreneurship amongst graduates. *European Journal of Soil Science, 10*(3), 419–434.

Raja, V. (2018, August 7). *12000 Households, 350+ Villages: How Crop Waste is Electrifying Rural India!* Retrieved from the better India: https://www.thebetterindia.com/155140/husk-power-system-renewable-energy-investment/

Robinson, P. B., Stimpson, D. V., Huefner, J. C., & Hunt, H. K. (1991). An attitude approach to the prediction of entrepreneurship. *Entrepreneurship Theory and Practice, 15*(4), 13–32. doi:10.1177/104225879101500405

Rural, B. P. O. (2012). *DesiCrew raises Rs 7 cr in Series B funding from responsAbility Ventures and Ventureast Tenet Fund.* Retrieved from NextBigWhat: https://nextbigwhat.com/desicrew-funding/

Sagie, A., & Elizur, D. (1999). Achievement motive and entrepreneurial orientation: a structural analysis. *Occupational and Organizational Psychology and Behavior, 20*(3), 375–387. doi:10.1002/(SICI)1099-1379(199905)20:3<375::AID-JOB884>3.0.CO;2-Y

Saxena, S. (2012). Problems Faced By Rural Entrepreneurs And Remedies To Solve It. *IOSR Journal of Business and Management, 3*(1), 23–29. doi:10.9790/487X-0312329

Sharma, M., Chaudhary, V., Bala, R., & Chauhan, R. (2013). Rural entrepreneurship in developing countries: Challenges, problems and performance appraisal. *Global Journal of Management and Business Studies, 3*(9), 1035–1040.

Shivani, S., Mukherjee, S. K., & Sharan, R. (2006). Socio-cultural influences on Indian entrepreneurs: The need for appropriate structural interventions. *Journal of Asian Economics, 17*(1), 5–13. doi:10.1016/j.asieco.2006.01.002

Shrimali, G., & Dhanaraj, C. (2014, July 18). *Case Summary: Husk Power Systems.* Retrieved from ISBINSIGHT: https://isbinsight.isb.edu/case-summary-husk-power-systems/

Smallbone, D., & Welter, F. (2006). Conceptualising entrepreneurship in a transition context. *International Journal of Entrepreneurship and Small Business, 3*(2), 190–206. doi:10.1504/IJESB.2006.008928

Stathopoulou, S., Psaltopoulos, D., & Skuras, D. (2004). Rural entrepreneurship in Europe: A research framework and agenda. *International Journal of Entrepreneurial Behaviour & Research*, *10*(6), 404–425. doi:10.1108/13552550410564725

Steyaert, C. (2007). 'Entrepreneuring' as a conceptual attractor? A review of process theories in 20 years of entrepreneurship studies. *Entrepreneurship and Regional Development*, *19*(6), 453–477. doi:10.1080/08985620701671759

Suan, C. T., Ai, Y. J., Raman, K., Loon, K. W., & Tanumihardja, J. (2011). Entrepreneurial intentions among university students. *Business & Management Quarterly Review*, *2*(3), 33–38.

Sundar, K., & Srinivasan, T. (2009). Rural Industrialisation: Challenges and Proposition. *Journal of Social Science*, *20*(1), 23–29.

Taormina, R. J., & Lao, S. K. M. (2007). Measuring Classical Entrepreneurial Motivation, Personality and Environmental Influences. *International Journal of Entrepreneurial Behaviour & Research*, *13*(4), 200–221. doi:10.1108/13552550710759997

The Story Behind the Data. (2020). Retrieved from desicrew: https://desicrew.in/about/

Thomas, A. S., & Mueller, S. L. (2000). A case for comparative entrepreneurship: Assessing the relevance of culture. *Journal of International Business Studies*, *31*(2), 287–301. doi:10.1057/palgrave.jibs.8490906

Urbano, D., & Turró, A. (2013). Conditioning factors for corporate entrepreneurship: An in (ex) ternal approach. *The International Entrepreneurship and Management Journal*, *9*(3), 379–396. doi:10.100711365-013-0261-8

Utsch, A., & Rauch, A. (2000). Innovativeness and initiative as mediators between achievement orientation and venture performance. *European Journal of Work and Organizational Psychology*, *9*(1), 45–62. doi:10.1080/135943200398058

Weber, P. C., & Geneste, L. (2014). Exploring gender-related perceptions of SME success. *International Journal of Gender and Entrepreneurship*, *6*(1), 15–27. doi:10.1108/IJGE-04-2013-0038

Wood, S. L., & Swait, J. (2002). Psychological indicators of innovation adoption: Cross-classification based on need for cognition and need for change. *Journal of Consumer Psychology*, *12*(1), 1–13. doi:10.1207/S15327663JCP1201_01

Yang, K. C. (2005). Exploring factors affecting the adoption of mobile commerce in Singapore. *Telematics and Informatics*, *22*(3), 257–277. doi:10.1016/j.tele.2004.11.003

Young, M., & Flores, I. (2011). Characteristics and Needed Assistance of Hispanic Women Business Owners: Emerging Entrepreneurs. *Small Business Institute Journal*, *7*, 80–105.

Young, N. (2010). Business networks, collaboration and embeddedness in local and extra-local spaces: The case of port Hardy, Canada. *Sociologia Ruralis*, *50*(4), 392–408. doi:10.1111/j.1467-9523.2010.00521.x

Zacharakis, A. L. (1997). Entrepreneurial entry into foreign markets: A transaction cost perspective. *Entrepreneurship Theory and Practice*, *21*(3), 23–40. doi:10.1177/104225879702100302

Zolin, R., Stuetzer, M., & Watson, J. (2013). Challenging the female underperformance hypothesis. *International Journal of Gender and Entrepreneurship*, *5*(2), 116–129. doi:10.1108/17566261311328819

ADDITIONAL READING

Asabi, M. O. (2017). Entrepreneurship Development: A Panacea for Rural Development in Nigeria. *African Journal of Management*, *2*(3), 135–147.

Audretsch, D. B., Bönte, W., & Keilbach, M. (2008). Entrepreneurship capital and its impact on knowledge diffusion and economic performance. *Journal of Business Venturing*, *23*(6), 687–698. doi:10.1016/j.jbusvent.2008.01.006

Noseleit, F. (2013). Entrepreneurship, structural change, and economic growth. *Journal of Evolutionary Economics*, *23*(4), 735–766. doi:10.100700191-012-0291-3

Nwankwo, F. O., & Okeke, C. S. (2017). Rural Entrepreneurship and Rural Development in Nigeria. *Africa's Public Service Delivery and Performance Review*, *5*(1), 1–7.

Sharma, M., Chaudhary, V., Bala, R., & Chauhan, R. (2013). Rural entrepreneurship in developing countries: Challenges, problems and performance appraisal. *Global Journal of Management and Business Studies*, *3*(9), 1035–1040.

Sharma, M., Vandana, C., Rajni, B., & Ranchan, C. (2013). Rural Entrepreneurship in Developing Countries: Challenges, Problems and Performance Appraisal. *Global Journal of Management and Business Studies*, *3*(9), 1035–1040.

Shivani, S., Mukherjee, S. K., & Sharan, R. (2006). Socio-cultural influences on Indian entrepreneurs: The need for appropriate structural interventions. *Journal of Asian Economics*, *17*(1), 5–13. doi:10.1016/j.asieco.2006.01.002

Thomas, A. S., & Mueller, S. L. (2000). A case for comparative entrepreneurship: Assessing the relevance of culture. *Journal of International Business Studies*, *31*(2), 287–301. doi:10.1057/palgrave.jibs.8490906

KEY TERMS AND DEFINITIONS

Entrepreneurship: The process of discovering new designs and techniques of combining resources.

Impediments: Barriers to entrepreneurship.

Innovation: Any proposed theory or design that blends existing knowledge, practices, procedures, systems, and skills to do something new.

Rural: The areas challenged by paucity of funds, lack of infrastructure facilities in terms of transportation, warehousing, and electricity; unavailability of information and communication technologies, skilled human resources, and technology.

Rural Entrepreneurship: An attempt to create the management for risk-taking appropriate to encash the opportunities, as well as to mobilize human, material, and financial resources to fulfil the project in rural areas.

Rural Innovation: Any proposed theory or design that blends existing knowledge, practices, procedures, systems, and skills to do something new in the rural context.

Rural Innovators: The new design initiators for the rural sector.

Chapter 4
Digital Innovation in Small Firms of Rural Canada

Suchit Ahuja
Concordia University, Canada

Yolande E. Chan
https://orcid.org/0000-0003-4040-9778
Queen's University, Canada

ABSTRACT

Unless there are systemic investments in digitization of rural economies, rural entrepreneurs will suffer, and digital innovation activity will remain modest. Nonetheless, the authors do find examples of digital innovation practiced by firms in rural economies. These firms successfully fostered growth and revitalization due to co-evolution of business and digital strategies, investments in technology, and digitization of business processes. In this chapter, using three such small, rural firms in Ontario, Canada, the co-evolution of business and digital technology strategies and related performance impacts are described by using the lens of "digital ecodynamics," which is defined as the holistic confluence among environmental factors, capabilities, and digital technologies—and their fused dynamic interactions unfolding as an ecosystem. The focus on the development of resources and capabilities that are critical for the survival of the firms and the local ecosystem centered around a business incubator that supports and sustains them.

INTRODUCTION

Rural communities are key to Canada's economy, culture, and social fabric. They work with urban centres to make our country the successful, prosperous place that it is. Rural communities are an integral part of the Canadian economy, contributing to the tourism, high-tech, and manufacturing sectors. They are on the front lines of Canada's resource economy. Through the Rural Economic Development Strategy, the Government of Canada supports strong and resilient rural communities as an integral part of the Canadian economy. - Infrastructure Canada, 2019[1]

DOI: 10.4018/978-1-7998-4942-1.ch004

Today, digital strategy, technologies, business models, processes, and content are integrated into almost all aspects of business and society. The technologies in themselves do not necessarily provide business advantages but must be combined with other firm resources as well as infrastructure that is available within the ecosystem of the firm to address business problems in innovative ways (Bharadwaj, 2000; El Sawy & Pereira, 2013; Nambisan et al., 2017). Used imaginatively, digital technology can "rapidly create new sources of competitive advantage and concatenate a series of temporary advantages over time" (Tanriverdi et al., 2010, p. 822). Technology investments can spur innovation and increase competitiveness. Some firms use digital technologies to drive their business strategies, facilitating innovation and creating business value. As business activities are digitized or performed electronically, firms can share information with, and respond flexibly to, suppliers and customers; they can reduce cycle times, control quality, and improve customer satisfaction (Tanriverdi et al., 2010).

Although we see the rapid adoption of digital technologies within large firms, startups, and small and medium enterprises (SMEs) in urban areas, the extant literature points to the slow adoption and limited diffusion of the same digital technologies to rural areas, often referred to as the "urban rural digital divide" (Hindman, 2000; Pham & Massey, 2018; Salemink et al., 2017). Rural areas are known to suffer from resource constraints, infrastructure scarcity, seasonality of business, lack of access to local and global markets, etc. (Hindman, 2000; Mair et al., 2012). The same trend applies to digital technologies as well. Unless there are systemic investments in digitization of rural economies, entrepreneurs in rural areas suffer and innovation activity remains largely curtailed (Salemink et al., 2017). Past research on rural areas underlines how they are often described as "passive" and lacking the vibrancy and dynamism that is often attributed to urban areas (Graziano, 2020). However, recent research has shown that on the contrary, rural areas are active on the innovation and entrepreneurship fronts and are often plugged into global networks (Graziano, 2020). This shift has been driven, to a large extent, by the pervasiveness of the digital technologies, platforms, and global ecosystems that leverage broadband connectivity, local technology and human resources, and underlying economic efficiencies provided by rural areas to develop digital products, services, and business models (Muñoz & Kimmitt, 2019).

Nonetheless, we do find some examples of digital innovation in rural economies where governments make the right policy and investment decisions to foster growth and revitalization (Chan & Ahuja, 2015; Chan, Krishnamurthy, and Desjardins, 2020). This is often done by creating innovation ecosystems that create synergy among local actors, resources, infrastructure, customers, and markets. To foster such digital ecosystems in rural areas and to provide rural businesses with equal opportunity to access digital services, the Canadian government has created the "Connect to Innovate" strategy to invest $585 million by 2023 and bring high-speed Internet to 975 rural and remote communities in Canada, including 190 Indigenous communities (Innovation, Science, and Economic Development Canada, 2019). Most rural areas consist of challenging geography and smaller populations that present barriers to private sector investment in building, operating, and maintaining infrastructure, thereby limiting the scale and scope of digital innovation that can be undertaken in such areas. Surprisingly, rural small firms in Canada often experience challenges and physical, digital, and social constraints that are like those experienced by firms in low-income economies or emerging markets (Ahuja and Chan, 2019). Therefore, it is important to correctly assess the needs of digital businesses in such areas and develop the appropriate digital, physical, and social infrastructure required by rural firms and communities.

In this chapter, we describe the co-evolution of business and digital technology strategies, investments in technology, the digitization of business processes, and related performance impacts. We use the lens of "digital ecodynamics" which is defined as the holistic confluence among environmental factors, business capabilities, and digital technologies—and their fused dynamic interactions unfolding as an ecosystem adapted from (El Sawy et al., 2010). We focus on small firms that are critical to the prosperity of most economies (Pickernell et al., 2013; Storey & Greene, 2010) and are embedded within rural ecosystems.

BACKGROUND

Canada has over one million small businesses, and 98% of all Canadian businesses have fewer than 100 employees (Innovation, Science, and Economic Development Canada, 2019). These firms employ about 48% of Canada's labor force and are responsible for nearly 50% of the Canadian GDP (Innovation, Science, and Economic Development Canada, 2019). With such significant contributions to the economy, there is growing emphasis on research that focuses on unique aspects of small businesses and their transformation as well as digitalization (Salemink, Strijker, & Bosworth, 2017). Our chapter responds to such calls to study emerging trends in digital business strategy (Bharadwaj et al., 2013), specifically in the context of small firms. The scope of digital business strategy has evolved, and IT and business strategies are increasingly fused together (Bharadwaj et al. 2013). The embedded nature of IT across the business value chain and the dependencies of dynamic capabilities on lower order competencies and resources. The speed of digital business strategy is rapid, and firms must develop capabilities to respond to fast-changing market conditions. Therefore, we emphasize the use of asset-light and flexible IT systems and services as new sources of business value creation are leveraged. As a result, even small businesses are forced to develop digital business strategies that facilitate new business models and serve new markets.

We use two primary theoretical lenses in our understanding, analyses, and explanations. First, we utilize the resource-based view (RBV) of the firm, which is a well-established and extensively used theoretical perspective in the field of strategic management (Barney, 2001). RBV posits that firms possess and exploit resources to gain competitive advantage. There have been criticisms centered around the focus of RBV on "resources" while ignoring the role of the manager, the firm's contextual understanding, its network and social connections that influence decision making, and its constantly changing external business environment (Arend & Bromiley, 2009). This is also the view in the entrepreneurship literature, where the entrepreneur plays a significant role in the formulation and execution of business strategy (Nambisan et al., 2019). However, there have been very few studies that focus on the role of both digital resources and digital entrepreneurs in a small business context. We address this gap in this chapter. Furthermore, several studies show that digital resources can be used to increase firm innovation and other aspects of firm performance (Nambisan et al., 2017). Similarly, related studies have shown how firms develop capabilities based on strategic exploitation of their digital resources, especially the set of readily available and easily deployable SMAC (Social media, Mobile apps, Analytics, Cloud computing) resources (El Sawy & Pereira, 2013). Other studies highlight that in uncertain and turbulent environments, dynamic capabilities (Teece et al., 2016) that build on ordinary capabilities to provide firms with strategic agility and flexibility are important for sustained competitive advantage and drive firm performance (Nambisan et al., 2017). Second, we use the lens of "digital ecodynamics" which is defined as the holistic confluence among environmental factors, business capabilities, and digital technologies—and their fused dynamic interactions unfolding as an ecosystem (El Sawy et al., 2010). Digital ecodynamics is a systemic phenomenon involving complex interactions among the triad of environmental turbulence, dynamic capabilities, and digital systems; the tight fusion among the three elements almost to the point of inseparability requires a "holistic" approach (El Sawy et al., 2010). We describe the co-evolution of business and digital technology strategies, investments in technology, the digitization of business processes, and related performance impacts.

Furthermore, our examination of digital innovation in small firms focuses attention on entrepreneurship in a new context of digital innovation. Previous studies in entrepreneurship suggest moving towards understanding the nature, richness, and dynamics of entrepreneurship by moving beyond the individual entrepreneur (Nambisan et al., 2017). We emphasize the transformational role that digital technologies play in entrepreneurship today (Nambisan et al., 2017). We explore small firms, revealing new insights from a joint perspective of digital strategy, IT capabilities and entrepreneurial activity. The novelty of our findings lies at the intersection of these research domains, where emphasis is given to both the role of digital entrepreneurs and newer, enabling technology capabilities that transcend traditionally established boundaries of firms, markets, and social environments (Bharadwaj et al., 2013; El Sawy & Pereira, 2013). We describe the internal strategies and technologies of small firms, while also demonstrating the influence of their external ecosystems. We show how, by participating in ecosystems, firms accrue benefits through spillover effects and shared knowledge. We also show how digital entrepreneurs make conscious efforts to return value to their ecosystems. We highlight the pivotal role played by local actors and entities including entrepreneurs, government agencies, venture firms, individual investors, and regional incubators in fostering, supporting, and scaling digital SMEs in rural areas (Chan & Farrington, 2019; Chan et al., 2020). The collective interplay among these entities leads to regional innovation, economic development, job creation, and social impact. However, in previous studies these entities have not been studied holistically and the focus has only been on one or two entities. Taking a digital ecodynamics perspective, we can focus on the relationships, processes, resources, technologies, and outcomes that are shared across the rural ecosystem while conducting an in-depth examination of each individual firm. In this way, we highlight both internal and external aspects of small firms.

METHODOLOGY

In our study, we closely examine seven small firms in a rural region of southern Ontario, Canada. We use a case study approach to explore issues and create a framework to study digital innovation in rural small firms. To obtain expert input, we conducted a total of 19 in-depth interviews with founders, owners and managers of small, technology-intensive Ontario firms. To enhance the validity of our findings, a case study database was created. Interview questions were pilot tested, and all interviews were audio-taped and transcribed. Initial codes were created using the interview guidelines and new codes added as the research progressed. All transcripts were coded by the researchers and high inter-rater agreement was ensured. Company websites were examined, and company documents filed. In this way, multiple sources of evidence were used (Yin, 2017). We used NVivo 9 software (www.qsrinternational.com) and MAXQDA 10 software (www.maxqda.com) to assist with data analysis and employed principles of "analytical generalizability" (Yin, 2017) to assist with theorizing.

We selected seven recently launched firms that faced significant resource challenges, operated in difficult business environments, and had technology platforms as core components of their business models. They varied widely in their histories, capabilities, resources, digital technologies, and ecosystems. Our intent was to understand their business models, technology solutions, digitized processes, products, services, and firm performance. Most of the firms had links to a regional business incubator or innovation center. In the business incubator, space could be leased, and access to technology and human capital resources (e.g., mentors) was provided, at a low cost. In this way, critical resources and capabilities could be rapidly acquired (Tamasy, 2007). We conducted interviews with knowledgeable incubator managers, business mentors, and technical staff. In this paper, we highlight three contrasting small businesses; all three had received assistance from the innovation center. We call the firms eProductions, eTireCo, and eCourseCo and describe them below.

eProductions: Disrupting the Media Industry with Lean IT Agility

eProductions was started in 1998 to produce TV shows for larger media clients looking to buy high quality TV content for showcasing the Home and Living genre. Dave had worked in the media industry in a big city for a few years and wanted to raise a family in a better neighborhood where he could enjoy a better quality of life. Seeking a better work-life balance, Dave moved with his family to a small town not too far from the city and started eProductions. While working for the large media company, Dave had noticed the shift in technology and the use of the internet for production management and communication purposes. Furthermore, TV, camera, storage, and production technology and related business processes were also changing. It was a generally turbulent time for the media industry.

Dave knew that in the small town he would incur lower overall operating costs, lower taxes, and significantly lower employee salaries. This would enable him to run his business more efficiently and help him compete with bigger, more established production studios. Essentially, Dave's plan was to disrupt the business of the larger production houses with a boutique model of production, by offering fast, cheap, and good customer service, remain lean and cater to unique needs of his customers. To achieve this, he deployed latest technology but in an affordable manner by constantly negotiating contracts and amortizing the costs of bulky IT infrastructure. eProductions also used communication and collaboration technologies to work with externally contracted production units, camera persons, editors, executive producers, etc. These technologies include VOIP, FTP, Skype, social media, virtual delivery systems for transmitting the television shows directly to the internet, and additionally using high-definition cameras and other cutting-edge equipment.

Although the business does not have a defined or documented business strategy, it has clearly positioned itself as a micro-television production company with quicker reaction times to customer demands than any of its larger competitors. It focuses on agility by responding to all requests within 12 hours and working as an extension of its clients. Furthermore, it has hired highly skilled staff and keeping its internal business processes loosely structured and flexible. It is an early adopter of technology and expands or upgrades technology based on the recommendations of its staff and new hires who possess the latest skills. The informal knowledge sharing between its internal employees and externally hired contract workers drives continuous improvement and co-creation of superior client-specific content.

eProductions measures its performance by the efficiency of its operational and delivery processes. It strives to keep costs low by relying on its technology capabilities and remaining flexible with respect to its decision-making and operations. It is also flexible with its human resource management and hires pre- and post-production staff on contract basis. Furthermore, it augments all its operations with low-cost technology in order to remain competitive in its pricing and revenue models. It measures success by the growth of the number of shows it produces every year and strives to keep its staff satisfied and free of stress. Happiness and a sense of achievement among its staff is a key goal.

eTireCo: Establishing a New Digital Platform for Tire Sales

eTireCo is a mobile app for car dealers and makes it easier for them to sell tires. It is a subscription-based company that provides a SaaS-based application to its customers. Customers using eTireCo report tire sales improvement between 10% to 30%. The journey to making eTireCo successful was not straightforward for Chris, the CEO. Along the way, he had previously worked on developing a content management software suite for car dealerships and this experience proved to be immensely helpful with developing eTireCo. When eTireCo was starting out, GM was closing 200 dealerships and it was a difficult period for the automobile industry. eTireCo had no business development experience and in order to seek mentorship and business development guidance it moved its operations to an incubator in southern Ontario. The incubator was able to provide both technology and business expertise as well as help in developing connections with national-level dealerships across Canada. This is a key factor in the success of eTireCo.

With eTireCo, the goal was to develop a digital shelf-space for tires, very similar to aisle shelf-space in Walmart, and then have dealerships browsing on their tablets or smartphones in order to respond to a customer request for a quote. The time to respond to a request for quote would be reduced to 1-2 minutes. The strategy was to partner with a tire distributor and develop the software for inventory while allowing the distributor to promote the software to his clients (car dealerships). Then, he would partner with independent dealerships as well and provide the software to them for a subscription fee. This eco-system strategy proved to be so successful that in three years eTireCo was installed in about 300 car dealerships across North America. eTireCo follows a strategic path based on the daily decisions of its founders. Additionally, there are other important factors that lead to the success of this strategy.

First, eTireCo was developed by following an iterative methodology with prototypes provided to customers regularly. This co-creation strategy ensured that the product was not only compatible with the design and functional requirements of the customers but also provided additional capabilities that were above and beyond, by considering the feedback provided in previous iterations. Second, eTireCo could not afford to hire expensive software engineers in Canada for the initial design and development as it did not have the revenues to support more staff. It decided to outsource the design and development to software developers in India but decided to pay a bit more than the market rate in order to ensure a high quality of coding, design, and development. Once it had enough revenues, eTireCo hired an in-house software architect to improve and scale the code, so that it was ready to be expanded in order to support its customer growth. Finally, eTireCo had successfully put together a top management team which was focused on business development. The synergy within this team helped eTireCo focus on its goals and ensured that the product was moved rapidly from conceptualization to commercialization.

Although eTireCo was moving into the automobile industry, it wanted to have a strategy that is difficult to mimic. Therefore, it built a network of customers from the very beginning and began leveraging the strengths of this network by making them a stakeholder in the design and development of the product. Furthermore, it also built solid business relationships with its customers by providing free user training to staff at the car dealerships and tire distributors. It has always focused on keeping its operating costs low and moving its operations from a big city to a rural location was part of this strategy. The salaries it paid to its 11 employees were much lower and its overhead expenses were much lower. As a result, it could focus on improving the quality of its core product/service.

eTireCo is focused on diversifying its business by partnering with more national-level dealerships and signing on more tire distributors. It measures its success by the number of customers it can bring onto its software platform and by the job satisfaction it provides to its employees. Overall, eTireCo attributes its success to its innovative use of a co-creation strategy with its customers and developing a core capability that enabled it to read between the lines of what the customer requirements are and then leveraging its technical capabilities to go above and beyond those requirements.

eCourseCo: Creating a Platform for Digitization of College Courseware

eCourseCo is a firm which digitizes course materials and enables sharing and social media integration. It also focuses on mobility and in addition to desktop software and an app for mobile devices. Simon, the founder, was passionate about creating software for the education industry and eCourseCo has allowed him to convert his passion into a product. The initial strategy was to quickly develop the product for the iPhone and iPad and partner with a technical college. Simon, the founder, sought the help of a business incubator in the region in order to be able to access his potential market. The incubator successfully helped eCourseCo get its first big break. However, in order to crack the higher education industry, which was the original industry eCourseCo wanted to target, it would have to further develop its product based on the feedback it was receiving from its first customer. This is where it made a critical error in judgment. Instead of taking the product through iterations, it started rapidly adding requested features in the hope that it will impress the large university client it was targeting. eCourseCo started investing heavily into the product and added capabilities such as HTML5 compatibility, integrated video and audio, calendar functionality, etc. This turned out to be a severe drain on the firm and caused a shortage on the operating budget. This is also because its first client was still not a paying client and no revenue was being generated by the firm.

Simon realized his mistake and then readjusted his strategy. It was decided that no more development on the technology will take place until eCourseCo has a strong client relationship in place. eCourseCo also broadened its target market by trying to expand to private K-12 schools in the area. This would provide more flexibility with respect to maintaining a dual revenue stream and the software requirements were not very different, therefore requiring minimum rework. It also learned the hard way that large public universities in the higher education industry are massive bureaucracies where RFP processes take a long time. For a startup like eCourseCo, this was an unsustainable option. Similarly, private schools were easier to sell to because their decision-making process was faster. Furthermore, universities had not matured in their in-class high-tech requirements. Students in only a handful of departments and programs were expected to be using iPads in class, while instructors were also not very savvy with the use of mobile devices for teaching purposes. In a way, the technology was ahead of the requirements of its target market.

Nevertheless, this futuristic technology also was a competitive advantage for eCourseCo. It had built on an innovative technology platform, which is HTML 5, which none of its competitors such as Learning Management Systems and Education Content Delivery Systems were providing. Instructors and students could literally drag content onto the course and it also synchronized the content for everyone. The calendar layout made it an especially useful part of course planning and delivery. The social media interaction elements supported out-of-class engagement between the instructors and students. The product was customer centric and flexible to adapt to any educational environment. These were real technical strengths of eCourseCo that needed to be leveraged while marketing its product and services.

eCourseCo measures its performance based on the number of contracts it can setup with educational institutes in the region. It wants to gain credibility and establish a long-term paying client, before advancing to the next stage of development. It is also targeting private K-12 schools to augment its revenues.

Simon recognizes the role of the business incubator in helping him get access to his market and in bypassing several layers of bureaucratic structures. Furthermore, in hindsight eCourseCo realized through influential members of the incubator that it did not have to be a part of the RFP process in order to get its product at the university. This was a major learning point for Simon, and he is thankful for being a part of the business incubator. He has also realized that for eCourseCo to be successful, it needs to be part of a network or ecosystem, with participants that are not only interested in the product/service but are also stakeholders in the success of the firm. eCourseCo plans to move in this direction as soon as it has established a solid foundation.

FINDINGS

These companies illustrate several important principles. Below, we summarize key observations on drivers of firm investment in digital technology, the co-evolution – and even fusion – of business and technology strategies, the creation of digital ecosystems, and firm and ecosystem performance.

Prioritization of Investments in Digital Technology

For eProductions, the cost of its technology had decreased significantly since the inception of the firm. The equipment for video processing, the hardware, and some software applications had become much more affordable. In addition, the firm's business model relied on worker mobility. The flexibility of having only a few full-time staff and hiring additional contract staff as needed on a project-by-project basis helped eProductions repurpose its investment in HR to invest in core digital technologies such as the HD cameras and other broadcasting equipment that were still expensive. It reduced its overhead operational expenses by moving to a rural location and freed up capital for technology investments. The overhead expenses of the firm were a third of that of its competitors in larger cities. The firm also differentiated itself as being agile, able to respond to client needs quickly and effectively. The capabilities and structures that supported these sensing and responding competencies required, and helped justify, the investments in digital technologies.

In a market driven by low profit margins and intense competition, eTireCo had developed a digital platform and fostered an ecosystem where both tire distributors and car dealerships required the TireApp to compete in their respective markets. eTireCo sold subscription services to both tire distributors and car dealerships. It maintained high levels of service and support and iteratively developed the platform with inputs from users. It developed a capability to use its technology platform to drive sales in the market. Its value proposition was that it tailored its technology product to the needs of its customers and provided exceptional service and support. eTireCo depended on its established business relationships to drive the adoption of its technology platform. It focused on both ends of its value chain – the dealerships/independents and the tire distributors. This gave its digital platform a source-to-market view of the industry. Being the first mover in this space, it was able to capture a large market share. It developed a SaaS product that was mobile device friendly. For eTireCo, the technology was the business. Investments in software development were simply viewed as business investments.

eCourseCo was an early adopter of HTML5. It organized the delivery of entire courses around a digital calendar and provided related apps and desktop support. Digitization of content was necessary for ease of information storage and retrieval. eCourseCo focused on customer needs, enabling professors and students to see, design, and configure course content according to their preferences. It seized the opportunity to change a paper-based "course packs" culture in higher education in the region. eCourseCo used outsourcing to develop its software products. As the founder stated, "we built the technology and invested heavily in it at the beginning, and now we have a great horse. Now we just need to find a bunch of people to ride it." At eCourseCo, the technology was ahead of, and drove, the business opportunities.

New Business Models Enabled by Digital Technologies

At eProductions, early adoption of new HD technology created business opportunities and competitive advantage. Although this was perhaps risky, as making the investments did not automatically result in new opportunities, it was the combination of the technology strategy with a business strategy that seized business opportunities that resulted in firm success. eProductions invested in emerging technology before its competitors, developed internal technology capabilities, and accessed competencies of external contractors to exploit sources of competitive advantage. Despite its rural location, eProductions exploited Internet-based technologies for communication and collaboration in order to engage its ecosystem and create and maintain superior customer relationships.

eTireCo built a digital platform to co-create TireApp with its customers, and so was able to refine its sensing and responding capabilities to a greater extent than any of its competitors. As the founder stated, "it's almost like the customer is programming for you. The closer you can get to that, especially for a B2B product, the higher your chances of success." At eTireCo, the digital technology enabled the firm to continuously hear from customers and incorporate feedback into TireApp. There was continual innovation and continual growth in market penetration and business success.

At eCourseCo, the "software was literally the first in Canada that was helping executive education institutions deliver their courses or their content online like that." The company strategy was to find one or more big clients (e.g., universities) that they could penetrate. It wanted to build strong, deep client relations, one customer at a time, tailoring the software as it went, and making it easy for clients to adopt its products. eCourseCo was willing to be flexible and to innovate continuously in order to lead in its market. As the founder stated, "On the iPad we built an app, which basically could take content in a course pack and organize it all together and you could make notes on the course pack. Really the platform and the capabilities of the platform that we employed, that's made the technology hard to copy." Because the software ran on Android, iPad, and web browsers, it was device independent. The product was "first out the gate" and would be difficult to match or beat. eCourseCo's use of SaaS and its mobile-first strategy meant that no other content management system or learning management system had similar capabilities. In this way, eCourseCo led the way using its technology. It also survived because of its technical agility. After an unsuccessful round of targeting universities, eCourse rapidly modified its software to serve other markets such as private high schools. These markets were more profitable and easier to penetrate. Using its technical agility, eCourseCo created new competitive opportunities.

All three firms that we studied relied heavily on digital technologies, with several focusing on maximizing cost efficiencies and the ability to scale rapidly and effectively using cloud-based platforms. Their early adoption of digital technology, and technical agility, created business opportunities and competitive advantages. eProductions invested heavily in advanced Hi-Def technology and used Internet-based content distribution. eTireCo used IT to provide learning opportunities and support value co-creation with customers. eTireCo and eCourseCo used technology to iterate versions of their products and services. There was continuous learning, business model adjustment, business product development and innovation. These firms kept changing their business/technology offerings to address new customer needs and to provide services that none of their competitors could provide. By using the technology to drive non-stop product enhancements and nimbleness, they not only "stayed in the game" but led the pack.

Co-Evolution of Business Strategy and Digital Capabilities

At eProductions, the digital technology strategy had three components – the IT infrastructure and equipment required for company operations, the HR skills required to creatively leverage the IT systems, and the underlying processes and capabilities that supported both the technology and the staff. As the founder stated, "It is a combination of the content (which is our business), the technology or the Internet and our people that allows you to collaborate and manage. That experience is only going to continue to get richer and richer." The business strategy was dependent on effective operations, competitive tactics – such as sensing and responding to changing customer demands – and strategically co-evolving the business and IT to remain dynamic and flexible in a turbulent market. Although the business and technology strategy were not explicitly documented, they were very integrated. Without a flexible strategy for hiring contractual staff and supporting them with appropriate technology and systems, eProductions could not achieve its high-performance levels.

The founder at eTireCo claimed that the business and technology strategy were inseparable. The technology was the product/service. It also supported an ecosystem, facilitating the intensive involvement of customers in the product design process that resulted in major value co-creation. Training to customers was also provided through webinars, Skype, GoTo Meeting, etc. Technology helped customers "adopt [TireApp] and put it in their organization, and once it's in and it's stuck, they can't get rid of it." As the founder indicated, "we actually end up getting more feedback and constructive feedback from our customer support people, who actually work with the shoppers and the people every day. So [our customers define] the technology strategy. It's nice to bring a solid vision to the whole organization … Without the business end of it, without the actual business connections, the customers, everything I've built over two years, I mean, there's nothing [TireApp] can really do, and [we] don't want to do that." Outsourcing some of the system development was necessary because of limited company resources. However, eTireCo was switching to an in-house approach (via hiring a software architect) to scale the application. The decision-making involved continuous inter-twining of business and technology choices.

The platform that eCourseCo designed and its capabilities were hard to copy. The platform was unique and addressed a niche market but also supported flexibility and customization. The technology and its products were interdependent. When looking for feedback to evolve its platform, eCourseCo likely should have taken small iterations, but initially decided to wait to release its primary product until it had met all major needs of its first university client. This negatively impacted the firm's cash reserves. It had to rapidly modify its products and look for new markets (private schools) where these products would be well-received. It was a classic case of how intertwined the technology and business strategies needed to be, and how things could go badly wrong if there was misalignment.

In summary, we see that at eProductions, the business strategy was shaped by, and dependent on, the digital technology and the Internet which enabled the firm to sense and respond to changing customer opportunities in a dynamic market. At eTireCo and eCourseCo, the technology was the product, delivery platform, service channel, communication mechanism and ecosystem foundation. Changes in the business automatically meant adjustments in the technology and vice versa.

Performance Beyond Profits: Care and Well-being of Employees and Communities

eProductions measured its performance by the efficiency of its operational and delivery processes. It measured success by the growth of the number of shows it produced every year. "We have had enormous growth, and again this year we went up another 100%. The plan is to just keep growing the business." eProductions also aimed to keep its staff satisfied and experiencing only reasonable amounts of stress. Quality of life, happiness and a sense of achievement among its staff were key goals. As the founder stated, "You could be making a crap load of money but if every night you are going to be feeling sick to your stomach because you are stressing, that is not success."

eTireCo measured its performance by the number of customers using its software platform and by the job satisfaction of its employees. It focused on internal system performance and paid constant attention to improving customer-centric applications in cost effective ways. System performance drove customer satisfaction. eTireCo monitored customer engagement, customer relationship management (CRM) levels, TireApp usage, TireApp change requests, employee satisfaction and profitability. eCourseCo measured its performance by monitoring the number of contracts with educational institutions in the region. eCourseCo tracked product adoption, user growth, client relationships, costs and profitability.

In summary, as the businesses evolved, they paid attention to a range of measures of success, including individual employee quality of life, technology/system quality, customer satisfaction, profitability and the health of the ecosystem.

DIGITAL INNOVATION IN RURAL SMALL FIRMS: A RESEARCH FRAMEWORK

We used the case data inductively to create a framework (Figure 1) to inform research and practice. Key framework elements include founder characteristics, digital resources and capabilities, firm capabilities, incubator capabilities, risk mitigation mechanisms, and firm performance. These are described below.

Founder Characteristics

The research framework highlights the background and experiences of the founder. In the small firms we studied, most company founders were still the CEOs (even with eProductions, founded in 1998). Most of the founders either had several years of work experience in the industry or had gained knowledge about the industry through family members, prior to starting their firms. Their backgrounds and experience provided the founders with valuable insights and insider perspectives about their industries. For instance, they knew of problems plaguing their industries and opportunities that could be exploited. Furthermore, most founders made the decision to launch their small firms based on trigger events or conditions. These triggers ranged from personal considerations such as seeking a better quality of life for their families or better work-life balance, to basic cost considerations for operating a business such as the need to move to a rural/semi-urban location to reduce operating costs. Additionally, they understood industry turbulence, saw technology opportunities, and sensed the changing demands of customers, looking for customized service offerings at lower prices. The founders could conceptualize new, different business models.

Figure 1. Research Framework

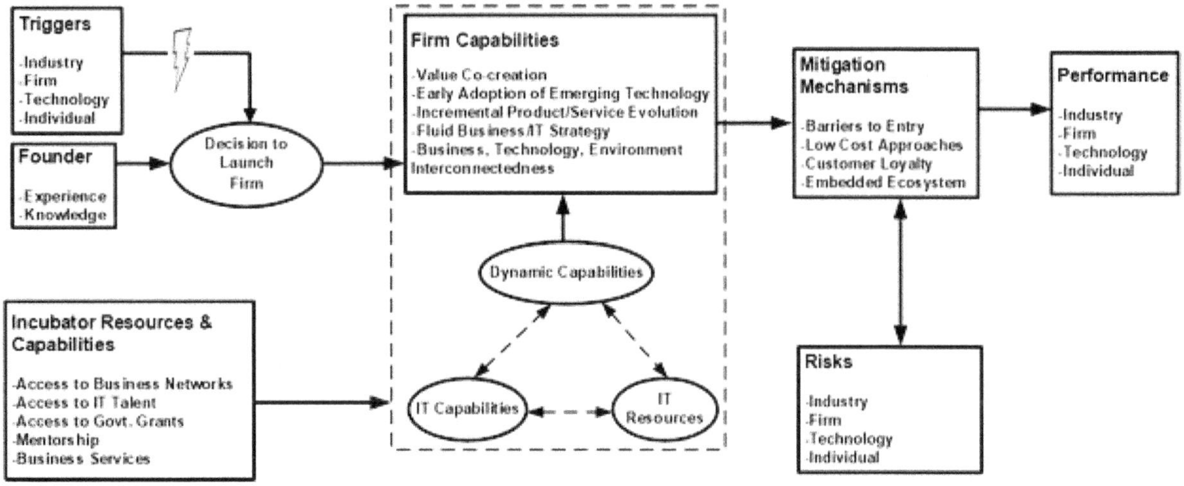

Digital Resources and Digital Capabilities

The digital resources and capabilities of these firms were interdependent and tightly integrated. The interaction between resources and capabilities has been depicted in the framework with two-way dotted arrows. The IT resources included the following: 1) SMACIT infrastructure, which represents emerging IT such as Social media, Mobile apps, Analytics, Cloud computing, and the Internet of Things (Ross 2014). Instead of investing in expensive infrastructures, the firms relied on modular, nimble, scalable and ubiquitous systems that allowed them to remain flexible and to adapt to changing requirements. These systems and technologies ranged from Amazon's Web Services (AWS) and Microsoft's Azure Cloud platform all the way to using open source development languages, Google Apps platform for email, and Skype for communications. 2) Digital communications that involved the use of mobile chat apps, Skype, and other applications to stay in touch with team members and clients. 3) Skilled IT employees: The firms depended on the skills and expertise of new IT employees/contract staff to develop evolving systems. Employees who understand how IT could be leveraged for business success were especially valuable. 4) IT-enabled intangibles (Bharadwaj, 2000) which are complementary (Rehm & Goel, 2017) and ancillary benefits that the firm can take advantage of while it deploys its core IT resources. For example, social interaction among vendors, IT employees and customers were supported by using electronic communications media. This social interaction improved internal project management and communications.

Digital capabilities were strategically developed by the firms and played a crucial role in exploiting the available resources for competitive advantage. Several IT capabilities were developed for this purpose. 1) In order to take advantage of the SMACIT technologies, the firms developed an IT leveraging capability (El Sawy et al., 2010), which enabled them to leverage emerging technologies for specific purposes. For example, one firm might use the cloud to build an online transaction platform, while another might use it to store data files. 2) Two of the firms focused on data digitization and invested resources in building a digitization capability. As a result, they designed digital platforms that were at the leading edge of current technologies and had no competing platforms in their industries. 3) The firms also knew when to outsource key activities. With changing technology and business needs, it was impossible for firms to possess all skills and technical knowledge in-house, especially with limited budgets and tight deadlines. As a result, some firms maintained a superior outsourcing/contract management capability as they augmented their internal staffing needs with contract workers with the right skills and expertise. Using the right IT hiring platforms (online platforms such as Taleo, Kenexa, Freelancer, and LinkedIn) and partnering with the right contract firms for skilled workers was important for developing this capability. 4) The firms demonstrated high business process adaptability. They were responsive to changing customer requirements and offered customizable solutions in order to remain competitive. As a result, these firms remained flexible and adaptable, and altered their business processes as business needs changed. None of the firms used resource-intensive or inflexible project management systems or business process management systems. They relied on the decision-making skills of the founder and key employees to adapt to various business situations. 5) support and training for key customers allowed customer assistance to be delivered remotely, without the need to travel to customer locations. This helped lower costs and provided customers with instant access to support when technical issues emerged. 6) The firms took advantage of emerging technologies such as mobile and cloud computing, and developed capabilities to design products and services for ubiquitous use across mobile and web platforms. For this, a right fit among IT skills, technology architecture, and business strategy was required. However, these capabilities could not be tightly coupled as the firms needed to maneuver to adjust to changing and dynamic environments. In this way, firms developed impressive dynamic capabilities.

Firm Dynamic Capabilities

Dynamic capabilities are higher order capabilities supported by underlying, simpler resources and capabilities (Teece et al., 2016). Dynamic capabilities allowed the firms to be flexible in changing business conditions and operated at strategic and tactical levels. This is why, in the framework, dynamic capabilities are shown as being dependent on core IT capabilities and IT resources but supporting or influencing firm-level capabilities. Dynamic capabilities can be developed by reconfiguration and recombination of IT capabilities and IT resources. The interactions are complex and difficult to separate. The firms we studied displayed at least three distinct dynamic capabilities. 1) Agility, which is the ability to sense changes in the business environment, respond effectively to such changes, and make rapid decisions to ensure that competitive advantage is maintained (Bharadwaj et al., 2013), helped the firms respond to changing customer, business, and technological demands. It was an important capability from a strategic standpoint because it directly related to the founders' goals to keep their firms nimble and responsive to customer demands, ensuring they could compete against larger firms. 2) The firms had dynamic knowledge management capabilities or the capacity to quickly acquire, exploit, and assimilate knowledge related to projects, customers, and technological changes from both internal and external sources and use it to improve future products/services as well as interactions with customers. 3) Dynamic human resource (HR) capabilities were also visible. With the growing complexity of technology and business, it was difficult for small firms with limited resources to hire skilled employees in-house.

In order to address this challenge, firms established a dynamic HR capability where they relied on a trusted HR partner for outsourcing. Firms followed the current trend of "upsourcing", which involves hiring the right people, with the right skills, at the right time. This process was complex. Therefore, establishing relationships in the market with firms and people who understood the firm's contractual and project requirements was extremely important. Although the small firms addressed the development of IT capabilities and dynamic capabilities based on resource availability well, they did not wish to outlay a lot of resources on important but standard operational issues such as ensuring legal compliance, accounting, and tax filing. Here, eTireCo, and eCourseCo sought assistance from a regional incubator. Next, we discuss the incubator's capabilities.

Incubator Resources and Capabilities

The incubator in the region where these firms are located provided low-cost business support services. A key service – founder mentorship – was provided by seasoned business development experts and venture capitalists. The founders of the firms acknowledged the role of the mentors in helping overcome various business challenges. The incubator also leased physical space to firms, and provided access to services such as legal advising, accounting, marketing, HR management, and business executive coaching. The incubator also partnered with a technical institute/college in the region where they recruited IT and other employees for the firms. They also recruited from call centers and IT development offices of larger firms in the region. Their semi-urban location helped them access IT and managerial talent at lower costs than in big cities. Furthermore, the incubator also provided small firms with access to government grants that provided rebates for hiring young, local employees. This helped keep HR costs low and translated into lower prices of products and services for customers. Finally, eTireCo, and eCourseCo benefited from accessing the business networks of the mentors. This helped them establish themselves and their firms as "known brands" in the region. This was an important incubator service because it provided visibility across business circles and helped firms get some of their first paying customers. As a founder stated, "An institution like the Innovation Center that has the resources … and the support with the community … makes it a huge motivator for an entrepreneur like myself to continue to develop our company there."

Mitigation of Risks

Once the firms began to aggressively pursue growth, profitability, and other performance-oriented aspects of the business, they faced a challenge common to small firms – limited resources and constraints that restricted their ability to scale at will. It became important to maintain a balance between pursuing growth opportunities and maintaining the existing level of business, revenues, and relationships that had been carefully built during earlier phases. The firms faced pressures from both internal and external sources. First, firms faced risks due to ongoing changes in the industry and shifts in technology, including the evolution of more sophisticated systems and processes disrupting current generation technologies. This was even more applicable for firms at the leading edge of IT that were dependent on emerging IT for their success. The firms also faced challenges from competitors who could copy their technological capabilities and leapfrog them to the market, especially when they were larger, incumbent firms. Second, as they diversified and pursued new customers, the firms faced challenges with respect to managing internal costs of operations, employee wages, etc. There were also some concerns regarding lack of adoption of certain products/services, e.g., due to the introduction of competing products/services, which added to the pressure to tread carefully by balancing growth plans in new areas with the reality of resource constraints. Third, despite the rapid growth at times, the founders and employees wished to keep work-life balance as a priority and maintain a cordial working atmosphere.

In order to manage these constraints and risks, the firms adopted various strategies and mechanisms. Interviewees discussed how they constantly endeavored to lower operational costs and find resources such as funding, skilled employees, and management guidance. They sought to adopt low-cost approaches to ensuring financial and business sustainability. For example, they did not invest in the most cutting-edge technology for non-mission critical needs. They might use the incubator resources instead. Furthermore, even the acquisition strategy for new, required technology was based on affordability and amortization of costs over a reasonable period of time. Next, the firms were consciously engaged in building barriers for entry for new competitors. The firms were aware that rapidly evolving technology was subject to imitation, substitution, and acquisition by competitors. Therefore, they engaged in building embedded ecosystems or networks of trust and loyalty with current customers. By providing anytime training and support free of cost, they aimed to win over the trust of current customers and expand their footprint in the industry through word of mouth. As a result, they created non-technological barriers of entry which were difficult to imitate and even more difficult to substitute. Without a network of customers, any new competitor would find it difficult to sell even a better technological product/service. The firms were actively engaged in not just the technical and profitability sides of their businesses, but also paid attention to social and human aspects. This was reflected in our framework from the trigger events, to the risks and mitigation mechanisms, and in the performance criteria that these firms used.

Performance and Innovation Outcomes

We detected four different levels of firm performance. 1) At the industry level, for firms using digital platforms, it was important to gain acceptance from, and have their technology adopted by, their customers. They also sought active partnerships and alliances with other firms to further increase the usefulness of the ecosystem and their customer base. The firms sought to make positive ecosystem impacts. 2) At the firm level, business performance was tracked using traditional measures such as growth, profitability, low costs, and customer satisfaction, but also ecosystem-related measures such as customer well-being, employee well-being, and across-the-board innovation. 3) At the technology level, firms wanted to ensure that their IT was robust, accessible, and scalable. In addition, they monitored technical metrics such as time spent using the system, customer interaction, paying customer conversion, and IT-driven innovation. From a broader ecosystem perspective, the firms displayed a keen sense of wanting to use technology to provide better experiences for their customers, ensure security and privacy, reduce errors, and save customer time and costs. 4) At a personal level, firms monitored work-life balance as a measure of individual success and were deeply interested in providing positive working environments for their employees. They were also concerned about employee health and welfare. They also were concerned about the well-being of individuals within their ecosystems, e.g., focusing on developing and strengthening relationships with suppliers and customers, even if it led to increased time, effort and costs.

CONCLUSION

In almost all countries, the Internet is changing the ways in which firms compete and providing very new business opportunities. The only end to business opportunity is our imagination. Similarly, in most countries, small firms are the backbone of the economy (Pickernell et al. 2013). Increasing competitiveness and innovation of rural small firms is critical for economic and social success of nations and communities. Although our study is limited by its exploratory nature and focus on Canadian firms, our findings are potentially useful to managers of small firms, wherever they may be geographically located.

We invite practitioners to use the framework when launching or repositioning small digital technology-enabled firms.

In this chapter, we have responded to the call to study emerging trends in digital business strategy. We recognize that the scope of digital innovation has evolved, and IT and business strategies are increasingly fused together (El Sawy et al., 2010; Nambisan et al., 2017). We emphasize the embedded nature of digital technologies across the business value chain and we acknowledge that the speed of digital innovation is rapid, and firms must develop capabilities to respond to fast-changing market conditions. We provide a framework for studying rural entrepreneurship that moves beyond the individual entrepreneur but acknowledge his/her contributions towards fostering digital innovation in ecosystems despite suffering from scarcity of resources and other challenges. This chapter draws together leading academic research on digital innovation and entrepreneurship in the context of rural firms (El Sawy et al., 2010; Tanriverdi et al., 2010). It provides important, practical research on rural small firms, business development, and ecosystem development (Tamasy, 2007). Studies on digital ecodynamics provide "an energizing vision for IS strategy research" and have the potential to reshape "strategic management research and practice in a turbulent and digitized world" (Bharadwaj et al., 2013; El Sawy et al., 2010) We have examined the co-evolution of business and technology strategies and their execution, as well as small firm innovation (Bharadwaj et al., 2013; El Sawy et al., 2010).

This chapter makes important theoretical contributions to understanding how RBV can be extended to digital resources and capabilities and how digital capabilities can be inter-related with firm dynamic capabilities (Teece et al., 2016). Thus, we establish stronger linkages between RBV and the emergent digital innovation literature and provide empirical evidence in the context of digital entrepreneurship in rural Canada. Furthermore, we highlight how digital innovation and entrepreneurship has moved well beyond the traditional boundaries of the firm and is embedded in ecosystems (Nambisan et al., 2019) that consist of complex physical, digital, and social relationships among participants and entities, usually centered around a focal entity (incubator) that orchestrates the activities within and outside the ecosystem (Chan et al., 2020; Ahuja and Chan, 2017). While most previous research seeks to highlight one or two aspects of digital innovation and entrepreneurship within rural firms, we use the "digital ecodymanics" perspective as an appropriate theoretical lens to provide a holistic view of the various nuts and bolts that enable digital innovation by exploiting underlying resources and capabilities, and more importantly, drive the co-evolution of the business strategies and digital capabilities of the firms. This results in a comprehensive research framework that captures the breadth and depth of our investigation of these firms.

This chapter also provides rich insights to practitioners, entrepreneurs, and policy makers regarding factors that fuel and inhibit digital innovation and entrepreneurship in small, rural firms in Canada. The chapter provides "on-the-ground" and "real world" examples of how rural entrepreneurs make business and technology decisions and how their businesses contribute to the economic growth and development of rural economies. It also highlights the crucial role of business incubators and other business services in supporting rural entrepreneurship and innovation – both digital and physical. Although previous research has shown the importance of providing support and services for startups through business incubators, this is among the first studies to focus on the role of such incubator(s) in a rural setting specifically to promote digital innovation and entrepreneurship. The findings of this study can guide local, provincial, and federal governments regarding policy decisions for making investments in rural businesses and communities. Finally, the chapter illustrates that rural entrepreneurs emphasize performance beyond profits alone. They also support their employees, give back to the local community, create opportunities locally, and willingly contribute to sustaining and improving the overall health and well-being of the ecosystem.

REFERENCES

Ahuja, S., & Chan, Y. E. (2019). Frugal innovation and digitalisation: A platform ecosystem perspective. In *Frugal Innovation* (pp. 89–107). Routledge. doi:10.4324/9780429025679-5

Ahuja, S., & Chan, Y. E. (2017). Resource orchestration for IT-enabled Innovation. *Kindai Management Review*, *5*(1), 78–96.

Arend, R. J., & Bromiley, P. (2009). *Assessing the dynamic capabilities view: Spare change, everyone?* Sage Publications Sage UK.

Barney, J. B. (2001). Is the resource-based "view" a useful perspective for strategic management research? Yes. *Academy of Management Review*, *26*(1), 41–56.

Bharadwaj, A., El Sawy, O. A., Pavlou, P. A., & Venkatraman, N. (2013). Digital business strategy: Toward a next generation of insights. *Management Information Systems Quarterly*, *37*(2), 471–482. doi:10.25300/MISQ/2013/37:2.3

Bharadwaj, A. S. (2000). A resource-based perspective on information technology capability and firm performance: An empirical investigation. *Management Information Systems Quarterly*, *24*(1), 169–196. doi:10.2307/3250983

Chan, Y., & Ahuja, S. (2015). *Digital Ecodynamics in Small Firms: Using Information Technology to Compete. Thirty Sixth International Conference on Information Systems*, Fort Worth, TX.

Chan, Y. E., Ahuja, S., Denford, J. S., Henfridsson, O., & Levallet, N. (2020). Digital Innovation and Entrepreneurship: The Challenges of an Ecosystem Perspective. Academy of Management Proceedings, 2020(1), 15203. doi:10.5465/AMBPP.2020.15203symposium

Chan, Y. E., & Farrington, C. J. (2018). Community-based research: Engaging universities in technology-related knowledge exchanges. *Information and Organization*, *28*(3), 129–139. doi:10.1016/j.infoandorg.2018.08.001

Chan, Y. E., Krishnamurthy, R., & Desjardins, C. (2020). Technology-Driven Innovation in Small Firms. *MIS Quarterly Executive*, *19*(1), 39–55. doi:10.17705/2msqe.00024

El Sawy, O. A., Malhotra, A., Park, Y., & Pavlou, P. A. (2010). Seeking the Configurations of Digital Ecodynamics: It Takes Three to Tango. *Information Systems Research*, *21*(4), 835–848. doi:10.1287/isre.1100.0326

El Sawy, O. A., & Pereira, F. (2013). *Business Modelling in the Dynamic Digital Space*. Springer Berlin Heidelberg., doi:10.1007/978-3-642-31765-1

Graziano, T. (2020). Rural Entrepreneurship, Innovation, and Technology: Narratives From the Italian AgriFood Startup Ecosystem. In Handbook of Research on Agricultural Policy, Rural Development, and Entrepreneurship in Contemporary Economies (pp. 334-353). IGI Global.

Hindman, D. B. (2000). The Rural-Urban Digital Divide. *Journalism & Mass Communication Quarterly*, *77*(3), 549–560. doi:10.1177/107769900007700306

Innovation, S., & the Economic Development Canada. (2019). *Key Small Business Statistics – November 2019*. Available at: https://www.ic.gc.ca/eic/site/061.nsf/vwapj/KSBS_Nov-2019_En_Final_5.pdf/$file/KSBS_Nov-2019_En_Final_5.pdf

Mair, J., Martí, I., & Ventresca, M. J. (2012). Building Inclusive Markets in Rural Bangladesh: How Intermediaries Work Institutional Voids. *Academy of Management Journal*, *55*(4), 819–850. doi:10.5465/amj.2010.0627

Muñoz, P., & Kimmitt, J. (2019). Rural entrepreneurship in place: An integrated framework. *Entrepreneurship and Regional Development*, *31*(9-10), 842–873. doi:10.1080/08985626.2019.1609593

Nambisan, S., Lyytinen, K., Majchrzak, A., & Song, M. (2017). Digital innovation management: Reinventing innovation management research in a digital world. *Management Information Systems Quarterly*, *41*(1), 223–238. doi:10.25300/MISQ/2017/41:1.03

Nambisan, S., Wright, M., & Feldman, M. (2019). The Digital Transformation of Innovation and Entrepreneurship: Progress, Challenges and Key Themes. *Research Policy*, *48*(8), 103773. doi:10.1016/j.respol.2019.03.018

Nambisan, S., Zahra, S. A., & Luo, Y. (2019). Global platforms and ecosystems: Implications for international business theories. *Journal of International Business Studies*, *50*(9), 1464–1486. Advance online publication. doi:10.105741267-019-00262-4

Pham, L., & Massey, B. (2018). Effective Digital Participation: Differences in Rural and Urban Areas and Ways Forward. In M. Dezuanni, M. Foth, K. Mallan, & H. Hughes (Eds.), *Digital Participation through Social Living Labs* (pp. 315–332). Chandos Publishing. doi:10.1016/B978-0-08-102059-3.00017-4

Pickernell, D., Senyard, J., Jones, P., Packham, G., & Ramsey, E. (2013). New and young firms: Entrepreneurship policy and the role of government–evidence from the Federation of Small Businesses survey. *Journal of Small Business and Enterprise Development*, *20*(2), 358–382. doi:10.1108/14626001311326770

Rehm, S.-V., & Goel, L. (2017). Using information systems to achieve complementarity in SME innovation networks. *Information & Management*, *54*(4), 438–451. doi:10.1016/j.im.2016.10.003

Salemink, K., Strijker, D., & Bosworth, G. (2017). Rural development in the digital age: A systematic literature review on unequal ICT availability, adoption, and use in rural areas. *Journal of Rural Studies*, *54*, 360–371. doi:10.1016/j.jrurstud.2015.09.001

Storey, D. J., & Greene, F. J. (2010). *Small business and entrepreneurship*. Financial Times/Prentice Hall.

Tamasy, C. (2007). Rethinking technology-oriented business incubators: Developing a robust policy instrument for entrepreneurship, innovation, and regional development? *Growth and Change*, *38*(3), 460–473. doi:10.1111/j.1468-2257.2007.00379.x

Tanriverdi, H., Rai, A., & Venkatraman, N. (2010). Research commentary—Reframing the dominant quests of information systems strategy research for complex adaptive business systems. *Information Systems Research*, *21*(4), 822–834. doi:10.1287/isre.1100.0317

Teece, D., Peteraf, M., & Leih, S. (2016). Dynamic capabilities and organizational agility: Risk, uncertainty, and strategy in the innovation economy. *California Management Review*, *58*(4), 13–35. doi:10.1525/cmr.2016.58.4.13

Yin, R. K. (2017). *Case Study Research and Applications: Design and Methods*. SAGE Publications.

ADDITIONAL READING

Ashmore, F. H., Farrington, J. H., & Skerratt, S. (2017). Community-led broadband in rural digital infrastructure development: Implications for resilience. *Journal of Rural Studies*, *54*, 408–425. doi:10.1016/j.jrurstud.2016.09.004

Bhatti, Y., & Prabhu, J. (2019). Frugal innovation and social innovation: linked paths to achieving inclusion sustainably. Handbook of Inclusive Innovation.

Chan, Y. E., Dixon, J. A., & Dukelow, C. R. (2013). *Revitalizing rural economies: A guide for practitioners*. McGill-Queen's Press-MQUP.

Koutsouris, A. (2010, July). The emergence of the intra-rural digital divide: A critical review of the adoption of ICTs in rural areas and the farming community. In *9th European IFSA Symposium* (Vol. 4, No. 7).

Larimo, J. A., Marinov, M. A., Marinova, S. T., & Leposky, T. (2020). *International Business and Emerging Economy Firms*. Springer International Publishing. doi:10.1007/978-3-030-27285-2

McMurray, A. J., & De Waal, G. A. (Eds.). (2019). *Frugal Innovation: A Global Research Companion*. Routledge. doi:10.4324/9780429025679

Porter, M. E., Ketels, C. H., Miller, K., & Bryden, R. (2004). Competitiveness in rural US regions: Learning and research agenda. Institute for Strategy and Competitiveness, Harvard Business School, 1-17.

Roberts, E., Anderson, B. A., Skerratt, S., & Farrington, J. (2017). A review of the rural-digital policy agenda from a community resilience perspective. *Journal of Rural Studies*, *54*, 372–385. doi:10.1016/j.jrurstud.2016.03.001

KEY TERMS AND DEFINITIONS

Capabilities: Capabilities are the accumulated knowledge and skills that enable a firm to coordinate its activities and deploy resources advantageously.

Digital Ecodynamics: Digital Ecodynamics is a systemic phenomenon involving complex interactions among the triad of environmental turbulence, dynamic capabilities, and digital systems.

Digital Innovation: Digital innovation refers to the application of digital technology to existing business problems. Digital innovation can include development of a new technology strategy in an existing business context, adoption and implementation of a new software or platform, and evolution from analog to digital processes.

Dynamic Capabilities: The firm's ability to integrate, build, and reconfigure internal and external resources and capabilities to address rapidly changing environments.

Founder: The founder of a startup is usually the creator of the company (usually to solve a problem) and seeks market validation by building a minimum viable product (MVP), i.e. a prototype, to develop and validate their business models.

Resource-Based View (RBV): The resource-based view (RBV) is a managerial framework used to determine the strategic resources a firm can exploit to achieve sustainable competitive advantage.

Startup: A startup is a company or project begun by an entrepreneur to seek, develop, and validate a scalable economic model.

Chapter 5
SMEs Internationalization Through Electronic Commerce: Benefits, Disadvantages, and Barriers

Michael Cook
Charles Sturt University, Australia

Sophia Duan
https://orcid.org/0000-0002-8235-0092
RMIT University, Australia

Branka Krivokapic-Skoko
https://orcid.org/0000-0003-3373-7124
Charles Sturt University, Australia

ABSTRACT

This study explores the benefits, disadvantages, and barriers for the internationalization of regional small and medium-sized enterprises (SMEs) through the adoption of electronic commerce (e-commerce). Interviews were conducted with directors of ten Australian regional SMEs for exploring their use of e-commerce in the internationalization process. This led to the identification and validation of benefits, disadvantages, and barriers for the internationalization of regional SMEs with the use of e-commerce. A better understanding of these benefits, disadvantages, and barriers would help e-commerce stakeholders develop appropriate strategies and policies for driving the adoption of e-commerce for the internationalization of regional SMEs.

INTRODUCTION

Internationalization is the expansion of economic activities across national borders (Ruzzier, et al., 2006). Organizations of all sizes aim to expand their international operations to achieve vital growth, increase entrepreneurial knowledge and reinforce financial efficiency. Electronic commerce (e-commerce) refers

DOI: 10.4018/978-1-7998-4942-1.ch005

to any form of business transaction in which parties interact electronically rather than through direct contact (Grandon and Pearson, 2004). It has emerged as an enabling tool for the internationalization of organizations mainly due to its benefits, especially to small-and-medium-sized enterprises (SMEs), including strengthened customer relationships, ease of reaching targeted markets, improved efficiency, reduced costs, and greater competitive advantage (Duan et al., 2012; Deng et al., 2020).

Realizing that e-commerce is a major source of competitive advantage as well as a cost-effective way for the internationalization of SMEs, governments actively assist SMEs with expanding and growing their businesses through the development of policies and programs to improve economic conditions for SMEs. In Australia, for example, key initiatives were introduced that worth a $5.3 billion (ASBAS, 2019; Duan, 2020). Such initiatives have created a sound environment for supporting Australian SMEs financially and promoting the adoption of e-commerce for their respective internationalization.

SMEs in regional areas are affected by circumstances inherent to their location. Regional areas are defined as geographical areas located outside metropolitan centers and major cities (ABS, 2018). Regional areas are characterized by high unemployment, a shortage of skills, limited access to resources and a lack of infrastructure (MacGregor and Kartiwi, 2010). SMEs are significant regional development agents. This is especially the case in regional Australia where SMEs constitute approximately 95% of all businesses in services and industry sectors (ABS, 2018).

The Internet has become an important tool to facilitate the process of internationalization in enterprises. As an enabler, e-commerce has the potential to facilitate organizational change in regional SMEs allowing them to compete and operate in a global environment. As a result, SMEs are no longer confined by geography, rather the internet has permitted SMEs the ability to move from time to space variables.

The promising e-commerce outlook and continuous support from governments (Duan, 2020) provide a sound opportunity for SMEs in the regional areas to internationalize using e-commerce with low cost. The adoption of e-commerce in Australian SMEs, however, is disappointing, evidenced by the relatively low levels of participation in the e-commerce relevant activities by Australian SMEs (Deng et al., 2019). Only 51% of Australian SMEs, for example, take orders online in 2017, among which 11% are specifically targeting international customers (ABS, 2018). A better understanding of benefits, disadvantages and barriers for the adoption of e-commerce for internationalization in regional SMEs is highly needed.

This research aims to investigate the benefits for regional SMEs by using e-commerce for internationalization, as well as to examine the disadvantages and barriers that regional SMEs need to overcome to benefit from the e-commerce adoption in the internationalization process. To achieve this, the research question is proposed as follows:

How do regional SMEs perceive e-commerce in terms of benefits, disadvantages and barriers to adoption for internationalization?

A literature review was undertaken to explore the benefits, disadvantages and barriers to SME internationalization through the adoption of e-commerce. The review forms the basis for this research and guided development of interview questions. Ten regional SMEs in Australia were then selected as case studies. Semi-structured interviews were conducted to obtain rich information for analysis. Through comprehensive 'within-case analysis' and 'cross-case comparison,' several benefits, disadvantages and barriers were identified, and their implications discussed.

In what follows, the next section presents a review of the related literature. Next, the research design and methodology discussed followed by the research findings. Finally, conclusion section concludes the paper with a discussion of the results and areas of future research.

LITERATURE REVIEW

Benefits of e-Commerce Adoption

For regional SMEs to successfully internationalize, an understanding of both benefits to be gained and barriers to be overcome is required. Table 1 presents a summary of the benefits of e-commerce adoption, although not necessarily limited to regional SMEs. Many of the advantages of e-commerce adoption can be considered intangible and are only realized after a period (MacGregor and Kartiwi, 2010). This idea is based on learning, efficiency and cost advantages.

Table 1. Advantages of e-commerce adoption

Advantages	Sources
Access to market knowledge	(Damanpour, 2001); (Berry and Kai-uwe Brock, 2004); (Knight and Cavusgil, 2004)
Reduce disadvantage	(Berry and Kai-uwe Brock, 2004)
Reduce uncertainty	(Damanpour, 2001); (Berry and Kai-uwe Brock, 2004)
Reduce transaction costs	(Damanpour, 2001); (Bertschek and Fryges, 2002); (Berry and Kai-uwe Brock, 2004)
Increase transaction efficiency	(Bowden, et al., 2001); (Damanpour, 2001); (Bertschek and Fryges, 2002); (Osarenkhoe, 2009)
Access new customers	(Bowden, et al., 2001); (Damanpour, 2001); (Pavic, et al., 2007); (Osarenkhoe, 2009)
Enhance company image	(Bowden, et al., 2001)
Faster response time	(Bowden, et al., 2001); (Chong, 2008)
Develop networks	(Damanpour, 2001); (Stansfield and Grant, 2003)
Identify new markets	(Stansfield and Grant, 2003); (Bamberry, 2006)
Achieve economies of scale	(Bamberry, 2006)
Compete against larger firms	(Chong, 2008); (MacGregor and Kartiwi, 2010)

Studies have found that e-commerce has a positive effect on the accumulation of information (Knight and Cavusgil, 2004), which can reduce the perceived disadvantages and uncertainties associated with SMEs (Berry and Kai-uwe Brock, 2004). It has also been suggested that e-commerce can reduce transaction costs and free up resources that can be redirected to areas where they can be utilized more effectively (Berry and Kai-uwe Brock, 2004). E-commerce has also been found to have a positive effect on the efficiency of established business processes and increasing market transparency (Bertschek and Fryges, 2002; Raymond, 2001). Further studies have shown that e-commerce has the potential to create efficiencies from automation of transactions, advantages in identifying new market intermediaries, the consolidation of demand and supply, as well as changes in the extent of the vertical integration of companies that were not possible a few years ago (Bertschek and Fryges, 2002; Osarenkhoe, 2009). This allows SMEs to compete globally without having to physically contact business partners and customers, demonstrate products to potential customers, and rapidly facilitate the transaction of payment (Osarenkhoe, 2009).

Through the internet's ability to overcome geographical boundaries (Pavic et al., 2007), SMEs are able to achieve economies of scale and thus expand further into domestic markets and potentially internationalize (Bamberry, 2006). This acts as a way of securing competitive advantage because it is a cost-effective way of reaching global customers and competing effectively against larger firms (MacGregor and Kartiwi, 2010). A study conducted by Bowden et al. (2001) further elaborated on the intangible benefits noting that e-commerce had an impact on (1) enhancing company image (2) improving information exchange (3) faster response time (4) providing access to potential customers and (5) creating new opportunities. Another study by Harrigan, Ramsey and Ibbotson (2010) found that SMEs utilizing e-commerce are reaping greater benefits than their ad-hoc counterparts through its ability to open up new markets and level the playing field between SMEs and larger firms (Chong, 2008). Kendall and Kendall (2001) summarized this best by noting that e-commerce is an elaboration of traditional business models that provides value to both the customer and business (Kendall and Kendall, 2001).

Disadvantages of e-Commerce Adoption

Research has shown that a variety of internal and external disadvantages exist for the adoption of e-commerce in SMEs. Macgregor and Kartiwi (2010) found that significant disadvantages included reduced flexibility, increase in security concerns, doubling of work and deterioration of relations with business partners.

A study conducted by Bertschek and Fryges (2002) elaborated on the internal disadvantages and found that e-commerce required a significant amount of organizational commitment. This is in relation to implementing various technical requirements, the reorganization of work processes and adaptation of logistic and inventory systems. Whilst Lawson et al. (2001) found the added cost of e-commerce adoption to be exacerbated through the high cost of consultants and the lack of government programs to support its implementation.

Additionally, research conducted by Stansfield and Grant (2003) found that e-commerce has a considerable impact on the external environment noting that the adoption of e-commerce can lead to increased competition. It was also suggested that SMEs face difficulties in managing traditional customer and supplier relations given the lack of personalized contact in e-commerce (Harrigan, Ramsey, and Ibbotson, 2010). Table 2 presents a summary of the disadvantages of e-commerce adoption, which may be a factor in regional businesses

Table 2. Disadvantages of e-commerce adoption

Disadvantage	Source
Reduced flexibility	(MacGregor and Kartiwi, 2010)
Security	(Lawson, et al., 2001); (MacGregor and Kartiwi, 2010)
Increase in workload	(MacGregor and Kartiwi, 2010)
Deterioration of relations	(Harrigan, et al., 2010); (MacGregor and Kartiwi, 2010)
Organizational restructuring	(Bertschek and Fryges, 2002)
Increased threats and competition	(Stansfield and Grant, 2003)
Cost of consultants	(Lawson, et al., 2001)
High financial requirements	(MacGregor and Kartiwi, 2010)
Large range of e-commerce options	(MacGregor and Kartiwi, 2010)

Barriers to e-Commerce Adoption

A study conducted by MacGregor and Kartiwi (2010) found that barriers to e-commerce adoption could be characterized as external supply and demand barriers, and internal resource and human barriers. In an earlier study conducted by MacGregor and Vrazalic (2005), barriers to adoption were classified into organizational and environmental categories. Thus, barriers deemed significant could include a lack of technical resources, the complexity of e-commerce, and difficulty in measuring the rate of return.

Similarly, Braun (2002) noted the need for compatibility of the product being sold and other barriers such as fear of isolation, competitor use, alienating intermediaries, uncontrolled growth, lack of technological expertise and lack of strategic definition (Braun, 2002). Stansfield and Grant (2003) noted the lack of IT support and IT expertise as being critical in determining the propensity to adopt e-commerce. Whilst Lawson, Alcock and Cooper (2001) identified four barriers to adoption including security concerns, cost of consultants, lack of government incentives and lack of IT expertise. These barriers are confirmed in other studies (Barry and Milner, 2002; Martin and Matlay, 2001; McCole and Ramsey, 2005; Pavic, et al., 2007).

Chong (2008) expanded on the environmental impacts of the lack of critical mass in consumers using the internet. Their studies concluded that critical mass was required for benefits to be fully recognized. As a result of the lack of widespread acceptance, potential users of e-commerce technology may resist the push to adopt e-commerce technology. This is because customers have been slow to adopt e-commerce, and as a result, the benefits perceived by SMEs have been slow to manifest (Chong, 2008). The barriers are summarized in Table 3.

Table 3. Barriers to adoption

Barriers	Sources
Lack of product compatibility	(Braun, 2002); (MacGregor and Vrazalic, 2005)
Fear of isolation	(Braun, 2002)
Competitor use	(Braun, 2002)
Alienating intermediaries	(Braun, 2002)
Uncontrolled growth	(Braun, 2002)
Lack of expertise	(Braun, 2002); (Barry and Milner, 2002); (Stansfield and Grant, 2003); (Chong, 2008); (Lawson, et al., 2001); (Martin and Matlay, 2001); (MacGregor and Kartiwi, 2010)
Lack of strategic definition	(Braun, 2002)
Lack of time	(McCole and Ramsey, 2005); (Barry and Milner, 2002); (Bowden, et al., 2001); (MacGregor and Kartiwi, 2010)
Unwillingness to change	(McCole and Ramsey, 2005)
Disadvantage	(McCole and Ramsey, 2005); (MacGregor and Kartiwi, 2010)
Lack of trust	(McCole and Ramsey, 2005); (MacGregor and Kartiwi, 2010)
High costs	(Bowden, et al., 2001); (Chong, 2008); (Lawson, et al., 2001); (MacGregor and Vrazalic, 2005)
No critical mass	(Bowden, et al., 2001); (Chong , 200 8)
Security concerns	(MacGregor and Vrazalic, 2005); (MacGregor and Kartiwi, 2010)
Lack of government support	(Lawson, et al., 2001)

RESEARCH METHOD

To answer the research question, ten case studies of SMEs across regional New South Wales, Australia were conducted. As the research question is largely exploratory, a qualitative case study approach is the most appropriate research method (Yin, 2017). The qualitative case study allows for access to deeper levels of understanding of new or complex phenomena by yielding a high level of detail, which serves the exploratory aim of this research. Compared to quantitative research, which is more confirmatory than exploratory, the knowledge gained through qualitative investigation is more informative and richer, therefore offering an enhanced understanding (Yin, 2017).

To capture a holistic viewpoint and enhance research validity, this study has drawn upon multiple sources of evidence, including semi-structured interviews, on-site unobtrusive observations and comprehensive reviews of business reports and databases. Semi-structured interviews were used as the main data collection method in this study. Additional face-to-face interviews were conducted with four key informants for the purpose of context building and triangulation. This included interviews with representatives from the Riverina Business Enterprise Centre, the NSW Department of Industry and Austrade.

To ensure validity in the analysis, and to provide a better understanding of each company's background, preparation work such as a review of key documents (i.e. business reports, news, whitepapers and archival records), was carried out before and after the interviews. Where possible on-site unobtrusive observations were also conducted to obtain contextual information and reinforce data triangulation. Notes were taken during the observations, while interviews were audio-recorded, transcribed and documented to enhance research reliability (Yin, 2017).

Table 4. Nature of e-commerce adoption

	Western Plains Winery	Breakout Furniture	Gypsy Beans	Liberty Lights	Origami Paper Supplies	Sigma Consulting	Top Gun Bioscience	Dose Wines	Bags4bags	Applique Haberdashery
Website design and purpose										
Static website	x					x	x	x		
Shopping cart		x	x	x	x			x	x	x
Online brochure	x	x								
Social media presence and use										
Facebook			x		x	x		x	x	
Twitter					x	x		x		
YouTube				x		x		x	x	
LinkedIn						x		x		
e-Commerce focus and development										
Cloud Computing						x	x	x		
Business-to-Business (B2B)	x		x	x	x		x	x		x
Business-to-Consumer (B2C)	x	x	x	x	x	x		x	x	x
Search Engine Optimization (SEO)						x	x	x	x	
IT Consultant	x		x		x		x		x	x
Perceived growth after adoption										
High growth after adoption			x			x	x	x		x
Medium growth after adoption		x		x	x					
Low growth after adoption	x								x	

Analysis of the information collected was based on 'within-case analysis' and 'cross-case comparison' (Miles and Huberman, 1994), which is the treatment of each case as a separate study (Yin, 2017). This includes the use of the interview data to construct word tables that will assist in the identification and analysis of emerging patterns, similarities and differences in the case studies.

The use of unstructured analysis will aid in the construct of word tables. Three steps were followed in this research: (i) Grouping of data based on tags which identify sets of common information, (ii) Creation of categories which list, compare tags and (iii) Characterization of similarities in the data.

Coding of responses was also used to assess the richness of the data. Coding includes Manifest, Latent and Global categories as described by Aberbach and Rockman (2002) to allow for an assessment of the suitability of the data and determine the richness of the information gathered through the interview process. Findings were triangulated across multiple data sources, and clarifications from participants after the interviews were sought as required to ensure accuracy.

FINDINGS

The following sections present the findings.

Nature of e-Commerce Adoption

Table 4 shows the nature of e-commerce adoption by the case studies. This includes information on the type of website design, the adoption of social media, the focus of the business and the perceived impact of e-commerce adoption on the growth of the business.

The nature of the website developed by the case studies was determined to be of two types; the static website, or the website as a point of sale. Four case studies had developed the static website, using it as a method of conveying information. This was particularly relevant for services SMEs (*Sigma Consulting* and *Top Gun Bioscience*), which determined use of the website as a point of sale was not practical. The participant from Top Gun bioscience noted this implication:

We aren't so much you're 'hang your website out there and take orders on the web' type of guys. It's super complex stuff, it takes a long time... the website won't ever function as a commercial structure for us.

The use of the website as a point of sale was more prominent in small business case studies. In those case studies where this was relevant, the point of sale aspect was used to supplement a 'bricks and mortar' operation or was used as a means of facilitating the sale of the new inventive or innovative product. Interestingly, the use of a website as a point of sale for the larger company was only adopted as a method of maintaining the link between the company and the customer. The participant from *Dose Wines* stating that:

B2C is almost non-existent for us because we sell to retailers not to customers so B2C is minuscule. The reason we do it is primarily to maintain a relationship with customer.

Social media was also identified as one of the means of e-commerce adoption by SMEs. Among others, Facebook proved to be the most popular site due to personal use by the business owner. The benefits of social media adoption included its ease of use, ability to communicate instantly with inquiries from customers and as a low-cost tool of advertising. The small business case studies tended to use Facebook as the primary social media site whilst the *Sigma Consulting* and *Dose Wines* (services and large company case studies) utilized all the social media sites listed above. The participant from *Origami Paper Supplies* noted the benefits of social media:

We started off with Facebook as a marketing tool...It was a great way for us to show people the type of business we had and to show them the products, and to engage with people because of the comments and the way that you can have that backwards and forwards interaction on Facebook.

However, some of the case studies (*Western Plains Winery, Breakout Furniture, Liberty Lights, Top Gun Bioscience,* and *Applique Haberdashery)* were still skeptical of social media as a business tool. The reasons include the use of social media as a personal space that should be free from advertising, a lack of understanding, not being suited to the targeted demographic, and a lack of time in facilitating its development.

Of the different functions of e-commerce, most small case studies used it as a means of supporting consumer transactions. In some cases, this method was adopted to supplement the income from other means whilst in the case of *Dose Wines*, the B2C component was maintained to preserve the link between the company and the individual consumer. Use of e-commerce as a B2C function did not register with *Top Gun Bioscience* due to the external factors of the industry in which they operate. In that case, it was not practical to operate e-commerce as a B2C function due to the nature of their work and their industry, rather e-commerce was used to establish credibility and trust as opposed to a point of sale:

Our clients don't shift suppliers that often, there's a fair bit of regulatory bind attached.

E-commerce use as a B2B function was prominent in most case studies of all sizes. The small business case studies primarily used e-commerce as a communication tool with suppliers of their products. In the services case studies, B2B focused on communication and the dissemination of information between the various parts of the value chain. On the other hand, *Dose Wines* utilized the B2B function as the primary operative means of e-commerce. *Dose Wines* had used e-commerce to automate almost every aspect of their business operations including logistics, accounting, business analytics and marketing.

People think of B2B as just a transaction- make an order. We've actually not automated that in your e-commerce, but we've actually automated all of the heavy liftings, but the 10% is still traditional and the 90% has been converted over where all the work was.

Cloud computing is another theme that emerged from the case studies especially in the case of the services businesses and *Dose Wines*. Cloud computing was an effective tool for the sharing of information between the business and their clients. Cloud computing is maintained as an efficient system for the storage and handling of data between the business and their clients. The participants from *Dose Wines* stated the benefits of cloud computing on the efficient operation of the company:

We've got to communicate... we've got to get the wine shipment overseas, we've got to get a lot of stuff to customers...the real work is actually all the logistics about getting through the transport, the shipping, the clearances, all the government stuff, the quality analysis...transport bits, so all of that is handled in a cloud-based system.

Although the small business case studies expressed a desire to embrace cloud-based computing, the limitations are mainly associated with infrastructure as noted by *Top Gun Bioscience:*

We've had limitations around cloud computing because of the infrastructure...there's a pipe or a thing that runs through Dubbo ... and apparently if you're in the right one or two suburbs of Dubbo you've got access ... if you're not then bad luck. So, the infrastructure in part is physically here, how accessible it is I don't know, but is it severely limiting, no.

Regarding the perceived impact of e-commerce adoption on the business, all case studies had noted a growth impact of varying degrees. Perceived low growth was experienced by *Western Plains Winery* and *Bags4Bags* who both attributed this to poor marketing of the site. *Western Plains Winery* mentioned that:

It's a slow start, I'm hopeful that it will improve ... I've just got to keep putting it out there to people to let them know that it's there.

Case studies that experienced a medium range of growth include *Breakout Furniture, Liberty Lights and Origami Paper Supplies*. Two of the case studies had acknowledged that a focus on the bricks and mortar aspect of the business had been the core part of its business operations; however, growth was still experienced in the online component of the business. The participant from *Origami Paper Supplies* noted the impact of e-commerce adoption on their business:

In the couple of months that we've had the website we've had a few thousand dollars' worth of sales so that's a few thousands of dollars, we wouldn't have had, so I call it successful.

Case studies that experienced a perceived high rate of growth include *Gypsy Beans, Sigma Consulting, Top Gun Bioscience, Dose Wines* and *Applique Haberdashery*. In the case of *Dose Wines*, the adoption of e-commerce had facilitated the growth of the company from a medium-sized enterprise to a large company, whilst in other cases, growth through e-commerce had been unexpected. The participant from *Applique Haberdashery* noted the impact of high and unexpected growth on the firm and e-commerce as a facilitator of this growth:

The website was getting overloaded, we were having too many people on there… it was starting to seriously not go well… it was time-consuming, it was frustrating for the girls because it couldn't happen quick enough, and it just wasn't built for the amount of traffic that we were expecting.

The amount of growth in the case studies can be attributed to greater consumer access to the business as a result of maintaining an online presence. It should be noted that the level of growth is from the perspective of the business owner.

Advantages

Table 5 shows the perceived advantages derived from e-commerce adoption within the case studies.

Table 5. Advantages of e-commerce adoption

	Western Plains Winery	Breakout Furniture	Gypsy Beans	Liberty Lights	Origami Paper Supplies	Sigma Consulting	Top Gun Bioscience	Dose Wines	Bags4bags	Applique Haberdashery
E-commerce as a marketing tool	x	x	x	x	x	x	x	x	x	x
Overseas Inquiries	x		x	x		x	x	x		x
Instant Communication	x	x	x				x			
Survivability	x	x		x		x	x		x	x
Network by social media						x			x	
Supply chain consolidation		x	x	x	x				x	
Speed and Efficiency	x	x		x		x		x		
Ease of Administration	x									x
Site for Bona Fides				x		x	x		x	x
Established Credibility			x	x		x	x			
Develop Trust						x	x			
Access to Larger Markets	x	x	x	x	x	x	x	x	x	x
Increased Confidence	x	x		x	x					
Facilitate Customer Service	x			x		x				
Encourage Word of Mouth		x	x	x		x	x	x	x	
Time Saver	x	x					x	x		
Respond to Inquiry	x		x	x		x	x			
Ease in Finding Clients				x		x	x	x		
E-commerce a Cost Saver	x	x				x		x	x	x

Within these case studies, several different advantages appeared. The most significant factor that emerged in all small business case studies was the ability to use e-commerce as a low-cost marketing tool. In almost all the case studies, e-commerce as a marketing tool was linked to social media adoption as the main form of communication with customers and the products of the business. The owner of *Origami Party Supplies* noted the impact of e-commerce as a marketing tool stating:

It comes back to marketing because it's just letting people know we're here and what we've got. But basically, we just cranked it up, the website, and stuck a note on Facebook, started putting our website on our ads.

While the owner of *Gypsy Beans* noted the impact of social media as a powerful tool to share information about its products:

The bottom line is I've embraced it [social media] ...I've seen the potential of the benefits that social media can have because people, especially the generation coming through, really feed off that. I'll give you an example, we had a new cake, a passionfruit cheesecake, and I told the girls just send it out on Facebook...and within a week that cake sold out...and the amount of people who said they read it off Facebook it was weird.

In the medium and larger enterprise case studies, the use of social media emerged as the main tool. For *Dose Wines* the ability to communicate the company brand and link specific marketing campaigns to the customer, which they characterized as an advantage in e-commerce adoption:

We've had this idea in terms of the internet was a good way to communicate with customers... we run something like 20 [domains] for either Dose Wines as a company overall but then we have a lot of brand-specific sites. So [sites] for things like our Emeri Wine, it has two [sites] – a domestic one and a US one.

However social media was not registered as the main tool with *Top Gun Bioscience,* rather the use of the website and SEO appeared as the main components of e-commerce devoted to marketing:

So, for us in our digital marketing strategy, it will be the whole LinkedIn, blogs, update the website, enhance our SEO work.

Social media use by SMEs is also a phenomenon recognized by the state government. A key informant noted the increased awareness of social media by businesses and its continued proliferation as a tool for disseminating information and communication:

I see businesses using it [e-commerce] to almost its fullest ability. A lot of them have Facebook and a lot of them have twitter, and they use these tools as best they can to get in touch with contacts.

Another significant factor that emerged was the ability to access larger markets. This was prominent in all case studies, and in some situations, it allowed SMEs to operate in areas without a significant capacity for supporting the business. *Breakout Furniture* noted the capability to operate from *Cowra* without critical mass within the town:

I reckon is it allows you to sell into a bigger market than you would just having a shopfront sitting in Cowra... if you're buying something and you're just relying on Cowra it might sit around for bloody 12 months before you can sell it.

This was also the case for the SMEs that were established around an innovative and inventive product. *Bags4Bags* and *Liberty Lights* both highlighted the impact of e-commerce as an important tool in ensuring the survivability of the business, as well as the usefulness of e-commerce in marketing their product outside the local region:

If it hadn't been for the internet this wouldn't have been successful. The internet has been pivotal in the whole set up of the operation. And I thought to myself if I had been doing this the way it was done 10-20 years ago, then it wouldn't have had happened. And I think people in my type of scenario who have this unique product, and then to do it through the internet is the way to go.

In the case of business operations, the main findings included the ability to communicate instantly with clients, speed and efficiency, the ability to respond to an inquiry and the use of e-commerce as a cost saver. *Dose Wines* used e-commerce as the next innovative step towards greater efficiency:

If you don't do it your competitors will so it's just another piece of this constant… it's the current piece of getting more efficient, you know in the past there was mechanization… we've put larger volumes through stainless steel tanks, we have mechanical presses … so at each generation and at each era, there's been a way of making things more efficient.

Of significance is the impact of e-commerce in the services case studies – *Top Gun Bioscience* and *Sigma Consulting*. The main contribution is the ability to allow clients to research the bona fides of the business. This is significant in establishing the trust and credibility of the business in the eyes of the potential client. Therefore, services case studies spent more time ensuring a more expert look to convey a sense of professionalism within the business. *Top Gun Bioscience* noted this:

We only came to understand about 5 or 6 six years ago that the world was looking at a web presence first to check your bona fide… without a decent web presence, we have probably been inquiries without even knowing it, even though the business could've been far more substantial than its web presence so that's when we worked out that web presence is critical.

The participants noted the impact of e-commerce adoption on their personal development. This relates to increasing confidence in doing business and being more readily able to make business decisions without regard for the impact on others. The participant from *Origami Paper Supplies* noted the increased confidence in making business decisions especially in being able to be more selective of the types of products they sell and the suppliers they choose:

When we started the business we really had no idea what we were doing and I think we were trying to be all things to all people, but now I realize that we can be a bit discerning and just stock what we want to stock… so coming to that realization has empowered us to streamline our supplier list, [which] we are cutting down constantly as we get more confident about what we are doing and more confident in our business.

Disadvantages

The most significant disadvantage in relation to e-commerce adoption is the perceived reliance on a system dependent operation. Many of the case studies operated solely on the internet whilst others noted that e-commerce was the significant tool for communicating products to customers and if a fault occurred in the system, then business operations would not be possible. The participant from *Western Plains Winery* noted that:

If something goes wrong like your computer breaks down or you lose your wireless connection then you can't do a thing, business stops so that's always one big disadvantage to the whole thing. If your computer or your printer or your fax stops then that's it no more work.

The participant from *Liberty Lights* noted complete reliability on the internet as the fundamental operating tool for the business. The participant also noted the vital nature of the internet in establishing the business in the first place, where the internet worked as the key enabler for the establishment of the business, and ensured the viability and survivability of the business:

Internet connection is paramount. Before the internet and If I had done this 10 years without the internet, then it just wouldn't happen. It would've just been a good idea gone down the tubes because I couldn't [communicate].

E-commerce was identified as a major cost in the case studies across all sizes. In some cases, the decision to implement e-commerce was the first major cost for the business and was subsequently planned and budgeted. In some cases, e-commerce implementation had a considerable impact on the financial health of the business. The participant from *Gypsy Beans* noted:

The website is very out of date, but back in '03 or thereabouts, even earlier, that was a happening website. We paid in excess of 12 grand back then. Talk about being ripped off, the fact of the matter is that 7-8 years ago, e-commerce was still in its infancy, it was very much a part of businesses that weren't really being embraced or understood, but we could see the potential.

In the case of *Top Gun Bioscience*, the significant cost and risk with implementing e-commerce was reduced through government grants. The high cost is also associated with the belief that creating a professional appearance is necessary to build the credibility of the business:

How do we invest in getting it world-class? It's got to be world-class and we've got to make investments to make it world-class. So with enough money we can do anything on this planet, it's just having enough to do the job efficiently so again we'll go to the best providers we know in Australia to have this work done and it's just then how to cost effectively do it.

For *Dose Wines*, in order to reduce the cost of maintaining and updating the e-commerce system, open-source software was used during initial implementation. It should be noted where the cost of implementing e-commerce systems was that those case studies that had faced large costs had implemented e-commerce by engaging IT consultants.

Table 6. Disadvantages of e-commerce adoption

	Western Plains Winery	Breakout Furniture	Gypsy Beans	Liberty Lights	Origami Paper Supplies	Sigma Consulting	Top Gun Bioscience	Dose Wines	Bags4bags	Applique Haberdashery
System Dependent Operation	x			x		x	x	x	x	x
E-commerce a Major Cost	x		x	x			x	x		x
Need to Market the Site	x	x			x	x			x	
A Need to Generate Traffic	x					x		x	x	
Maintain Quality of Information in the Network	x						x		x	
No Disadvantages		x								

Another identified disadvantage was the need to generate traffic by constantly marketing the website. This was prevalent but not limited to the small business case studies where efforts to market the website were met with mixed results. The participant from *Western Plains Winery* mentioned the need to market their website in order to establish the name of the business in what was perceived as a saturated advertising space.

Five per cent of our turnover would be off the website, but that's probably because it's quite new. I've done one email blast to our database that we collect here at the counter to say that they [customers] can now buy our wine online through our website, and I put a link so that... [which] only initiated one sale. So, I don't know, people say that they order online a lot and there's a lot of online shopping going on, but I suppose there's a lot to choose from and you really must get your name out there.

The participant from *Sigma Consulting* also mentioned the need to market their website constantly in order to generate traffic. The proactive nature of constantly marketing the website can be perceived as a disadvantage but essential in attracting new clients. The overall perception being that simply establishing a website as the marketing tool is not adequate without the work of marketing the website to the potential client.

I think the only disadvantage would be ... you mentally expect the website to magically bring you more clients rather than doing basic marketing... For example, say I was in a retail shop in some backstreet of Bathurst and I put my sign out the front and I sat inside my shop all day, and wondered why no one came in. You've got to be out there getting traffic to your website.

The idea of constant marketing as a means of establishing and growing a network is also noted in a key informant interview. Although e-commerce use is increasing, the difficulty is in marketing the business, particularly in a saturated environment, rather than the use of e-commerce technology:

You have most organizations that are internet users, email users; they'd have other sorts of technology operating in their business. I think it's more getting your markets and actually making the connections. That's the obstacle.

Overall, the disadvantages of e-commerce adoption can be associated with the system-dependent operation, the initial cost of implementing e-commerce and the constant need to market websites and generate traffic to the website. This is particularly an issue where markets have been established outside the local region as well as the size of the enterprise, which can significantly affect the ability to invest in the development of e-commerce platforms.

Barriers

Table 7 presents the barriers of e-commerce adoption within the case studies.

In terms of small business case studies, the most significant factor is the lack of IT knowledge. This is in relation to the building and design of websites, although not necessarily with the maintenance of a social media presence. In all of the case studies that did experience a lack of IT knowledge as a barrier (*Western Plains Winery, Gypsy Beans, Liberty Lights, Sigma Consulting, Top Gun Bioscience, Breakout*

Furniture, Bags4Bags, Origami Paper Supplies, and Applique Haberdashery) some form of external knowledge was engaged through the use of an IT consultant whereas those that were well established and had resources to invest (such as *Dose Wines*) had developed internal IT capabilities.

Table 7. Barriers to e-commerce adoption

	Western Plains Winery	Breakout Furniture	Gypsy Beans	Liberty Lights	Origami Paper Supplies	Sigma Consulting	Top Gun Bioscience	Dose Wines	Bags4bags	Applique Haberdashery
Lack of IT Knowledge	x		x	x		x	x			x
Time Barrier	x				x				x	x
Lack of Guidance	x		x	x					x	
Family Barrier			x						x	x
Lack of IT Infrastructure	x		x	x			x	x		
Start-up Capital			x	x					x	x
Difficulty with IT Consultant					x				x	x

The participant from *Western Plains Winery* noted this as a significant problem to be addressed. This was further characterized as part of their personal development:

Probably our biggest barrier is our lack of IT knowledge, that's our own personal problem.

A key informant from the NSW Department of Industry also noted the impact of a lack of IT knowledge on the propensity to adopt e-commerce. This is primarily associated with a fear of security derived from myths and 'urban truths':

I find that there are some people who are really fearful of trading online. They don't trust PayPal; they've heard all the urban myths or urban truths about people getting their money out of their bank accounts. So, they've been quite hesitant and there are some businesses here that still don't have a web presence at all.

A lack of IT infrastructure also presented itself as a barrier in case studies across all sizes. This presented itself as the main factor in determining the complexity of the e-commerce systems adopted. Although in all cases, this barrier can be attributed to the location of the case studies being either out of town or in an area with an overall lack of access to IT infrastructure. In the case of *Top Gun Bioscience* and *Dose Wines*, a lack of infrastructure prevented the development of cloud computing systems, as well as adoption and use of tools such as videoconferencing:

We've stuck to our own services in the meantime until Telstra catches up, so cloud computing can become effective in the future for us… It's not effective in the short-term because of infrastructure.

For the small business case studies that noted this as the main barrier (*Western Plains Winery, Liberty Lights* and *Gypsy Beans*), all were in areas with relatively poor access in terms of infrastructure, speed and reception. To counter this, the case studies had either come to situations where a compromise had to be made on the design and functionality of the website to ensure speed or to operate in two areas: Greenthorpe and Young in the case of *Gypsy Beans* and Oberon and Sydney in the case of *Liberty Lights*. The participant from *Liberty Lights* noted the difficulty accessing adequate infrastructure:

I basically spend my time half here (Oberon) and half there (Sydney). If I was trying to do it totally from here. Even though I have a satellite connection, the breakup is so severe you can't hold a conversation, so I schedule myself. When I have to make a phone call I do it from Sydney.

A lack of infrastructure was noted as a barrier in key informant interviews. A Key Informant from a major government department noted the need for substantial improvement in physical IT infrastructure. This was stated as essential in the further dissemination of information between the government and the businesses as well as between the businesses themselves:

In terms of IT ... it's certainly looking to improve with things like broadband coming through. Certainly, the work that I do with Austrade, for example, we provide webinars which allow business to access information and updates via the web and so any improvements in access and speed will enable further dissemination of information... It's there like road and rail, it certainly [has room to] improve.

Other barriers that can be linked include a lack of guidance and difficulty in working with IT consultants. Case studies noted that a lack of guidance can be tied to lack of IT knowledge. In this regard, this barrier refers to the variety of options that exist for e-commerce adoption, and the choice of the right program to meet the needs of the business.

In these situations, the case studies had engaged IT consultants, however many of the case studies noted the difficulty in working with IT consultants in relation to the compromise of its website designs. Origami Paper Supplies noted the fact that this impacted on the timeframe for implementing e-commerce:

I had hoped to have it up and running within three months, but we had to wait for software, the shopping cart that our developer wanted to use was about to have a new release and so he wanted to wait until the new release came and it was always, next week, next week, next week.

Time constraints and family commitments also emerged as major barriers to the small business case studies (*Western Plains Winery, Gypsy Beans, Origami Paper Supplies, Bags4Bags* and *Applique Haberdashery*). In these cases, the participants had young families that restricted the extent to which business decisions could be made, such as travelling overseas to meet suppliers. In some circumstances, the business was run as a husband-wife team, which subsequently placed limitations on their time resources. The participant from *Applique Haberdashery* mentioned these factors:

The other area to go to is Europe, we haven't been asked to go across to a couple of trade shows in Europe and we have competitors that go there and we need to do that, but we've got to wait for the kids to get a bit older, so maybe a couple of years or so.

DISCUSSION

The impact of the advantages can differ based on the context of the individual case study. The larger case studies were more attuned to advantages associated with increasing the speed and efficiency of the business, use of e-commerce as a cost-saver, and its use as a method of attracting new customers, which is particularly important for these businesses considering the limited customer base, and therefore demand for their product, in their local area. This is associated with the transition from B2C to B2B e-commerce processes. For the services case studies, the advantages can be related to the ability to allow potential clients to research the business and attract new clients. Therefore, e-commerce was used as a way of enhancing company image, developing trust and credibility. For the smaller enterprises, the advantages associated with e-commerce adoption include access to larger markets, the ability to develop their business networks, as a cost saver and as a means of ensuring the survivability of the business. This is particularly important in the regional context where limited and localized markets may not be conducive to business operations.

These results indicate that the advantages of e-commerce adoption associated with larger businesses can be linked to increased efficiencies in the internal process of running the business. Advantages associated with e-commerce adoption for the smaller business can be linked to the external operations of the business in terms of accessing new markets and in its use as a marketing tool. For all case studies, the ability to access new markets and potential clients and suppliers outside their local area is a key driver in the adoption of e-commerce.

Disadvantages derived from the results include the system-dependent operations, the cost of e-commerce adoption, a need to market websites, and a need to manage the quality of information being communicated. In the regional context, where low quality infrastructure and limited market and supply opportunities have greater significance, these disadvantages may have a greater impact on regional SMEs, services SMEs, as opposed to SMEs operating in metropolitan areas.

Reduced flexibility, security concerns and increased workloads did not render as significant barriers in most case studies. In many cases, the process of maintaining e-commerce systems was relatively simple and did not have a significant impact on the running of the business. Increased workloads can be linked to the need to market websites in order to generate traffic, however, instant communication made this a simple operation.

Deterioration of business partner relations are no longer seen as a key disadvantage, in fact, in many cases, the opportunity e-commerce presented in strengthening relations in the business network was noted. The data we collected indicate that the importance of physical contact was acknowledged as crucial to establishing business relationships. E-commerce was used as a means of strengthening the relationship, particularly over long distances and over a period. It should be noted the e-commerce adoption in any means does not replace physical contact.

Organizational restructuring is not seen as a disadvantage of e commerce adoption. In some cases, the businesses identified e-commerce as an integral part of their operations from its establishment, therefore little restructuring was required. However, the system-dependent operation of the businesses is seen as a major disadvantage given the importance of e-commerce in facilitating business processes. In the regional context, system-dependent operations and low-quality infrastructure present a considerable risk to an enterprise.

High financial requirements and the cost of consultants are not listed as a significant disadvantage in adopting e-commerce. Many case studies noted the use of free software and internet-based programs to facilitate e-commerce operations. This had a considerable impact on reducing the cost of implementing and maintaining e-commerce. The use of non-financial assistance through government programs also had an influence in alleviating these costs and the cost of consultants. For the larger case studies, the disadvantages are still relevant especially in relation to the use of external IT consultants and costs associated with software licenses. In the larger case studies, this was reduced using open-source software and through the development of internal capabilities.

Fear of isolation, lack of product compatibility, alienating intermediaries, unwillingness to change, and no perceived critical mass was not identified in any of the interview data as barriers to e-commerce adoption. In many cases, e-commerce was adopted because of the appropriateness of the product and regardless of the availability of critical mass. Often, no critical mass in the local environment was a key driver for adopting e-commerce.

Lack of IT knowledge is revealed as a considerable barrier to e-commerce adoption. However, the significance of this barrier is eroded given the readily available source of IT consultants in both the private and public sectors. Often, the level of IT knowledge developed from personal experience with internet programs helped alleviate concerns with a lack of IT knowledge. Other cases simply avoided this barrier either through personal training or by exploiting the skills of other people.

The regional SMEs included in this study were aware of the risks associated with uncontrolled growth; however, this is not necessarily in relation to e-commerce adoption but rather internationalization. This barrier was more prominent with the smaller case studies rather than the larger case studies. In the smaller case studies, this barrier was mitigated through limiting the marketing campaign in order to control the levels of growth experienced by the business, or alternatively, plans were in place to cope with future high growth.

Time constraints are of relevance to the case studies. This is particularly true for the smaller case studies rather than the larger case studies due to family commitments. As a result, e-commerce designs in the business have been compromised in order to facilitate the needs of the family. This factor is highly influenced by the owner context of the business where the time barrier can be mainly associated with younger business owners rather than the older business owners.

Lack of trust was not mentioned as a considerable barrier by most of the case studies. This interpretation can be related to the owner context of the participants who were of an innovative nature. It was mentioned from Key Informant interviews that a lack of trust still exists in the regional business communities, however, this mainly concerns the older business owners.

High costs as a barrier less of a factor in e-commerce adoption. However, it was noted as a considerable cost to those SMEs that acted as first movers, who preempted these costs in their budget planning. Many of the SMEs noted the reduced cost of software packages, consultants and free online internet programs that can be used to facilitate business operations.

CONCLUSION

This research makes theoretical and practical contributions to the field. Theoretically, this research contributes to the existing e-commerce adoption research by extending the scope to the regional SMEs in their internationalization process. Practically, the implications of the study are useful for government organizations and business development organizations for developing appropriate strategies and policies for promoting the adoption of e-commerce for the internationalization of SMEs in regional areas. For regional SMEs, a recognition of benefits, risks and barriers that they face in the internationalization process via e-commerce will enable regional SMEs to more effectively plan their participation and future activities and realize the benefits of e-commerce.

The research has some limitations when assessing the generalizability of the results. First, being of a qualitative nature, the interpretation of the results is subject to the researcher's exploration of the data. Therefore, in order to confirm the results presented in this study, a wider quantitative study should be conducted. Secondly, the small sample size and the limited range of industries represented in the study attract caution when generalizing the results in a wider context. It should be noted that the majority of the cases were classed as small enterprises therefore the strength of the results in terms of medium- and large-sized enterprises may be of lesser standing. Finally, research was only conducted with SMEs from regional NSW, Australia, therefore caution should be exercised when generalizing the results in other regional areas and even applying them to metropolitan SMEs and SMEs in other countries.

An expansion of the study into other geographical areas and a further categorization of the SMEs could be the focus of future research. This is required as current literature tends to categorize SMEs regardless of the environment they operate in and the complex contextual permutations in which they exist. Further research in other regional areas would also assist in determining the generalizability of the results. This can be enhanced using quantitative research to validate the qualitative results. A quantitative approach will also allow a greater scope of questions to clarify points discovered in this study. This includes assessing the validity of the advantages, disadvantages, and barriers for the internationalization of regional SMEs with the use of e-commerce.

REFERENCES

Aberbach, J., & Rockman, B. (2002). Conducting and coding elite interviews. *PS, Political Science & Politics*, *35*(4), 673–676. doi:10.1017/S1049096502001142

ABS (Australia Bureau of Statistics). (2018). *Summary of IT Use and Innovation in Australia Business, 2016-2017.* http://www.abs.gov.au

ASBAS. (2019). *Australian Small Business Advisory Services (ASBAS) Digital Solutions*. https://www.business.gov.au/Expertise-and-Advice/Australian-Small-Business-Advisory-Services-ASBAS-Digital-Solutions

Bamberry, G. (2006). The influence of technology on regional development: Case studies from the riverina region. *Australiasian Journal of Regional Studies*, *12*(2), 173–190.

Barry, H., & Milner, B. (2002). SMEs and electronic commerce: A departure from the traditional prioritisation of training? *Journal of European Industrial Training*, *26*(7), 316–326. doi:10.1108/03090590210432660

Berry, M., & Brock, J. K.-U. (2004). Marketspace and the internationalization process of the small firm. *Journal of International Entrepreneurship*, *2*(3), 187–216. doi:10.1023/B:JIEN.0000032773.32304.a6

Bertschek, I., & Fryges, H. (2002). *The adoption of business-to-business e-commerce: Empirical evidence for German companies*. Discussion Paper No. 02-05, Centre for European Economic Research (ZEW), Mannheim.

Bowden, S., Clark, D., Corner, P., Gibb, J., Kearins, K., & Pavlovich, K. (2001). *Adoption and implementation of e-business in New Zealand: preliminary results*. Paper presented at the 9th NZSMS Annual Conference, Hamilton.

Braun, P. (2002). Networking tourism SMEs: E-commerce and e-marketing issues in regional Australia. *Information Technology & Tourism*, *5*(1), 13–23. doi:10.3727/109830502108751028

Chong, S. (2008). Success in electronic commerce implementation: A cross-country study of small and medium-sized enterprises. *Journal of Enterprise Information Management*, *21*(5), 468–492. doi:10.1108/17410390810904247

Damanpour, F., & Damanpour, J. A. (2001). E-business e-commerce evolution: Perspective and strategy. *Managerial Finance*, *27*(7), 16–33. doi:10.1108/03074350110767268

Deng, H., Duan, S. X., Jie, D., & Fu, J. (2019). An efficiency-based approach for selecting electronic markets in sustainable electronic business: A SME's perspective. *Sustainability*, *11*(7), 1858. doi:10.3390u11071858

Deng, H., Duan, S. X., & Luo, F. (2020). Critical determinants for electronic market adoption: Evidence from Australian small- and medium-sized enterprises. *Journal of Enterprise Information Management*, *33*(2), 335–352. doi:10.1108/JEIM-04-2019-0106

Duan, X., Deng, H., & Corbitt, B. (2012). Evaluating the critical determinants for adopting e-market in Australian small-and-medium sized enterprises. *Management Research Review*, *35*(3/4), 289–308. doi:10.1108/01409171211210172

Duan, S. X. (2020). An examination of e-market adoption in Australian SMEs. *Small Enterprise Research*, *27*(1), 23–38. doi:10.1080/13215906.2019.1687321

Grandon, E. E., & Pearson, J. M. (2004). Electronic commerce adoption: An empirical study of small and medium US businesses. *Information & Management*, *42*(1), 197–216. doi:10.1016/j.im.2003.12.010

Harrigan, P., Ramsey, E., & Ibbotson, P. (2010). Critical factors underpinning the e-CRM activities of SMEs. *Journal of Marketing Management*, 1–27.

Kendall, J., & Kendall, K. (2001). A paradoxically peacefull coexistence between commerce and ecommerce. *Journal of Information Technology Theory and Application*, *3*(4), 1–6.

Knight, G. A., & Cavusgil, S. T. (2004). Innovation, organizational capabilities, and the born-global firm. *Journal of International Business Studies*, *35*(2), 124–141. doi:10.1057/palgrave.jibs.8400071

Lawson, R., Alcock, C., & Cooper, J. (2001). *e-Business adoption by manufacturing SMEs in regional Australia*. Paper presented at the 14th Bled Electronic Commerce Conferece, Bled, Slovenia.

MacGregor, R. C., & Vrazalic, L. (2005). A basic model of electronic commerce adoption barriers: A study of regional small businesses in Sweden and Australia. *Journal of Small Business and Enterprise Development*, *12*(4), 510–527. doi:10.1108/14626000510628199

MacGregor, R. C., & Kartiwi, M. (2010). Perception of barriers to e-commerce adoption in SMEs in a developed and developing country: A comparison between Australia and Indonesia. *Journal of Electronic Commerce in Organizations*, *8*(1), 61–82. doi:10.4018/jeco.2010103004

Martin, L., & Matlay, H. (2001). "Blanket" approaches to promoting ICT in small firms: Some lessons from the DTI ladder adoption model in the UK. *Internet Research: Electronic Networking Applications and Policy*, *11*(5), 399–410. doi:10.1108/EUM0000000006118

McCole, P., & Ramsey, E. (2005). A profile of adopters and non-adopters of ecommerce in SME professional service firms. *Australasian Marketing Journal*, *13*(1), 36–48. doi:10.1016/S1441-3582(05)70066-5

Osarenkhoe, A. (2009). An integrated framework for understanding the driving forces behind non-sequential process of internationalization among firms. *Business Process Management Journal*, *15*(2), 286–316. doi:10.1108/14637150910949498

Pavic, S., Koh, S. C. L., Simpson, M., & Padmore, J. (2007). Could e-business create a competitive advantage in UK SMEs? *Benchmarking: An International Journal*, *14*(3), 320–351. doi:10.1108/14635770710753112

Raymond, L. (2001). Determinants of web site implementation in small businesses. *Internet Research: Electronic Networking Applications and Policy*, *11*(5), 411–422. doi:10.1108/10662240110410363

Ruzzier, M., Hisrich, R. D., & Antoncic, B. (2006). SME internationalization research: Past, present, and future. *Journal of Small Business and Enterprise Development*, *13*(4), 476–497. doi:10.1108/14626000610705705

Stansfield, M., & Grant, K. (2003). An investigation into issues influencing the use of internet and electronic commerce among small-medium sized enterprises. *Journal of Electronic Commerce Research*, *4*(1), 15–33.

Yin, R. K. (2017). *Case study research and applications: Design and methods*. Sage publications.

ADDITIONAL READING

Abebe, M. (2014). Electronic commerce adoption, entrepreneurial orientation and small-and medium-sized enterprise (SME) performance. *Journal of Small Business and Enterprise Development*, *21*(1), 100–116. doi:10.1108/JSBED-10-2013-0145

Bell, J., & Loane, S. (2010). New-Wave'Global Firms: Web 2.0 and SME Internationalisation. *Journal of Marketing Management*, *26*(3-4), 213–229. doi:10.1080/02672571003594648

Bose, T. K. (2016). Critical success factors of SME internationalization. *Journal of Small Business Strategy*, *26*(2), 87–109.

Camra-Fierro, J., Centeno, E., Al-Hyari, K., Al-Weshah, G., & Alnsour, M. (2012). Barriers to internationalisation in SMEs: Evidence from Jordan. *Marketing Intelligence & Planning*, *30*(2), 188–211. doi:10.1108/02634501211211975

Eduardsen, J. (2018). Internationalisation Through Digitalisation: The Impact of E-Commerce Usage on Internationalisation in Small-and Medium-Sized Firms. *International Business Research, 13*, 159–186.

Holmberg, M., & Holmström-Szugalski, M. (2017). Internationalization through E-Commerce: Exploring percieved risks and understanding the challenges ahead.

Jones, P., Packham, G., Beckinsale, M., Jahanshahi, A. A., Zhang, S. X., & Brem, A. (2013). E-commerce for SMEs: Empirical insights from three countries. *Journal of Small Business and Enterprise Development, 20*(4), 849–865. doi:10.1108/JSBED-03-2012-0039

Zaied, A. N. H. (2012). Barriers to e-commerce adoption in Egyptian SMEs. *International Journal of Information Engineering and Electronic Business, 4*(3), 9–18. doi:10.5815/ijieeb.2012.03.02

KEY TERMS AND DEFINITIONS

E-Commerce: Any form of business transaction in which parties interact electronically rather than through direct contact.

Internationalization: Internationalization is the expansion of economic activities across national borders.

Perceived Advantage: The perception of the positive consequences that are caused by the adoption of e-commerce for internationalization.

Perceived Barrier: A SME's assessment of the obstacles to the adoption of e-commerce for internationalization.

Perceived Risk: A combination of uncertainty and seriousness to the adoption of e-commerce for internationalization.

Regional Areas: Geographical areas located outside metropolitan centers and major cities.

SMEs: SMEs in Australia are the organization with less than 200 employees.

Chapter 6
An Application of the "Amplifying Casual Looping" Model to Manor House Management

José Luís Braga
https://orcid.org/0000-0001-7668-5200
Polytechnic Institute of Tomar, Portugal

Marta Dionísio
https://orcid.org/0000-0002-4654-3399
Polytechnic Institute of Tomar, Portugal

ABSTRACT

This chapter attempts to explain the main strategies adopted by the hosts of manor houses when they engage in lodging activities. The present research draws on 53 non-structured interviews made to owners/hosts of housing tourism facilities (HT). The methodological approach used is classic grounded theory (CGT). CGT encompasses a set of strict research procedures leading to concepts which explain what is going on in the HT substantive area. Within this context, the authors reveal a theoretical code, designated as 'amplifying casual looping', which the authors believe has the merit of effectively conceptualizing the substantive codes generated by us. This causal model broadens in both directions: positive (virtuous circle) and negative (vicious circle).

INTRODUCTION

Housing tourism (HT), as a type of accommodation, was implemented as a pilot project in 1978, and put into practice in four territories: Ponte de Lima, Vouzela, Castelo de Vide and Vila Viçosa (Pereiro, 2018). Its creation was aimed at fighting regional asymmetries in the national territory and offering

DOI: 10.4018/978-1-7998-4942-1.ch006

differentiated hotel capacity in areas where it was scarce. In 1982, through Order No. 102/82, the HT program started (Silva, 2009).

In compliance with the Portuguese legislation currently in force (Decree-Law no. 80/2017, 30th June), 'housing tourism enterprises are establishments of a family nature installed in old private properties that, due to their architectural, historical or artistic value, are representative of a particular epoch, namely palaces and manors, which can be located in rural or urban spaces' (CENTER, 2020a).

In fact, HT has been contributing to restore countless houses of erudite heritage, gaining recognition and consideration by the populations of the places in which it operates, also contributing to the 'return to the origins' of countless families once installed in urban areas and for the emergence of new types of tourism in rural areas (Braga, 2016). In addition, together with the rural tourism (RT), HT contributed, definitely, to the diversification of the tourist offer; the reduction of seasonality; cooperation between local actors; the boost of tourism animation projects and the provision of services that support tourism activities, which led to an awareness of entities and institutions regarding their social, economic and environmental impacts (Silva, 2010).

HT is performed in manor houses – some of them dating back to the 15th and 16th centuries – which requires a big effort from the owners to preserve their original character. Hence, this chapter intends to explain the main strategies used by owners to solve the problems they face in this activity. Our research shows that when owners put a lot of effort in being competent hosts, they are more able to preserve their house. By contrast, if they do not engage to the full extent with HT, they will struggle to keep the house repaired.

According to CGT principles, the research process here deployed enables us to understand what is happening in HT lodging facilities. This chapter highlights a theoretical code (an 'amplified casual looping' model) that emerged during the analysis stage of our doctoral dissertation (Braga, 2016) and which helps to understand the main concern of the hosts: the transmission of the property (the manor house) to the next generation in the best possible condition.

This chapter will make a brief foray into the history of HT in Portugal, from its origins to the present. Then, it will be analysed the specificities of this type of tourism; the methodology used for the collection and analysis of empirical data; the results achieved and, by way of conclusion, the discussion, and other final considerations.

BACKGROUND

The Beginnings

Some of the manor houses that constitute the HT offer have remote origins. Several of them belong to families whose lineage descends from the first nobility of the kingdom of Portugal. This fact explains its concentration in the North of Portugal and, mainly, in Ponte de Lima (Stoop, & Sotto Mayor, 2015). Since their construction - which often dates to the 17th and 18th centuries - these houses have had numerous functions, the last of which has been welcoming tourists since the 1980s (Silva, 2012).

HT, in its origins, is indelibly associated with a desire to return to the countryside, which dates to the European Romantic Movement of the dawn of nineteenth century (Jepson & Sharpley, 2018). It demonstrates the desire of some layers of the population to retrieve their rural origins or constitutes an escape from the hurried and exhausting way of life in the city, reinvigorating or forming affective bonds with the rural world.

As a matter of fact, rural tourism, at first, was restricted to a privileged class and was subject to the existence of secondary residences, which, in the past, had constituted the first home of families of aristocratic origins - to which belonged the individuals who had left the country side to live in the cities and who returned in the summer season or during the grape harvest (Menezes, 2000).

On the other hand, the promotion of this type of tourism by public organizations sought to prevent the increasing depopulation of rural areas and the concomitant weakening of agricultural activities. It should be also added the need to diversify tourist flows, taking them to destinations in the interior to avoid the excessive predominance of 'sun and beach' tourism.

Martins (2012) recalls this aspiration from the 1st National Congress of Tourism in 1936. On this occasion, three trends loomed:

1. The verification of the touristic relevance of the interior of the country, even though it lacks a clear materialization of this interest;
2. The requalification of under-occupied buildings, aiming at the recovery of the architectural heritage;
3. The generation of accommodation through the adaptation of available rooms for a timely occupation by tourists.

The subsequent stage combines the territorial component with the three perspectives described above. In fact, there was an urgent need to select the area or areas most appropriate for the implementation of RT. Thus, the manor houses in Basto and Ponte de Lima regions impose themselves, although other alternatives are suggested, making it evident as an imperative, the creation of an area where a pilot experience would take place.

The first expression of interest by government authorities in rural areas is made by António Ferro, then director of the National Propaganda Secretariat, through Law No. 31.259 of May 1st, 1941, which creates the *Inns* (i.e. *Pousadas de Portugal*). These accommodations consisted of hotel units installed in historic buildings or monuments (e.g. castles, convents or monasteries) or in appealing scenic locations.

Three decades later, in the early 1970s, the intention to adapt castles, manors and buildings of classical architecture remains, but belonging to private individuals, a heritage in which the northern part of Portugal is fertile. However, this aspiration does not obtain the approval of the then General-Director of Tourism, who favours Ribatejo as an ideal territory to carry out the pilot experience, due to its proximity to the capital (see Figure 1).

In fact, as Cavaco (1999) says, accordingly to what had been happening in other European countries, in the early 70's, rural tourism started to be considered by the responsible authorities as a product to be put into practice and commercialize in a way to attract national and international customs with purchasing power, what will affect alternative tourism based on humanized landscapes. Therefore, according to Godinho (2004), we can trace the origins of RT back to a time earlier, 1957, to the Treaty of Rome (which established the European Economic Community) and the creation of the CAP (Common Agricultural Policy).

However, despite the 1970s having witnessed the creation of the first and only national park in Portugal in this period, car ownership was still limited to a small fraction of the Portuguese population, who mostly lived in the coast urban areas. At this time, rural areas and small towns were visited only by a few tourists who went there on bus tours. Thus, these areas languished due to the combined effect of depopulation, large-scale emigration and an aging population (Menezes, 2000).

Therefore, HT emerged as a new way of accommodation that was based on the use of rooms belonging to private houses. This modality had the virtue of offering accommodation in regions where it was null or scarce. Cavaco refers to '*re-functionalization*' (Braga, 2016) as follows:

The first modern forms of rural tourism involved families that are well rooted in the region and who own houses by inheritance, sometimes already quite degraded, that are very costly to recover and that are hardly financed by their current owners and a size that is not appropriate for today's families, even considering it extended to three generations.

Its adaptation to tourism presupposed, in addition to the recovery works, those of general re-modelling and creation of infrastructures, particularly the expansion of rooms, the building of bathrooms and leisure equipment (Cavaco, 1999, p. 299).

The activity benefited from the commitment of Maria Laura Achemann, who, in the late 1970s, began to travel around Portugal, gaining followers and 'taking root in a tourist practice that we were not used to' (Fernandes, 1983, p. 26). Godinho corroborates this opinion regarding the then employee of the General-Directorate for Tourism: 'the country lacks the recognition to this Lady for her role in the implantation of RT in Portugal and for her inexhaustible struggle for its dynamism in all places where it was necessary to fight' (2004, p. 93). On the other hand, Pina, in the tourism radiography he made in Portugal in the 20th century, reports, as follows, the implementation of HT in our country, after having long been established in Austria, Germany, France, England and Switzerland:

Launched in 1977 by Luís Filipe Madeira, when he held the position of Secretary of State for Tourism, Housing Tourism would, however, be boosted by the department itself of the General-Directorate for Tourism, which had the heroic support of Maria Laura Achemann, who had a wide knowledge of the hospitality sector. Originally, it had been introduced to complement, in a dispersive and expeditious way, the country's accommodation capacity, momentarily stagnated by the economic regression. However, favoured with attractive credit lines, Housing Tourism gradually became self-programmed with the inclusion of numerous manor houses, starting to develop itself, mixed with some voluntarism, in a sense that already has little to do with the initial conception, substantially enriched in the course of the process (Pina, 1988, p. 190).

HT came to replace the custom that prevailed in the bathing and thermal areas of Portugal to rent private rooms to vacationers. Therefore, it was possible to see the old habit of fishermen, who in the summer moved into tents and rented their rooms, a custom that also extended itself to other social classes. This primitive housing tourism, based on the improvisation of the populations, was mainly carried out by families who did not have the resources to stay in hotels and pensions and was characteristically seasonal. Consequently, this activity escaped the tourist circuits and travel agency programs, as well as the scope of the competent authorities.

However, the institutionalization of HT aimed at something different. On one hand, it was intended to provide infrastructures to the places where traditional hospitality did not settle, neither the old *housing tourism*. These were particularly inland and mountain areas, 'the great "landscapes" that tend to attract new layers of tourists, saturated with consecutive years of beach' (Fernandes, 1983, p. 26).

Figure 1. Proposals of pilot experience areas (Martins, 2013)
Source: (Martins, 2013, p. 9)

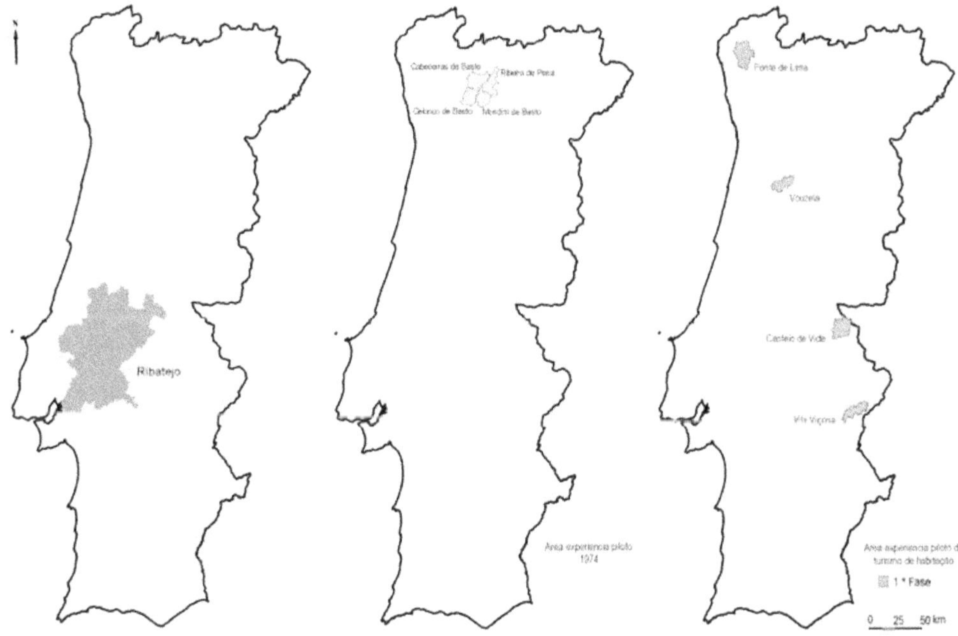

Consolidation

In Portugal, the first proposed regulation of the HT dates, therefore, from May 1978, and was inscribed in Regulatory Decree No. 14/78, of 12th May. This document seeks to establish, for the purpose of inventorying and disseminating in the tourist market, a register of private accommodation that can be used as accommodation for tourists, namely private rooms, dwelling houses, and apartments. Registration would be freely requested by the owners to the General-Directorate for Tourism (GDT), that would decide on its suitability for the intended purpose (Silva, 2009).

Fernandes quotes a warning issued by the City Council of Arcos de Valdevez on March 30th, 1979, which was considered paradigmatic by GDT employees:

In order to solve the serious problem of lack of accommodation for tourists in this municipality, it is public that the registration for private accommodation able to be used by the tourists, namely rooms in private houses, dwelling houses and apartments, is open.

The service to be provided will include, in addition to the use of the bedroom and bathroom with the respective clothing equipment, the provision of breakfast when necessary.

If there is a need to carry out construction works and improvements, the owner or tenant may request, through the City Council, financial support from the State.

The attention of interested people is drawn to the importance of this initiative, which has an impact on the county's economy, both in terms of the hospitality industry and of commerce in general, and that of households that are in a position to join, as it can be seen as an important financial aid.

The initiative is available for the entire municipality, and information may be requested from the City Council (Fernandes, 1983, p.27-28).

In the same year, following the creation of the pilot experience area in Ponte de Lima, Casa do Outeiro became the first HT project in the region. The implementation of HT in the North-West of the country was, to a large extent, associated with a discourse to promote the tradition and architectural heritage of great value in inland rural areas and to stimulate the development of Portugal inland, especially following the population exodus of the 1960s.

If, in the early days of the HT, only four pilot areas of high natural, social and heritage potential were considered, already endowed with some tourism development, soon afterwards, other areas of the inland were contemplated, which also have some virtues, but lacking a significant offer and suitable for commercial accommodation, even though already crossed by some flows, as it happened with the Douro Valley and, subsequently, with the entire national territory.

In 1982, through the Legislative Order No. 102/82, of 24th June, the '*Turismo de Habitação*' (HT) program was introduced, which as we saw above, aimed at increasing the accommodation capacity where it was almost non-existent or reduced, both in quality and quantity terms and, likewise, favouring the tourist and socio-economic development of these areas, establishing a means of conservation of the national artistic-architectural heritage with the adaptation of old, palatial or manor homes for a tourism of quality.

At this time, priority areas were determined: the regions of Minho, Basto and Vale do Douro, the natural parks of Peneda-Gerês and Serra da Estrela and the medieval villages of Sortelha, Marvão, Óbidos and Monsaraz. At the same time, it was favoured the scrutiny of other areas with potential (Silva, 2009).

Through Decree-Law No. 423/83, of December 5th, the expression 'housing tourism' is legally established and the offer of HT is promoted by sanctioning its 'public utility', which gives the related units, access to financing through the Tourism Fund. It is also in 1983 that RT will feature in the national statistical universe.

In the same year, the Housing Tourism Association (TURIHAB), a non-profit organization, based in the village of Ponte de Lima, is founded. TURIHAB has a reservation centre, but it is also responsible for the quality of services provided by HT houses (Menezes, 2000). The certification process that was implemented by this association 'also contributed to promote the characteristics of accommodation' (Martins, 2013, p. 10).

On March 5th and 6th of that same year, the Alto Minho Tourism Region (RTAM), sponsored by the Municipality of Ponte de Lima, carried out the First Housing Tourism Days with the objective of 'tidying a little bit the house up, because the TH was beginning to thrive and well, concretely, in the Municipality of Ponte de Lima and it was necessary to give it the right direction' (Sampaio, 2012, p. 177). In 1984, the Second Days of Housing Tourism would take place.

Through Decree-Law No. 251/84, of 25th July, the scope of the HT is extended beyond the exploitation of tourist accommodation, to 'services of tourism interest in the fields of animation, crafts, culture, sport and leisure for tourists' (Cavaco, 1999, p. 294-295).

Likewise, the properties that joined the HT were classified according to modalities A or B, according to the quality of the construction of the main building:

A. When referring to a manorial-type building/manor, mansion house/palatial house or single-family house, with architectural value, large dimensions, quality furniture and decoration and suitable sanitary facilities;
B. It concerns the building located in a rural environment, rustic type or with notorious regional specificities and with appropriate household and decoration, in addition to functional sanitary facilities (Sampaio, 2012).

On March 16th, 1984, RTAM will introduce a Central Reservation, signing the 1st Protocol with TURIHAB. Sampaio (2012) confirms that, one year later, regarding the RT Product Life Cycle, the discovery (exploration) phase of what is new was inaugurated. In this period, tourists looking for this type of development would be allocentric (Plog, 1974).

The official RT modalities benefited from the Tourism Investment Financing System (SIFIT) - which provided the attribution of non-refundable subsidies (Braga & Lopes, 2020) - and from the direct financing of the Tourism Fund (funds that came from fees on gambling). The recognition of the tourist utility given the location, equipment and service provided, in the same way, facilitated access to credit and tax exemptions (transfer tax, municipal tax) (Cavaco, 1999).

In 1986, through Decree-Law No. 256/86, of 27th August, the designation of '*Turismo no Espaço Rural*' (Rural Tourism)' was officially instituted, expanding the scope of 'Housing Tourism'. Therefore, two new types of accommodation are created: Rural Tourism (TR) and Agritourism (AG). Silva (2009) also mentions that, in that same year, through the Legislative Order nº 86/86, of September 23rd, the terms of the loans to be granted by the Tourism Fund to HT, RT and AG are established, having been determined that the financing can't exceed 50% of the investment in fixed capital in the portion aimed at the tourist exploration (Silva, 2009).

Regarding the spatial distribution of the HT units, it reflected, at that time, the preponderance of Ponte de Lima and accused the proximity of the Peneda-Gerês National Park, as well as the absence of State Inns. In the same way, Alto-Douro was beginning to show itself with its vineyards and their inherent tangible heritage.

The publication of Regulatory Decree No. 5/87, of January 14th, will define what HT, RT and AG specifically are. Thus, HT is defined as:

Activity of interest for family oriented tourism, which consists of providing accommodation in houses that simultaneously serve as residence for their owners and fulfil the requirements of Housing Tourism - use of old houses, manor houses, palatial houses or residences of recognized architectural value, with adequate dimensions, quality furniture and decoration.

Sampaio also adds that the practice of HT could include the special classification of "old houses":

When practiced on classified properties of international, national, regional or local value, and others that, due to their epoch, architectural, historical or artistic value, are considered to be "old houses" by the General Directorate of Tourism after hearing the Portuguese Institute of Cultural Heritage (Sampaio, 2012, p.177).

The same regulation also sets the maximum number of rooms. In the RT, the figure is six, and in this case, as well as in the HT and the AG, it cannot exceed six in the main building and 10 with the accommodation in the annexes. In addition, rural tourists should contact sweets, wines, festivals from the agricultural calendar and farming. Additionally, the houses where they were staying should be marked with an identification plate.

Soon after, the Legislative Order nº 20/87, of February 24th, established the forms of relationship between guests and owners and mentioned some of the complementary activities of leisure and animation that are likely to be promoted, namely water sports, hunting and fishing.

In 1988, it was created another national non-profit association, whose activity is aimed at 'supporting, disseminating and promoting Rural Tourism, representing the interests of the owners of tourist accommodation units, duly licensed, in its various modalities' (PRIVETUR, 2013).

Five years later, in 1993, TURIHAB, intending to revitalize Manor Tourism, creates the brand *Solares de Portugal* (Portugal Manors), during the 1st National Meeting of Housing Tourism. This brand currently constitutes a network that expands itself throughout the national territory (CENTER, 2020).

In 1997, Decree-Law No. 256/86, of 27th August, is replaced by Decree-Law No. 169/97, of 4th July, which 'provides a new legal framework for activities associated with RT' (Silva, 2009, p.52). On the other hand, the legislation distinguishes accommodation modalities (housing tourism, rural tourism, agritourism, village tourism and countryside houses) from tourist enterprises (rural hotels and rural camping sites). Unlike what happens with countryside houses and village tourism, in HT and in other types of accommodation, as well as in rural hotels, the residence of entrepreneurs during the service period is mandatory.

On the other hand, Regulatory Decree No. 37/97, of 25th September, establishes the minimum requirements for the facilities and functioning of private homes as RT units, aiming to guarantee the comfort and safety of users, without questioning the particularities of the establishments. This regulation also sets the maximum and minimum number of rooms in the houses of HT, incorporated or not in the main building: from 3 to 10. Cavaco, in turn, lists other criteria that the HT should meet:

It is always necessary to have a living room reserved for guests; in each room it can only be installed two single beds or one double bed, being the maximum capacity of two-person rooms (exception in the case of children). Each room must have a window; adequate furniture and equipment; in the housing tourism its minimum area is 12m² and 10m², respectively, whether with two beds or a double bed and if with a single bed, values that fall to 9m² and 7m² in the other rural tourist houses; if there are private rooms, their minimum area is 12m²; bathrooms are private in housing tourism (Cavaco, 1999, p. 297).

The regulations also compelled the HT promoters to provide information in the rooms in Portuguese, English, and another foreign language. These reports should include the services provided, meals, areas and equipment for visitors and the location of medical, nursing and pharmacy services. The HT promoter should also be ready to provide information about:

Regional tourist, historical, ethnographic, cultural, gastronomic and landscape heritage, means of public transport or roads, and must ensure lunch and dinner [...] when there is no restaurant less than 5 km away, based on traditional cuisine menus and regional products, this in addition to light meals and breakfast (Ibidem).

In addition, establishments should be identified with classification plates, present in Ordinance No. 1070/97, of 23rd October. The typical symbol of RT is preserved, of a green tree on a white rectangle, and the initials HT, RT, AG, VT, RH, CH are added depending on the specificity of the accommodation: housing tourism, rural tourism, agritourism, village tourism, rural hotel, country house, respectively (see Figure 2).

Figure 2. Housing tourism id plate (Seripex, 2015)
Source: (Seripex, 2015)

Nowadays

Since 1974, there has been an affirmation of local authority and local agents to the detriment of central power, whose hegemony was a prerogative of the previous regime. Corresponding to this trend enunciated by Martins (2013), the Decree-Law nº 54/2002, of March 11th, transfers the process of licensing and permission for the execution of urban operations of houses and enterprises related to RT to municipalities. At the same time, the Regional Directorates for Economy reserve to themselves the prerogatives previously performed by the GDT (e.g. sanction the designation and classification according to the type of accommodation).

This regulation is replaced by the 2008 diploma. The Decree-Law No. 39/2008, of March 7th, divides the units, previously under the sphere of RT, into two types of tourist establishments:

1. HT enterprises;
2. RT enterprises.

In the same diploma, HT is defined as: 'family establishments installed in old private properties that, due to their architectural, historical or artistic value, are representative of a certain time, namely palaces and manors, being located in rural or urban spaces'. It is also stated that HT enterprises should not exceed 15 accommodation units.

On the other hand, the classification, the setting of the maximum capacity and the licensing of the functioning, as well as the execution of construction works in these establishments, with the exception of rural hotels, remain under the jurisdiction of the municipalities, safeguarding the binding opinion of the Portugal Tourism, IP (Silva, 2009).

This legislative text makes the HT of RT projects autonomous, the former being able to be in rural or urban areas. For Sampaio (2012), at this stage, the life cycle of the RT product reaches the stage of consolidation (being accordingly expected an increase of psychocentric tourists).

Nevertheless, RT was poorly spread throughout the Portuguese territory, inaugurating the 'local accommodation' modality in 2008, also with the purpose of recognizing some indistinct units that were not part of the common typologies that have been developed over 30 years.

On the other hand, Ordinance No. 937/2008, of August 20th, establishes the minimum requirements that HT and RT establishments must comply with. In accordance with this regulation, the HT family nature 'is characterized by the residence of the owner or operating entity or his/her representative in the housing tourism enterprises during the functioning period'.

Currently, both RT and HT are regulated by Decree-Law No. 80/2017, of June 30th (CENTER, 2020a).

MAIN FOCUS OF THE CHAPTER

In an extremely simplified way, we can argue that the HT provides a stay in a manor house, as well as the cohabitation and socializing with the owners of the house. The latter is also assumed as a repository of national and regional identity. However, HT is distinguished from RT, since it is a manifestation of cultural tourism that occurs mainly in rural areas. At HT, the cultural product is essentially the accommodation in a house of classical architecture. In other words, this type of offer values the eminently rural geographical situation of the house, its historical heritage, and its small size, which influences the way in which the reception takes place. The service at HT is, for Cavaco (1999, p. 294), 'always personalized, unprofessional, domestic and familiar'.

In fact, as our theorization shows (Braga, 2016), the owners of these houses see in HT a way of conserving and sustaining family homes, creating conditions for others - not just themselves and their families - to assign them value. Some of these houses are even classified as properties of municipal or public interest (Braga & Lopes, 2020). HT also allows cultural exchange, which benefits not only the tourists, but the promoters of the activity themselves (Silva, 2012).

In the case of *Solares de Portugal* brand, established by TURIHAB, the enterprises are also manor homes, many of them owned by the same family for several centuries, dating back to its foundation in the 17th and 18th centuries. There are few HT units located in small palaces, *chalets* or villas from the end of the 19th century or the beginning of the 20th century. The houses covered by the brand were divided into three groups: Manor Houses; Farms and Estates, and Rustic Houses, thus ensuring the highest level of quality and hospitality.

Thus, *Manor Houses* are elegant and majestic houses, most of them from the 17th and 18th centuries. Its architecture is erudite, combining several styles that materialize different episodes of the Portuguese history - the African, Indian and Brazilian influences that witnessed the country's imperialist past are notable. *Farms and Estates* are, as the name implies, estates and farms that are situated in a rural and atmosphere setting. The main houses in this section comprise several architectural styles, ranging from classic to rustic. Finally, the *Rustic Houses* are characterized by their type of building, simple architectural style and construction provided by regional materials. Its size is smaller and contains unpretentious, practical and comfortable furniture (Corfu & Kastenholz, 2008).

The HT also conveys an 'ideology of the authentic and the singular', which emphasizes the differentiation and specificity of the expressions 'of tangible culture of local matrix, an economic niche that is environmentally and heritage friendly. Tourism that wants small-scale and sustainable proximity in form and concept '(Rodrigues, 2013). This concept is opposed to mass and globalized tourism, on a large scale, which acts to the detriment of local interests, being the ones established outside the large housing centres marginalized by the tourism industry.

In other words, the success of the concept lies in the fact that it consubstantiates an alternative form of tourism, contrary to urban and bathing massification, and enhances unique destinations driven by the pastoral-style ideas of returning to the countryside, but, essentially, by the exaltation of the singular and nonreplicable character of places and houses.

With the introduction of this segment, it was also intended to offer accommodation capacity without the need for large investments, avoiding the construction of large, low-profit hotel units. High-end tourism was sought in the interior of the country, thus contributing to the preservation of heritage. Regarding this last point, João d'Abreu de Lima, former Mayor of Ponte de Lima, who was sworn in because of the 1976 municipal elections, declared in 1993 the following:

There was also the circumstance that this new type of tourism brought specifically the attraction of allowing the restoration of old houses, old manor houses, some in ruins, others already tired and resources spent in the construction and its interiors, thus saving a valuable and beautiful heritage, which few or no regions have with the profusion, differences, beauty and architectural harmony that is found in the municipality of Ponte de Lima and throughout the Lima Valley. Loans were offered at good rates and reimbursement terms, which was of interest to the owners of these homes (apud Martins, 2013, p. 10).

Regarding the furniture of the houses, the manor houses present, according to Silva (2010, p. 34), 'crystals, silverware, tapestries, school pictures, coats of arms, family portraits and rooms with iron beds with the Crown of the King and D. Maria, D. Luís, D. José and canopy'. In the more rustic style HT houses, the decoration uses traditional materials for domestic use - namely iron pots, handicrafts, earthenware and traditional ceramics, irons, gasometers, fireplaces - agricultural tools, as well as country-inspired paintings. As for the rooms, it's visible the presence of iron beds, cupboards built into the wall and stone floors.

Tradition is inseparable from HT, so devotional objects could not be absent. Therefore, oratories, crucifixes and religious iconography are usually found in the chapels of manors and mansion houses.

This decoration seeks to mimic the old way of life, emphasizing the authenticity of the scenery. In fact, most of these houses have been in the possession of the same family for several generations, or even since they were built. The HT is also a way for the guest to get in touch with the former nobility of the province, with high social status. For Rodrigues:

Family homes appear to us integrated in complex processes of memory elaboration based on experience and the existence of a lived and felt past, as a great moment of a lineage, where the right to memory is configured as a virtue or among the most powerful social groups, or at least, with a sense of home and family (Rodrigues, 2013, p.1201).

Silva (2010) also reveals that, together with the historical and traditional objects, the HT houses contain equipment that is characteristic of modern life: television, telephone, electricity, running water, basic sanitation, central heating and properly equipped bathrooms.

The HT also has the virtue of allowing a more direct knowledge of the country and its people, with the tourist being able to integrate their daily life and share his/her worldviews. Fernandes (1983, p. 28) also added that 'throughout the country, a huge variety of sensations and experiences can be discovered and lived through this form of tourism'.

As we saw above, HT houses can be in urban or rural areas, although the second situation is, notoriously, the most common one. It is, therefore, an alternative tourism, which diverges from the mass tourism because it tends to be 'locally controlled, of a family nature, of small scale and in harmony with the physical, social and cultural environment of the host communities, in which the guest is accommodated in the host's house) '(Silva, 2010). In the case of alternative tourism, the guest is welcomed, without mediation, at the host's home, benefiting from the services and logistics that exist in the house.

Interestingly - and still according to Silva (2009) - about a third of the rooms and beds provided by RT units are in structures attached to the main house. These secondary constructions originally had agricultural functions as caretakers' houses, stables, porches, cattle ranches, and storage shops. There is, therefore, a "*re-functionalization*" that favours tourism over agriculture. Thus, these apartments, which have independent access and which, as explained in our theory (Braga, 2016), seek to intensify the privacy of the host family and guests, have equipment, such as kitchens or 'kitchenettes, independent access, small, private, autonomous, functional living-dining room '(Cavaco, 1999).

Also according to Cavaco (1999, p. 297), these houses are very often located in farms and have their leisure areas, such as' lawns, boxwood and myrtle gardens, secular groves, with prestigious species (cypresses, cedars, palm trees, Japanese trees, camellias, azaleas), parks, boulevards, lakes and fountains, water tanks to which others have been added, such as swimming pools, saunas, solariums, etc.'

The HT, in addition to the accommodation, must include breakfast. Approximately one third of the RT houses, according to Silva (2009), serve other meals, namely lunches or dinners for guests, with a significant part, even though three times smaller, serving meals indiscriminately. In accordance with the law, the meal service includes typical regional dishes, and is often made with products from the properties where the houses are located.

To supplement the income from HT, a substantial part of the houses makes the investment profitable and pays for the risk of the enterprise, the dedication and sacrifice that the modality requires, carrying out forms of animation that complement the product offered. This corresponds to the desire to lessen the harmful consequences of the diminished average occupancy rates, fleeting stays, and the seasonality inherent to the modality.

The HT comprises complementary activities of animation, such as swimming pools, tennis courts, hunting and fishing and nautical activities, horse riding, visits, and tours. Many of them take place outside the HT property, through an informal partnership with the service providers. Another way of supplementing income - which our theory has also made evident - are the events that many of these houses hold together with accommodation: rental of spaces for parties, weddings, baptisms, colloquia and conferences and, sometimes, for the shooting of films and soap operas (Silva, 2009).

As far as prices are concerned, these are not legally fixed and, of course, vary depending on the reservation made for the high season (Carnival, Easter, August, Christmas and New Year) or for the low season.

Regarding the treatment, sometimes there is the intense friendly relationships between hosts and guests. There is, very often, the idea in HT that the guest has a special status, which is not that of a common tourist, since he shares knowledge, affections, memories, and experiences with the host family. However, Silva (2010, p. 37) sees in this relationship a 'hosting commodification process', in which there is an inversion of the traditional relationship of hospitality, as material exchange and economic profit are privileged. Such a situation can degenerate welcoming into a false friendship or even subservience. Of course, the nature of the host-guest relationship varies from house to house. Rodrigues is also in line with criticisms of the housing commodification:

Unfortunately, in some the commercial and economic side of the tourist activity is considered, where hospitality is a kind of cosmetic and advertising euphemism. Where the relations between host and guest are essentially commercial and distant, typical of a commercial host that provides a service in exchange for a value that is charged and paid by the tourist (Rodrigues, 2013, p. 1208).

METHODOLOGY

The research methodology used in the present study was CGT, which is a methodological approach that allows the generation of theories from the data taken from the studied reality. Its development was due to the pioneering work of American sociologists Barney G. Glaser and Anselm Strauss in the 1960s of the 20th century and this is today one of the most popular research strategies in the world (Birks & Mills, 2011). In this text we propose ourselves to demonstrate the usefulness of the CGT methods to find out what is happening in the substantive area of HT, an activity that has contributed to the enhancement of regional identity and to the cohesion of the national territory.

This methodology allows an unprecedented approach, which escapes from the ethnographic method that has prevailed in studies developed so far in the substantive area of HT. CGT does not aim at description like ethnography, but at conceptualization. CGT favours the notion of dialogues between equals, rather than a hierarchical relationship between interviewer and interviewee. This method also has the potential of not being limited to a unit of analysis, since the categories that result from it are generalized 'to be applicable to a multitude of diverse daily situations within the substantive area, not just to a specific type of situation (Glaser & Strauss, 1967, p. 237). According to Birks and Mills (2011), the use of CGT methods is more appropriate when: (a) little is known about the study area; (b) the generation of a theory with explanatory power is the intended result; (c) in the research situation, it is inserted an inherent process that is likely to be explained through the CGT methods.

Therefore, CGT allows you to develop a theory. Tourism, as a discipline, needs its own theories, independent of those from other areas of knowledge. CGT seeks to understand the action in a substantive area from the point of view of the actors involved. The theory will explain the owners' main concern and how it is resolved and processed. Continuous resolution is the central variable. The main objective of the

CGT researcher is to discover the central category once this resolves the main concern. This achievement marks the end of the first phase of analysis. The investigation process is characterized by a spiral, that is, as an investigator develops the theory, he can revisit phases according to the needs.

Taking this into account, the process consists of (Braga & Scott, 2015; Scott, 2007): (i) data collection and open coding; (ii) writing memos throughout the study; (iii) selective coding; (iv) theoretical sampling; (v) theoretical coding; (vi) sorting, and (vii) writing. Three examples of open coding elicited from the hosts interviews are shown below (table 1). On table 2, one example of a memo about a code and its relationship with other codes is provided.

Table 1. Open coding sample

Concept	Quote
Achievement	*All kinds of people are received, those you like and those you have less pleasure in receiving.*
Auscultation	*We talk to them for the first time and know it soon. They are very frontal. That is when I realize that they want to be as isolated as possible. It is very easy for them to define what they want. The direct approach is the best: we can ask.*
Dedication	*On Saturdays and Sundays there was no maid. My wife and I had to give breakfast. Sometimes there were 6 to 8 people of different nationalities. It was a drag to take things there [points to the old caretaker's house, which was the place where he received customers]. My wife was becoming a housekeeper for Housing Tourism.*

Source: (Braga, 2016)

Table 2. Memo sample

Concept	Memo
Partnerships	*It is possible that the hosts, to occupy the accommodation divisions, must establish partnerships with mass reservation centres, aimed towards the sensitive and insensitive customer to the Accommodation Exploration Modality [i.e. Housing Tourism]. It is also possible that the massification in the market makes the houses abandon the traditionalist style of accommodation in favour of the progressive one to increase their occupation and consequently their self-sustainability. Niche reservation centres do not seem to be able to occupy the house at a time when the economic context is negative and this can lead to the adhesion of houses to mass reservation centres, which may bring more insensitive customers.*

Source: (Braga, 2016)

Overall, the research question at CGT is not substantiated in a statement that identifies the phenomenon to be studied. The research problem, as well as the related issues, emerge and guide the theoretical sampling. The focus of the research is defined following the open coding, data collection through theoretical sampling and the application of the method of constant comparative analysis (Glaser, 1992).

As for the type of interviews that we conducted with owners/hosts of HT, these were mainly face-to-face (48), but also by phone (3) and email (2). Regarding the geographical origin of the houses, the vast majority are in the old province of Minho (34). A residual number can be found in Douro Litoral (4), Trás-os-Montes and Alto Douro (3), Beira Litoral (4), Beira Alta (1), Ribatejo (1), Alto Alentejo (2), Baixo Alentejo (3), Algarve (1) and Azores (2) - note that the total number of houses counted is fifty-five since one of the interviewees is the owner of three HT, two on the Azores islands and one in the Algarve region.

If we consider the sampling by district, we have Viana do Castelo where the largest number of houses is concentrated (21), followed by Braga (12), Porto (5), Aveiro (4), Beja (3), Vila Real (2), Évora (2), Ponta Delgada (1), Horta (1), Faro (1), Viseu (1), Santarém (1) and Bragança (1) - the same distortion factor above mentioned maintains its effectiveness in this case.

Figure 3. Housing Tourism Units in Portugal (© 2015, Oficina do Mapa. Used with permission)
Source: (Braga, 2016)

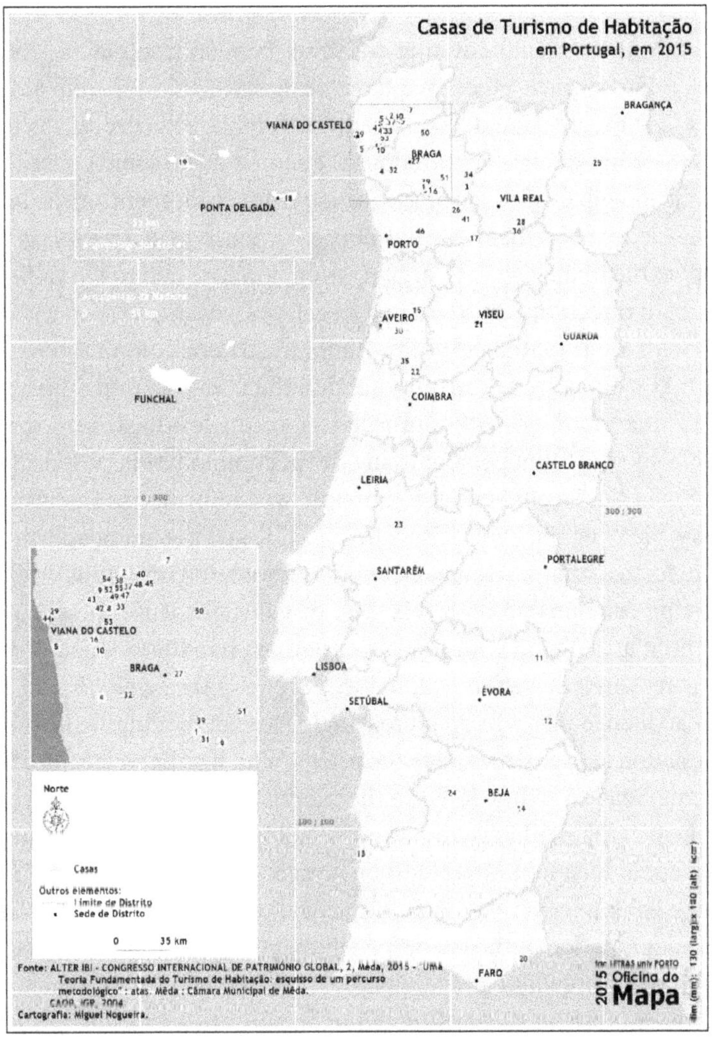

SOLUTIONS AND RECOMMENDATIONS

The theoretical integration in CGT is based on the classification of memos according to analytical rules, however, always considering the theoretical codes. However, the theoretical framework of CGT is not elaborated beforehand. The researcher only classifies the categories and properties of his/her memos, through similarities, as well as the conceptual relationships and ordinances that arise from the analysis.

During the process, certain patterns emerge and will be adjusted to the scheme, being the analytical rules, the only guideline that the analyst has (Planes, Miras & Requena, 2006).

Therefore, the analyst must remain receptive to what emerges and gains relevance throughout the CGT process, but particularly for the theoretical codes in the writing phase. It is about applying a range of analytical schemes to the data to increase its abstraction. These are the ways in which the substantive codes and the data they express are interrelated.

Theoretical codes come from all fields of knowledge and theoretical perspectives: social psychology, philosophy, organizational theory, economy, political science, history, biochemistry and so on (Glaser, 2005).

Economy provides the theoretical code that we think best conceptualizes the way the substantive codes generated by us relate to each other. We have designated this theoretical code as an 'amplified casual looping' model (see Figures 4 and 5) (Glaser, 2005, p. 9). This process is described by Glaser in the following way: as the consequences continuously become causes and causes continuously become consequences, we are faced with evolutions or involutions of recrudescent seriousness. Glaser lists social situations in which this scheme applies: marital abuse or abuse of authority as the abuse intensifies. This model is also applicable to the growing organizational failure and to the falling-in-love. The causal model is amplified in both directions: positive and negative (Ibidem).

The same happens with a substantial part of the theoretical codes of our theory. Therefore, according to the model in amplified vicious cycle causality model, the non-vocational host will be less willing to dedicate himself to HT, therefore, he will approach the guests less, listening, consequently, also less, what will make him less successful in personalizing the accommodation proposal and valuing it. It also happens that, since he is not dedicated enough, the host will informalize the accommodation proposal and narrow its visibility, pleasing only guests sensitive to HT, and not being able to attract guests insensitive to HT, who require formalization (Braga, 2016). Therefore, the host will have difficulties in helping and extending the hosting relationship with this type of guests because the presented accommodation proposal is basic and little articulated with the surroundings. In addition, accommodation assessments will start to become increasingly negative, leading to a break in the reputation of the house, which will lead to periods of low affluence that will be increasingly extended, with the host being obliged to close or lessen the accommodation capacity or reduce the prices, which will reduce the economic sustainability of the house and, in time, lead to a slowdown in the rate of recovery. This will require recoveries with increasingly high intensities that will have to be supported by the host's increasingly depleted equity. If the host does not have enough capital, there will be a great deal of uncertainty in the continuity of the house (or the debt to the bank to cover the costs of restoration) which, in the end, may lead to a break in the transmission or the degradation of the property's authenticity. This situation will lead to a less fulfilment of the host, which will imply less and less dedication to the HT unit, which will result in its end.

In sharp contrast, we can foresee a causal model in an amplified virtuous cycle causality model: the vocational host is more dedicated to the HT, approaching more the guests and, in this way, listening more and better. As a result of a better listening, the host will know if guests want more autonomy or more proximity. Likewise, the host will be more able to personalize the hosting proposal - because he/she has management skills, dynamism, creativity, linguistic competence and interpersonal skills, something that the non-vocational host lacks -, valuing it as it is his/her duty. In addition, the host will be willing to formalize the HT, increasing its visibility to attract, also, HT insensitive guests. Consequently, the host will be more likely to help and extend the hosting relationship as he/she offers a diverse and well-articulated with the surroundings accommodation proposal. Pleased with the hosting proposal, guests will evaluate it favourably, contributing this positive assessment for an increase in the reputation of the house.

Therefore, the host will notice that the periods of high influx are more and more extended and that, to accommodate the guests, he/she will have to open or increase more and more the accommodation capacity (availability that, if not well managed, may lead to the weakening of the family attachment to the house). As guests run into increasing numbers, the host will raise prices as his/her hosting capacity is limited. As a consequence of his/her effort, the host will witness an increase in the economic sustainability of the HT, which will lead to an increase in the pace of recovery of the house as a higher intensive recovery isn't needed. In this way, the host will see his/her own capital increased (avoiding resorting to the bank to obtain capital for the restoration of the house) and will be increasingly sure of the continuity of the house (much more if the transmission is linearized, favouring a child, or harmonizing transmission, creating a family society). So, because the house has been recovered, with an unscathed identity and the necessary formalization for the pursuit of HT - and because the house has a good reputation - the host will be fulfilled and will be able to increase his/her dedication to HT.

FUTURE RESEARCH DIRECTIONS

We can see lines of investigation that deserve to be pursued. Namely, using the CGT to learn about the inheritance transmission strategies of housing tourism owners, aiming, thus, to produce legislation that facilitates the inheritance, avoiding family disputes that, frequently, lead to the destruction of these manors. On the other hand, we believe that it is essential to draw up an inventory of the tourist resources of the surroundings of the houses of HT, seeking to create tourist products that bring together transportation, tourist entertainment, gastronomy, attractions and events and that are likely to prolong the stay of guests in the houses of Housing Tourism.

CONCLUSION

This chapter highlights a theoretical code that, in our opinion, constitutes an entirely original contribution to the literature regarding HT and, inherently, a valid allowance for the heritage and rural tourism state of the art.

Although Silva's previous works (2009, 2010) on HT have been exhaustive in the study of this tourist activity niche, the present approach contributes to the state of the art by making evident the need for hosts to adopt a proactive strategy in their approach to the management of this type of tourism.

From our point of view, the two models highlighted in this text allow the action of the host to be guided so that he can improve his/her performance by further personalizing the service he/she provides to guests and strengthening contact with them, because only then will he/she be able to meet their expectations, providing them with better experiences and thus satisfying them; which, in turn, will lead to an improvement in the reputation of his/her accommodation and an improvement in its economic sustainability. Only then will it be possible for the host to have the house recovered and ready to be passed on to future generations. The vicious cycle model highlights the harmful effects of the host's lack of dedication to the management of these enterprises.

Figure 4. Amplified vicious cycle causality model (Braga, 2016)
Source: (Braga, 2016)

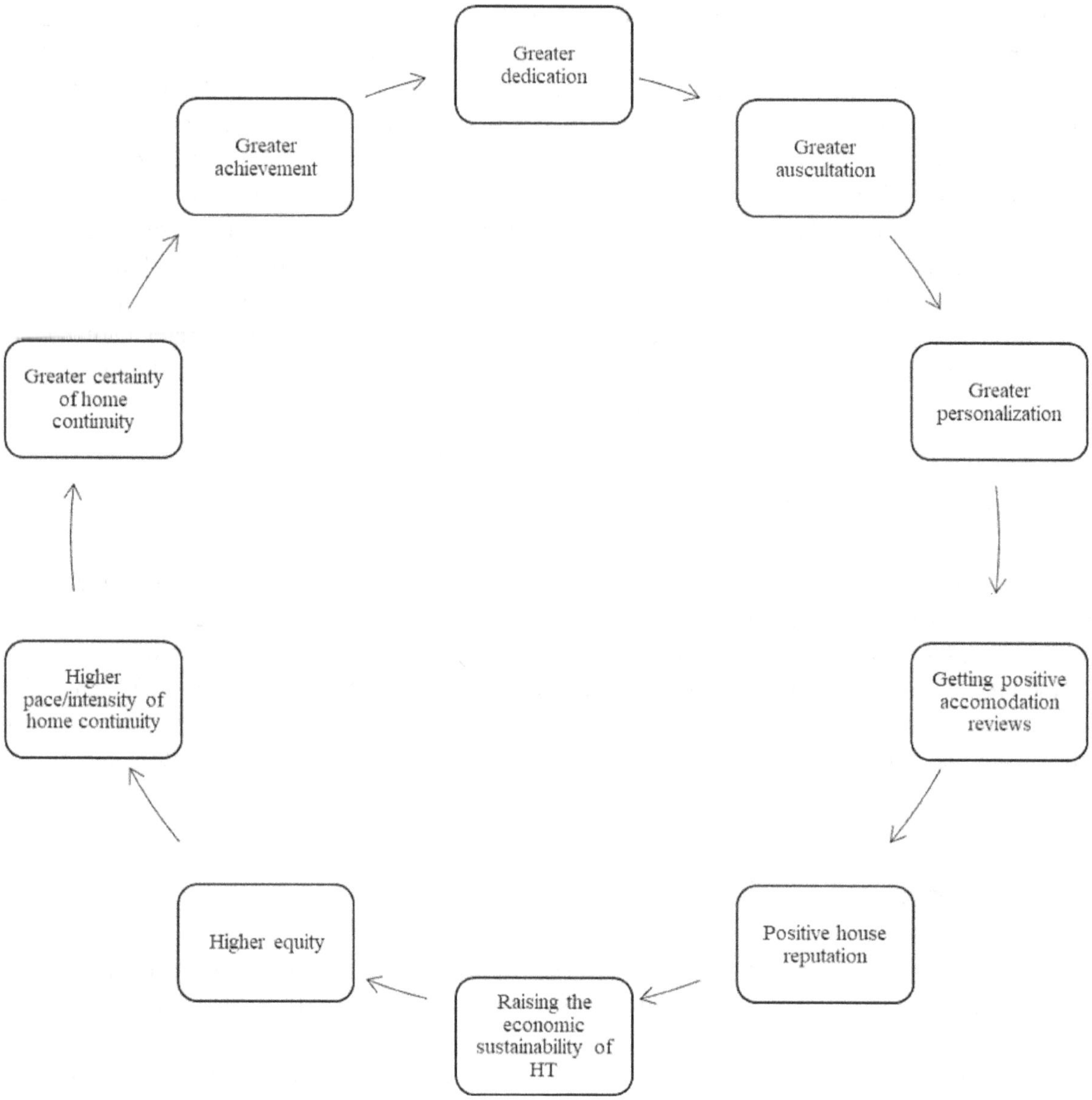

Nevertheless, our theory has some limitations, such as our difficulty in delimiting the analysis of data to a smaller number of properties and categories, what Glaser calls parsimony and scope (Braga, 2016). In addition, the integration of our theory proved to be painful, since we produced a bank of memos that was too extensive, many of which proved to be more descriptive than conceptual. Thus, the integration of the generated theory with the literature in the substantive area could have been more incisive.

In this chapter we apply the CGT methodology, which contemplates a set of rigorous research procedures leading to the emergence of conceptual categories that, in turn, explain a significant part of the behaviour learned in the substantive area of HT.

Figure 5. Amplified virtuous cycle causality model (Braga, 2016)
Source: (Braga, 2016)

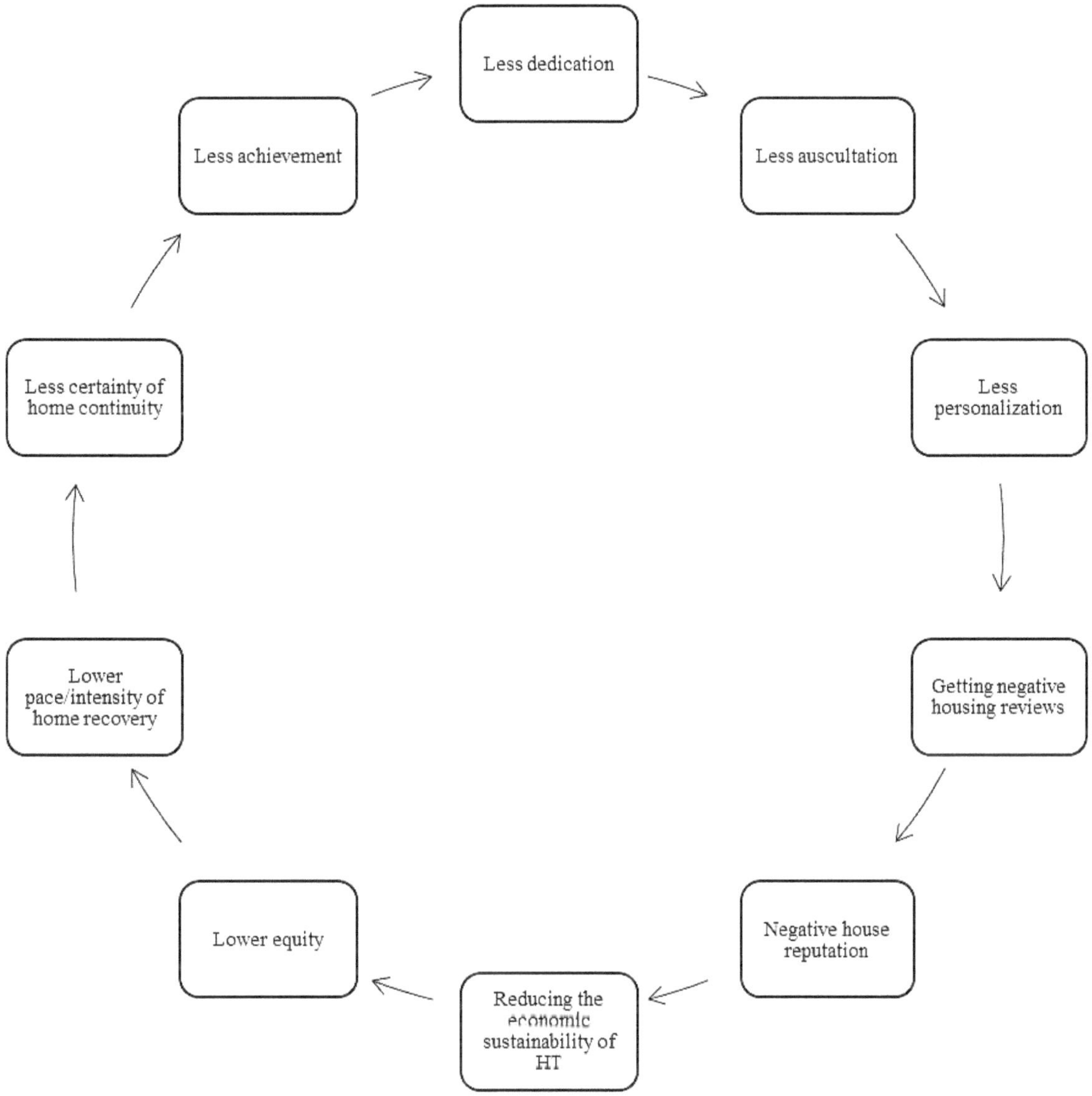

In this context, we revealed a theoretical code, called 'amplifying casual looping', which, we believe, has the merit of effectively conceptualizing the substantive codes generated by us. This causal model, as we have seen, is amplified in both directions: positive (virtuous circle) and negative (vicious circle).

Therefore, and as a result of the analysis of the schemes proposed above, we can conclude that a host of a HT house, if he intends to make it profitable, must be dedicated to the activity (having linguistic competence, interpersonal skills, being able to value the hosting, have technological competence, be dynamic, creative and have management skills, among others skills). If the host of HT feels that she/he does not have these faculties, he must pass the testimony to a continuing host of the same family or choose a legal framework in which his/her role is secondary. The owner who wants to join the HT, but who does not want to be sufficiently involved, must grant the exploration to a branch company, or hire a professional host. The host must, therefore, dedicate himself to the HT being aware that he will have to sacrifice his family life and leisure time to devote time and work to the modality.

REFERENCES

Birks, M., & Mills, J. (2011). *Grounded Theory: A Practical Guide* (1st ed.). Sage Publications Inc.

Braga, J. (2016). *Refuncionalizando a Casa Solarenga: uma Grounded Theory* (Doctoral dissertation). Universidade de Santiago de Compostela, Santiago de Compostela. Retrieved from: https://minerva.usc.es/xmlui/handle/10347/14805

Braga, J., & Lopes, J. (2020). The Public Sector's Role in Fostering Development in Low-Density Areas: The Case of Housing Tourism. In D. Kala & S. Bagri (Eds.), *Global Opportunities and Challenges for Rural and Mountain Tourism* (pp. X–X). IGI Global. doi:10.4018/978-1-7998-1302-6.ch012

Cavaco, C. (1999). *Desenvolvimento rural: Desafio e utopia*. Centro de Estudos Geográficos da Universidade de Lisboa.

CENTER - Centro Nacional do Turismo no Espaço Rural. (2020a). *Legislação Turismo de Habitação e Turismo no Espaço Rural.* Retrieved from: http://www.center.pt/PT/estudos.php

CENTER - Centro Nacional do Turismo no Espaço Rural. (2020b). *Encontros do Turismo de Habitação e do Turismo no Espaço Rural.* Retrieved from: https://www.center.pt/PT/encontros.php

Corfu, A., & Kastenholz, E. (2008). The opportunities and limitations of the internet in providing a quality tourist experience: The case of "Solares de Portugal". *Journal of Quality Assurance in Hospitality & Tourism*, *6*(1-2), 77–88. doi:10.1300/J162v06n01_06

Decree nº 5/87 de 14 de janeiro da Presidência do Conselho de Ministros. Diário da República I série nº 11. Retrieved from: http://www.oasrn.org/upload/apoio/legislacao/pdf/tur587.pdf

Fernandes, J. (1983, August). Turismo de Habitação: Férias tranquilas nas regiões onde rareia a hotelaria clássica. *Revista de Ação Regional e Local.*, *4*(23), 26.

Glaser, B. (1992). *Basics of Grounded Theory analysis*. Sociology Press.

Glaser, B. (2005). *The Grounded Theory perspective III: Theoretical coding*. Sociology Press.

Glaser, B., & Strauss, A. (2008). *The discovery of Grounded Theory: Strategies for qualitative research. 3ª Reimp*. Aldine Transaction. (Original work published 1967)

Godinho, M. (2004). O Turismo em Espaço Rural (TER) em Portugal. Problemas e desafios para o futuro. *Revista de Turismo e Desenvolvimento, 1*(1), 91-93. Retrieved from: https://dialnet.unirioja.es/servlet/articulo?codigo=3548517

Jepson, D., & Sharpley, R. (2018). More than sense of place? Exploring the emotional dimension of rural tourism experiences. In B. Lane & E. Kastenholz (Eds.), *Rural Tourism: New Concepts, New Research, New Practice* (pp. 25–46). Routledge. doi:10.4324/9781315111865-2

Lemos, F., & Farhangmehr, M. (2007). Tourism marketing and management: The case of Pousadas vs. Solares de Portugal. *Revista Turismo e Desenvolvimento, 7/8*, 117.

Martins, L. (2013). O "alojamento local" – entre o impulso da novidade e a maturidade do turismo rural português. *Proceedings – Conferência Vale do Douro: Desenvolvimento Rural e Ordenamento Turístico*. Retrieved from: https://sigarra.up.pt/fpceup/pt/pub_geral.pub_view?pi_pub_base_id=43899&pi_pub_r1_id=

Menezes, F. (2000). *Tourism as an Agent of rural development: Construction of programmes and institutional forms of implementation: a case study of LEADER I in Vale do Lima (in NW Portugal)* (Master's dissertation). Retrieved from: http://www.center.pt/imprensactr/estudo_788.pdf

Pereiro, X. (2018). Abordagem exploratória do turismo rural de Trás-os-Montes e Alto Douro (Portugal). *Analise Social, 53*(226), 58–87. http://analisesocial.ics.ul.pt/documentos/n226a03.pdf

Pina, P. (1988). *Portugal: o turismo no século XX*. Lucidus.

Planes, V., Miras, R., & Requena, A. (2006). *Teoría Fundamentada Grounded Theory: El desarrollo de teoría desde la generalización conceptual* (1st ed.). Centro de Investigaciones Sociológicas.

Plog, S. (1974). Why Destination Areas Rise and Fall in Popularity. *The Cornell Hotel and Restaurant Administration Quarterly, 14*(4), 55–58. doi:10.1177/001088047401400409

PRIVETUR – Associação Portuguesa de Turismo Rural. (2013). *Turismo Rural.pt. Quem somos*. Retrieved from: http://www.turismorural.pt/pt/quem-somos/

Rodrigues, F. (2013). O Turismo de Habitação no Douro – para uma antropologia da hospitalidade nas casas de turismo. *Proceedings – Congresso Internacional da Casa Nobre – Um Património para o Futuro, Arcos de Valdevez, 3*, 1195-1209.

Sampaio, F. (2012). O turismo rural integrado e as rotas dos vinhos. In A. Cardoso, & S. Trilho (Eds.), *Proceedings – Congresso Internacional Vinhas e Vinhos, Arcos de Valdevez*. Porto: Câmara Municipal de Viana do Castelo.

Scott, H. (2007). *The Temporal Integration of Connected Study into a Structured Life: A Grounded Theory* (Unpublished Doctoral Dissertation). University of Portsmouth, Portsmouth.

Seripex. (2015). *Housing Tourism ID Plate*. Retrieved from: http://www.seripex.com/placas_classificativas/placas_classificativas.htm

Silva, L. (2009). *Casas no Campo: Etnografia do Turismo Rural em Portugal*. ICS.

Silva, L. (2010). Perspectiva antropológica do turismo de habitação. *Pasos: Revista de Turismo y Patrimonio Cultural, 8*(1), 31-46. Retrieved from: http://www.pasosonline.org/Publicados/8110/PS0110_3.pdf

Silva, S. (2012). *Ponte de Lima – Património histórico e turismo: As Casas Senhoriais ("Casas Antigas") como espaços de Turismo de Habitação* (Master's dissertation). Universidade do Porto, Porto. Retrieved from: https://sigarra.up.pt/flup/pt/pub_geral.show_file?pi_doc_id=13966

Stoop, A., & Sotto Mayor, J. (2015). *Arquitectura Senhorial do Minho*. Caminhos Romanos.

ADDITIONAL READING

Azevedo, C. (1988). *Solares Portugueses: Introdução ao Estudo da Casa Nobre*. Livros Horizonte.

Braga, J. (2019). *Refuncionalizando a Casa Solarenga: Uma Grounded Theory*. Novas Edições Académicas.

Gómez, V. (2001). *Turismo en el espacio rural*. Editorial Popular.

Kastenholz, E., Carneiro, M., Eusébio, C., & Figueiredo, E. (Eds.). (2016). *Meeting Challenges for Rural Tourism through Co-Creation of Sustainable Tourist Experiences*. Cambrige Scholars Publishing.

Lane, B., & Kastenholz, E. (Eds.). (2017). *Rural Tourism: New Concepts, New Research, New Practice*. Routledge.

Sharpley, R., & Sharpley, J. (1997). *Rural Tourism: An Introduction*. Routledge.

Silva, L., & Leal, J. (2015). Rural tourism and national identity building in contemporary Europe: Evidence from Portugal. *Journal of Rural Studies*, *38*, 109–119. doi:10.1016/j.jrurstud.2015.02.005

Stoop, A. (1989). *Stately homes and country houses in the vicinity of Lisbon*. Civilização.

Stoop, A. (2007). *Living in Portugal*. Flammarion.

KEY TERMS AND DEFINITIONS

Agritourism: Modality of tourism integrated in Rural Tourism carried out in private houses inserted in agricultural holdings, which allow the monitoring and knowledge of agricultural activities or participation in the work carried out there.

Classical Grounded Theory: Also known as Glaserian, an inductive method originated by Barney Glaser and Anselm Strauss, which, following a methodological division between the two, was developed exclusively by the first North American sociologist. This research strategy aims at the systematic generation of theory through an interactive investigation process that leads to the emergence of conceptual categories.

Housing Tourism: Modality of accommodation in manor houses and palaces of architectural, historical, and artistic value and refined interiors, which, in Portugal, takes the designation of *Turismo de Habitação*. In this accommodation, which can be in rural or urban areas, the owner is typically present during the guests' stay and offers a personalized service.

Manor House: Noble family home, usually of large dimensions and erudite architecture, which, in Portugal, can date back to the 17th and 18th centuries.

Ponte de Lima: One of the oldest villages in Portugal, founded even before the formation of the Portuguese State (1143), which is located in the northwest of the Iberian Peninsula, namely in the district of Viana do Castelo. It constituted one of the 4 pilot zones for Housing Tourism. The Housing Tourism Association (TURIHAB) is based in this municipality.

Pousadas de Portugal: Chain of hotel establishments, created in 1941 on the initiative of António Ferro, director of the National Propaganda Secretariat, during the dictatorial period of the New State. The Inns are historical monuments, castles, convents, and monasteries owned mainly by the Portuguese State that are recovered and adapted to the function of tourist accommodations.

Rural Tourism: Type of alternative tourism, different from mass tourism that allows the guest to enjoy customs, values, cultural and gastronomic practices, characteristics of rural communities. This type of tourism includes a set of complementary activities and services for tourist entertainment and is distinguished by providing a personalized welcome.

TURIHAB – Housing Tourism Association: Cooperative organization that aims to recover and preserve the heritage associated with family tradition and the identity of the manor and rustic houses that have been converted into tourist developments.

Chapter 7
Empowering Marginalized Women Through Entrepreneurship:
Breaking the Barrier

Faraha Nawaz
University of Rajshahi, Bangladesh

ABSTRACT

The purpose of this chapter is to analyze some positive life changes happened through micro-finance-driven entrepreneurship development among a sample of marginalized women in Bangladesh. The chapter is based on both primary and secondary data collected from two villages in Rajshahi district in Bangladesh. The author argues that when poverty is reduced, women are better able to meet their practical gender needs; however, they are not empowered unless they are also able to meet their strategic gender needs. The author also argues in this chapter that although entrepreneurship development empowers women, it cannot bring empowerment to all women equally at all levels. In the concluding remarks, the author contends that although many women are empowered at the household level, very few are empowered at the community level.

INTRODUCTION

Bangladesh is one of the most densely populated countries in the world. It is also characterized by extreme poverty and inequality (Lefton, 2013). Gender discrimination and disempowerment of women are among the root causes of this situation. Neither the government nor the market has been able to reverse this and meet the welfare needs of most of the population. When non-government organizations (NGOs) began operating, one of their prime methodologies was to empower impoverished women through entrepreneurship development by offering them collateral-free loans called 'microfinance.' However, the role of microfinance in this area has been a matter of intense debate and controversy. Research on microfinance reveals a paradox, for it has both positive and negative impacts on poverty and women's

DOI: 10.4018/978-1-7998-4942-1.ch007

empowerment. This debate is particularly fierce when the role that NGOs play in the advancement of women's empowerment is taken into consideration.

Positive views are held by researchers such as Rahman (2010, p. 44), who argue that microfinance[1] has appeared as a new paradigm through which NGOs have supported the empowerment of poor women by considerably expanding their activities through strategies such as group formation, credit delivery, savings, insurance, training, and advocacy. Rahman views microfinance as a response to the increasing poverty created through the process of globalization. In addition to poverty alleviation, microfinance has also been a tool for strengthening the role of women in Bangladesh. Rankin (2002) suggests that microfinance organizations foster democratic participation within microfinance groups, and this promotes collective decision making (p. 13). Through the group formation and participation process, women can develop leadership abilities and personal networks.

Basargekar (2010) argues that microfinance brings positive effects by raising women's levels of awareness about social issues and decision- making rights as a way of improving their wellbeing (pp. 25-43). Similarly, other researchers have found some improvement in women's individual capacities such as community mobility and decision making. Sanyal (2009, p. 529) suggests that women's membership in microfinance groups may improve their individual capacity and facilitate their collective empowerment. Some supporters of NGOs consider women's empowerment purely from an economic perspective and believe that women can simply be empowered if they are economically developed. They argue that NGOs have concentrated their efforts on women's economic development by involving the women in income-generating activities and providing them with training, credit and other inputs and that the financial support given by NGOs is beneficial to women and ensures their empowerment in rural Bangladesh (Shailo, 1994, p. 18).

Another study conducted by Institute of Social Studies Trust (2009) examined the impact of microfinance in reducing domestic violence against women. An analysis of data relating to the impact of microfinance indicates that it contributes considerably towards the economic empowerment of women. The data revealed that despite only 5% of respondents claiming to have benefited directly by the disbursement of microfinance, others benefitted indirectly as a result of their involvement in Self Help Groups. Bhattacharya, Bedi and Chhachhi (2009) conducted research on the nexus between marital violence and women's employment in North Indian villages. They gathered wide-ranging data relating to the impact of women's paid work on spousal violence. Their research suggests that there is a positive relationship between women's employment and the reduction of violence against women. They found that women's engagement in paid work was associated with a sharp reduction of spousal violence.

On the other hand, the impact of microfinance institutions on disadvantaged women is subject to a long-standing dispute. Daley-Harris argues that Bangladesh is the world's most saturated microfinance market and that the impact of this microfinance is highly controversial. For example, in 1965, Thailand's per capita income was 50% higher than that of Bangladesh. By 2004, it had risen to almost 600% higher than Bangladesh. More importantly by 2002, Thailand had pushed the $1 per day poverty rate down to only 2%. So, Indonesia and Thailand achieved their success even though there were no extensive microfinance institutions for serving the poor (Pollin, Feffer & Daley-Harris, 2007, p. 3).

Several studies reveal that the repayment rates of Grameen Bank's loans do not match those claimed by the bank. Moreover, there is no serious supervision of bank policies and this enables the bank to delay defaults and hide problem loans. Other studies found that NGO programs overlook the extremely poor women who make up a significant percentage of their potential clients. The functional coverage of NGOs is fragmented as the number of poor women in an area is dependent on the service capacity of the NGOs rather than the actual needs of the area. Sometimes NGOs are accused of being new agents for expanding neo-imperialism. Western donors meet their own interests through NGOs and establish patron client relationships that hinder social revolution (Begum, 2003, p. 77).

It is evident that empowering women is a key to addressing poverty and inequality, and that microfinance provides a tool for this purpose (Lefton, 2013). Whilst many studies have already been undertaken in the area of microfinance, very few have focused on its impact on women's empowerment, especially from the perspective of generating social capital side by side with financial capital as an essential outcome. Whilst I agree with researchers who put forward both positive and negative arguments regarding microfinance based on their empirical research, it is timely to strengthen and extend the current debate and discourse by highlighting both the tangible and intangible aspects of microfinance and its influence on women in certain circumstances. I have attempted to achieve this by addressing the various socio-economic factors within and beyond microfinance that could make a difference to the transformation of gender power relations. I have also focused on all aspects of empowerment: economic, social, psychological and political in the larger context of the institutional relationships that take place across the household, market, community and state levels. The paper also addresses some policy implications based on the findings of the research. This core objective of this chapter is to analyze some positive life changes among Bangladeshi marginalized women through micro-finance driven entrepreneurship development.

BACKGROUND

Although NGOs have recently gained prominence in development discourse, this is not a recent phenomenon. There is a long history of international voluntary assistance to provide welfare services to the poor (Korten, 1991). In the colonial period, groups of volunteer families and other land based elite groups appeared spontaneously to support vulnerable people in natural disasters like flood, famine and epidemics. These groups ceased to exist once the situation improved. They shared an ethical value of taking care of their *Proja*[2] in distress (Ahmed, 1999, p. 12).

Gradually efforts were made primarily by Christian missionaries to institutionalize the charity work and social welfare activities in Bangladesh. They often set up hospitals, schools, orphanages and so forth in remote and poverty-stricken areas. Many such centers have now been in operation for over hundred years and have progressively become known as NGOs. In the pre- liberation period, most of the NGOs were missionaries from other countries. Of these, one of the longest operating was organized by the Baptist Missionary Society and it has been in existence since 1794. The longest running local NGO is the Kumudini Welfare Trust, which began its operation in 1944 (Ahmed, 1999, p. 11).

Although NGOs have been working in traditional ways since the British colonial period, they radically transformed their role after the Bangladesh Liberation War of 1971. This nine-month war devastated the country, causing extensive destruction to the physical, social and economic infrastructure. The Government faced the uphill task of providing aid to the war-affected peoples and rehabilitating the damaged infrastructure. During this time a number of NGOs emerged to respond to the massive need for relief and rehabilitation activities. The following quote from Ahmed (1999) captures this:

There could be no mistaking the needs following the devastating natural disasters in 1970 and the war of liberation which left a shattered economy and infrastructure and millions of refugees but at the same time, a resolute new nation which the people would build together. NGOs were requested to respond to the efforts at relief, rehabilitation and national reconstruction and respond they did. Many international NGOs and voluntary organizations extended their helping hands to assist Bangladesh (p. 12).

Primarily, NGOs emerged as charitable and voluntary organizations. Over time their activities slowly transitioned from relief and rehabilitation to developing welfare programs to promote development by introducing microcredit schemes. These projects followed on from community and sustainable systems development, as the Government of Bangladesh did not have adequate capacity to deal with challenges confronting it. NGOs mostly commenced their involvement by targeting groups of poor people from similar socio-economic backgrounds. Initially the target group was the dispossessed poor, both male and female. Then, in response to the global issue of gender inequality, they shifted the emphasis to providing programs for women only. Gradually, financial sustainability became a dominant issue in microcredit programs when these emerged as a development tool to alleviate poverty via international development agencies such as the World Bank, the United Nations Capital Development Fund, etc. (Rahman, 2010, p. 13).

NGOs have now become the main providers of microcredit in Bangladesh. Collateral-free microcredit programs have been the main catalyst for alleviating poverty and empowering women. Today's use of the expression 'microfinancing' has its roots in the 1970s when microcredit pioneer, Dr. Mohammad Yunus, introduced the Grameen Bank model. Since then, the NGO sector has achieved remarkable recognition for developing a model of microcredit that introduced collateral-free loans to rural poor women as a key strategy for alleviating poverty (Mahtab, 2007, p. 82). The Grameen Bank also promoted social and financial discipline by emphasizing activities relating to education, family planning and public health through its social and environmental development programs. These activities were aimed at enabling the rural poor to become more productive and improve their standard of living (Kabir, 2002 cited in Siddiquee & Faroqi, 2009, p. 248).

Encouraged by the success of the Grameen Bank, a large number of NGOs such as the Bangladesh Rural Advancement Committee (BRAC), the Association for Social Advancement (ASA) and Proshika, also provided collateral-free small loans to the poor aimed at poverty alleviation in Bangladesh (Mahtab, 2007, p. 82). This brought a new wave of microcredit initiatives and innovations into the sector. The BRAC began experimenting with loans to poor people, especially women, and gradually the idea was replicated by some local NGOs as well (Begum, 2003, p. 61). The *Palli Karma Shhayok Foundation* (PKSF), a non-profit company created by the Bangladesh Parliament, sponsored credit programs where 82% of the beneficiaries were women. Credit facilities widened the capacity of rural women to become involved in both farming and non-farming activities. Most studies reveal that the credit was mostly used for generating self-employment (Rahman, 1996; Hossain, 1988; Lovell, 1992; Ray, 1987; and Yunus, 1983, cited in Sarkar, 2000, p. 3). This reduced poverty and empowered the women.

Bangladesh is known as the birthplace of microcredit. A few experimental programs were commenced in Bangladesh after 1971 whereby the poor were given small loans to invest in micro business. This kind of microcredit was offered based on solidarity group lending, with each member taking group responsibility and providing a guarantee for the loan repayments. The origins of group-based microcredit in its recent practical manifestation can be linked with numerous organizations founded in Bangladesh including, the Grameen Bank. Microfinance emerged as a constant global effort to address poverty and gender discrimination throughout the world especially in third world countries. Nevertheless, the question remains as to why microfinance is assumed to be a role model for development throughout the world. One possible answer is that microfinance serves unmet global needs since two-thirds of the global population has no access to banking services. Microfinance is the only strategy whereby banking services without collateral are provided to the doorsteps of poor people. It is the only approach which focuses especially on poor women rather than men, providing them with the opportunity to work as a gateway or entry way for the rest of the household. The family and children receive the greatest benefit when the mother of the family earns money.

Bangladesh is characterized by gender inequality. This is not unique to any region or country, but it sometimes takes on different forms that result in different consequences. The gender norms and practices that prevail in a patriarchal country like Bangladesh keep women isolated from the outside world. This is a country that restricts women to undertaking purely reproductive roles or sometimes productive roles that can be carried out largely within the home. Women's domestic and family work is essential, yet it is unpaid, ignored and rarely considered to be of the same value as work that is primarily undertaken by men (Efroymson et al., 2007, p. 28).

In Bangladesh, women are raised with messages that convey their lack of value and capability in comparison with men. The patriarchal culture and social norms place them in a position of subordination and oppression in their families, neighborhoods and communities. Their upbringing trains them to be good mothers and wives and to perform all household chores perfectly. Bangladesh is a classic patriarchal society where women are expected to live and stay in their husbands' homes when they marry. This is often a long distance from where they were born and grew up and they are treated with very little respect (Kabeer et al., 2013, p. 2). Thus, women in Bangladesh are underprivileged and oppressed, not only by the family but right up to the state level, and this is totally unacceptable. Gender equality and women's empowerment is not only a development issue but also a human rights and social justice issue.

The overall development of a country is not possible without gender mainstreaming. Women comprise half the total population of Bangladesh and the development of the country will not progress unless they are fully involved in the development process (Goswami, 1998). In order to be rid of the curse of poverty and to progress development, male supremacy and the oppression and domination of women need to cease, and strategies must be put in place to advance the empowerment process from the household to the state level. One of the experimental tools being applied to empower women is the microfinance developed by NGOs in Bangladesh. Since the Second World War, a number of global development models have been adopted to facilitate the development of underdeveloped countries. In 1976 microfinance was introduced in Bangladesh as one of these global development models. As women were the most vulnerable members of the community, the microfinance programs were essentially women-focused with the vision of increasing their empowerment as a fundamental approach towards furthering the overall development of the country (Shehabuddin, 1992, p. 71).

Gradually, microfinance programs have been replicated all over the world. Despite microfinance being adopted as a most promising development tool, previous literature highlights the existence of two extremely polarized views regarding the impact of microfinance on women. The critics argue that credit money will work as an exploitative mechanism to abuse innocent rural women while the advocates argue that microfinance will improve the economic condition of rural women which will in turn improve their social position. These conflicting views motivated the researcher to undertake the current study. The study explores the question of whether microfinance is an effective way to move women from positions of subordination and discrimination and facilitate their empowerment. It describes how women's subordinated positions could be improved, as well as exploring why and how women experience personal transformation. The interest in women's empowerment began with the issue of women's self-perception and how changes in their sense of self might lead to changes in their ability to stand up for their rights in the context of microfinance.

In this book chapter, an in-depth qualitative research approach has been adopted. Two villages from the Rajshahi district were chosen for the study, based on their suitability in terms of location, ease of availability of the programs in the villages, duration of the programs, the number of women beneficiaries and transport facilities. The study areas were representative as both NGOs have been operating in the selected villages for more than ten years. The women borrowers were chosen through a purposive network sampling method. Both primary and secondary sources of data were used in the study. Primary data were collected from microfinance borrowers, their family members (mostly husbands), government officials, NGO officials and community leaders. Data were validated through crosschecking one respondent's views with the other and primary data were also crosschecked with secondary data. Secondary data were collected from various publications, books, articles, websites and NGO reports. When collecting data, an interpretive epistemological position guided the choice of applying qualitative methods such as in-depth interviews, focus group discussions and observation. Case stories were also obtained through in-depth interviews with women borrowers. Data were validated by applying triangulation data collection methods and this chapter also provides details of the data analysis techniques that were used.

MAIN FOCUS OF THE CHAPTER

Issues, Controversies, Problems

Empowerment is a multi-dimensional concept. It has been used in many different contexts and by many different organizations in the fields of education, health, social work and psychology, as well as in the work of feminist and development organizations. It is, therefore, essential to describe the background, meaning, theories and models of empowerment. Empowerment can be described as a process whereby people become able to organize themselves to increase their own self-reliance, to assert their independent right to make choices and to control resources that will assist them to challenge and eliminate their own subordination (Malhotra et al., 2002). Pilla (1995) also defines empowerment as an active, multidimensional process that enables women to realize their full identity and power in all spheres of life (cited in Nawaz, F., 2010, p. 64). Power is not a commodity to be transacted. It has to be acquired and needs to be exercised, sustained and preserved. It is not possible for one person to empower another. People can only empower themselves.

Cheston and Kuhn (2002) argue that empowerment covers two important aspects: choice and power (p. 12). A person must have options to choose from and have the power to choose from the available options. As mentioned earlier, the current research goes beyond the financial paradigm of empowerment which focuses only on the choice component of empowerment and ignores the power component. Both choice and power components of empowerment are applied in the thesis. When compared to their previous circumstances, microfinance has increased women's options for choice by offering them collateral free loans; however, this does not necessarily imply that they have gained power of choice. It is, therefore, worthwhile to look at both aspects of empowerment. The concept of women's emancipation emerged in the Indian sub-continent during the nationalist movement against colonial British rule. During the 1970s and 1980s feminists came up with the concept of empowerment to address the gender imbalance that existed in the control and distribution of resources. In rural Bangladesh, society not only treats women as inferior, but the women also perceive themselves to be inferior. The empowerment process lies, therefore, in women's ability to exercise choice by freeing themselves of their inferiority complex.

Krishna (2003) emphasizes the importance of women having effective economic choices in their lives (cited in Bali, 2006, p. 9), while Malhotra, Schule and Boender (2002) argue that women's empowerment must include access to options, choice, control and power (p. 5). Saraswathy, Panicker and Sumi (2008) argue that women's empowerment is a continuous process whereby powerless women become conscious of their situation and organize themselves to improve it and gain access to opportunities (p. 190). This results in women taking control over their own lives, setting their own agendas, gaining skills, solving problems and developing self-reliance. However, Mayoux (2000a) maintains that the power of women to make decisions at a policy or political level is one of the key elements of women's empowerment (p. 9). This paper explores beyond the narrow minimalist evaluation of microfinance rather it looks at whether and how microfinance empowers women through entrepreneurship development by utilizing microloans.

An entrepreneur can be defined as one who initiates and establishes an economic activity or enterprise. Entrepreneurship thus refers to the general trend of setting up new enterprises in a society (Begum, 1993). The International Labor Organization (ILO, 1984, cited in Islam and Aktaruzzaman, 2001) defines an entrepreneur as a person with a set of characteristics that typically includes self-confidence, result-oriented, risk taking, leadership, originality and future-oriented. Khanka (2002) referred to women entrepreneurs as those who innovate, imitate or adopt a business activity. Given that entrepreneurship is the set of activities performed by an entrepreneur, it could be argued that being an entrepreneur precedes entrepreneurship. In any case, the entrepreneurial definitions described above highlight the aspects of risk-taking, innovating and resource organizing.

Burzyńska et. al. (2018) argued that entrepreneurs are businessmen who realize new business opportunities by taking risk. They introduce innovations and new ideas that determine socio-economic development. They stated that the concept of entrepreneurship is immanently linked to the development of the economy, which is achieved through establishment of new enterprises, their successive development, creation of new resources, markets, technologies, products and services, processes and transactions, thus contributing to creation of value. In addition to looking at concepts and characteristics of entrepreneurship, it is also possible to look at the main features of entrepreneurship, which are given as (i) being an economic agent, (ii) being creative, (iii) taking and bearing risk, (iv) being innovative, and (v) being dynamic.

Entrepreneurship may be regarded as what entrepreneurs do. In other words, entrepreneurship is the act of being an entrepreneur. It is a process of involving various actions to be undertaken to establish an enterprise. Some have referred to entrepreneurship as risk bearing while others view it as innovating, and still others consider it thrill-seeking (Khanka, 2002). Entrepreneurship is the key to small business development. A country may have resources, but the problem of development is to put these resources into the process of production. This can only be made possible through initiatives by some people or organization (Hossain and Rahman, 1999). Entrepreneurship plays a vital role in the growth and development of any country, especially of a poverty-ridden country like Bangladesh. The development of a country depends not only on the human resources but also on the proper utilization of all the resources. Entrepreneurship development is a powerful instrument to activate the forces of socio-economic development of a country. Development of entrepreneurship can solve acute problems like unemployment, underemployment, disguised employment etc. (Saha, 1995). Microcredit refers to small loans that are provided to the poor, especially women, to stimulate entrepreneurship[3]. The term microcredit has been replaced by microfinance in recent times due to its wider role, as microfinance adds the provision of savings and insurance services to that of credit. Some organizations also include training and other services such as health and education (Abed, 2000, p. 14).

The microfinance movement has often been referred to as a second revolution in credit theory and policy. The first revolution was focused on microcredit taking into consideration structural barriers such as information asymmetries, lack of collateral, high cost, high risk and systematic market bias when providing savings and credit services to the poor. The second revolution focused on the microfinance program. Because microcredit programs mainly provided a small loan-oriented service, the promoters of the second revolution describe the microcredit approach as only satisfying the interests of lenders rather than developing products that met the customers' needs. This narrow 'lender focused' approach was transformed with the introduction of the second revolution (Woller, 2002, p. 1). The paper demonstrates to what extent and if so, then how rural women become empowered through their involvement in different entrepreneurial activities by utilizing microloans.

As microfinance provided by NGOs have assumed wider roles, there has been simultaneous growth in the debate and controversy surrounding them, not only in Bangladesh but also globally. Different schools of thought have emerged to explain the controversy surrounding the role of Microfinance. Modernization theorists hold positive views regarding the function of NGOs. From the positive point of view, it is argued that NGOs have a constructive association with the state and have emerged in order to help the state perform different developmental activities (Holloway, 1998, p. 20).

Rankin (2002) suggests that microfinance organizations foster democratic participation within microfinance groups, and this promotes collective decision making (p. 13). Through the group formation and participation process, women can develop leadership abilities and personal networks. Basargekar (2010) argues that microfinance brings positive effects by raising women's levels of awareness about social issues and decision -making rights as a means of improving their wellbeing (pp. 25-43). Similarly, other researchers have found some improvement in women's individual capacities such as community mobility and decision-making. Sanyal (2009) suggests that women's membership in microfinance groups may improve their individual capacity and facilitate their collective empowerment (p. 529). Some supporters of NGOs consider women's empowerment purely from an economic perspective and believe that women can simply be empowered if they are economically developed. They argue that NGOs have concentrated their efforts on women's economic development by involving the women in income- generating activities and providing them with training, credit and other inputs and that the financial support given by NGOs is beneficial to women and ensures their empowerment in rural Bangladesh (Shailo, 1994: 18).

Sarumathi and Mohan (2011) also conducted research on the role of micro-finance on women's empowerment. Their study was carried out in the Pondicherry region of India and it revealed a gradual increase in all three aspects of empowerment amongst women because of their participation in microfinance programs. From interactions with the women, it was found that they were also more empowered socially and psychologically because of their participation in self-help groups arising out of micro finance programs. In another study in Bahawalpur, Pakistan, Nawaz, Jahanian and Manzoor (2012) found that micro-credit drives women's empowerment in a positive direction because women feel empowered at personal, economic and family levels after using micro-credit in various income generating activities. They argued that economic empowerment of women further drives increasing empowerment at other levels.

On the contrary, researchers who have a negative view of microfinance programs have often criticized the contribution of NGOs, considering their endeavors as repetitious and their activities as largely insignificant (Islam & Hussain, 1993). Ahmed (1993) claims that strong national and international backing has encouraged NGOs to defy decisions of the state by setting their own agendas (p. 20).Haque (2006 cited in Nawaz, 2013: 88) has made the observation that the influence of NGOs has increased in most developing nations over recent years. It is quite conceivable that NGOs have become a formidable force in Bangladesh, affecting the political and economic environment and the power and legitimacy of the government. They are the alternative voice who frequently expresses their opinions against the power of political society and the state.

Haque and Itohara (2009) have undertaken research to explore the effects on women's empowerment of participation in micro-credit programs in Bangladesh. The results of the study reveal that only 21% of the women respondents experienced a positive effect on their empowerment with the remainder reporting no improvement. However, amongst those women who felt more empowered, 69% were active members of micro-credit programs. Another study published in the same year by Rahman et al. (2009) using a case study from Bangladesh, also identified some factors influencing the level of empowerment experienced by female micro-credit borrowers. They concluded that education provided women with the tools to make positive decisions for their lives. Hence, micro-finance is not enough to empower women unless it is combined with education. Such debate and paradox in the literature inspired the author to conduct an in-depth study of women borrowers to explore and understand whether micro-finance has had a favorable impact on their empowerment through creating social capital.

Therefore, opinions vary about the ability of microfinance programs to empower women. While some researchers agree that the effects are positive, others disagree, and the true impact seems to depend on how microfinance programs are implemented. For example, Cons and Paprocki (2008) disagree that microfinance empowers women on the grounds that it has the negative effect of increasing dowries. Women are forced to take out loans as the only alternative means of paying these increased dowries for their daughters. Some female borrowers fall into a cycle of debt and must use a microcredit loan from one organization to meet the interest obligations of another. The authors also argue that microfinance institutions often judge the performance of their field officers by the number of repayments they have been able to secure. As a result, the field officers sometimes use coercive and violent tactics to collect monies owed by borrowers (p. 3). Findings relating to the impact of microfinance on the incidence of domestic violence are also conflicting.

In summary, among the various programs launched by NGOs, at the world-wide level microfinance is regarded as a development model, but despite this global renown, it has not been free from criticism. The debate is particularly fierce when the role of microfinance in empowering women is taken into consideration. There is hardly any consensus on its role in women's empowerment and this inspired me to conduct research in this field.

The paper aims to analyze how women become empowered by getting them involved in entrepreneurial activities through microcredit supplied by NGOs. When considering women's involvement in entrepreneurial activities, it is important to determine whether women have access to resources and whether they have participated in entrepreneurial activities. It is also worthwhile to consider any changes that microfinance has brought about in gendered allocation and utilization of resources which, in a patriarchal society like Bangladesh, is generally under the male's favor and control. To explore the impact of microfinance on gendered distribution and utilization of resources, two questions were important to consider: who has access to what type of employment (home or local market based)? How? The study suggests that microfinance provides the opportunity for women to have access to and make use of resources.

For assessing the impact of microfinance in facilitating women's involvement in entrepreneurial activities, it is important to know how many women were involved in entrepreneurial activities before and after joining the microfinance groups. The following table demonstrates respondents' opinions about their involvement in entrepreneurial activities.

Table 1. Respondent's opinions about their involvement in entrepreneurial activities

Respondents Involvement in entrepreneurial activities	Number and Percentage
Involvement in entrepreneurial activities before being involved in entrepreneurial activities	01(2.5%)
Involvement in entrepreneurial activities after being involved in entrepreneurial activities	37 (92.5%)
No Involvement in entrepreneurial activities	02(5%)
Total	40 (100%)

Source: Nawaz, F. (2020)

Primary data reveals that only one (2.5%) woman from the selected respondents was involved in entrepreneurial activities before her enrolment in the program while 37 (92.5%) stated that they had an association in entrepreneurial activities after their involvement in microfinance. Two (5%) indicated no involvement in entre. Therefore, the majority of respondents indicated either a direct or indirect involvement in entrepreneurial activities after joining and receiving microcredit from NGOs. The study shows a positive relationship between training and independent non-farm income generating activities at local market. The women who did not receive training were unable to launch businesses at market level on their own, due to a lack of courage, confidence, accounting knowledge and business operating skills, while those who had received long-term skills-based training and financial literacy, launched independent businesses. Some of them assisted their husbands in business by providing information they had gained from training, while others worked as co-workers in their husbands' businesses.

From in-depth interviews and focus group discussions, it was revealed that most of the women would not have started any entrepreneurial activities unless they had received training from the NGOs. Following the skill-based training and financial literacy offered under the microfinance program, the women engaged in income generating activities related to their skills. The interviews with the women highlighted the outcome that their family income was increased to some extent after they became involved in microfinance program.

The field investigation reveals that time spent in a microfinance program plays a vital role in women's proactive involvement in entrepreneurial activities. Those who are involved in the microfinance program for a comparatively longer time confirm that they are engaged in independent market-oriented income generating activities such as petty business, tailoring, poultry farm, grocery shop keeping, dairy farm with credit money at the community level and consequently make a good economic contribution to their families. They also state that the training offered by NGOs was very useful for the utilization of loans and making profits. However, those who spent relatively less time in entrepreneurial activities and had no training were either involved in homestead entrepreneurial activities such as cattle rearing, poultry farming, sewing, dairy farming, cow dung processing and *katha* (hand-stitched quilt) making or worked as assistants in their husbands' businesses having little or limited involvement in the business operation. The study indicates that the women choose on-the-homestead entrepreneurial activities because they must look after their families. So, women's domestic and family responsibility does not allow them to choose to work far away from their home.

The research indicates most of the women beneficiaries are involved in traditional home-oriented income generating activities such as livestock rearing, *katha* sewing, paddy husking, poultry and post harvesting activities. Some who are long term borrowers, and who received skill-based training, are now involved in small trading and marketing goods. But not all women had the opportunity to be trained, ultimately leading them to choose some easy home-based income generating activities. From the above discussion women's involvement in microfinance promotes their income generating activities either at the household or the community level. In terms of the women's ability to meet their strategic needs, this finding allowed me to present a continuum of cases from the least empowered women through to the most empowered. However, although microfinance enabled women to have improved access to resources, it is crucial to look at whether the women had control over those resources.

The study confirms that 65% of women borrowers pass either the full amount or a portion of their loan to their husbands. Despite having access to resources, these women have limited or no control over their loan utilization. Nevertheless, 35% of women respondents are involved in some non-farming income generating activities either separately or jointly with their husbands. These women not only have access to their loan but also have either partial or full control over its utilization.

SOLUTIONS AND RECOMMENDATIONS

The following policy recommendations are primarily based on views gathered from women and community leaders.

1. The primary research suggests that sustainable life transformations for women can only be achieved if all women clients can utilize their money independently, effectively and efficiently. Therefore, an important policy suggestion is to introduce financial literacy training as a compulsory component of the process that must be incorporated by all NGOs/MFIs. This will enable women to utilize credit money more productively and, most importantly, to do this independently.
2. Microfinance programs operated by NGOs must be properly monitored in order to overcome the problem of over-indebtedness and multiple borrowing. A wider use of technology, client support services and cost-effective operating procedures would facilitate the sustainability of microfinance programs.
3. The women who performed best in the study received credit plus other services from NGOs, and so it is important that NGOs place more focus on a credit plus approach. such as health, education, and legal aid that will foster more sustainable and complete life changes for marginalized women.
4. The findings of the study revealed that BRAC has recently introduced a monthly loan repayment collection policy and this has not been appreciated by the clients. NGOs should consider holding meetings more frequently, on a weekly basis. This would allow clients to meet more often and would also provide more opportunities for them to make their repayments.
5. Another important policy suggestion is to introduce separate loan schemes for the extremely poor who have no assets, so that they can use their loan more efficiently. One possible solution for the poorest of the poor could be the provision of non-interest emergency loans.

6. The microcredit regulatory authority (MRA) has recently made a ruling on the interest rate for all NGOs operating their microfinance programs in Bangladesh. To ensure the improved welfare of women in the long term, it is important for both NGOs to review their interest rate policies. I propose that the rate of interest rate/service charge needs to be calculated using the 'declining balance method' as this would be a more effective way of assisting women to escape from poverty and inequality in the long term.

Moreover, the domestic burden for women in rural areas needs to be reduced. This could be achieved by the state offering free childcare opportunities at the village level and by encouraging women to stand up for their rights and insist that other family members share the burden of domestic work. In addition, more job opportunities need to be created for women, not only in the rural villages but also in semi-urban and urban areas. I argue that women's empowerment will not be achieved at the community, market and state levels until the unfairness of their unpaid reproductive role is challenged. The government, media and NGOs need to work together with a common aim of promoting gender equality and women's empowerment in all sectors of the country. A comprehensive and holistic approach is required to change the gender biased attitudes and mind sets that still exist at all levels of the community.

FUTURE RESEARCH DIRECTIONS

The current research has undertaken a critical evaluation of the effects of microfinance on women's empowerment. However, social capital can also be created through microfinance groups and women can use their group networks in narrowly restricted way. This could have a detrimental impact on the empowerment of women. Future researchers could explore this aspect as another means of investigating the intangible outcomes of microfinance. Furthermore, the current research has focused on a national and a local NGO only. There are many local NGOs in Bangladesh who are actively operating their microfinance programs, but their contribution has always been out of focus. Future research could be conducted on these local NGOs and their microfinance programs. The study was also restricted to two villages only. Similar research could also be conducted with wider coverage in a similar socio-economic context.

CONCLUSION

To conclude, the field data suggests that the women who had greater access and control over income and expenditure following their involvement in microfinance, with their husbands now preferring to discuss the utilization of the loan with them. They jointly made decisions concerning both using the loan and arrangements for repayment. These women cover 35% of the total respondents. This positive finding about women's control over income and expenditure was verified by their husbands. Males also acknowledged that their partners had acquired improved skills in accurately managing their income. These women, therefore, were comparatively more economically empowered than those who were involved in home based small scale entrepreneurial activities. Accordingly, it can be said that in some cases microfinance driven entrepreneurial activities have brought about some positive changes for women with respect to their ability to exercise control over household income and expenditure. The chapter presented a continuum of cases from the least empowered to the most empowered women in terms of their ability to control loan utilization, income and expenditure. The women who had access to markets and were involved in local trade associations had more control over their household income and expenditure They were more economically empowered than the women in the other groups because they had a greater say and control over resources. While many women respondents were able to meet their basic needs, not all of them were able to improve their strategic needs.

REFERENCES

Abed, F. H. (2000). *Microfinance NGOs in Bangladesh: Growth, impact, challenges*. Paper presented at the Asian Regional Conference on the potential and limitations of economic initiatives in grassroots development - Current issues and Asian experiences, Rajendrapur, Bangladesh.

Ahmed, M. (1993). *Growth of industrial entrepreneurship in Bangladesh: A study of bank financed engineering industries* (Unpublished doctoral dissertation). University of Rajshahi - Bangladesh.

Bali, S. R. (2006). *Microfinance and women's empowerment: Evidence from the Self-Help Group Bank Linkage Programme in India. Sida*. Division for Market Development.

Basargekar, P. (2010). Measuring effectiveness of social capital in microfinance: A case study of urban microfinance program in India. *International Journal of Social Enquiry*, *3*(2), 25–43.

Bayulgen, O. (2008). Muhammad Yunus, Grameen Bank and the Nobel Peace Prize: What political science can contribute to and learn from the study of microcredit. *International Studies Review*, *10*(3), 525–547. doi:10.1111/j.1468-2486.2008.00803.x

Begum, A. (2003). *Government-NGO interface in development management: Experiences of selected collaboration models in Bangladesh*. A. H. Development Publishing House.

Bhattacharya, M., Bedi, A. S., & Chhachhi, A. (2009). *Marital violence and women's employment and property status: Evidence from North Indian villages*. Discussion Paper No. 4361, Institute for the Study of Labour, Bon, Germany.

Cheston, S., & Kuhn, L. (2002). Empowering women through microfinance. In S. Daley-Harris (Ed.), *Innovations in microfinance for the poorest families* (pp. 167–228). Kumarian Press.

Cheston, S., & Kuhn, L. (2002). Empowering women through microfinance. In S. Daley-Harris (Ed.), *Innovations in microfinance for the poorest families* (pp. 167–228). Kumarian Press.

Cons, J., & Paprocki, K. (2008). The limits of microcredit - A Bangladeshi case. *Food First Backgrounder*, *14*(4), 7–11.

Efroymson, D., Biswas, B., & Ruma, S. (2007). *The economic contribution of women in Bangladesh through their unpaid labour*. Retrieved January 24, 2020 from http://healthbridge.ca/Bangladesh%20summary%20report%20final.pdf

Goswami, A. (1998). Empowerment of women in Bangladesh. *Journal of Empowerment*, *5*, 45–70.

Haque, M., & Itohara, Y. (2009). Women empowerment through participation in micro-credit programme: A case study from Bangladesh. *Journal of Social Science*, *5*(3), 244–250.

Holloway, R. (1998). *Supporting citizens initiatives: Bangladesh's NGOs and society*. Practical Action Publishing Ltd. doi:10.3362/9781780446066

Islam, M. N., & Hussain, S. (1993). Rural development programs and the role of NGOs in Bangladesh. In M.A Quddus (Ed.), Rural development in Bangladesh: Strategies and experiences. Comilla, Bangladesh: Bangladesh Academy for Rural Development (BARD).

Islam, T. (2007). *Microcredit and poverty alleviation*. Ashgate Publishing Ltd.

Kabeer, N. (2001). Resources, agency, achievements: Reflections on the measurement of women's empowerment. In A. Sisask (Ed.), Discussing women's empowerment: Theory and practice (pp. 17-59). Swedish International Development Agency.

Kantor, P. (2003). Women's empowerment through home-based work: Evidence from India. *Development and Change*, *34*(3), 425–445. doi:10.1111/1467-7660.00313

Korten, D. C. (1991). The role of nongovernmental organizations in development: Changing patterns and perspectives. In S. Paul & A. Israel (Eds.), *Nongovernmental organizations and the World Bank*. World Bank Publications.

Lefton, R. (2013). *Gender equality and women's empowerment are key to addressing global poverty.* Retrieved March 26, 2020 from http://www.americanprogress.org/issues/poverty/news/2013/03/11/56097/gender-equality-and-womens-empowerment-are-key-to-addressing-global-poverty/

Mahtab, N. (2007). *Women in Bangladesh: from inequality to empowerment*. A. H. Development Publishing House.

Malhotra, A., Schule, S. R., & Boender, C. (2002). *Measuring women's empowerment as a variable in international development.* Background paper prepared for the World Bank workshop on poverty and gender: New Perspective.

Mayoux, L. (2000a). *Microfinance and the empowerment of women: A review of key issues*. Retrieved December 02, 2013 from http://www.ilo.org/wcmsp5/groups/public/--ed_emp/documents/publication/wcms_117993.pdf

MkNelly, B., & McCord, M. (2001). Credit with education. *Impact Review No. 1: Women's Empowerment. Freedom from Hunger*.

Molla, M. (1982). Credit problems of the rural disadvantaged in Bangladesh. *Journal of Bank Porikrama*, *7*(1), 59–64.

Nawaz, F. (2011). *Strengthening awareness among rural adolescent girls in Bangladesh: A case study on adolescent development program of BRAC*. Lambert Academic Publishing.

Nawaz, F. (2013). Bargaining with poverty: An empirical review on some rural women in Bangladesh. *Studies on Home and Community Science*, *7*(2), 87–94. doi:10.1080/09737189.2013.11885397

Nawaz, N., Jahanian, A., & Manzoor, S. W. (2012). Empowering women through microcredit: A case study of Tameer Microfinance Bank, Bahawalpur. *Journal of Economics and Sustainable Development, 3*(6), 17–21.

Pollin, R., Feffer, J., & Daley-Harris, S. (2007). *Debate on microcredit.* Retrieved May 28, 2014, from http://fpif.org/debate_on_microcredit/

Rahman, A. (1999). Microcredit initiative for equitable and sustainable development: Who pays? *World Development, 27*(1), 67–82. doi:10.1016/S0305-750X(98)00105-3

Rahman, A. K. M. M. (2010). *NGO and development: Myth and reality.* AH Development Publishing House.

Rankin, K. (2002). Social capital, microfinance and the politics of development. *Feminist Economics, 11*(8), 1–24. doi:10.1080/13545700210125167

Sanyal, P. (2009). From credit to collective action: The role of microfinance in promoting women's social capital and normative influence. *American Sociological Review, 74*(4), 529–550. doi:10.1177/000312240907400402

Saraswathy, A. K. P., Panicker, K. S. M., & Sumi, M. (2008). Micro credit and women empowerment: A study in India. *International Journal of Global Business, 1*(1), 184–213.

Sarkar, A. R. (2000). *Women in microcredit and their empowerment: Case study of BRAC societies under Sherpur Upazila of Bogra District. Bogra.* Tajma Art Press.

Sarumathi, S., & Mohan, K. (2011). Role of microfinance in women's empowerment; An empirical study in Pondicherry region rural SHGs. *Journal of Management and Science, 1*(1), 1–10.

Shailo, I. (1994). Genesis and growth of NGOs: Their achievements and success in national development. *Alternative Development Journal, 4*(13), 18–20.

Shehabuddin, R. (1992). *Empowering rural women: The impact of Grameen Bank in Bangladesh.* Grameen Bank.

Siddiquee, N., & Faroqi, M. (2009). Holding the giants to account? Constraints on NGO accountability in Bangladesh. *Asian Journal of Political Science, 17*(3), 243–264. doi:10.1080/02185370903403434

Sobhan, R. (1997). The political economy of micro credit. In G. D. Wood & I. Sharif (Eds.), *Who needs credit? Poverty and finance in Bangladesh* (pp. 131–144). Zed Books.

Woller, G. (2002). Introduction to the second microfinance revolution: Creating customer centered microfinance institutions. *Journal of International Development, 16*(2), 1–5.

ADDITIONAL READING

Nawaz, F. (2013). Bargaining with poverty: An empirical review on some rural women in Bangladesh. *Studies on Home and Community Science*, *7*(2), 87–94. doi:10.1080/09737189.2013.11885397

Nawaz, F. (2015). Microfinance, Financial Literacy, and Household Power Configuration in Rural Bangladesh: An Empirical Study on Some Credit Borrowers. *Voluntas*, *26*(4), 1100–1121. doi:10.100711266-015-9585-z

Nawaz, F. and Mclaren Helen (2016). Silencing hardship: Bangladeshi women, microfinance and reproductive work, *Social Alternatives: Silence as a power*, 35(1):19-25

Nawaz, F. (2017). Conscientization among rural women: A case of Bangladesh, In Nilan (Eds) 'Conscientization', Routledge, Taylor and Francis Group, New York

Nawaz, F. (2019). *Microfinance and Women's empowerment in Bangladesh: Unpacking the Untold Narratives*. Palgrave Macmillan Publishing. doi:10.1007/978-3-030-13539-3

Nawaz, N., Jahanian, A., & Manzoor, S. W. (2012). Empowering women through microcredit: A case study of Tameer Microfinance Bank, Bahawalpur. *Journal of Economics and Sustainable Development*, *3*(6), 17–21.

Zafarullah, H., & Nawaz, F. (2019). Pathways to Women's Empowerment in Bangladesh: Employment and Microfinance as Interventions. *Journal of Asian Education and Development Studies*, *8*(4), 387–404. doi:10.1108/AEDS-11-2018-0168

KEY TERMS AND DEFINITIONS

Economic Empowerment: Economic empowerment focuses on the 'power to' dimension of power relationships, where 'power to' refers to higher access to credit and savings and other economic resources.

Empowerment: Empowerment can be defined as transformation of power relations at various levels of the society.

Entrepreneurship: An entrepreneur is a person who has possession of a new enterprise, venture, idea or becomes involved in income-generating activities and assumes significant accountability for the inherent risks and the outcome.

Microcredit: Microcredit refers to small loans that are provided to the poor, especially women, to stimulate entrepreneurship.

Microfinance: The term microcredit has been replaced by microfinance in recent times due to its wider role, as microfinance adds the provision of savings and insurance services to that of credit.

Practical Gender Needs: Practical gender needs as being shared by household members, but women often identified this as their specific need. It includes water provision, health care provision, opportunities or earning an income to provide for the household, provision of housing and basic services and distribution of food.

Strategic Gender Needs: Strategic gender needs relate to the gender division of labour, power, control as well as issues such as legal rights, domestic violence, equal wages and women's control over their own bodies.

ENDNOTES

1 Currently microcredit has changed into microfinance due to its wider dimensional functions which include a wide range of financial and organizational services.

2 *Proja* is a Bengali term for tenants; it refers to a person who holds or possesses for a time lands or tenements of another, usually for rent

3 Entrepreneurship is the act of being an entrepreneur - one who undertakes an endeavour. An entrepreneur is a person who has possession of a new enterprise, venture, idea or becomes involved in income-generating activities and assumes significant accountability for the inherent risks and the outcome.

Chapter 8
The ICT Adoption in AMUL:
An Easy, Innovative, Self-Sustainable Approach for Rural Regions

Pranav D. Desai
https://orcid.org/0000-0001-5196-9872
Indukaka Ipcowala Institute of Management, FMS, Charotar University of Science and Technology, Changa, India

ABSTRACT

The adoption of information communication technologies (ICT) in rural regions of Gujarat by the Gujarat Cooperative Milk Marketing Federation Limited (GCMMFL) can be considered as an iconic practice in the dairy industry in India. It is typically assumed that the efforts associated with the investment of ICT in rural area are not as effective as expected, though in the case of Amul, it was proved otherwise. Amul is a dairy farming company that produces a variety of milk products and GCMMF takes responsibility of distributing and marketing of the products of it. Amul has been a forerunner of rural India's adoption of ICT in dairy industry. This chapter shares the success story of Amul and how they utilized ICT in the dairy industry. The application of IT enabled Amul to get better control for the accumulated milk from scattered suppliers. The Amul case is a prime example for the enabling role of the technology for innovation.

INTRODUCTION

The Indian economic system has seen the biggest boost in agriculture, manufacturing and the offerings sector in the past few years. Specifically, in India, dairy farming has been rehearsed as one of the main income generating sources in the rural areas. During the past few years, each household unit in these international locations appeared after its 'family dairy animals' or encouraged to conduct dairy farming. The substantial cost of milk creation, troubles of sanitation became major problems for dairy manufacturers. During such a period, a company named Amul, introduced a way to overcome major problems with dairy production. The introduction of new information and communication technological solutions helped Amul to provide solutions for dairy farmers and also obtain an appropriate return

DOI: 10.4018/978-1-7998-4942-1.ch008

for their work. The creators of Amul encouraged the collaboration of farmers and helped them to build their skills and introduced a mutually beneficial arrangement. The association and implementation of new model to collaborate with the suppliers of milk (the farmers in this scenario) made effective contribution to founders and visionaries of Amul in the advancement of the Indian Dairy Farming scenario. The "Green Revolution" in India guaranteed the wellbeing of the people in rural regions and confirmed continued support. Parallelly, A "White Revolution" has been headed out to generate a subsidiary profits for rural dairy farmers of Gujarat, India. The technological infrastructure introduced by Amul provided greater efficiencies to milk treating centers and milk merchandise. The introduction of information and communication technologies has also enabled the availability of products and availability of distribution structures that enables the effective distribution for Amul to reach close to billion consumers.

GCMMF, is India's one of the largest dairy product marketing company with annual business (2019-20) of around US $ 5.1 Billion. The organization is involved in acquisition of approx. 23 million liters of milk for each day from around 18,600 city milk beneficial social orders. This includes 18 section associations protecting 33 areas, and more than 2.7 million milk providing individuals.

This company is considered as the role model for various dairy cooperative societies in the Gujarat area in India. The company is prominently recognized with the brand name of 'AMUL,' among the consumers and the other competitors. The most prominent characteristic of this brand is that it intends to offer profitable approaches to the farmers and furthermore maintain high customer satisfaction and customer engagement through different methods such as offering different objects which are suitable incentive for cash. The model followed by Amul has not been completely been imitated by dairy producers in India and it has been considered as a proven model for recreation in parts of the world. The structure is exclusively working for advertising and marketing for the brand products of 'Amul' and 'Sagar'. This structure is also one of the largest structures in India which includes more than sixty-one Sales Offices and has a vast vendor support that includes ten thousand carriers and more than 11 lakh retailers. This brand offers a range of products that include traditional Indian desserts, ghee, milk, Pizza cheese, Ice-cream, chocolates, milk powder, well-being drinks, spread, cheddar, Paneer and many more.

GCMMF was a small company which was a gift of a co-operative revolution initiated with villages in single digit and around 250 liters of milk in 1946. The success of Amul model commenced with the motto of "Bypassing the intermediaries." By cutting down the intermediaries, they were able to ensure a proper price for the rural dairy farmers. One of the biggest problems faced by the dairy farmers is that due to intermediaries, they were unable to gain a profit out of their dairy businesses. By introducing a new model, Amul, resolved one of the largest problems faced by the rural dairy farmers.

In Figure 1, the distribution network of Amul is provided.

Figure 1. The anand pattern

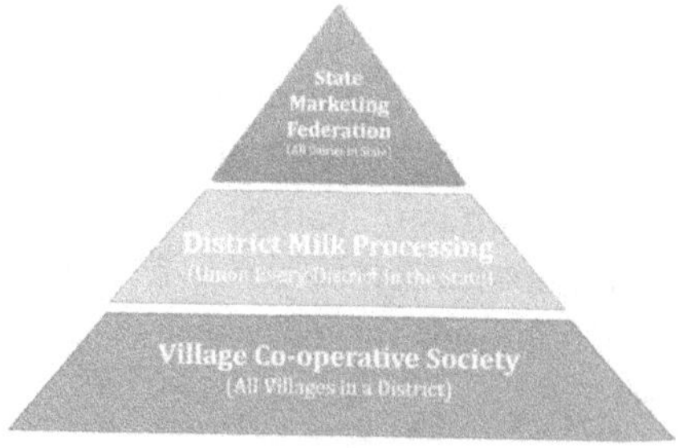

The Anand sample is one of a suggestion of Amul that consists of the Dairy Co-Operative societies at village stage and a dispensation unit, recognized as "Union" at district level, as shown in Figure 1. As depicted, the collective farmers prospered and conventional the idea of Co-Operative societies and replicated to a number of different areas of Gujarat and India as well. For high-quality advertising and distribution of the merchandise of the milk unions, Gujarat Co-operative Milk Marketing Federation (GC-MMF) used to be shaped in 1973. GCMMF is the sole marketer for the whole varies of Amul products. Initially, they had been solely milk powder and butter. Later it is long-drawn-out considerably to cowl different merchandise such as – ice creams, pizza, ghee, cheese, chocolates, shrikhand, paneer and so on. These made Amul the main meals company in India. The revised shape of GCMMF is proven in Fig.2.

Figure 2. The anand pattern – revised structure

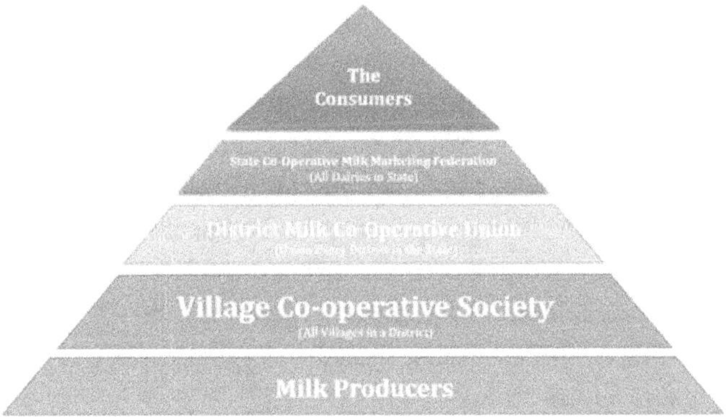

BACKGROUND

The cooperative structure proposes a type of association that is broadly predominant in creating nations including India. It has incredible potential as an instrument of provincial advancement. Co-activity as a moral standard has been praised everywhere throughout the world since days of yore. As a method of social conduct, it is show in innumerable exercises of individuals performed to accomplish a shared objective. From the philosophical point of view, co-activity and its inverse, rivalry, are two essential propensities of human conduct and both co-exist in each person. Co-activity can rise under profoundly assorted circumstances and in like manner there are a few speculations / recommendations that look to clarify why individuals do and don't co-work.

The source of formal co-activity as a co-usable association is followed to Europe, especially, England, France and Germany, in the mid-nineteenth century. In 1844, a gathering of individuals in Rochdale, England, framed the Rochdale Society of Fair Pioneers to acquire higher wages from their managers. This system developed into the model for comparative stores also, related ventures all through the world. Around a similar time, Fourier built up ——phalanxes|| in France and Raiffeisen and Schulze spearheaded and actualized the possibility of co-employable banks in Germany. In this way, in other European nations additionally, co-agents developed fundamentally as individuals' reaction to their misuse by moneylenders and merchants. With the rise of co-employable development in Europe, the International Co-usable Collusion (ICA) was set up in 1895. Its primary obligation was to organize the exercises of partnered co-usable organizations in different pieces of the world. Foundation of socialism in USSR and therefore in other nations was instrumental in advancing government-coordinated, or parasternal cooperatives. Some co-agents fizzled, and some others succeeded. Notwithstanding their disappointments and shortcomings, co-agents have made do after some time and now control noteworthy portions of business sectors in many created and creating nations including market-situated economies. For instance, in USA, cooperatives order 70 percent of the liquid milk showcase, 80 percent of the new organic products showcase, 35 percent of farming credit of different types, and 30 for every penny of the grains and oilseeds showcase.

In most developing countries which includes India, co-agents had been superior by using their administrations as contraptions of united states improvement. In India, due to the fact of the English inheritance, the co-usable kind of affiliation was once conceived in 1904 ensuing upon the order of the Co-employable Credit Societies Act.

In this way, a regularly entire act, the Co-usable Societies Act, used to be approved in 1912. This Act gave, entomb alia, for the manufacturing of the put up of Recorder of Co-usable Societies, enrolment of co-usable social orders for one of a kind purposes, and review. Under the Montaque-Chelmsfort Reforms affected in 1919, co-activity became into a Provincial Subject and the areas had been permitted to make their personal co-employable laws. Under the Government of India Act 1935, ——co-usable societies|| have been handled as a State Subject. In request to inspire the basis of co-agents having enrolment from greater than one Province, the Government of India ordered the Multi-Unit Cooperative Societies Act, 1942. Later a step by step a ways achieving Central enactment, the Multi-State Co-Usable Societies Act, 1984, was once ordered through Parliament so as to merge a variety of legal guidelines overseeing comparable kinds of agreeable social orders.

After India executed Independence in August 1947, co-agents anticipated greater distinguished centrality as an instrument of monetary turn of activities and grew to become into a essential piece of India's Five Year Plans. The All India Rural Credit Overview Committee Report, 1954 prescribed a coordinated way to deal with useful savings and accentuated the requirement for realistic deposit co-employable social orders by using increasing their territory of activity, empowering rustic reserve funds, and differentiating their business. The Committee likewise counseled that the authorities ought to add to the provide capital of the co-agents. In 1958, the National Development Council (NDC) embraced a Resolution on National Strategy on Co-agents. Accordingly, in January 1959, the Working Group on Co-usable Policy set up through the Ministry of Food and Agriculture, Administration of India, advised an define for actualizing the NDC's Goal. The Government of India has when you consider that given full-size monetary, specialized and regulatory assist to co-agents each legitimately and by way of implication thru State governments.

However, professional measurements on milk introduction indicates a substantial increment in milk introduction beginning with the Seventies underneath OF software over the tiers in previous two decades, the precision of the insights has been examined with the aid of a few researchers. Mergos and Alderman (1987) assessed the effect of Operation Flood (OF) in two World Bank-supported dairy enhancement ventures, one every in Madhya Pradesh and Karnataka. They observed that milk advent had improved at the regular gradual tempo of round 7 percentage for every annum in the Project zones beneath OF versus non-of regions. In an ongoing document based on the available hypothetical and experimental confirmations, Mergos (1997) inspected the floor reality of increment in milk advent and direct impact

OF on milk creation. The investigation conceded that the instant impact OF on milk advent improvement had been humble and proven that 25 percentage to 50 percentage of increment in acquisition by using OF was once probable due to the fact of exchanging. It likewise upheld that milk introduction increment in the state was once actual and no proof was once on hand to exhibit in any case. As we would like to think, there is presently sufficient proof handy to assist the rationalization that a tremendous phase of the gradual milk advent carried out after the beginning of 0F should be ascribed to increased flexibly of targeted adjusted steers feed, higher creature social insurance plan and the board, getting ready and education of milk makers, and worthwhile maker price of milk all gave below OF.

Nalini Kumar (1997:34) whilst exploring the writing on OF, mainly in the post-1987 period, noticed that OF had produced a voluminous and disputable writing. He seen that a ton of proof on OF was once both recounted and depended on territory express contextual analyses. Absence of observational facts furthermore, logical meticulousness maintains on being an actual restrict of the reachable proof on OF application impacts. Pundits have even puzzled the exactness of authority value determinations of milk creation. Be that as it may, there is sufficient proof to exhibit that there has been good sized improvement in the dairy area. Gigantic trade in the dairy economy, extensive showcasing machine and increased per capita accessibility of milk regardless of the excessive increment in populace are ample pointers of the development.

At first, Operation Flood, similar to some other effective improvement program, had pulled in a great deal of analysis, for the most part from a gathering of social researchers working under the sponsorship of the Institute of Social Studies, at The Hague. For model, Doornbos et al. (1990:283, 284, 293 and 294) have watched, entomb alia, that (a) the accessibility of dairy help to India under OF permitted the Indian specialists to keep up the supposed exchange costs of skim milk powder and spread oil at a level underneath the household creation cost; (b) with the exemption of some development districts, the huge increment in milk obtainment under OF could be because of a move in showcasing channels, i.e., ranchers exchanging their deals from ghee dealers to co-agents, as opposed to any sizeable increment in milk creation. They presume that in spite of the fact that dairy co-agents may have expanded the salary winning chances of the landed milk makers, they absolutely have not decreased the overall imbalances intrinsic in nearby financial structures. Likewise, it was felt that whatever salary additions may have been determined by peripheral and little rancher makers have barely made any huge gouge in the serious issues of destitution and ailing health. In our supposition, it isn't right that the exchange costs of skim milk powder and spread oil were ever beneath the degree of household creation cost. In actuality, as we have referenced before in this paper, an intentional exertion was made under Activity Flood to guarantee that the maker cost of milk is fixed at a level which takes care of the expense of creation as well as gives a sensible edge to the maker. The methodology was to give the imperative motivator through the milk cost and sponsored information sources and administrations to the maker to increment milk creation.

THE OPERATIONS OF COOERATIVE SOCITY

The village milk co-operative is a society of predominant milk producers formed underneath the guidance of a supervisor or milk furnishes officer of the Co-operative Dairy Union (District stage Co-operative proudly owning the processing plant).

Figure 3. Co-operative society model of amul

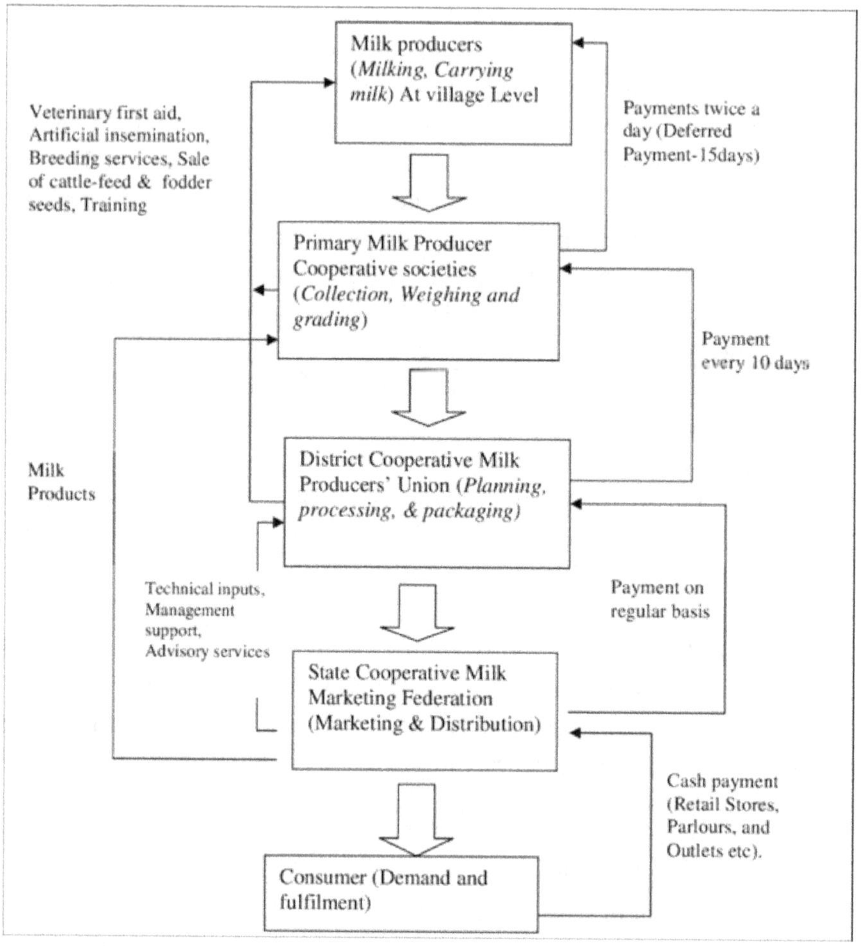

Challenges in Indian Dairy Farming

Precision Dairy (PD) speaks to an advancement, as opposed to unrest in overseeing dairy frameworks. The utilization of new advancements basically gives more noteworthy data, and in more detail, for ranchers settling on the executive's choices. The likely volume of new data elevates the requirement for ranchers to have a strong ranch arranging process, the purpose of gathering more information without an arranging and dynamic structure to support its utilization. There is a scope of ranch the executives arranging forms and a procedure depicted by previous research with regards to NZ dairy cultivating contains arranging, usage, and control stages.

One of the contextual investigation ranchers utilized a comparable, however progressively characterized approach based around steps of 'plan, measure, oversee, and audit'. He applied this way to deal with most parts of the business and could do as such with various timetables, week by week, month to month, the lactation, the lifetime of the dairy animals. Where he saw most profit by PD was in quick input on his arranging and usage forms too as his administration techniques.

The significance of good homestead the board arranging practice in the effective utilization of PD innovations features a test while considering industry-great D&E venture. Deciding the most suitable portion of financing in this zone can be seen regarding the various scales at which issues happen.

At the homestead level industry RD&E can conceivably connect with private innovation organizations around innovation structure, establishment, reconciliation, and preparing. It is at this scale privately owned businesses have the most grounded possible job in innovation plan and on-ranch support, with industry RD&E associations giving autonomous exploration, administration around best practice, and summed up expansion.

Figuring out how to utilize the new innovations is a crucial piece of the usage procedure and building learning systems is a likely strategy to advance learning. Innovation providers gave a large portion of the preparation accessible to contextual analysis ranchers, utilizing an assortment of approaches remembering one-for one help, infrequent client gatherings, telephone backing, and far off PC get to. The test for these preparing exercises was in engaging ranchers to proactively learn and consider instructions to utilize their new frameworks. Client bunches appeared the most mainstream strategy for learning, yet as indicated by the organizations these gatherings had variable degrees of participation. Potential purposes behind this might be identified with absence of recognition among ranchers that the gatherings lead to positive results, or that the degree of learning was pitched at early clients rather than further developed clients. One rancher remarked:

'The best thing about those is simply discovering what others are doing. So, we gain from one another. I believe they're all in a comparable situation as far as really what data is in there, however a few people are clearly more PC proficient and jumped into somewhat further and discovered a few odds and ends that are valuable.' There was little cooperation between ranch specialist co-ops, for example, advisors what's more, veterinarians, and PD frameworks. There is critical potential for administration suppliers, for example, Vets, nutritionists, and agronomists to improve their administration offering by utilizing the information gathered through PD as well as help their customers get more from the frameworks. These specialist organizations can include information also, setting to information being created through milk meters, movement sensors, or field meters.

INTEGRATION OF INFORMATION TECHNOLOGY

In addition, Amul Dairy, Vidya Dairy and your Federation, 17-part associations are determining advantages of utilizing SAP for professional interactions. The Federation has likewise gained excellent ground on the execution of the Amul Automatic Milk Collection System (AMCS) application at Village Dairy Cooperative Societies. Even more about 11,000 town social orders are canvassed in the venture up to this point. The application has absorbed the Cow-to-Consumer (C2C) IT Value Chain. Regularly, in excess of 11 lakh Short Message Services (SMS) are being sent to drain makers sharing data on the quality and amount of milk poured. The versatile based applications are conveyed for milk ranchers/ maker individuals, association/society the executives and the administrative group pioneers/individuals to get to AMCS information whenever it might suit them.

Review of the ICT Platform

Milk creation is a significant spine of the daily practice of India, as milk is one of the prime wellsprings of proteins and calcium for a to a great extent vegan populace. Dairying conveys a vocation for many Indian ranchers and beneficial salary for an enormous number of country families just as means for ladies to take an interest in the financial action in rustic regions. India turned into the biggest maker of milk in 1999 and the credit goes to the committed endeavors of the worth included co-employable development augmentation by the National Dairy Development Board (NDDB).

The co-usable development, began at Amul Dairy in Gujarat, has been recreated to in excess of 70,000 towns in around 200 locales of India. The dairy area started to utilize in excess of 4000 PCs in rustic areas for handling milk purchasing/selling exchanges in a reliable and straightforward methods and uncovered 500000 individuals every day to its advantages.

AMUL AMCS (Automatic Milk Collection System)

Amul AMCS model is an outright solution to Village Dairy Cooperative Societies that embarks digital revolution in dairy industry. The salient features of the system are like largest IT Integration of Dairy Industry with Cashless & Organized Societies on a Common Digital Platform. This has been designed for Farmers and Milk Unions to smoothen up the largest dairy industry in India. This model was initiated with a prime goal to collectively deliver the farmers, a single platform to collaborate. It is believed that the Indian dairy enterprise will surpass all different giant dairy manufactures in the world.

Figure 4. Amul AMCS (automatic milk collection system)

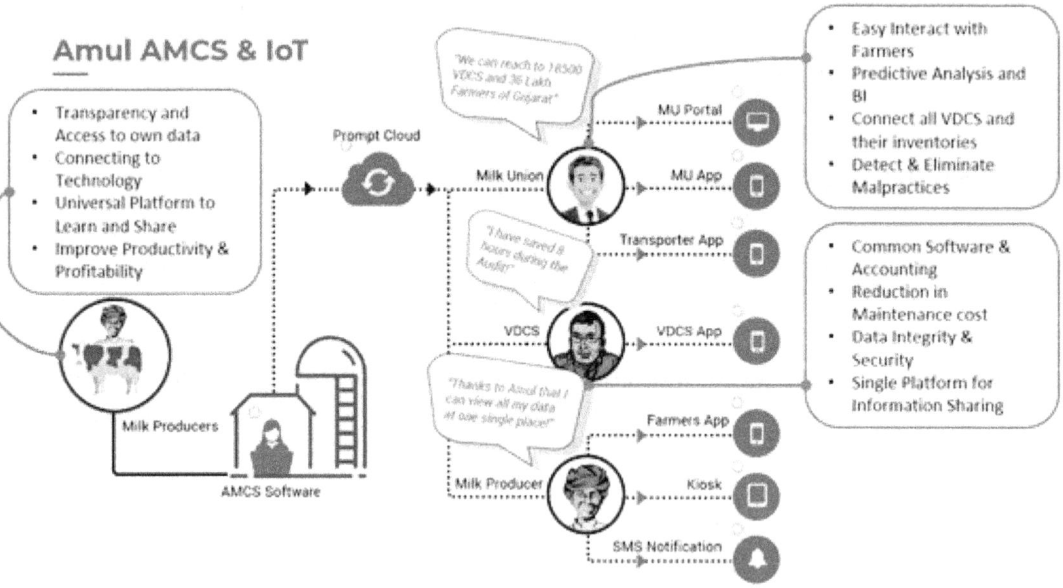

The milk procurement process with involvement of three major stakeholders, farmers, milk agreeable social orders, and milk associations. To interface and every one of them in a solitary stage and achieve straightforwardness, AMCS gives a few instruments.

An appeared in Fig 4, It empowers co-employable structure rancher to monitor his whole commitments and receivables. It additionally contributes an amount of milk he is providing for the milk society in the two meetings, the measure of fat and SNF, sum credited in his record, total passbook of his financial balance, think about how much milk he gave a month ago/year, the fat SNF was there and how much steers feed did he purchase from milk society. It gives adequate and exact data of exchanges with milk social orders conferring simple business the board. The prime goal of such activities is to connect with each of the 18,500-town agreeable social orders through this application. It will empower the framework to interface ranchers and their town to an item made out of his milk being sold anyplace in India. Amul AMCS activities is viewed as amazingly earth-shattering undertaking in Cow to Consumer process.

A brought together information the executives framework is intended to halfway keep up at one spot for information examination, milk creation estimation in any region or town or course, to distinguish and break down milk creation variety particularly dependent on occasional and changes in climatic conditions and for future milk creation estimations. Prior to building up the stage, authorities needed to travel and visit every town to meet ranchers to talk about their interests and fathom them. Rather than the equivalent, Amul AMCS Helps to Connect all partners that can make it serene to screen, all exercises going on in any locale or town situated at one spot and dependent on the equivalent, the essential activities can be taken. This likewise makes conceivable to oversee and react to ranchers' complaints and issues midway. Cashless Society is one of the protuberant prominent components that Amul AMCS offers is Cashless Society. Beforehand, payments to farmers were deposited on a weekly or bi-monthly basis. Due to Digital India initiative, it will become easy to deposit money directly into farmers' accounts, linked to milk society's bank account. Moreover, farmers will receive instant notifications whenever payment credited to their accounts. Henceforth, AMCS project stands extremely important for all these activities. An important member of the co-operative society, milk producer, basically a farmer, can keep track of his contribution and all the essential information useful for future decision making, altogether proving to be favorable. The ultimate beneficiaries of this project will be all the participants / members of the co-operative structure like farmers, district union officers, and the Federation.

Materials and Methods

The regular annual rainfall stages between 51 and 102 cm. Based on the climatic variation, Gujarat is divided into eight agro-climatic zones via the Agriculture and Co-operation Department, Government of Gujarat:

1. Lower Southern Gujarat
2. Upper southern Gujarat
3. Middle Gujarat
4. Northern Gujarat
5. Bhal & coastal area
6. Southern Saurashtra
7. Northern Saurashtra, and
8. North-western zone.

Each zone diverges from the other in terms of its habitat, flora, climate, soil and rainfall. These differences in the zones results in the diverse groups of organisms, thus making it a potential site for carrying out the present study.

To identify the performance of the ICT Adoption in Amul the study steered in two purposively selected agro-climatic zones, Middle Gujarat zone and Upper Southern Gujarat zone of Gujarat state. There were 18 and 19 milk collection routes respectively. Four routes from each zone were selected by stratified random sampling technique.

Around16 dairy cooperative societies have been selected randomly, consisting of two societies from each selected route. The societies should have been registered for last 3 years was the minimum criteria for their selection. 16 primary milk producers or member farmers, who were supplying milk to cooperative society at least 180 days in one year, were selected randomly.

In Total, 160 respondents have been selected from 16 societies as a sample. The primary data have been collected through meeting then in person and detailed have been collected through the structured questionnaire. Outcome / Performance of cooperative societies was measured by using the index developed by Singh (1995) which was suitably modified to fit the present study. The secondary data required for measuring performance were collected from secretaries of the selected societies. The procedure used for calculating the performance by using above mentioned index is explained as under. The preferences of societies were measured in two steps. In first step, score of each indicator was calculated and in the second step, the performance score of each co-operative society was calculated. The indicator score was gathered by summation of key score got under each indicator multiplied by its weightage. Lastly, the performance scores were obtained by summation of indicator scores of each co-operative society. Procedure for calculation of indicator score and performance score of DCSs is represented as under:

1. Calculation of the Indicator Score (IS)

The score of individual indicators was calculated by the following formula:

$$IS = \Sigma\, KS \times W$$

where, IS represents the indicator score and KS represents the key score, and

$$\Sigma\, KS = \Sigma\, Ksi \text{ and } \Sigma\, Ksi = Ks1 + Ks2 + Ks3$$

where, Ks1, is the key score for the first year; Ks2, is the key score for the second year; Ks3, is the key score for the third year, and W, is the weightage assigned to the indicator.

2. Computing the Performance Score (PS) of Dairy Co-operative Societies (DCSs)

The performance score (PS) of each DCS was calculated by the following formula:

$$PS = \Sigma\, ISi$$

where, Σ ISi= Is1+ Is2 + Is3 + Is4 where, Is1, is the indicator score of first indicator of DCSs; Is2, is the indicator score of second indicator of DCSs; Is3, is the indicator score of third indicator of DCSs; Is4, is the indicator score of fourth indicator of DCSs.

The performance percentage of DCSs was calculated by dividing the performance score of each society by the maximum possible performance which in our case was 123 and then multiplying by 100.

Performance of dairy co-operative societies: The Middle Gujarat zone is having an organized network of milk collection center as compared to other players in the state. The Middle Gujarat zone has 18 defined routes to collect the milk from 354 village level milk producer cooperative societies.

Table 1. Performance of DCSs of middle gujarat and upper southern gujarat zone

Milk Cooperatives Societies	Middle Gujarat Zone		Upper Southern Gujarat Zone	
	Performance Score	Performance Percentage PS/MPS x 100	Performance Score	Performance Percentage PS/MPS x 100
1	62	50.40	63	51.22
2	95	77.23	60	48.78
3	70	56.91	60	48.78
4	66	53.66	59	39.84
5	57	46.34	58	47.15
6	55	44.71	53	43.09
7	52	42.28	44	35.72
8	53	43.09	46	37.40
Mean	63.75	51.83	54.12	44.00

PS – Performance Score, MPS – Mean Performance Score

The close perusal of data presented in Table 1 show the performance scores and performance percentage of DCSs in two zones of J&K. The performance percentage of cooperative societies in Middle Gujarat zone ranged from 42.28 to 77.23%, with the mean performance percentage of 51.83%. The

Table 2. Indicator wise performance of zones

Indicators	Weightage	Performance in Middle Gujarat Zone		Performance in Upper Southern Gujarat Zone	
		Score	%	Score	%
Yearly increase or decrease in membership over a period of three years	1	61	50.83	80	66.67
Yearly average of milk price in rupees per liter paid to the members over a period of three years	4	128	33.33	96	25.00
Average quantity of milk collection in liters per member per year over a period of three years	3	243	84.37	159	52.21
Percentage of households covered by a VLMPCS in a year in the whole village over a period of three years	2	68	35.42	123	66.12

performance of cooperatives in Upper Southern Gujarat zone ranged from 35.77 to 51.22%, with mean performance percentage of 44.00% only which was lower compared to that of Middle Gujarat zone. The reasons for better performance of DCSs in Middle Gujarat zone might be due to the cumulative effect of factors like socio-personal, economic and psychological characteristics of member farmers and management committee members.

The mean performance gap, which is 100 minus mean performance percentage, calculated for co-operative societies of Middle Gujarat zone was 48.17% and in Upper Southern zone was 56.00%. The excessive values for the overall performance hole point out that there is a lot of scope in enhancing the enactment of the model. The overall performance of dairy co-operative societies was once additionally assessed indicator wise, to spotlight the relative significance of specific indicators. The indicator wise performance percentage is presented in Table 2. The co-operative societies in Middle Gujarat were performing better with respect to indicators; average milk collection per member and average milk price per liter paid to members, yearly over a period of 3 years.

The reason for this better performance of DCSs in Middle Gujarat was the more productivity of mulch animals and more average price for their milk because their milk mainly came from buffalo. But the co-operative societies in Upper Southern Gujarat zone were performing better with respect to indicators, change in membership and percentage change in households covered in village yearly over a period of 3 years and started to inculcate ICT practices penetratingly than Middle Gujarat zone. The probable reasons for this might be less marketed surplus available with co-operative members and less involvement of other marketing channels in the study area.

FUTURE DIRECTIONS

The changes in the Indian dairy enterprise have been giant whether examined the usage of farm numbers, farm size, productivity, or adoption of scientific techniques. From 2000 to 2020, common dairy farm measurement grew by 37.5% in cows, and cow productiveness accelerated 8.2%. Thus, the figures no longer solely exhibit increase in farm size. However additionally mean in-creased intensity, as cow productiveness multiplied whilst land inputs had been deemphasized. Technology adoption developments have been specifically striking. Over the period, will increase had been considered in the use of computerized take-offs, milking three instances daily, and genetic selection. Somewhat stunning used to be that no considerable modifications had been discovered in different technological innovations, administration practices, and systems, such as udder washers, DHIA membership, computerized feed shipping systems, computerized milking systems, the use of a nutritionist, or grazing, though many accelerated in phrases of share of milk produced as small farms exited whilst giant adopters endured farming. Reasons past the scope of this learn about can also give an explanation for why every of these technologies, administration practices, or manufacturing structures remained particularly steady over the duration of study, and every point deserves sizeable lookup to decide influences on farm profitability or other reasons stopping extra farmers from adopting. Adopters of every one of the technologies, administration practices, and manufacturing structures (besides grazing) have a tendency to be adopters of the different technologies, practices, and systems. This suggests at least two things. First, the applied sciences complement one every other and may also be used in a usual structures approach. Second, every used to be used extra significantly with the aid of large farms, so there show up to be big economies of measurement related with adoption of each. This suggests that as farm sizes proceed to grow, large farms will be the adopters of these technologies, whether or now not they are technically complementary with one another.

There are monstrous open doors in including the innovation in dairy cultivating, yet we need to temper that with a portion of the real world and understand that applying it isn't in every case simple and it needs to bode well. Notwithstanding, there are difficulties that innovation could help dairy makers. The accessibility of financially savvy innovation can be one of the difficulties. One innovation that has increased more intrigue has been the spread of programmed calf feeders as they permit calves to have increasingly visit dinners, Sensor advances have likewise been all the more broadly acknowledged. Probably the most well-known utilizations for wearable sensor innovation have been to follow heat cycles and the time a cow spends eating and ruminating. Estimating rumination and the time a dairy animal spends eating gives information on the metabolic wellbeing of the crowd and the cow. Setting up an approach to quantify milk parts could be an approach to record information like physical cell tally and milk fat, which have been followed two years, he said. Be that as it may, it could likewise permit makers a method of following progesterone or beta-hydroxybutyrate (BHB) levels, which identify with fruitfulness and dairy animals' wellbeing, individually. Picture investigation innovation may give an approach to record data like cow's body condition score and the group's wholesome status. Non-wearable sensors could convey an economy of scale as they can follow different creatures instead of one.

The significant purposes behind the non-selection or suspension of these advancements were: no accessibility of administration; absence of information among ranchers; and withdrawal of free/sponsored administrations by government. The interdependency of the dairy esteem chain exercises and the key specialized and business difficulties of coordinating RFID innovation inside the entire dairy esteem chain. Investigating key encouraging elements which will increment RFID selection inside the said esteem chain ought to likewise be remembered for future examination.

Besides, most dairy items are products what's more, separating or following them utilizing RFID at different levels (thing box-bed levels) could be testing and not financially savvy. In expansion, the milk from different homesteads can be blended (e.g., during the assortment or potentially preparing/fabricating), along these lines, it would be helpful to research how RFID innovation could be utilized to distinguish from which milk a given cheddar is made. Other territories for future examination into the utilization of RFID in the dairy industry include: evaluating the effect of feed sources on other dairy exercises; following separated dairy cattle into meat markets; deciding the business esteem of RFID thing labelling inside the dairy esteem chain; and assessing the effect of RFID thing labeling in the following and following of dairy items for improved client wellbeing inside nation and between nations.

Notwithstanding investigating the effect of RFID innovation on business parts of dairy cultivating, future exploration could likewise examine its sociological suggestions by receiving, for instance, a word related viewpoint. A word related viewpoint is inferred from word related science, another individual from the social sciences, which produces information and comprehension about occupation, the ordinary things individuals do to involve their time (counting paid work) and the socio-social, geo physical and political impacts that shape occupation. Applying a word related point of view could encourage an investigation of the effect of the presentation of RFID innovation on the control of dairy cultivating, and feature impacts upon the propensities, jobs, customs of dairy ranch proprietors and their representatives, on plan and utilization of the work place, and in general pontoon of basic exchanges and communications that happen on a regular schedule on the dairy ranch. Given the RFID innovation is yet to be utilized in Australian dairy cultivating for an enormous scope, and that no different investigations on dairy cultivating have embraced a word related viewpoint, it is from the presentation of RFID. Be that as it may, other word related science exploration would show that there would be an incentive in assessing the impact of RFID on laborer fulfilment, wellbeing related work capacity, and working environment structure.

Inspecting the on-going friend audited writing on the utilization of RFID in the dairy business has recognized a range of business applications, some industry-explicit issues just as future territories of examination.

DISCUSSION

The IT operations at Amul are embedded with the foundations of collaboration, co-operation and co-evolution as opposed to the conflict, conformation and opposition method observed. Amul has become and established as a trendsetter in the entire dairy operations. Even though Automated Milk Collection Centers and Dairy Information System Kiosk tasks phases are still underway to streamline its supply chain, Amul as a company has delivered a lot of advantages to the rural community. Unlike the competitors of Amul, the uniqueness is that Amul has facilitated the rural populace to become empowered.

Agricultural Universities and Government Agencies are collaborating with Amul to embed IT initiatives at GCMMF. Amul has seen the potential of implementing new IT initiatives to get maximum out of their businesses and they are keen on initiating such information technology projects. The journey of hypothesizing and executing an ICT platform for a dairy enterprise is an exceptionally difficult assignment. The reason for this, is that Amul, a dairy manufacturing company, has a dispersed architecture. The quintessential elements that contributed to the success of this task is worth investigating.

Firms that are able to overcome the reluctance of deploying IT for reaching operational excellence in rising economies reap much benefits. Most corporations digitalize their daily operations in order to minimize the operational costs and achieve better production outcomes. At Amul, IT has helped them for facts sharing and evaluating complicated trade-offs whilst making selections for dealers. The extra strong style in these economies is the use of IT for managing the boundary between the market and the provider of products and services.

In this chapter, by utilizing the case study AMUL, we have introduced a strong commercial enterprise mannequin that work in massive rising economies characterized through underdeveloped rural markets, infrastructure and suppliers. The Cooperative shape with interconnecting association as in GCMMF is one instance of success in managing such complicated supplier chain. The long-term undertaking in such instances is to deliver greater benefits to individuals in the rural communities and extend their capabilities.

REFERENCES

Baviskar, B. S. (1998). *Dairy Co-operative rural development in Gujarat. Resources Institutions and Strategies: Operation Flood and Indian Dairying* (M. Doornbos & K. N. Nair, Eds.). Stage Publications.

Blayney & Manchester. (2000). Large Companies Active in Changing Dairy Industry. *Food Review, 23*(2), 8-13.

Buttriss, J. L. (2013). Food reformulation: The challenges to the food industry. *The Proceedings of the Nutrition Society, 72*(1), 61–69. doi:10.1017/S0029665112002868 PMID:23228239

Chandra Sekhara, P. (2002). *Private Extension: Indian Experience, Pro-Farmer Private extensions*. Manage.

Khan, S. (2002). *ICT as an instrument to leverage: The millennium development goals*. UN ICT Task Force.

Kumar, A., & Shah, J. (2016). Dairying as an instrument for ensuring socioeconomic and nutritional security in rural India. *Indian Journal of Agricultural Economics*, *71*(1), 78–89.

Patel, A. S. (1988). *Co-operative Dairying and Rural Development: A Case Study of AMUL*. In B. S. Baviskar & D. W. Attwood (Eds.), *Who Shares? Cooperatives and Rural Development* (pp. 362–377). Oxford University Press.

Randhawa, S. S. (2016). Technological innovations in dairy farming as a tool to boost rural income in Punjab, India. *Journal of Advances in Dairy Research*.

Sidhu, R. S., & Bhullar, A. S. (2004). Changing structure of the farm economy in Punjab: Impact of livestock on income and employment. *Indian Journal of Agricultural Economics*, *59*, 578–587.

Sidhu, R.S., & Singh, S. (2004). Agricultural wages and employment in Punjab. *Econ & Pol Wkly, 39*.

Singh, K., & Pundir, R. S. (2000). *Co-operatives and Rural Development in India*. Institute of Rural Management, Anand. https://www.irma.ac.in/pdf/randp/ 979_76324.pdf

Singh, P., & Kumari, B. (2017). Importance of livestock sector in doubling farmers income by 2022. *International Journal of Economic Development*, *13*(2a), 136–140.

Singh, R. K. H., & Chandar, A. K. (2015). Impact of dairy cooperatives on income and employment in rural areas of Meghalaya. *Indian Journal of Dairy Science*, *68*, 173–179.

ADDITIONAL READING

Bowonder, B., Raghu Prasad, B. R., & Kotla, A. (2005). ICT application in a dairy industry: The e-experience of Amul. *International Journal of Services Technology and Management*, *6*(3-5), 241–265. doi:10.1504/IJSTM.2005.007410

International Institute for Communication and Development IICD. 2014. ICT Solutions for Inclusive Agricultural Value Chains, (May).

ITU. (2013). *International Telecom Union Annual Report 2013*. Measuring the Information Society.

Kuma, B. 2012. Market Access and Value Chain Analysis of Dairy Industry in Ethiopia: The Case of Wolaita Zone A Dissertation Submitted to the School of Agricultural Economics and Agribusiness, School of Graduate Studies, In Partial Fulfillm.

Levi, M., Naveh, G., Berman, S., Fink, L., Altmann, W., Leber, M., and Weber, C. 2012. Collaborative Manufacturing Network for Competitive Advantage D9. 1 – Evaluation Framework (Public), 1–26.

Masuki, K., Kamugisha, R., & Mowo, J. 2010. Role of mobile phones in improving communication and information delivery for agricultural development: Lessons from South Western Uganda. ICT and Development - Research Voices from Africa. International Federation for Information Processing (IFIP), Technical Commission 9 – Relationship Between Computers and Society. Workshop at Makerere University, Uganda. 22-23 March 2010, (March), 1–13.

Okello, J. J., Kirui, O., Njiraini, G. W., & Gitonga, Z. (2011). Drivers of use of information and communication technologies by farm households: The case of smallholder farmers in Kenya. *Journal of Agricultural Economics*.

Rashid, A., & Elder, L. (2009). *Mobile phones and development: An analysis of IDRCsupported projects*. The Electronic Journal of Information Systems.

United States Agency for International Development (USAID). 2013. Uganda Mobile Money Assessment and Case Study Examining Cash Payment Streams and Uganda Mobile Money Study. United States Agency for International Development., (February), 1–71.

KEY TERMS AND DEFINITIONS

Cooperative Movement: Assortment of overall associations, established to give shared help with monetary endeavors to support their individuals.

Dairy Farming: Class of agribusiness for long haul creation of milk, which is prepared (either on the homestead or at a dairy plant, both of which might be known as a dairy) for inevitable offer of a dairy item.

National Dairy Development Board (NDDB): In 1965, NDDB used to be registered underneath the Societies Registration Act, the Charitable Trust Act and the Public Trust Act. Consistent with its mannequin and mandate, NDDB headquarters had been set up at Anand. The mandate of NDDB is to replicate Anand Pattern Dairy Cooperatives in different part of the nation its now well-known Operation Flood (OF) program.

Operation Flood (OF): The Operation Flood (OF) program applied by way of National Dairy Development Board (NDDB) performed a key position in bringing about this transformation.

Precision Dairy Farming: Applications of innovations to quantify physiological, behavioral, and creation pointers on singular creatures to improve the board methodologies and homestead execution.

RFID Technology: Uses electromagnetic fields to naturally recognize and follow labels connected to objects. A RFID label comprises of a minuscule radio transponder; a radio collector and transmitter.

Wearable Technology: Wearable innovation, wearables, style innovation, tech frocks, or design gadgets are brilliant electronic gadgets (electronic gadget with small scale controllers) that are worn near and additionally on the outside of the skin, where they distinguish, break down, and transmit data concerning for example body signals, for example, indispensable signs, as well as encompassing information and which permit now and again prompt biofeedback to the wearer.

Chapter 9
Rural Entrepreneurship in Vietnam:
Identification of Facilitators and Barriers

Thanh-Thuy Nguyen
https://orcid.org/0000-0002-4833-6908
RMIT University, Australia

Javad Shahreki
Multimedia University, Malaysia

Pham Van Hong
Dai Nam University, Vietnam

Nguyen Van Tung
Ho Chi Minh University of Transport, Vietnam

ABSTRACT

Rural Vietnam can be defined in three settings that include agriculture, rural development, and rural livelihoods, in which the agriculture has played a critical role in Vietnam's economy, contributing 20% to the GDP and 40% to the working population. This chapter attempts to identify the facilitators and potential barriers to rural entrepreneurship in Vietnam by following a qualitative research design examining the literature. Further, the chapter particularly attempts to identify the facilitators and potential barriers to develop rural entrepreneurship in the high-tech context. The analysis of the study illustrates the two most critical facilitators for rural entrepreneurship in Vietnam as "enterprise capitals" and "innovation including technology." Further, the study also highlighted barriers such as "limited access to distribution channels" and "limited access to business support and technology."

DOI: 10.4018/978-1-7998-4942-1.ch009

INTRODUCTION

Vietnam is an agricultural nation with the mainland of more than 331,699 km^2 of which the context of rural can be seen in three settings, including agriculture, rural development and rural livelihoods (Powell et al., 2011). In this context, agricultural entrepreneurship plays a significant role in rural business. Further, this contributes to Vietnam's economy with more than ten million hectares of agricultural produced land area, making up one-third of Vietnam's economy. Vietnam agriculture sector's growth rate was comparable to India, Bangladesh and Bhutan in the Asia-Pacific region (Statista, 2020). The agriculture sector contributes around 20 per cent to the gross domestic products (GDP) annually while employing 40 per cent of the working population in Vietnam (Vietnam-Briefing, 2018), while total rural sector accounted for 15.34 and 15.28 per cent of the country's GDP in 2017 and 2018, respectively (Statista, 2020). Production of rural businesses has increased drastically in the latest years through various challenges, for instance, market price instabilities, natural tragedies and pandemics, etc. (Nguyen et al., 2014).

Vietnam's farm production has not received a solidly competitive edge in both domestic and foreign markets, partly resulted from lack of high technologies implemented in the business (Asia-News-Monitor, 2018). The term "high tech agriculture" was defined by Vietnam high-tech laws (Article 19, Section 1) which is a broad concept referring to a wide range of new technical tools for accelerating the adoption of high and new technologies that can improve the performance of farming practices and farm management. However, in the last ten years, only 29 agricultural manufacturing zones with 192 enterprises have involved high technology in their production among thousands of entrepreneurs and agricultural zones (GSO, 2018), which is a relatively insignificant ratio. Therefore, high tech agriculture development has been promoted by both Vietnam's government and entrepreneurs as a necessary direction for improving domestic farm produce and competing with imported products (Vietnam-Briefing, 2018). It is a solid belief that agriculture enterprises and households in rural regions have benefited and will benefit from the application of high tech and the adoption of international standards.

This chapter, hence, attempts to answer two critical questions:

1. What are facilitators supporting Vietnam's rural entrepreneurship in this digital era? And
2. What contextual constraints exist, preventing the impact of digitalization in rural entrepreneurship activities in Vietnam?

Supporting this content, the background of this study includes a review of the literature regarding the prominence of rural entrepreneurship to rural development and the economic context in Vietnam's history concerning the digital era. A few rural entrepreneurship frameworks are discussed, considering the implementation of these conceptual frameworks in the current studies. Later, the research methodology and the research outcomes from a national interview content analyzing, following by an investigating of the discoveries, implications, and the study's limitations, to conclude the section.

BACKGROUND

Digital Era and Its Challenges

In recent decades, the traditional economy has been facing a global shift to a digital era speeded by digital technologies. Characterized by technology which increases the speed and breadth of knowledge turnover within the economy and society, the Digital Era has been perceived as the development of an evolutionary system. This system has a very high knowledge turnover and decreases human controls (Shepherd, 2004). In this era, under the massive influence of the internet and digital technologies such as cloud computing, the Internet of Things, mobile devices and virtual reality to name as a few, there has been a proliferation of digital ventures (Ansong & Boateng, 2019). In other words, the implications of the digital era are enormous, both socially and economically, as technological functionality with more knowledge-based (Shepherd, 2004). It does not create value-added to only our everyday lives, but also to the way businesses are operated. Bukht & Heeks (2017) asserted that the digital economy plays a vital role in economic output, which originated exclusively or principally from digital technologies, using a business model based on digital goods or services.

Under the impact of digital technologies, newly established enterprises using them receive immense benefits due to the transaction costs reduced, and efficiency increased (La¨tti, 2016). On the one hand, the digital ecosystem allows businesses to benefit from a collection of the networks of internet, machines, computers, people, etc. that can perform complex operations (i.e. data mining and advanced data analytics). On the other hand, digital technologies allow small and medium enterprises (SMEs) to manage more efficiently their international operations and business. At the same time, the transportation cost is reduced with higher frequency and reliability. Besides, human capital has also become more mobile with more elaborate capabilities. That is why enterprises in the digital economy tend to implement business models in which digital technologies will change the firm's business activities, and the way revenues generated (Veit et al., 2014).

Nevertheless, the digital revolution likewise creates enormous challenges for enterprises. Under the academic perspective, some of them are the explosion of data and social media, the proliferation of channels, and the shift in consumer demographics, etc. (Leeflang et al., 2014). Another academic research discovers that the issues are coming from the lack of resources, including worker skills, economic resources, as well as time management and privacy issues (Berg et al., 2018). However, under the industrial perspective, main obstacles faced by companies in the digital age come from the business's understanding the need to change, lack of a clear vision for a digital customer journey, ineffective gathering and leveraging of customer data, and inflexible technology stack and development processes (Tiersky, 2018). These challenges must be thoroughly considered when doing business in the digital era.

Rural Entrepreneurship

Components of Rural Business and its Roles in Economy

During the most recent decades, the rural entrepreneurship has expanded and been considered as a venture (Henry & McElwee, 2014). Defra (2004) argued that there was no precise definition of rural entrepreneurship or in other words, agricultural business. Therefore, the concept specified by the Her Majesty's Stationery Office (HMSO) was suggested. In this concept, the rural company in England is a business displayed at a location defined as rural. So far, the agricultural enterprise has tended to be associated with land-based companies, for instance, farms or agricultural-related services (McElwee, 2006; McNally, 2001). However, in the State of the Countryside report 2005 in England, the rural was divided into three clusters by using the population's metric of sparsity to classify a rural area into six types (Defra, 2004). In EU, the European Union (EU, 2008) defined that more than 91 per cent of the territory of the EU is 'rural' where are homes to more than 56 per cent of the EU's population. More recently, Henry & McElwee (2014) illustrated that a rural enterprise reflects three main characteristics, which are (1) setting in rural as the primary location, (2) employing labors within a specific distance to the workplace, and (3) adding value to the gross value-added (GVA).

Rural entrepreneurship has been well identified as a crucial apparatus for the evolution of agricultural development in developed countries (OECD, 2006). Dabson (2001) claims that rural entrepreneurship can be used for tackling vital economic problems within rural areas in the United States. Henderson (2002) argues that rural entrepreneurship contributes significantly to the increase of local earnings and prosperity, as well as provides the connection between the agricultural community and the broader and global economy. The rural entrepreneurship in the United States, through its based development, play its essential part in promoting human growth, rural vigor, local entrepreneurship and economic development (Gladwin et al., 1989; Macke & Markley, 2006). Additionally, Driga et al. (2009) confirm that rural entrepreneurship promotes rural development more than merely economic and employment increase. In Central and Eastern European countries, rural entrepreneurship is believed as an essential tool for seizing obstacles to the growth of fringe areas. It also is a source of income to create viable rural economies and societies (Davis & Pearce, 2000; Labrianidis, 2006). Another study in developing nations announces that rural entrepreneurship makes up around 25 per cent of full-time rural employment and 40 per cent of rural incomes (Haggblade et al., 2002). Hence, to conclude the crucial role of rural entrepreneurship in nurturing rural inhabitants and in offering a substantial economic option to rural poverty.

Drivers and Barriers of Rural Entrepreneurship Development to High-Tech Agriculture

Discussing on the drivers or facilitators supporting rural entrepreneurship, many authors propose different factors as drives and barriers for entrepreneurship development. Many relevant studies agreed that capital is a driver for the development of agricultural enterprises, even though there are different concepts of "capital" developed and named such as business capital, social capital or environment capital (Agarwal et al., 2004; Falconer, 2000; Finke & Bosworth, 2016; Mcelwee, 2008; McElwee & Atherton, 2013), even though there are different concepts of "capital" developed and named such as business capital, social capital or environment capital. Another vital driver named "infrastructure investment" includes transportation and logistics network infrastructure (Delalić & Oruč, 2014; McElwee & Atherton, 2013). This driver is different from the driver named "mobility", which means the flexibility to switch and apply specific developing models to similar rural regions (Maskell et al., 1998; McElwee & Atherton, 2013). Innovation, including technology, is listed as another driver which can promote rural development through rural enterprises (HM-Treasury, 2001; McElwee & Atherton, 2013; Zaremohzzabieh et al., 2015).

Surprisingly, "human resource and skills training" and "geography and travel distance" are listed as both drivers and barriers in many researches. It means these factors can either boost up the rural entrepreneurship business (Delalić & Oruč, 2014; Finke & Bosworth, 2016; HM-Treasury, 2001; Lourenço et al., 2014; McElwee & Atherton, 2013) or draw them back (Delalić & Oruč, 2014; Maskell et al., 1998; McElwee & Atherton, 2013; McElwee & Bosworth, 2010).

Table 1. The drivers and barriers to the development of rural entrepreneurs

Drivers	Barriers
Enterprise capitals (Agarwal et al., 2004; Falconer, 2000; Finke & Bosworth, 2016; Mcelwee, 2008; McElwee & Atherton, 2013)	Limited access to distribution channel (Delalić & Oruč, 2014; Finke & Bosworth, 2016; Mcelwee, 2008; McElwee & Atherton, 2013)
Infrastructure investment (Delalić & Oruč, 2014; HM-Treasury, 2001; McElwee & Atherton, 2013)	Capital requirement of entry (Delalić & Oruč, 2014; Gasson, 1998; McElwee & Atherton, 2013; Rantamäki-Lahtinen, 2002)
Innovation including technology (HM-Treasury, 2001; McElwee & Atherton, 2013; Zaremohzzabieh et al., 2015)	Economy of scale (Kupiainen, 2000; Morris, 2019; McElwee & Bosworth, 2010; McElwee & Atherton, 2013)
Mobility (Maskell et al., 1998; McElwee & Atherton, 2013)	Legislation and regulations (European Commission, 2008; Falconer, 2000; McElwee & Atherton, 2013; Powell et al., 2011)
Geography and travel time (Finke & Bosworth, 2016; McElwee & Atherton, 2013)	Geography and travel time (Finke & Bosworth, 2016; Maskell et al., 1998; McElwee & Atherton, 2013)
Human resource and skills training (Delalić & Oruč, 2014; HM-Treasury, 2001; Lourenço et al., 2014; McElwee & Atherton, 2013; McElwee et al., 2006)	Human resource and skills (Delalić & Oruč, 2014; Lexology, 2018; McElwee & Bosworth, 2010; McElwee & Atherton, 2013)
	Limited access to business support & technology (Finke & Bosworth, 2016; Morris, 2019; Lowe & Talbot, 2000; McElwee, 2004; McElwee & Atherton, 2013)

Source: Literature

Discussing the limitations to create negative impacts on rural entrepreneurship, limited access to distribution channel (DC) is an obvious challenge to rural business development because it restricts the infrastructure or transport network connecting the rural region to the hubs (Delalić & Oruč, 2014; Finke & Bosworth, 2016; Mcelwee, 2008; McElwee & Atherton, 2013). Similarly, limited access to business support provided by the region or state governments can slow-down the business in rural areas (Finke & Bosworth, 2016; Lowe & Talbot, 2000; McElwee, 2004; McElwee & Atherton, 2013). High requirement of capital entry when founding a rural business is listed as another barrier (Delalić & Oruč, 2014; Gasson, 1998; McElwee & Atherton, 2013; Rantamäki-Lahtinen, 2002). The economy of scale may drive enterprises focusing on their business in non-rural regions which rapidly gain profits, rather than investing in a new rural area (Kupiainen, 2000; McElwee & Bosworth, 2010; McElwee & Atherton, 2013). Finally, a complicated legislation and regulations system may weaken the rural business to even less rewarding (EC, 1996; Falconer, 2000; McElwee & Atherton, 2013; Powell et al., 2011).

Table 1 summarizes the involving literature and authors into six drivers and seven barriers confronting the entrepreneurs in rural development. On top of that, the revolution of Industry 4.0 happened during recent years has generated a significant impact in societies, including agriculture and rural development. Regarding this change, Morris (2019) states that the most significant problem in the agricultural sector is to make a moving step towards investment in new digital technologies. This conclusion is correlated with high expenses for farmers in a short-term perspective. However, it can increase revenues and substantially protect the environment in the long term. The drivers and barriers of confronting the entrepreneurs in rural development, therefore, are presented in Table 1, in which two factors named "human resource and skills" and "geography and travel time" can be either drivers or barriers, based on the case studies.

A Snapshot of Rural Vietnam

The Role of the rural sector in Vietnam's economy

In the opinion of Powell et al. (2011), rural Vietnam contains both positive and negative indicators defined in three mentioned settings, named agriculture, rural development and rural livelihoods.

Regarding agriculture, the successful economic development over the past two decades has enabled the evolution of Vietnam's economy from primarily agriculture-based marketplace to an industry-based one. However, the rural sector still makes up a significant role in Vietnam's economy, in which the land area for agriculture accounted for 39.28 per cent of Vietnam's total land area in 2016. The agriculture sector made up 39.8 per cent of the overall labor market, means approximately 20.47 million employed workers in 2018 (Statista, 2020). Although under a variety of challenges, such as market instabilities, natural tragedies and outbreaks, to name as a few, the production of agriculture and involving areas has increased drastically in current years. National statistics indicated that Vietnam's most principal crop, means rice, has reached the consumption of 22 million metric tons in 2018 and 2019, ranking it in fifth place just after China, India, Indonesia and Bangladesh (Statista, 2020). This outcome resulted from the extensive application of new technology in improving productivity and maintaining the sustainability of the entire agricultural sector.

Infrastructure investment in rural areas is progressing in Vietnam, illustrated by Powell et al. (2011). From the early 2000s, the improvement in the capacity of irrigation and drainage system has contributed to agricultural production and the livelihoods of rural inhabitants. Until 2018, there has been 98.8 per cent of rural households having electricity while all rural areas have been provided schools, medical centers and telecommunication services, etc. (GSO, 2018).

Rural livelihoods play an essential role in Vietnam communities in which rural people accounted for over 70 per cent in 2008 and 64.1 per cent in 2018 of the total population (World Bank, 2018), in which 54 per cent of the rural residents employed in agriculture, forestry and aquaculture and fishery (Powell et al., 2011). The average income of rural communities has risen almost fourfold in the last ten years (GSO, 2018). Besides, medical treatment has been assessed more easily for rural people. More rural students have participated in higher education through different supporting policies of government such as rural student loan at the favorable interest rate, and tuition fee exempted program, etc. Consequently, the education system and level of high professional skills in rural Vietnam have been improving rapidly.

Snapshot of Vietnam's Rural Enterprises: from Traditional to High-Tech

The number of enterprises investing directly in agriculture has increased triple times over the past three years, from approximately 3,000 to 11,800 enterprises. They spread across regions and fields from production to processing and consumption of agricultural products. Many large enterprises have invested in this area to raise the value of agricultural output (Vietnam-Communist-Party-News, 2019). Nevertheless, there have been quite a few researches on Vietnam rural entrepreneurship during the ten recent years.

One recent representative of researches on Vietnam rural entrepreneurs is the study of Brünjes & Diez (2016), in which they examined a variety of rural entrepreneurs in Vietnam and conclude that the underemployment, risks and shocks in agriculture production can lead to low income and poverty. Besides, local market potentials or new business are considered as perceived opportunities rather than technical upgrading and innovation. The paper of Le & Raven (2015), as a collaborated research with

Women's Union of Vietnam, PeaceTrees Vietnam and an NGO based in Seattle, USA, analyzed the impact of variables on the experiences of success and motivational factors in rural Vietnam's women entrepreneurs. Another study on female entrepreneurs in rural Vietnam by Nguyen et al., (2014) indicated that the policies on pro-entrepreneurship of government, supported by the interventions of the private sector, have had an influence on rural Vietnam. However, rural females in Vietnam are still constrained by societal predispositions, financial restrictions, and limited educational opportunities in entrepreneurship. Sohns & Diez (2018) explained Vietnam's rural micro-entrepreneurship, using the multilevel analysis to analyze the effects of descriptive factors at a variety of concentrations. Their study found the evidence to prove that the individual level controls both the opportunity-driven, and the necessity driven in rural entrepreneurship of Vietnam. In contrast, the regional level only has a substantial influence on opportunity-driven entrepreneurship. These papers did not discuss the drivers and barriers to Vietnam rural entrepreneurs directly; however, the research outcomes, technically, are like those of international literature above.

Although the agricultural sector in Vietnam has reached a terrific growth in ten recent years, as mentioned, rural Vietnam still has been facing issues and challenges. These issues are listed in "Vietnam National Conference to promote businesses investing in agriculture 2018" by Minister Nguyen Chi Dung of Ministry of Plan and Investment (MOST, 2018), on behalf of the Vietnamese government. The government has offered and promoted through different government-funded packages to attract more entrepreneurs to establish in rural regions using high-tech agriculture.

The term "high tech agriculture enterprises", defined by the new Vietnam High-tech Laws (Article 19, Section 1), includes four categories characterized by (1) types of the high-tech implemented, (2) product's quality and productivity, (3) research activity outcomes, and (4) labor qualifications, environment-friendly and energy efficiency. In 2019, there are approximately 11,400 agricultural cooperatives in Vietnam. Still, only 29 agrarian production zones and 192 organizations implementing high-tech in their business and production process. These enterprises are locating mainly in Thai Nguyen, Bac Ninh, Vinh Phuc, Lam Dong, Ho Chi Minh city and Mekong Delta region, which creates leading high-tech areas of agricultural cooperatives (GSO, 2018).

RESEARCH METHODOLOGY

Mentioned by Morris et al., (2001), understanding entrepreneurship through frameworks helps regularly establish the entrepreneurship's field because it delivers an outline converting the concept into order, tolerates the organizing of variables to identify interactions. Nguyen et al., (2014) review three well-known frameworks which are (1) The Global Entrepreneurship Monitor (GEM) framework, (2) The GEM Model of Entrepreneurship and (3) Community Context, which provides a practically conceptual foundation to investigate the female entrepreneurship in rural Vietnam. This study's framework using community context is presented in Figure 1 to explore the facilitators and constraints of high-tech rural entrepreneurship in Vietnam.

This study adopts a qualitative research design which examines the phenomena that guide rural entrepreneurs in Vietnam under the impact of the revolution of the Industry 4.0 to answer the research questions, by identifying and reviewing the potential facilitators and constraints to the rural entrepreneurship development in this setting. The study, therefore, firstly sets a framework to compare the list of facilitators or drivers defined in the literature to the practices in rural entrepreneurs in Vietnam. Secondly, the study examines the constraints exist that might prevent the impact of digitalization in agricultural entrepreneurship activities in Vietnam.

Figure 1. Steps followed in reviewing the literature

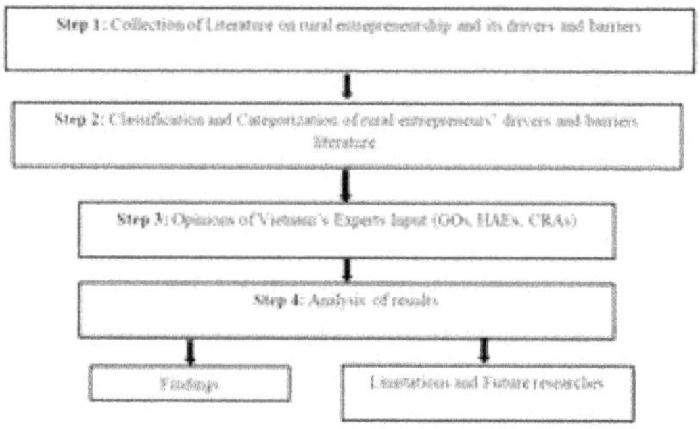

Data Collection

The study uses the dataset collected by a national research project on rural entrepreneurs' opinion surveys during 2017-2019 funded by the Ministry of Agriculture and Rural Development (MARD), Vietnam. This project's outcomes and dataset were published; however, merely focusing on the needs of Vietnam rural development and the growth of rural entrepreneurs. The study, therefore, comprehends the content of interviews about the drivers of Vietnam rural entrepreneurship and high technology. Data collection includes eight interviews with government representatives in the Ministry of Agriculture and Rural Development (MARD) and Vietnam Chamber of Commerce and Industry (VCCI), and 26 interviews with managers in rural entrepreneurs. Among these 26 interviews, six ones were with managers in high-tech agriculture enterprises locating in rural regions in the North (Lao Cai, Phu Tho), Centre (Nam Dinh, Nghe An) and South (Can Tho, Tien Giang, Dong Nai, Ba Ria-Vung Tau) of Vietnam, plus the Vietnam national statistics in the last five years.

Methodology

The mentioned project uses a snowball technique to establish interviews with open-ended questions. The research hence uses the text analysis software Nvivo 12 to analyze and encode all the data. The pre-pinpointed themes of rural entrepreneurship drivers, barriers and high-tech impacts were employed to organize the coded responses via an open coding scheme (Pham et al., 2019). The interviewees were separated into three groups named "Government officers" who mainly belong to the MARD and region governments (Eight of GOs), "High-tech agriculture entrepreneurs" (Six of HAEs) and "Common rural entrepreneurs" (20 of CREs). Because all interview content shared is in the Vietnamese language, two Vietnamese researchers in the research team translated the interviewing transcripts to English.

RESEARCH FINDINGS AND DISCUSSIONS

The study analyses the research findings following the content of the interviews, means the group of factors to decide the drivers and barriers of Vietnam rural entrepreneurship to implement high-tech.

Enterprise Capitals and Capital Requirement of Entry

The first and foremost essential drivers promoting Vietnam rural entrepreneurship, mentioned by 100 per cent of interviewees, is the business capital. Following Vietnam General Statistical Office (GSO, 2018), the total investment in the agricultural sector quadrupled in 2018 (US$ 10.5 trillion), in which the average business capital of farming enterprises in 2018 was US$ 1.8 billion per enterprise. The increase of capital investment has promoted the number of rural enterprises investing directly in agriculture, from approximately 3,000 to 11,800 enterprises in the past three years. These interview's outcomes share the same perspectives to Falconer (2000), Agarwal et al., (2004), McElwee & Atherton (2013), Finke & Bosworth (2016) and Mcelwee (2008). However, while some authors may consider the concept "capital" in several perspectives, likely business capital, human resource capital or environment capital, the interviewees in Vietnam only conferred to the business capital perspective.

The business capital is the most important factor to establish a high-tech agriculture business. Without it, there is no future for the high-tech ones (*100% agreed by GOs, HAEs, CREs, 2018*).

If discussing the success of capital attraction of high-tech enterprises in the context of rural cooperatives, the picture is not bright. The government of Vietnam has announced several supporting policies and incentive schemes to encourage private and local rural businesses to shift towards high-tech agriculture application. For instance, the loan package worth US$4.4 billion for high tech implementation approved by the government in March 2017. This loan package permits the national banks providing capital to high-tech agriculture enterprises at almost zero per cent interest rate. In contrast, other sectors bear the interested rates from nine per cent to twelve per cent per year at the time. However, only 192 high tech rural enterprises were founded, accounting for 1.63 per cent. Among those, only 44 high tech enterprises were successful in calling foreign investment within the last five years, accounting for 0.4 per cent (GSO, 2018).

There is no strict requirement of the capital of entry, while rural business receives quite many supports from the government. Therefore, the requirement of capital entry is not the barrier in Vietnam, as all the agricultural enterprises here receive a capital entry reduction comparing to other businesses.

Innovation Including Technology

Taking about the impact of innovation and technology in agriculture business, all GOs and HAEs concur that they significantly increase the quality and quantity of the products, which brings business trade to a higher-level success in both export markets and the stock market. (HM-Treasury, 2001; McElwee & Atherton, 2013; Zaremohzzabieh et al., 2015). Nevertheless, only 45 per cent of CREs agree with this conclusion and have the willingness to implement innovation and high-tech in their agriculture operation, even though they said there are still obstacles in recognition and marketing of applied technology products in agriculture. Other CREs mentioned that in a developing country like Vietnam, high-tech agriculture products would have a higher price which means less competitive in the market. Under the circumstances, they prefer to focus on the traditional agriculture techniques producing more organic products, in which they also claim that it is "another type of high tech" in farming. The rest would like to keep their business operation in at no change.

Innovation and high technology applied in agriculture boost the enterprises' business providing products in higher quality and larger quantity to the market (*100% GOs, 100% HAEs and 45% CREs, 2019*).

High-tech at this moment requires a huge extra investment which increases our price in the market while our businesses depend on the buyers' decision. We prefer to focus more on traditional techniques for organic products (*40% CREs, 2019*)

There is a vital notification here that many rural enterprises interviewed are still using a basic IT system, such as computers, standard internet system with conventional technology in communications generally. Two CRE does not even reach the mechanization yet, but still using the fixed phone, light bulb, and the combustion engine in their farming operations.

Infrastructure Investment vs Geography and Travel Time

Answering the question of what if the current infrastructure and the transport network support the rural entrepreneurs and high-tech agriculture business, the interviewees showed ambiguous perspectives on how the government should invest in the rural infrastructure. However, all GOs, HAEs and CREs agreed that the current infrastructure in rural regions such as transport system and irrigation had not been developed well. As the situation in all over Vietnam, the transport system is still fragmented and incompetent (Nguyen, 2016), especially in rural regions, leaving this potential facilitator becoming the existed constrain for Vietnam high-tech agricultural enterprises. The Vietnam rural businesses are specifically in need of better infrastructure, more distribution centers and a well-connected transport network to cut down their logistics costs and to provide better services to their customers, likely shorten transporting time. That is why the HAEs usually built their own distribution centers to meet customer services' requirement, even though the cost of DC operation is quite high.

Even though the infrastructure and transport network are much more developed than ten years ago, the growth rate of infrastructure is still lower than the rate of economic growth in these years (*100% GOs, HAEs, CREs, 2018*).

All rural enterprise operations are conducted in rural and/or remote areas, means geography and travel time constrains. Fragmented and incompetent infrastructure and transport networks only worsen the business opportunities of the rural business. (*62.5% GOs, 50% HAEs, 60%CREs, 2018*)

Legislation and Regulations vs Economy of Scale

The next question is if the rural business receives any support from the government or there is any drawback in legislation and regulations in rural development in Vietnam? The interviewed GOs mentioned that from 2018, the government had published Decree 57/2018/ND-CP, which focuses on policies and incentives to attract more high-tech investments in agriculture and rural areas. It promotes land rights and rents, taxes' reductions and exemptions, and provides the financial support following provincial and national development programs for research and development (R&D) as well as technology transferred. Besides, the state government has endorsed a master plan on improving high-tech agriculture zones by 2020 through 2030, in which large scale and modern agriculture production methods by R&D are implemented to increase the quality of rural production and reduce costs. By 2030, least ten more hi-tech agricultural zones are targeted to be built in six provinces named Lao Cai, Phu Tho, Son La, Nam

Dinh, Nghe An and Hanoi. Also, in the government plans, by 2020, the country will have at least 500 hi-tech agricultural cooperatives, plus will increase the high-tech agricultural production value by five times (Statista, 2020). As the target, around 60 per cent of the high-tech agricultural cooperatives will locate in production centers such as Mekong River Delta, Red River Delta, Central Highlands. Roughly 30 to 40 per cent of them will implement automation technology models and biotechnology from the current 17 per cent.

Relating the government plan, HAEs and CREs likewise agreed that the government had provided enormous support on legislation and regulations, which indeed enhances the increasing number of rural enterprises.

There are supporting regulations and policies to rural enterprises recently, such as tax reduction, low interest rate loan, low land renting fee, etc. The high-tech agriculture enterprises in rural regions even receive a higher tax discounted but still not attractive enough for such a huge investment. (*100% GOs, HAEs, CREs, 2019*)

Mobility vs Economy of Scale

In terms of mobility, the interviewees did not provide much information. However, all interviewees reflected that the linkages between the Vietnam rural enterprises and the international and domestic buyers should be increased for the complete improvement of the value chain. On top of that, the planning for agricultural land use, especially the preparation of raw material areas for agriculture, has not been implemented effectively and is still lacking stability.

Rural enterprises require a large land area however the master plan of the government has changed from time to time, which is unstable for the enterprises to decide to invest more (*100% CREs, 2019*).

Human Resource and Labor Skills

Human resource (HR) and labor skills are the last theme to be discussed, which also the most challenge for high-tech agriculture enterprises in rural regions. It is a general understanding among GOs, HAEs and CREs that the human resources in rural areas are now mostly low-level, free and highly fragmented as well as have not been trained in the progress of technology and techniques. Moreover, the transition of significant volumes of agricultural land to other commercial purposes such as industrial zones, tourism sites or new urban areas has led to a substantial increase in the high unemployment rate in rural Vietnam. This situation requires new training programs implemented, and then the enterprises can utilize these labors successfully.

Entrepreneurs thought it is the responsibility of the province's government to promote such a kind of training, or at least to call for collaboration between the enterprises and the government for the practice. Some managers suggested that the government should invite experienced experts in other countries having high-tech agricultures such as Japan, South Korea, Israel, etc. to develop training programs for high-tech farming practices to support local producers.

The province government should open vocational training centers or training programs for the labors working for high-tech corporations and business in rural regions. (66% HAEs, 75%CREs, 2019)

The enterprises should have knowledge in the area they are doing business, such as water protection, biotech, and new material technology. If the local producers plan to implement high-tech farming, they should be educated well about the benefits and challenges of high-tech farming. (62.5% GOs, 2019)

Table 2 summarizes the facilitators and barriers in developing high-tech agriculture entrepreneurship in Vietnam.

Table 2. Facilitators and barriers in developing high-tech agriculture entrepreneurship in Vietnam

Name	Literature		Vietnam	
	Drivers	*Barriers*	*Drivers*	*Barriers*
Enterprise capitals	x		x	
Capital requirement of entry		x	x	
Innovation including technology	x		x	
Infrastructure investment	x			x
Geography and travel time	x	x	x	x
Legislation and regulations		x	x	
Economy of Scale		x		x
Mobility	x			x
Human resource and skills training	x	x	x	x
Limited access to distribution channel		x		x
Limited access to business support & technology		x		x

In the table, the white rows illustrate the similar findings between the literature and this study, while the dark rows present the disparity of the findings between them.

Some of the study outcomes share the comparable findings to the literature review, in which two drivers named "Enterprise capitals" and "Innovation including technology" are the most critical facilitators in promoting rural enterprises, even though there are diverse understandings about the concept of "high-tech". The study likewise finds three other similar barriers to rural business development named "Economy of Scale", "Limited access to distribution channel" and "Limited access to business support & technology", as mentioned in the literature review. Two other indicators, named "Geography and travel time" and "Human resource and skills Training", are considered as both drivers and barriers for Vietnam rural entrepreneurs. Therefore, Vietnam government is suggested to promote these indicators significantly by planning more distribution centers in rural regions as well as providing support for HR training programs in these regions.

Surprisingly, the drivers named "Capital requirement of entry" and "Legislation and regulations" are listed as facilitators in Vietnam rural development while they are barriers in other studies. In contrast, the drivers named "Infrastructure investment" and "Mobility" in literature are considered as barriers to Vietnam rural business, due to the significant limitation of infrastructure investment and mobility programs.

IMPLICATIONS AND RECOMMENDATIONS

Theoretical Implications

This study contributes to rural entrepreneurship development by conducting a comprehensive literature analysis and interview analysis to identify facilitators and barriers to rural entrepreneurship in Vietnam.

This study demonstrates the identical understandings with other studies in literature by highlighting the most important facilitators to promote the rural entrepreneurship development likely "Enterprise Capitals" (Agarwal et al., 2004; Falconer, 2000; Finke & Bosworth, 2016; Mcelwee, 2008; McElwee & Atherton, 2013) and "Innovation including Technology" (HM-Treasury, 2001; McElwee & Atherton, 2013; Zaremohzzabieh et al., 2015). Besides, the study agreed with literature content that three barriers to rural entrepreneurship development are "Economy of Scale" (Kupiainen, 2000; Morris, 2019; McElwee & Bosworth, 2010; McElwee & Atherton, 2013), "Limited access to distribution channel" (Delalić & Oruč, 2014; Finke & Bosworth, 2016; Mcelwee, 2008; McElwee & Atherton, 2013), and "Limited access to business support & technology" (Finke & Bosworth, 2016; Lexology, 2018; Lowe & Talbot, 2000; McElwee, 2004; McElwee & Atherton, 2013).

The studies likewise noticed that there are factors which can be driven as either facilitators or barriers, depending on the economic status of the country, named "Geography and Travel time" (Finke & Bosworth, 2016; McElwee & Atherton, 2013), and "Human Resource and Skills Training" (Delalić & Oruč, 2014; McElwee, 2006; McElwee & Atherton, 2013).

Additionally, the study promotes the theory by clarifying the differences leading to the decision of facilitators and barrier in an emerging country generally and Vietnam particularly. They are "Capital requirement of Entry" and "Legislation and Regulations" which are confirmed as facilitators in Vietnam rural entrepreneurship development while defined as barriers in other studies (Delalić & Oruč, 2014; European Commission, 1996; Falconer, 2000; Gasson, 1998; McElwee & Atherton, 2013; Powell et al., 2011; Rantamäki-Lahtinen, 2002). In contrast, the other drivers listed in the literature as "Infrastructure Investment" (Delalić & Oruč, 2014; HM-Treasury, 2001; McElwee & Atherton, 2013) and "Mobility" (Maskell et al., 1998; McElwee & Atherton, 2013) are considered as challenges or barriers to Vietnam rural entrepreneurship due to the limitation of infrastructure investment and mobility programs in rural regions.

Finally, the study contributes to the qualitative research literature by focusing more on understanding the nature of research problems (Strauss & Corbin, 1994), which is the issues surrounding rural entrepreneurship development practices in Vietnam in our case. By using a relative number of in-depth interviews, the study helps to understand the reality of the world of rural entrepreneurship through description and interpretation of people's experiences. This method allows researchers to have a more ingrained viewpoint and more understanding of the phenomena (Gordon, 2008). Likewise, the paper contributes to the literature by describing the facilitators and barriers in rural entrepreneurship development in Vietnam by examining the practices of both high-tech agriculture enterprises and traditional rural business. The willingness to invest in high-tech, therefore, primarily hinges on the strategy of the organizations in the value of implementing high technology.

Practical Implications

The study presents practical implications in rural entrepreneurship development in emerging countries generally, and Vietnam particularly. From the interview content, taking a step-in high-tech investing has remained a significant challenge in the rural agriculture enterprises. Even though it increases yields and protect the environment significantly in the long term, it is associated with high costs and therefore high prices for the products. At present, Vietnam's agriculture sector is nonetheless in its initial stages of technology development, or other words, the digitalization. However, there is an increasing number of rural enterprises beginning to embrace digital technology and big data innovations in their farming business. Note that there are many rural businesses prefer to focus on traditional agriculture techniques to produce more organic products, which is another efficient way to promote rural farming development. Though it is not in the same context of "high technology development" defined by the Vietnamese government.

As pointed out in the study, the practices in Vietnam contribute an impact to the rural entrepreneurship development in emerging countries. Even with active support of the government in tax reduction and loans with zero per cent of interest, the agricultural enterprises still hesitate to invest in high-tech development due to many insecure or even risky circumstances such as the fluctuation of the market or the dependent on the power of the buyers, etc. This situation opens more opportunities for future researches in this field.

Besides, a decent collaboration, between the public sector, industry players and the agriculture business community, is significantly crucial for the implementation of high-tech agriculture in Vietnam. In particular, the national government and decision-makers should utilize the transportation network connecting to DCs in rural regions as well as the underlying digital base for rapidly increasing data flows.

Lastly, the government and the enterprises should plan solutions to promote human resource development and training for high tech operations in rural regions drastically.

FUTURE RESEARCH DIRECTIONS AND CONCLUSION

This paper explores the current practices of rural entrepreneurship development in rural Vietnam by analyzing the interview content of 26 agricultural enterprises in rural regions and eight government officers about the advantages, drivers and challenges in rural entrepreneurship development, plus an in-depth literature review. The findings demonstrate a visible government's strategy to promote rural high-tech development; however, there are still barriers to implementing this strategy. Taking advantages from this support, rural entrepreneurs can make a preferable loan as the business capitals and invest in innovation and technology. However, this support cannot guarantee the success of the agricultural business in Vietnam, but the success partly depends on the market and the power of the buyers. That is why many rural enterprises use very rudimentary technology in their farming operations and are reluctant to invest in higher technology for better productivity and cleaner products. On the other trend, some rural enterprises avoid investing by switching to traditional farming techniques for organic products, which are increasingly preferred in the market. The authors, therefore, recommend some corresponding actions and practices which can be implemented practically to overcome the existing problems to enhance the rural entrepreneurship development in Vietnam, given the different types of the rural enterprises and the Vietnamese government.

The limitations of the study come from the nature of the methodology, in which the participants mainly shared their perspectives on drivers and barriers to their business development answering the questions "what", "why" and "how" which explain why the rural entrepreneurship did not take the support from the government. In contrast, the other group of interviewees share about the government supporting policies. However, they have not shared the actual impacts of high technology on their business, or if some small and medium enterprises would accept and can handle the upcoming technology changes. The interviewees also do not share the reasons why the government only focuses on the financial support directly to the business using legislation and regulations, but not the national plan to improve infrastructure and human resource development in the rural regions.

Hence, future studies ought to investigate how high-tech can change and enhance agricultural operations in emerging countries, especially small and medium enterprises (SMEs). Besides, the study may need to switch from small sample interview size to a more extensive collected survey to generalize the findings on a larger scale. Thus, subsequent studies will conduct quantitative surveys to validate the findings and establish a model for better replication in different markets.

REFERENCES

Agarwal, S., Courtney, P., Errington, A., Moseley, M., & Rahman, S. (2004). *Determinants of relative economic performance of rural areas. Final research report prepared for DEFRA*. University of Plymouth and Countryside and Community Research Unit.

Ansong, E., & Boateng, R. (2019). Surviving in the digital era – business models of digital enterprises in a developing economy. *Digital Policy, Regulation & Governance, 21*(2), 164–178. doi:10.1108/DPRG-08-2018-0046

Asia-News-Monitor (2018). Vietnam: Vietnam commits to realising GMS high-tech agriculture priority. *Asia News Monitor.*

Berg, V., Birkeland, J., Pappas, I. O., & Jaccheri, L. (2018). The Role of Data Analytics in Startup Companies: Exploring Challenges and Barriers. In *Challenges and Opportunities in the Digital Era*. Springer. doi:10.1007/978-3-030-02131-3_19

Brunjes, J., & Diez, J. A. (2016). Obtaining non-farm wage employment in rural Vietnam. *Asia Pacific Viewpoint, 57*(2), 263–279. doi:10.1111/apv.12116

Bukht, R., & Heeks, R. (2017). *Defining, conceptualising and measuring the digital economy. Development Implications of Digital Economies (DIODE). No. 68*. University of Manchester. Retrieved from www.gdi.manchester.ac.uk/research/publications/working-papers/di/

Dabson, B. (2001). Supporting Rural Entrepreneurship. *E-Proceedings of Rural and Agriculture Conference, 2001*, 35–47.

Davis, J., & Pearce, D. (2001). The rural non- farm economy in central and eastern Europe. In Z. Lerman & C. Csaki (Eds.), *The Challenge of Rural Development in the EU Accession Process*. World Bank.

Defra, D. (2004). Rural strategy. Report of Department for Environment Food and Rural Affairs.

Delalić, S., & Oruc, N. (2014). Determination of Firm Growth: A Study of Rural SMEs in Bosnia-Herzegovina. *Journal of Economic & Social Studies*, *4*(1), 5–23. doi:10.14706/JECOSS11411

Driga, O., Lafuente, E., & Vaillant, Y. (2009). Reasons for the relatively lower entrepreneurial activity levels of rural women in Spain. *Sociologia Ruralis*, *49*(1), 70–96. doi:10.1111/j.1467-9523.2008.00475.x

European Commission. (2008). *Rural Development Policy 2007-2013*. Retrieved from https://enrd.ec.europa.eu/enrd-static/fms/pdf/BEC22A59-E570-413B-5A9B-682D3306E183.pdf

Falconcer, K. (2000). Farm-level constrains on agri-environmental scheme participation: A transactional perspective. *Journal of Rural Studies*, *16*(3), 379–394. doi:10.1016/S0743-0167(99)00066-2

Finke, H., & Bosworth, G. (2016). Exploring the character of rural businesses: Performing change and continuity, Local Economy. *The Journal of the Local Economy Policy Unit*, *31*(5), 619–636. doi:10.1177/0269094216655407

Gasson, R. (1998). Educational qualification of UK farmers: A review. *Journal of Rural Studies*, *14*(4), 487–498. doi:10.1016/S0743-0167(98)00028-X

Gladwin, C. H., Long, B. F., Babb, E. M., Beaulieu, L. J., Moseley, A., Mulkey, D., & Zimet, D. J. (1989). Rural entrepreneurship: One key to rural revitalization. *American Journal of Agricultural Economics*, *71*(5), 1305–1314. doi:10.2307/1243127

Gordon, R. D. (2008). Qualitative Approaches. In S. R. Clegg & J. R. Bailey (Eds.), *International Encyclopedia of Organization Studies*. SAGE Publications. doi:10.4135/9781412956246.n457

GSO. (2018). *Vietnam General Statistical Office. Statistic data of 2018*. Retrieved from http://www.gso.gov.vn/SLTK/Menu.aspx?rxid=0d2b0d9f-8bb1-4718-a9e9-06bfb58be14d&px_language=vi&px_db=11.+Y+t%E1%BA%BF%2C+v%C4%83n+h%C3%B3a+v%C3%A0+%C4%91%E1%BB%9Di+s%E1%BB%91ng&px_type=PX

Haggblade, S., Hazell, P. B. R., & Reardon, T. A. (2002). Strategies for stimulating poverty- alleviating growth in the rural nonfarm economy in developing countries. In *Environment and Production Technology Division, International Food Policy Research Institute (IFPRI) and Rural Development Department*. World Bank EPTD Discussion Paper No. 92.

Henderson, J. (2002). Building the rural economy with high-growth entrepreneurs. *Economic Review-Federal Reserve Bank of Kansas City*, *87*, 45–75.

Henry, C., & McElwee, G. (2014). Defining and Conceptualising Rural Enterprise. In *Exploring Rural Enterprise: New Perspectives on Research, Policy & Practice*. Emerald. doi:10.1108/S2040-724620140000004001

Treasury, H. M. (2001). *Productivity in the United Kingdom: 3 – The Regional Dimension. Report*. HM Treasury.

Kupiainen, K. (2000). *Performance of Small Rural Enterprises*. Agricultural Economics Research Institute Report, 239.

Labrianidis, L. (2006). Fostering entrepreneurship as a means to overcome barriers to development of rural peripheral areas in Europe. *European Planning Studies*, *14*(1), 3–8. doi:10.1080/09654310500339067

La¨tti, R. (2016). *Value Creation and Strategy in the Hyperconnected World the Current Wave of Digitalization. Explained through the Study of Finnish Forerunner Companies*. Aalto University.

Le, Q., & Raven, P. (2015). Woman entrepreneurship in rural Vietnam: Success and Motivation factors. *Journal of Developing Areas*, *49*(2), 57–76. doi:10.1353/jda.2015.0024

Leeflang, P., Verhoef, P., Dahlström, P., & Freundt, T. (2014). Challenges and solutions for marketing in a digital era. *European Management Journal*, *32*(1), 1–12. doi:10.1016/j.emj.2013.12.001

Lourenço, F., Sappleton, N., Dardaine-Edwards, A., Mcelwee, G., Cheng, R., Taylor, D., & Taylor, A. (2014). Experience of entrepreneurial training for female farmers to stimulate entrepreneurship in Uganda. *Gender in Management*, *29*(7), 382–401. doi:10.1108/GM-05-2013-0054

Lowe, P., & Talbot, H. (2000). *Providing advice and information in support of rural microbusinesses.* Centre for Rural Economy Research Report. University of Newcastle. Newscastle upon Tyne.

Maskell, P. H., Eskelinen, I., Hannibalsson, A., Malmberg, J., & Vatne, E. (1998). *Competitiveness, Localised Learning and Regional development. Specialization and Prosperity in Small Open economics.* Routledge. doi:10.4324/9780203276921

Mcelwee, P. D. (2008). Forest environmental income in Vietnam: Household socioeconomic factors influencing forest use. *Environmental Conservation*, *35*(2), 147–159. doi:10.1017/S0376892908004736

McElwee, G. (2004). *A segmentation framework for the farm sector.* Paper presented at 3rd Rural Entrepreneurship Conference. University of Paisley.

McElwee, G. (2006). Farmers as entrepreneurs: Developing competitive skills. *Journal ofDevelopmental Entrepreneurship*, *11*(3), 187–206. doi:10.1142/S1084946706000398

McElwee, G., Pyysia¨inen, J., Anderson, A., & Vesala, K. (2006). Developing the entrepreneurial skills of farmers: Some myths explored. *International Journal of Entrepreneurial Behaviour & Research*, *12*(1), 2139.

McElwee, G., & Bosworth, G. (2010). Exploring the Strategic Skills of Farmers Across a Typology of Farm Diversification Approaches. *Journal of Farm Management*, *13*(12), 819–838.

McElwee, G., & Atherton, A. (2013), Rural Entrepreneurship. In World Encyclopedia of Entrepreneurship. Edward Elgar Publishing Limited.

McNally, S. (2001). Farm diversification in England and Wales: What can we learn from the farm business survey. *Journal of Rural Studies*, *17*(2), 47–57. doi:10.1016/S0743-0167(00)00050-4

Morris, M. H., Kuratko, D. F., & Schindehutte, M. (2001). Towards integration: Understanding entrepreneurship through frameworks. *The International Journal of Entrepreneurship and Innovation*, *2*(1), 35–49. doi:10.5367/000000001101298765

Morris, D. (2019). Vietnam Agriculture Farming 4.0 - Issues and Solutions - Impact of the Major Trade Agreements CPTPP. *EUVNFTA and Investment Protection Agreement*. Retrieve from https://www.lexology.com/library/detail.aspx?g=5b12a52a-97ed-4672-8def82e297450659.%20Retrieved%20on%20 Dec%2021,%202019 on Jun 15, 2020.

MOST. (2018). *Ministry of Sciences and Technology, Vietnam*. Retrieved from https://www.most.gov.vn/vn/tin-tuc/15274/nong-nghiep-thong-minh--co-hoi-va-thach-thuc-cho-nong-nghiep-viet-nam.aspx

Nguyen, T. T. (2016). An investigation of the Vietnamese shipping industry and policy recommendations for profound participation into ASEAN integration. *The Asian Journal of Shipping and Logistics*, *32*(2), 81–88. doi:10.1016/j.ajsl.2016.05.001

Nguyen, C., Frederick, H., & Nguyen, H. (2014). Female entrepreneurship in rural Vietnam: An exploratory study. *International Journal of Gender and Entrepreneurship*, *6*(1), 50–67. doi:10.1108/IJGE-04-2013-0034

OECD. (2006). *The New Rural Paradigm: Policies and Governance*. OECD Report, Directorate for Public Governance and Territorial Development. Retrieved from https://www.oecd.org/cfe/regional-policy/thenewruralparadigmpoliciesandgovernance.htm

Pham, H. C., Nguyen, T. T., McDonald, S., & Tran-Kieu, N. Q. (2019). Information sharing in Logistics Firms: An Exploratory Study of the Vietnamese Logistics Sector. *The Asian Journal of Shipping and Logistics*, *35*(2), 87–95. doi:10.1016/j.ajsl.2019.06.001

Powell, N., Swartling, Å. G., & Minh Ha, H. (2011). The national policy landscape: The legacy and the present situation. In N. Powell, Å. G. Swartling, & H. Minh Ha (Eds.), *Stakeholder Agency in Rural Development Policy: Articulating Cogovernance in Vietnam*. World Agroforestry Centre ICRAF.

Rantamaki-Lahtinen, L. (2002). Finnish pluriactive farms – the common but unknown rural enterprises. In H. W. Tanvig (Ed.), *Rurality, Rural Policy and Politics in a Nordic-Scottish Perspective. Working paper 1/02*. Danish Centre for Rural Research and Development.

Shepherd, J. (2004). *Social and Economic Transformation in the Digital Era*. IGI Global. doi:10.4018/978-1-59140-158-2.ch001

Sohns, F., & Diez, R. J. (2018). Explaining micro entrepreneurship in rural Vietnam—A multilevel analysis. *Small Business Economics*, *50*(1), 219–237. doi:10.100711187-017-9886-2

Statista. (2020). Available at https://www.statista.com/topics/5653/agriculture-in-vietnam/

Strauss, A., & Corbin, J. (1994). Grounded Theory Methodology. In N. K. Denzin & Y. S. Lincoln (Eds.), *Handbook of Qualitative Research*. SAGE Publications.

Tiersky, H. (2018). *Navigating digital transformation*. Retrieved from https://www.cio.com/article/3179607/5-top-challenges-to-digital-transformation-in-the-enterprise.html

Veit, D., Clemons, E., Benlian, A., Buxmann, P., Hess, T., Kundisch, D., & Spann, M. (2014). Business models. *Business & Information Systems Engineering*, *6*(1), 45–53. doi:10.100712599-013-0308-y

BriefingV. (2018). Retrieved from https://www.vietnam-briefing.com/news/need-high-tech-farming-vietnam.html/

Vietnam Communist Party News. (2019). Retrieved from http://dangcongsan.vn/thoi-su/so-luong-doanh-nghiep-dau-tu-vao-nong-nghiep-tang-3-lan-541807.html

Work Bank. (2018). *Trade Economics*. Retrieved from https://tradingeconomics.com/vietnam/rural-population-percent-of-total-population-wb-data.html

Zaremohzzabieh, Z., Samah, B., Muhammad, M., Omar, S., Bolong, J., Hassan, M., & Shaffril, H. (2015). A Test of the Technology Acceptance Model for Understanding the ICT Adoption Behavior of Rural Young Entrepreneurs. *International Journal of Business and Management*, *10*(2), 158–169. doi:10.5539/ijbm.v10n2p158

ADDITIONAL READING

Finkle, T. A., & Timothy, O. (2014). Entrepreneurship in the Digital Era: Creating Your Own Online Business. *Entrepreneurship Education and Pedagogy*, *2*(2), 133–150. doi:10.1177/2515127418820680

He, X. (2019). Digital entrepreneurship solution to rural poverty: Theory, practice and policy implications. *Journal of Developmental Entrepreneurship*, 24(1), 1-32 (1950004)

Hsieh, Y. J., & Wu, Y. J. (2019). Entrepreneurship through the platform strategy in the digital era: Insights and research opportunities. *Computers in Human Behavior*, *95*, 315–323. doi:10.1016/j.chb.2018.03.033

Joshi, M. P., Kathuria, R., & Sidhartha, D. (2019). Corporate Entrepreneurship in the Digital Era: The Cascading Effect through Operations. *The Journal of Entrepreneurship*, *28*(1), 4–34. doi:10.1177/0971355718810554

Pappas, M., Drigas, A., Papagerasimou, Y., Dimitriou, H., Katsanou, N., Papakonstantinou, S., & Karabatzaki, Z. (2018). Female Entrepreneurship and Employability in the Digital Era: The Case of Greece. *Journal of Open Innovation: Technology, Market, and Complexity*, *4*(2), 1–15. doi:10.3390/joitmc4020001

Pělucha, M., & Kasabov, E. (2020). Rural Development in the Digital Age: Exploring Neo-Productivist EU Rural Policy. New York Routledge. ISBN 978-0-367-35658-3 (hbk). ISBN 978-0-429-34098-7 (ebk)

Sikora, A. R., Terry E. R., Vlek., P., & Chitj, J. (2020). *Transforming agriculture in southern Africa: constraints, technologies, policies and processes*. Routledge, Taylor & Francis Group.

Ziyae, B., Sajadi, S., & Mobaraki, M. (2014). The deployment and internationalization speed of e-business in the digital entrepreneurship era. *Journal of Global Entrepreneurship Research*, *4*(1), 1–11. doi:10.118640497-014-0015-2

KEY TERMS AND DEFINITIONS

Barrier: The factor prevents or blocks the movement of the objective content.

Digital Era: The era that is under a massive influence of the Internet and digital technologies such as cloud computing, the Internet of Things, mobile devices, and virtual reality.

Facilitator: The factor supports the movement of the objective content.

High-Tech: A technology at the cutting edge, means the most advanced technology at the time.

High-Tech Agriculture: The term refers to a wide range of new technical tools for accelerating the high-tech adoption that can improve the performance of farming practices and farm management.

High-Tech Rural Entrepreneurship: The enterprises in rural areas implement high-tech in their operation and management to improve their product's quality and productivity, mainly in agriculture. These enterprises also focus on research activity outcomes, and labor qualifications, environment-friendly and energy efficiency.

Qualitative Research: A kind of research that relies on unstructured and non-numerical data, in which the data may take the form of fieldnotes of the researcher from his/her observation, interviews, documents, including material objects, etc.

Rural Entrepreneurship: An entrepreneurship which ensures value addition to rural resources in rural areas engaging largely rural human resources.

Chapter 10
Strategic Use of Agriculture Information System by Agripreneurs in Rural Economies:
Current Role and Future Prospects

Krishnadas R.
https://orcid.org/0000-0001-9420-5012
SASTRA University (Deemed), India

Renganathan R.
SASTRA University (Deemed), India

ABSTRACT

The penetration of digital technologies has opened new avenues to integrate rural farmers into a new digitally driven agri-food system. Digitalization is fundamentally changing the way of the agricultural technologies and such new technologies help farmers, manufacturers, retailers, and customers in their daily activities. The development of digital technologies with the presence of information systems is essential in altering the mode of business processes. However, on the other hand, the differences between rural and urban technological facilities broadens due to a lack of information access. To bridge the rural and urban divide, technologies can play an important role among rural entrepreneurs. This chapter is an attempt to investigate the agricultural entrepreneurs or agripreneurs use of agricultural information systems to implement innovative approaches in dynamic market conditions.

DOI: 10.4018/978-1-7998-4942-1.ch010

INTRODUCTION

Based on the current estimate of the United Nations (2018), the worldwide population is set to reach 9.3 billion by 2050. Most of the population expansion is set to occur in rural areas. The advancement of digital technology is so fast that all employment fields need to be coordinated to speed up development (United Nations, 2018). The 4th Industrial Revolution will act as a powerful to bringing-out disruption with the help of digital technologies. The development of new digital technologies with the presence of digital media is very essential in altering the mode of business processes (Mckinsey, 2019). Innovations through digital technologies will alter several sectors including the agriculture sector (World Economic Forum, 2016). Digitalization is fundamentally changing the way agricultural technology is utilized and it also helps in aiding the farmers, manufacturers, retailers, customers, and the broader agricultural sector to a greater extent. Farmers are prompting new digital and advanced technologies that are altering the way they conduct farming activities (FAO, 2019). Every intervention that aims to increase productivity, reduce costs, improve water use efficiency, disseminate information on efficient farm practices, or unify agricultural markets will demand the deployment of appropriate technology. The penetration of digital technologies has opened new avenues to integrate rural entrepreneurs into a new digitally driven agri-food system (USAID, 2018).

According to Okediran & Ganiyu (2019), agriculture is an information-intensive industry where there is a continual need for updated information about agricultural inputs, market information, and logistics. Glendenning and Ficarelli (2012) suggested that agricultural education, research, and development of extension activities are the important inputs that are possible through digital technologies. Rural entrepreneurship majorly influences various issues like economic development, employment, food, and social security (FAO, 2017). Palacios et al. (2015) emphasized that to develop rural areas and to prevent rural migration, the promotion of digital inclusion among rural entrepreneurs is sine qua non for developing countries. The access to information and technology gap between rural and urban areas broadens due to lack of information access and it affects the marginalized communities in the rural areas across developing countries (Ye & Yang, 2020).

As human beings, farmers are keen on updating what are the best practices in agriculture and they constantly seek developments in research and technology. Farmers are eager to learn expertise, in particular in the modern agricultural sector, to become mentally powerful and capable of embracing modern agriculture methods. For this, farmers need accurate and valuable information as early as possible. Growth in the ICT sector has led to the transformation of carrying out business activities. Agricultural Information Systems play a key role to fight poverty, achieving food security, and providing information that creates opportunities for poor people. According to the FAO (2019), to provide a competitive advantage for rural agricultural entrepreneurs, digitalization plays a vital role to access global markets and to have an efficient distribution of products.

This chapter emphasizes the importance of agricultural information systems for agricultural development and identifies the benefits and challenges of the current systems for the agripreneurs. This chapter also helps in finding some of the factors influencing the adoption and use of agri information systems. The strategic use and prospects of agricultural information system applications are the other objectives of the chapter. Finally, the general conclusions about agricultural information systems are emphasized and implications for better usage are suggested. In this chapter, an introduction to various information systems used in agriculture is provided. The next section in the chapter is the background of the rural entrepreneurship, the benefits and challenges of agripreneurs are discussed.

ENTREPRENEURS

Schumpeter (1965) defined entrepreneurs as "individuals who exploit market opportunity through technical and organizational innovation." An entrepreneur is a dedicated and innovative person, who often explores new ways to develop and grow his company. Enterprise is an interaction between attitudes, activities, and aspirations which are inherently dynamic and vary from one stage to another in economic growth (Acs, 2010). An entrepreneur is a person who passionately searches for potential prospects in his company. Zimmerer & Scarborough (2005) hold that entrepreneurs are new businesses or innovations built for productivity and development in the presence of uncertainty and risk. An entrepreneur is a person who is open to opportunities for trade. The entrepreneur should classify customers and suppliers and act as a bridge where the intermediate role is to generate profit (Deakins & Freel, 2006). In general, entrepreneurs face constraints on financial capital and liquidity (Blanchflower & Oswald, 1998). Yet their work is more fulfilled than workers and their flexibility is much greater (Benz & Frey, 2008).

Rural Entrepreneurship – Benefits and Challenges

Rural development is more synonymous with entrepreneurship more than ever before. It is an effort to develop effective risk management opportunities and mobilization of human, information, and capital resources for the implementation of rural projects (Saxena, 2012).

Benefits of Rural Entrepreneurship

There are numerous benefits that can be reaped through rural entrepreneurship (FAO, 1997). Major benefits from rural entrepreneurship can be achieved and it is best described below as follows:

- **Employment Opportunities:** The development of industrial units in rural areas through rural entrepreneurship is the source for income creation and generation of employment opportunities.
- **Regional Growth:** The regional development in a balanced way can be possible through the rural entrepreneurship can scatter the concentration of major industrial units in urban areas.
- **Prevention of Migration of Rural Population:** There are disparities in income for rural and urban people. Rural entrepreneurship will pave the way in developing infrastructural facilities like roads, power, bridges, etc. It prevents the migration of people from rural to urban areas.
- **Empowering Rural Youth:** Rural entrepreneurship can empower the rural youth and expose them to various avenues to adopt entrepreneurship.
- **Improved Standard of Living:** The literacy rate of the rural population can be improved by rural entrepreneurship. The education and self - employment will flourish the local community and thereby increasing their standard of living.

Challenges faced by Rural Entrepreneurs

In comparison with the urban areas, rural areas are in some way disadvantaged; enormous economic production differences exist between these areas (Smallbone, 2009). There are several challenges that are faced by rural entrepreneurs. Financial and marketing risks are the primary reason for farmers to engage in uneconomical activities (Tan et al., 2008). Management risk, marketing risk, and lack of funding/

financing are the other possible risks associated with rural entrepreneurs (Stathopoulou, Psaltopoulos, & Skuras, 2004).

- **Financial Problems:** The major problem for rural entrepreneurs is to arrange funds for working capital. The capacity of small-scale business activities in rural areas is under threat due to altering global environmental conditions. Rapid urbanization with an increase in population growth creates a rise in demand. Due to substantial drift challenges, the capacities of outmoded small-scale industries are under risk (Salas et al., 2007).
- **Marketing Problems:** Urban entrepreneurs and large-sized organizations pose a major threat to rural entrepreneurs. The rural entrepreneurs incur the high cost of production due to high input costs. The rural entrepreneurs face the problem of fixing the standards and maintaining them (Jayadatta, 2017). The new enterprises cannot afford to spend on marketing expenditures and advertising since they lack financial resources. The presence of middlemen also hinders their future growth. Transportation facilities and distribution facilities also add woes to marketing problems in rural areas. Moreover, agricultural products are not standardized and graded (FFTC Agricultural policy platform, 2017).
- **Management Problems:** Rural entrepreneurs face a challenging task in the procurement of raw materials (Ghosh, 2013). Warehousing and storage are the other risks faced by rural entrepreneurs. Rural entrepreneurs also suffer majorly due to a lack of technical knowledge. Lack of training facilities and other extensive services are the other hurdles for the development of rural entrepreneurship.
- **Human Resource Problems:** Lower literacy rate is also one of the problems faced by rural entrepreneurs and they should devise strategies to overcome it. Lack of suitable workers high suitable skills is the other challenge in rural areas and is unable to find workers with high skills. Rural entrepreneurs are generally supposed to be less innovative in their thinking abilities. Hence, rural youth very little options and opportunities (OECD, 2010).

AGRI ENTREPRENEURS

Agripreneurship refers to entrepreneurship in agriculture. Dollinger (2003) defines entrepreneurship in agriculture as the emergence of an innovative economic organization for progress or development in agriculture in uncertain conditions. Agricultural entrepreneurs generate business through their farms. They earn income through farming activities. Agri-entrepreneurs are passionate about their job and they are ready to take the risk to improve their business and to earn profits through agricultural activities. The entrepreneurial way is a suitable way for many small-scale farmers, and it is increasingly necessary to produce for markets and profits. Agripreneurship is mostly influenced by the economic, educational, and cultural situation (Singh, 2013).

Challenges for Agricultural Entrepreneurs

The global population is poised to grow by about 9.6 billion in the year 2050 from 7.6 billion in 2018 (UN DESA, 2019). With the increasing population leading to rapidly growing food demand, it is critical to building efficiencies in agriculture to achieve food security. According to Greyson (2018), there are a significant number of people living in developing countries in rural areas and depend on the activities of the agro-economy. Rural Entrepreneurs have lesser access to information & market, inputs, financing, and training compared to their urban counterparts. Lower smartphone penetration in the rural areas and high cost of the internet combined with poor network coverage are the hindrances for the use of mobile agricultural applications (World Bank, 2017). Agriculture inputs like seeds, fertilizers, chemicals for crop protection, farm equipment, credit services, which are essentially required for crop production(Sheahan & Barrett, 2017). Adoption of quality seeds, rapid farm mechanization, the growing area under irrigation, and easy availability of institutional credit are the key supply-side drivers. Several challenges are faced by the food and agricultural sector.

Agricultural entrepreneurs have developed their farm businesses, may encounter the challenges such as (i) risk related to market, (ii) access to finance and credit, (iii) access to information, (iv) bargaining power is low, (v) susceptibility to economic uncertainty and (vi) access to training and related challenges (FAO, 2012).

- **Risk Related to Market:** Generally producing for local markets has several risks associated which ultimately leads to low prices for the produce. Farmers need to evaluate the risks associated with these aspects while choosing markets to sell their produce. They should have a combination of both international and local markets to increase their profitability. Farm Markets are dynamic, diverse, and are not completely predictable. Improved market involvement offers rural entrepreneurs more opportunities.
- **Access to Finance and Credit:** It is another foremost challenge faced by agricultural entrepreneurs. They are usually ignorant of sources of finance and they are stuck by with local moneylenders for borrowing. Their access to credit is less because they lack collateral, have no credit history and they have lower income. They should have sufficient knowledge about interest rates and repayments.
- **Access to Information:** Information access is very vital for making a profitable business. Agripreneurs in rural markets face difficulty in accessing information related to diverse information such as weather conditions prevailing in the region, knowledge on market prices, quality of seeds, fertilizers, farm equipment, etc. Digital technologies in addition to the traditional informational sources are vital for the agricultural entrepreneurs to access the information which can make them successful
- **Bargaining Power is Low:** Small-scale entrepreneurial farmers usually have lesser bargaining power. Their production is less and hence their negotiation power is also less. The agricultural entrepreneurs must purchase inputs and equipment at a higher price since they have lesser bargaining power. The same scenario is applicable to their bargaining power in the marketplace and they are forced to sell at lower prices for their produce.
- **Susceptibility to Economic Uncertainty:** Unexpectedly low crop yields, fluctuations in the prices for inputs and products, increasing interest rates, and additional market add vows to the agricultural entrepreneurs. Such variations may lead to reduced profits in the agricultural sector. Agricultural entrepreneurs run a substantial risk and find it difficult to overcome these economic shocks.
- **Access to Training and Related Challenges:** Inculcating the entrepreneurship characteristics and making a successful farmer is not an easy task. It requires training and access to knowledge. The market participation of Small-scale farmers is very less and needs to be addressed. Not all

farmers can be successful from common programs intended to nurture entrepreneurship. A suitable training program should be designed exclusively for cultivating business and entrepreneurial skills.

BACKGROUND

Bryant (1989) suggested that rural entrepreneurs are primary decision-makers because they are incorporated into the socio-economic environment. Akca, Sayili, & Esengun (2007) argued that when it comes to the development process, rural entrepreneurs lag their urban counterparts. To bridge the rural & urban divide ICT can play an influential role among rural entrepreneurs. Agricultural entrepreneurship through digital technologies is a way by which farmers can capitalize on their culture and region to diversify existing business practices. The creation of information systems and their use consists of integrated for online access and the efficient management and administration of information systems. The importance of computer-based technologies and knowledge in the agricultural and food sectors is the importance of information systems. These systems contribute to the decision-making and management of knowledge (Silerová and Lang, 2006). The horizontal transfer of information among similar farms remained very essential. Several researchers suggested that new agricultural information sources are required, and they anticipated that the use of computerized databases will increase in the future.

Substantial details are required in information system processes, system function engagement, and operation. Particularly, the knowledge needs of rural entrepreneurs and the organizations participating in these operations need to be explored (Demiryurek et al., 2008). Many studies have illustrated a lack of conventional printing and library knowledge systems to rural farmers and the rural population, who are typically illiterate and relatively distant from formal information sources. New technology scientists say that technology can overcome this obstacle by supplying information and thermal people with the aid of modern information technologies. The next section in this chapter will elaborate on various agricultural information systems as well as introduce some of the factors influencing the adoption and use of these information systems.

AGRICULTURAL INFORMATION SYSTEMS

According to Roling (1988), the agricultural information system (AIS) is a system for generating, transforming, consolidating, receiving, and transferring agricultural information in a way that synergistically characterizes the utilization of knowledge of the farmers. A comprehensive research tool for collecting, creating, exchanging information, and using this knowledge to improve productivity is provided by the AIS (Talug, 1990). Ahmadvand and Karami (2011) stated that AIS focus on three important aspects: First, it must be available to small and marginal consumers who have low income. Second, it is built in the context of the limitations of access to land and water supplies to maximize production with a growing population. Third, it is used to prevent the accentuation of climate change, technologies that will allow and better manage the use of capital and externalities in agricultural development. Policymakers, program managers, agricultural scientists, government planners, farmers, and other stakeholders will get benefitted through agri-business information (Zaman, 2002). He further added that AIS will allow the smaller landholding farmers to compete with larger farmers.

Mistr (2007) stressed that the potential of information systems must be designed in AIS with user-friendly tools and portals. At each point in the cycle, farmers have various kinds of information requirements. Such provisions include the forecasting weather conditions, agricultural methods, supplies, prices, and the control of diseases in crops. Information networks are meant to provide these knowledge requirements to the growers. They can obtain information from a varietal of sources, among others, or from the same social network. While the mainstream economic theory suggests that communication is expensive, and the knowledge is neither symmetrical nor costly. This is partly because knowledge is accessible through conventional methods, such as television, radio, or newspaper. The role of Information Technology in agriculture is also to resolve asymmetries in knowledge and provide stakeholders with accuracy in information. Tremendous potential for data processing and information building in agricultural systems is provided by Information Technology (Sonka, 2015).

Role of Information Systems in Agriculture

The competence of ICT with regard to agriculture can be surveyed comprehensively under two headings: (a) as a direct tool for commitment to agricultural productivity and (b) as an indirect tool for farmers to make them educated and well informed to make imperative choices which will have a positive effect in agriculture and allied activities are led. The indirect benefits of ICT for agripreneurs are significant and remains unexplored. For taking decisions, the farmer requires timely and reliable sources of information inputs. At present, the agripreneurs depend on inputs from conventional sources which are slow and unreliable. For making decisions, they critically require convenient and dependable sources of information ideas. Thus, this information not merely useful for them but also makes them competitive due to changing environmental conditions.

Digital Divide

Although nearly half of the people worldwide already use the Internet, it is overwhelming in developing countries. Only one in seven people in the least developed countries use the Internet (ITU, 2016) and the variations between rural and urban (though trends vary from country to country) tend to be quite distinct. Educated users prefer to utilize more digital technology, such as e-commerce, entertainment, electronic banking, and public utilities. The digitization of agri-food systems entails the possibility of differential distribution of potential benefits across rural and urban areas, between gender and the population of young people. In urban areas, 'physical environments' (resources, expertise, networks) have always been better established relative to rural areas. In tandem with foreign urbanization patterns and the developments of medium-size towns, digitization is theoretically rising current inequalities between rural-urban communities (UN DESA, 2018) and societies in the digital transition phase.

Digital Literacy

According to UNESCO, Digital literacy is the use of relevant digital devices and connected technologies to access, manage, integrate, communicate, evaluate, and understand through economic and social life participation. It comprises of competencies such as computer literacy, ICT literacy, information, and media literacy. Digital inclusion is a way to empower people through ICT, but the existing digital divide due to differential access to ICT tools, low digital literacy, and lack of sustainable usage are the hindrances to digital inclusion. 'Digital literacy' is critical for using digital technologies. Unlike in many developed countries, where people regularly use advanced technologies and digital skills in day-to-day lives, ICT knowledge, and skills are low in underdeveloped countries (Upadhyaya, 2019). In recent times, the rapid development of ICTs has provided a new platform for micro-enterprises, to reach clients globally. Increasingly, digital literacy will be a requirement in agriculture and allied training will be required (Neirotti, Raguseo, & Paolucci, 2018). Swati (2019) suggested that entrepreneurs should develop and nurture a culture of market creation and not market development. There is a lot of untapped potential for value creation at the lower level of the pyramid.

Digital transformation has the potential to deliver significant economic, social, and environmental benefits. Krushna, Misra, and Patra (2013) argued that digital inclusion will support the rural entrepreneurs by providing better assistance along with technical training and it will empower them to offer better services. Digital inclusion is a significant aspect and acts as an economic catalyst in the era of the Industrial Revolution 4.0 (Horváth and Szabó, 2019). Digital integration of the nation requires a transformation at the grassroots and entrepreneurs in the rural areas and act as an agent for this transformation. The concept of digital inclusion will progress and creates new trends in emerging rural markets which paves the way for product development and diversification of products. To develop rural areas, promotion of digital inclusion can be considered as an important strategy. Rural entrepreneurs should use the convenience of digital technology to expand their commercial markets. In Rural entrepreneurship, the use of the Internet should be promoted which will benefit them. In addition, the use of e-marketing media is extremely important, particularly in the business, investment, banking, agricultural industries (Aishah, 2017). Digital inclusion can be recognized as a technology evolution by which entrepreneurs mobilize software systems and innovate technological fusion, which enables companies to revolutionize their business models with respect to manufacturing and production services (Lee et al., 2018). In the next section of the chapter, the benefits of the adoption and use of agricultural information systems are discussed.

BENEFITS OF INFORMATION SYSTEMS USAGE IN AGRICULTURE

According to FAO (2017), AIS is the most accessible application for many farmers, especially people living in rural areas. The roles played by the AIS help to keep getting advanced and there is a necessity to monitor uninterruptedly and categorize new progress, to prioritize applications for enhancing farmers' income. The use of digital technology can help lower the costs, assist farmers to make more precise decisions and improve access to information, and markets. Agricultural information interacts with and influences agricultural productivity in a variety of ways. It can help inform decisions regarding land, labor, livestock, capital, and management. The technical advances through AIS will offer rural entrepreneurs in building productive and cost-effective growing and marketing systems (Gorla, 2009). Agricultural productivity can arguably be improved by relevant, reliable, and useful information and knowledge. The number of issues and opportunities related to advanced technology. Farm size, data analytics and management gap, education and research gaps, business development, and employment are some of the important factors.

- **Information on crops** - Farm details are gathered and submitted to the internet: field types, field land area, harvest date, yields, etc. The information is evaluated for statistical reviews and tables which farmers can access with ordinary web browsers through the internet. Based on the details, farmers can create their development plans.

- **Information on production techniques** - Output knowledge produced by agricultural testing institutes and agricultural development stations can be collected and incorporated. Rural entrepreneurs may use the internet and other platforms to acquire these details.
- **Information on production equipment and agricultural inputs** - The Information is obtained from firms supplying field processing machines, and other farm goods, crops, and other inputs. Rural Entrepreneurs are equipped with the knowledge collected in this way.
- **Market Information** - Dařena (2007) argued that the information systems model to marketing and established marketing information systems offer to support and accomplish marketing activities. Information about different agricultural products will assist the rural entrepreneurs in securing the best prices for their goods. In order to reorient farmers' output to markets where better prices are anticipated, market knowledge practices should be checked on the various markets and encouraged. The reports provide useful statistics on some of the main import and export industries. Information Technology will enable the production of forecast details in subsequent years on key agricultural products. This will allow the producers and merchants to determine when their goods are priced higher.
- **The other information of interest for farmers and their families** - Example of this kind of knowledge includes weather predictions, credit quality, and specialist guidance on the conservation of crops in good condition, etc. Although, there are few questions regarding the beneficial impact of increased information processing in agriculture and individual farmers, information gathering, and delivery remains to be complicated and costly. Information System gives all stakeholders in the agricultural sector the capacity to expand the quantity of knowledge accessible to all potential consumers and cut costs of transmitting the information (Rafi, 2017). These frameworks can play a significant role in potential agricultural development operations. Such applications include mobile interactions are a clear illustration of Information Technology usage in agriculture. In the next section in the chapter, the strategic use and prospects of agricultural information system applications are discussed.

STRATEGIC USE OF AGRICULTURAL INFORMATION SYSTEMS

Dawar Sanjay (2015) highlighted that an efficient agricultural model is the most critical factor to achieve profitable and sustainable growth in the rural market. Agriculture is an important segment which is fundamental for the endurance of present-day man. Agriculture has evolved the way of life, and without them, the existence cycle is not possible. The produce from agriculture promotes exchange between the nations. In this way, it brings revenue for agripreneurs. By adjusting and utilizing information technology, everybody reaps benefits through the association, and it helps to improve agrarian development. The nature of the Agricultural Information System contributes to underestimation amongst end-users of the importance of centrally provided information which, to a great extent, provides raw material to several intermediaries (Vidanapathirana, 2012). Governmental support is essential for the success of AIS as information about several public resources, including climate, weather, soil, and water apart from information about national policies on labour laws, ownership, and insurance is involved (Lu et al., 2015). The Agriculture Information Systems can be used as a resource for collecting knowledge regarding market (prices), meteorological forecasts, guidance from agricultural experts, etc.

Role of Innovation for Rural Entrepreneurs

In the contemporary business ecosystem, the inclusion of digital technologies is essential to improve innovation among rural entrepreneurs. Innovation is seen as a complex process, based on interactive network learning. Innovation is important for the competitiveness of enterprises and industrial sectors. Digital technologies have lowered information-related production costs and changed the characteristics of innovation. (Nylén and Holmström, 2015) Harnessing the potential of Agri Information system successfully requires combining different technologies used for varying purposes into coherent systems. The use of digital technologies by agricultural entrepreneurs will make them more competitive & innovative which will serve as a platform to enhance their livelihood (Ganguly, 2017). Technology-based companies that may include new ventures are the main tools with which new information and knowledge from the field of agriculture, science, technology, and engineering that result in meaningful economic benefits (Fang et al., 2016). The digital business allows, products to reach out to the world quickly and cheaply and this they attribute to the power of the internet (Evans, 1999). As money is scarce, rural people need to be offered such goods that provide immediate value creation. Also, an environment where consumers have easy access to technology will act as a catalyst in the adoption process. The entrepreneurs should develop and nurture a culture of market creation and not market development. There is a lot of untapped potential for value creation at the lower level of the pyramid, especially in rural areas. The consumers have awareness about brand and value. Today business consumers are getting connected and networked. Agricultural entrepreneurs are said to be a new group of innovators in the rural landscape, especially in the emerging markets. The rural segment with the help of digital technology advocates as a useful tool for capacity building in the future and requires suitable research and policy decisions for understanding their needs (Goyal, 2014).

Prospects of Agricultural Information System Applications in Agribusiness

Agripreneurs can adopt new technologies through AIS. Agricultural production is significantly contributed by Agricultural information services and in turn, it will improve the standard of living of the farmers. Zylbersztajn (2017) suggested that the methodologies to study agri-business processes have demonstrated a trend in the transformation from individual markets to chains, channels, and system prospects. Hoang, Castella, and Novosad (2006) explored how the operation of social networks in rural areas of developed countries as the properties of individuals and households and control access to knowledge, research, and development benefits. Most of the rural farmers depend on local knowledge for improved farming systems. The literacy level is important to access authentic information about farming activities. The farming process generally involves the number of decisions that require diverse information such as weather conditions prevailing in the region, knowledge on market prices, quality of seeds, fertilizers, farm equipment, etc. Progressions in the information and communication technologies offer an opportunity to exploit information and knowledge to expand production in agriculture particularly for developing and agrarian countries (Lwoga, 2010).

ROLE OF AGRICULTURAL INFORMATION SYSTEMS TO ENHANCE PRODUCTIVITY

The pressures of urban lifestyles paved the way to a "counter-urbanization" pattern. This has made to mounting concentration in the rural areas. The lower cost of launching new products and processes using the Internet and online platforms facilitates versioning and experimenting products for differentiated customers. In order to empower rural entrepreneurs, the power of digital technology plays a crucial role. The digital drive is bringing about digital inclusion for digital empowerment assisted by digital infrastructure for digital delivery of services. Agricultural entrepreneurs should unceasingly find ways to improve efficiency, productivity, reduce costs, and increase their profitability. Farmers have to increase their productivity with the low initial costs of the investments. Things like purchasing lesser inputs and materials, using more on-farm resources, and making better use of equipment and machinery. They should reduce ownership costs by sharing the resources. Agricultural knowledge operates in numerous ways to enhance agricultural output. It can help to guide land, work, livestock, capital, and management decisions. It is possible to increase farm performance by enabling appropriate, accurate, and valuable knowledge and information (Jones et al., 2017). Digital technologies will direct the selection of crops and production, promote the selection of loans and insurance, and offer environmental guidance, disease-related assistance, and in-house and export data in real-time. The farmers in rural economies need to implement innovative approaches to rural markets and demand for better food quality. Nevertheless, most of the area lies untapped for technology and creativity. ICTs applications are becoming popular now. E-governance with knowledge, can establish accountability and enhance governance in agriculture policies.

Innovations will accelerate growth, prosperity, and resilience, but they cannot eliminate human and social progress (Omar et al., 2018). Through technical advances, farmers can grow more effectively with less manpower and reach higher yields by utilizing fewer inputs. However, developments in farming technology contribute significantly to a more sustainable farming system which promotes quality improvement and less usage of resources. Food and nutrition technical developments are helping millions of people around the world to enhance their safety and well-being. According to the World Bank (2020), agricultural production is essential to poverty reduction. Agricultural efficiency is a driver for the increased cost of produce, employment and incomes, and industries that connect with the farming industry. The technology remains important for current food protection threats. The current function of technology is either to improve agricultural development or to restrict or mitigate externalities such as land and water loss and pollution. This is why technology has become more efficient. Although smallholder farmers face great challenges, a number of creative institutional models emerge which allow small-scale farmers to profit from the value-chain-dominated 'modern agriculture' (Loeper, 2018). These include establishing selling farmer/producer organizations, promoting contract production, creating supply chains for products of high value by an effective combination of private. Presently, rural entrepreneurs depend on conventional sources of information for decision inputs from which are not reliable and are very slow. There is a need for new digital technologies backed with information systems that are not only valuable but essential to remain competitive due to the changing environment. Technologies implemented through information systems will be helpful in harvesting, transporting, storage processes, and to distribute farm outputs in a highly efficient way and helps to reduce wastage. Digital Information systems will benefit the farmers to have a strong preference for prices offered by the main market and to realize realistic returns from retailers and wholesalers. This section of the chapter dealt with the role of agriculture information systems in enhancing productivity are discussed.

CONCLUSION

Connecting the rural community and its members to the world through digital technology is becoming increasingly vital for community strength for growth and social development. An environment where consumers have easy access to technology will act as a catalyst in the adoption process. The rural entrepreneurs should develop and nurture a culture of market creation and not market development. There is a lot of untapped potential for value creation at the lower level of the pyramid. The adoption of Agricultural Information Systems (AIS) is easier to implement for larger farmers. This causes differences between large and small-scale farmers, with a matching disparity among developed and developing countries. Farmers are instigating new digital and advanced technologies that are altering the way they farm and digitalization that is fundamentally changing the way agricultural technology and input suppliers relate with farmers, manufacturers, retailers, customers, and the broader agricultural sector. The use of Digital information systems will also enable farmers to compete in various situations of excellence and empower them in various stages of the value chain. Rural small and marginal holdings in agriculture are vital for increasing agriculture growth, food security and to improve the global economy. Through the penetration of internet services, disseminating agri-related information across wide areas can be made simpler. Agricultural Information Systems will assist the farming communities to fulfil the greater objective by empowering them and helpful in facilitating the extension services which will address global food security, economic development and thereby improving their overall welfare. The Agricultural Information Systems would be helpful for the farmers to make use of the latest technologies & methods and contribute to economic development across the globe. It is challenging in rural countries to transmit new agricultural technologies to a single farmer within a short period. If the farmers are empowered with Agri Information technologies, the livelihood opportunities for rural people would be enhanced. The establishment of information centers is important for easy access and productive use of agricultural information in this digital era. These information centers may supply rural farmers with the desired agrarian knowledge in a way that they can understand.

REFERENCES

Acs, Z. J. (2010). Entrepreneurship and Economic Development: The Valley of Backwardness. *Annals of Innovation & Entrepreneurship*, *1*(1), 5641. doi:10.3402/aie.v1i1.5602

Ahmadvand, M., & Karami, E. (2011). Factors Influencing the Success of Agricultural Information Systems: A Factor Analysis. *Journal of Agricultural Science and Technology*, *5*(1), 101–108.

Aishah. (2017). Approach to the use of e-marketing medium among entrepreneurs' women. *Journal of Global Business and Social Entrepreneurship*, 47–57.

Akca, H., Sayili, M., & Esengun, K. (2007). Challenge of Rural People to Reduce Digital Divide in the Globalized World: Theory and Practice. *Government Information Quarterly*, *24*(2), 404–413. doi:10.1016/j.giq.2006.04.012

Benz, M., & Frey, B. S. (2008). Being Independent Is a Great Thing: Subjective Evaluations of Self-Employment and Hierarchy. *Economica*, *75*(298), 362–383. doi:10.1111/j.1468-0335.2007.00594.x

Blanchflower, D. G., & Oswald, A. J. (1998). What Makes an Entrepreneur? *Journal of Labor Economics, 16*(1), 26–60. doi:10.1086/209881

Bryant, C. R. (1989). Entrepreneurs in the Rural Environment. *Journal of Rural Studies, 5*(4), 337–348. doi:10.1016/0743-0167(89)90060-0

Dařena, F. (2007). Global Architecture of Marketing Information Systems. *Agricultural Economics, 53*(9), 432–440.

Das, K., Rama, H. M., & Patra, M. R. (2013). *E-Governance and Digital Inclusion: Creating Smart Rural Women in India Service Oriented Architecture View Project.* Digital India View Project E-Governance and Digital Inclusion: Creating Smart Rural Women in India.

Deakins, D., & Freel, M. (2006). *Entrepreneurship and small firms* (4th ed.). McGraw-Hill.

Demiryurek, K., Erdem, H., Ceyhan, V., Atasever, S. & Uysal, O. (2008). Agricultural information systems and communication networks: the case of dairy farmers in Samsun province of Turkey. *Information Research, 13*(2), paper 343.

Dollinger, M. J. (2003). *Entrepreneurship – Strategies and Resources* (International Edition). Pearson.

Evans, P. (1999). *Blown to Bits: How the New Economics of Information Transforms strategy*. Harvard Business School Press.

Fang, J., Zhu, X., Wang, C., & Shangguan, L. (2016). Applications of DNA Technologies in Agriculture. *Current Genomics, 17*(4), 379–386. doi:10.2174/1389202917666160331203224 PMID:27499686

Ganguly, K., Gulati, A., & von Braun, J. (2017). *Innovations spearheading the next transformations in India 's agriculture*. ZEF Centre for Development Research, University of Bonn.

Ghosh, S. (2013). Entrepreneurship: An overview of the issues and challenges in the context of rural development in India. *Business Spectrum, 1*(2).

Glendenning, C. J., & Ficarelli, P. (2012*). The relevance of content in ICT initiatives in Indian agriculture.* IFPRI Discussion paper No 1180.

Gorla, N. (2009). A Survey of Rural E-Government Projects in India: Status and Benefits. *Information Technology for Development, 15*(1), 52–58. doi:10.1002/itdj.20064

Goyal, S. K. (2014). Agricultural Mechanization for Sustainable Agricultural and Rural Development in Eastern U. P. - A Review. *Agriculture for Sustainable Development, 2*(1), 192 198.

Greyson, K. A. (2018). Agribusiness System Hub for Rural Agricultural Cooperative Societies in Developing Countries. *Computer Science and Information Technology, 6*(1), 63–69. doi:10.13189/csit.2018.060403

Hoang, L. A., Castella, J. C., & Novosad, P. (2006). Social Networks and Information Access: Implications for Agricultural Extension in a Rice Farming Community in Northern Vietnam. *Agriculture and Human Values, 23*(4), 513–527. doi:10.100710460-006-9013-5

Horváth, D., & Szabó, R. Z. (2019). Driving Forces and Barriers of Industry 4.0: Do Multinational and Small and Medium-Sized Companies Have Equal Opportunities? *Technological Forecasting and Social Change*, *146*, 119–132. doi:10.1016/j.techfore.2019.05.021

Jayadatta, S. (2017). *Major Challenges and Problems of Rural Entrepreneurship in India*. Academic Press.

Jones, J. W., Antle, J. M., Basso, B., Boote, K. J., Conant, R. T., Foster, I., Godfray, H. C. J., Herrero, M., Howitt, R. E., Janssen, S., Keating, B. A., Munoz-Carpena, R., Porter, C. H., Rosenzweig, C., & Wheeler, T. R. (2017). Toward a New Generation of Agricultural System Data, Models, and Knowledge Products: State of Agricultural Systems Science. *Agricultural Systems*, *155*, 269–288. doi:10.1016/j.agsy.2016.09.021 PMID:28701818

Lee, Yun, Pyka, Won, Kodama, Schiuma, Park, Jeon, Park, Jung, Yan, Lee, & Zhao. (2018). How to Respond to the Fourth Industrial Revolution, or the Second Information Technology Revolution? Dynamic New Combinations between Technology, Market, and Society through Open Innovation. *Journal of Open Innovation: Technology, Market, and Complexity*, *4*(3), 21.

Lu, Y., Lu, Y., Wang, B., Pan, Z., & Qin, H. (2015). Acceptance of Government-Sponsored Agricultural Information Systems in China: The Role of Government Social Power. *Information Systems and e-Business Management*, *13*(2), 329–354. doi:10.100710257-014-0235-6

Lwoga, E. T. (2010). Bridging the Agricultural Knowledge and Information Divide: The Case of Selected Telecenters and Rural Radio in Tanzania. *The Electronic Journal on Information Systems in Developing Countries*, *43*(1), 1–14. doi:10.1002/j.1681-4835.2010.tb00310.x

Mistr, M. (2007). *The Czech Republic's emerging agricultural information and advisory services*. 18th European Seminar on Extension Education: Supporting Viable Rural Communities, Prague, Czech University of Life Sciences.

Mohd Rafi, A. F. (2017). Entrepreneurial psychology: The role of motivation in business creation new E-Commerce. *Journal of Business and Social Development*, 49-59.

Neirotti, P., Raguseo, E., & Paolucci, E. (2018). How SMEs Develop ICT-Based Capabilities in Response to Their Environment: Past Evidence and Implications for the Uptake of the New ICT Paradigm. *Journal of Enterprise Information Management*, *31*(1), 10–37. doi:10.1108/JEIM-09-2016-0158

Nylén, D., & Holmström, J. (2015). Digital Innovation Strategy: A Framework for Diagnosing and Improving Digital Product and Service Innovation. *Business Horizons*, *58*(1), 57–67. doi:10.1016/j.bushor.2014.09.001

Okediran, O. O., & Ganiyu, R. A. (2019). E-Agriculture Reviewed: Theories, Concepts and Trends. *FUOYE Journal of Engineering and Technology*, *4*(1), 125–130. doi:10.46792/fuoyejet.v4i1.366

Omar, F. I., Dimyati, H. A., Ahmad, N., & Khairuddin, S. M. H. S. (2018). Digital Inclusion Among Entrepreneurs of Small and Medium. *Journal of Education and Social Sciences*, *9*(2), 90–97.

Palacios-Lopez, A., Christiaensen, L., & Kilic, T. (2015). *How Much of the Labor in African Agriculture is Provided by Women?* World Bank Policy Research Paper 7282. World Bank.

Röling, N. G. (1988). *Extension Science. Information System in Agricultural Development*. Cambridge University Press.

Salas, S., Chuenpagdee, R., Seijo, J. C., & Charles, A. (2007). Challenges in the Assessment and Management of Small-Scale Fisheries in Latin America and the Caribbean. *Fisheries Research*, *87*(1), 5–16. doi:10.1016/j.fishres.2007.06.015

Sanjay, Raghuram, & Vineet. (2015, Mar. 16). Winning the trust of rural consumers. *Business Standard, The Strategist*.

Saxena, S. (2012). Problems Faced by Rural Entrepreneurs and Remedies to Solve It. *IOSR Journal of Business and Management*, *3*(1), 23–29. doi:10.9790/487X-0312329

Schumpeter, J. A. (1965). Economic Theory and Entrepreneurial History. In H. G. Aitken (Ed.), *Explorations in enterprise*. Harvard University Press.

Sheahan, M., & Barrett, C. B. (2017). Ten Striking Facts about Agricultural Input Use in Sub-Saharan Africa. *Food Policy*, *67*, 12–25. doi:10.1016/j.foodpol.2016.09.010 PMID:28413243

Silerova, E., & Lang, K. (2006). Information systems - tool for changing our future. *Agricultural Economics –. Czech*, *52*, 447–450.

Singh, A. P. (2013). Strategies for Developing Agripreneurship among Farming Community in Uttar Pradesh, India. *Academicia: An International Multidisciplinary Research Journal*, *3*(11), 1–12.

Smallbone, D. (2009). Fostering Entrepreneurship in Rural Areas. In J. Potter & A. R. Hofer (Eds.), *Strengthening entrepreneurship and economic development in East Germany: lessons from local approaches* (pp. 161–187). OECD.

Sonka, S. (2015). Big data: From hype to agricultural tool. *Farm Policy Journal*, *12*(1), 1–9.

Stathopoulou, S., Psaltopoulos, D., & Skuras, D. (2004). Rural Entrepreneurship in Europe: A Research Framework and Agenda. *International Journal of Entrepreneurial Behaviour & Research*, *10*(6), 404–425. doi:10.1108/13552550410564725

Swati Bisht, N. P. (2019). Digital Entrepreneurship and The Bottom of The Pyramid- A Conceptual Framework. *International Journal on Recent Trends in Business and Tourism*, 33-42.

Talug, C. (1990). *Agricultural research-development and the examination of extension services for agricultural productivity*. MPM Publishing.

Tan, S., Heerink, N., Kruseman, G., & Qu, F. (2008). Do Fragmented Landholdings Have Higher Production Costs? Evidence from Rice Farmers in Northeastern Jiangxi Province, P.R. China. *China Economic Review*, *19*(3), 347–358. doi:10.1016/j.chieco.2007.07.001

Upadhyaya, L. (2019). Digital Inclusion: Strategies to Bridge Digital Divide in Farming Community. *Journal of Agriculture Science and Technology*, 1079–1089.

Vidanapathirana, N. P. (2012). *Agricultural information systems and their applications for development of agriculture and rural community, a review study*. Paper presented at the 35th Information Systems Research Seminar in Scandinavia – IRIS 2012, Sigtuna, Sweden.

von Loeper, W. J., Drimie, S., & Blignaut, J. (2018). The Struggles of Smallholder Farmers: A Cause of Modern Agricultural Value Chains in South Africa. In *Agricultural Value Chain*. InTech. doi:10.5772/intechopen.75710

Ye, L., & Yang, H. (2020). From Digital Divide to Social Inclusion: A Tale of Mobile Platform Empowerment in Rural Areas. *Sustainability*, *12*(6), 2424. doi:10.3390u12062424

Zaman, M. A. 2002. *Present Status of Agricultural Information Technology Systems and Services in Bangladesh*. Retrieved from http//jsai.or.jp/afita/afita-conf/2002/part 1/p075.pdf

Zimmerer, T.W. & Scarborough, N.M. (2005). *Essentials of Entrepreneurship and Small Business Management*. Pearson.

Zylbersztajn, D. (2017). Agribusiness Systems Analysis: Origin, Evolution and Research Perspectives. *Revista ADM*, *52*, 114–117.

ADDITIONAL READING

Bishop-Sambrook, C. (2005). Contribution of farm power to smallholder livelihoods in sub-Saharan Africa. *Agricultural and Food Engineering Technical Report*.

Kazeem, A. A., Dare, A., Olalekan, O., Abiodun, S. E., & Komolafe, T. L. (2017). Attitudes of farmers to extension trainings in Nigeria: Implications for adoption of improved agricultural technologies in Ogun state southwest region. *Journal of Agricultural Sciences*, *62*(4), 423–443. doi:10.2298/JAS1704423K

Kizilaslan, N. (2006). Agricultural information systems: A national case study. *Library Review*, *55*(8), 497–507. doi:10.1108/00242530610689347

Okewu, E., & Okewu, J. (2015). Curbing Insecurity in Sub-Saharan Africa Through ICTs for Development (ICT4D) Paper presented at the 15th European Conference on eGovernment, Portsmouth, UK.

Omar, F. I., Dimyati, H. A., Ahmad, N., & Khairuddin, S. M. H. S. (2018). Digital Inclusion Among Entrepreneurs of Small and Medium. *Journal of Education and Social Sciences*, *9*(2), 90–97.

Ommani, A. R. (2005). Information and Communication Technology (ICT) for Agricultural Information Dissemination (policy development of Agricultural Information Disseminationof developing countries). [to Persian]. *Dehati Journal*, *24*(2), 18–27.

Tarhini, A., Elyas, T., Akour, M. A., & Al-Salti, Z. (2016). Technology, demographic characteristics and e-learning acceptance: A conceptual model based on extended technology acceptance model. *Higher Education Studies*, *6*(3), 72–89. doi:10.5539/hes.v6n3p72

Upadhyaya, L. (2019). Digital Inclusion: Strategies to Bridge Digital Divide in Farming Community. *Journal of Agriculture Science and Technology*, 1079–1089.

KEY TERMS AND DEFINITIONS

Agriculture Information System (AIS): It is a system for generating, transforming, consolidating, receiving, and transferring agricultural information in a way that synergistically characterizes the utilization of knowledge by the farmers.

Digital Technology: These are electronic tools, systems, devices, and resources that generate, store or process data. Well known examples include social media, online games, multimedia, and mobile phones.

E-Agriculture: The philosophy emphasizing on the need to transfer knowledge and experience in the use of ICT in agriculture.

Farm Management Information Systems: A planned system of collecting, processing, storing, and disseminating data in a form needed to carry out farm-related operational functions.

Information and Communications Technology (ICT): It is an extension term IT that emphasizes the role of unified communication, integration of communication between computers, and the business technology, middleware, storage and audio-visual systems required for users to access, store, transmit and control information.

Innovation System: It is defined as a new way of doing something, ranging from changes in the way we think to the way we produce new products or use new processes or procedures.

Technology Transfer: The process of disseminating new technologies and other practical applications that largely result from research and development (R&D) efforts in different fields of agriculture.

Chapter 11
Capability Maturity Model for Agricultural Supply Chain Management Software

Saliya Nugawela
Swinburne University of Technology, Australia

Darshana Sedera
Southern Cross University, Australia

ABSTRACT

Compared to the supply chain management of other business domains, agricultural supply chain management is affected with issues such as diversity of production and demand, the bulkiness of produce, perishability, seasonality, harvest uncertainty, and climate complexity. These issues are more prominent in rural agricultural sector. Availability of mature supply chain management processes and systems can enhance the productivity of rural agricultural communities. This chapter proposes a five-stage capability maturity model for the implementation and maintenance of supply chain management processes in farm management information systems. The capability maturity model is a valuable aid to determine the digitized supply chain process' ability to consistently and continuously achieve improvement and organizational objectives. The model is proposed based on the findings of the analysis of 121 supply chain management software in the farming sector, the Capability Maturity Model by the Software Engineering Institute, and the Supply Chain Process Management Maturity Model.

INTRODUCTION

Successfully managing the agricultural supply chains is essential to the development of the rural economy. In this chapter, we propose a maturity model for supply chain management processes of farm management software. Improving the performance and effectiveness of existing supply chain management processes is paramount to the development of rural agriculture. Thus, a maturity model can aid in figuring out the current level of the supply chain digitization and contribute to enhancing the processes to the next level.

DOI: 10.4018/978-1-7998-4942-1.ch011

Agriculture is the science and art of cultivating plants and keeping animals by people for food and raw materials. Agriculture covers various sectors such as crop cultivation, animal husbandry, dairying, fisheries, agroforestry, organic farming, vertical farming, and other associated activities (FAO, 2017). Agriculture is one of the most critical areas of human activity worldwide (Lokuge et al. 2016a). As the growing global population is expected to surpass the 9 billion mark by 2050, the demand has heightened for increased production of nutritious food to meet the ever-increasing demand and ensure food security. Thus, placing pressure on already-fragile resources (FAO, 2017; World Bank, 2017; Kaloxylos et al, 2012).

Especially in developing countries, agriculture plays a vital role in the economy (Sedera and Lokuge 2017). It accounts for most of the rural employment, directly or indirectly. Improvements in agriculture productivity results in farmers' income rise, food prices fall, freed labor for additional employment, rural economic growth and sustainable management of natural resources (FAO, 2017; Chhachhar & Hassan, 2013; Duncombe, 2018; World Bank, 2017). In the current competitive business environment, a farm can survive financially and be sustainable only when it is well managed (Husemann & Novkovic, 2014). Farmers and related stakeholders face a significant challenge in effectively managing information generated both internally and externally to improve the efficiency of operations, reduce environmental impact and comply with various quality standards (Sørensen et al, 2010b).

The widespread and increasing use of computers and the dramatic increase in the uptake of the Internet have improved and eased the process of handling information generated in a farm environment (Lokuge and Sedera 2014a; Lokuge and Sedera 2014b; Sørensen et al, 2010a). The study conducted by Carrer et al (2010) among citrus farms in Brazil has found that the most efficient farms in the sample are already ahead in the process of adoption of Information Systems (IS) for production planning and control.

Farmers can use IS to match cropping practices to climatic trends, use resources sustainably, cope with productivity threats, apply latest farming techniques, increase production through optimizing input use, make more timely decisions, labour savings, improve market access, manage finances, and comply with regulations (Dufty & Jackson, 2018; World Bank, 2017; Esfahani & Asadiye, 2009; FAO, 2016). Thus, attempting to enhance the farm processes through sophisticated information and communication developments (Barmpounakis et al, 2015; Eitzinger et al, 2019). Many consider IS as the new revolution that will modernize farming and guarantee food security. In developed economies, innovations such as the Internet of Things, Cloud Computing and Big Data has already revolutionized farming (FAO, 2017; FAO, 2018; Lokuge and Sedera 2014c; Lokuge and Sedera 2016; World Bank, 2017).

Farm Management Information Systems (FMIS) are a specialized category of Management Information Systems (MIS) solutions. FMIS is defined as a planned system for collecting, processing, storing, and disseminating data in the form needed to carry out a farm's operations and functions (Fountas et al, 2015). An FMIS is essentially a Management Information System (MIS) for the agriculture sector (Tummers et al, 2019). These FMISs have evolved from simple record keeping software into complex systems that can manipulate large amounts of data and provide decision support capabilities (Paraforos et al, 2016).

The management of agricultural production is both qualitatively and quantitatively confronted with deciding under uncertainty, changing market demands, prices instability, climate change, lack of knowledge management, and capital availability (Borodin et al, 2016; Mittenzwei et al, 2017).

The rest of this chapter is organized as follows: The next section describes the relationship between the rural communities and the agricultural supply chain management. This is followed by a brief overview of the agricultural supply chain management software, the study motivation, SCM processes in FMIS, Supply Chain Process Management Maturity Model (SCPM3) and the Capability Maturity Model

(CMM). The next section explains the methodology followed. Next, the capability maturity model for implementation and maintenance of supply chain management processes in farm management information systems is described. Finally, the conclusion is presented.

RURAL COMMUNITIES AND AGRICULTURAL SUPPLY CHAIN MANAGEMENT (ASCM)

Agricultural production makes up a significant part of the world economy and provides the raw material for many industries (Shukla & Jharkharia, 2013). Agricultural Supply Chain Management (ASCM) includes a set of activities from farm to points of final consumption including farming, harvesting, processing/production, testing, packaging, warehousing, transportation, distribution and marketing (Tsolakis et al, 2014). IS are important in conceptualizing, designing and developing innovative ways for making the ASCM more efficient and responsive. It enables the farmers and consumers to integrate the entire supply chain process of agricultural production, improving the efficiency and responsiveness (Routroy & Behera, 2017). Under the growing evolution and complexity of the agricultural sector and the challenges it faces, managing agricultural supply chains efficiently has become important (Borodin et al, 2016).

Due to its association with food security, employment generation and poverty reduction, agriculture remains an essential economic activity worldwide (Adjei, Kosoe & Forkuor, 2017). In most developing countries, agriculture plays a vital role in the economy (Chhachhar, 2013) and the majority of the rural population depending on agriculture-related activities (Sørensen, Kateris, & Bochtis, 2019). As an example, in Africa, between 60 and 80 per cent of the region's rural population is employed in agriculture (FAO, 2018, p. vii). Agriculture generates jobs, improves incomes, contribute to poverty eradication and promotes economic growth in rural areas (FAO, 2017, p. viii). Rural agriculture contributes to food security, foreign exchange earnings and provides raw materials for agro-based industries in the region. But the sector is faced with the challenges such as access to markets, knowledge, new technology and skills, new inputs, emerging value chains and other opportunities (Sylvester, 2013, p. iii). Rural development is a comprehensive and multidimensional concept aims at the development of agriculture, allied activities and human resources in rural areas to improve the quality of life and economic welfare of people living in villages (Ghadiyali, Lad, & Dhodiya, 2018).

In many agricultural, rural communities, the low availability of timely and needed information has disadvantaged farmers to sell their harvests below fair price (Miller, Saroja & Linder, 2013, p. 1). Proper use of Market Information Systems (MIS) (an integral part of SCM) can promote agricultural development among small-scale producers, enhance transparency, enhance competitiveness, reduce information asymmetries, improve market efficiency, improve food security, signal emerging food problems, and facilitate policy and planning decisions. MIS can contribute to strengthening the bargaining power of rural farmers (Fonteneau & Khalil, 2017, p. V).

Agricultural supply chains have become a significant building block for the rural development (Marsden, Banks & Bristow, 2000). Johnson & Hofman (2004, p.3) emphasize that rural communities must become more 'market smart'. To do that, rural enterprises should be able to forecast, interpret and respond to supply signals from domestic and global markets. This allows them to capitalize on consumer preferences. To achieve the linking of rural farmers with markets, supply chains should overcome challenges such as vulnerability to natural disasters, new pests, and political instability.

Based on a survey carried out in the rural regions of Europe, Marsden, Banks & Bristow (2000) suggest that sustainable rural development through the evolution of reconfigured supply chains must be based upon both institutional support and associational development. The growing global demand for food has opened new opportunities for rural farmers. However, according to Mkhabela (2007), rural farmers' capability to utilize the opportunity is hindered due to their lack of access to markets, capital, inputs, technology, and extension services.

Proper supply chain management is linked to the success in rural agribusiness. The study conducted by Collins & Lim-Camacho (2005) among fifteen rural agribusiness supply chains demonstrates that "in new rural industries, firms with medium to high levels of supply chain management thinking, planning and implementation are more successful in terms of creating value and achieving competitive advantage than those with lower levels of supply chain management thinking, planning and implementation."

A STATUS REPORT ON AGRICULTURAL SCM SOFTWARE

In agriculture and other industries, the effectiveness and performance of the supply chain is a significant factor that determines the level of profitability (Vanathi & Swamynathan, 2013). Maturity Models are based on the conception that people, processes, and organizations gradually progress to a higher level of capability/effectiveness following a process of development, which encompasses an evolutionary sequence of phases (Gomes & Romão, 2018). High-level of process maturity results in high-level of performance. The higher level of maturity enables higher performance (Vanathi & Swamynathan, 2013). The maturity model depicts a sequence of stages that form an expected, desired, or logical path from an initial to a target maturity state (Poeppelbuss et al, 2011). The maturity model acts as an instrument to facilitate organizational management, including the management of information systems functions (Carvalho, Rocha & Abreu, 2016). Maturity model defines an essential framework for identifying the capabilities of an IS in an organization. The maturity model enables the organization's ability to plan and implement actions that allow them to advance to a higher maturity stage and thus stimulate and guide the development of their IS capabilities to achieve the proposed objectives of the IS (Gomes & Romão, 2018).

The Study Motivation

There is a lack of literature related to the maturity of digitization for ASCM software in specific and FMIS in general. Our research focuses on the development of a Capability Maturity Model for Implementation and Maintenance of Supply Chain Management (SCM) Processes in Farm Management Information Systems.

The following four research questions guide the development of the maturity model:

- What maturity models are available for IS?
- Which maturity model is most dominant in the IS domain?
- What are the agricultural supply chain processes?
- What are the maturity models available for SCM?

This chapter presents the preliminary results of identifying the maturity models of IS necessary for the specific requirements of the agricultural supply chain. The model we developed will be tested through a case study done in a farming organization with complete SCM processes.

Supply Chain Management Processes in FMIS

Lambert, Cooper & Pagh (1997), states the supply chain means the integration of key business processes carried out by all consecutive suppliers of products and providers of services and information that add value for customers and stakeholders. According to Szymczak (2013), a supply chain is a flow of material, information and financial data. At earlier stages of the supply chain, materials are semi-finished products, subcomponents, parts, production materials and work-in-progress (unfinished products). At the final stage of the supply chain, which focuses on distribution, the material is considered as the finished product to be marketed. Flow management requires information that helps plan, organize and control the flow of resources between consumers and suppliers. Financial data flows occur in the supply chain as a result of purchase and sales transactions concluded between supply chain links.

An analysis conducted by Cooper, Lambert & Pagh (1997) and Croxton et al (2001) pinpoint eight basic supply chain processes: customer relationship management, customer service level management, demand management, order fulfilment, manufacturing flow management, procurement management, product development and commercialization, and returns management.

The subject of Supply Chain Management (SCM) has been examined thoroughly and in detail in the academic literature with numerous published books and research papers. Also, the SCM processes are successfully digitized with many SCM software solutions available in the market (Lokuge and Sedera 2017; Lokuge et al. 2016b; Sedera and Lokuge 2017). However, this does not conclude that the unique problems faced in agricultural SCM have been explored. As long as supply chains continue to evolve and change, there will be a need for additional exploration and digitization.

Unlike supply chains in other business domains, the agriculture supply chain has not improved in the last few decades (Naik & Suresh, 2018). Some unique issues in agriculture supply chains are long queued time during peak harvest season, rapidly growing production needs, the uncertain quality of produce, health and safety aspects, perishable nature of the produce, high fluctuations in demand and prices, managing the large amount of wastage created in the agriculture supply chain, post-harvest loss, massive produce spoilage/contamination, effects of extreme weather conditions, high level of production uncertainty, increasing use of emerging technologies, mechanical damages, temperature management, poor logistical support services, complex food safety regulatory environment, and production of goods without purchase orders. (Kamble et al, 2020; Naik & Suresh 2018; Negi & Anand 2015; Routroy & Behera 2017; Chandrasekaran & Raghuram 2014; Roekel et al, 2002)

Supply Chain Process Management Maturity Model (SCPM3)

"The lack of industrialization, inadequacy of the management, information inaccuracy, and inefficient supply chains are the significant issues in an agri-food supply chain (Kamble et al, 2020, p. 179)." The increasing use of emerging technologies such as internet of things, the blockchain and big data technologies in the agriculture supply chains are driving the agricultural supply chain towards a digital supply chain environment that is data driven (Kamble et al, 2020; Lokuge et al. 2016b; Lokuge et al. 2019; Sedera et al. 2016; Sedera et al. 2001). Supply chain processes have developmental stages that can be clearly defined, managed, measured and controlled over time. The higher level of process maturity can provide better control of the results, more accurate forecasting and more effectiveness in achieving goals (Lockamy & McCormack 2004; Poirier & Quinn 2004). Supply chain process maturity influences the business processes of a company and affects its performance (McCormack & Johnson 2001; McCormack et al, 2009). More mature supply chain processes result in companies reducing costs faster than their less mature peers and achieving higher profit margins (Hofmann & Reiner 2006). De Oliveira et al (2012), propose a five-level Supply Chain Process Management Maturity Model (SCPM3). Information is an essential driver for the success of SCPM3 (Kamble et al, 2020). The description of the different levels of the SCPM3 is presented in Table 1.

Table 1. Levels of supply chain process management maturity model (SCPM3) (Kamble et al. 2020; de Oliveira et al. 2012)

Level	Description
I (Foundation)	Focused on building an underlying structure. Sourcing is the focus area.
II (Structure)	Distribution and demand planning processes get structured.
III (Vision)	Planning, source, make, deliver is viewed distinctly. Focus on the development of cross-functional teams and supply chain integration.
IV (Integration)	Firms focus on establishing long-term collaborative relationships with all their supply chain stakeholders. Strategic planning team focus on selecting supply chain partners and building long-term relationships with stakeholders.
V (Dynamics)	Supply chain attains a high level of integration. Firm's take control of demand and capacity constraints by establishing a pull system through the development of a close relationship with customers.

Capability Maturity Model (CMM)

Capability Maturity Model (CMM) was developed by SEI (Software Engineering Institute) at Carnegie Mellon University in 1991 and updated in 1993 as version 1.1 based on the study and data collected from various organizations, members of industry and government who had worked as a vendor with the U.S Department of Defense (DoD). In CMM, the term maturity refers to improving organizations' processes continually. The intention of developing the framework was to help software organizations improve their software process maturity and how to evolve toward a culture of software excellence. The model achieves this by serving as a set of guidelines against which an organization can determine its current process maturity. Furthermore, the model can be used to identify the few issues most critical to software quality and process improvement (Chaudhary & Chopra, 2017; Baumert & McWhinney, 1992; Paulk et al, 1993a; O'Regan, 2010). Capability levels apply to process improvement achievement in individual process areas. Maturity levels apply to process improvement achievement in multiple process areas. The CMM contains five levels of software process maturity: Initial, Repeatable, Defined, Managed, and Optimizing (Table 2).

According to Baumert & McWhinney (1992), an organization at the Initial Level has few stable software processes and lacks a stable environment for developing and maintaining software. An organization at the Repeatable Level has stable processes in place for planning and tracking the software project enabling a stable, managed working environment. An organization at the Defined Level has a standard process for developing and maintaining software across the organization. An organization at the Managed Level sets carefully well-defined consistent processes and quantitative quality goals for software products. An organization at the Optimizing Level has the means to identify weak process elements and strengthen them for continuous process improvement.

Table 2. The five levels of software process maturity (Paulk et al. 1993a)

Level	Description
1) Initial	The software process is characterized as ad hoc, and occasionally even chaotic. Few processes are defined, and success depends on individual effort.
2) Repeatable	Basic project management processes are established to track cost, schedule, and functionality. The necessary process discipline is in place to repeat earlier successes on projects with similar applications.
3) Defined	The software process for both management and engineering activities is documented, standardized, and integrated into a standard software process for the organization. All projects use an approved, tailored version of the organization's standard software process for developing and maintaining software.
4) Managed	Detailed measures of the software process and product quality are collected. Both the software process and products are quantitatively understood and controlled.
5) Optimizing	Continuous process improvement is enabled by quantitative feedback from the process and from piloting innovative ideas and technologies.

METHODOLOGY

Using a systematic literature review protocol, we referred the published research papers, books, case studies, farm-related websites (government, commercial and research), and FMIS product descriptions to identify the farm processes. Then, we clustered the farm processes under nine categories (Nugawela & Sedera, 2020). A similar classification was observed in Fountas et al (2015). The identified farm process categories in FMIS are Farm Field Activity Management, Finance and Accounting, Supply Chain Management, Report Generation, Farm Equipment Management, Quality Control, Support for Different Farming Types, Modern Technology Support, and Farm Labour Management.

In the second phase of the study, we have examined 184 FMIS modules (Table 5 -Appendix) from 130 vendors (Nugawela & Sedera, 2020). Both crop and livestock farming software were considered. The selection of FMIS was limited for the software which has English language support. We selected software vendors from the United Kingdom, United States, Canada, Australia, New Zealand, France, Italy, The Netherlands and India which provide the application in English and have an English-based website and product descriptions. For searching the FMIS software, we used specific keywords such as farm management systems, farm management information systems, farm software, agricultural information systems, e-agriculture, agtech software and livestock management systems. We consequently aggregated the gathered information in a table comprising all relevant data concerning the FMIS module and the farm processes supported. We attached particular attention to correctly identifying the farm processes supported by the FMIS module and assigning the relevant process cluster.

Out of the 184 software modules analyzed, 121 modules (65.76%) supported 'supply chain management' processes. As the third phase of the study, we performed a detailed analysis of Agricultural Supply Chain Management (ASCM) Processes in FMIS. The list of processes identified is given in Table 3. During the investigation, we referred the product descriptions, customer reviews and free/trial versions to identify how SCM processes integrate with the other software features/systems and how successful the SCM processes are in supporting the farm activities.

In parallel, we also explored information systems maturity models studies. Therein, we first used the keywords "Maturity model", and queried academic publication databases with no time constraints. By observing, first the journal and conference publications, next available book chapters, we identified several Capability Maturity Models (CMM). Several publications relevant to IS maturity model in general and health care IS maturity model in specific were selected (Jansen, 2020; Becker, Knackstedt & Stein 2010; Carvalho, Rocha & Abreu, 2016; Gomes & Romão, 2018; Matrane et al, 2015;Poeppelbuss et al, 2011; Proença & Borbinha, 2016; Tarhan et al, 2019). However, we were unable to find any maturity model relevant to FMIS. The paper published by Poeppelbuss et al (2011), regarding Maturity models in information systems research suggests that the Capability Maturity Model (CMM) is the most dominant foundation of past IS research on maturity models.

We applied the Procedure Model for the Maturity Model Development proposed by Becker, Knackstedt & Pöppelbuß (2009) and Becker, Knackstedt & Stein (2010) to develop the maturity model for digitization of ASCM processes. This approach is a flowchart-oriented procedure model comprising eight phases interconnected by decisions and control flows. Their approach is based on the seven guidelines for design science proposed by Hevner et al (2004). The flowchart for the Procedure Model Followed for the Maturity Model Development is given in Figure 1.

Figure 1. Procedure Model Followed during the Maturity Model Development (adapted from Becker, Knackstedt & Pöppelbuß (2009) and Becker, Knackstedt & Stein (2010))

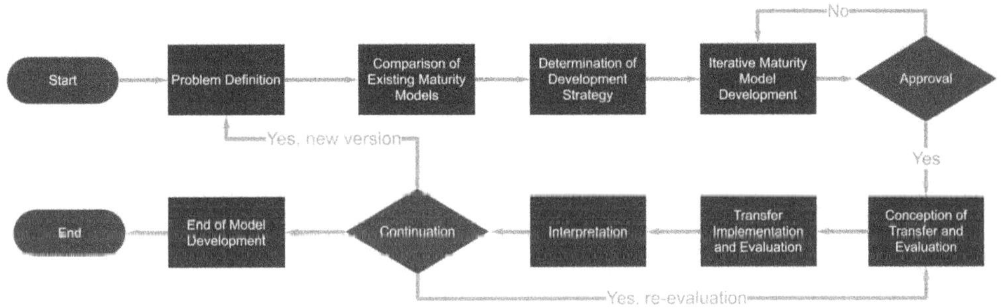

In order to complete the model development process, we need to conduct case studies in farm organizations where the SCM processes are digitized. That will be the next phase of this research.

Based on the analysis of 121 Farm Management Information Systems (out of 184 total FMIS analyzed), we have identified the Agricultural Supply Chain Management Processes listed in Table 3.

Table 3. Supply chain management processes in FMIS

SCM Process	Number of FMIS supporting the process	SCM Process	Number of FMIS supporting the process
Storage management	72	Facilitating crop recall activities	22
Re-ordering management	35	Management of a labelling system to control the produce	47
Scheduling and tracking of inventory	110	Management of purchases	121
Warehouse management	55	Marketing of crops harvested	73
Traceability of inventory items	63	Manage inventories	121
Inventory accountability management	21	Loading & Delivery Tracking	67
Quantity adjustment according to the farmers' plan	87	Order Booking and Tracking	121
Managing the supply of Agrochemicals and fertilizers	90	Order & Dealer Management	121
Managing the supply of seeding and planting materials	90	Produce Packing Traceability Records	45
Monitoring and management of Nursery	12	Maintain Shipping & Receiving Records	121
Management of orders	121	Informing the farmer of available markets and prevailing prices	32
Packing management	45	Keep up with animal purchase and sales	56
Commodity price tracking	32		

Order, inventory, purchases and shipping management facilities were present in all analyzed software. Realtime market data support was available through mobile apps in 32 applications. Agricultural product-related tracking features were available in half the applications analyzed. Nursery management and crop recall activities were supported only by a few software. This area needs more process digitization. The software which supported warehouse management, chemical and fertilizer management, packing and marketing had advanced features implemented.

CAPABILITY MATURITY MODEL FOR IMPLEMENTATION AND MAINTENANCE OF SCM PROCESSES IN FMIS

Based on the understanding of the Supply Chain Management process implementation in 121 Farm Management Information Systems (out of 184 total FMIS analyzed), Capability Maturity Model guidelines and Supply Chain Process Management Maturity Model (SCPM3); we have developed a Capability Maturity Model for Implementation and Maintenance of Supply Chain Management Processes in Farm Management Information Systems.

Development of our model starts with the problem definition. What supportive tools are required to assess the as-is situation of the implementation and maintenance of ASCM processes of an FMIS in a farming company, derive and prioritize improvement measures and subsequently control the progress of their implementation?

In the second phase, (1) we conducted a literature review to identify existing maturity models devoted to information systems, (2) we analyzed 121 ASCM software carefully. The literature review indicated that the CMM is the most widely used Maturity Model in the IS domain. The analysis of software provided the foundation to identify the digitized ASCM processes, customer feedback, level of integration with other systems, required quality standards and need for further innovation.

In the third phase, we needed to determine how the model is to be transferred to the farming domain. We decided to conduct a case study in a large-scale farming company with well-established ASCM processes and in-house software development capabilities. This will be done as the second phase of our research in future. As part of the case study, we will collect and analyze empirical quantitative data related to the model and use as the basis for the decision on the further development of our capability maturity model.

The remaining phases of the procedure model followed during the maturity model development (Figure 1), will be conducted during the second phase of the research, along with the case study.

Table 4. Capability maturity model for implementation and maintenance of supply chain management (SCM) processes in farm management information systems

Capability Maturity Level	Level Parameter Description
1) Initial (Foundation)	Focus is on implementing or managing the basic SCM processes. Misaligned expectations. Lack of foundation to build trust and create value. Ad Hoc Processes. No measurement and analysis of process performance. SC processes are not integrated with other systems. Lack the software quality assurance.
2) Repeatable (Structure)	Focus is on structuring the implementation and management of basic SCM processes. Plan for SC information sharing with other systems. Tracking, measurement, analysis and quality assurance processes are implemented. Basic project management processes are established to track cost, schedule, and functionality.
3) Defined (Vision)	Focus on integrating the SC processes with other systems. Integrated software management. Establish the intergroup coordination within the organization. All processes are well documented and standardized. Use an approved process within the organization for developing and maintaining SCM software. Reviews are conducted aiming at improving processes.
4) Managed (Integration)	All SCM processes are integrated with the other systems in the organization. Focus on integrating the organization's systems with the systems of external supply chain stakeholders. Detailed measures of the SCM software process and product quality are collected.
5) Optimizing (Dynamics)	High level of integration of SCM software processes is achieved both within the other systems of the organization and with the systems of external supply chain stakeholders. Continuous SCM process improvement is performed through quantitative feedback from the processes. Established system for detection and prevention of errors. Established systems for SCM software change management. Full implementation of software quality assurance procedures. Innovative ideas for SCM are identified and tested.

Level 1: Initial (Foundation): This level represents the worst-case scenario in the implementation and maintenance of SCM Processes in FMIS. It is characterized by a focus on implementing or man-

aging the basic SCM processes, misaligned expectations, lack foundation to build trust and create value, Ad Hoc Processes, no measurement and analysis of process performance, non-integrated SC processes and lack of software quality assurance.

Level 2: Repeatable (Structure): To reach this level, structuring the implementation and management of basic SCM processes needs to be established. Should start planning for SC information sharing with other systems. Tracking, measurement, analysis and quality assurance processes should be implemented. Basic project management processes should be established to track cost, schedule, and functionality.

Level 3: Defined (Vision): To reach this level, steps must be taken on integrating the SC processes with other systems in the organization. It is characterized by integrated software management, intergroup coordination within the organization, documented and standardized processes, using approved process within the organization for developing and maintaining SCM software and conducting reviews aiming at improving processes.

Level 4: Managed (Integration): When this level is reached, all the SCM process are appropriately integrated with the other systems in the organization. Management should focus on integrating the organization's systems with the systems of external supply chain stakeholders. Detailed measures of the SCM software process and product quality should be collected.

Level 5: Optimizing (Dynamics): Upon reaching this level, a high level of integration of SCM software processes is achieved both within the other systems of the organization and with the systems of external supply chain stakeholders. Continuous SCM process improvement should be performed through quantitative feedback from the processes. This level is also characterized by the establishment of systems for detection and prevention of errors, systems for SCM software change management, full implementation of software quality assurance procedures and testing innovative ideas for SCM process improvement.

CONCLUSION

Information Systems have become a strategic part of organizations, contributing effectively to align business processes with strategies, increasing productivity and effectiveness (Matrane et al, 2015). Implementing software with high quality, rapid time to market, high user satisfaction, and low costs continue to be a significant challenge (Ply et al, 2012). Application of information systems in rural agricultural supply chain management: enhance traceability; increase efficiency and predictability; reduce spoilage, responds to quality standards requirements; and allow large buyers track, manage, pay, and reward small producers (Asenso-Okyere & Mekonnen, 2012).

Within various business domains and industries, maturity models are introduced as guides and reference frameworks for information system (IS) management (Carvalho et al, 2019). The maturity model-based assessment can be used to measure the current maturity level of a particular aspect of an organization in a meaningful way. Thus, enabling stakeholders to identify strengths and areas to improve, and accordingly plan what to do in order to reach higher maturity levels (Proença & Borbinha, 2016; Tarhan et al, 2019).

Following a Maturity model would enhance the credibility of the company, provide a logical path to improvement, improve technical and management practices, leads to higher quality of software, reduces the cost of maintenance and incidences of defects, leads to a culture of improvement, and have the support and understanding of business and defining services in business rather than IT terms (O'Regan, 2010; Hirschheim, Welke & Schwarz, 2010).

One of our largest challenges in this research work was to develop a maturity model in a field that is governed by a high level of uncertainty and lack of widespread adoption. According to Jansen (2020), while there is a rapid increase in publications of new maturity models, there is little literature that mainly discusses the development of maturity models.

The Capability Maturity Model for Software provides software organizations with guidance on how to gain control of their processes for developing and maintaining software and how to evolve toward a culture of software engineering and management excellence. The CMM was designed to guide software organizations in selecting process improvement strategies by determining current process maturity and identifying the few issues most critical to software quality and process improvement. By focusing on a limited set of activities and working aggressively to achieve them, an organization can steadily improve its organization-wide software process to enable continuous and lasting gains in software process capability (Paulk et al, 1993a). CMM is widely considered the most prevalent Software Process Innovations (SPIs) reference model in use globally (SEI 2010). Another significant advantage of the CMM is, it does not dictate the use of a particular software development methodology or the adoption of specific development tools and technologies (Ply et al, 2012).

Based on our study, we propose a CMM with five maturity levels representing a distinct stage of software process capability for SCM software implementation and maintenance (Table 4). In the initial stage of maturity, organizations use essential SCM software components. As the organization matures to the second stage, structured implementation, information sharing, tracking and quality assurance begins to emerge. As the initiatives continue, in the third stage, the company moves into the defined stage and begins supporting SCM processes with services such as integrated software management, process documentation and reviews for improvement. Next, they move into the quantitatively managed stage where the focus is on achieving vital objective measures, which allows the farm organization to create a service architecture designed to promote flexibility and agility. Finally, during the optimized stage, business processes have created that lead to an adaptive architecture.

The supply chains have different needs depending upon their maturity levels, and hence it is challenging to propose a generalized solution that may work for all the situations (Cadez & Guilding, 2008). In order to evaluate the usefulness of our maturity model for the ASCM software implementation and maintenance, we need to implement it in a real-life setting and prove whether the model provides the projected benefits. For this purpose, our aim is to apply the model to a substantial number of existing ASCM software and evaluate its applicability and the feasibility of the collected results. This will be conducted as the next stage of the research. The main goal of further research planned in farming organizations is the stabilization of the maturity model and the dissemination into practice. Finally, we want to gather the opinion of managers and employees who uses ASCM software and perform a qualitative and quantitative analysis of the proposed maturity model.

Based on the literature review, there seems to be a lack of research done in the field of maturity models linked to the Farm based Information Systems. There are several maturity models available for Management Information Systems. However, none of the models captures the unique requirements of an agricultural organisation. The need to develop maturity models for information systems are even higher for agricultural organisations based in rural areas as they face more unique issues.

REFERENCES

Adjei, P. O. W., Kosoe, E. A., & Forkuor, D. (2017). Facts behind the myth of conservative rurality: Major determinants of rural farmers' innovation adoption decisions for sustainable agriculture. *GeoJournal*, *82*(5), 1051–1066. doi:10.100710708-016-9728-9

Asenso-Okyere, K., & Mekonnen, D. A. (2012). The importance of ICTs in the provision of information for improving agricultural productivity and rural incomes in Africa. *African Human Development Report. UNDP Sponsored research Series.*

Barmpounakis, S., Kaloxylos, A., Groumas, A., Katsikas, L., Sarris, V., Dimtsa, K., Fournier, F., Antoniou, E., Alonistioti, N., & Wolfert, S. (2015). Management and control applications in Agriculture domain via a Future Internet Business-to-Business platform. *Information Processing in Agriculture*, *2*(1), 51–63. doi:10.1016/j.inpa.2015.04.002

Baumert, J., & McWhinney, M. (1992). *Software Measures and the Capability Maturity Model* (CMU/SEI-92-TR-025). http://resources.sei.cmu.edu/library/asset-view.cfm?AssetID=11715

Becker, J., Knackstedt, R., Lis, L., & Stein, A. (2010). Towards a maturity model for research portals. *ECIS 2010 Proceedings*, (38). http://aisel.aisnet.org/ecis2010/38

Becker, J., Knackstedt, R., & Pöppelbuß, J. (2009). Developing maturity models for IT management. *Business & Information Systems Engineering*, *1*(3), 213–222. doi:10.100712599-009-0044-5

Borodin, V., Bourtembourg, J., Hnaien, F., & Labadie, N. (2016). Handling uncertainty in agricultural supply chain management: A state of the art. *European Journal of Operational Research*, *254*(2), 348–359. doi:10.1016/j.ejor.2016.03.057

Cadez, S., & Guilding, C. (2008). An exploratory investigation of an integrated contingency model of strategic management accounting. *Accounting, Organizations and Society*, *33*(7-8), 836–863. doi:10.1016/j.aos.2008.01.003

Carrer, M. J., de Souza Filho, H. M., Batalha, M. O., & Rossi, F. R. (2015). Farm Management Information Systems (FMIS) and technical efficiency: An analysis of citrus farms in Brazil. *Computers and Electronics in Agriculture*, *119*, 105–111. doi:10.1016/j.compag.2015.10.013

Carvalho, J. V., Rocha, Á., & Abreu, A. (2016). Maturity models of healthcare information systems and technologies: A literature review. *Journal of Medical Systems*, *40*(6), 131. doi:10.100710916-016-0486-5 PMID:27083575

Carvalho, J. V., Rocha, Á., van de Wetering, R., & Abreu, A. (2019). A Maturity model for hospital information systems. *Journal of Business Research*, *94*, 388–399. doi:10.1016/j.jbusres.2017.12.012

Chandrasekaran, N., & Raghuram, G. (2014). *Agribusiness supply chain management*. CRC Press. doi:10.1201/b16704

Chaudhary, M., & Chopra, A. (2017). *CMMI for Development*. Apress. doi:10.1007/978-1-4842-2529-5

Chhachhar, A. R., & Hassan, M. S. (2013). Information communication technology for agriculture development. *The Journal of American Science*, *9*(1), 85–91.

Collins, R., & Lim-Camacho, L. A. (2005). *Unlocking successful new rural industries: is supply chain management the key?: final report to the Rural Industries Research and Development Corporation. RIRDC Publication*. Rural Industries Research and Development Corporation.

Cooper, M. C., Lambert, D. M., & Pagh, J. D. (1997). Supply chain management: More than a new name for logistics. *International Journal of Logistics Management*, *8*(1), 1–14. doi:10.1108/09574099710805556

Croxton, K. L., Garcia-Dastugue, S. J., Lambert, D. M., & Rogers, D. S. (2001). The supply chain management processes. *International Journal of Logistics Management*, *12*(2), 13–36. doi:10.1108/09574090110806271

De Oliveira, M. P. V., McCormack, K., & Trkman, P. (2012). Business analytics in supply chains–The contingent effect of business process maturity. *Expert Systems with Applications*, *39*(5), 5488–5498. doi:10.1016/j.eswa.2011.11.073

Dufty, N., & Jackson, T. (2018). *Information and communication technology use in Australian agriculture*. Australian Bureau of Agricultural and Resource Economics and Sciences.

Duncombe, R. (Ed.). (2018). *Digital Technologies for Agricultural and Rural Development in the Global South*. CABI. doi:10.1079/9781786393364.0000

Eitzinger, A., Cock, J., Atzmanstorfer, K., Binder, C. R., Läderach, P., Bonilla-Findji, O., Bartling, M., Mwongera, C., Zurita, L., & Jarvis, A. (2019). GeoFarmer: A monitoring and feedback system for agricultural development projects. *Computers and Electronics in Agriculture*, *158*, 109–121. doi:10.1016/j.compag.2019.01.049 PMID:31007323

Esfahani, L. P., & Asadiye, Z. S. (2009, December). The role of information and communication technology in agriculture. In *2009 First International Conference on Information Science and Engineering* (pp. 3528-3531). IEEE. 10.1109/ICISE.2009.1282

Fonteneau, F., & Khalil, C. (2017). Buidling agricultural market information systems: a literature review. *Buidling agricultural market information systems: a literature review.*

Food and Agriculture Organization (FAO) of the United Nations. (2016). *E-Agriculture Strategy Guide (Piloted in Asia-Pacific countries)*. http://www.fao.org/3/a-i5564e.pdf

Food and Agriculture Organization (FAO) of the United Nations. (2017). *Information and Communication Technology (ICT) in Agriculture, A Report to the G20 Agricultural Deputies*. http://www.fao.org/3/a-i7961e.pdf

Food and Agriculture Organization (FAO) of the United Nations. (2018). *Guidelines on the use of remote sensing products to improve agricultural crop production forecast statistics in sub-saharan African countries. Food and Agriculture Organization of the United Nations*. FAO.

Fountas, S., Carli, G., Sørensen, C. G., Tsiropoulos, Z., Cavalaris, C., Vatsanidou, A., Liakos, B., Canavari, M., Wiebensohn, J., & Tisserye, B. (2015). Farm management information systems: Current situation and future perspectives. *Computers and Electronics in Agriculture*, *115*, 40–50. doi:10.1016/j.compag.2015.05.011

Ghadiyali, T., Lad, K., & Dhodiya, J. (2018). Design and Development of the Agricultural Model: A Way to Connect Farmer Community to Agriculture Market for Betterment of Rural Development. In *ICT Based Innovations* (pp. 51–62). Springer. doi:10.1007/978-981-10-6602-3_6

Gomes, J., & Romão, M. (2018). Information system maturity models in healthcare. *Journal of Medical Systems*, *42*(12), 235. doi:10.100710916-018-1097-0 PMID:30327955

Hevner, A. R., March, S. T., Park, J., & Ram, S. (2004). Design science in information systems research. *Management Information Systems Quarterly*, *28*(1), 75–105. doi:10.2307/25148625

Hirschheim, R., Welke, R., & Schwarz, A. (2010). Service-oriented architecture: Myths, realities, and a maturity model. *MIS Quarterly Executive*, *9*(1).

Hofmann, P., & Reiner, G. (2006). Drivers for improving supply chain performance: An empirical study. *International Journal of Integrated Supply Management*, *2*(3), 214–230. doi:10.1504/IJISM.2006.008594

Husemann, C., & Novković, N. (2014). Farm management information systems: A case study on a German multifunctional farm. *Economics of Agriculture, 61*(297-2016-3594), 441-453.

Jansen, S. (2020). A focus area maturity model for software ecosystem governance. *Information and Software Technology*, *118*, 106219. doi:10.1016/j.infsof.2019.106219 PMID:32490064

Johnson, G. I., & Hofman, P. J. (2004). Agri-product supply-chain management in developing countries. In *Agri-product supply-chain management in developing countries. Proceedings of a workshop, Bali, Indonesia, 19-22 August 2003.* Australian Centre for International Agricultural Research (ACIAR).

Kaloxylos, A., Eigenmann, R., Teye, F., Politopoulou, Z., Wolfert, S., Shrank, C., ... Nicole, H. (2012). Farm management systems and the Future Internet era. *Computers and Electronics in Agriculture*, *89*, 130–144. doi:10.1016/j.compag.2012.09.002

Kamble, S. S., Gunasekaran, A., & Gawankar, S. A. (2020). Achieving sustainable performance in a data-driven agriculture supply chain: A review for research and applications. *International Journal of Production Economics*, *219*, 179–194. doi:10.1016/j.ijpe.2019.05.022

Kolukısa Tarhan, A., Garousi, V., Turetken, O., Söylemez, M., & Garossi, S. (2020). Maturity assessment and maturity models in health care: A multivocal literature review. *Digital Health*, *6*, 2055207620914772.

Lambert, D. M., Cooper, M. C., & Pagh, J. D. (1998). Supply chain management: Implementation issues and research opportunities. *International Journal of Logistics Management*, *9*(2), 1–20. doi:10.1108/09574099810805807

Lockamy, A. III, & McCormack, K. (2004). The development of a supply chain management process maturity model using the concepts of business process orientation. *Supply Chain Management*, *9*(4), 272–278. doi:10.1108/13598540410550019

Lokuge, S., & Sedera, D. (2014a). Deriving Information Systems Innovation Execution Mechanisms. In *Australasian Conference on Information Systems*. Auckland, New Zealand: AIS.

Lokuge, S., & Sedera, D. (2014b). Enterprise Systems Lifecycle-Wide Innovation. In *Americas Conference on Information Systems (AMCIS 2014)*. Savannah, GA: AIS.

Lokuge, S., & Sedera, D. (2014c). Enterprise Systems Lifecycle-Wide Innovation Readiness. In *Pacific Asia Conference on Information Systems*. Chengdu, China: AIS.

Lokuge, S., & Sedera, D. (2016). Is Your IT Eco-System Ready to Facilitate Organizational Innovation? Deriving an IT Eco-System Readiness Measurement Model. In *International Conference on Information Systems*. Dublin, Ireland: AIS.

Lokuge, S., & Sedera, D. (2017). Turning Dust to Gold: How to Increase Inimitability of Enterprise System. In *Pacific Asia Conference on Information Systems*. Langkawi, Malaysia: AIS.

Lokuge, S., Sedera, D., Atapattu, M., & Samaranayaka, D. (2016a). Exploring the Role of IS in Agriculture: Creating an Agenda Towards Agri-Informatics. In *Pacific Asia Conference on Information Systems*. Chiyai, Taiwan: AIS.

Lokuge, S., Sedera, D., & Grover, V. (2016b). Thinking inside the Box: Five Organizational Strategies Enabled through Information Systems. In *Pacific Asia Conference on Information Systems*. Chiyai, Taiwan: AIS.

Lokuge, S., Sedera, D., Grover, V., & Xu, D. (2019). Organizational Readiness for Digital Innovation: Development and Empirical Calibration of a Construct. *Information & Management*, *56*(3), 445-461.

Marsden, T., Banks, J., & Bristow, G. (2000). Food supply chain approaches: Exploring their role in rural development. *Sociologia Ruralis*, *40*(4), 424–438. doi:10.1111/1467-9523.00158

Matrane, O., Talea, A., Okar, C., & Talea, M. (2015). Towards A new maturity model for information system. *International Journal of Computer Science Issues*, *12*(3), 268.

McCormack, K., Willems, J., Van den Bergh, J., Deschoolmeester, D., Willaert, P., Štemberger, M. I., ... Vlahovic, N. (2009). A global investigation of key turning points in business process maturity. *Business Process Management Journal*, *15*(5), 792–815. doi:10.1108/14637150910987946

McCormack, K. P., & Johnson, W. C. (2001). *Business process orientation: Gaining the e-business competitive advantage*. CRC Press.

Miller, C., Saroja, V. N., & Linder, C. (2013). *ICT uses for inclusive agricultural value chains*. Food and Agriculture Organization of the United Nations.

Mittenzwei, K., Persson, T., Höglind, M., & Kværnø, S. (2017). Combined effects of climate change and policy uncertainty on the agricultural sector in Norway. *Agricultural Systems*, *153*, 118–126. doi:10.1016/j.agsy.2017.01.016

Mkhabela, T. (2007). Linking farmers with markets in Rural South Africa: Rural Development and poverty alleviation through supply chain management. Pretoria: National Agricultural Marketing Council (NAMC), Market and Economic Research Centre (MERC).

Naik, G., & Suresh, D. N. (2018). Challenges of creating sustainable agri-retail supply chains. *IIMB Management Review*, *30*(3), 270–282. doi:10.1016/j.iimb.2018.04.001

Negi, S., & Anand, N. (2015). Issues and challenges in the supply chain of fruits & vegetables sector in India: A review. *International Journal of Managing Value and Supply Chains*, *6*(2), 47–62. doi:10.5121/ijmvsc.2015.6205

Nugawela, S., & Sedera, D. (2020). *Analysis of Farm Management Information Systems: Opportunities and Pathways for Future Value*. PACIS.

O'Regan, G. (2010). *Introduction to software process improvement*. Springer Science & Business Media.

Paraforos, D. S., Vassiliadis, V., Kortenbruck, D., Stamkopoulos, K., Ziogas, V., Sapounas, A. A., & Griepentrog, H. W. (2017). Multi-level automation of farm management information systems. *Computers and Electronics in Agriculture*, *142*, 504–514. doi:10.1016/j.compag.2017.11.022

Paulk, M. C., Curtis, B., Chrissis, M. B., & Weber, C. V. (1993a). *Capability Maturity Modelfor Software, Version 1.1*. Tech ReportCMUSEI-93TR-24, Software Engineering institute, Carnegie Mellon University, Pittsburgh, PA.

Paulk, M. C., Weber, C. V., Garcia, S. M., Chrissis, M. B., & Bush, M. (1993b). *Key practices of the capability maturity model, Version 1.1. Software Engineering institute*. Carnegie Mellon University.

Ply, J. K., Moore, J. E., Williams, C. K., & Thatcher, J. B. (2012). IS employee attitudes and perceptions at varying levels of software process maturity. *Management Information Systems Quarterly*, *36*(2), 601–624. doi:10.2307/41703469

Poeppelbuss, J., Niehaves, B., Simons, A., & Becker, J. (2011). Maturity models in information systems research: Literature search and analysis. *Communications of the Association for Information Systems*, *29*(1), 27.

Poirier, C. C. (2004). How are we doing? A survey of supply chain progress. *Supply Chain Management Review*, *8*(8), 24-31.

Proença, D., & Borbinha, J. (2016). Maturity models for information systems-a state of the art. *Procedia Computer Science*, *100*, 1042–1049. doi:10.1016/j.procs.2016.09.279

Roekel, J. V., Kopicki, R., Broekmans, C. J., & Boselie, D. M. (2002). Building agri supply chains: issues and guidelines. *A guide to developing agricultural markets and agroenterprises*.

Routroy, S., & Behera, A. (2017). Agriculture supply chain. *Journal of Agribusiness in Developing and Emerging Economies*, *7*(3), 275–302. doi:10.1108/JADEE-06-2016-0039

Sedera, D., & Lokuge, S. (2017). The Role of Enterprise Systems in Innovation in the Contemporary Organization. In R. G. Galliers & M.-K. Stein (Eds.), *The Routledge Companion to Management Information Systems* (p. 608). The Routledge. doi:10.4324/9781315619361-21

Sedera, D., Lokuge, S., Grover, V., Sarker, S., & Sarker, S. (2016). Innovating with Enterprise Systems and Digital Platforms: A Contingent Resource-Based Theory View. *Information & Management*, *53*(3), 366–379.

Sedera, D., Rosemann, M., & Gable, G. (2001). Using Performance Measurement Models for Benefit Realization with Enterprise Systems - the Queensland Government Approach. In *European Conference on Information Systems*. Bled, Slovenia: AIS.

SEI. (2010). *Process Maturity Profile: CMMI® for Development SCAMPISM Class A Appraisal Results 2010 Mid-Year Update. Software Engineering Institute*. Carnegie Mellon University.

Shukla, M., & Jharkharia, S. (2013). Agri-fresh produce supply chain management: A state-of-the-art literature review. *International Journal of Operations & Production Management*, *33*(2), 114–158. doi:10.1108/01443571311295608

Sørensen, C. A. G., Kateris, D., & Bochtis, D. (2019). ICT Innovations and Smart Farming. In M. Salampasis & T. Bournaris (Eds.), *Information and Communication Technologies in Modern Agricultural Development. HAICTA 2017. Communications in Computer and Information Science* (Vol. 953). Springer.

Sørensen, C. G., Fountas, S., Nash, E., Pesonen, L., Bochtis, D., Pedersen, S. M., Basso, B., & Blackmore, S. B. (2010a). Conceptual model of a future farm management information system. *Computers and Electronics in Agriculture*, *72*(1), 37–47. doi:10.1016/j.compag.2010.02.003

Sørensen, C. G., Pesonen, L., Fountas, S., Suomi, P., Bochtis, D., Bildsøe, P., & Pedersen, S. M. (2010b). A user-centric approach for information modelling in arable farming. *Computers and Electronics in Agriculture*, *73*(1), 44–55. doi:10.1016/j.compag.2010.04.003

Sylvester, G. (2013). *Information and communication technologies for sustainable agriculture-indicators from Asia and the Pacific*. Rap Publication, (2013/14).

Szymczak, M. (Ed.). (2013). *Managing towards supply chain maturity: Business process outsourcing and offshoring*. Springer.

Tsolakis, N. K., Keramydas, C. A., Toka, A. K., Aidonis, D. A., & Iakovou, E. T. (2014). Agrifood supply chain management: A comprehensive hierarchical decision-making framework and a critical taxonomy. *Biosystems Engineering*, *120*, 47–64. doi:10.1016/j.biosystemseng.2013.10.014

Tummers, J., Kassahun, A., & Tekinerdogan, B. (2019). Obstacles and features of Farm Management Information Systems: A systematic literature review. *Computers and Electronics in Agriculture*, *157*, 189–204. doi:10.1016/j.compag.2018.12.044

Vanathi, R., & Swamynathan, R. (2013). A study on adoption of supply chain maturity model for enhancement of supply chain performance in industries. *Life Science Journal*, *10*(2), 1921–1925.

World Bank. (2017). ICT in agriculture: connecting smallholders to knowledge, networks, and institutions: e-sourcebook. International Bank for Reconstruction and Development, The World Bank.

ADDITIONAL READING

Becker, J., Knackstedt, R., & Pöppelbuß, J. (2009). Developing maturity models for IT management. *Business & Information Systems Engineering*, *1*(3), 213–222. doi:10.100712599-009-0044-5

Borodin, V., Bourtembourg, J., Hnaien, F., & Labadie, N. (2016). Handling uncertainty in agricultural supply chain management: A state of the art. *European Journal of Operational Research*, *254*(2), 348–359. doi:10.1016/j.ejor.2016.03.057

Chandrasekaran, N., & Raghuram, G. (2014). *Agribusiness supply chain management*. CRC Press. doi:10.1201/b16704

Collins, R., & Lim-Camacho, L. A. (2005). *Unlocking successful new rural industries: is supply chain management the key?: final report to the Rural Industries Research and Development Corporation. RIRDC Publication*. Rural Industries Research and Development Corporation.

Duncombe, R. (Ed.). (2018). *Digital Technologies for Agricultural and Rural Development in the Global South*. CABI. doi:10.1079/9781786393364.0000

Ghadiyali, T., Lad, K., & Dhodiya, J. (2018). Design and Development of the Agricultural Model: A Way to Connect Farmer Community to Agriculture Market for Betterment of Rural Development. In *ICT Based Innovations* (pp. 51–62). Springer. doi:10.1007/978-981-10-6602-3_6

Hofmann, P., & Reiner, G. (2006). Drivers for improving supply chain performance: An empirical study. *International Journal of Integrated Supply Management*, *2*(3), 214–230. doi:10.1504/IJISM.2006.008594

Kamble, S. S., Gunasekaran, A., & Gawankar, S. A. (2020). Achieving sustainable performance in a data-driven agriculture supply chain: A review for research and applications. *International Journal of Production Economics*, *219*, 179–194. doi:10.1016/j.ijpe.2019.05.022

Lockamy, A. III, & McCormack, K. (2004). The development of a supply chain management process maturity model using the concepts of business process orientation. *Supply Chain Management*, *9*(4), 272–278. doi:10.1108/13598540410550019

Routroy, S., & Behera, A. (2017). Agriculture supply chain. *Journal of Agribusiness in Developing and Emerging Economies*, *7*(3), 275–302. doi:10.1108/JADEE-06-2016-0039

KEY TERMS AND DEFINITIONS

Agriculture: Agriculture is the art and science of cultivating the soil, growing crops and raising livestock to provide food, wool, and other products.

Farm Management Information System: A management information system (MIS) for the agriculture sector used for collecting, processing, storing, and disseminating data in the form needed to carry out a farm's operations and functions.

Information System: An integrated set of hardware, software, infrastructure and trained personnel organized for collecting data, storing data, processing data, and distributing information.

Management Information System: An information system that aid in management decision-making by facilitating the coordination, control, analysis, and visualization of information in an organization.

Maturity Model: A maturity model is a tool that facilitates the assessment of the current status of a process and encourages figuring out what needs to be done in order to improve the performance and effectiveness to achieve the next level.

Supply Chain: A supply chain is a system of producers, consumers, activities, information, and resources aimed at distributing a specific product to the final buyer.

Supply Chain Management: The active management of the flow of goods and services from point of origin to point of consumption.

APPENDIX

Table 5. FMIS software

Conservis	Vinetel	Herd Manager	Digital Horses
Climate FieldView	Cropwin	Herdwatch	PigKnows
Agworld	FarmLife	EasyKeeper	Go360
AgVantage	Probityfarms	Pro Feeder	Modisar
smartfarm	AgCinect	Pro Med	John Deere
smartrisk	Farm Files Crops	Pro Mini	OMNIAFARM
mwarehouse	Farm Files Livestock	Pro Pasture	Agricolarum
smartsales	Farmplan Gatekeeper	Pro Harvest	AgWare
Harvest Profit	Farmplan Livestock	Ranch Manager	AGCOMMAND
Granular Insights	Farmplan Business & accounts	EZ-Ranch Cattle Software	AGCO CONNECT
Granular Business	ProSoftXP	Farmwizard Beef Manager	AUTO-GUIDE™ 3000
Croptracker Farm Management	AgExpert Field	Farmwizard Milk Manager	CLIMATE FIELDVIEW™
Croptracker Cultivation	Smart Fertilizer Management	Farmwizard Sheep Manager	TASK DOC
Croptracker Orchard Management	Tea Garden Software	Porcitec	FENDT LOGISTICS
Croptracker Harvest Quality Vision	Adviroguard	Ovitec	Blue skies accounting
Farmbrite	Pet Tiger	Cunitec	AgExpert Accounting
EasyFarm	FarmERP	Genet-Assist	Wheelman Pro
Agrivi	iCropTrak	Cow Sense Suite	Agricultural Data Systems
AgriXP Farm LogBook & Weather	FieldX	PigCHAMP	AgTerra
Cropolis	Phoenix	CattleMax	Argos
Plantator System	Farm Production Manager	CattleLink	Ag Leader SMS
Agrimap	Ekylibre	feedIT	Agfiniti
AFS Connect	ExactFarming	animalManagement	AGROCOM
Agroptima	SourceTrace - Datagreen	deliverIT	Crop Recording
FarmLogics OutGrowers	CropRecords	MeatSys	Fairport PAM
FarmLogics Value Chain	Soft.Farm	Integrafarm	Famous ERP
FarmLogics Campo	AgroScout	Today's Rancher	VitSmarter
FarmLogics ERP	Gtp.agri	DairyQuest	PanAgro
Farmer Core	Gtp.farm	GoatPRO	Greenlight Grower Management
Farmer Fit	Gtp.serra	HeiferPRO	MSSB Consulting
Farmer Pro	Gtp.eno	RationPRO	Pear Agri
AgVision Grain	Gtp.CE	DairyComp	Produce Magic
iAgri	Gtp.TS	FeedComp	PROGIS
Produce Inventory Control System	CSAware	ParlorComp	Basf
Land.db	Agricolus	DairyLive	Agri Open Data
LandMagic	agtoolsindustry	AgriTech Analytics	AGRIS
CitrusPro	Agroop	BoviSync	CenterPoint Accounting
Feed Supervisor	DecipherAg	Pig Production Management System	Chetu Farm Management
Hoof Supervisor	DecipherGo	AgroVision CropVision	FarmLogs
Truck Supervisor	PreAgri	AgroVision CowVision	PickTrace
FarmLogic	Regen Farmer	PigVision	AgriWebb
AgSquared	farmOS	AgroVision Poultry	GreenFingers
Agrinavia	CropTrails	Kingswood Herd	Agriculture ERP
Tend Smart Farm	PANTHEON Farming	HerdMASTER	Vistex
Agri Tracking Systems	Farm Matters	CowCalf Herd Management	Spokane
Farm Manager Pro	Maximix	Digital Swine	trecker.com

Chapter 12
From Lean Towards Frugal Product Development

Caglar Ucler
Ozyegin University, Turkey

Ravi Kumar Gupta
https://orcid.org/0000-0003-4419-8111
CAD Lab, Department of Mechanical Engineering SAMM, Manipal University Jaipur, India

ABSTRACT

Frugal innovation is considered as a disruptive growth strategy for businesses that focuses on the utilization of limited resources of rural areas. Similarly, lean management targets to develop new products in accordance with the customer requirements while managing the wastage. The purpose of this chapter is to highlight a pathway to frugal product development through lean management experiences. This is particularly of interest to developing territories and rural areas due to their innate characteristics. The analysis highlighted that innovation ideas have high diffusion rates if the product configuration is properly conducted. Despite the common objectives of lean and frugal development, this chapter investigates distinguishing features and conducts a comparison of both methodologies in order to provide specific guidance for companies that follow lean management to capture the benefits of frugal product development.

INTRODUCTION

The adoption of innovation ideas in developing or rural territories can be rapid with high diffusion rates. This is particularly common among large companies, but the main problem lies with the product configuration, which must be set correctly. Such large companies entering rural markets as a leader can deliver innovative products. However, when corporations are not responding to the local context and need, even the minimum viable products derived from mature markets cannot succeed in developing territories. Instead, successful new product development for developing markets must incorporate innate needs of the context to shape innovative solutions, which in turn respects local requirements and leaves

DOI: 10.4018/978-1-7998-4942-1.ch012

out all unnecessary elements within an economizing strategy. This process of reducing the complexities and cost of the production is called as frugal innovation and resulting products can even find their way back into developed territories in the form of reverse innovation.

Consequently, frugal innovation is desired by many firms but is considered as a new and developing concept. It is rather a disruptive growth strategy for more business and social value. Developing territories are promising a large potential because of the growth of their middle class (Tiwari et al., 2014). Similarly, rural areas which are getting more accessible with new technologies are promising a high potential as well. In both developing and developed areas, simple utilitarian products are preferred over heavily configured products and companies are trying to become leaders in developing innovative products or services (Schumpeter, 1950). Thus, there is a competition against time. In addition, there are many companies targeting these markets, which are mimicking each other's products and services. However, pervasive social inequalities are restraining the widespread diffusion of innovation in developing territories (Greenhalgh et al., 2008, p. 61).

When it comes to diffusion of innovative ideas, there are many factors affecting the diffusion, which are intrinsic to the country, the context of the product and the market. Hence, companies from developed territories setting their only goal to minimize the cost, are mostly failing. The product should be cost effective, but it also must be suitable and applicable for local needs. This requires interaction with the local market to transform the minimum viable requirements into the product, which is covered in the lean practices.

Since frugal product development is reducing the consumption of already limited resources of rural areas, there is an analogy to lean product development. Lean is a mature product centric methodology, where no waste is allowed. So, it can be applied to processes and products. Then, lean product development integrates all suppliers within standardization to inspect a wide spectrum of alternate solutions that variation is reduced. This requires the evaluation of all processes for waste. However, lean management is also missing some important aspects such as (i) the interaction is not good enough since the iteration with the customer is not emphasized, (ii) the utilization level remains low, and (iii) the product development cycles are simply too long.

As a result, experiences of proven method "Lean Product Development" along with the newer concept of "Frugal Product Development" can be utilized to ensure success in developing territories. A product is something that can be offered to a market for attention, acquisition, use or consumption that might satisfy a want or need. Creating a product covers the complete process of converting all market requirements then to streamline all efforts to form a viable product, which can then be brought to the target market. This is usually made iteratively to fulfill the requirements and satisfy targeted customers. Consequently, there are product development phases within one product as well as successive products with modifications or additions driving the product towards maturity. Only when the novel or diverse characteristics provide added value to the end user, the product becomes successful. These new or different characteristics may be technology driven or market driven. Product development may involve modifying an existing product or creating an entirely new product that meets a newly defined customer requirement.

The development of a product from the scratch is occasionally expensive and has less confidence as compared to existing products and takes more time. The development of a product by the modification of existing products and functionalities is less expensive and has more confidence that it can be easily introduced to the market. Hence, it is beneficial to introduce an existing successful product to a different markets. This is one of the innovation practices followed by many companies.

There are many challenges based on culture, geography, political systems, demographic, psychographic and behavioralists aspects, which become important in such rural markets. Furthermore, the technology can either be a constraint or generate further requirements in developing territories, when not leveraged adequately. Not all rural areas have the same technological readiness, and sometimes there is no acceptance of such advanced products. In such instances, frugal development is the best way to support the developers.

On top of this, the product development must be realized in a short time subject to cost reduction for competitive advantage. For such instances, lean product development is a common method utilized. It emphasizes less of everything, for example, less resources, less work-in-process, less time, and less cost, to produce a product. In fact, lean product development involves the identification and elimination of seven elements of waste as overproduction, waiting, transporting, over-processing, inventory, wasted motion, rework and defects that production on demand only can be utilized. This implies just-in-time (JIT), customer involvement, continuous simplification of processes for minimum stock and work-in-process, optimization of the usage of manufacturing resources (Burton, 2001; Pyzdek, 2003; Mynott, 2012).

Lean might deliver a cost optimized product for developed markets. However, shifting purchasing behaviors of distinct markets particularly in developing markets drive different expectations which lead to entirely different products at different times and markets. Again, frugal innovation is proposed as the correct business strategy to assist companies to rethink their existing product design and production procedures when facing ambitious encounters, especially in emerging markets. There, it is important to stress out that Frugal is defined as answering to severe resource limitations with products having extreme cost rewards compared to existing solutions.

The services and products achieved by 'Frugal Innovation' need not to be of inferior quality but fulfill only as many requirements as necessary and must be provided cheaply (Bhatti, 2012). This means that companies should develop products and services for emerging markets with acceptable quality or functions to fit customer's needs solely without any extras, and meanwhile the products and services should be low cost. This requires totally new products and implies that the lean versions of existing products simply will not work there. Therefore, traditional products and services with complex characteristics commonly see in matured markets should be restructured to become attractive according to frugal standards. Some products or services must also be established from the scratch in the local area to capture the needs and features of the regional market (Zeschky et al., 2011).

All in all, it is fair to say that lean and frugal have one common formula: they both look at reduction of unnecessary items and waste. However, frugal product development focuses on the right combination of frugal criteria to satisfy needs whereas lean product development emphasizes providing low cost products and services.

Despite the common objectives of lean and frugal, there are distinguishing features as well. In this book chapter, we investigate these two product development methods, to understand whether these two product development strategies are contrasting each other or supporting each other. Their differences are also explained in this chapter along with their historical importance so that Frugal Innovation and Lean manufacturing principles are analyzed and presented with examples from literature. A pathway to frugal is enlightened herewith and discussed how a frugal product can be achieved from lean experiences. Consequently, first the method is explained briefly, followed by the explanation of the elements of lean product development. Then, Frugal Product Development is explained. After that, a comparison is made in the results section, which are complemented with recommendations to effectively incorporate frugal into lean organizations.

BACKGROUND

This book chapter necessitated from the need to succeed in rural and/ or developing territories, which requires the understanding of the frugal product development. In the section below, we introduce both lean product development and frugal product development and then we compare them both. While we compare the results, the results obtained by the ProRegio (2015) which focused on frugal product development are applied here. Further, we conducted a literature review to understand both lean product development and frugal product development. When conducting the literature review, we conducted the keyword serach. The keywords such as lean, frugal, was utilized for the literature review. Frugal Product Development was reviewed by using the key words frugal and product development or frugal innovation and product development consolidating in the frugal attributes. Then, the knowledge from the ProRegio (2015) Project was used to explain to distinguish frugal innovation from standard innovation. After that, the tacit experience of the authors was converted explicitly to a comparison of lean and frugal to support the implementation of frugal by lean adopters.

LEAN PRODUCT DEVELOPMENT

Lean Manufacturing has been evolved from the efforts of Taichii Ohno at Toyota Motor Company resulting in the Toyota Manufacturing System (TMS). It is challenging all activities and processes continuously (Ohno, 1988), where all processes without added value shall be eliminated with the aid of specifications, early customer integration, simplicity by the involvement at all organizational levels (Spear and Bowen, 1999). In other words, lean is focusing on workflow, customer value and the elimination of waste aiming at the pull of value adding processes by the customer (Sanders et al., 2016). Then, the continuous pull production throughout the participating supply chain results in JIT production, which is particularly utilized by continuous flow with step time reduction, statistical process control, and employee involvement (Shah and Ward, 2007).

Lean applications can be seen widely in both, manufacturing and service deployment (Sanders et al., 2016). When the principles of lean are applied to product development, it is designated as Lean Product Development. This embodies the whole new product development process: lean product development covers ideation, assessment of ideas, concept development and evaluation and product detailing until the delivery of the product to the manufacturing (Rauch et al., 2016). Targets of lean product development can be defined either from the outcome-oriented perspective as to achieve a better quality and functionality of products (Mynott, 2012), or from the process-oriented perspective to reduce waste and to increase added value in new product development (Liker and Morgan, 2006). Lee and Chang (2010) proposed a lean design process with seven steps as (i) product definition with the integration of the Voice of Customer (VOC), (ii) product line optimization respecting expecting resources and planning a roadmap, (iii) target cost determination with value engineering, (iv) translation of requirements into specifications, (v) design at system level, (vi) design at detail level with design of experiments, and (vii) production preparation process (3P) incorporating JIT.

Consequently, lean product development involves continuous improvement, standardization, visual management, flow and pull principle, zero-failure principle, leadership and people, frontloading in an integrated product development (IPD) environment to avoid errors of sequential design (Pessôa and Trabasso, 2017). There, Womack and Jones (2003) describe that the enclosure of all stake holders in lean product development enables a consequent value stream leading towards perfection. This leads towards the Elements of lean product development as seen in Table 1.

Table 1. Elements of lean product development

Element	Description
Culture	Excellence is supported and the improvement becomes persistent. Technology is facilitated for the adaptation of new processes. "Simple visual communication" is used.
Knowledge management	All possibilities are compared with standardized data. Organizational learning is enabled with standard methods and tools. Distinct solutions are understood and applied by all engineers. Detailed checklists and standards have to be used to assess product performance. Suppliers are a contributing part of the product development process. Continuous improvement and therefore a continuous learning are essential.
Organizational structure	All managers have to be able to do the technical engineering job by themselves. Leading roles have to mentor primarily. Promotions and rewards are based on competence and capabilities. "value-centered systems" are key for development processes. Both, functional as well cross-functional capabilities are key.
Process	"key integration events" are facilitated to pull work. All milestones tracked precisely. Set based development with various alternatives is used, where only performers are continued. The process of the development is to utilize levels. Standardization is applied everywhere possible.
Tools and technology	The tools are not solely enabling lean; it is solely about how these tools are used.

Source: (Womack and Jones, 2003; Cleveland, 2006)

FRUGAL PRODUCT DEVELOPMENT

Frugal implies a new way of conceptualizing. Such as in design thinking, it embodies a new approach for product development. Frugal innovation is proposed as a business strategy to assist companies rebuild their existing product design and production processes, when facing competitive encounters. A product is considered as frugal if only frugal attributes are addressed in a precise proportion as required. The frugal attributes are Functional, Robust, User-friendly, Growing, Affordable & Local. Consequently, a frugal product addresses all these attributes and is unique for a specific region or targeted market, cut specifically for local requirements.

In general, the term "frugal innovation" refers to a process under which the complexities of an innovation occur to reduce the cost of goods and provide products with lower prices in a high-volume market. This idea is known as "juggad" in India, "zizhuchuangxin" in China, "gambiarra" in Brazil and "jua kali" in Kenya. The English concept can be DIY (do-it-yourself) or "make do and mend". It is essentially finding a means to an easy and quick solution to a problem.

As in lean, frugal innovation or frugal engineering is about reduction of the complexity and thus the cost of products. This also covers the way of how they are being produced. Generally, frugal is understood as the elimination of the non-essential features from the products to sell them in developing countries, i.e. to succeed in low to mid-income market segments. This is partially correct. While the lean configuration of the streamlined requirements is essential, the development of totally new approaches for the product are required, which mostly ends up with totally new designs rather than downsized existing products.

There, frugal services and products need not to be of lower quality, but they must be provided cheaply (Bhatti, 2012). Designing products for such countries or market segments does call for an increased durability and reliance on unconventional distribution channels. Globalization and rising incomes in developing countries do drive the eagerness of large firms for frugal innovation. Targeting the so-called "overlooked consumers", firms from industrialized countries hope to attain a high volume and consequent profit despite "razor-thin" profit margins.

Consequently, frugal products are low-end to mid-end products or services sold largely in developing marketplaces, which occasionally may find their way to developed marketplaces in the form of reverse innovation (Govindarajan and Ramamurti, 2011; Zeschky et al., 2014). Frugal products can be defined based on the frugal attributes which are found in almost all the industries (Berger, 2013). The definition of these attributes is given in Table 2.

Table 2. Frugal attributes

Attributes	Description
Functional	Product performance is mid to low, focused on key features.
Robust	Products are robust and maintenance friendly.
User-friendly	Products are simple and easy-to-use, also concerning first-time usage.
Growing	Markets are growing and large production volumes enable economies of scale.
Affordable	Products are low-priced and offer good "value for money".
Local	Products are mainly sold in emerging marketplaces and tailored to local necessities.

Source: (Berger, 2013)

First, the product has to focus solely on key features, which is the functionality aspect. Then, all frugal products have to be robust and user-friendly. Since the emerging markets require high output numbers, the frugal products must be designed for large production volumes that they can support the growth of the market. All these must be realized in an affordable way, resulting in local cut products tailored for developing or rural markets.

Thus, the developed product to say "frugal product" must address FRUGAL attributes namely Functional, Robust, User-friendly, Growing, affordable and Local. These attributes can be respected within variable acceptable ranges for a targeted market. There, it is challenging to identify the optimal values of these attributes that they are simultaneously contributing to the product. Successful development of such a product with a sweet spot provides a lot of opportunities to attract innovation.

The need for frugal innovation comes from three basic constraints of the emerging markets, namely market affordability, resource constraints or scarcity and institutional voids or complexities (Figure 1). First, the ability of the population to afford the products is key in frugal that market affordability constraints have largely been reflected targeting the wide population at the bottom of the pyramid (Prahalad, 2012). Market affordability detects the target cost as an independent design parameter that is required to be achieved during the development of a product. Basically, it is for the understanding of customer affordability. Achieving affordable product to emerging markets especially in rural areas is challenging and needs the redesign or the rethinking of the features and their organization in the considered product. Affordable convenience is an important factor influencing low-income consumer demand for a variety of basic products and products with basic characteristics or features. The additional features and improved quality may be added to the product based on the market affordability. Market affordability is a dynamic aspect, and it is affected the by the purchasing power of customers. That is the reason, product features and quality are varied across different markets and geographical regions. It is interesting that technologies and capabilities developed for the bottom may have the opportunity to 'move up in the pyramid' and challenge prevailing capabilities too often which are developed first for the top-of-the-pyramid markets (London and Hart, 2004). Then, the fundamental economic problem of having apparently unrestricted human wants in a world of limited resources embodies the second constraint (Figure 1). It states that society does not have enough productive resources to meet all human wants and needs. Constraints of resources during the product/ service development are either based on the inability to procure or on the control of the workforce (Schumpeter, 1934; Shane and Venkataraman, 2000). Resource constraint product development is to develop new products that use minimal resources and are affordable to a larger market (Sharma and Iyer, 2012). Conventional approaches for product development do not consider the type and extent of resources used in the product development. Rather, frugal product development is driven by resource scarcity and tends to use the least possible resources in developed products that find a suitable fit with the targeted market. This can give rise to various ideas to redevelop existing products and also to promote the use of indigenous tools and techniques. Then another constraint is embodied by institutional voids or complexities (Figure 1), which are defined "as the lack of institutional facilities, norms, and regulations needed for a well-functioning economy" (North, 1990). Especially bottom of the pyramid markets is characterized by institutional voids with regard to market-facilitating institutions or pre-conditions for markets. There is an incomplete separation of formal politics, informal politics, and economic activity affecting the realization as well the consumption of products and services.

Figure 1. Frugal Innovation Constraints: Understanding the Context and Challenges
Source: (Own derivation)

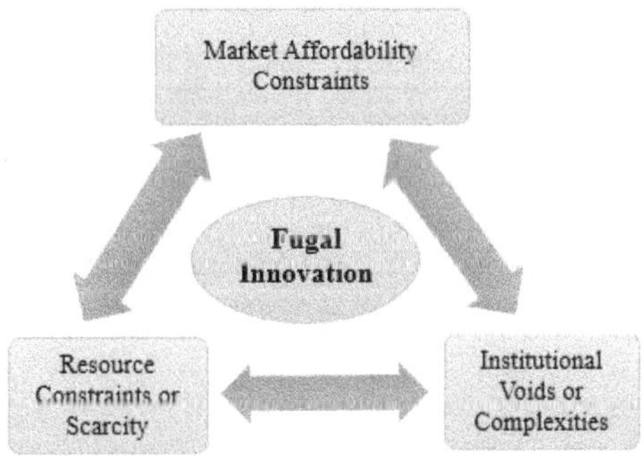

Despite these challenges, and perhaps also because of them, local and international entrepreneurs and firms in emerging markets are producing innovations, which are resolving local needs with local context, and at the same time profiting to the extent that they can expand to neighboring developing nations and even beyond socioeconomic borders to developed markets (Khanna and Palepu, 2006; Khanna, 2008).

According to Bound and Thornton (2012) and ProRegio (2015), the main reasons for frugal products and services are

- Deleveraging and lackluster growth in developed economies (Barclay, 2014),
- Environmental constraints.
- Needs of rapidly ageing societies (Mukerjee, 2012).
- Large growing market size of developing and emerging economies (Forbes, 2011).
- Push of new technologies enabling dramatic cost reductions.

Consequently, the development of frugal products is inevitable and plays an important aspect for western companies. Delivering a totally new market the growth potential of the sales of frugal products is significantly larger than products for mature markets. Frugal product development is not simply an interrogation of technological simplification of existing products subject to be promoted at lower prices. In-order to attain long-term achievement, companies must consider the above six key product attributes (see Table 2) and also to align the full value chain to precise market necessities. There, the main success factors are a complete knowledge of marketplaces and customer requirements, which shall be converted to innovation. However, frugal innovation is different from "standard" innovation in that a comparison is given in Table 3.

Table 3. Frugal innovation vs. Standard innovation

Factors	Frugal Innovation	"Standard" Innovation
Environment	Institutional voids and resource limitations	High quality institutions and slack resources
Cost	Low-cost input and low-cost output	High-cost input and high-cost output
Diffusion Approach *(in what way does the innovation spread through a specific population or social system)*	Bottom-up approach	Top-down approach
Users *(end-users of the product)*	Late majority, laggards: Low income, limited education	Innovators, early adopters: High incomes, high education
Sources *(type of companies, change in perception, demographic changes etc. that lead to innovation)*	Entrepreneurs, family business groups, social movements	Entrepreneurs, large organizations
Process *(the execution of a new or significantly enhanced product development)*	Open, distributed	Closed
Characteristics	Mainly architectural	Mainly component

Source: (Bhatti, 2012)

Consequently, the criteria for frugal innovation can be summarized as considerable cost reduction, attention on core functionalities and optimized performance level (Weyrauch and Herstatt, 2006). To achieve these criteria, the ten Core Competencies of Frugal Innovation were established by the Frugal Innovation Lab at Santa Clara University as: (Basu et al., 2013)

- *Ruggedization: designed for harsh physical environments (e.g., heat, moisture, pests);*
- *Lightweight: portable for varying transport possibilities;*

- *Mobile Enabled Solutions: connectivity anytime, anywhere;*
- *Human Centric Design: easy-to-use, intuitive designs that require little to no prior knowledge or training to utilize;*
- *Simplification: minimalist features and functional requirements;*
- *New Distribution Models: non-conventional channels & access;*
- *Adaptation: leveraging existing products, inputs & services;*
- *Use of Local Resources: sourcing without importing equipment and materials, utilize indigenous tools and material;*
- *Green Technologies: powered by renewable resources;*
- *Affordability: low initial and operation costs.*

The competencies are the basis for making powerful contributions to greater global sustainability, including greater inclusiveness and social equity. Their role in evaluating new technologies and processes for consumers in emerging economies will enable them to become more and more important and influential in the global market landscape over the next 5-10 years (Basu et al., 2013).

By reducing the need to resources, frugal innovation supports growth and becomes eventually disruptive. This also increases the social value beside the growth of the business and the consumption of capital and time is reduced. Consequently, Western companies follow the examples in emerging markets such as India and China that they tend to adopt frugal innovation in developed economies (Radjou and Prabhu, 2014; Gupta et al., 2017). Today there are even examples of Frugal innovation applied to aircraft production using modular product development approach (Belkadi et al., 2017) where modular product architectures with frugal attributes on the modules and parameters considered (Gupta et al., 2017).

Many people can associate frugal innovation with only inexpensive products with a low technology. However, it is far more than this. There are distinct features of frugal innovation, which are worth being explored in detail. First of all, frugal innovation is about making better products, the sole target is not price advantage. Then, services can be frugal as well. Most importantly, frugal is based on the re-modelling rather than the reduction of features. At last but not the least, low cost does not necessarily imply low technology, frugal innovation can utilize or facilitate cutting edge technology as well (Bound and Thornton, 2012).

Frugal innovation is for the high end and mid end of both, the developed markets as well emerging markets as shown in Figure 2.

Figure 2. Market segments with frugal innovation connection - Source: (ProRegio, 2015)

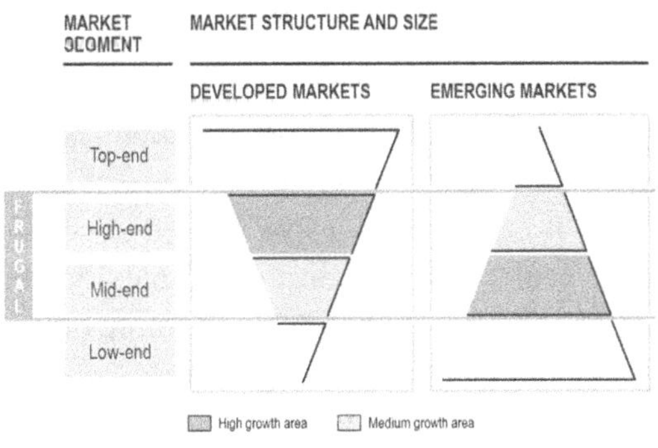

The most common example in the literature regarding frugal innovation is the Tata Nano car (Figure 3 and Table 4) (Gandikota, 2014). Remarkable efforts in the development of the Nano car are reducing the insignificant features keeping in mind the general population and local conditions in India and then redesigning in modules to meet the exact requirements. There is a lot of emphasis on using indigenous tools and techniques for manufacturing. Then, the Indian Mangalyaan spacecraft for Mars was developed 3 times faster. This included spending that was 10 times less than what NASA had designed, through the reuse of existing components ("The Economic Times", 2014). It reached the Martian orbit in September 2014. The Mars Orbiter Mission (MOM), also referred as Mangalyaan, costs only $74 million, about $25 million less than the Hollywood film Gravity, making it the most economically successful interplanetary mission in history. India is the first country to have successfully attempted its first mission to Mars ("The Economic Times", 2014). Mangalyaan is an excellent example of frugal innovation as a technological demonstration. Other notable examples of frugal innovation are ChotuKool Fridge, Foldscope, MittiCool Refrigerator, Nokia 1100, Solar light bulb, Sorghum beer, Haier's Mini Magical Child washing machine, Siemens' Fetal Heart Monitor (FHM) device, GE's $800 portable electrocardiogram (ECG) machine so as to include frugal attributes as per the requirements of the targeted market.

GE's health care laboratory in Bangalore (India) built a hand-held ECG machine called the Mach 400. Multiple buttons on traditional ECGs was reduced to four buttons. The heavy printer was replaced by smaller gadget used in portable ticket machine. The Mach 400 is small enough to fit in a small backpack. It can be operated on battery or the main power supply.

Figure 3. Tata Nano as example of frugal innovation
Source: ("The Economic Times", 2014)

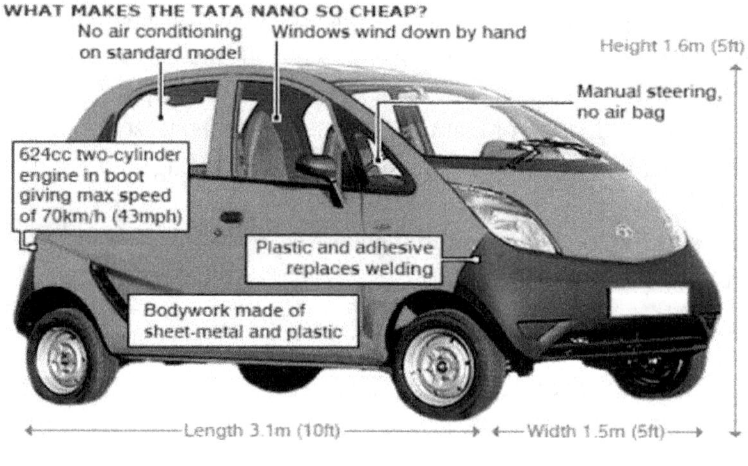

Frugal innovation is a "clever" way for product development, which is challenging the traditional approach of western companies thinking that higher amounts of resources during the development necessarily achieve better results. It is not necessarily required to convert lots of natural resources into expensive products with a high level of sophistication and complexity. This is mainly based on two simple reasons. First, the American as well European consumers are more budget oriented that they do not want over engineered products which are costly. Then, natural resources are getting scarcer that products inevitably are getting expensive (Radjou and Prabhu, 2014). This is the point where frugal meets lean.

Table 4. Mangalyaan spacecraft and Tata Nano as examples of frugal innovation

Frugal Attributes	Tata Nano	Mangalyaan Spacecraft
Functional	Small Wheels and Mounting; Three nuts per wheel; No airbag in standard version; Two-cylinder engine giving max-speed of 70 km/h;	Mangalyaan was equipped with 5 instruments, bringing down its payload mass to 15 kg;
Robust	-	Indigenous materials and innovative technology prioritize over imports, keeping design simple;
User-friendly	Provides only one wing mirror; Windows wind down by hand; No air-conditioning on standard model;	-
Growing	Possible to add some of the required additional features and related modules (4 models are available in market)	-
Affordable	Initial market launch price, Rs. 100,000 (approx. $1,400);	Cost: $74 million only. The most economical successful interplanetary mission in history. Same basic structure and systems as the lunar orbiter, saving time and money. Instead of launching straight into the Trans-Martian trajectory, it was initially launched into Earth's orbit, after that it used gravity and its own propulsion systems to arrive at Mars' orbit. This ended the launch fuel and cost efficiently.
Local	Developed by an Indian company and sold in the India market (product of a considerable network of relationships (Tiwari and Herstatt, 2012))	Designed and developed by the Indian Space Research Organization (ISRO).

Source: (Own derivation)

RESULTS AND RECOMMENDATIONS

Historically, the lack of resources, the difficulties concerning the affordability of the population and the institutional voids were the main drivers for triggering the frugal innovation. It was simply that lower income classes within the developed countries had the need of being able to access cheaper but equally functional solutions. As an answer frugal development emerged, which is focusing mainly on the essential requirements. Therefore, the frugal product can be defined, in general, as the kernel of a technical solution without any extra, i.e. non-necessary, features or functionalities in the product/ service. This is totally in-line with lean.

Lean is moreover a philosophy, which is traditionally guiding the manufacturing management, whereas frugal is concerned with the product itself. Hence inventory, load leveling, and standardization are not included in frugal. Consequently, there are no frugal competence centers with distinct processes and tools and technologies distinguishing from other facilities.

However, frugal is open to lean. A general comparison of lean and frugal product development is summarized especially for practitioners in Table 5. In summary, frugal attributes are considered as per the requirements whereas lean attributes are considered to minimize wastage in material and time. When they are practiced together, there is a high potential to succeed in developing rural markets.

Table 5. Comparison of lean and frugal product development

	Lean	Frugal (as per the requirements)
Functional - Individualization/ Customization	Not considered	Yes
Robust	Yes	Yes
User-friendly	Not considered	Yes
Growing - Expanding Product Range	Not considered	Yes
Growing – Expanding Product Market to Different Regions	Not considered	Yes
Growing – Expanding Product Market to Wide Range of Customers	Not considered	Yes
Affordable	Not considered	Yes
Local - Culture	Not considered	Yes
Local - Geography	Not considered	Yes
Local - Political System	Not considered	Yes
Local - Demographic	Not considered	Yes
Local - Psychographic	Not considered	Yes
Local- Behavioralists	Not considered	Yes
Customer value focus	Yes	Yes
Waste elimination	Yes	Not considered
Only required features	Yes	Yes
Inventory	Yes	Not considered
Load leveling	Yes	Not considered
JIT	Yes	Yes
Process Focus & Reengineering	Yes	Yes
Strategic planning	Not considered	Yes
Continuous improvement	Yes	Yes
Competence center	Yes	Not considered
Standardization	Yes	Not considered
All stakeholders	Yes	Yes

Source: (Own derivation)

In detail, frugal as well the lean development both are delivering a robust product focusing the customer value i.e. the VOC to achieve only the minimum set of features. Thus, in both cases the production has to be set respectively, where JIT and process focus, and reengineering are important. Consequently, continuous improvement can be achieved by respecting all stakeholders' perspectives. However, some production related constraints and planning is not respected by frugal, while it mainly focuses on the product. Under the bottom line, lean innovation advocates to create a lot less waste, whereas frugal innovation advocates a lot of fewer extra features or no extra features. This is how the companies have to develop their products cut for rural or developing markets. Frugal product development is a way to explore and build customer's experiences around the product (Gupta et al., 2018). As a customer is using the product, customer's experiences and preferences are instantiated which simplifies the product and supports lean as well. Then, this can be used in changing the product and functionalities as the way the customer uses it and according to the inputs of stakeholders from the supply chain. Hence, the knowledge management of lean is in fact supported by frugal product development. This is important in understanding how the customer really is behaving with the product with the use context in the given environment that it can be reflected in the product development. Consequently, the academic contribution is the crystallization of the fact that lean and frugal support each other.

Moreover, the 4th industrial revolution talks about the use of different sensors, connectivity, artificial intelligent techniques, machine learning, machine to machine communication and so on to develop smart factories and smart management of resources (Pisching et al., 2015). This is especially a trend topic of the research and the frugal adaptation requires a high level of interaction. Industry 4.0 aims to produce a highly flexible model for developing personalized digital products and services in the production phase to enable interaction between people, products and devices in real time (Albert, 2015). Therefore, it is important to connect real customers and use the environment in the product development stages. This is common for both the lean and frugal product development, for which strategies are needed for integrating customers along with their use context and environment into the product development virtually and remotely, which is further setting future research directions.

CONCLUSION

Many companies are attracted by the growth of the emerging markets. Those companies willing to succeed in rural or developing territories must differentiate their products, address the needs of the local communities, without any additional costs. Furthermore, economizing strategies must be utilized only to lower product prices, but not to generate totally new price classes. In order to minimize the complexities in their product development and relate to the local needs, companies could possibly transform their existing lean capabilities into frugal. In such instances, frugal product development is considered as the key process of simplifying the complexity and dramatically reduce the cost of goods or services and ease their production.

Whereas, the lean product development integrates all suppliers within standardization to inspect a wide spectrum of alternate solutions so that variation is reduced, frugal enables new perspectives. While lean requires the evaluation of all processes for alternative solutions and reduction of waste, frugal gives totally new products which best suit in a lean environment. Consequently, aspects such as cost reduction by integrating suppliers and manufacturing systems to reduce waste and processing time are totally in line with frugal. Therefore, lean product development can be evaluated with the frugal aspects and integrating customers evaluations lead to frugal product respecting the lean product development or say lean-frugal product. This is the major managerial impact of this chapter. Frugal attributes are considered as per the requirements or evaluated whereas lean attributes are considered to minimize wastage in material and time. Therefore, lean and frugal product development support each other.

The academic contribution of this book chapter is on the interaction and transformation of lean and frugal product development. As stated before, a combined product development approach using lean and frugal innovations and optimization along with global product development parameters is needed to deliver the right product, at the right time, for the right location (targeted market/region), in the right proportions (features). The remote interaction with the product user, i.e. the customer, is an area for further research as well.

REFERENCES

Albert, M. (2015). *Seven things to know about the Internet of Things (IoT) and Industry 4.0.* Modern Machine Shop.

Barclay, C. (2014). Using frugal innovations to support cybercrime legislations in small developing states: Introducing the cyber-legislation development and implementation process model (CyberLeg-DPM). *Information Technology for Development, 20*(2), 165–195. doi:10.1080/02681102.2013.841630

Basu, R. R., Banerjee, P. M., & Sweeny, E. G. (2013). Frugal Innovation - Core Competencies to address Global Sustainability. *Journal of Management for Global Sustainability, 2*(2), 63–82. doi:10.13185/JM2013.01204

Belkadi, F., Gupta, R. K., Natalizio, S., & Bernard, A. (2017). Modular Architectures Management with PLM for the Adaptation of Frugal Products to Regional Markets. *14th IFIP international conference on product lifecycle management.*

Berger, R. (2013). *Frugal Products: Study Results.* Roland Berger Strategy Consultants. http://www.rolandberger.com/media/pdf/Roland_Berger_Frugal_products_20130212.pdf

Bhatti, Y.A. (2012). *Challenges of frugal innovation and role of business models.* Presentation material. Santa Clara University, Engineering for developing world class.

Bound, K., & Thornton, I. (2012). *Our Frugal Future: Lessons from India's Innovation system.* Nesta.

Burton, T. T. (2001). *Is this a Six Sigma, lean, or Kaizen Project?* Breakthrough.

Cleveland, J. (2006). Toyota's other system -this one for product development. *Automotive Design & Production, 118*(2), 18–22.

Forbes. (2011). *Why Invest in Emerging Markets?* Author.

Gandikota, V. (2014). *The Curious Case of TATA Nano car. The Nordic Frugal Innovation Society.* TNFIS.

Govindarajan, V., & Ramamurti, R. (2011). Reverse innovation, emerging markets, and global strategy. *Global Strategy Journal, 1*(3-4), 191–205. doi:10.1002/gsj.23

Greenhalgh, T., Robert, G., Bate, P., Macfarlane, F., & Kyriakidou, O. (2008). *Diffusion of innovations in health service organisations: a systematic literature review.* John Wiley & Sons.

Gupta, R. K., Belkadi, F., & Bernard, A. (2017). Evaluation and management of customer feedback to include market dynamics into product development: Satisfaction Importance Evaluation (SIE) model. *21st International Conference on Engineering Design.*

Gupta, R. K., Ucler, C., & Bernard, A. (2018). Extension of the Virtual Customer Inspection for Distant Collaboration in NPD. *2018 IEEE International Conference on Engineering, Technology and Innovation*, 1–7. 10.1109/ICE.2018.8436333

Khanna, T. (2008). *Billions of Entrepreneurs — How China and India Are Reshaping Their Futures-And Yours*. Harvard Business School.

Khanna, T., & Palepu, K. G. (2006). Emerging Giants: Building World-Class Companies in Developing Countries. *Harvard Business Review*, *84*(10), 60–72.

Lee, M. C., & Chang, T. (2010). Developing a lean design for Six Sigma through supply chain methodology. *International Journal of Productivity and Quality Management*, *6*(4), 407–434. doi:10.1504/IJPQM.2010.035891

Liker, J. K., & Morgan, J. M. (2006). The Toyota Way in Services: The Case of Lean Product Development. *The Academy of Management Perspectives*, *20*(2), 5–20. doi:10.5465/amp.2006.20591002

London, T., & Hart, S. L. (2004). Reinventing Strategies for Emerging Markets: Beyond the Transnational Model. *Journal of International Business Studies*, *35*(5), 350–370. doi:10.1057/palgrave.jibs.8400099

Mukerjee, K. (2012). Frugal innovation: the key to penetrating emerging markets. *Ivey Business Journal*, *76*(4).

Mynott, C. (2012). Lean Product Development: A Manager's Guide. London, UK: The Institution of Engineering and Technology (IET).

North, D. (1990). *Institutions, Institutional Change and Economic Performance*. Cambridge University Press. doi:10.1017/CBO9780511808678

Ohno, T. (1988). *Toyota production system: beyond large-scale production*. Productivity Press.

Pessôa, M., & Trabasso, L. G. (2017). *The Lean Product Design and Development Journey: A Practical View*. Springer International Publishing. doi:10.1007/978-3-319-46792-4

Pisching, M. A., Diolin, F. J., Filho, J. S., & Miyagi, P. E. (2015). Service composition in the cloud-based manufacturing focused on the Industry 4.0. *IFIP International Federation for Information Processing*, *2015*, 65–72.

Prahalad, C. K. (2012). Bottom of the pyramid as a source of breakthrough innovations. *Journal of Product Innovation Management*, *29*(1), 6–12. doi:10.1111/j.1540-5885.2011.00874.x

ProRegio. (2015). Customer-driven design of product-services and production networks to adapt to regional market requirements: Deliverable D1.4: Market requirements regarding frugal innovation for products and product-services. Horizon2020 under GA-Nr. 636966. Patras, Greece: Laboratory for Manufacturing Systems and Automation (LMS).

Pyzdek, T. (2003). *The Six Sigma Handbook: A Complete Guide for Green Belts, Black Belts and Managers at All Levels*. McGraw-Hill.

Radjou, N., & Prabhu, J. (2014). 4 CEOs Who Are Making Frugal Innovation Work. *Harvard Business Review*, *28*(4), 1–6.

Rapoza, K. (2011). *What Makes Emerging Markets Great Investments?* http://www.forbes.com/pictures/eglg45gdjd/why-invest-in-emerging-markets-2/

Rauch, E., Dallasega, P., & Matt, D. T. (2016). The way from Lean Product Development (LPD) to Smart Product Development (SPD). *Procedia CIRP*, *50*, 26–31. doi:10.1016/j.procir.2016.05.081

Sanders, A., Elangeswaran, C., & Wulfsberg, J. (2016). Industry 4.0 implies lean manufacturing: Research activities in Industry 4.0 function as enablers for lean manufacturing. *Journal of Industrial Engineering Management*, *9*(3), 811–833. doi:10.3926/jiem.1940

Schumpeter, J. (1950). *Capitalism, Socialism and Democracy*. Harper and Row.

Schumpeter, J. A. (1934). *The Theory of Economic Development*. Harvard University.

Shah, R., & Ward, P. T. (2007). Defining and developing measures of lean production. *Journal of Operations Management*, *25*(4), 785–805. doi:10.1016/j.jom.2007.01.019

Shane, S., & Venkataraman, S. (2000). The Promise of Entrepreneurship as A Field of Study. *Academy of Management Review*, *25*(1), 217–226.

Sharma, A., & Iyer, G. R. (2012). Resource-constrained product development: Implications for green marketing and green supply chains. *Industrial Marketing Management*, *41*(4), 599–608. doi:10.1016/j.indmarman.2012.04.007

Spear, S., & Bowen, H. K. (1999). Decoding the DNA of the Toyota production system. *Harvard Business Review*, *77*(5), 96–106.

The Economic Times. (2014). *Mars Mission: India creates history as Mangalyaan successfully enters Mars orbit in first attempt.* http://economictimes.indiatimes.com/news/science/mars-mission-india-creates-history-as-mangalyaan-successfully-enters-mars-orbit-in-first-attempt/articleshow/43299562.cms

Tiwari, R., & Herstatt, C. (2012). Frugal Innovation: A Global Networks' Perspective. Die Unternehmung (Swiss Journal of Business Research and Practice), 66(3), 245-274.

Weyrauch, T., & Herstatt, C. (2017). What is frugal innovation? Three defining criteria. *Journal of Frugal Innovation*, *2*(1), 1. doi:10.118640669-016-0005-y

Womack, J. P., & Jones, D. T. (2003). *Lean thinking*. Free Press.

Zeschky, M., Widenmayer, B., & Gassmann, O. (2011). Frugal innovation in emerging markets. *Research Technology Management*, *54*(4), 38–45. doi:10.5437/08956308X5404007

Zeschky, M. B., Winterhalter, S., & Gassmann, O. (2014). From cost to frugal and reverse innovation: Mapping the field and implications for global competitiveness. *Research Technology Management*, *57*(4), 20–27.

ADDITIONAL READING

Agarwal, N., & Brem, A. (2012, June). Frugal and reverse innovation-Literature overview and case study insights from a German MNC in India and China. In 2012 18th International ICE Conference on Engineering, Technology and Innovation (pp. 1-11). IEEE. 10.1109/ICE.2012.6297683

Belkadi, F., Vlachou, E., Gupta, R. K., Zogopoulos, V., Kaya, M., Bernard, A., ... Bayrak, I. K. (2018). Modularity as a support for frugal product and supplier network co-definition under regional market constraints: A mirroring hypothesis application. *International Journal of Production Research*, *56*(20), 6575–6590.

Bessant, J., & Tidd, J. (2007). *Innovation and entrepreneurship*. John Wiley & Sons.

Bhatti, Y. A. (2012). What is frugal, what is innovation? Towards a theory of frugal innovation. Towards a Theory of Frugal Innovation (February 1, 2012).

Buergin, J., Belkadi, F., Hupays, C., Gupta, R. K., Bitte, F., Lanza, G., & Bernard, A. (2018). A modular-based approach for Just-In-Time Specification of customer orders in the aircraft manufacturing industry. *CIRP Journal of Manufacturing Science and Technology*, *21*, 61–74.

Cooper, R. (2017). Supply chain development for the lean enterprise: interorganizational cost management. Routledge.

Cusumano, M. A., Nobeoka, K., & Kentaro, N. (1998). *Thinking beyond lean: how multi-project management is transforming product development at Toyota and other companies*. Simon and Schuster.

Gupta, R. K., Belkadi, F., Buergy, C., Bitte, F., Da Cunha, C., Buergin, J., ... Bernard, A. (2018). Gathering, evaluating and managing customer feedback during aircraft production. *Computers & Industrial Engineering*, *115*, 559–572.

Hossain, M. (2018). Frugal innovation: A review and research agenda. *Journal of Cleaner Production*, *182*, 926–936. doi:10.1016/j.jclepro.2018.02.091

Mourtzis, D., Vlachou, E., Zogopoulos, V., Gupta, R. K., Belkadi, F., Debbache, & A., Bernard, A. (2018). Customer feedback gathering and management tools for product-service system design. Procedia CIRP, 67, 577-582.

Rao, B. C. (2013). How disruptive is frugal? *Technology in Society*, *35*(1), 65–73. doi:10.1016/j.techsoc.2013.03.003

Schipper, T., & Swets, M. (2012). *Innovative lean development: how to create, implement and maintain a learning culture using fast learning cycles*. CRC Press. doi:10.1201/b10254

KEY TERMS AND DEFINITIONS

Behavioralists: Explaining events by observing and analyzing the behavior of individuals.

Emerging: (Here) rising, developing.

Frugal: In general, economical; here, functional, robust, user-friendly, growing, affordable, and local.

Innovation: Either a new idea converted to a product or service which is actively marketed (object innovation), or the change of the way of doing things (subject innovation).

JIT: Just in time. A strategy to reduce the inventory streamlining the supply chain with the production schedule.

Lean: In general, healthy animal without fat; here, without any unnecessary waste.

New Product Development: Complete process of bringing a new product to the market involving ideation in the fuzzy front end, the development of this idea, further design of the product respecting the production constraints, the implementation and commercialization.

Psychographic: Qualitative methodology of studying customers based on psychological characteristics and traits such as values, desires, goals, interests, and lifestyle choices.

Rural: Outside of the urban area, that is, countryside.

Chapter 13
An Advancement to the Grameen Bank Model

Khushboo Deepakkumar Bhatt
Charotar University of Science and Technology, India

Manali Pinank Vin
Symbiosis International University, India

ABSTRACT

This chapter proposes the concept of the Grameen Bank initiated by Muhammad Yunus as a prototype for promoting rural entrepreneurship within the under-developed rural community governed by the digital portal. There are many factors that were considered important for the shift from microfinance to financial inclusion when proposing the model. One of the key factors is what is happening with data in general and our ability through digitization to have a more comprehensive understanding of the needs of the poor community. The Grameen model is considered as an advanced empathetic financial service that is appropriate for the needy poor women located in rural locations. By analyzing prior literature on Grameen model, in this chapter, an advancement to the existing Grameen model is proposed.

INTRODUCTION

Grameen Bank, a Bangladeshi bank which was established by financial analyst Muhammad Yunus as a way of improving the lives of rural population and providing little advances to poor people. The Grameen (Bengali: "Rural") model, contrived by Yunus in 1976. This model depends on gatherings of five planned borrowers who meet consistently with Grameen Bank field administrators. Ordinarily, two of the five imminent borrowers are conceded advances. If after a trial time frame, the initial two borrowers meet the terms of reimbursement, at that point credits are conceded to the rest of the gathering individuals. Grameen bank was transformed into a free bank in 1983; headquartered in Dhaka, Bangladesh, it has in excess of 2,200 branches in Bangladesh. The Grameen model symbolize a proficient method for helping the poor and rural population by giving them chances to support themselves. It was identified that of 97 percent of Grameen's advance beneficiaries have been ladies.

DOI: 10.4018/978-1-7998-4942-1.ch013

Bangladesh is one of the poorest and overpopulated nations in the world, and population of women in that nation are among the poorest of poor people. In the late 1970s, a man played out a supernatural incident there. With a couple of credits out of his pocket in 1976, Professor Yunus demonstrated to himself that even the most distressed could haul themselves out of horrendous destitution. By planting a vegetable garden, exchanging dairy animals, or opening a little shop, these ladies could possibly make an advantage, feed their family and pay back their advance with intrigue. He then took this to indicate Rome, where the International Fund for Agricultural Development (IFAD) had recently been established, with the understanding of neediness moderation in the poorest nations. With his interest, he impacted IFAD that an advance to the Grameen Bank, as he called his business undertaking, would be a decent resource and particularly supportive to decrease destitution in Bangladesh.

Microcredit projects in Bangladesh are sorted out by non-government organizations (NGOs), state-claimed business banks, private business banks, Grameen Bank, and concentrated projects of a few services of Bangladesh government. Microcredit has created a new extension in Bangladesh in both rural and urban areas. In terms of rural development, the role of micro-credit is very important and in rural Bangladesh, the effect of micro-credit is huge. The government has proposed rural development administration under which, Micro-credit operations, research-oriented organizations, and close monitoring on expected Micro-credit outcomes and interprets the report are conducted. The government policy on Micro-credit also covers the stakeholder's involvement by providing maps and flowcharts. The Bangladesh Rural Development Board (BRDB) is also under the Ministry of Local Government, Rural Development and Cooperatives. This is one of the biggest administration institutions set up by the Government of Bangladesh which is specifically engaged with local advancement and poverty mitigation exercises in Bangladesh. The poverty alleviation project is also a government-funded program.

This project aims to shape casual gatherings, give ability for preparing for independent work, collection of claim capital through thrift stores, the supply of small-scale credit for money earning exercises, bring issues to light, re-establish the certainty of poor people, human asset advancement, up-keeping condition and guaranteeing the manageability. Grameen Bank has turned around regular financial practice by expelling the requirement for guarantee and made a financial framework dependent on shared trust, responsibility, cooperation and innovativeness. Grameen Bank gives credit to the least fortunate of the poor in Bangladesh, with no guarantee. At Grameen Bank, credit is a financially savvy weapon to battle neediness and it fills in as an impetus in the overall improvement of financial states of the poor who have been kept outside the financial circle on the ground. Professor Muhammad Yunus, the founder of "Grameen Bank" contemplated that if money related assets can be made accessible to the needy with terms and conditions that are suitable and sensible. "The microfinance sector is not only helping the poor in rural areas to generate some income, but it also promotes entrepreneurship and help them to become entrepreneurs, said the Nobel peace prize winner and founder of Grameen Bank of Bangladesh Muhammad Yunus.

In an interview with CNBC-TV18, Yunus, who is known as a pioneer of the microcredit concept, said the microfinance sector in India would double the size in the next five years and become a significant economic entity. "Rural areas always provided the labour to the city. I don't think, after micro credit, that would be the scenario. The scenario will be that they would be dealing with their own economy, building their own economy as entrepreneurs. I think microcredit has transformed the whole idea of what the urban and rural relationship would be." According to facts and figures uploaded on the official website, "As of, November 2019, it has 9.60 million individuals, 97 percent of whom are women. With 2,568 branches, Grameen Bank offers types of assistance in 81,678 towns, covering in excess of 93 percent of the all-out towns in Bangladesh."

The aim of this chapter is to showcase a different approach or an advancement of Grameen Bank Model i.e., the E-Grameen Model which can perform all the business-related processes in support to smoothen the operational process of the traditional Grameen Bank Approach. Moreover, as a part of extension of the model, to indicate, track and analyse the overall performance and activities under the E-Grameen model, a Data Dashboard system will be suggested. In this chapter, the authors have followed the descriptive methodology to write the context of the scenario. Authors have collected and analysed past articles, books, publications regarding the Grameen Bank and provided insights on the Grameen model. In this book chapter, the authors propose an advanced Management Information System (MIS) based model which can trace the data of all the stakeholders and can help to provide one common dashboard for all.

MICRO FINANCE AND CREDIT LENDING MODEL

This section provides an overview to the microfinance and the credit lending models used in India as well as across the world. Moreover, the philosophy related to Grameen Bank is been discussed.

Microfinance institutions are the oldest financial institutions in the world, but with time they have adapted to the changes, and have started using various credit lending models. Microfinance services are provided with different methods. A total of 14 models are existing. which include associations, bank guarantees, community banking, cooperatives, credit unions, Grameen, group, individual, intermediaries, NGOs, peer pressure, ROSCAs, small business, and village banking models. The models are loosely related with each other, and most good and sustainable microfinance institutions have features of two or more models in their activities.

The Microfinance lending models vary in the legal forms, in the channels and methods of delivery, in the governance structure, in the approach to sustainability and in the approach to microfinance where the funds are sourced from, and how the money is governed.

The following Credit Lending Models are being used by the Microfinance Institutions:

- **Associations:** This is where the object community forms an 'association' through which different microfinance (and other) activities are initiated. Such activities may include savings. Associations or groups can be composed of youth, or women; they can form around political/religious/cultural issues; can create support structures for microenterprises and other work-based issues. In some countries, an 'association' can be a legal body that has certain improvement such as a collection of fees, insurance, tax breaks and other protective measures. Distinction is made between associations, community groups, people's organizations, etc. on one hand (which are mass, community based) and NGOs, etc. which are external organizations.
- **Bank Guarantees:** As the name suggests, a bank guarantee is used to access a loan from a commercial bank. This guarantee may be arranged externally (through a donor/donation, government agency etc.) or internally (using member savings). Loans obtained may be given directly to an individual, or they may be given to a self-formed group. Bank Guarantee is a form of capital guarantee scheme. Guaranteed funds may be used for various purposes, including loan recovery and insurance claims. Several international and UN organizations have been creating international guarantee funds that banks and NGOs can subscribe to, to on lend or start microcredit program.

- **Community Banking**: The Community Banking model essentially treats the entire community together unit and establishes semi-formal or formal institutions through which microfinance is dispensed. Such institutions are usually formed by extensive help from NGOs and other organizations, who also train the community members in various financial activities of the community bank. These institutions may have savings components and other income-generating projects included in their structure. In many cases, community banks also are a part of larger community development program which use finance as an inducement for action.
- **Cooperatives:** A co-operative is an autonomous association of persons united voluntarily to satisfy their common economic, social, and cultural needs and aspirations through a jointly owned and democratically controlled enterprise. Some cooperatives include member-financing and savings activities in their mandate.
- **Credit Unions:** A depository financial institution may be a unique member-driven, self-help financial organization. it's organized by and comprised of members of a specific group or organization, who comply with save their money together and to form loans to every other at reasonable rates of interest. The members are people of some common bond: working for an equivalent employer; belonging to an equivalent church, union, social fraternity, etc.; or living/working within the same community. A credit union's membership is hospitable all who belong to the group, no matter race, religion, colour or creed. A depository financial institution may be a democratic, not-for-profit financial cooperative. Each is owned and governed by its members, with members having a choose the election of directors and committee representatives.
- **Grameen:** The Grameen model emerged from the poor-focused grassroots institution, Grameen Bank, started by Prof. Mohammed Yunus in Bangladesh. It essentially adopts the subsequent methodology: A bank unit is about up with a Field Manager and variety of bank workers, covering a neighbourhood of about 15 to 22 villages. The manager and workers start by visiting villages to familiarize themselves with the local milieu during which they're going to be operating and identify prospective clientele, also as explain the aim, functions, and mode of operation of the bank to the local population. Groups of 5 prospective borrowers are formed; within the first stage, only two of them are eligible for, and receive, a loan. The group is observed for a month to ascertain if the members are conforming to rules of the bank. as long as the primary two borrowers repay the principal plus interest over a period of fifty weeks do other members of the group become eligible themselves for a loan. due to these restrictions, there's substantial group pressure to stay individual records clear. during this sense, collective responsibility of the group is collateral on the loan.
- **Group:** The Group Model's basic philosophy lies within the incontrovertible fact that shortcomings and weaknesses at the individual level are overcome by the collective responsibility and security afforded by the formation of a gaggle of such individuals. The collective coming together of individual members is employed for variety of purposes: educating and awareness building, negotiation power, peer pressure etc.
- **Individual:** this is often a simple credit lending model where micro loans are given on to the borrower. It doesn't include the formation of groups or generating peer pressures to make sure repayment. The individual model is, in many cases, a neighbourhood of a bigger 'credit plus program, where other socio-economic services like skill development, education, and other outreach services are provided.
- **Intermediary:** Intermediary model of credit lending position may be a 'go-between' organization between the lenders and borrowers. The intermediary plays a critical role of generating credit

awareness and education among the borrowers (including, in some cases, starting savings program. These activities are geared towards raising the 'credit worthiness' of the borrowers to A level sufficient enough to form them attractive to the lenders. The links developed by the intermediaries could cover funding, program links, training and education, and research. Such activities can happen at various levels from international and national to regional, local and individual levels. Intermediaries might be individual lenders, NGOs, microenterprise/microcredit program, and commercial banks (for government financed program). Lenders might be government agencies, commercial banks, international donors, etc.

- **Non-Governmental Organizations**: NGOs have emerged as a key player within the field of microcredit. they need played the role of intermediary in various dimensions. NGOs are active in starting and participating in microcredit program. This includes creating awareness of the importance of microcredit within the community, also as various national and international donor agencies. they need developed resources and tools for communities and microcredit organizations to watch progress and identify good practices. they need also created opportunities to find out about the principles and practice of microcredit. This includes publications, workshops and seminars, and educational program.
- **Peer Pressure:** Peer pressure uses moral and other linkages between borrowers and project participants to make sure participation and repayment in microcredit program. Peers might be other members during a borrower's group (where, unless the initial borrowers during a group repay, the opposite members don't receive loans. Hence pressure is placed on the initial members to repay); community leaders (usually identified, nurtured and trained by external NGOs); NGOs themselves and their field officers; banks etc. The 'pressure' applied are often within the sort of frequent visits to the defaulter, community meetings where they're identified and requested to comply etc.
- **Rotating Savings and Credit Associations**: Rotating Savings and Credit Associations (ROSCAs) are essentially a gaggle of people who close and make regular cyclical contributions to a standard fund, which is then given as a payment to at least one member in each cycle. for instance, a gaggle of 12 persons may contribute Rs. 100 (US$33) per month for 12 months. The Rs. 1,200 collected monthly is given to at least one member. Thus, a member will 'lend' money to other members through his regular monthly contributions. After having received the payment amount when it's his turn (i.e. 'borrow' from the group), he then pays back the quantity in regular/further monthly contributions. Deciding who receives the payment is completed by consensus, by lottery, by bidding or other agreed methods.
- **Small Business**: The prevailing vision of the 'informal sector' is one among survival, low productivity and really little value added. But this has been changing, as more and more importance is placed on small and medium enterprises (SMEs) – for generating employment, for increasing income and providing services which are lacking. Policies have generally focused on direct interventions within the sort of supporting systems like training, technical advice, management principles etc.; and indirect interventions within the sort of an enabling policy and market environment. A key component that's always incorporated as a kind of common denominator has been finance, specifically microcredit – in several forms and for various uses. Microcredit has been provided to SMEs directly, or as a neighborhood of a bigger enterprise development program, alongside other inputs.
- **Village Banking:** Village banks are community-based credit and savings associations. They typically contain 25 to 50 low-income individuals who are seeking to enhance their lives through self-

employment activities. Initial loan capital for the village bank may come from an external source, but the members themselves run the bank: they choose their members, elect their own officers, establish their own by-laws, distribute loans to individuals, collect payments and savings. Their loans are backed, not by goods or property, but by moral collateral: the promise that the group stands behind each individual loan.

Though these models have their own model specific strengths and weaknesses, they have demonstrated to provide financial services to the unorganized sector with effective outreach. Majority of the microfinance institutions offer and provide credit on a solidarity-group lending basis without collateral. There is also a range of other methodologies that MFIs follow. Some MFIs start with one methodology and later move or diversify to another methodology so that they do not exclude certain socio-economic categories of clients. So, it becomes important to have a basic understanding of methodologies and activity of Credit Lending Models.

GRAMEEN BANK

The philosophy of the Grameen Bank is simple: that the widespread availability of credit can solve many issues in undeveloped areas and that individuals in the undeveloped areas often have the best ideas and the most powerful means to develop them. The objective of the Grameen-style programs is to get local people to run businesses and keep them going after the aid agencies have left. Grameen Bank proverb is: "If you give a man a fish you feed him for a day. If you teach him to fish, you feed him for a lifetime." Another objective of Grameen-style program is to improve the status of women and help them start businesses, so they delay having children and don't contribute to overpopulation.

Yunas told Atlantic Monthly, "You look at the tiniest village, and the tiniest person in that village, a very capable person, a very intelligent person. You only have to create the proper environment to support these people so that they can change their lives." Yunas developed three main criteria for borrowers: 1) the loans had to be repaid on time: 2) only the poorest, landless villagers were eligible; and 3) most of the money would be lent to women."

One reason for the bank's success is its system of self-regulation, everyone who takes out a loan becomes a member of a five-person borrowing group, a 40-member center and attend meetings every week. Groups share responsibility for the loan repayments and defaults. If one member of the group fails to pay the entire group loses their loan. This means that members are careful to pick new members who, without fail, will pay back their loans. If all five members repay their loan quickly, they are guaranteed access to credit for the rest of their lives.

THE BENEFITS OF GRAMEEN BANK MODEL

- **Directed to poor:** This model focuses on the poor dependent on specific criteria, for example, size of the land holding, state of the house, and salary of the family units. Its objective includes the alleviation of poverty of the rural poor through credit and social intermediation.

- **Entryway step administration:** Bank goes to customers rather than customers to bank right now. All the budgetary administrations are conveyed through ordinary gatherings in the network. This has made the way for all the poor for monetary administrations.
- **Security less:** Loans are by and large dispensed without insurance. Customers who can't give insurance or satisfy the few reports required by different banks can get advances from Grameen. It accepts that the poor are bankable, so it rather centers around the income and customer's reimbursement history, not on the physical guarantee, for example, land and building.
- **Rehashed and expanded volume of credits:** The advance payment technique of Grameen is in cycle. Each cycle contains 1 to 1.5 years' timeframe. The credit cycle is rehashed and the volume of the advance increments in each cycle. This makes workable for the customers to reimburse the advance in various portions.
- **Great reimbursement:** Repayment rate above 95% in Grameen. It is a result of the philosophy and solid control in the framework.
- **Concentrate on ladies:** Grameen customers are only ladies. This has added to ladies strengthening and is a comprehensive framework.
- **Quickly developing:** Grameen has been discovered quickest for outreach development. This is because of strategy (simple access to advance, simple reimbursement plan, entryway step administration, and so forth.) and solid monetary order received by the framework.
- **Overseen by banking proficient:** as opposed to a helpful and CBO model, Grameen is overseen by banking experts. Grameen has a banking society which guarantees supportability and practicality of the program.
- **Effect on underestimated gatherings:** The Grameen program has a positive effect on the lives of poor people. Grameen has expanded mindfulness on wellbeing and instruction among the network individuals. It has been discovered to be strong on improving the living state of the underestimated gatherings. The entrance and command over assets and support of ladies on dynamic has improved through the Grameen program.

STAKEHOLDERS

The stakeholders of Grameen Bank are described below:

Figure 1. Stakeholders of grameen bank model
Source: Millennium Bank Report

Customers

Retail Bankers: Customers use the Bank's services. The Bank's stability depends greatly on their preferences. Almost every family who opens the account would enjoy the Bank's services. Bank in turn accumulates over half of the population's savings and acts as a lender in the economy when needed.

Corporate: Enterprises and businesses that contribute significantly to the national Gross Domestic Product have accounts opened with the Bank.

Local Communities and the Society

The bank should ensure active engagement with society (local communities). Its activity is inextricably linked to the social and environmental spheres in which it operates, this results in goodwill and trust from the local communities towards the bank and helps the bank prosper.

Employees

Bank will play a pivotal role in generating employment in the rural areas. The officers are the Bank's core asset, they interact with customers and form the Bank's reputation, support the development of its infrastructure, and ensure the implementation of the Bank's strategy and business missions. This also can result in upliftment of the rural areas towards a developed nation.

Shareholders and investors

The Bank is a public company with its securities traded all on local, regional, nation and in future maybe even the foreign markets. Shareholders' influence is determined by the applicable laws, and the Bank's corporate governance practice. The Bank strives to increase its market capitalization and is interested in transparent and open interaction with its shareholders.

Government

The Bank is a major taxpayer and participates in the implementation of essential state projects and programs, both federal and regional. The Government, represented by its authorities and companies where it has a participating interest, is an important partner and a customer of the Bank.

MICRO FINANCE OPEN SOURCE (MIFOS) MODEL

Mifos X is a hearty center financial stage that is conveyed by means of the cloud or facilitated on premise. Mifos X is fueled by the Apache Fineract stage and gives a suite of web and versatile applications that can be designed and reach out to address the issues.

Features of MIFOS

Figure 2. The Micro Finance Open Source (MIFOS) Model

- **Portfolio Management**: Advancement and Agility are basic in monetary administrations. The concentrated item setup motor backings a tremendous scope of credit, store, and offer based items for gatherings, people or organizations permitting to improve on the fly and quickly react to client requests.

- **Customer Management**: Owning the relationship with the client is basic. The client account is at the focal point of Mifos X permitting to exceptionally recognize, know, and survey the danger of the client and join any kind of money related assistance or gather any sort of information for them.
- **Business Management**: Productivity and Transparency are essential to prosperity. Mifos X gives a hearty bookkeeping bundle that completely coordinates with the portfolio and can go about as an independent framework for the whole broad record. Pentaho joining gives endeavor level business knowledge and the simplicity of making altered reports.
- **Portable Delivery and Enablement**: The eventual fate of budgetary consideration is advanced and prepared to assist with going versatile. Mifos X gives a rich arrangement of staff and clients confronting versatile applications for field-based and branchless tasks and self-administration cooperation's from clients. The hearty self-administration APIs and web snares structure permits you to go branchless and quickly coordinate with portable cash and computerized monetary administrations.

THE INFORMATION AND COMMUNICATION TECHNOLOGY (ICT) CHALLENGES OF SMALL MICRO FINANCE INSTITUTIONS (MFIS)

Most software for MFIs is highly customized and developed by and for large organizations, often with significant financial support from donors, and not with the needs of smaller rural organizations in mind. In addition, most solutions are proprietary (or built on top of proprietary technology), which means their owners charge licensing fees for use of the software and control who can make changes to it. This lack of competition can lead to high costs for training and customization. Cost is one factor that prevents access to the technology especially for smaller and remote organizations that cannot afford the required capital investment or pay to modify existing packages to suit their needs.

Moreover, the list of obstacles, specific to these small organizations goes on:

- Lack of skilled staff to support the Management Information System.
- Lack of local IT support and services environment for after-sale service, training, and support
- Lack of budget to procure and update/upgrade technology
- Technology needs are too diverse to warrant the usefulness of an off the-shelf package and existing solutions require costly modifications or are too sophisticated.
- High need for localization (language of interface, iconography, etc.)

In the section to follow, we will elaborate why we see Free and Open Source Software as a solution that has the potential of tackling the problems and challenges just illustrated.

A HOLISTIC ECOSYSTEM FOR MICROFINANCE

Successful Free/Open Source Software (FOSS) projects are community-based collaborative efforts in which participants benefit from the aggregate contributions more than they would from individual proprietary investments. In the case of microfinance, a FOSS ecosystem would enable the development of a core software platform that could be customized to fit the needs of large as well as small MFIs. Such an ecosystem will comprise the following elements: Microfinance institutions - Large MFIs have the resources to invest in development of a core software solution. They would benefit from pooling of resources and sharing of expertise and are able to attract donor funding for such technology development projects. Since access to the core solution is free of charge, and modifications are equally shared with the community, small MFIs would get access to a software solution that addresses their needs at low cost. In addition, they would equally benefit from sharing expertise with other small MFIs.

FRAMEWORK FOR IMPACT SCRUTINY

Other than the advancement and increment in outreach that can all the more effectively be accomplished by the utilization of Free an Open-Source Software (FOSS) and ICTs by and large, we want to cause to notice the difficulties that accompany it; one must not overlook that the complete access to money related administrations isn't really all that is required particularly by poor people. Issues, for example, making, additional administrations and market linkages are vital. The achievement of the usage of FOSS arrangements can't absolutely be estimated by quantities of individuals came to. Often, appraisals of new innovations or execution of programming focus on the start of the chain, which means specifically on changes in the MFI and its tasks, and not adequately on the advantages it brings to the clients. Concentrate lies ordinarily on MFIs adaptability in activities and announcing, manageability.

These evaluations have a place with the way of thinking regularly alluded to as the "middle person" school (Hulme, 2000) and related with the Ohio State University School's investigations of provincial accounts. While all these are significant perspectives that will most assuredly be influenced, we see the significance in surveying who has the advantages and how, and thus follow the expected recipient way of thinking, getting as far down the effect chain as would be prudent (Hulme, 2000). One has to know how the poor arrangement with the choices given to them and whether Microfinance helped them to improve their way of life. In what tails we spread out how the impact of a program on clients came to can be evaluated at moderately minimal effort. Given that an intermittence happens in time-measurement, which is plainly characterized, the proposed system is the before-after structure, additionally called interfered with time-arrangement plan. These strategies can be enhanced with an extra information assortment exertion, including control gatherings, yet henceforth likewise greater expenses.

The principle situation in evaluating the impact of any intercession is straightforward: one for the most part looks at two individuals, one getting the mediation and the other not. On the off chance that the two individuals are the very same, other than their intercession status, at that point the distinction between their results of intrigue, (for example, pay) can be produced as the results of the mediation. On the off chance that the people vary, contrasts in result can't be simply credited to the intercession. Also, obviously, it is difficult to have the very same individuals and henceforth surveying the effect requires making a deduction about the results that would have been watched for program members had they not taken an interest frequently alluded to as the potential-result way to deal with causality.

The control reactions (results) originate from the period before the mediation, the treated reactions originate from the time after. From this develops the 'before-after (BA) estimator, which can pleasantly be applied in the current setting. All together for this strategy to be pertinent, longitudinal information on results estimated when a program for an individual who takes an interest should be accessible. In the wake of clarifying the strategy we will really expound on which factors are required and oftentimes as of now exists and consequently no extra exertion must be placed into information assortment.

AN ADVANCED GRAMEEN BANK MODEL

Customers in Unbanked Rural Centers have no access to banking in their vicinity and had to travel to nearby towns for their banking needs. The launch strategies for URCs were executed keeping in mind the customer needs and their financial requirements for a better tomorrow. The concept of doorstep account opening using Aadhar authentication on a hand-held device was a new experience for rural residents. This seamless service of Grameen Bank can be developed without any paperwork hassles and was welcomed and appreciated by the residents.

The Bank can get involved in educating and guiding URC customers on how to manage their savings better and enabling them to become financially empowered. The Bank may offer customized affordable and accessible financial services to Small and Marginal Farmers and other rural customers enabling them to improve their income levels and savings. Differentiated marketing tools through Farmers Clubs assisted by NABARD will be used to improve visibility of branches and business. Customized products will have repayment aligned to cash flows and dairy loans as a component shall be offered to dairy farmers to maintain it on a monthly basis. The Bank should focus on products such as Dairy loans, Composite Agriculture Loans, Kisan Credit Card and two-wheeler loans in rural areas. The Grameen Bank should be positioned as a preferred financial services provider with these customized products and services and TAT (Turn Around Time) driven convenient branches in availing loans and depositing disposable income.

Digital marketing & PR has played an integral role to highlight the bank's presence on the web and in national media. On the digital front, Google location mapping should be developed for all branches to ensure each bank branch has its presence on digital and to enable seamless user navigation. Sarvajal (Sarvajal leases its water purification technology/equipment to a local entrepreneur who becomes the franchise owner) has established real-time online monitoring of the drinking water infrastructure which enables viability of distributed remote operations, quality control and streamlined maintenance services. Sarvajal leases its water purification technology/equipment kind of Water Automated Teller Machine (ATM) to a local entrepreneur who becomes the franchise owner. They pay a fee that represents a proportion of the cost of the filtration unit, they also provide training, marketing material, sustained services & maintenance for each franchisee. Owners take up responsibility for distribution ATM cards to customers also they give rechargeable facilities to customers, they provide clean water to the underserved consumer at an affordable price of 1 Rs. /litre, they are working on 3 points approaching affordability, accessibility & purity. The Grameen Bank should take up initiatives for upliftment of rural Population with the use of latest ICT.

The Grameen Bank can work closely with low-income customer segments often referred to as micro-entrepreneurs and economically active poor. However, there was always a need to become a specialized bank in order to provide a full range of banking products & services to low income households.

Technology and banking channels can be the core drivers of customer service at Grameen Bank. Robust portfolio quality is an outcome of sound risk mitigation tools imbibed in the field processes and credit policies which are reviewed and revised periodically.

Figure 3. The Advanced Grameen Bank model

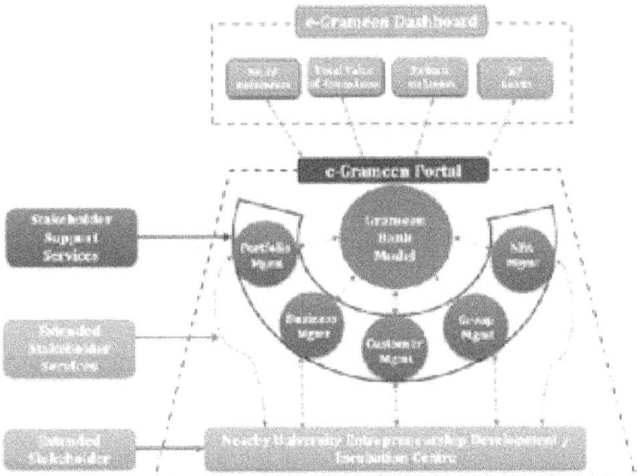

e-Grameen performs all business-related processes in support to smoothen the operational processes of the Grameen Bank. The e- Grameen portal will monitor the Core and Extended stakeholders as shown in the given above model. The portal will make it possible to track the performance of each activity of the stakeholders.

As shown in figure, the existing model of Grameen Bank is having stakeholder support services like Portfolio Management, Business Management, Customer Management, Group Management and Non-Performing Asset (NPA) Management. For effective monitoring of the performance of the micro loan, the extended stakeholder will be engaged in the process. In this model, we have suggested nearby *University Entrepreneurship Development / Incubation Centre* to enrich and monitor the stakeholder support services of Grameen Bank.

The extended model also suggests the e-Grameen Dashboard to have a quick view of the current performance of the micro loan. The dashboard indicates the performance of overall activities in categorization of the four major numbers of borrowers, Total value of Gross Loans, Return on Loan and non-performing Loans.

CONCLUSION

The subject of ICTs in microfinance is critical, on the grounds that its key objective is the expansion of advantages to needy, rural individuals. While this objective is important to many developing nations, particularly developed nations are in promising positions. India for instance has incredible involvement in fruitful microfinance ventures yet are feeling the squeeze to broaden the advantages and improve living states of its numerous provincial poor. What's more these nations have generally all around created ICT areas and programming advancement limits, and this nearby accessibility of abilities presents a chance to make the moderate and versatile programming arrangement that is required by the little rustic MFIs in creating nations.

The public sector can play a significant role in supporting the dispersion of microfinance administrations to poor people, by supporting/financing community-oriented programming advancement for MFIs, encouraging information arranges between MFIs, bringing issues to light of the benefits of a synergistic methodology that is based on FOSS. Simultaneously, this is a period of chance for the private segment, both huge MFIs just as little neighborhood associations and specialist organizations who could bolster and keep up the IT foundation of little remote associations. The authors have focused on the significance of giving moderate and fitting innovation to build effort of all-encompassing microfinance administrations to the exceptionally poor. Simultaneously authors are careful with regards to the quantifiable effect of such intercession. It stays an urgent research need to discover progressively about the people that are being come to and the effect on their living conditions, to abstain from likening straightforward increment in quantities of customers with genuine effect on employment. This must be accomplished through deliberately structured checking and progressing assessment endeavors.

To begin with, it is critical to know 'who' is being come to and consider the Trade-off between expanding effort and arriving at poor people. The authors of the study contend that this exchange is significant and that it is the motivation behind why a various arrangement of organizations is required: huge foundations that can serve poor people and not all that unadulterated for a huge scope and little and nearby establishments that focus on the extremely poor. Strategy creators need to consider the extraordinary help that these littler establishments may require since their activities are battling to become self-practical. So as to build the quantity of such little associations, governments should bring down boundaries of section right now. This should be possible through altering the administrative system or offering help and administrations. The authors of the study contend that the improvement of a FOSS Management Information System (MIS) for these littler associations would encourage their scaling up and permit them to actualize stricter assessment and detailing guidelines, which thus would empower access to contributor subsidizing. What's more, the government ought to energize the coordinated effort between MFIs of various sizes and at various phases of improvement. Giving a typical innovation stage and norms for trade of information would incredibly encourage this procedure.

In order to track the records of the numbers of borrowers, Total value of Gross Loans, Return on Loan and non-performing Loans, the Artificial Intelligence and Machine Learning Based Model can be developed and utilized. In particular, advanced Dashboard system having with a unique identification code for all the access holder of the Grameen Bank Model would add value. This unique ID could showcase the status of funds provided to the account holder as well as can trace the data related to the usage of the funds.

REFERENCES

Arsenault, N. (2003). *Answering the Top 5 Myths about Selecting Software for Microfinance Institutions.* White Paper.

Asian Development Bank. (2000). *The Role of central Banks in Microfinance in Asia and the Pacific.* Asian Development Bank.

Cascio, J. (2006). *Open Source Microcredit, Revisited.* The Tech Bloom Collaborative and Emergent Technologies, posted at February 10, 2006)2:44pm, accessed August 8,2006 21:06pm at http://www.worldchanging.com/archives/004095.html

CGAP. (2005). *Funding Microfinance Technology.* CGAP Donor Brief No. 23.

Coleman, B. E. (2002). *Microfinance in Northeast Thailand: Who benefits and how much?* ERD Working Paper Series No.9.

Dailey-Harris, J. (2005). *State of the microcredit Summit Campaign Report 2005.* The Microcredit Summit Campaign, Washington, DC.

Foster, D. (2005). *What C.E.O.s Need To Know About Software Selection.* MicroSave Briefing Note # 43.

Ghosh, R. A. (2003). Licence fees and GDP per capita: The case for open source in developing countries. *First Monday, 8*(12). http://www.firstmonday.org/issues/issue8 12/ghosh/index.html

Ghosh, R. A. (2005). *Free/Libre/Open Source Softwarefor developing countries: skills, employment and costs.* Paper presented at USUARIA 2005, 2nd National Congress on Software Libre, Argentina.

Heckman, J. J., & LaLonde, R. J. (1999). The Economics and Econometrics of Active Labor Market Programs, Prepared for the Handbook of Labor Economics, Volume III, Orley Ashenfelter and David Card, editors. doi:10.1016/S1573-4463(99)03012-6

Hulme, D. (2000). *Is microcredit Good for Poor People?* A note on the dark side of MicroFinance. Accessible from http: microsave.org.

Ketley, R. & Duminy, B. (2003). *Meeting the Challenge The Impact of Changing Technology on Micro-Finance Institutions (MFIs).* MicroSave Briefing Note # 21.

Lee, M.-J. (2005). *Micro-Econometrics for Policy, Program and Treatment Effects.* Oxford University Press Inc. doi:10.1093/0199267693.001.0001

Mainhart, A. (1999). *Management Information System for Microfinance: An Evaluation Framework.* U.S. Agency for International Development, Bureau for Global Programs, Center for Economic Growth and Agricultural Development, Office of Microenterprise Development, through funding to the Microenterprise Best Practices (MBP) Project, contract number PCE-C-00-96-90004-00.

Morduch, J. (1998). *Does Microfinance Real ly Help the Poor? New Evidence on Flagship Programs in Bangladesh.* MacArthur Foundation project on inequality working paper, Princeton University, draft.

Nichter, S., Goldmark, L., & Fiori, A. (2002). *Understanding Microfinance in the Brazilian Context.* BNDES.

Parikh, T. (2005). *'Rural Microfinance Service Delivery: Gaps, Inefficiencies and Emerging Solutions.* University of Washington.

Pitt, M., & Khandker, S. (1998). The Impact of Group-Based Credit Programs on Poor Households in Bangladesh: Does the Gender of Participants Matter? *Journal of Political Economy, 106*(5), 958–996.

Prasad, G. (2001). *Yes, you can do Business with Open Source.* Accessed August 9, 2006 at http://www.zdnetindia.com/techzone/linuxcentre/stories/32999.html

Rao, K. M. (2004). *Microfinance Institutions in India.* Presented at the APRACA Seminar at Manila on Regulation of MFIs.

Raymond, E. S. (2000). *The Cathedral and The Bazaar*. Available from http://www.catb.org/ esr/writings/cathedral-bazaar/cathedralbazaar/

Regy, P. V., & Mahajan, V. (2006). IT at BASIX: Successes and Failures, a Retrospective. *Information Development*, *IV*(5).

Sanchez, E. C. (2003). *Microfinance and technology: the way to greater financial access*. Accessed 1 August 2006 at http://www.itmatters.com.ph/features.php?id=091503

Schmidt, J. P. (2006). *Free & Open Source Software for Microfinance: Increasing Efficiency and Extending Benefits to the Poor*. Academic Press.

Steve, L. (2005). *Model Credit Buerau Open Source Solution Being tested in Morocco, submitted on July 3, 2005 9:00*. Accessed August 8, 2006 21:09 on http://www.nextbillion.net/newsroom/2005/07/03/model-creditbureau-open-source-solution-being-tested-in-morocco

Waterfield, C., & Ramsing, N. (1998). Handbook for Management Information Systems for Microfinance Institutions. CGAP Technical Tool Series No. 1, February 1998. Augsburg.

ADDITIONAL READING

A.-R. K. El- Dalabeeh. (2013). The role of financial analysis ratio in evaluating performance (case study : National chlorine industry). *Interdisciplinary Journal of Contemporary Research in Business*, *5*(2), 13–29.

Asian Development Bank. (2000). *The Role of central Banks in Microfinance in Asia and the Pacific*. Asian Development Bank.

Foster, D. (2005) 'What C.E.O.s Need To Know About Software Selection, MicroSave Briefing Note #43.

Hossain, M. (1988). *Credit for Alleviation of Rural Poverty: The Grameen Bank in Bangladeh." Research Report 65*. Washington, D.C.: International Food Policy Research Institute.

Hulme, D. (2000) 'Is microcredit Good for Poor People? A note on the dark side of MicroFinance, accessible from http: microsave.org.

Akuamoah Boateng, I., & Agyei, A. (2013). Microfinance in Ghana: Development, success factors and challenges. *International Journal of Academic Research in Accounting Finance and Management Sciences*, *3*(4), 153–160.

Appiahene, P., & Missah, Y. M. "Predicting the operational efficiency of banks in the presence of information technology investment," in Proceedings of the International Conference on Artificial Intelligence and Soft Computing (ICAISC), pp. 6–11, Academics World, Munich-Germany, 2019.

Pitt, M., & Khandker, S. (1998). 'The Impact of Group-Based Credit Programs on Poor Households in Bangladesh: Does the Gender of Participants Matter¿. *Journal of Political Economy*, *106*(5), 958–996.

Prasad, G. (2001) Yes, you can do Business with Open Source, FreeOS.com, July 26, 2001, accessed August 9, 2006 at http://www.zdnetindia.com/techzone/linuxcentre/stories/32999.html

Raymond, E. S. (2000), 'The Cathedral and The Bazaar, Available from http://www.catb.org/ esr/writings/cathedral-bazaar/cathedralbazaar/, last accessed September 2006.

Rural Banks. 2018, http://bog.gov.gh

Yaron, J. 1992. Succeed Rural Finance Institution. World Bank Discussion Paper No. 150. Washington, D.C.

KEY TERMS AND DEFINITIONS

Artificial Intelligence: Artificial intelligence, sometimes called machine intelligence, is intelligence demonstrated by machines, unlike the natural intelligence displayed by humans and animals.

Credit Union: A credit union is a unique member-driven, self-help financial institution.

ICT: Information and communication technology.

Micro Credit: Microcredit is the extension of very small loans to impoverished borrowers who typically lack collateral, steady employment, or a verifiable credit history.

Micro Finance: Microfinance refers to the arrangement of monetary administrations to low-pay customers, including shoppers and the independently employed (Ledgerwood, 2000).

Micro Funding: Projects that are too small to gain support from mainstream venture capital firms can be linked to a group of investors willing to take a chance on your project through Micro Funding. Micro Funding allows you, as an entrepreneur, to network with investors and managers to grow your business to the next level.

MIFOS: Micro finance open source.

NPA: Non-Performing Assets. A nonperforming asset (NPA) refers to a classification for loans or advances that are in default or in arrears.

Stakeholders: A person with an interest or concern in something, especially a business.

Chapter 14
Engaging With Stakeholders for Developing an Effective Entrepreneurial Ecosystem in Universities Based in Rural Setup

Pranav D. Desai
https://orcid.org/0000-0001-5196-9872
Indukaka Ipcowala Institute of Management, FMS, Charotar University of Science and Technology, Changa, India

ABSTRACT

This chapter proposes a new model that promotes and develops an entrepreneurial ecosystem in universities based in rural setup. The entrepreneurial universities could accomplish the status as an innovative environment center by collaborating with new businesses. Universities in rural areas can introduce business training, college business hatcheries, and college endeavor government-common society cooperation that enabled entrepreneurial behaviors. The target of a business college filling in as a pioneering entrepreneurial eco-system development center is to animate financial advancement, produce work, and make imaginative innovation-based endeavors or acting as an administration organization. While these services can be provided through a university, a university in a rural set up has an opportunity to act as a center for the economic development in rural areas. Attention is set on the need to create solid coordinated effort among key partners for making progress in building a viable enterprising system.

INTRODUCTION

In Indian market, development of new companies has improved in recent times. Specifically, the emergence of various home-developed unicorn businesses is popular across the nation. One of the significant sponsors prompting this advancement has been the super financing that has been blasted through the

DOI: 10.4018/978-1-7998-4942-1.ch014

greater part of these unicorn businesses between 2014 to 2019. This has been in accordance with the worldwide pattern as well. Indeed, even the hopeful unicorn businesses have had a good run during this period. The patterns of speculations proposed that speculators need to enter as an early financial specialist, even before the beginning of the firm.

From a general review, India seems to be a flourishing under-infiltrated buyer driven market with an extension for exponential development. Web infiltration and its expanding significance will drive most of the organizations. Because of the shopper socioeconomics, with China being outside the field of play, India offers the biggest speculation opportunity that the world is peering toward. This is regardless of the large number of operational, administrative and tax assessments that encompass the business condition in India. Be that as it may, 2019 has ended up being a year offering somewhat of a rude awakening to everyone and reclassified the elements as it were. The year likewise set the pace for the following stage in the advancement of the start-up eco system. The development in dynamic that should unmistakably come in at this stage would be a positive development taking the start-up space in India towards more prominent statures, as it merits.

The bigger issues tormenting the organizations, for example, is the chaotic and divided Indian market, absence of clear and straightforward approach activities, absence of framework, absence of information and presentation, difficulties in working together. The system and course of guidelines should be refreshed and received according to the occasions. The correct arrangement matter declarations by legislators can be a push. In conditions such as these, professional changes declarations are required to give the truly necessary force to the general business condition in the nation in the start-up space.

To make mindfulness and building a pioneering situation, a great deal of accentuation should now be given to making foundation for tutoring new companies. Different partners, for example, the legislature, corporates, instructive establishments and others should hold hands to assemble a superior environment for youngsters. We comprehend that the Commerce Ministry is intending to assemble an online entrance for data sharing among different partners including hatcheries/quickening agents, heavenly attendant financial specialists, venture capital (VC) assets and government offices. We likewise comprehend that other such activities are in the pipeline and turned out at the appointed time. The objective of this book chapter is to introduce the key ideas and bits of knowledge from building an effective eco system through the collaboration with a university network. The study also focuses on the advancement of academic institutes towards an accomplishment of the "Innovative Perfect." This chapter analyze the joint effort of various stake holders, alongside seeking after a third crucial territorial/national monetary improvement activities (Philpott et al., 2011). The expression "pioneering business college" is in the future utilized as an intermediary for the "innovative college" to suit the setting of a business college that is freely organized, oversaw, supported, and staffed, with instructing faculty for the most part.

The concept of an "Entrepreneurial Eco System" is used as a broader term aiming specifically to academic institutions, business enterprise training, college brooding, and partner joint effort, with academic institutions. The emerging concept of an Entrepreneurial Ecosystem can be seen as, "the association of restricted social systems, speculation capital, colleges, and dynamic financial strategies that make conditions strong of development-based endeavors." It has been set up that the segments of enterprise instruction, business hatching, and framing organization courses of action among partners within and outside the University, are crucial for developing effective and fruitful environment for Entrepreneurship.

The setting of an excellent, dynamic environment for nonstop learning and activity focused on critical thinking and inventive administration and business is a need for today's education system. The study focuses on a group of academic institute leaders that are thinking about the improvement of innovative entrepreneurship systems and how to set up within academic environment, hatchery supporters, directors, and graduates who are examining propelling an innovation or administration business. In the same light, it targets potential scholarly businessmen, particularly those engaged with business colleges and innovation offices, just as the more extensive business and scholastic networks. Numerous hypotheses and definitions are referred for innovative entrepreneurial eco-system. In none of the case, there is no intelligible hypothesis supporting to the different components of an innovative environment.

BACKGROUND

Entrepreneurial ecosystems systems show an interconnected network between different segments that help each other in bringing forth new business visionaries. New business visionaries can rise and create not just in view of the gallant, skilled, and visionary individual (businessman). New organizations likewise emerge since they are in a situation or "Entrepreneurial Eco-System " that permits them to be simple and strong in beginning a business. A helpful enterprising environment is required in bringing forth imminent new businessmen. The legislature firmly energizes the introduction of businessmen among the younger generation. The legislature understands the job of businessmen in deciding the advancement of a country has been demonstrated by a few developed nations, for example, America, Japan, and neighboring nations, for example, Singapore, Malaysia, and Thailand.

At present, the quantity of business visionaries in Indonesia is still exceptionally constrained. This can be seen from the aftereffects of which shows that the new Indonesia has around 1.65 present of businessmen from an all-out populace of 250 million. As indicated by Miron et al. (1961), this number has not arrived at the perfect number of two present of the populace. Particularly when contrasted with the United States a long way behind since it has arrived at in excess of 12 present of the populace become business visionaries. Besides, Japan has in excess of 10 present of businessmen, even close by nations, for example, Singapore, Malaysia, and Thailand each have 7 present, 5 present and 3 present of the all-out number of business visionaries. In light of exploration results, colleges have a significant job in bringing forth planned new business visionaries. Since college graduates have far more extensive bits of knowledge and can create imaginative models as an arrangement to turn into a businessman. In accordance with the exploration, a business visionary will have the option to prevail as indicated by Alistair et al. (2012) in the event that they have creative capacities and the information on enterprise.

How significant the job of colleges is in bringing forth imminent businessmen, the college as indicated by Mack et al. (2016) must have the option to make a favorable enterprising eco-framework. The job of every part in the environment, for example, staff as per Hayter et al. (2018) is required in adding to the interpersonal organization of imminent business visionaries. While the arrangement determinants are an increasingly prevailing variable in making an enterprising environment. Policymakers as per Hermanto and Suryanto (2017) will have the option to synergize the segments in the enterprising environment. More exhaustively, Mueller et al. (2014) clarified that school is simply the correct condition to cultivate social imagination, fearlessness, and opportunity to create. The job of schools is significant in the improvement of environments. Business enterprise will affect understudies during and after they complete training.

Different specialists Guerrero et al. (2016) accentuates the commitment of colleges in advancing development and enterprising exercises. Wai Boh et al. (2016) found a side project system for business visionaries from enterprising environments at colleges. Entrepreneurship eco-system will be increasingly favorable on the off chance that they can investigate the job of segments from formal and casual systems, physical and social framework. Likewise, every part should have the option to give benefits and duplicate the environment.

As per Isenberg (2011a), a pioneering environment comprises of components that can be assembled into six spaces: helpful culture, encouraging strategies and authority, accessibility of committed money, significant human capital, adventure well-disposed markets for items, and wide arrangement of institutional and infrastructural underpins.

Prahalad (2005) gives a definition to an innovative entrepreneurial eco-system, which as per him environments empower people, organizations, and networks to join viably to produce monetary riches and flourishing. The unprecedented quality of the entrepreneurial eco-system is to unite partners who are regularly determined by different objectives and desires.

While Aldrich et al. (1989) clarify that enterprising entrepreneurial eco-systems are described by the privately-run company and good examples, assorted economies, solid business foundation, accessible venture capital, strong innovative culture, and open arrangements that support business creation. The pioneering environment cannot just go about as an impetus in quickening financial advancement from a steady economy however can likewise go about as a main player as far as sparing an economy confronting a sharp decrease. The social effect on the advancement of an enterprising environment can't be disregarded. There is a requirement for models that perceive people without disregarding social factors that are outside the ability to control of people. A solitary structure is required in view of the character and conduct of people, political frameworks and laws, social traditions identified with the national culture from which they begin (Lee and Peterson, 2000).

Previous studies portray in detail modern framework that encourages and represses enterprise. Framework incorporates institutional courses of action to control and normalize new advances, enrichment reserves, open information, logical premise, financing components, and an assortment of a skilled workforce, just as exploration and responsibility for improvement, production, advertising, and appropriation capacities. The utilization of the entrepreneurial eco-system as per Cohen (2006) traces nine primary elements which are the fundamental segments, including casual systems, formal systems, colleges, government, proficient administrations and backing, capital administrations, and the ability pool. Isenberg (2011a), proposed a model for entrepreneurial eco-system comprising of thirteen elements, including administration, government, culture, examples of overcoming adversity, human capital, money related capital, enterprise associations, training, framework, financial groups, systems, bolster administrations, early clients. They incorporate government partners, instructive foundations, money related establishments, media, and systems.

The aim of this article is to present the key concepts and insights from literature related to the question of building a university entrepreneurial ecosystem centered in rural region upon the development of an aspiring university business school as the hub of the ecosystem.

The article further examines empirically, the progress of business schools toward the achievement of an "entrepreneurial ideal", which is described as embracing the triple helix model of university industry-government collaboration, along with pursuing a third mission of regional/national economic development initiatives. The term "entrepreneurial business school" is hereafter used as a proxy for the "entrepreneurial university" to suit the context of a university business school that is independently structured, managed, funded, and staffed, with teaching personnel mainly recruited from business as adjunct lecturers, and with a board of predominantly business sector members.

LITERATURE REVIEW

Previous studies reveal that, the academic institutions have been delineated as 'standard incubation centers' and are in center of the advancement and innovativeness. Not for all the Universities, it is possible to continuously proficient, proactive and inventive in attracting accomplices, allowing them to be a contributory performer to the system of innovation. The regional impacts of such innovative contribution through academic institution, for instance, development Transfer Offices, ensured advancement, turn far from the academic institutions. The wide importance has been observed for insightful business undertaking, and neighborhood endeavor, anyway all are clearly unequivocally interrelated. The venturesome school thought can be fathomed at the institutional level; while insightful business undertaking suggests the activities and occupations endeavors for making spearheading thinking, exercises, associations and availability of seed money. During studies, the endeavor has been observed as a key errand to promote the employments, improving business undertaking, instructing and data exchange practices within imaginative territory.

The concept of an "entrepreneurial ecosystem" is used in this article as an umbrella term to cover the related components of entrepreneurial universities, entrepreneurship education, university incubation, and stakeholder collaboration, with particular focus on university + industry + government + civil society participation in a quadruple helix system. The relatively new notion of an entrepreneurial ecosystem can be viewed as, "the union of localized cultural networks, investment capital, universities, and active economic policies that create environments supportive of innovation-based ventures". Although research in this field is recent, it has been established that the components of entrepreneurship education, business incubation, and forming partnership arrangements among stakeholders within universities and with external players, are vital to building successful ecosystems.

The setting for our research is a small developing middle-income country in the Caribbean whose major university's business school mission is to provide "a world-class, dynamic environment for continuous learning and action aimed at problem-solving and innovative management and business". The article targets an audience of university administrators that are contemplating the development of entrepreneurial ecosystems and how to establish entrepreneurial universities, incubator sponsors, managers, and graduates who are contemplating launching a technology or service business. As well, it targets potential academic entrepreneurs, especially those involved in business schools and technology departments, as well as the wider business and academic communities.

Many theories and definitions are cited in relation to entrepreneurial ecosystems, entrepreneurial universities, and their third mission of economic development through participation in triple helix collaboration, tertiary-level entrepreneurship education, university-based incubation, and key stakeholder collaboration. However, there is no generally agreed upon definition, nor coherent theory that integrates the various elements of an entrepreneurial ecosystem. Rather the tendency is to import policies and practices from successful ecosystems while disregarding the relevant cultural and economic features of the local setting. Against this theoretical background, this article builds on the core concept of the triple helix of Etzkowitz and Leydesdorff, by applying the extended concept of the 'quadruple helix' of university + industry + government + civil society collaboration. The latter brings the community element forward with a collaborative network as the essential role of universities.

Building University-Based Entrepreneurial Ecosystems

It is considered that the pioneering entrepreneurial eco-systems are based on eight explicit factors:

1. Access to business sectors
2. Satisfactory human asset limit
3. Proper financing from different sources
4. Bolster instruments containing counsellors / Mentors
5. Organizing game plans, proficient administrations, and hatcheries or quickening agents
6. A Business well-disposed condition
7. Institute level enterprise instruction and preparing that advances a culture of enterprise, thought age, and graduates with an endeavor direction,
8. A philosophy that is associated to the research, business visionaries and the overall / holistic development.

Concession to the environment columns focuses on the move in corporate viewpoints to focus upon individuals, systems, and establishments, in light of the view that "Business visionaries make new worth, composed through the assortment in the administration modes, empowered with limited to the particular setting of an academic institutions". It is contended that there is no single way to making a pioneering entrepreneurial eco-system, and that fairly the procedure includes various stages that are not well characterized as the college continues through them. It is in like manner questionable whether the idea is relevant to all districts, or progressively proper to areas where emotionally supportive networks as of now under the development phase. In contrast to the same, the important aspect of a university based entrepreneurial eco-system, capable enough to support the primary level business units.

Enterprising Institutions

The idea of the developing entrepreneurship within the University students starts with the capacity building of the University staff. The crucial point of creating and dispersing information relies upon the structure of the specific University. In recent time, academic institutions felt obligated to create income, which prompted the third strategic changing over its endeavors into financial advancement exercises, for example, "innovation move that supports the transformation of new age technology to uplift the living standards. The result of developing entrepreneurial eco system within Universities reflects through the collaboration with industry and government. Such efforts imply through moderately free activities, a half-breed association that manages the strains between outside connections and autonomy for achieving destinations. Various studies have unfolded the structures for the innovative Entrepreneurial eco system for Universities. Out of such many have practiced a domain, inside which the advancement of pioneering attitudes and practices are inserted, empowered, upheld, boosted, and remunerated" (Hannon, 2013). In this manner, what is required at pioneering colleges is business enterprise training.

Enterprise Training

The investigation of initiative has picked up driving force during recent years and is presently basic in numerous establishments of higher learning. The pattern focuses to utilizing experiential learning procedures, including experienced businessmen, using exercises from disappointment, receiving enterprise as a work on, preparing in circumstance distinguishing proof, and adjusting substance to social settings. The role of Universities for incitement of monetary act and business creation is recognized, yet the role of academic institutions in developing the innovative establishments, making novel pursuits, and cultivating successful connections keeps on being discussed (Davey et al., 2016). Right now, was underlined that "enterprise is not just for the picked rare sorts of people who can distinguish business openings in the commercial center, produce a marketable strategy, give the fundamental money related capital and assemble another endeavor" (Blenker et al., 2012). At the end of the day, more individuals at colleges can be doing it and examining it than have attempted up until now.

Institutes / Colleges are considered as "pioneering" when they embrace an enterprising point of view in instructing and discovering that joins a mixed and intelligent methodology. Among the primary driver is building an innovative society as a basic bone of the new age. Inserting enterprise concentrates within educational institutions shown progressively saw as methods for encouraging innovative conduct and outlooks in ventures and innovative mind-sets within the students. Thusly, critical thinking leads in deal with more extensive social worth creation, act mindfully with financial specialists and key partners, practice ecological manageability and moral conduct, perceive the network's stake in the accomplishment of the endeavor, and give suitable compensations to capable enterprise.

The Academic Institution Brooding

The activities for developing entrepreneurship spirit into revenue driven hatcheries encouraged by the accessibility of investment, in light of possibilities of benefit. The development was continued in the mid-2000s, even the monetary downturn of 2008 in any case. A few sorts of hatcheries rose by different orders free business, territorial, organization inside, college partnered, virtual hatcheries, blended, innovation. The characterizing attributes of budding entrepreneurs were arrangement of workstations, office support, available financing, start-up specialized help, and prologue to business systems.

Various research on Entrepreneurship development models by Universities have been viewed as pushing agent for the improvement of supportable innovative entrepreneurial systems, while instances of brooding activities in little creating nations colleges are commonly dismissed. Hatcheries reliably perceived as enterprising advancement benefits that try to extend the efforts for developing new undertakings for focusing on the defenselessness during early phase of improvement. All the additional focuses on the regular motivation behind university hatcheries working inside an enterprising entrepreneurial eco-system was portrayed as being "to advance business, development, the formation of early phase ventures. Early stage ventures pursuits regularly rise as University projects, which are to some degree uncommon, yet add needs to get into developing applications, innovation and draw in the innovator in an advancement procedure.

University Business Incubation

The idea of business brooding as a college activity goes back to the last part of the 1950s. During the 1980s, the activity developed into revenue driven hatcheries encouraged by the accessibility of investment, because of possibilities of benefit. The extension was continued in the mid-2000s, even the monetary downturn of 2008 in any case. A few sorts of hatcheries rose by different classifies autonomous business, territorial, organization inner, college partnered, virtual hatcheries, blended, innovation, social, and essential exploration. The characterizing qualities of early hatcheries were arrangement of workstations, office support, available subsidizing, start-up specialized help, and prologue to business systems. Right now, hatcheries are considered "a deliberate, orderly exertion to sustain new firms in the beginning phase of their movement in a controlled domain", and are seen as a powerful procedure which offers "a mix of foundation, improvement bolster procedures and mastery expected to defend against disappointment and steer incubate firms into a development way". This procedure has prompted a move in need to hatchery administrations with get to broadband, Wi-Fi, and arranged PCs, meeting rooms, and in any event, coaching. There is a developing group of examination on college drove hatcheries that are viewed as impetuses for the improvement of manageable college based innovative biological systems, while instances of brooding activities in little creating nations colleges are commonly ignored. Subsequently, this article speaks to a huge commitment around there by refreshing and adding to past work. Hatcheries are reliably seen as enterprising improvement benefits that look to expand the pool of new undertakings and to address their weakness in the beginning phase of advancement. All the more explicitly, the basic motivation behind college hatcheries working inside an enterprising environment was depicted as being "to advance business, advancement, the production of new firms, and monetary turn of events. New pursuits regularly rise as college side projects, which are to some degree uncommon, yet at the same time add to the commercialization of innovation and draw in the creator in the advancement procedure.

Stakeholder Collaboration: From Triple to Quadruple Helix Model

The achievement of advancement frameworks depends on solid linkages among the scholarly community/colleges, industry, and state/government, whose connections structure the triple helix model of coordinated effort. With the rise of "information economies", the adequacy of triple helix joint effort in conveying the normal measure of advancement and financial improvement was addressed. This prompted the expansion of a fourth helix, involving the media, inventive enterprises, culture, values, ways of life, and workmanship, stretching out the idea to a fourfold helix framework. These entertainers comprised some portion of the more extensive network occupied with making "new information, innovation and advancement meeting both monetary and cultural needs". In such manner, the expansion of the triple helix to the fourfold helix, was intended to recognize the basic job of the overall population and network for accomplishing the information destinations and development strategies. This occurs through a more concentrated field of joint effort inside a territorial advancement arrange concentrated on information serious turn of events. This article contends that reinforcing the current partner shared endeavors, is basic to the advancement of an incipient enterprising biological system center point. The fruitful instance of iMinds was portrayed as an activity to connect college exploration to business needs, and to build up an atmosphere helpful for dynamic new businesses and new pursuits. This atmosphere speaks to another model of an enterprising biological system that includes open joint effort with key partners, "concentrated participation and cooperation, human and social capital turn of events, overflow impacts, and shared fortification", that is, one that reflects the activity of fourfold helix interrelationships.

THE PROPOSED EYE MODEL

Figure 1. The eye model

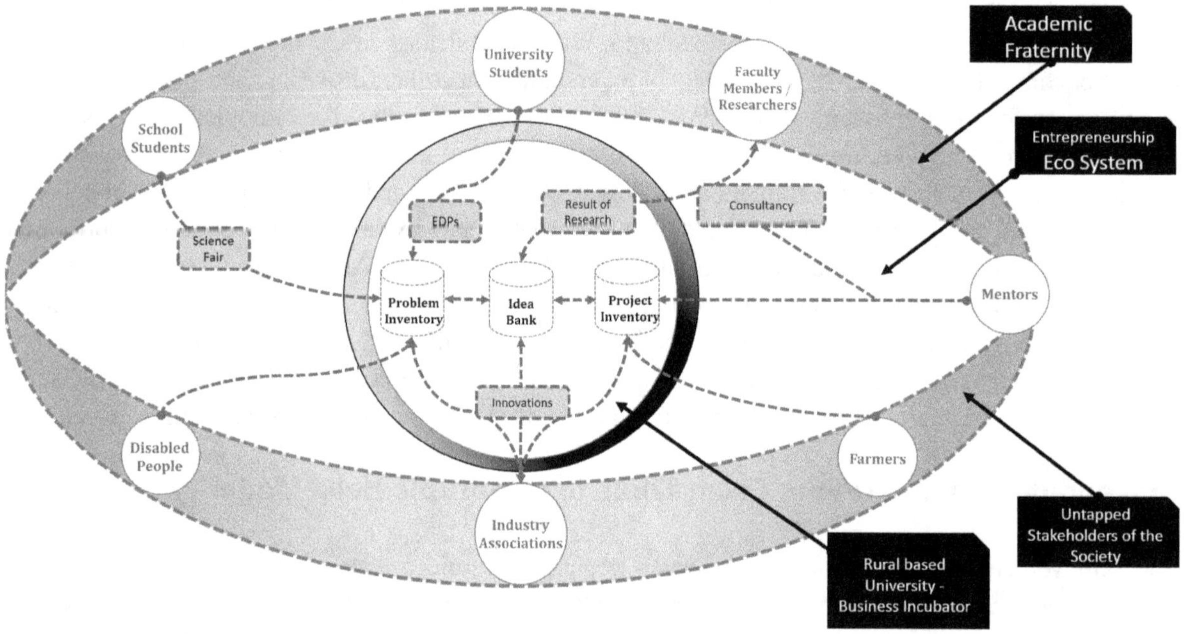

For connecting with partners however advanced instruments for creating powerful pioneering entrepreneurial eco-system in colleges situated in country region, the Eye model have been created. To improve the capacity of start-up originators and business visionaries and their administration and innovation, the hatchery ought to permit the undertaking to put their essential spotlight on building up their item or innovation. This guarantees the hatchery is basically worried about the hindrances to passage related with progress, for example, financing, attainability, and access to physical offices important to business work. With the help of the hatchery, the hazard to the beginning up and venture is diminished and consistent change to development can be practiced. By advancing the development of the beginning up and little endeavor, the essential aftereffect of the hatchery becomes to expand the achievement pace of the related ventures.

The capacity of the Business Incubator is to create business visionaries and unite the different segments of the little undertaking and start-up eco system into an engaged focus where assets can affect, and the financial advancement of the network can occur. From the figure demonstrated as follows, businessmen can emerge out of different sources, for example, colleges, organizations, and cultural associations. They bring aptitudes and properties from their encounters that make them ready to frame a serious undertaking. What's more, there ought to be impetuses to the businessmen to take hazards and contribute their time, vitality, and riches into the venture. On the opposite side, a few unique sorts of administrators can work the Business Incubator. They give the degree of help and compelling administrations that will carry an incentive to the business visionaries. Therefore, the monetary impacts can be acknowledged in the network and past.

Figure 2. Functions of entrepreneurship centre at rural based University

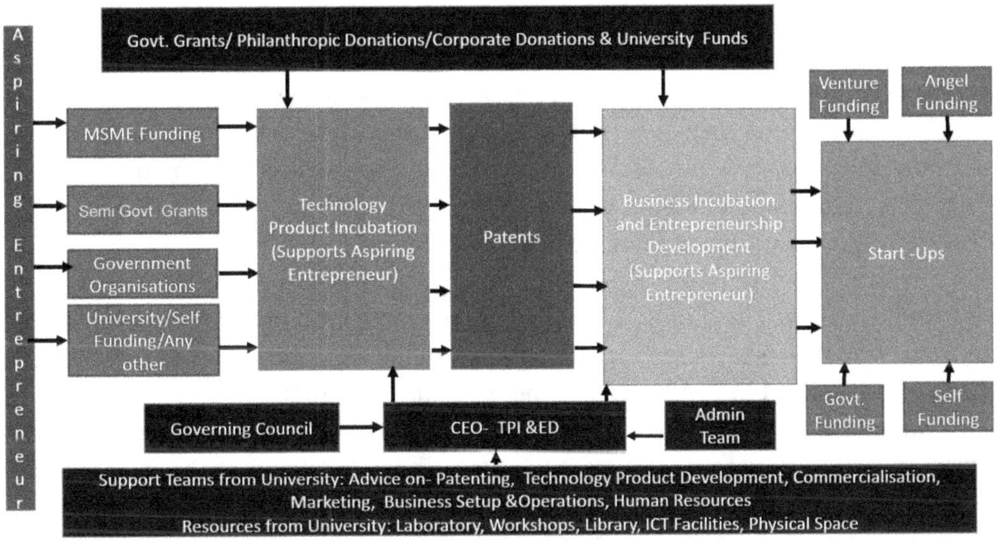

The Coordinator of the hatching place will be answerable for dealing with the business hatchery focus to play out the genuine business hatchery activity, giving the vital administrations to new companies and ventures. The administrators of the business hatcheries get monetary help from financial specialists into the business hatcheries. The beginning up and little undertakings are the organizations that can add to territorial or national financial advancement and carry development to the network. The speculator segment of the working framework is the focal and neighborhood governments, universities, Chamber of Commerce, the private endeavors, and so on that help the activity with financing and construct the Incubator center. The Investor underpins exercises identified with new companies and private ventures and manages the Business Incubator Centre through the activity of the Supervisory Committee. What's more, these financial specialists are anticipating naturally visible impacts, for example, animating the economy if the speculator is openly financed, or on account of private speculators by holding value of promising organizations and anticipating the returns of future profits or value deal.

The procedure model of a business hatchery's working framework can be extraordinary, so various attributes exist contingent upon the built up objective and physical area. You can see the Incubator working framework through the perspective of the destinations and methodology. The Incubator working framework is planned to characterize the connection between and the components that influence the essential operational exercises of the Incubator endeavors.

ROLE OF ICT IN DEVELOPING EFFECTIVE ECOSYSTEM

While the Entrepreneurship Centre at Rural based University makes demonstrable progress on its development goals and invested in basic infrastructure, opportunities to improve remain. The ICT based strategy and development efforts have been impactful, but there is still much to accomplish, as can be described by two overarching themes. First, the Ecosystem needs to create a foundation for success. Development strategies have contributed to that goal, but its digital markets and the resources required to build the ecosystem (human capital, investment, networks) must be cultivated. Secondly, the leadership of ecosystem building should transition from the government to the Entrepreneurship Centre at Rural based University. For the review process, the ecosystem canvas can used to capture ecosystem insights from stakeholders across seven pillars. A summary of stakeholder assessment of each pillar offers a useful overview of the ecosystem at Entrepreneurship Centre at Rural based University:

- **Vision and Strategy:** The country ICT strategies have created a foundation for the ICT innovation ecosystem, while adequately engaging ministries and stakeholders. However, leveraging private sector engagement and leadership can further stimulate progress.
- **Infrastructure and Programs:** As mentioned above, the government investment in fiber optic cable improved the country's ICT infrastructure. However, access to that infrastructure is constrained by cost, limited awareness, and last mile solutions. Additionally, soft infrastructure development outside of capital city is limited.
- **Talent and Champions:** Country A has a talent gap across multiple categories—technical, soft, and support skills. A key contributor is the lack of hands-on training available through the education system, which leads to graduates who have low levels of experience and knowledge. However, changes are underway to update university curricula and introduce ICT training into secondary education. The ecosystem has also done a good job of importing talent into the country.
- **Capital and Resources**: In country A, there are few investment resources for start-ups and growing companies. Government contracts and international development funding are the predominant sources of support, although there are some international investment resources. Initiatives to improve the investing landscape include creating a national investment fund.
- **Markets and Networks:** Country a size and its population's limited engagement with ICT means that its digital markets are also limited. However, given the strong environment for doing business, there are opportunities for the country to establish regional leadership through membership in the regional communities However, existing networks should be recognized as stakeholders and ICT clusters need further growth and enrichment.
- **Culture and Communities**: Entrepreneurial interest among young people is strong and communities have emerged to support that interest. But culturally, risk tolerance is low due to the conservative culture and limited ability to absorb financial risk.
- **Policy and Regulation**: Actors in the public sector own their ecosystem-building roles, as have the ministries, which are engaged in the country's development strategies. However, there is room for building partnerships.

There are three main implications for the ecosystem insights described above. They are as follows:

1. The Incubation Centre should create a new framework for policy experimentation.

2. Stakeholders need to recognize their roles and invest in policy outcomes. Not only should stakeholders in the ICT innovation ecosystem take their roles seriously, they need to be invested in policy outcomes. To accomplish this, better tools for understanding the ecosystem as well as identifying and sharing good practices are required to get engaged.
3. Learning from good practices developed domestically and internationally is critical. There are many good practices within the country and abroad that can be applied to build the local ecosystem. Adopting such practices is a critical element of policy experimentation. To maximize impact and relevance, key actors should focus on those that relate to the recommendations for the country's ecosystem, specifically.

EVALUATION CRITERIA

Figure 3. The evaluation criteria for the selection of the projects

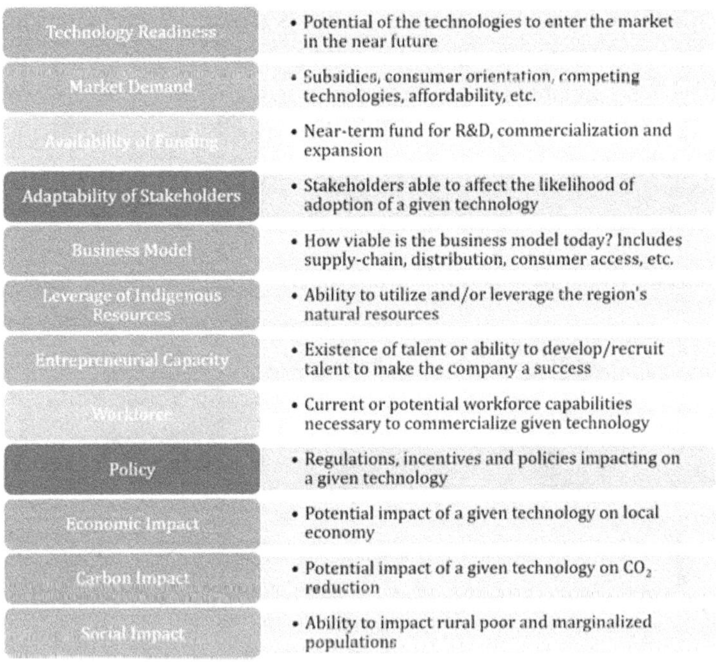

The Pace by Pace Approach

Pace 1: The Awareness In this stage, raising and group building, including the set-up of a task group, a work plan, and the beginning of mindfulness raising exercises to advance the hatch venture.

Pace 2: The Feasibility Study. This stage explores the Feasibility of the start-up venture. Toward the finish of this stage, the beginning up groups should know whether there is adequate, request from planned business visionaries for the sort of foundations and bolster benefits that a college based brooding place gives. Right now, is likewise essential to see whether and how partners will bolster the improvement and activity of things to come brooding focus.

Pace 3: The Business Plan. The result from the possibility study gives the premise to the strategy. Right now, solid model is explained determining in words and in money related figures the sort of help that can be given by the specialists to address the issues of its clients; how the gatherings will be composed and worked; and how the entirety of this can be financed. The field-tested strategy helps the beginning up groups to get financing and is a guide for the supervisory crew on the most proficient method to execute the orderly procedure of big business advancement.

Pace 4: Implementation. This stage considers the choice of fitting hatchery staff and incorporates many uncommon preparing measures, which constructs the limit of things to come hatchery staff to work the business and to help its customers.

Stakeholder engagement is a fundamental component of materiality assessments, which are then used to inform sustainability strategy, reporting, and disclosure. Without input from key stakeholder groups, any approach to sustainability will be limited by an organization's self-interest and inward focus.

BSR™ is a global non-profit organization that works with its network of more than 250 member companies and other partners to build a just and sustainable world. From its offices in Asia, Europe, and North America, BSR™ develops sustainable business strategies and solutions through consulting, research, and cross-sector collaboration. They have published a five-step guide to stakeholder engagement in 2011. They have also updated the guide as a response to developments over the last seven years, all of which necessitate a far clearer focus on stakeholder trust by corporations.

Figure 4. The Five-step approach to stakeholder engagement

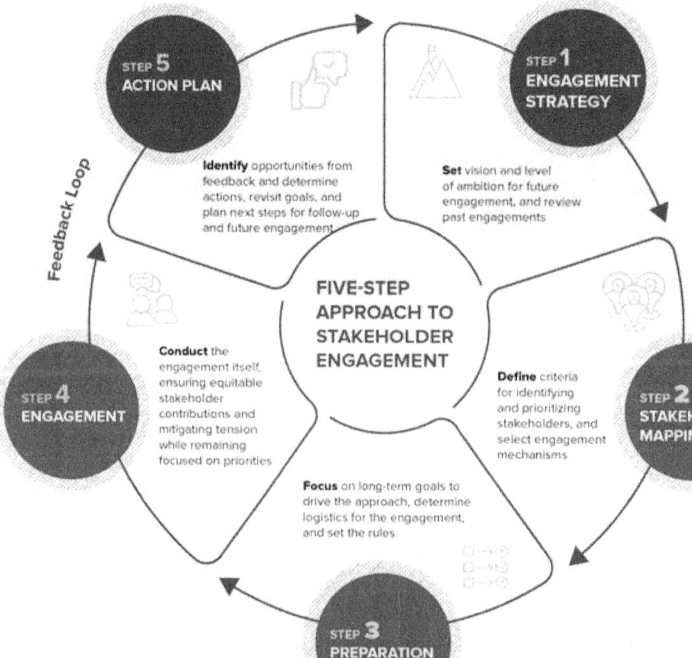

1. **Engagement Strategy**: Set vision and level of ambition for future engagement and review past engagements.
2. **Stakeholder Mapping**: Define criteria for identifying and prioritizing stakeholders and select engagement mechanisms.
3. **Preparation**: Focus on long-term goals to drive the approach, determine logistics for the engagement, and set the rules.
4. **Engagement**: Conduct the engagement itself, ensuring equitable stakeholder contribution and mitigating tension while remaining focused on priorities.
5. **Action Plan**: Identify opportunities from feedback and determine actions, revisit goals, and plan next steps for follow-up and future engagement.

CONCLUSION

The article attempted to give understanding into the possibility of school based venturesome eco frameworks. These rely upon making creative schools, joining venture guidance in the instructive plans, developing school drove business incubation centers as new interest improvement mechanical assemblies, and expanding accomplice joint exertion as a "fourfold helix" system. The makers endeavored a definite examination of a school-based business school importance to fill in as a venturesome situation community as logical examination, considering insider action exploration to check progress towards the enterprising eco-framework targets.

The key finishes came to are according to the accompanying: The structure of a suitable school venturesome condition is a long stretch endeavor that solicitations bolstered thought considering how universities work in storage facilities counter to effective joint exertion. The improvement of an ambitious business school, especially with respect to a touch of making country, addresses a huge test considering small financing, human resource limit, totally committed power, and a juvenile spearheading society.

The fundamental of introducing endeavor preparing in the instructive program of business schools has expanded moderate affirmation (inside the UWI structure). Sponsorship for agonizing exercises are required to be reluctant. Inadequate money related resources and greatness organization have exemplified the equivalent. The answer for the equivalent is towards strengthening interrelationships between accomplices the joining into genuine applications. Enterprising Eco framework weaknesses can incite unsatisfactory degrees of significant worth for graduating innovative undertakings. These judgments highlight a prerequisite for propelling progressively noticeable joint exertion among individuals developing the University as an innovative eco-framework focus point. An exact overview of the investigation focused on that collaboration among school and industry was the authoritative factor in vitalizing headway. Strengthening key accomplice facilitated exertion, particularly about a fourfold helix strategy, as proposed in the article, in this way prescribes express exercises that should be looked for after eagerly. Prime among these are: To sum up, we acknowledge that the headway of continuously thought and wide participation among accessories and individuals is plausible, and that looking for after the movement things proposed above will go far to improving social orders' synergistic results in building a school based venturesome condition place.

Enterprise offices are sitting in a specific specialty inside and past the pioneering college of giving instructing and commitment that is supported by investigation into business. Associations with their areas stream the two different approaches, including a maintained communication and connections between office individuals and territorial pioneering entertainers. Business divisions are doing a broader scope of crucial, including both formal and casual relationships for making an amazing environment at academic institution. This study requires an inversion of that pattern and sets the ground for additional examination concerning business offices, and in fact different kinds of offices not yet caught in the writing, as key drivers of local financial improvement inside and past the idea of the innovative Universities.

REFERENCES

Abreu, M., & Grinevich, V. (2013). The nature of academic entrepreneurship in the UK: Widening the focus on entrepreneurial activities. *Research Policy*, *42*(2), 408–422. doi:10.1016/j.respol.2012.10.005

Acs, Z. J., Braunerhjelm, P., Audretsch, D. B., & Carlsson, B. (2009). The knowledge Spillover Theory of Entrepreneurship. *Small Business Economics*, *32*(1), 15–30. doi:10.100711187-008-9157-3

Audretsch, D., & Keilbach, M. (2008). Resolving the knowledge paradox: Knowledge-spillover entrepreneurship and economic growth. *Research Policy*, *37*(10), 1697–1705. doi:10.1016/j.respol.2008.08.008

Audretsch, D. B. (2014). Networking among Women Entrepreneurs. Audretsch, D.B. From the entrepreneurial university to the university for the entrepreneurial society. *The Journal of Technology Transfer*, *39*(3), 313–321. doi:10.100710961-012-9288-1

Baldini, N., Fini, R., Grimaldi, R., & Sobrero, M. (2014). Organisational Change and the Institutionalisation of University Patenting Activity in Italy. *Minerva*, *52*(1), 27–53. doi:10.100711024-013-9243-9

Boh, W. F., De-Haan, U., & Strom, R. (2007). Assessing the Regional Economic Development Impacts of Universities: A Review of Current Approaches. International Regional Science Review -. *International Regional Science Review*, *30*(1), 20–46. doi:10.1177/0160017606296731

Cohen, J. (2006). Social, emotional, ethical and academic education: Creating a climate for learning, participation in democracy and well-being. *Harvard Educational Review*, *76*, 201–237. www.hepg.org/her/abstract/8. doi:10.17763/haer.76.2.j44854x1524644vn

Etzkowitz, H. (2003). Research Groups As 'Quasi-Firms': The Invention of the Entrepreneurial University. *Research Policy*, *32*(1), 109–121. doi:10.1016/S0048-7333(02)00009-4

Etzkowitz, H., Webster, A., Gebhardt, C., & Terra, B. (2000). The Future of the University and the University of the Future: Evolution of Ivory Tower to Entrepreneurial Paradigm. *Research Policy*, *29*(2), 313–330. doi:10.1016/S0048-7333(99)00069-4

Feldman, M., Feller, I., Bercovitz, J., & Burton, R. (2002). Equity and the Technology Transfer Strategies of American Research Universities. *Management Science*, *48*(1), 105–121. doi:10.1287/mnsc.48.1.105.14276

Goddard, J., Kempton, L., & Vallance, P. (2013). *The civic university: Connecting the Global and the Local*. Academic Press.

Gordon, I., Hamilton, E., & Jack, S. (2011). A study of a university-led entrepreneurship education programme for small business owner/managers. *Entrepreneurship and Regional Development*, *2011*. Advance online publication. doi:10.1080/08985626.2011.566377

Gregorio, D., & Shane, S. (2003). Why Do Some Universities Generate More Start-ups Than Others? *Research Policy*, *32*(2), 209–227. doi:10.1016/S0048-7333(02)00097-5

Guerrero, M., Urbano, D., & Alain, F. (2016). Entrepreneurial activity and regional competitiveness: Evidence from European entrepreneurial universities. *The Journal of Technology Transfer*, *41*(1), 105–131. doi:10.100710961-014-9377-4

Hayter, C., Nelson, A., Zayed, S., & O'Connor, A. (2018). Conceptualizing academic entrepreneurship ecosystems: A review, analysis and extension of the literature. *The Journal of Technology Transfer*, *43*(4), 1039–1082. Advance online publication. doi:10.100710961-018-9657-5

Hermanto, B., & Suryanto, S. E. (2017). Entrepreneurship Ecosystem Policy in Indonesia. *Mediterranean Journal of Social Sciences*, *8*(1), 110–115. doi:10.5901/mjss.2017.v8n1p110

Isenberg, D. (2011a). The entrepreneurship ecosystem strategy as a new paradigm for economy policy: principles for cultivating entrepreneurship. Babson Entrepreneurship Ecosystem Project, Babson College.

Lee, S., & Peterson, S. (2000). Culture, entrepreneurial orientation, and global competitiveness. *Journal of World Business*, *35*(4), 401–416. doi:10.1016/S1090-9516(00)00045-6

Mack, E., & Mayer, H. (2015). The evolutionary dynamics of entrepreneurial ecosystems. *Urban Studies (Edinburgh, Scotland)*, *53*. Advance online publication. doi:10.1177/0042098015586547

Miron D, McClelland DC (1961). The Impact of Achievement Motivation Training on Small Businesses. *California Management Review, 21*(4), 13-28. doi:10.2307/41164830

Mueller, S., & Anderson, A. (2014). Understanding the entrepreneurial learning process and its impact on students' personal development: A European perspective. *International Journal of Management Education*, *12*(3), 500–511. Advance online publication. doi:10.1016/j.ijme.2014.05.003

Phan, P., Siegel, D., & Wright, M. (2005). Science Parks and Incubators: Observations, Synthesis and Future Research. *Journal of Business Venturing*, *20*(2), 165–182. doi:10.1016/j.jbusvent.2003.12.001

Philpott, K., Dooley, L., O'Reilly, C., & Lupton, G. (2011). The entrepreneurial university: Examining the underlying academic tensions. *Technovation*, *31*(4), 161–170. doi:10.1016/j.technovation.2010.12.003

Prahalad, C. K. (2005). Learning to Lead. *Vikalpa*, *30*(2), 1–10. doi:10.1177/0256090920050201

Pugh, R., Lamine, W., Jack, S., & Hamilton, E. (2018). The entrepreneurial university and the region: What role for entrepreneurship departments? *European Planning Studies*, 1–21. doi:10.1080/09654313.2018.1447551

Rothaermel, F., Agung, S., & Jiang, L. (2007). University Entrepreneurship: A Taxonomy of the Literature. *Industrial and Corporate Change*, *16*(4), 691–791. doi:10.1093/icc/dtm023

Simons, H. (2009). *Case Study Research in Practice*. Academic Press.

ADDITIONAL READING

Davey, T., Hannon, P., & Penaluma, A. (2016). Entrepreneurship Education and the Role of Universities in Entrepreneurship: Introduction to the Special Issue. *Industry and Higher Education*, *30*(3), 171–182. doi:10.1177/0950422216656699

DeCleyn, S. H., Gielen, F. & Coppens, J. 2013. Incubation Programs from Public Research Organizations as Catalysts for Open Business Ecosystems. *Technology Innovation Management Review*, April 2013: 29-34.

Kunttu, L. (2017). Educational Involvement in Innovative University-Industry Collaboration. Technology *Innovation. Management Review*, *7*(12), 14–22.

Lahikainen, K., Kolhinen, J., Ruskovaara, E., & Pihkala, T. (2019). Challenges to the Development of an Entrepreneurial University Ecosystem: The Case of a Finnish University Campus. *Industry and Higher Education*, *33*(2), 96–107. doi:10.1177/0950422218815806

Malecki, E. J. (2017). Entrepreneurship and entrepreneurial ecosystems. *Geography Compass*, *12359*, 1–21. Retrieved October 12, 2018, from wileyonlinelibrary.com/journal/gec3

Naia, A., Baptista, R., Januário, C., & Trigo, V. (2014). A Systematization of the Literature on Entrepreneurship Education. *Industry and Higher Education*, *28*(2), 79–96. doi:10.5367/ihe.2014.0196

Philpott, K., Dooley, L., O'Reilly, C., & Lupton, G. (2011). The Entrepreneurial University: Examining the Underlying Academic Tensions. *Technovation*, *31*(4), 161–170. doi:10.1016/j.technovation.2010.12.003

Rae, D. (2010). Universities and Enterprise Education: Responding to the Challenges of the New Era. *Journal of Small Business and Enterprise Development*, *17*(4), 591–606. doi:10.1108/14626001011088741

KEY TERMS AND DEFINITIONS

Business Hatchery: It helps new and new businesses to create by offering types of assistance, for example, the board preparing or office space.

Business Incubation Process: A remarkable institutional game plan that is fundamentally worried about creating pioneering society in a network.

Business Incubator: Hatching focus gives a totally different startup environment for the youthful business visionary. Following might be the definition A stage where thought can be sustained into feasible business. Where you can get some master coaching. Assists with discovering starting assets and systems administration. Even though they help, however the new businesses need to accomplish their own work generally, they ought not hang tight for hatching focus yet should begin working any place and at whatever point they can.

Entrepreneurial Ecosystem: The social and financial circumstance influencing nearby or territorial business enterprise. Organizations situated inside spots filling in as hatcheries for innovativeness, advancement, and business enterprise have a more prominent possibility of progress.

Grassroots E&I Movement: A grassroots development, regularly determined by understudies and graduated class in organization with the provincial pioneering network.

Roles of the Faculty Champions: The conventional job of these people differed generally, from an understudy head to a college President. In any case, they shared a typical conviction of the significance of business enterprise for the college and the area, just as a lot of individual associations with industry and the local pioneering network that would demonstrate basic to the college's rise as an innovative focus, especially during the 'startup' period of the establishment's E&I advancement.

Seed Money: Known as seed subsidizing or seed capital, is a type of protections offering in which a financial specialist puts capital in a new business in return for a value stake or convertible note stake in the organization.

Chapter 15
Theoretical Opportunities for Rural Innovation and Entrepreneurship Research

Sachithra Lokuge
https://orcid.org/0000-0003-4558-687X
RMIT University, Australia

ABSTRACT

Even though rural entrepreneurship and rural innovation have been studied for decades, the advent of social media, mobile, analytics, cloud computing, and internet of things—also referred to as digital technologies—has provided new opportunities and challenges for this vast discipline. As a result of the advent of digital technologies, we see new business models, new processes, products, and services emerging in the market. Such opportunities challenge the orthodox view of IT use and innovation, opening new avenues for researches, and challenges the existing theoretical understanding. This chapter is an attempt to understand the existing literature on rural innovation and entrepreneurship in information systems discipline and to identify opportunities for rural entrepreneurship and innovation in the digital era.

INTRODUCTION

The advent of digital technologies has provided unprecedented opportunities for all organizations across the globe, including those that could not afford to invest extensively in technologies that lead innovations (Nambisan 2013; Nylén and Holmström 2015; Sedera et al. 2016; Yoo et al. 2012). The innate characteristics of digital technologies such as cost effectiveness, ease of acquisition, ease of learning, ease of deployment and ease of management have made it easy for any organization to innovate using technologies (Lokuge and Sedera 2018; Nylén and Holmström 2015; Sedera and Lokuge 2017). Similarly, the advent of such technologies has created myriad opportunities for innovation and entrepreneurial activities in the rural areas (Cui et al. 2019; Li et al. 2019; Lokuge et al. 2016). While researchers such as Salemink et al. (2017) highlight the disparities of rural versus urban with regard to digital infrastructure, less attention has been paid to the opportunities available for minimizing the fundamental disadvantages in rural

DOI: 10.4018/978-1-7998-4942-1.ch015

communities using digital technologies. As per Newbery et al. (2017), studying rural innovation and entrepreneurship will not only be valuable to academia, but it will add value to the practitioners such as rural communities, governments, small business holders and not-for-profit organizations in alleviating poverty, empowering women, improving economic conditions and minimizing the power disparities. Considering the advantages of contributing to such an interdisciplinary research area like rural innovation and entrepreneurship, the objective of this book chapter is to investigate the theoretical frameworks utilized in rural innovation and entrepreneurship studies in information systems (IS) context and thereby identify possible future research areas for IS researchers.

While researchers have studied the use of digital technologies in the developing countries context (e.g., Thaker et al. 2017; Venkatesh et al. 2016a; Venkatesh et al. 2016b), the context rurality is different to the context of developing countries. Therefore, it is important to define rurality in order to understand rural innovation and rural entrepreneurship. Most of the studies attempt to define rurality through social, economic and ecological components. For example, according to Dabson (2005) rurality can be defined through the differences in economy, values, environment and atmosphere. Further, studies such as Cloke (2006) conceptualize rurality using areas where most of the agricultural activities happen. While dissenting to the conceptualization of Cloke (2006), Newbery et al. (2017) proposes conceptualizing rurality through contextual factors such as peripherality from the center, uneven levels of development in terms of poverty, inequality and access to resources. Considering the prior conceptualizations, in this book chapter, rurality will be theorized by following the view of Stathopoulou et al. (2004), whereby rurality is determined through the three components such as geographic, social and economic.

According to Newbery et al. (2017), rural innovation and entrepreneurship plays a key role in promoting economic advances, providing more job opportunities and enhancing the livelihood of communities in the rural areas. Considering its importance, this book chapter is an attempt to contribute to the academia by providing an analysis on the extant theoretical frameworks on rural innovation and entrepreneurship. Through an archival analysis of major IS journals, this book chapter attempt to provide future research areas for IS researchers.

The remainder of this book chapter proceeds as follows. First, an overview to rural innovation and entrepreneurship is provided. Then, details of the literature review process are provided under the research methodology section. The analysis section provides the results of the literature review and a summary of theoretical foundations utilized in extant literature on rural innovation and entrepreneurship. Then, the theoretical framework for future research is provided. Finally, this article concludes by paving a path with an outlook on our next scholastic direction.

RURAL INNOVATION AND ENTREPRENEURSHIP

This section provides an overview to rural innovation and rural entrepreneurship literature. In order to provide an overarching view of rural innovation and entrepreneurship, not only IS research, but also management, innovation and entrepreneurship disciplines have been studied in this section.

Rural Innovation

Prior research alludes innovation to be a complex subject due to its mystical nature of its creation and adoption within an organization (Van de Ven 1986). Considering its importance and relevance, innovation has received attention of both academics and practitioners (Ahuja et al. 2016; Kohli and Melville 2019; Lokuge et al. 2019; Tan et al. 2016a). Innovation is considered as lifeblood or the survival mechanism for organizations in the contemporary competitive world (Leifer et al. 2000; Lewis et al. 2002; Utterback 1994). Though innovation is an extensively studied area, researchers posit various interpretations regarding innovation (Baregheh et al. 2009; Sears and Baba 2011). For example, there is a continuous debate among scholars in identifying innovation as a totally new idea or an imitation (Ruttan 1959). For most organizations, the term 'innovation' does not resonate with the 'new-to-the-world' concept. Researchers such as Lai et al. (2009) and Lyytinen and Rose (2003) argue that innovation need not be a totally new concept to the world and could even be considered as an imitation of something already used elsewhere, but new to the unit of adoption. For majority of organizations, innovation is not always an invention (Utterback 1971). As such, in this book chapter the latter conceptualization of innovation as an 'imitation of something already used elsewhere, but new to the unit of adoption' is followed. Following this, rural innovation is defined as the creation and implementation of new ideas or solutions, new to the unit of adoption, that deal with rural context (Sonne 2010).

When rural innovation is considered as an innovation, such conceptualization provides an opportunity to study it through widely classified typologies of innovation such as product innovation, process innovation, technical innovation and administrative innovation (Benner and Tushman 2003; Damanpour 1987; Damanpour 1991). Since the rurality in rural innovation encompasses its impacts on the social systems, as Pato (2015) suggested there are further extensions that are available for researchers when studying rural innovation. Further, with the advent of digital technologies, the accessibility to these technologies have provided unprecedented opportunities for small business owners in rural regions to innovate like resourceful counterparts. As a result, there is an opportunity for IS researchers to provide their expertise in digital innovation, innovation readiness, digital technology use, technology-led innovation and innovation adoption in the rural context.

Rural Entrepreneurship

Nambisan (2017, p. 1029) states that "digital technologies have transformed the nature of uncertainty inherent in entrepreneurial processes and outcomes as well as the ways of dealing with such uncertainty." Such discourses highlight the very nature of digital technologies and how they are changing the way entrepreneurs initiate their new business ideas. The relatively inexpensive, on-demand, functionally oriented, flexible digital technologies provide entrepreneurs with more opportunities to innovate (Lokuge and Sedera 2016; Lokuge et al. 2018; Nylén and Holmström 2015; Zittrain 2006). Such characteristics of digital technologies curtail the traditional barriers for entrepreneurship (Nambisan 2017). As such, rural communities are provided with an opportunity to become entrepreneurs (Tan et al. 2016b). Prior IS researchers have investigated common issues in IT use in developing countries (Leong et al. 2017; Leong et al. 2016b). In addition, such researchers have focused their attention on entrepreneurship in the growth stage of the entrepreneurial lifecycle (Tumbas et al. 2017; Wright and Stigliani 2013). Further, with the advent of new technologies such as mobile and social media, it is interesting to investigate how entrepreneurs in rural areas have utilized these platforms to identify new opportunities (Fischer and Reuber 2014). As such, the use of digital technologies in rural entrepreneurship context is an important yet, under-studied topic in the IS discipline.

The rural areas are inherently challenged with heterogeneous economic structures, government instability, weak and unstable economic institutions and limited skills and knowledge regarding business and technologies (Ernst 2002; Gupta 2013; Sedera et al. 2014; Tate et al. 2013). However, entrepreneurial activities play an important role in sustaining the socio-economic growth in rural areas (Pato 2015; Xiao et al. 2013). While rural entrepreneurship has been a much discussed topic of interest among researchers (Gaddefors and Anderson 2019; Newbery et al. 2017; Pato and Teixeira 2016; Wortman Jr 1990; Zahra 2007), most of the research on rural entrepreneurship has been conducted by relating rural context to entrepreneurship (Gaddefors and Anderson 2019). However, Stathopoulou et al. (2004) suggest that the geographic, social and economic contextual factors will provide different theoretical implication from this unique entrepreneurial genre. As such, it is interesting to analyze the nature of studies conducted in IS regarding rural entrepreneurship. Given the importance of rural entrepreneurship, it is important to understand theoretical foundations applied in the extant literature. By doing so, this book chapter attempt to provide new areas of research for rural entrepreneurship.

RESEARCH METHODOLOGY

This section of the book chapter details the methodology used in collating, synthesizing and analyzing the rural innovation and entrepreneurship literature. It outlines the search strategy and the journals reviewed for the analysis. The review of literature on rural innovation and entrepreneurship includes studies published between 1st of January 2009 to 31st of December 2019. Table 1 lists all journal outlets in IS used for the literature review. The selection of journals was inspired by the basket of eight journals list. Table 2 includes references of all the papers reviewed in the archival analysis from 2009 – 2019. The selection of the papers preferred inclusion, over exclusivity. In here, while searching for papers, even though the objective is to identify the application of digital technologies in the rural context, no specification was made for identifying papers on digital technologies in the rural context. That allowed us to canvass substantial body of developing literature. Each article identified through the search was read in its entirety and the relevance was determined. The most relevant papers were identified and then the theoretical frameworks of the papers were identified. The following keywords were used in the search "rural, developing nation*, developing countr*, developing econom*." The papers that were published from 2009 – 2019 in the last decade was considered for the analysis. However, for 2009, no paper related to rural innovation or entrepreneurship was found. At the end, the study included 22 papers that were considered relevant for the analysis.

Table 1. Journals taken for the analysis

Acronym	Journal Name
MISQ	Management Information Systems Quarterly
ISR	Information Systems Research
JMIS	Journal of Management Information Systems
JAIS	Journal of Association for Information Systems
JIT	Journal of Information Technology
ISJ	Information Systems Journal
JSIS	Journal of Strategic Information Systems
EJIS	European Journal of Information Systems

Table 2. Details of the papers taken for the analysis

Year	Reference	Count
2010	(Okoli et al. 2010)	1
2011	(Brown and Thompson 2011; Datta 2011)	2
2013	(Dobson et al. 2013; Foster and Heeks 2013; Tarafdar et al. 2013; Venkatesh and Sykes 2013)	4
2014	(Sanner et al. 2014; Venkatesh et al. 2014)	2
2015	(Sandeep and Ravishankar 2015a; Sandeep and Ravishankar 2015b; Singh et al. 2015)	3
2016	(Leong et al. 2016a; Venkatesh et al. 2016a)	2
2017	(Bernardi et al. 2017; Cui et al. 2017)	2
2018	(Slavova and Karanasios 2018)	1
2019	(Chipidza and Leidner 2019; Cui et al. 2019; Karanasios and Slavova 2019; Li et al. 2019; Pethig and Kroenung 2019)	5

Table 2 details all details of the papers taken for the analysis.

Table 3. Breakdown of the papers taken for the analysis

Journal	2019	2018	2017	2016	2015	2014	2013	2012	2011	2010	2009
MISQ	0	0	0	1	1	0	1	0	0	0	0
ISR	0	0	0	1	0	0	1	0	0	0	0
JMIS	0	0	0	0	0	0	0	0	0	0	0
JAIS	1	1	1	0	0	1	0	0	0	0	0
JIT	0	0	0	0	0	0	2	0	0	0	0
ISJ	2	1	0	0	1	1	0	0	1	0	0
JSIS	1	0	1	0	1	0	0	0	0	0	0
EJIS	0	0	0	0	0	0	0	0	1	1	0

Analysis

This section provides the results of the analysis. Table 3 below depicts the number of papers used for the archival analysis. Out of the 22 papers, most of the papers were on e-commerce adoption in the rural context. Except for 4 papers, all 18 papers followed a case study approach.

Additionally, an analysis based on the country where data is sourced from was conducted. For example, India, where 69% of the population live in rural areas had only 6 studies related to rural innovation and entrepreneurship in the sample. China was the second most frequently referred country, followed by Ghana, Kenya, Georgia and Australia. Overall, the results of the analysis highlights that there is a clear lack of focus on rural context and lot of opportunities for researchers to conduct new research.

In addition, the theories that have been applied was identified and Table 4 provides a summary of all the theories used in the review. Based on the analysis, 16 theories/frameworks were identified. The Arab policy and IT (APIT) model (Hill et al. 1998) was not considered for the analysis as it is not a theory. Activity theory (Leont'ev 1978) was the most commonly used theory in the sample. In addition to this, Resource orchestration perspective (Sirmon et al. 2011) and Frame theory (Cornelissen and Werner 2014) were commonly applied by researchers. The analysis of the sample highlighted that, most studies employed organizational-level theories and that only a handful of studies considered individual or group-level theories. The predominant focus on employing organizational level theories is understandable given that the overall focus of rural innovation initiatives tends to be at the organizational level. However, by focusing on individual-level adoption, proliferation, management and the benefits of rural entrepreneurship initiatives, practitioners could get better insights.

FUTURE RESEARCH DIRECTIONS

Figure 1 provides the proposed framework for studying rural innovation and entrepreneurship using digital technologies. Figure 1 summarizes the future research areas for rural innovation and entrepreneurship literature.

When considering the theories utilized in rural innovation and entrepreneurship context in IS discipline, it is evident that IS researchers have myriad of opportunities in this area. For example, when considering theories such as the technology diffusion theory of Rogers (1995), even though this has been used in rural innovation context, this theory requires a rethink. As per Brown and Thompson (2011) an organic process subject to market push-pull mechanisms, is not sufficient for rural innovation context as in the rural context, not only the organizational level factors, but also many other individual and societal factors hinder the diffusion of rural innovation. Investigation of such factors will add value not only to the academia, but also to the practitioners. In addition, technology acceptance model (Davis 1989), theory of planned behavior (Ajzen 1991) and theory of reasoned action (Ajzen and Fishbein 1973) can be extended to rural innovation context, applying to the rurality context. The technology acceptance model (Davis 1989) provides theoretical explanation to better understand the innovation adoption behaviors of individuals (Salim et al. 2014). The individuals in a rural context differs from economical, geographical and social aspects. As such, IS researchers could identify new factors that affects the adoption behavior of the rural community. The UTAUT (Venkatesh et al. 2003) can also be extended by similar to technology acceptance model (Davis 1989). Similarly, the innovation diffusion in rural community can be affected by different contextual factors as such, Rogers's innovation diffusion theory too can be applied to generate new insights.

Table 4. Identified theories in the analysis

Theory	Explanation/paper brief	Reference
Activity theory (Leont'ev 1978)	As per activity theory, human activity is considered as a subject (a person or a group) acting upon an object (the problem, situation, or focus of the activity), with the activity being mediated by means of material artifacts. The artifact is also referred to as tools. In this paper, by applying activity theory, the paper highlights how changes in the information and communication technologies among smallholder farmers in Ghana, led to a process of hybridization of information practices. The study also investigates the changes introduced as a result of using information and communication technologies.	(Slavova and Karanasios 2018)
	This paper applies activity theory to examine how development actors within the Ghanaian agricultural sector endorse information technology in their day-to-day farming practices in the rural areas.	(Karanasios and Slavova 2019)
	The paper applies activity theory to understand the role of governments in rural China in managing rural e-commerce ecosystems and the impact of such ecosystems on poverty alleviation.	(Li et al. 2019)
Actor network theory (Callon 1999)	The theory posits that networks comprise of both social and technical parts and these elements are treated as inseparable by the theory. This paper utilizes actor network theory to explain ecommerce adoption in a rural context, which can be considered as an innovation. By utilizing actor network theory and unified theory of acceptance and use of technology, the paper proposes a global information technology adoption model.	(Datta 2011)
Effectuation theory (Sarasvathy 2001)	This theory describes how social entrepreneurs act in resource constrained environments. In a resource-constrained environment, the entrepreneurs follow an intuitive decision-making process, sometimes disregarding the rational choices on offer. This paper applies effectuation theory to understand the process of impact sourcing, investigate motivational triggers of impact sourcing entrepreneurship, the entrepreneurial actions underpinning different phases of venture creation and the positive institutional-level influences on impact sourcing of Indian companies. This theory has been widely used in entrepreneurship studies.	(Sandeep and Ravishankar 2015b)
Frame theory (Cornelissen and Werner 2014)	Frame theory posits that frames are socio-cognitive structures that individuals use to make sense of the world. Through these frames, policymakers understand the problems and identify possible solutions. This paper through the application of frame theory, investigates how incongruent frames evolve over time in IS innovation and what implications and changes the adoption of IS have on innovation processes in the rural healthcare innovation setting.	(Bernardi et al. 2017)
	By applying frame theory, this paper investigates how impact sourcing ventures frame their activities to marginalized communities. The paper provides an overview to the difficulties faced by impact sourcing ventures in operationalizing their strategic intent and how different and diverse framings are used by impact sourcing ventures to influence the local rural community.	(Sandeep and Ravishankar 2015a)
Innovation diffusion theory (Rogers 1995)	The innovation diffusion theory explains why, and at which rate new ideas and technologies spread. The theory posits that the innovators are eager to adopt new technologies; however, individuals who are risk-averse, cautious and skeptical are more likely to be laggards, in terms of adopting technology compared to innovators. Usually there is a general mistrust among governments and communities in rural areas. As such, there is a reluctance among rural communities in adopting eGovernment initiatives, which can be considered as an innovation for the rural communities.	(Venkatesh et al. 2014)
Institutional theory (DiMaggio and Powell 1983)	Institutional factors have been applied to understand e-government policies and initiatives undertaken by the Government of Jamaica. The institutional theory provides the theoretical underpinning to understanding the socially constructed evolving logics that give meaning to organizational actions. This theory has been applied in understanding technological innovations. In this paper, the institutional theory is applied to understand a rural telehealth innovation and to understand the organizational transformations and path constitution patterns.	(Brown and Thompson 2011)
Market efficiency theory (Kendall and Dearden 2018)	The market efficiency theory has been applied to investigate the use of contemporary technologies such as mobile technologies in agri-business to get agriculture related information, market information and to identify market trends. The theory posits that the key problem of the farmer is the inability to gain a fair price for their products. According to the theory, the adoption of technologies for agriculture can enhance the participation of the farmers and thereby can get a greater income for their produce.	(Karanasios and Slavova 2019)
Path constitution theory (Van de Ven and Poole 1995)	This theory combines path dependence and path creation perspectives. Path dependence focuses on historically embedded, contingent processes that are beyond the control of the actors. Path creation focuses on mindful contributions from powerful actors. The paper applies path dependence and path creation perspectives to understand how technological innovation paths constitute in organizational contexts.	(Singh et al. 2015)
Postcolonial theory (Adam and Myers 2003)	The theory provides an understanding to the ways in which colonialism continues to affect the former colonies after political independence. The theory emphasizes the negative effects of power asymmetries on development projects in former colonies (developing countries). The asymmetric power relationship can be applied to the rural context as well. This theory can be applied to the rural context as this covers contextual factors such as culture, leadership, identity and power that defines the rurality. This can be applied to both rural innovation and entrepreneurship context.	(Chipidza and Leidner 2019)

continued on following page

Table 4. Continued

Theory	Explanation/paper brief	Reference
Resource orchestration perspective (Sirmon et al. 2011)	Resource orchestration theory extends the resource based view (Barney 1991) by proposing that resources alone might not have rare, inimitability, valuable, non-substitutable characteristics that promote competitive advantage. However, orchestration of resources can provide such characteristic which may lead to gain competitive advantage. This paper applies orchestration perspective to investigate how social entrepreneurs in rural China orchestrate resources to achieve social innovation and it explains the processes for achieving social innovations in the rural context.	(Cui et al. 2017)
	This paper investigates community capability, a capability developed through a lead user's individual capability and the interactions between bundling product and e-commerce knowledge resources by rural community members and structuring institutional and legal resources by the local government. The authors further investigated the relationship between the individual capability of a lead user and the interactions between the resource orchestrations of different stakeholders and community capability using the resource orchestration perspective.	(Cui et al. 2019)
Social identity theory (Tajfel 1981)	Social identity theory postulates that social category (e.g., nationality, political affiliation) with which an individual feels a sense of belonging provides a definition of that individual. However, an individual may feel belonging to multiple social categories. Through the application of this theory and social markedness theory, the paper suggests two mechanisms by which functional limitations affect a digitally disadvantaged person's adoption decision. They are: (i) technology perceptions (i.e., perceived usefulness, perceived ease of use, and perceived access barriers), and (ii) marked status awareness (i.e., stigma consciousness).	(Pethig and Kroenung 2019)
Social markedness theory (Brekhus 1998)	Social markedness theory holds the view that social actors actively perceive one side of a contrast while ignoring the other side as epistemologically unproblematic. In the paper, marked individuals are considered as those who are digitally advantaged. Through the application of this theory and social identity theory, the paper provides two mechanisms by which functional limitations affect a digitally disadvantaged person's adoption decision. They are: (i) technology perceptions and (ii) marked status awareness.	(Pethig and Kroenung 2019)
Social network theory (Wasserman and Faust 1994)	Social network theory provides a theoretical lens to understand how individuals' ties with others in a given network. This paper applied social network theory to understand the benefits of a digital divide intervention that is influenced by the power and the actors in the network.	(Venkatesh and Sykes 2013)
Theory of market separations (Bartels 1968)	The market separations theory describes barriers in the flow of goods, information, and money that obstruct the market exchanges between producers and consumers. The theory provides four types of disconnections between producers and consumers. They are: Spatial, Temporal, Informational, and Financial. By utilizing this theoretical perspective, the paper investigates how and why ICT-enabled innovations in products and processes deployed for market development at the bottom of the pyramid (individuals whose income is less than $2 per day), enable developmental outcomes through reduction of market separations.	(Tarafdar et al. 2013)
Unified theory of acceptance and use of technology (UTAUT) (Venkatesh et al. 2003)	The unified theory of acceptance and use of technology theory was developed through a review and union of the constructs of eight models such as theory of reasoned action, technology acceptance model, motivational model, theory of planned behavior, a combined theory of planned behavior/technology acceptance model, model of PC utilization, innovation diffusion theory, and social cognitive theory. The UTAUT attempts to explain user intentions to use an IS and subsequent usage behavior. According to UTAUT, four key constructs such as performance expectancy, effort expectancy, social influence, and facilitating conditions are considered as determinants of usage intention and behavior.	(Datta 2011)

While the development of new theories such as power parity theory (Chipidza and Leidner 2019) is applicable to developing nations and ICT4D (information and communication for development), the asymmetry in power can be applied to the rural innovation and entrepreneurship context as well. For example, even in a developed nation, the rural areas have disparity in resources, infrastructure and skills. As such, IS researchers could apply their expertise in contributing to academia and practice.

For rural entrepreneurship context, the application of chauffeur theory (Markus 2001) can add value. As per chauffeur theory (Markus 2001), the leaders are not only information coordinators, but also ecosystem orchestrators and the source of motivation. Since in a rural context, the entrepreneur is faced with resource limitations, this can be applied to understand the rural entrepreneurs' behavior.

Figure 1. Rural innovation and entrepreneurship future research areas

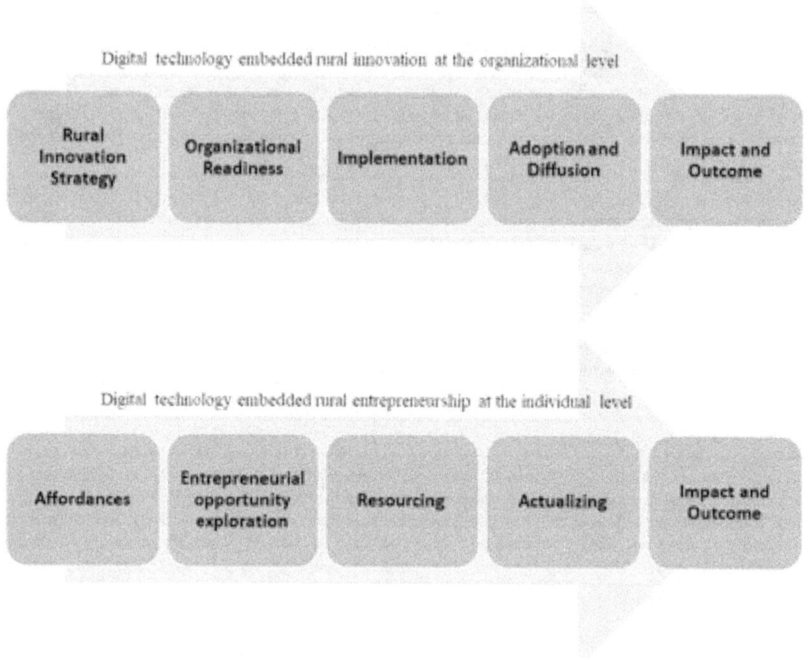

Affordances captures the positivity the stakeholders have towards entrepreneurship and how they perceive digital technology in the context of rural entrepreneurship. The entrepreneurial exploration, resourcing, actualizing, can be applied to assess rural entrepreneurship. With the advent of digital technologies, it is interesting to see how these technologies affect each of these important aspects of entrepreneurship in the rural context.

Future studies of rural innovation and entrepreneurship can consider the below areas as well:

- **Rural innovation modes:** there are three types of innovation modes discussed in literature. For example, incremental, quantum, and disruptive innovation. The incremental innovation refers to gradual improvements. The quantum innovation refers to a major improvement to an existing initiative that displaces current understanding (Maxwell 2009). The disruptive innovation as the name suggests is a major improvement to an existing initiative. Similarly, researchers can identify different rural innovation modes and contextual factors for such innovation modes.
- **Rural innovation and entrepreneurship contextual factors:** Most of the rural innovation and entrepreneurship research to date has focused on studying adoption factors. The IS researchers could identify new contextual factors considering the novelty of the rurality context by conducting case studies and surveys.
- **Rural innovation strategies:** The IS researchers can utilize their years of expertise in technology led strategies, resource-based view and strategic management literature in identifying new strategies for rural context. Further, the role of the technology in rural innovation and entrepreneurship, leadership and the management of strategies for successful innovation can be further studied.
- **Dimensions of rural innovation and entrepreneurship:** prior research on innovation generally distinguish innovation by the speed of the innovation process and its frequency to deliver innova-

tions to the market (Benner and Tushman 2003). Innovation speed can be defined as the duration of the ideation and the commercialization of an innovation (Kessler and Chakrabarti 1996). Innovation frequency determines how often an organization introduces and delivers new products and services to the market (Pettigrew et al. 2001). Similar concepts can be applied to rural innovation and entrepreneurship context to add value to academia and practitioners.

CONCLUSION

In reviewing the academic papers, it was evident that rural innovation and entrepreneurship have not yet received its due diligence. In almost all countries around the world, there are rural areas where there is lack of infrastructure, lack of resources and geographically distant from the urban areas. According to World Bank, in 2015 45% of the population resides in rural communities in the world. Even though, the impact of rural innovation and entrepreneurship is high, this concept is new to many countries and communities. With the advent of digital technologies rural communities similar to urban communities are provided with myriad opportunities for innovation and entrepreneurial activities (Cui et al. 2019; Li et al. 2019). The objective of this book chapter was to investigate the application of digital technologies in rural innovation and entrepreneurship in information systems (IS) context and thereby identify the future research areas for IS researchers. To identify the theoretical opportunities, this book chapter analyzed papers on rural innovation and entrepreneurship published in top IS journals from 2009-2019. Based on the analysis, 16 theories/frameworks were identified and only 15 theories were utilized for the analysis. While most of these theories are on organizational level, there are lot of opportunities for future research areas. For example, there is an opportunity for IS researchers to provide their expertise in digital innovation, innovation readiness, digital technology use, technology-led innovation and innovation adoption in the rural context. Also, they can utilize different methodologies to assess the rural context as well (Sedera et al. 2003; Sedera et al. 2001). Further, the researchers can investigate environmental factors, organizational factors, technological factors and individual factors that affect rural innovation and entrepreneurship. Through the review of literature, it was evident that in IS outlets, none of the papers investigated innovation using digital technologies. As such, it was clear that there is a huge opportunity for IS researchers to contribute to research on rural innovation and entrepreneurship using digital technologies. Further, this book chapter provided a framework that can be utilized for IS researchers for identifying future research areas in rural innovation and entrepreneurship.

REFERENCES

Adam, M. S., & Myers, M. D. (2003). Have You Got Anything to Declare? In *Organizational Information Systems in the Context of Globalization* (pp. 101–115). Springer. doi:10.1007/978-0-387-35695-2_7

Ahuja, S., Chan, Y., & Denford, J. (2016). IT-Enabled Innovation and Improvisation in Canadian Smes: A Qualitative Comparative Analysis. In *Americas Conference on Information Systems*. San Diego: AIS.

Ajzen, I. (1991). The Theory of Planned Behavior. *Organizational Behavior and Human Decision Processes*, *50*(2), 179-211.

Ajzen, I., & Fishbein, M. (1973). Attitudinal and Normative Variables as Predictors of Specific Behavior. *Journal of Personality and Social Psychology*, *27*(1), 41-57.

Baregheh, A., Rowley, J., & Sambrook, S. (2009). Towards a Multidisciplinary Definition of Innovation. *Management Decision*, *47*(8), 1323-1339.

Barney, J. (1991). Firm Resources and Sustained Competitive Advantage. *Journal of Management*, *17*(1), 99-120.

Bartels, R. (1968). The General Theory of Marketing. *Journal of Marketing*, *32*(1), 29-33.

Benner, M.J., & Tushman, M.L. (2003). Exploitation, Exploration, and Process Management: The Productivity Dilemma Revisited. *Academy of Management Review*, *28*(2), 238-256.

Bernardi, R., Constantinides, P., & Nandhakumar, J. (2017). Challenging Dominant Frames in Policies for IS Innovation in Healthcare through Rhetorical Strategies. *Journal of the Association for Information Systems*, *18*(2), 81–112.

Brekhus, W. (1998). A Sociology of the Unmarked: Redirecting Our Focus. *Sociological Theory*, *16*(1), 34-51.

Brown, D.H., & Thompson, S. (2011). Priorities, Policies and Practice of E-Government in a Developing Country Context: Ict Infrastructure and Diffusion in Jamaica. *European Journal of Information Systems*, *20*(3), 329-342.

Callon, M. (1999). Actor-Network Theory—the Market Test. *The Sociological Review*, *47*(1), 181-195.

Chipidza, W., & Leidner, D. (2019). A Review of the Ict-Enabled Development Literature: Towards a Power Parity Theory of Ict4d. *The Journal of Strategic Information Systems*, *28*(2), 145-174.

Cloke, P. (2006). Conceptualizing Rurality. In P. Cloke (Ed.), *Handbook of Rural Studies*. Sage. doi:10.4135/9781848608016.n2

Cornelissen, J.P., & Werner, M.D. (2014). Putting Framing in Perspective: A Review of Framing and Frame Analysis across the Management and Organizational Literature. *Academy of Management Annals*, *8*(1), 181-235.

Cui, M., Pan, S.L., & Cui, L. (2019). Developing Community Capability for E-Commerce Development in Rural China: A Resource Orchestration Perspective. *Information Systems Journal*, *29*(4), 953-988.

Cui, M., Pan, S.L., Newell, S., & Cui, L. (2017). Strategy, Resource Orchestration and E-Commerce Enabled Social Innovation in Rural China. *The Journal of Strategic Information Systems*, *26*(1), 3-21.

Dabson, B. (2005). Entrepreneurship as a Real Community and Economic Development Strategy. In *Rural policy research institute & Truman school of public affairs*. University of Missouri.

Damanpour, F. (1987). The Adoption of Technological, Administrative, and Ancillary Innovations: Impact of Organizational Factors. *Journal of Management*, *13*(4), 675-688.

Damanpour, F. (1991). Organizational Innovation: A Meta-Analysis of Effects of Determinants and Moderators. *Academy of Management Journal*, *34*(3), 555-590.

Datta, P. (2011). A Preliminary Study of Ecommerce Adoption in Developing Countries. *Information Systems Journal*, *21*(1), 3-32.

Davis, F.D. (1989). Perceived Usefulness, Perceived Ease of Use, and User Acceptance of Information Technology. *MIS Quarterly*, (13), 319-340.

DiMaggio, P., & Powell, W.W. (1983). The Iron Cage Revisited: Collective Rationality and Institutional Isomorphism in Organizational Fields. *American Sociological Review*, *48*(2), 147-160.

Dobson, P., Jackson, P., & Gengatharen, D. (2013). Explaining Broadband Adoption in Rural Australia: Modes of Reflexivity and the Morphogenetic Approach. *MIS Quarterly*, *37*(3), 965-991.

Ernst, D. (2002). Global Production Networks and the Changing Geography of Innovation Systems. Implications for Developing Countries. *Economics of Innovation and New Technology*, *11*(6), 497-523.

Fischer, E., & Reuber, A.R. (2014). Online Entrepreneurial Communication: Mitigating Uncertainty and Increasing Differentiation Via Twitter. *Journal of Business Venturing*, *29*(4), 565-583.

Foster, C., & Heeks, R. (2013). Innovation and Scaling of Ict for the Bottom-of-the-Pyramid. *Journal of Information Technology*, *28*(4), 296-315.

Gaddefors, J., & Anderson, A.R. (2019). Romancing the Rural: Reconceptualizing Rural Entrepreneurship as Engagement with Context(s). *The International Journal of Entrepreneurship and Innovation*, *20*(3), 159-169.

Gupta, A.K. (2013). Tapping the Entrepreneurial Potential of Grassroots Innovation. *Stanford Social Innovation Review*, *11*(3), 18-20.

Hill, C.E., Loch, K.D., Straub, D., & El-Sheshai, K. (1998). A Qualitative Assessment of Arab Culture and Information Technology Transfer. *Journal of Global Information Management*, *6*(3), 29-38.

Karanasios, S., & Slavova, M. (2019). How Do Development Actors Do "Ict for Development"? A Strategy-as-Practice Perspective on Emerging Practices in Ghanaian Agriculture. *Information Systems Journal*, *29*(4), 888-913.

Kendall, L., & Dearden, A. (2018). Towards Alternate Theories of Change for M4ard. In R. Duncombe (Ed.), *Digital Technologies for Agricultural and Rural Development in the Global South* (pp. 92–103). CABI. doi:10.1079/9781786393364.0092

Kessler, E.H., & Chakrabarti, A.K. (1996). Innovation Speed: A Conceptual Model of Context, Antecedents and Outcomes. *Academy of Management Review*, *21*(4), 1143-1191.

Kohli, R., & Melville, N.P. (2019). Digital Innovation: A Review and Synthesis. *Information Systems Journal*, *29*(1), 200-223.

Lai, E.L.-C., Riezman, R., & Wang, P. (2009). Outsourcing of Innovation. *Economic Theory*, *38*(3), 485-515.

Leifer, R., McDermott, C. M. G., Peters, L.S., Rice, M.P., & Veryzer, R.W. (2000). Radical Innovation: How Mature Companies Can Outsmart Upstairs. Boston, MA: Harvard Business School Press.

Leong, C., Tan, B., Xiao, X., Tan, F.T.C., & Sun, Y. (2017). Nurturing a Fintech Ecosystem: The Case of a Youth Microloan Startup in China. *International Journal of Information Management*, *37*(2), 92-97.

Leong, C.M.L., Pan, S.-L., Newell, S., & Cui, L. (2016a). The Emergence of Self-Organizing E-Commerce Ecosystems in Remote Villages of China: A Tale of Digital Empowerment for Rural Development. *MIS Quarterly*, *40*(2), 475-484.

Leong, C. M. L., Pan, S. L., Zhu, K., & Cui, L. (2016b). Digitally Enabled Grassroots Enterpreneurship for Rural Development. In *Pacific Asia Conference on Information Systems*. Chiyai, Taiwan: AIS.

Leont'ev, A. N. (1978). *Activity, Consciousness, and Personality*. Prentice-Hall.

Lewis, M.W., Welsh, M.A., Dehler, G.E., & Green, S.G. (2002). Product Development Tensions: Exploring Contrasting Styles of Project Management. *Academy of Management Journal*, *45*(3), 546-564.

Li, L., Du, K., Zhang, W., & Mao, J.Y. (2019). Poverty Alleviation through Government-Led E-Commerce Development in Rural China: An Activity Theory Perspective. *Information Systems Journal*, *29*(4), 914-952.

Lokuge, S., & Sedera, D. (2016). Is Your IT Eco-System Ready to Facilitate Organizational Innovation? Deriving an IT Eco-System Readiness Measurement Model. In *International Conference on Information Systems*. Dublin, Ireland: AIS.

Lokuge, S., & Sedera, D. (2018). The Role of Enterprise Systems in Fostering Innovation in Contemporary Firms. *Journal of Information Technology Theory and Application, 19*(2), 7-30.

Lokuge, S., Sedera, D., Atapattu, M., & Samaranayaka, D. (2016). Exploring the Role of IS in Agriculture: Creating an Agenda Towards Agri-Informatics. In *Pacific Asia Conference on Information Systems*. Chiyai, Taiwan: AIS.

Lokuge, S., Sedera, D., Grover, V., & Xu, D. (2019). Organizational Readiness for Digital Innovation: Development and Empirical Calibration of a Construct. *Information & Management*, *56*(3), 445-461.

Lokuge, S., Sedera, D., & Nanayakkara, S. (2018). Innovate or Copy: A Qualitative Document Analysis to Entrepreneurship in Developing Countries. In *European Conference on Information Systems*. Portsmouth, UK: AIS.

Lyytinen, K., & Rose, G.M. (2003). The Disruptive Nature of Information Technology Innovations: The Case of Internet Computing in Systems Development Organizations. *MIS Quarterly*, *27*(4), 557-596.

Markus, L. (2001). Toward a Theory of Knowledge Reuse: Types of Knowledge Reuse Situations and Factors in Reuse Success. *Journal of Management Information Systems*, *18*(1), 57-93.

Maxwell, I. E. (2009). *Managing Sustainable Innovation: The Driver for Global Growth*. Springer. doi:10.1007/978-0-387-87581-1

Nambisan, S. (2013). Information Technology and Product/Service Innovation: A Brief Assessment and Some Suggestions for Future Research. *Journal of the Association for Information Systems*, *14*(4), 215-226.

Nambisan, S. (2017). Digital Entrepreneurship: Toward a Digital Technology Perspective of Entrepreneurship. *Entrepreneurship Theory and Practice*, *41*(6), 1029-1055.

Newbery, R., Siwale, J., & Henley, A. (2017). Editorial: Rural Entrepreneurship Theory in the Developing and Developed World. *International Journal of Entrepreneurship and Innovation*, *18*(1), 3-4.

Nylén, D., & Holmström, J. (2015). Digital Innovation Strategy: A Framework for Diagnosing and Improving Digital Product and Service Innovation. *Business Horizons*, *58*(1), 57-67.

Okoli, C., Mbarika, V.W., & McCoy, S. (2010). The Effects of Infrastructure and Policy on E-Business in Latin America and Sub-Saharan Africa. *European Journal of Information Systems*, *19*(1), 5-20.

Pato, L. (2015). Rural Entrepreneurship and Innovation: Some Successful Women's Initiatives. In *55th Congress of the European Regional Science Association*. Lisbon, Portugal: European Regional Science Association (ERSA).

Pato, M.L., & Teixeira, A.A. (2016). Twenty Years of Rural Entrepreneurship: A Bibliometric Survey. *Sociologia Ruralis*, *56*(1), 3-28.

Pethig, F., & Kroenung, J. (2019). Specialized Information Systems for the Digitally Disadvantaged. *Journal of the Association for Information Systems*, *20*(10), 1412-1446.

Pettigrew, A.M., Woodman, R.W., & Cameron, K.S. (2001). Studying Organizational Change and Development: Challenges for Future Research. *Academy of Management Journal*, *44*(4), 697-713.

Rogers, E. M. (1995). Diffusion of Innovations (4th ed.). New York: Free Press.

Ruttan, V.W. (1959). Usher and Schumpeter on Invention, Innovation, and Technological Change. *The Quarterly Journal of Economics*, *73*(4), 596-606.

Salemink, K., Strijker, D., & Bosworth, G. (2017). Rural Development in the Digital Age: A Systematic Literature Review on Unequal Ict Availability, Adoption, and Use in Rural Areas. *Journal of Rural Studies*, *54*, 360–371. doi:10.1016/j.jrurstud.2015.09.001

Salim, S. A., Sedera, D., Sawang, S., & Alarifi, A. (2014). Technology Adoption as a Multi-Stage Process. In *Australasian Conference on Information Systems (ACIS)*. Auckland, New Zealand: ACIS.

Sandeep, M., & Ravishankar, M. (2015a). Impact Sourcing Ventures and Local Communities: A Frame Alignment Perspective. *Information Systems Journal*, *26*(2), 127-155.

Sandeep, M., & Ravishankar, M. (2015b). Social Innovations in Outsourcing: An Empirical Investigation of Impact Sourcing Companies in India. *The Journal of Strategic Information Systems*, *24*(4), 270-288.

Sanner, T.A., Manda, T.D., & Nielsen, P. (2014). Grafting: Balancing Control and Cultivation in Information Infrastructure Innovation. *Journal of the Association for Information Systems*, *15*(4), 220-243.

Sarasvathy, S.D. (2001). Causation and Effectuation: Toward a Theoretical Shift from Economic Inevitability to Entrepreneurial Contingency. *Academy of Management Review*, *26*(2), 243–263.

Sears, G.J., & Baba, V.V. (2011). Toward a Multistage, Multilevel Theory of Innovation. *Canadian Journal of Administrative Sciences*, *28*(4), 357-372.

Sedera, D., Gable, G., & Chan, T. (2003). Survey Design: Insights from a Public Sector-ERP Impact Study. In *Proceedings of the 7th Pacific Asia Conference on Information Systems*. Adelaide, Australia: Association for Information Systems.

Sedera, D., & Lokuge, S. (2017). The Role of Enterprise Systems in Innovation in the Contemporary Organization. In R. G. Galliers & M.-K. Stein (Eds.), *The Routledge Companion to Management Information Systems* (p. 608). The Routledge. doi:10.4324/9781315619361-21

Sedera, D., Lokuge, S., Grover, V., Sarker, S., & Sarker, S. (2016). Innovating with Enterprise Systems and Digital Platforms: A Contingent Resource-Based Theory View. *Information & Management*, *53*(3), 366–379.

Sedera, D., Lokuge, S., Krcmar, H., Srivastava, S.C., & Ravishankar, M.N. (2014). The Future of Outsourcing in the Asia-Pacific Region: Implications for Research and Practice—Panel Report from Pacis 2014. *Communications of the Association for Information Systems*, *35*(1), 317-331.

Sedera, D., Rosemann, M., & Gable, G. (2001). Using Performance Measurement Models for Benefit Realization with Enterprise Systems - the Queensland Government Approach. In *European Conference on Information Systems*. Bled, Slovenia: AIS.

Singh, R., Mathiassen, L., & Mishra, A. (2015). Organizational Path Constitution in Technological Innovation: Evidence from Rural Telehealth. *MIS Quarterly*, *39*(3), 643-665.

Sirmon, D.G., Hitt, M.A., Ireland, R.D., & Gilbert, B.A. (2011). Resource Orchestration to Create Competitive Advantage Breadth, Depth, and Life Cycle Effects. *Journal of Management*, *37*(5), 1390-1412.

Slavova, M., & Karanasios, S. (2018). When Institutional Logics Meet Information and Communication Technologies: Examining Hybrid Information Practices in Ghana's Agriculture. *Journal of the Association for Information Systems*, *19*(9), 775-812.

Sonne, L. (2010). Pro-Poor, Entrepreneur-Based Innovation and It's Role in Rural Development. In *UNU-MERIT Paper Series*. United Nations University.

Stathopoulou, S., Psaltopoulos, D., & Skuras, D. (2004). Rural Entrepreneurship in Europe: A Research Framework and Agenda. *International Journal of Entrepreneurial Behavior & Research*, *10*(6), 404-425.

Tajfel, H. (1981). *Human Groups and Social Categories: Studies in Social Psychology*. Cambridge University Press.

Tan, F. T. C., Ky, D., & Tan, B. (2016a). Toward a Process Theory of IT-Enabled Frugal Innovation: The Role of Organizational Bricolage in Koufu Singapore. In *Pacific Asian Conference on Information Systems*. AIS.

Tan, F.T.C., Tan, B., & Pan, S.L. (2016b). Developing a Leading Digital Multi-Sided Platform: Examining IT Affordances and Competitive Actions in Alibaba.Com. *Communications of the Association for Information Systems*, *38*(36), 738–760.

Tarafdar, M., Singh, R., & Anekal, P. (2013). Impact of Ict-Enabled Product and Process Innovations at the Bottom of the Pyramid: A Market Separations Perspective. *Journal of Information Technology*, *28*(4), 279-295.

Tate, M., Sedera, D., McLean, E., & Burton-Jones, A. (2013). Information Systems Success Research: The "Twenty Year Update?" Panel Report from Pacis, 2011. *Communications of the Association for Information Systems*, *34*, 1.

Thaker, J.K., Chakrawal, A., & Goyal, P. (2017). A Study of Innovative Attitude of Indian Entrepreneurs of Various Industries in the Context to Educational and Economic Background. *International Research Journal of Multidisciplinary Studies*, *3*(6), 1-10.

Tumbas, S., Berente, N., & vom Brocke, J. (2017). Digital Capabilities for Buffering Tensions of Structure, Space, and Time During Entrepreneurial Growth. In *International Conference on Information Systems*. AIS.

Utterback, J.M. (1971). The Process of Technological Innovation within the Firm. *The Academy of Management Journal*, *14*(1), 75-88.

Utterback, J. M. (1994). *Mastering the Dynamics of Innovation*. Harvard Business School Press.

Van de Ven, A.H. (1986). Central Problems in the Management of Innovation. *Management Science*, *32*(5), 590-607.

Van de Ven, A.H., & Poole, M.S. (1995). Explaining Development and Change in Organizations. *Academy of Management Review*, *20*(3), 510-540.

Venkatesh, V., Bala, H., & Sambamurthy, V. (2016a). Implementation of an Information and Communication Technology in a Developing Country: A Multimethod Longitudinal Study in a Bank in India. *Information Systems Research*, *27*(3), 558-579.

Venkatesh, V., Morris, M.G., Davis, G.B., & Davis, F.D. (2003). User Acceptance of Information Technology: Toward a Unified View. *MIS Quarterly*, *27*(3), 425-478.

Venkatesh, V., Rai, A., Sykes, T.A., & Aljafari, R. (2016b). Combating Infant Mortality in Rural India: Evidence from a Field Study of Ehealth Kiosk Imlementations. *MIS Quarterly*, *40*(2), 353-380.

Venkatesh, V., & Sykes, T.A. (2013). Digital Divide Initiative Success in Developing Countries: A Longitudinal Field Study in a Village in India. *Information Systems Research*, *24*(2), 239-260.

Venkatesh, V., Sykes, T.A., & Venkatraman, S. (2014). Understanding E-Government Portal Use in Rural India: Role of Demographic and Personality Characteristics. *Information Systems Journal*, *24*(3), 249-269.

Wasserman, S., & Faust, K. (1994). *Social Network Analysis: Methods and Applications*. Cambridge University Press. doi:10.1017/CBO9780511815478

Wortman, M.S. (1990). Rural Entrepreneurship Research: An Integration into the Entrepreneurship Field. *Agribusiness*, *6*(4), 329-344.

Wright, M., & Stigliani, I. (2013). Entrepreneurship and Growth. *International Small Business Journal*, *31*(1), 3–22.

Xiao, X., Califf, C.B., Sarker, S., & Sarker, S. (2013). Ict Innovation in Emerging Economies: A Review of the Existing Literature and a Framework for Future Research. *Journal of Information Technology*, *28*(4), 264-278.

Yoo, Y., Boland Jr, R.J., Lyytinen, K., & Majchrzak, A. (2012). Organizing for Innovation in the Digitized World. *Organization Science*, *23*(5), 1398-1408.

Zahra, S.A. (2007). Contextualizing Theory Building in Entrepreneurship Research. *Journal of Business Venturing*, *22*(3), 443-452.

Zittrain, J.L. (2006). The Generative Internet. *Harvard Law Review*, *119*(7), 1974–2040.

ADDITIONAL READING

Gaddefors, J., and Anderson, A.R. 2019. "Romancing the Rural: Reconceptualizing Rural Entrepreneurship as Engagement with Context (S)," The International Journal of Entrepreneurship and Innovation (20:3), pp 159-169.

Gupta, A.K. 2013. "Tapping the Entrepreneurial Potential of Grassroots Innovation," Stanford Social Innovation Review (11:3), pp 18-20.

Kohli, R., and Melville, N.P. 2019. "Digital Innovation: A Review and Synthesis," Information Systems Journal (29:1), pp 200-223.

Nambisan, S. 2017. "Digital Entrepreneurship: Toward a Digital Technology Perspective of Entrepreneurship," Entrepreneurship Theory and Practice (41:6), pp 1029-1055.

Pato, L. 2015. "Rural Entrepreneurship and Innovation: Some Successful Women's Initiatives," in: *55th Congress of the European Regional Science Association*. Lisbon, Portugal: European Regional Science Association (ERSA).

Pato, M.L., and Teixeira, A.A. 2016. "Twenty Years of Rural Entrepreneurship: A Bibliometric Survey," Sociologia Ruralis (56:1), pp 3-28.

Wortman Jr, M.S. 1990. "Rural Entrepreneurship Research: An Integration into the Entrepreneurship Field," Agribusiness (6:4), pp 329-344.

Yoo, Y., Boland Jr, R.J., Lyytinen, K., and Majchrzak, A. 2012. "Organizing for Innovation in the Digitized World," Organization Science (23:5), pp 1398-1408.

KEY TERMS AND DEFINITIONS

Digital Technologies: New technologies such as social media, mobile technologies, analytics, cloud computing and internet-of-things are considered as digital technologies.

Entrepreneurship: The discovery, evaluation, and exploitation of future goods and services.

Framework: A conceptual structure for explaining a phenomenon.

Innovation: Implementation of an idea whether pertaining to a device, system, process, policy, program or service that is new to the organization.

Rural Entrepreneurship: The discovery, evaluation, and exploitation of novel ideas in the rural context.

Rural Innovation: the creation and implementation of new ideas or solutions, new to the unit of adoption, that deal with rural context.

Theory: A system of ideas intended to explain a phenomenon.

Compilation of References

Abed, F. H. (2000). *Microfinance NGOs in Bangladesh: Growth, impact, challenges*. Paper presented at the Asian Regional Conference on the potential and limitations of economic initiatives in grassroots development - Current issues and Asian experiences, Rajendrapur, Bangladesh.

Aberbach, J., & Rockman, B. (2002). Conducting and coding elite interviews. *PS, Political Science & Politics*, *35*(4), 673–676. doi:10.1017/S1049096502001142

Abreu, M., & Grinevich, V. (2013). The nature of academic entrepreneurship in the UK: Widening the focus on entrepreneurial activities. *Research Policy*, *42*(2), 408–422. doi:10.1016/j.respol.2012.10.005

ABS (Australia Bureau of Statistics). (2018). *Summary of IT Use and Innovation in Australia Business, 2016-2017*. http://www.abs.gov.au

Acs, Z. J. (2010). Entrepreneurship and Economic Development: The Valley of Backwardness. *Annals of Innovation & Entrepreneurship*, *1*(1), 5641. doi:10.3402/aie.v1i1.5602

Ács, Z. J., Autio, E., & Szerb, L. (2014). National Systems of Entrepreneurship: Measurement issues and policy implications. *Research Policy*, *43*(3), 476–494. doi:10.1016/j.respol.2013.08.016

Acs, Z. J., Braunerhjelm, P., Audretsch, D. B., & Carlsson, B. (2009). The knowledge Spillover Theory of Entrepreneurship. *Small Business Economics*, *32*(1), 15–30. doi:10.100711187-008-9157-3

Adam, M. S., & Myers, M. D. (2003). Have You Got Anything to Declare? In *Organizational Information Systems in the Context of Globalization* (pp. 101–115). Springer. doi:10.1007/978-0-387-35695-2_7

Adeleke, A., Oyenuga, O. O., & Ogundele, O. J. K. (2003). *Business Policy and Strategy. Mushin*. Concept Publications Limited.

Adjei, P. O. W., Kosoe, E. A., & Forkuor, D. (2017). Facts behind the myth of conservative rurality: Major determinants of rural farmers' innovation adoption decisions for sustainable agriculture. *GeoJournal*, *82*(5), 1051–1066. doi:10.100710708-016-9728-9

Adomakoa, S., Opokub, R. A., & Frimpongc, K. (2018). Entrepreneurs' improvisational behavior and new venture performance: Firm-level and institutional contingencies. *Journal of Business Research*, *83*, 10–18. doi:10.1016/j.jbusres.2017.10.006

Agarwal, S., Courtney, P., Errington, A., Moseley, M., & Rahman, S. (2004). *Determinants of relative economic performance of rural areas. Final research report prepared for DEFRA*. University of Plymouth and Countryside and Community Research Unit.

Agbenyagah, A. T. (2018). Determining the risk & effect of selected social capital elements on rural entrepreneurship: Empirical study of two rural district municipalities. *Risk Government and Control: Financial Markets & Institutions*, *8*(1), 36–48.

Ahmadvand, M., & Karami, E. (2011). Factors Influencing the Success of Agricultural Information Systems: A Factor Analysis. *Journal of Agricultural Science and Technology*, *5*(1), 101–108.

Ahmad, Z. S., & Xavier, R. S. (2012). Entrepreneurial Environments and Growth: Evidence from Malaysia GEM data. *Journal of Chinese Entrepreneurship*, *4*(1), 50–64. doi:10.1108/17561391211200939

Ahmed, M. (1993). *Growth of industrial entrepreneurship in Bangladesh: A study of bank financed engineering industries* (Unpublished doctoral dissertation). University of Rajshahi - Bangladesh.

Ahuja, S., & Chan, Y. E. (2017). Resource orchestration for IT-enabled Innovation. *Kindai Management Review*, *5*(1), 78–96.

Ahuja, S., & Chan, Y. E. (2019). Frugal innovation and digitalisation: A platform ecosystem perspective. In *Frugal Innovation* (pp. 89–107). Routledge. doi:10.4324/9780429025679-5

Ahuja, S., Chan, Y., & Denford, J. (2016). IT-Enabled Innovation and Improvisation in Canadian Smes: A Qualitative Comparative Analysis. In *Americas Conference on Information Systems*. San Diego: AIS.

Aishah. (2017). Approach to the use of e-marketing medium among entrepreneurs' women. *Journal of Global Business and Social Entrepreneurship*, 47–57.

Ajzen, I. (1991). The Theory of Planned Behavior. *Organizational Behavior and Human Decision Processes*, *50*(2), 179-211.

Ajzen, I., & Fishbein, M. (1973). Attitudinal and Normative Variables as Predictors of Specific Behavior. *Journal of Personality and Social Psychology*, *27*(1), 41-57.

Akca, H., Sayili, M., & Esengun, K. (2007). Challenge of Rural People to Reduce Digital Divide in the Globalized World: Theory and Practice. *Government Information Quarterly*, *24*(2), 404–413. doi:10.1016/j.giq.2006.04.012

Albert, M. (2015). *Seven things to know about the Internet of Things (IoT) and Industry 4.0.* Modern Machine Shop.

Alvarez, S. A., & Busenitz, L. W. (2001). The Entrepreneurship of Resource-Based Theory. *Journal of Management*, *27*(6), 755–775. doi:10.1177/014920630102700609

Amorós, J. E., Bosma, N., & Levie, J. (2013). Ten years of Global Entrepreneurship Monitor: Accomplishments and prospects. *International Journal of Entrepreneurial Venturing*, *5*(2), 120–152. doi:10.1504/IJEV.2013.053591

Andersson, M., Baltzopoulos, A., & Lööf, H. (2012). R&D strategies and entrepreneurial spawning. *Research Policy*, *41*(1), 54–68. doi:10.1016/j.respol.2011.08.005

Ansong, E., & Boateng, R. (2019). Surviving in the digital era – business models of digital enterprises in a developing economy. *Digital Policy, Regulation & Governance*, *21*(2), 164–178. doi:10.1108/DPRG-08-2018-0046

Arend, R. J., & Bromiley, P. (2009). *Assessing the dynamic capabilities view: Spare change, everyone?* Sage Publications Sage UK.

Arsenault, N. (2003). *Answering the Top 5 Myths about Selecting Software for Microfinance Institutions.* White Paper.

Asabi, M. O. (2017). Entrepreneurship Development: A Panacea for Rural Development in Nigeria. *African Journal of Management*, *2*(3), 135–147.

ASBAS. (2019). *Australian Small Business Advisory Services (ASBAS) Digital Solutions.* https://www.business.gov.au/Expertise-and-Advice/Australian-Small-Business-Advisory-Services-ASBAS-Digital-Solutions

Asenso-Okyere, K., & Mekonnen, D. A. (2012). The importance of ICTs in the provision of information for improving agricultural productivity and rural incomes in Africa. *African Human Development Report. UNDP Sponsored research Series.*

Asian Development Bank. (2000). *The Role of central Banks in Microfinance in Asia and the Pacific.* Asian Development Bank.

Asia-News-Monitor (2018). Vietnam: Vietnam commits to realising GMS high-tech agriculture priority. *Asia News Monitor.*

Atherton, A. (2004). Unbundling Enterprise and Entrepreneurship: From Perceptions and Preconceptions to Concept and Practice. *The International Journal of Entrepreneurship and Innovation, 5*(2), 121–127. doi:10.5367/000000004773863273

Atterton, J., & Ward, N. (2007). Diversification and Innovation in Traditional Land-Based Industries. In S. Mahroum, J. Atterton, N. Ward, A. M. Williams, R. Naylor, R. Hindle, & F. Rowe (Eds.), Rural Innovation (pp. 12-23). NESTA.

Audretsch, D. B. (2014). Networking among Women Entrepreneurs. Audretsch, D.B. From the entrepreneurial university to the university for the entrepreneurial society. *The Journal of Technology Transfer, 39*(3), 313–321. doi:10.100710961-012-9288-1

Audretsch, D. B., Bönte, W., & Keilbach, M. (2008). Entrepreneurship capital and its impact on knowledge diffusion and economic performance. *Journal of Business Venturing, 23*(6), 687–698. doi:10.1016/j.jbusvent.2008.01.006

Audretsch, D., & Keilbach, M. (2008). Resolving the knowledge paradox: Knowledge-spillover entrepreneurship and economic growth. *Research Policy, 37*(10), 1697–1705. doi:10.1016/j.respol.2008.08.008

Baden-Fuller, C. (1995). Strategic Innovation, Corporate Entrepreneurship and Matching Outside-in to Inside-out Approaches to Strategy Research 1. *British Journal of Management, 6*(s1), S3–S16. doi:10.1111/j.1467-8551.1995.tb00134.x

Baldini, N., Fini, R., Grimaldi, R., & Sobrero, M. (2014). Organisational Change and the Institutionalisation of University Patenting Activity in Italy. *Minerva, 52*(1), 27–53. doi:10.100711024-013-9243-9

Bali, S. R. (2006). *Microfinance and women's empowerment: Evidence from the Self-Help Group Bank Linkage Programme in India. Sida.* Division for Market Development.

Bamberry, G. (2006). The influence of technology on regional development: Case studies from the riverina region. *Australiasian Journal of Regional Studies, 12*(2), 173–190.

Barbosa, L. G. F. (2013). Incubadora de empresas de base tecnológica: Perceção dos empresários quanto aos apoios recebidos. *Revista de Administração e Gestão, 10*(3), 208–229.

Barclay, C. (2014). Using frugal innovations to support cybercrime legislations in small developing states: Introducing the cyber-legislation development and implementation process model (CyberLeg-DPM). *Information Technology for Development, 20*(2), 165–195. doi:10.1080/02681102.2013.841630

Baregheh, A., Rowley, J., & Sambrook, S. (2009). Towards a Multidisciplinary Definition of Innovation. *Management Decision, 47*(8), 1323-1339.

Barmpounakis, S., Kaloxylos, A., Groumas, A., Katsikas, L., Sarris, V., Dimtsa, K., Fournier, F., Antoniou, E., Alonistioti, N., & Wolfert, S. (2015). Management and control applications in Agriculture domain via a Future Internet Business-to-Business platform. *Information Processing in Agriculture, 2*(1), 51–63. doi:10.1016/j.inpa.2015.04.002

Barney, J. (1991). Firm Resources and Sustained Competitive Advantage. *Journal of Management, 17*(1), 99-120.

Barney, J. B. (2001). Is the resource-based "view" a useful perspective for strategic management research? Yes. *Academy of Management Review*, *26*(1), 41–56.

Baron, R. A., & Henry, R. A. (2011). Entrepreneurship: The genesis of organizations. In APA handbook of industrial and organizational psychology, Vol 1: Building and developing the organization (pp. 241-273). American Psychological Association.

Barry, H., & Milner, B. (2002). SMEs and electronic commerce: A departure from the traditional prioritisation of training? *Journal of European Industrial Training*, *26*(7), 316–326. doi:10.1108/03090590210432660

Bartels, R. (1968). The General Theory of Marketing. *Journal of Marketing*, *32*(1), 29-33.

Basargekar, P. (2010). Measuring effectiveness of social capital in microfinance: A case study of urban microfinance program in India. *International Journal of Social Enquiry*, *3*(2), 25–43.

Baskerville, R. F. (2003). Hofstede Never Studied Culture. *Accounting, Organizations and Society*, *28*(1), 1–14. doi:10.1016/S0361-3682(01)00048-4

Basu, R. R., Banerjee, P. M., & Sweeny, E. G. (2013). Frugal Innovation - Core Competencies to address Global Sustainability. *Journal of Management for Global Sustainability*, *2*(2), 63–82. doi:10.13185/JM2013.01204

Baumert, J., & McWhinney, M. (1992). *Software Measures and the Capability Maturity Model* (CMU/SEI-92-TR-025). http://resources.sei.cmu.edu/library/asset-view.cfm?AssetID=11715

Baumgartner, D., Pütz, M., & Seidl, I. (2013). What Kind of Entrepreneurship Drives Regional Development in European? A Literature Review on Empirical Entrepreneurship Research. *European Planning Studies*, *21*(8), 1095–1127. doi:10.1080/09654313.2012.722937

Baumgartner, D., Schulz, T., & Seidl, I. (2013). Quantifying entrepreneurship and its impact on local economic performance: A spatial assessment in rural Switzerland. *Entrepreneurship and Regional Development*, *25*(3-4), 222–250. do i:10.1080/08985626.2012.710266

Baviskar, B. S. (1998). *Dairy Co-operative rural development in Gujarat. Resources Institutions and Strategies: Operation Flood and Indian Dairying* (M. Doornbos & K. N. Nair, Eds.). Stage Publications.

Bayulgen, O. (2008). Muhammad Yunus, Grameen Bank and the Nobel Peace Prize: What political science can contribute to and learn from the study of microcredit. *International Studies Review*, *10*(3), 525–547. doi:10.1111/j.1468-2486.2008.00803.x

Becker, J., Knackstedt, R., Lis, L., & Stein, A. (2010). Towards a maturity model for research portals. *ECIS 2010 Proceedings*, (38). http://aisel.aisnet.org/ecis2010/38

Becker, J., Knackstedt, R., & Pöppelbuß, J. (2009). Developing maturity models for IT management. *Business & Information Systems Engineering*, *1*(3), 213–222. doi:10.100712599-009-0044-5

Begley, T. M., & Tan, W. L. (2001). The socio-cultural environment for entrepreneurship: A comparison between East Asian and Anglo-Saxon countries. *Journal of International Business Studies*, *32*(3), 537–553. doi:10.1057/palgrave.jibs.8490983

Begum, A. (2003). *Government-NGO interface in development management: Experiences of selected collaboration models in Bangladesh*. A. H. Development Publishing House.

Belkadi, F., Gupta, R. K., Natalizio, S., & Bernard, A. (2017). Modular Architectures Management with PLM for the Adaptation of Frugal Products to Regional Markets. *14th IFIP international conference on product lifecycle management.*

Benner, M.J., & Tushman, M.L. (2003). Exploitation, Exploration, and Process Management: The Productivity Dilemma Revisited. *Academy of Management Review*, *28*(2), 238-256.

Benz, M., & Frey, B. S. (2008). Being Independent Is a Great Thing: Subjective Evaluations of Self-Employment and Hierarchy. *Economica*, *75*(298), 362–383. doi:10.1111/j.1468-0335.2007.00594.x

Berger, R. (2013). *Frugal Products: Study Results*. Roland Berger Strategy Consultants. http://www.rolandberger.com/media/pdf/Roland_Berger_Frugal_products_20130212.pdf

Berg, V., Birkeland, J., Pappas, I. O., & Jaccheri, L. (2018). The Role of Data Analytics in Startup Companies: Exploring Challenges and Barriers. In *Challenges and Opportunities in the Digital Era*. Springer. doi:10.1007/978-3-030-02131-3_19

Bernardi, R., Constantinides, P., & Nandhakumar, J. (2017). Challenging Dominant Frames in Policies for IS Innovation in Healthcare through Rhetorical Strategies. *Journal of the Association for Information Systems*, *18*(2), 81–112.

Berry, M., & Brock, J. K.-U. (2004). Marketspace and the internationalization process of the small firm. *Journal of International Entrepreneurship*, *2*(3), 187–216. doi:10.1023/B:JIEN.0000032773.32304.a6

Bertschek, I., & Fryges, H. (2002). *The adoption of business-to-business e-commerce: Empirical evidence for German companies*. Discussion Paper No. 02-05, Centre for European Economic Research (ZEW), Mannheim.

Bharadwaj, A. S. (2000). A resource-based perspective on information technology capability and firm performance: An empirical investigation. *Management Information Systems Quarterly*, *24*(1), 169–196. doi:10.2307/3250983

Bharadwaj, A., El Sawy, O. A., Pavlou, P. A., & Venkatraman, N. (2013). Digital business strategy: Toward a next generation of insights. *Management Information Systems Quarterly*, *37*(2), 471–482. doi:10.25300/MISQ/2013/37:2.3

Bhattacharya, M., Bedi, A. S., & Chhachhi, A. (2009). *Marital violence and women's employment and property status: Evidence from North Indian villages*. Discussion Paper No. 4361, Institute for the Study of Labour, Bon, Germany.

Bhatti, Y.A. (2012). *Challenges of frugal innovation and role of business models*. Presentation material. Santa Clara University, Engineering for developing world class.

Birdthistle, N. (2008). An Examination of Tertiary Students' Desire to Found an Enterprise. *Education + Training*, *50*(7), 552–567. doi:10.1108/00400910810909027

Birks, M., & Mills, J. (2011). *Grounded Theory: A Practical Guide* (1st ed.). Sage Publications Inc.

Blake, B. F., Neuendorf, K. A., & Valdiserri, C. M. (2005). Tailoring new websites to appeal to those most likely to shop online. *Technovation*, *25*(10), 1205–1214. doi:10.1016/j.technovation.2004.03.009

Blanchflower, D. G., & Oswald, A. J. (1998). What Makes an Entrepreneur? *Journal of Labor Economics*, *16*(1), 26–60. doi:10.1086/209881

Blayney & Manchester. (2000). Large Companies Active in Changing Dairy Industry. *Food Review*, *23*(2), 8-13.

Boh, W. F., De-Haan, U., & Strom, R. (2007). Assessing the Regional Economic Development Impacts of Universities: A Review of Current Approaches. International Regional Science Review -. *International Regional Science Review*, *30*(1), 20–46. doi:10.1177/0160017606296731

Borodin, V., Bourtembourg, J., Hnaien, F., & Labadie, N. (2016). Handling uncertainty in agricultural supply chain management: A state of the art. *European Journal of Operational Research*, *254*(2), 348–359. doi:10.1016/j.ejor.2016.03.057

Bound, K., & Thornton, I. (2012). *Our Frugal Future: Lessons from India's Innovation system*. Nesta.

Bowden, S., Clark, D., Corner, P., Gibb, J., Kearins, K., & Pavlovich, K. (2001). *Adoption and implementation of e-business in New Zealand: preliminary results*. Paper presented at the 9th NZSMS Annual Conference, Hamilton.

Braga, J. (2016). *Refuncionalizando a Casa Solarenga: uma Grounded Theory* (Doctoral dissertation). Universidade de Santiago de Compostela, Santiago de Compostela. Retrieved from: https://minerva.usc.es/xmlui/handle/10347/14805

Braga, J., & Lopes, J. (2020). The Public Sector's Role in Fostering Development in Low-Density Areas: The Case of Housing Tourism. In D. Kala & S. Bagri (Eds.), *Global Opportunities and Challenges for Rural and Mountain Tourism* (pp. X–X). IGI Global. doi:10.4018/978-1-7998-1302-6.ch012

Braun, P. (2002). Networking tourism SMEs: E-commerce and e-marketing issues in regional Australia. *Information Technology & Tourism*, *5*(1), 13–23. doi:10.3727/109830502108751028

Brekhus, W. (1998). A Sociology of the Unmarked: Redirecting Our Focus. *Sociological Theory*, *16*(1), 34-51.

BriefingV. (2018). Retrieved from https://www.vietnam-briefing.com/news/need-high-tech-farming-vietnam.html/

Brown, D.H., & Thompson, S. (2011). Priorities, Policies and Practice of E-Government in a Developing Country Context: Ict Infrastructure and Diffusion in Jamaica. *European Journal of Information Systems*, *20*(3), 329-342.

Bruneel, J., Ratinho, T., Clarysse, B., & Groen, A. (2012). The Evolution of Business Incubators: Comparing demand and supply of business incubation services across different incubator generations. *Technovation*, *32*(2), 110–121. doi:10.1016/j.technovation.2011.11.003

Brunjes, J., & Diez, J. A. (2016). Obtaining non-farm wage employment in rural Vietnam. *Asia Pacific Viewpoint*, *57*(2), 263–279. doi:10.1111/apv.12116

Bryant, C. R. (1989). Entrepreneurs in the Rural Environment. *Journal of Rural Studies*, *5*(4), 337–348. doi:10.1016/0743-0167(89)90060-0

Bukht, R., & Heeks, R. (2017). *Defining, conceptualising and measuring the digital economy. Development Implications of Digital Economies (DIODE). No. 68*. University of Manchester. Retrieved from www.gdi.manchester.ac.uk/research/publications/working-papers/di/

Burton, T. T. (2001). *Is this a Six Sigma, lean, or Kaizen Project?* Breakthrough.

Buttriss, J. L. (2013). Food reformulation: The challenges to the food industry. *The Proceedings of the Nutrition Society*, *72*(1), 61–69. doi:10.1017/S0029665112002868 PMID:23228239

Cadez, S., & Guilding, C. (2008). An exploratory investigation of an integrated contingency model of strategic management accounting. *Accounting, Organizations and Society*, *33*(7-8), 836–863. doi:10.1016/j.aos.2008.01.003

Callon, M. (1999). Actor-Network Theory—the Market Test. *The Sociological Review*, *47*(1), 181-195.

Candau, F., & Dienesch, E. (2015). Spatial distribution of skills and regional trade integration. *The Annals of Regional Science*, *54*(2), 451–488. doi:10.100700168-015-0662-4

Carrer, M. J., de Souza Filho, H. M., Batalha, M. O., & Rossi, F. R. (2015). Farm Management Information Systems (FMIS) and technical efficiency: An analysis of citrus farms in Brazil. *Computers and Electronics in Agriculture*, *119*, 105–111. doi:10.1016/j.compag.2015.10.013

Carvalho, J. V., Rocha, Á., & Abreu, A. (2016). Maturity models of healthcare information systems and technologies: A literature review. *Journal of Medical Systems*, *40*(6), 131. doi:10.100710916-016-0486-5 PMID:27083575

Carvalho, J. V., Rocha, Á., van de Wetering, R., & Abreu, A. (2019). A Maturity model for hospital information systems. *Journal of Business Research*, *94*, 388–399. doi:10.1016/j.jbusres.2017.12.012

Cascio, J. (2006). *Open Source Microcredit, Revisited.* The Tech Bloom Collaborative and Emergent Technologies, posted at February 10, 2006)2:44pm, accessed August 8,2006 21:06pm at http://www.worldchanging.com/archives/004095.html

Cavaco, C. (1999). *Desenvolvimento rural: Desafio e utopia.* Centro de Estudos Geográficos da Universidade de Lisboa.

CENTER - Centro Nacional do Turismo no Espaço Rural. (2020a). *Legislação Turismo de Habitação e Turismo no Espaço Rural.* Retrieved from: http://www.center.pt/PT/estudos.php

CENTER - Centro Nacional do Turismo no Espaço Rural. (2020b). *Encontros do Turismo de Habitação e do Turismo no Espaço Rural.* Retrieved from: https://www.center.pt/PT/encontros.php

CGAP. (2005). *Funding Microfinance Technology.* CGAP Donor Brief No. 23.

Chan, Y. E., Ahuja, S., Denford, J. S., Henfridsson, O., & Levallet, N. (2020). Digital Innovation and Entrepreneurship: The Challenges of an Ecosystem Perspective. Academy of Management Proceedings, 2020(1), 15203. doi:10.5465/AMBPP.2020.15203symposium

Chandra Sekhara, P. (2002). *Private Extension: Indian Experience, Pro-Farmer Private extensions.* Manage.

Chandrasekaran, N., & Raghuram, G. (2014). *Agribusiness supply chain management.* CRC Press. doi:10.1201/b16704

Chan, Y. E., & Farrington, C. J. (2018). Community-based research: Engaging universities in technology-related knowledge exchanges. *Information and Organization*, *28*(3), 129–139. doi:10.1016/j.infoandorg.2018.08.001

Chan, Y. E., Krishnamurthy, R., & Desjardins, C. (2020). Technology-Driven Innovation in Small Firms. *MIS Quarterly Executive*, *19*(1), 39–55. doi:10.17705/2msqe.00024

Chan, Y., & Ahuja, S. (2015). *Digital Ecodynamics in Small Firms: Using Information Technology to Compete. Thirty Sixth International Conference on Information Systems*, Fort Worth, TX.

Chaturvedi, A., & Goyal, S. (2012). Changing severity of impediments for entrepreneurs in India: An empirical analysis. *International Journal of Entrepreneurship and Small Business*, *16*(1), 1–32. doi:10.1504/IJESB.2012.046914

Chaudhary, M., & Chopra, A. (2017). *CMMI for Development.* Apress. doi:10.1007/978-1-4842-2529-5

Cheston, S., & Kuhn, L. (2002). Empowering women through microfinance. In S. Daley-Harris (Ed.), *Innovations in microfinance for the poorest families* (pp. 167–228). Kumarian Press.

Chhachhar, A. R., & Hassan, M. S. (2013). Information communication technology for agriculture development. *The Journal of American Science*, *9*(1), 85–91.

Chimucheka, T. (2012). Impediments to youth entrepreneurship in rural areas of Zimbabwe. *African Journal of Business Management*, *6*(38), 10389–10395.

Chipidza, W., & Leidner, D. (2019). A Review of the Ict-Enabled Development Literature: Towards a Power Parity Theory of Ict4d. *The Journal of Strategic Information Systems*, *28*(2), 145-174.

Chong, S. (2008). Success in electronic commerce implementation: A cross-country study of small and medium-sized enterprises. *Journal of Enterprise Information Management*, *21*(5), 468–492. doi:10.1108/17410390810904247

Cleveland, J. (2006). Toyota's other system -this one for product development. *Automotive Design & Production*, *118*(2), 18–22.

Cloke, P. (2006). Conceptualizing Rurality. In P. Cloke (Ed.), *Handbook of Rural Studies*. Sage. doi:10.4135/9781848608016.n2

Cohen, J. (2006). Social, emotional, ethical and academic education: Creating a climate for learning, participation in democracy and well-being. *Harvard Educational Review*, *76*, 201–237. www.hepg.org/her/abstract/8. doi:10.17763/haer.76.2.j44854x1524644vn

Coleman, B. E. (2002). *Microfinance in Northeast Thailand: Who benefits and how much?* ERD Working Paper Series No.9.

Collins, R., & Lim-Camacho, L. A. (2005). *Unlocking successful new rural industries: is supply chain management the key?: final report to the Rural Industries Research and Development Corporation. RIRDC Publication*. Rural Industries Research and Development Corporation.

Cons, J., & Paprocki, K. (2008). The limits of microcredit - A Bangladeshi case. *Food First Backgrounder*, *14*(4), 7–11.

Cooper, M. C., Lambert, D. M., & Pagh, J. D. (1997). Supply chain management: More than a new name for logistics. *International Journal of Logistics Management*, *8*(1), 1–14. doi:10.1108/09574099710805556

Corfu, A., & Kastenholz, E. (2008). The opportunities and limitations of the internet in providing a quality tourist experience: The case of "Solares de Portugal". *Journal of Quality Assurance in Hospitality & Tourism*, *6*(1-2), 77–88. doi:10.1300/J162v06n01_06

Cornelissen, J.P., & Werner, M.D. (2014). Putting Framing in Perspective: A Review of Framing and Frame Analysis across the Management and Organizational Literature. *Academy of Management Annals*, *8*(1), 181-235.

Cromie, S. (2000). Assessing entrepreneurial inclinations: Some approaches and empirical evidence. *European Journal of Work and Organizational Psychology*, *9*(1), 7–30. doi:10.1080/135943200398030

Crossan, M. M., & Apaydin, M. (2010). A Multi-Dimensional Framework of Organizational Innovation: A systematic Review of the Literature. *Journal of Management Studies*, *47*(6), 1154–1191. doi:10.1111/j.1467-6486.2009.00880.x

Croxton, K. L., Garcia-Dastugue, S. J., Lambert, D. M., & Rogers, D. S. (2001). The supply chain management processes. *International Journal of Logistics Management*, *12*(2), 13–36. doi:10.1108/09574090110806271

Cui, M., Pan, S.L., & Cui, L. (2019). Developing Community Capability for E-Commerce Development in Rural China: A Resource Orchestration Perspective. *Information Systems Journal*, *29*(4), 953-988.

Cui, M., Pan, S.L., Newell, S., & Cui, L. (2017). Strategy, Resource Orchestration and E-Commerce Enabled Social Innovation in Rural China. *The Journal of Strategic Information Systems*, *26*(1), 3-21.

Dabson, B. (2001). Supporting Rural Entrepreneurship. *E-Proceedings of Rural and Agriculture Conference*, *2001*, 35–47.

Dabson, B. (2005). Entrepreneurship as a Real Community and Economic Development Strategy. In *Rural policy research institute & Truman school of public affairs*. University of Missouri.

Dailey-Harris, J. (2005). *State of the microcredit Summit Campaign Report 2005*. The Microcredit Summit Campaign, Washington, DC.

Dalborg, C., Friedrichs, Y. V., & Wincent, J. (2012). Beyond the numbers: Qualitative growth in women's businesses. *International Journal of Gender and Entrepreneurship*, *4*(3), 289–315. doi:10.1108/17566261211264163

Damanpour, F. (1987). The Adoption of Technological, Administrative, and Ancillary Innovations: Impact of Organizational Factors. *Journal of Management*, *13*(4), 675-688.

Damanpour, F. (1991). Organizational Innovation: A Meta-Analysis of Effects of Determinants and Moderators. *Academy of Management Journal, 34*(3), 555-590.

Damanpour, F., & Damanpour, J. A. (2001). E-business e-commerce evolution: Perspective and strategy. *Managerial Finance, 27*(7), 16–33. doi:10.1108/03074350110767268

Dařena, F. (2007). Global Architecture of Marketing Information Systems. *Agricultural Economics, 53*(9), 432–440.

Das, K., Rama, H. M., & Patra, M. R. (2013). *E-Governance and Digital Inclusion: Creating Smart Rural Women in India Service Oriented Architecture View Project.* Digital India View Project E-Governance and Digital Inclusion: Creating Smart Rural Women in India.

Das, S. (2012). Entrepreneurship through Micro Finance in Northeast India: A Comprehensive Review of Existing Literature. *Information Management and Business Review, 4*(4), 168–184. doi:10.22610/imbr.v4i4.978

Datta, P. (2011). A Preliminary Study of Ecommerce Adoption in Developing Countries. *Information Systems Journal, 21*(1), 3-32.

Davis, F.D. (1989). Perceived Usefulness, Perceived Ease of Use, and User Acceptance of Information Technology. *MIS Quarterly,* (13), 319-340.

Davis, J., & Pearce, D. (2001). The rural non- farm economy in central and eastern Europe. In Z. Lerman & C. Csaki (Eds.), *The Challenge of Rural Development in the EU Accession Process*. World Bank.

DC Anusha. (n.d.). *DesiCrew Solutions.* Retrieved from ChangeMakers: https://www.changemakers.com/socialbusiness/entries/desicrew-solutions

De Oliveira, M. P. V., McCormack, K., & Trkman, P. (2012). Business analytics in supply chains–The contingent effect of business process maturity. *Expert Systems with Applications, 39*(5), 5488–5498. doi:10.1016/j.eswa.2011.11.073

Deakins, D., & Freel, M. (2006). *Entrepreneurship and small firms* (4th ed.). McGraw-Hill.

Decree nº 5/87 de 14 de janeiro da Presidência do Conselho de Ministros. Diário da República I série nº 11. Retrieved from: http://www.oasrn.org/upload/apoio/legislacao/pdf/tur587.pdf

Defra, D. (2004). Rural strategy. Report of Department for Environment Food and Rural Affairs.

Delalić, S., & Oruc, N. (2014). Determination of Firm Growth: A Study of Rural SMEs in Bosnia-Herzegovina. *Journal of Economic & Social Studies, 4*(1), 5–23. doi:10.14706/JECOSS11411

Demiryurek, K., Erdem, H., Ceyhan, V., Atasever, S. & Uysal, O. (2008). Agricultural information systems and communication networks: the case of dairy farmers in Samsun province of Turkey. *Information Research, 13*(2), paper 343.

Deng, H., Duan, S. X., Jie, D., & Fu, J. (2019). An efficiency-based approach for selecting electronic markets in sustainable electronic business: A SME's perspective. *Sustainability, 11*(7), 1858. doi:10.3390u11071858

Deng, H., Duan, S. X., & Luo, F. (2020). Critical determinants for electronic market adoption: Evidence from Australian small- and medium-sized enterprises. *Journal of Enterprise Information Management, 33*(2), 335–352. doi:10.1108/JEIM-04-2019-0106

Desai, V. (2007). *Small Scale Industries and Entrepreneurship*. Himalaya Publishing House.

DesiCrew's Saloni Malhotra's story…. (2015, April 21). Retrieved from Social EntrepreneurshipRevisited: https://socialentrepreneurshiprevisited.wordpress.com/2015/04/21/desicrews-saloni-malhotras-story/

Dijkstra, L., Garcilazo, E., & McCann, P. (2013). The economic Performance of European Cities and City Regions: Myths and Realities. *European Planning Studies*, *21*(3), 334–354. doi:10.1080/09654313.2012.716245

DiMaggio, P., & Powell, W.W. (1983). The Iron Cage Revisited: Collective Rationality and Institutional Isomorphism in Organizational Fields. *American Sociological Review*, *48*(2), 147-160.

Dobbs, M., & Hamilton, R. T. (2007). Small business growth: Recent evidence and new directions. *International Journal of Entrepreneurial Behaviour & Research*, *13*(5), 296–322. doi:10.1108/13552550710780885

Dobson, P., Jackson, P., & Gengatharen, D. (2013). Explaining Broadband Adoption in Rural Australia: Modes of Reflexivity and the Morphogenetic Approach. *MIS Quarterly*, *37*(3), 965-991.

Dollinger, M. J. (2003). *Entrepreneurship – Strategies and Resources* (International Edition). Pearson.

Dontigney, E. (2018, April 13). *What are the Theories of Entrepreneurship?* Retrieved August 1, 2020, from azcentral.: https://yourbusiness.azcentral.com/theories-entrepreneurship-23795.html

Driga, O., Lafuente, E., & Vaillant, Y. (2009). Reasons for the relatively lower entrepreneurial activity levels of rural women in Spain. *Sociologia Ruralis*, *49*(1), 70–96. doi:10.1111/j.1467-9523.2008.00475.x

Duan, S. X. (2020). An examination of e-market adoption in Australian SMEs. *Small Enterprise Research*, *27*(1), 23–38. doi:10.1080/13215906.2019.1687321

Duan, X., Deng, H., & Corbitt, B. (2012). Evaluating the critical determinants for adopting e-market in Australian small-and-medium sized enterprises. *Management Research Review*, *35*(3/4), 289–308. doi:10.1108/01409171211210172

Dufty, N., & Jackson, T. (2018). *Information and communication technology use in Australian agriculture*. Australian Bureau of Agricultural and Resource Economics and Sciences.

Duncombe, R. (Ed.). (2018). *Digital Technologies for Agricultural and Rural Development in the Global South*. CABI. doi:10.1079/9781786393364.0000

Dziallas, M., & Blind, K. (2019). Innovation indicators throughout the innovation process: An extensive literature analysis. *Technovation*, *80-81*, 3–29. doi:10.1016/j.technovation.2018.05.005

EC. (2013). *REDI: The Regional Entrepreneurship and Development Index – Measuring regional entrepreneurship Final report*. Brussels: EC.

Efroymson, D., Biswas, B., & Ruma, S. (2007). *The economic contribution of women in Bangladesh through their unpaid labour*. Retrieved January 24, 2020 from http://healthbridge.ca/Bangladesh%20summary%20report%20final.pdf

Eitzinger, A., Cock, J., Atzmanstorfer, K., Binder, C. R., Läderach, P., Bonilla-Findji, O., Bartling, M., Mwongera, C., Zurita, L., & Jarvis, A. (2019). GeoFarmer: A monitoring and feedback system for agricultural development projects. *Computers and Electronics in Agriculture*, *158*, 109–121. doi:10.1016/j.compag.2019.01.049 PMID:31007323

El Sawy, O. A., Malhotra, A., Park, Y., & Pavlou, P. A. (2010). Seeking the Configurations of Digital Ecodynamics: It Takes Three to Tango. *Information Systems Research*, *21*(4), 835–848. doi:10.1287/isre.1100.0326

El Sawy, O. A., & Pereira, F. (2013). *Business Modelling in the Dynamic Digital Space*. Springer Berlin Heidelberg., doi:10.1007/978-3-642-31765-1

Entrialgo, M., Fernández, E., & Vázquez, C. J. (2000). Characteristics of managers as determinants of entrepreneurial orientation: some Spanish evidence. *Enterprise and Innovation Management Studies, 1*(2), 187-205.

Erdem, F. (2001). A cultural approach toward risk taking propensity and tolerance for ambiguity of entrepreneurs. *Akdeniz IIBF Dergisi, 2*, 43–61.

Ernst, D. (2002). Global Production Networks and the Changing Geography of Innovation Systems. Implications for Developing Countries. *Economics of Innovation and New Technology, 11*(6), 497-523.

Escandón-Barbosa, D. M., Urbano, D., Hurtado-Ayala, A., Salas paramo, J., & Dominguez, A. Z. (2019). Formal institutions, informal institutions and entrepreneurial activity: A comparative relationship between rural and urban areas in Colombia. *Journal of Urban Management*. doi:10.1016/j.jum.2019.06.002

Eschker, E., Gold, G., & Lane, M. D. (2017). Rural entrepreneurs: What are the best indicators of their success? *Journal of Small Business and Enterprise Development, 24*(2), 278–296. doi:10.1108/JSBED-07-2016-0112

Esfahani, L. P., & Asadiye, Z. S. (2009, December). The role of information and communication technology in agriculture. In *2009 First International Conference on Information Science and Engineering* (pp. 3528-3531). IEEE. 10.1109/ICISE.2009.1282

Etzkowitz, H. (2003). Research Groups As 'Quasi-Firms': The Invention of the Entrepreneurial University. *Research Policy, 32*(1), 109–121. doi:10.1016/S0048-7333(02)00009-4

Etzkowitz, H. (2017). Innovation Lodestar: The entrepreneurial university in a stellar knowledge firmament. *Technological Forecasting and Social Change, 123*, 122–129. doi:10.1016/j.techfore.2016.04.026

Etzkowitz, H., Webster, A., Gebhardt, C., & Terra, B. (2000). The Future of the University and the University of the Future: Evolution of Ivory Tower to Entrepreneurial Paradigm. *Research Policy, 29*(2), 313–330. doi:10.1016/S0048-7333(99)00069-4

EU. (2016). *CORK 2.0 DECLARATION "A Better Life in Rural Areas"*. Retrieved from https://enrd.ec.europa.eu/sites/enrd/files/cork-declaration_en.pdf

European Commission. (2008). *Rural Development Policy 2007-2013*. Retrieved from https://enrd.ec.europa.eu/enrd-static/fms/pdf/BEC22A59-E570-413B-5A9B-682D3306E183.pdf

Evans, P. (1999). *Blown to Bits: How the New Economics of Information Transforms strategy*. Harvard Business School Press.

Falconcer, K. (2000). Farm-level constrains on agri-environmental scheme participation: A transactional perspective. *Journal of Rural Studies, 16*(3), 379–394. doi:10.1016/S0743-0167(99)00066-2

Fang, J., Zhu, X., Wang, C., & Shangguan, L. (2016). Applications of DNA Technologies in Agriculture. *Current Genomics, 17*(4), 379–386. doi:10.2174/1389202917666160331203224 PMID:27499686

Feldman, M., Feller, I., Bercovitz, J., & Burton, R. (2002). Equity and the Technology Transfer Strategies of American Research Universities. *Management Science, 48*(1), 105–121. doi:10.1287/mnsc.48.1.105.14276

Fernandes, J. (1983, August). Turismo de Habitação: Férias tranquilas nas regiões onde rareia a hotelaria clássica. *Revista de Ação Regional e Local., 4*(23), 26.

Fhlatharta, A. M. N., & Farrell, M. (2017). Unravelling the strands of 'patriarchy' in rural innovation: A study of female innovators and their contribution to rural Connemara. *Journal of Rural Studies, 54*, 15–27. doi:10.1016/j.jrurstud.2017.05.002

Finke, H., & Bosworth, G. (2016). Exploring the character of rural businesses: Performing change and continuity, Local Economy. *The Journal of the Local Economy Policy Unit, 31*(5), 619–636. doi:10.1177/0269094216655407

Fink, M., Loidl, S., & Lang, R. (2012). *Community-based entrepreneurship and rural development Creating favourable conditions for small businesses in central Europe*. Routledge Taylor & Francis Group. doi:10.4324/9780203108116

Firdhous, M., Ghazali, O., & Hassan, S. (2013). Cloud Computing for Rural ICT Development: Opportunities and Challenges. In *International Conference on Computing, Electrical and Electronic Engineering* (pp. 680-685). Khartoum: IEEE. 10.1109/ICCEEE.2013.6634022

Fischer, E., & Reuber, A.R. (2014). Online Entrepreneurial Communication: Mitigating Uncertainty and Increasing Differentiation Via Twitter. *Journal of Business Venturing*, *29*(4), 565-583.

Fisher, R., Maritz, A., & Lobo, A. (2014). Evaluating entrepreneurs' perception of success. *International Journal of Entrepreneurial Behaviour & Research*, *20*(5), 478–492. doi:10.1108/IJEBR-10-2013-0157

Fonteneau, F., & Khalil, C. (2017). Buidling agricultural market information systems: a literature review. *Buidling agricultural market information systems: a literature review.*

Food and Agriculture Organization (FAO) of the United Nations. (2016). *E-Agriculture Strategy Guide (Piloted in Asia-Pacific countries)*. http://www.fao.org/3/a-i5564e.pdf

Food and Agriculture Organization (FAO) of the United Nations. (2017). *Information and Communication Technology (ICT) in Agriculture, A Report to the G20 Agricultural Deputies*. http://www.fao.org/3/a-i7961e.pdf

Food and Agriculture Organization (FAO) of the United Nations. (2018). *Guidelines on the use of remote sensing products to improve agricultural crop production forecast statistics in sub-saharan African countries. Food and Agriculture Organization of the United Nations*. FAO.

Forbes. (2011). *Why Invest in Emerging Markets?* Author.

Fortunato, M. W.-P. (2014). Supporting rural entrepreneurship: A review of conceptual developments from research to practice. *Community Development (Columbus, Ohio)*, *45*(4), 387–408. doi:10.1080/15575330.2014.935795

Foster, C., & Heeks, R. (2013). Innovation and Scaling of Ict for the Bottom-of-the-Pyramid. *Journal of Information Technology*, *28*(4), 296-315.

Foster, D. (2005). *What C.E.O.s Need To Know About Software Selection.* MicroSave Briefing Note # 43.

Fountas, S., Carli, G., Sørensen, C. G., Tsiropoulos, Z., Cavalaris, C., Vatsanidou, A., Liakos, B., Canavari, M., Wiebensohn, J., & Tisserye, B. (2015). Farm management information systems: Current situation and future perspectives. *Computers and Electronics in Agriculture*, *115*, 40–50. doi:10.1016/j.compag.2015.05.011

Freedman, D. A. (2009). *Statistical Models: Theory and Practise*. Cambridge University Press. doi:10.1017/CBO9780511815867

Fritsch, M. (2008). How does new business formation affect regional development? Introduction to the special issue. *Small Business Economics*, *30*(1), 1–14. doi:10.1007/11187-007-9057-y

Fritsch, M. (2011). The role of new business in regional development: introduction and overview. In M. Fritsch (Ed.), *Handbook of research on entrepreneurship and regional development* (pp. 1–10). Edward Elgar Publishing Limited. doi:10.4337/9780857936493.00005

Fuster, E., Padilla-Meléndez, A., Lockett, N., & del-Águila-Obra, A. R. (2019). The emerging role of university spin-off companies in developing regional entrepreneurial university ecosystems: The case of Andalusia. *Technological Forecasting and Social Change*, *141*, 219–231. doi:10.1016/j.techfore.2018.10.020

Gaddefors, J., & Anderson, A.R. (2019). Romancing the Rural: Reconceptualizing Rural Entrepreneurship as Engagement with Context(s). *The International Journal of Entrepreneurship and Innovation, 20*(3), 159-169.

Gandikota, V. (2014). *The Curious Case of TATA Nano car. The Nordic Frugal Innovation Society.* TNFIS.

Ganguly, K., Gulati, A., & von Braun, J. (2017). *Innovations spearheading the next transformations in India 's agriculture.* ZEF Centre for Development Research, University of Bonn.

Gasson, R. (1998). Educational qualification of UK farmers: A review. *Journal of Rural Studies, 14*(4), 487–498. doi:10.1016/S0743-0167(98)00028-X

Ghadiyali, T., Lad, K., & Dhodiya, J. (2018). Design and Development of the Agricultural Model: A Way to Connect Farmer Community to Agriculture Market for Betterment of Rural Development. In *ICT Based Innovations* (pp. 51–62). Springer. doi:10.1007/978-981-10-6602-3_6

Ghosh, R. A. (2003). Licence fees and GDP per capita: The case for open source in developing countries. *First Monday, 8*(12). http://www.firstmonday.org/issues/issue8 12/ghosh/index.html

Ghosh, R. A. (2005). *Free/Libre/Open Source Softwarefor developing countries: skills, employment and costs.* Paper presented at USUARIA 2005, 2nd National Congress on Software Libre, Argentina.

Ghosh, S. (2013). Entrepreneurship: An overview of the issues and challenges in the context of rural development in India. *Business Spectrum, 1*(2).

Gladwin, C. H., Long, B. F., Babb, E. M., Beaulieu, L. J., Moseley, A., Mulkey, D., & Zimet, D. J. (1989). Rural entrepreneurship: One key to rural revitalization. *American Journal of Agricultural Economics, 71*(5), 1305–1314. doi:10.2307/1243127

Glaeser, E. L., Ponzetto, G. A. M., & Tobio, K. (2014). Cities, Skills and Regional Change. *Regional Studies, 48*(1), 7–43. doi:10.1080/00343404.2012.674637

Glaser, B. (1992). *Basics of Grounded Theory analysis.* Sociology Press.

Glaser, B. (2005). *The Grounded Theory perspective III: Theoretical coding.* Sociology Press.

Glaser, B., & Strauss, A. (2008). *The discovery of Grounded Theory: Strategies for qualitative research. 3ª Reimp.* Aldine Transaction. (Original work published 1967)

Glendenning, C. J., & Ficarelli, P. (2012). *The relevance of content in ICT initiatives in Indian agriculture.* IFPRI Discussion paper No 1180.

Goddard, J., Kempton, L., & Vallance, P. (2013). *The civic university: Connecting the Global and the Local.* Academic Press.

Godinho, M. (2004). O Turismo em Espaço Rural (TER) em Portugal. Problemas e desafios para o futuro. *Revista de Turismo e Desenvolvimento, 1*(1), 91-93. Retrieved from: https://dialnet.unirioja.es/servlet/articulo?codigo=3548517

Gomes, J., & Romão, M. (2018). Information system maturity models in healthcare. *Journal of Medical Systems, 42*(12), 235. doi:10.100710916-018-1097-0 PMID:30327955

Gordon, I., Hamilton, E., & Jack, S. (2011). A study of a university-led entrepreneurship education programme for small business owner/managers. *Entrepreneurship and Regional Development, 2011.* Advance online publication. doi:10.1080/08985626.2011.566377

Gordon, R. D. (2008). Qualitative Approaches. In S. R. Clegg & J. R. Bailey (Eds.), *International Encyclopedia of Organization Studies*. SAGE Publications. doi:10.4135/9781412956246.n457

Gorla, N. (2009). A Survey of Rural E-Government Projects in India: Status and Benefits. *Information Technology for Development*, *15*(1), 52–58. doi:10.1002/itdj.20064

Goswami, A. (1998). Empowerment of women in Bangladesh. *Journal of Empowerment*, *5*, 45–70.

Govindarajan, V., & Ramamurti, R. (2011). Reverse innovation, emerging markets, and global strategy. *Global Strategy Journal*, *1*(3-4), 191–205. doi:10.1002/gsj.23

Goyal, S. K. (2014). Agricultural Mechanization for Sustainable Agricultural and Rural Development in Eastern U. P. - A Review. *Agriculture for Sustainable Development*, *2*(1), 192–198.

Grandon, E. E., & Pearson, J. M. (2004). Electronic commerce adoption: An empirical study of small and medium US businesses. *Information & Management*, *42*(1), 197–216. doi:10.1016/j.im.2003.12.010

Graziano, T. (2020). Rural Entrepreneurship, Innovation, and Technology: Narratives From the Italian AgriFood Startup Ecosystem. In Handbook of Research on Agricultural Policy, Rural Development, and Entrepreneurship in Contemporary Economies (pp. 334-353). IGI Global.

Greenhalgh, T., Robert, G., Bate, P., Macfarlane, F., & Kyriakidou, O. (2008). *Diffusion of innovations in health service organisations: a systematic literature review*. John Wiley & Sons.

Gregorio, D., & Shane, S. (2003). Why Do Some Universities Generate More Start-ups Than Others? *Research Policy*, *32*(2), 209–227. doi:10.1016/S0048-7333(02)00097-5

Greyson, K. A. (2018). Agribusiness System Hub for Rural Agricultural Cooperative Societies in Developing Countries. *Computer Science and Information Technology*, *6*(4), 63–69. doi:10.13189/csit.2018.060403

Grimaldi, R., & Grandi, A. (2005). Business incubators and new venture creation: An assessment of incubating models. *Technovation*, *25*(2), 111–121. doi:10.1016/S0166-4972(03)00076-2

GSO. (2018). *Vietnam General Statistical Office. Statistic data of 2018.* Retrieved from http://www.gso.gov.vn/SLTK/Menu.aspx?rxid=0d2b0d9f-8bb1-4718-a9e9-06bfb58be14d&px_language=vi&px_db=11.+Y+t%E1%BA%BF%2C+v%C4%83n+h%C3%B3a+v%C3%A0+%C4%91%E1%BB%9Di+s%E1%BB%91ng&px_type=PX

Guerrero, M., Urbano, D., & Alain, F. (2016). Entrepreneurial activity and regional competitiveness: Evidence from European entrepreneurial universities. *The Journal of Technology Transfer*, *41*(1), 105–131. doi:10.100710961-014-9377-4

Guerrero, M., Urbano, D., Fayolle, A., Klofsten, M., & Mian, S. (2016). Entrepreneurial universities: Emerging models in the new social and economic landscape. *Small Business Economics*, *47*(3), 551–563. doi:10.100711187-016-9755-4

Gupta, A.K. (2013). Tapping the Entrepreneurial Potential of Grassroots Innovation. *Stanford Social Innovation Review*, *11*(3), 18-20.

Gupta, R. K., Belkadi, F., & Bernard, A. (2017). Evaluation and management of customer feedback to include market dynamics into product development: Satisfaction Importance Evaluation (SIE) model. *21st International Conference on Engineering Design*.

Gupta, R. K., Ucler, C., & Bernard, A. (2018). Extension of the Virtual Customer Inspection for Distant Collaboration in NPD. *2018 IEEE International Conference on Engineering, Technology and Innovation*, 1–7. 10.1109/ICE.2018.8436333

Gupta, V. K., Guo, C., Canever, M., Yim, H. R., Sraw, G. K., & Liu, M. (2014). Institutional environment for entrepreneurship in rapidly emerging major economies: The case of Brazil, China, India, and Korea. *The International Entrepreneurship and Management Journal, 10*(2), 367–384. doi:10.100711365-012-0221-8

Habiyaremye, A., Kruss, G., & Booyens, I. (2019). Innovation for Inclusive Rural Transformaton: The Role of the State. *Innovation and Development*, 1-14.

Haggblade, S., Hazell, P. B. R., & Reardon, T. A. (2002). Strategies for stimulating poverty- alleviating growth in the rural nonfarm economy in developing countries. In *Environment and Production Technology Division, International Food Policy Research Institute (IFPRI) and Rural Development Department*. World Bank EPTD Discussion Paper No. 92.

Hansemark, O. C. (1998). The effects of an entrepreneurship programme on need for achievement and locus of control of reinforcement. *International Journal of Entrepreneurial Behaviour & Research, 4*(1), 28–50. doi:10.1108/13552559810203957

Haque, M., & Itohara, Y. (2009). Women empowerment through participation in micro-credit programme: A case study from Bangladesh. *Journal of Social Science, 5*(3), 244–250.

Harpa, E. (2017). Macroeconomic Analysis of the Competitive Factors which Influence Innovation in Rural Entrepreneurship. *Procedia Engineering, 181*, 965–968. doi:10.1016/j.proeng.2017.02.494

Harrigan, P., Ramsey, E., & Ibbotson, P. (2010). Critical factors underpinning the e-CRM activities of SMEs. *Journal of Marketing Management*, 1–27.

Hayter, C., Nelson, A., Zayed, S., & O'Connor, A. (2018). Conceptualizing academic entrepreneurship ecosystems: A review, analysis and extension of the literature. *The Journal of Technology Transfer, 43*(4), 1039–1082. Advance online publication. doi:10.100710961-018-9657-5

Hayton, J. C., George, G., & Zahra, S. A. (2002). National culture and entrepreneurship: A review of behavioral research. *Entrepreneurship Theory and Practice, 26*(4), 33–52. doi:10.1177/104225870202600403

Heckman, J. J., & LaLonde, R. J. (1999). The Economics and Econometrics of Active Labor Market Programs, Prepared for the Handbook of Labor Economics, Volume III, Orley Ashenfelter and David Card, editors. doi:10.1016/S1573-4463(99)03012-6

Henderson, J. (2002). Building the rural economy with high-growth entrepreneurs. *Economic Review- Federal Reserve Bank of Kansas City, 87*, 45–75.

Henderson, J., Low, S. A., & Weiler, S. (2009). Drivers of Regional Entrepreneurship in Rural and Metro Areas. In N. Walzer (Ed.), *Entrepreneurship and Local Economic Development* (pp. 81–102). Rowman & Littlefield Publishers, Inc.

Henry, C., & McElwee, G. (2014). Defining and Conceptualising Rural Enterprise. In C. Henry & G. McElwee (Eds.), *Exploring Rural Enterprise: New Perspectives on Research, Policy and Practice* (pp. 1–8). Emerald Group Publishing Limited. doi:10.1108/S2040-724620140000004001

Hermanto, B., & Suryanto, S. E. (2017). Entrepreneurship Ecosystem Policy in Indonesia. *Mediterranean Journal of Social Sciences, 8*(1), 110–115. doi:10.5901/mjss.2017.v8n1p110

Hevner, A. R., March, S. T., Park, J., & Ram, S. (2004). Design science in information systems research. *Management Information Systems Quarterly, 28*(1), 75–105. doi:10.2307/25148625

Hill, C.E., Loch, K.D., Straub, D., & El-Sheshai, K. (1998). A Qualitative Assessment of Arab Culture and Information Technology Transfer. *Journal of Global Information Management, 6*(3), 29-38.

Hindman, D. B. (2000). The Rural-Urban Digital Divide. *Journalism & Mass Communication Quarterly*, *77*(3), 549–560. doi:10.1177/107769900007700306

Hirschheim, R., Welke, R., & Schwarz, A. (2010). Service-oriented architecture: Myths, realities, and a maturity model. *MIS Quarterly Executive*, *9*(1).

Hisrich, R., Langan-Fox, J., & Grant, S. (2007). Entrepreneurship Research and Practice: A call to Action for Psychology. *The American Psychologist*, *62*(6), 575–589. doi:10.1037/0003-066X.62.6.575 PMID:17874898

Hoang, L. A., Castella, J. C., & Novosad, P. (2006). Social Networks and Information Access: Implications for Agricultural Extension in a Rice Farming Community in Northern Vietnam. *Agriculture and Human Values*, *23*(4), 513–527. doi:10.100710460-006-9013-5

Hofmann, P., & Reiner, G. (2006). Drivers for improving supply chain performance: An empirical study. *International Journal of Integrated Supply Management*, *2*(3), 214–230. doi:10.1504/IJISM.2006.008594

Hofstede, G. (2001). *Culture's consequences: Comparing values, behaviors, institutions, and organizations across nations*. Sage.

Holloway, R. (1998). *Supporting citizens initiatives: Bangladesh's NGOs and society*. Practical Action Publishing Ltd. doi:10.3362/9781780446066

Hormiga, E., de Saá-Pérez, P., Díaz-Díaz, N. L., Ballesteros-Rodríguez, J. L., & Aguiar-Diaz, I. (2017). The influence of entrepreneurial orientation on the performance of academic research groups: The mediating role of knowledge sharing. *The Journal of Technology Transfer*, *42*(1), 10–32. doi:10.100710961-015-9463-2

Horváth, D., & Szabó, R. Z. (2019). Driving Forces and Barriers of Industry 4.0: Do Multinational and Small and Medium-Sized Companies Have Equal Opportunities? *Technological Forecasting and Social Change*, *146*, 119–132. doi:10.1016/j.techfore.2019.05.021

Hulme, D. (2000). *Is microcredit Good for Poor People?* A note on the dark side of MicroFinance. Accessible from http: microsave.org.

Husemann, C., & Novković, N. (2014). Farm management information systems: A case study on a German multifunctional farm. *Economics of Agriculture, 61*(297-2016-3594), 441-453.

Innovation, S., & the Economic Development Canada. (2019). *Key Small Business Statistics – November 2019*. Available at: https://www.ic.gc.ca/eic/site/061.nsf/vwapj/KSBS_Nov-2019_En_Final_5.pdf/$file/KSBS_Nov-2019_En_Final_5.pdf

Investopedia. (2019). *Research and Development (R&D)*. Retrieved from https://www.investopedia.com/terms/r/randd.asp

Isenberg, D. (2011a). The entrepreneurship ecosystem strategy as a new paradigm for economy policy: principles for cultivating entrepreneurship. Babson Entrepreneurship Ecosystem Project, Babson College.

Islam, M. N., & Hussain, S. (1993). Rural development programs and the role of NGOs in Bangladesh. In M.A Quddus (Ed.), Rural development in Bangladesh: Strategies and experiences. Comilla, Bangladesh: Bangladesh Academy for Rural Development (BARD).

Islam, T. (2007). *Microcredit and poverty alleviation*. Ashgate Publishing Ltd.

Ismail, N. (2017, December 11). *Rural Businesses See Digital Technology as Key to Growth but Face Skills and Training Barriers*. Retrieved August 9, 2020, from Information Age: https://www.information-age.com/rural-businesses-digital-technology-key-growth-123469962/

Jansen, S. (2020). A focus area maturity model for software ecosystem governance. *Information and Software Technology, 118*, 106219. doi:10.1016/j.infsof.2019.106219 PMID:32490064

Jayadatta, S. (2017). *Major Challenges and Problems of Rural Entrepreneurship in India*. Academic Press.

Jepson, D., & Sharpley, R. (2018). More than sense of place? Exploring the emotional dimension of rural tourism experiences. In B. Lane & E. Kastenholz (Eds.), *Rural Tourism: New Concepts, New Research, New Practice* (pp. 25–46). Routledge. doi:10.4324/9781315111865-2

Johnson, G. I., & Hofman, P. J. (2004). Agri-product supply-chain management in developing countries. In *Agri-product supply-chain management in developing countries. Proceedings of a workshop, Bali, Indonesia, 19-22 August 2003.* Australian Centre for International Agricultural Research (ACIAR).

Jones, J. W., Antle, J. M., Basso, B., Boote, K. J., Conant, R. T., Foster, I., Godfray, H. C. J., Herrero, M., Howitt, R. E., Janssen, S., Keating, B. A., Munoz-Carpena, R., Porter, C. H., Rosenzweig, C., & Wheeler, T. R. (2017). Toward a New Generation of Agricultural System Data, Models, and Knowledge Products: State of Agricultural Systems Science. *Agricultural Systems, 155*, 269–288. doi:10.1016/j.agsy.2016.09.021 PMID:28701818

Jordaan, J., Alderson, M., Warren-Smith, I., & Lehmann, M. (2003). Enterprise Development in Rural Communities: Experiences and Preliminary Results on the Use of an Integrated Demonstration and Training Business. *13th Global Conference on Internationalizing Entrepreneurship Education and Training.*

Kabeer, N. (2001). Resources, agency, achievements: Reflections on the measurement of women's empowerment. In A. Sisask (Ed.), Discussing women's empowerment: Theory and practice (pp. 17-59). Swedish International Development Agency.

Kaloxylos, A., Eigenmann, R., Teye, F., Politopoulou, Z., Wolfert, S., Shrank, C., ... Nicole, H. (2012). Farm management systems and the Future Internet era. *Computers and Electronics in Agriculture, 89*, 130–144. doi:10.1016/j.compag.2012.09.002

Kamble, S. S., Gunasekaran, A., & Gawankar, S. A. (2020). Achieving sustainable performance in a data-driven agriculture supply chain: A review for research and applications. *International Journal of Production Economics, 219*, 179–194. doi:10.1016/j.ijpe.2019.05.022

Kantor, P. (2003). Women's empowerment through home-based work: Evidence from India. *Development and Change, 34*(3), 425–445. doi:10.1111/1467-7660.00313

Karanasios, S., & Slavova, M. (2019). How Do Development Actors Do "Ict for Development"? A Strategy-as-Practice Perspective on Emerging Practices in Ghanaian Agriculture. *Information Systems Journal, 29*(4), 888-913.

Karimi, S. (2015). Rural entrepreneurship: Challenges and opportunities. *Journal of Entrepreneurship in Agriculture, 1*(3), 101–119.

Kendall, J., & Kendall, K. (2001). A paradoxically peacefull coexistence between commerce and ecommerce. *Journal of Information Technology Theory and Application, 3*(4), 1–6.

Kendall, L., & Dearden, A. (2018). Towards Alternate Theories of Change for M4ard. In R. Duncombe (Ed.), *Digital Technologies for Agricultural and Rural Development in the Global South* (pp. 92–103). CABI. doi:10.1079/9781786393364.0092

Kessler, E.H., & Chakrabarti, A.K. (1996). Innovation Speed: A Conceptual Model of Context, Antecedents and Outcomes. *Academy of Management Review, 21*(4), 1143-1191.

Ketley, R. & Duminy, B. (2003). *Meeting the Challenge The Impact of Changing Technology on MicroFinance Institutions (MFIs).* MicroSave Briefing Note # 21.

Khanna, T. (2008). *Billions of Entrepreneurs — How China and India Are Reshaping Their Futures-And Yours*. Harvard Business School.

Khanna, T., & Palepu, K. G. (2006). Emerging Giants: Building World-Class Companies in Developing Countries. *Harvard Business Review*, *84*(10), 60–72.

Khan, S. (2002). *ICT as an instrument to leverage: The millennium development goals*. UN ICT Task Force.

Knight, G. A., & Cavusgil, S. T. (2004). Innovation, organizational capabilities, and the born-global firm. *Journal of International Business Studies*, *35*(2), 124–141. doi:10.1057/palgrave.jibs.8400071

Koh, H. C. (1996). Testing hypotheses of entrepreneurial characteristics: A study of Hong Kong MBA students. *Journal of Managerial Psychology*, *11*(3), 12–25. doi:10.1108/02683949610113566

Kohli, R., & Melville, N.P. (2019). Digital Innovation: A Review and Synthesis. *Information Systems Journal*, *29*(1), 200-223.

Kolukısa Tarhan, A., Garousi, V., Turetken, O., Söylemez, M., & Garossi, S. (2020). Maturity assessment and maturity models in health care: A multivocal literature review. *Digital Health*, *6*, 2055207620914772.

Korsgaard, S., Müller, S., & Tanvig, H. W. (2015). Rural entrepreneurship or entrepreneurship in the rural - between place and space. *International Journal of Entrepreneurial Behaviour & Research*, *21*(1), 5–26. doi:10.1108/IJEBR-11-2013-0205

Korten, D. C. (1991). The role of nongovernmental organizations in development: Changing patterns and perspectives. In S. Paul & A. Israel (Eds.), *Nongovernmental organizations and the World Bank*. World Bank Publications.

Kotey, B., & Sorensen, A. (2014). Barriers to Small Business Innovation in Rural Australia. *Australian Journal of Regional Studies*, *2*(3), 405–429.

Kumar, A., & Shah, J. (2016). Dairying as an instrument for ensuring socioeconomic and nutritional security in rural India. *Indian Journal of Agricultural Economics*, *71*(1), 78–89.

Kupiainen, K. (2000). *Performance of Small Rural Enterprises*. Agricultural Economics Research Institute Report, 239.

La¨tti, R. (2016). *Value Creation and Strategy in the Hyperconnected World the Current Wave of Digitalization. Explained through the Study of Finnish Forerunner Companies*. Aalto University.

Labrianidis, L. (2006). Fostering entrepreneurship as a means to overcome barriers to development of rural peripheral areas in Europe. *European Planning Studies*, *14*(1), 3–8. doi:10.1080/09654310500339067

Lai, E.L.-C., Riezman, R., & Wang, P. (2009). Outsourcing of Innovation. *Economic Theory*, *38*(3), 485-515.

Lambert, D. M., Cooper, M. C., & Pagh, J. D. (1998). Supply chain management: Implementation issues and research opportunities. *International Journal of Logistics Management*, *9*(2), 1–20. doi:10.1108/09574099810805807

Lampadarios, E., Kyriakidou, N., & Smith, G. (2017). Towards a new framework for SMEs success: A literature review. *International Journal of Business and Globalisation*, *18*(2), 194–232. doi:10.1504/IJBG.2017.081954

Lang, R., Fink, M., & Kibler, E. (2014). Understanding Place-based Entrepreneurship in Rural Central Europe: A Comparative Institutional Analysis. *International Small Business Journal*, *32*(2), 204–227. doi:10.1177/0266242613488614

Larsson, E., Hedelin, L., & Garling, T. (2003). Influence of export advice on expansion goals of small businesses in rural Sweden (Global perspective). *Journal of Small Business Management*, *41*(2), 205–212. doi:10.1111/1540-627X.00076

Lawson, R., Alcock, C., & Cooper, J. (2001). *e-Business adoption by manufacturing SMEs in regional Australia*. Paper presented at the 14th Bled Electronic Commerce Conferece, Bled, Slovenia.

Lee, Yun, Pyka, Won, Kodama, Schiuma, Park, Jeon, Park, Jung, Yan, Lee, & Zhao. (2018). How to Respond to the Fourth Industrial Revolution, or the Second Information Technology Revolution? Dynamic New Combinations between Technology, Market, and Society through Open Innovation. *Journal of Open Innovation: Technology, Market, and Complexity, 4*(3), 21.

Leeflang, P., Verhoef, P., Dahlström, P., & Freundt, T. (2014). Challenges and solutions for marketing in a digital era. *European Management Journal, 32*(1), 1–12. doi:10.1016/j.emj.2013.12.001

Lee, H., Kelley, D., Lee, J., & Lee, S. (2012). SME survival: The impact of internationalization, technology resources, and alliances. *Journal of Small Business Management, 50*(1), 1–19. doi:10.1111/j.1540-627X.2011.00341.x

Lee, M. C., & Chang, T. (2010). Developing a lean design for Six Sigma through supply chain methodology. *International Journal of Productivity and Quality Management, 6*(4), 407–434. doi:10.1504/IJPQM.2010.035891

Lee, M.-J. (2005). *Micro-Econometrics for Policy, Program and Treatment Effects*. Oxford University Press Inc. doi:10.1093/0199267693.001.0001

Lee, S., & Peterson, S. (2000). Culture, entrepreneurial orientation, and global competitiveness. *Journal of World Business, 35*(4), 401–416. doi:10.1016/S1090-9516(00)00045-6

Lefton, R. (2013). *Gender equality and women's empowerment are key to addressing global poverty*. Retrieved March 26, 2020 from http://www.americanprogress.org/issues/poverty/news/2013/03/11/56097/gender-equality-and-womens-empowerment-are-key-to-addressing-global-poverty/

Leifer, R., McDermott, C. M. G., Peters, L.S., Rice, M.P., & Veryzer, R.W. (2000). Radical Innovation: How Mature Companies Can Outsmart Upstairs. Boston, MA: Harvard Business School Press.

Lekhanya, L. M. (2018). The digitalisation of Rural Entrepreneurship. In S. M. Brito (Ed.), Entrepreneurship - Trends and Challenges (pp. 36-63). Intech. doi:10.5772/intechopen.75925

Lemos, F., & Farhangmehr, M. (2007). Tourism marketing and management: The case of Pousadas vs. Solares de Portugal. *Revista Turismo e Desenvolvimento, 7/8*, 117.

Leong, C. M. L., Pan, S. L., Zhu, K., & Cui, L. (2016b). Digitally Enabled Grassroots Enterpreneurship for Rural Development. In *Pacific Asia Conference on Information Systems*. Chiyai, Taiwan: AIS.

Leong, C., Tan, B., Xiao, X., Tan, F.T.C., & Sun, Y. (2017). Nurturing a Fintech Ecosystem: The Case of a Youth Microloan Startup in China. *International Journal of Information Management, 37*(2), 92-97.

Leong, C.M.L., Pan, S.-L., Newell, S., & Cui, L. (2016a). The Emergence of Self-Organizing E-Commerce Ecosystems in Remote Villages of China: A Tale of Digital Empowerment for Rural Development. *MIS Quarterly, 40*(2), 475-484.

Leont'ev, A. N. (1978). *Activity, Consciousness, and Personality*. Prentice-Hall.

Le, Q., & Raven, P. (2015). Woman entrepreneurship in rural Vietnam: Success and Motivation factors. *Journal of Developing Areas, 49*(2), 57–76. doi:10.1353/jda.2015.0024

Lewis, M.W., Welsh, M.A., Dehler, G.E., & Green, S.G. (2002). Product Development Tensions: Exploring Contrasting Styles of Project Management. *Academy of Management Journal, 45*(3), 546-564.

Li, L., Du, K., Zhang, W., & Mao, J.Y. (2019). Poverty Alleviation through Government-Led E-Commerce Development in Rural China: An Activity Theory Perspective. *Information Systems Journal, 29*(4), 914-952.

Liker, J. K., & Morgan, J. M. (2006). The Toyota Way in Services: The Case of Lean Product Development. *The Academy of Management Perspectives, 20*(2), 5–20. doi:10.5465/amp.2006.20591002

Littunen, H. (2000). Entrepreneurship and the characteristics of the entrepreneurial personality. *International Journal of Entrepreneurial Behaviour & Research*, *6*(6), 295–310. doi:10.1108/13552550010362741

Lockamy, A. III, & McCormack, K. (2004). The development of a supply chain management process maturity model using the concepts of business process orientation. *Supply Chain Management*, *9*(4), 272–278. doi:10.1108/13598540410550019

Lokuge, S., & Sedera, D. (2017). Turning Dust to Gold: How to Increase Inimitability of Enterprise System. In *Pacific Asia Conference on Information Systems*. Langkawi, Malaysia: AIS.

Lokuge, S., & Sedera, D. (2018). The Role of Enterprise Systems in Fostering Innovation in Contemporary Firms. *Journal of Information Technology Theory and Application, 19*(2), 7-30.

Lokuge, S., Sedera, D., & Grover, V. (2016b). Thinking inside the Box: Five Organizational Strategies Enabled through Information Systems. In *Pacific Asia Conference on Information Systems*. Chiyai, Taiwan: AIS.

Lokuge, S., Sedera, D., Atapattu, M., & Samaranayaka, D. (2016). Exploring the Role of IS in Agriculture: Creating an Agenda Towards Agri-Informatics. In *Pacific Asia Conference on Information Systems*. Chiyai, Taiwan: AIS.

Lokuge, S., Sedera, D., Atapattu, M., & Samaranayaka, D. (2016a). Exploring the Role of IS in Agriculture: Creating an Agenda Towards Agri-Informatics. In *Pacific Asia Conference on Information Systems*. Chiyai, Taiwan: AIS.

Lokuge, S., Sedera, D., Grover, V., & Xu, D. (2019). Organizational Readiness for Digital Innovation: Development and Empirical Calibration of a Construct. *Information & Management, 56*(3), 445-461.

Lokuge, S., & Sedera, D. (2014a). Deriving Information Systems Innovation Execution Mechanisms. In *Australasian Conference on Information Systems*. Auckland, New Zealand: AIS.

Lokuge, S., & Sedera, D. (2014b). Enterprise Systems Lifecycle-Wide Innovation. In *Americas Conference on Information Systems (AMCIS 2014)*. Savannah, GA: AIS.

Lokuge, S., & Sedera, D. (2014c). Enterprise Systems Lifecycle-Wide Innovation Readiness. In *Pacific Asia Conference on Information Systems*. Chengdu, China: AIS.

Lokuge, S., & Sedera, D. (2016). Is Your IT Eco-System Ready to Facilitate Organizational Innovation? Deriving an IT Eco-System Readiness Measurement Model. In *International Conference on Information Systems*. Dublin, Ireland: AIS.

Lokuge, S., & Sedera, D. (2017). Turning Dust to Gold: How to Increase Inimitability of Enterprise System. In *Pacific Asia Conference on Information Systems*. Langkawi, Malaysia: AIS.

Lokuge, S., Sedera, D., & Nanayakkara, S. (2018). Innovate or Copy: A Qualitative Document Analysis to Entrepreneurship in Developing Countries. In *European Conference on Information Systems*. Portsmouth, UK: AIS.

London, T., & Hart, S. L. (2004). Reinventing Strategies for Emerging Markets: Beyond the Transnational Model. *Journal of International Business Studies*, *35*(5), 350–370. doi:10.1057/palgrave.jibs.8400099

Lourenço, F., Sappleton, N., Dardaine-Edwards, A., Mcelwee, G., Cheng, R., Taylor, D., & Taylor, A. (2014). Experience of entrepreneurial training for female farmers to stimulate entrepreneurship in Uganda. *Gender in Management*, *29*(7), 382–401. doi:10.1108/GM-05-2013-0054

Lowe, P., & Talbot, H. (2000). *Providing advice and information in support of rural microbusinesses*. Centre for Rural Economy Research Report. University of Newcastle. Newscastle upon Tyne.

Lowe, R., & Marriott, S. (2006). *Enterprise: Entrepreneurship and Innovation Concepts, Contexts and Commercialization* (1st ed.). Elsevier Ltd.

Lu, Y., Lu, Y., Wang, B., Pan, Z., & Qin, H. (2015). Acceptance of Government-Sponsored Agricultural Information Systems in China: The Role of Government Social Power. *Information Systems and e-Business Management, 13*(2), 329–354. doi:10.100710257-014-0235-6

Lwoga, E. T. (2010). Bridging the Agricultural Knowledge and Information Divide: The Case of Selected Telecenters and Rural Radio in Tanzania. *The Electronic Journal on Information Systems in Developing Countries, 43*(1), 1–14. doi:10.1002/j.1681-4835.2010.tb00310.x

Lyytinen, K., & Rose, G.M. (2003). The Disruptive Nature of Information Technology Innovations: The Case of Internet Computing in Systems Development Organizations. *MIS Quarterly, 27*(4), 557-596.

MacGregor, R. C., & Kartiwi, M. (2010). Perception of barriers to e-commerce adoption in SMEs in a developed and developing country: A comparison between Australia and Indonesia. *Journal of Electronic Commerce in Organizations, 8*(1), 61–82. doi:10.4018/jeco.2010103004

MacGregor, R. C., & Vrazalic, L. (2005). A basic model of electronic commerce adoption barriers: A study of regional small businesses in Sweden and Australia. *Journal of Small Business and Enterprise Development, 12*(4), 510–527. doi:10.1108/14626000510628199

Mack, E., & Mayer, H. (2015). The evolutionary dynamics of entrepreneurial ecosystems. *Urban Studies (Edinburgh, Scotland), 53*. Advance online publication. doi:10.1177/0042098015586547

Mahroum, S. (2007). Overview: Rural Innovation. In S. Mahroum, J. Atterton, N. Ward, A. M. Williams, R. Naylor, R. Hindle, & F. Rowe (Eds.), *Rural Innovation* (pp. 4–11). NESTA.

Mahtab, N. (2007). *Women in Bangladesh: from inequality to empowerment*. A. H. Development Publishing House.

Mainhart, A. (1999). *Management Information System for Microfinance: An Evaluation Framework*. U.S. Agency for International Development, Bureau for Global Programs, Center for Economic Growth and Agricultural Development, Office of Microenterprise Development, through funding to the Microenterprise Best Practices (MBP) Project, contract number PCE-C-00-96-90004-00.

Mair, J., Martí, I., & Ventresca, M. J. (2012). Building Inclusive Markets in Rural Bangladesh: How Intermediaries Work Institutional Voids. *Academy of Management Journal, 55*(4), 819–850. doi:10.5465/amj.2010.0627

Malerba, F., & McKelvey, M. (2020). Knowledge-intensive innovative entrepreneurship integrating Schumpeter, evolutionary economics, and innovation systems. *Small Business Economics, 54*(2), 503–522. doi:10.100711187-018-0060-2

Malhotra, A., Schule, S. R., & Boender, C. (2002). *Measuring women's empowerment as a variable in international development*. Background paper prepared for the World Bank workshop on poverty and gender: New Perspective.

MAMAOT. (2012). *Programa Rede Rural Nacional*. MAMAOT.

Markus, L. (2001). Toward a Theory of Knowledge Reuse: Types of Knowledge Reuse Situations and Factors in Reuse Success. *Journal of Management Information Systems, 18*(1), 57-93.

Marsden, T., Banks, J., & Bristow, G. (2000). Food supply chain approaches: Exploring their role in rural development. *Sociologia Ruralis, 40*(4), 424–438. doi:10.1111/1467-9523.00158

Martin, L., & Matlay, H. (2001). "Blanket" approaches to promoting ICT in small firms: Some lessons from the DTI ladder adoption model in the UK. *Internet Research: Electronic Networking Applications and Policy, 11*(5), 399–410. doi:10.1108/EUM0000000006118

Martins, L. (2013). O "alojamento local" – entre o impulso da novidade e a maturidade do turismo rural português. *Proceedings – Conferência Vale do Douro: Desenvolvimento Rural e Ordenamento Turístico*. Retrieved from: https://sigarra.up.pt/fpceup/pt/pub_geral.pub_view?pi_pub_base_id=43899&pi_pub_r1_id=

Maskell, P. H., Eskelinen, I., Hannibalsson, A., Malmberg, J., & Vatne, E. (1998). *Competitiveness, Localised Learning and Regional development. Specialization and Prosperity in Small Open economics*. Routledge. doi:10.4324/9780203276921

Mas-Verdú, F., Ortiz-Miranda, D., & García-Álvarez-Coque, J. M. (2016). Examining organizational innovations in different regional settings. *Journal of Business Research*, *69*(11), 5324–5329. doi:10.1016/j.jbusres.2016.04.132

Matrane, O., Talea, A., Okar, C., & Talea, M. (2015). Towards A new maturity model for information system. *International Journal of Computer Science Issues*, *12*(3), 268.

Maxwell, I. E. (2009). *Managing Sustainable Innovation: The Driver for Global Growth*. Springer. doi:10.1007/978-0-387-87581-1

Mayoux, L. (2000a). *Microfinance and the empowerment of women: A review of key issues*. Retrieved December 02, 2013 from http://www.ilo.org/wcmsp5/groups/public/--ed_emp/documents/publication/wcms_117993.pdf

McClelland, D. C. (1961). *The Achieving Society, D*. Van Norstrand Co Inc. doi:10.1037/14359-000

McCole, P., & Ramsey, E. (2005). A profile of adopters and non-adopters of ecommerce in SME professional service firms. *Australasian Marketing Journal*, *13*(1), 36–48. doi:10.1016/S1441-3582(05)70066-5

McCormack, K. P., & Johnson, W. C. (2001). *Business process orientation: Gaining the e-business competitive advantage*. CRC Press.

McCormack, K., Willems, J., Van den Bergh, J., Deschoolmeester, D., Willaert, P., Štemberger, M. I., ... Vlahovic, N. (2009). A global investigation of key turning points in business process maturity. *Business Process Management Journal*, *15*(5), 792–815. doi:10.1108/14637150910987946

McElwee, G. (2004). *A segmentation framework for the farm sector.* Paper presented at 3rd Rural Entrepreneurship Conference. University of Paisley.

McElwee, G., & Atherton, A. (2013), Rural Entrepreneurship. In World Encyclopedia of Entrepreneurship. Edward Elgar Publishing Limited.

McElwee, G. (2006). Farmers as entrepreneurs: Developing competitive skills. *Journal of Developmental Entrepreneurship*, *11*(3), 187–206. doi:10.1142/S1084946706000398

McElwee, G., & Atherton, A. (2011). Rural Entrepreneurship. In L. P. Dana & L.-P. Dana (Eds.), *World Encyclopedia of Entrepreneurship* (pp. 377–384). Edward Elgar Publishing. doi:10.4337/9781849808453.00048

McElwee, G., & Bosworth, G. (2010). Exploring the Strategic Skills of Farmers Across a Typology of Farm Diversification Approaches. *Journal of Farm Management*, *13*(12), 819–838.

McElwee, G., Pyysiä¨inen, J., Anderson, A., & Vesala, K. (2006). Developing the entrepreneurial skills of farmers: Some myths explored. *International Journal of Entrepreneurial Behaviour & Research*, *12*(1), 2139.

McElwee, G., & Smith, R. (2014). Researching rural enterprise. In A. Fayolle (Ed.), *Handbook of Research on Entrepreneurship* (pp. 307–334). Edward Elgar.

Mcelwee, P. D. (2008). Forest environmental income in Vietnam: Household socioeconomic factors influencing forest use. *Environmental Conservation*, *35*(2), 147–159. doi:10.1017/S0376892908004736

McNally, S. (2001). Farm diversification in England and Wales: What can we learn from the farm business survey. *Journal of Rural Studies, 17*(2), 47–57. doi:10.1016/S0743-0167(00)00050-4

Meijers, E. J., & Burger, M. J. (2017). Stretching the Concept of 'Borrowed Size'. *Urban Studies (Edinburgh, Scotland), 54*(1), 269–291. doi:10.1177/0042098015597642

Menezes, F. (2000). *Tourism as an Agent of rural development: Construction of programmes and institutional forms of implementation: a case study of LEADER I in Vale do Lima (in NW Portugal)* (Master's dissertation). Retrieved from: http://www.center.pt/imprensactr/estudo_788.pdf

Mian, S. (2011). University's involvement in technology business incubation: what theory and practice tell us? *International Journal of Entrepreneurship and Innovation Management, 13*(2), 113-121.

Mian, S. (2016). Business Incubations and Incubator Mechanisms. In P. Phan, S. Mian, & L. Wadid (Eds.), *Technology Entrepreneurship And Business Incubation: Theory, Practice, Lessons learned* (pp. 1–34). Imperal College Press. doi:10.1142/9781783269778_0001

Miller, C., Saroja, V. N., & Linder, C. (2013). *ICT uses for inclusive agricultural value chains.* Food and Agriculture Organization of the United Nations.

Minniti, M., & Naudé, W. (2010). Introduction: What Do We Know About the Patterns and Determinants of Female Entrepreneurship Across Countries? *European Journal of Development Research, 22*(3), 277–293. doi:10.1057/ejdr.2010.17

Miron D, McClelland DC (1961). The Impact of Achievement Motivation Training on Small Businesses. *California Management Review, 21*(4), 13-28. doi:10.2307/41164830

Mistr, M. (2007). *The Czech Republic's emerging agricultural information and advisory services.* 18th European Seminar on Extension Education: Supporting Viable Rural Communities, Prague, Czech University of Life Sciences.

Mittenzwei, K., Persson, T., Höglind, M., & Kværnø, S. (2017). Combined effects of climate change and policy uncertainty on the agricultural sector in Norway. *Agricultural Systems, 153*, 118–126. doi:10.1016/j.agsy.2017.01.016

Mkhabela, T. (2007). Linking farmers with markets in Rural South Africa: Rural Development and poverty alleviation through supply chain management. Pretoria: National Agricultural Marketing Council (NAMC), Market and Economic Research Centre (MERC).

MkNelly, B., & McCord, M. (2001). Credit with education. *Impact Review No. 1: Women's Empowerment. Freedom from Hunger.*

Mohd Rafi, A. F. (2017). Entrepreneurial psychology: The role of motivation in business creation new E-Commerce. *Journal of Business and Social Development*, 49-59.

Molla, M. (1982). Credit problems of the rural disadvantaged in Bangladesh. *Journal of Bank Porikrama, 7*(1), 59–64.

Morduch, J. (1998). *Does Microfinance Real ly Help the Poor? New Evidence on Flagship Programs in Bangladesh.* MacArthur Foundation project on inequality working paper, Princeton University, draft.

Moreira, A. C. (2015). Entrepreneurial Tourism: The cration of business opportunities in the Adrimag Region, Portugal. In L. Carvalho (Ed.), *Handobook of Research on Entrepreneurial Sucess and its impact on Regional Development* (pp. 376–404). IGI Global.

Morris, D. (2019). Vietnam Agriculture Farming 4.0 - Issues and Solutions - Impact of the Major Trade Agreements CPTPP. *EUVNFTA and Investment Protection Agreement.* Retrieve from https://www.lexology.com/library/detail.aspx?g=5b12a52a-97ed-4672-8def82e297450659.%20Retrieved%20on%20Dec%2021,%202019 on Jun 15, 2020.

Morris, M. H., Kuratko, D. F., & Schindehutte, M. (2001). Towards integration: Understanding entrepreneurship through frameworks. *The International Journal of Entrepreneurship and Innovation*, *2*(1), 35–49. doi:10.5367/000000001101298765

MOST. (2018). *Ministry of Sciences and Technology, Vietnam*. Retrieved from https://www.most.gov.vn/vn/tin-tuc/15274/nong-nghiep-thong-minh--co-hoi-va-thach-thuc-cho-nong-nghiep-viet-nam.aspx

Movahedi, R., & Yaghoubi-Farani, A. (2012). Analysis of the Barriers and Limitations for the Development of Rural Women's Entrepreneurship. *International Journal of Entrepreneurship and Small Business*, *15*(4), 469–487. doi:10.1504/IJESB.2012.046476

Mueller, S., & Anderson, A. (2014). Understanding the entrepreneurial learning process and its impact on students' personal development: A European perspective. *International Journal of Management Education*, *12*(3), 500–511. Advance online publication. doi:10.1016/j.ijme.2014.05.003

Mukerjee, K. (2012). Frugal innovation: the key to penetrating emerging markets. *Ivey Business Journal*, *76*(4).

Müller, S. (2013). *Entrepreneurship and Regional Development: On the interplay between agency and context* (PhD thesis). Department of Business Administration, Aarhus University, Aarhus.

Müller, S. (2016). A progress review of entrepreneurship and regional development: What are the remaining gaps? *European Planning Studies*, *24*(6), 1133–1158. doi:10.1080/09654313.2016.1154506

Muñoz, P., & Kimmitt, J. (2019). Rural entrepreneurship in place: An integrated framework. *Entrepreneurship and Regional Development*, 1–32. doi:10.1080/08985626.2019.1609593

Murray, L. B., & MacMillan, I. C. (1988). Entrepreneurship: Past Research and Future Challenges. *Journal of Management*, *14*(2), 139–161. doi:10.1177/014920638801400202

Mwatsika, C. (2015). Entrepreneurship development and entrepreneurial orientation in rural areas in Malawi. *African Journal of Business Management*, *9*(9), 425–436. doi:10.5897/AJBM2014.7552

Mynott, C. (2012). Lean Product Development: A Manager's Guide. London, UK: The Institution of Engineering and Technology (IET).

Nacu, C. M., & Avasilcai, S. (2014). Technological Ecopreneurship: Conceptual Approaches. *Procedia: Social and Behavioral Sciences*, *124*, 229–235. doi:10.1016/j.sbspro.2014.02.481

Naik, G., & Suresh, D. N. (2018). Challenges of creating sustainable agri-retail supply chains. *IIMB Management Review*, *30*(3), 270–282. doi:10.1016/j.iimb.2018.04.001

Nambisan, S. (2013). Information Technology and Product/Service Innovation: A Brief Assessment and Some Suggestions for Future Research. *Journal of the Association for Information Systems*, *14*(4), 215-226.

Nambisan, S. (2017). Digital Entrepreneurship: Toward a Digital Technology Perspective of Entrepreneurship. *Entrepreneurship Theory and Practice*, *41*(6), 1029-1055.

Nambisan, S. (2017). Digital Entrepreneurship: Toward a Digital Technology Perspective of entrepreneurship. *Entrepreneurship Theory and Practice*, *41*(6), 1029–1055. doi:10.1111/etap.12254

Nambisan, S., Lyytinen, K., Majchrzak, A., & Song, M. (2017). Digital innovation management: Reinventing innovation management research in a digital world. *Management Information Systems Quarterly*, *41*(1), 223–238. doi:10.25300/MISQ/2017/41:1.03

Nambisan, S., Wright, M., & Feldman, M. (2019). The Digital Transformation of Innovation and Entrepreneurship: Progress, Challenges and Key Themes. *Research Policy*, *48*(8), 103773. doi:10.1016/j.respol.2019.03.018

Nambisan, S., Zahra, S. A., & Luo, Y. (2019). Global platforms and ecosystems: Implications for international business theories. *Journal of International Business Studies*, *50*(9), 1464–1486. Advance online publication. doi:10.105741267-019-00262-4

Nawaz, F. (2011). *Strengthening awareness among rural adolescent girls in Bangladesh: A case study on adolescent development program of BRAC*. Lambert Academic Publishing.

Nawaz, F. (2013). Bargaining with poverty: An empirical review on some rural women in Bangladesh. *Studies on Home and Community Science*, *7*(2), 87–94. doi:10.1080/09737189.2013.11885397

Nawaz, N., Jahanian, A., & Manzoor, S. W. (2012). Empowering women through microcredit: A case study of Tameer Microfinance Bank, Bahawalpur. *Journal of Economics and Sustainable Development*, *3*(6), 17–21.

Negi, S., & Anand, N. (2015). Issues and challenges in the supply chain of fruits & vegetables sector in India: A review. *International Journal of Managing Value and Supply Chains*, *6*(2), 47–62. doi:10.5121/ijmvsc.2015.6205

Neirotti, P., Raguseo, E., & Paolucci, E. (2018). How SMEs Develop ICT-Based Capabilities in Response to Their Environment: Past Evidence and Implications for the Uptake of the New ICT Paradigm. *Journal of Enterprise Information Management*, *31*(1), 10–37. doi:10.1108/JEIM-09-2016-0158

Newbery, R., Siwale, J., & Henley, A. (2017). Editorial: Rural Entrepreneurship Theory in the Developing and Developed World. *International Journal of Entrepreneurship and Innovation*, *18*(1), 3-4.

Newman, A., Obschonka, M., Schwarz, S., Michael, C., & Nielsen, I. (2019). Entrepreneurial Self-efficacy: A systematic Review of teh Literature on its Theoritical foundations, measurmenet, antecedents and outcomes and an agenda for future research. *Journal of Vocational Behavior*, *110*, 403–419. doi:10.1016/j.jvb.2018.05.012

Nguyen, C., Frederick, H., & Nguyen, H. (2014). Female entrepreneurship in rural Vietnam: An exploratory study. *International Journal of Gender and Entrepreneurship*, *6*(1), 50–67. doi:10.1108/IJGE-04-2013-0034

Nguyen, T. T. (2016). An investigation of the Vietnamese shipping industry and policy recommendations for profound participation into ASEAN integration. *The Asian Journal of Shipping and Logistics*, *32*(2), 81–88. doi:10.1016/j.ajsl.2016.05.001

Nichter, S., Goldmark, L., & Fiori, A. (2002). *Understanding Microfinance in the Brazilian Context*. BNDES.

Nie, P., Ma, W., & Sousa-Poza, A. (2020). The Relationship between Smatrphone use and Subjective Well-being in Rural China. *Electronic Commerce Research*. Advance online publication. doi:10.100710660-020-09397-1

Nijkamp, P. (2009). *Entrepreneurship, development, and the spatial context*. Retrieved from Helsinki: Nulty, D. D. (2008). The adequacy of response rates to online and paper surveys: what can be done? *Assessment & Evaluation in Higher Education*, *33*(3), 301–314.

North, D. (1990). *Institutions, Institutional Change and Economic Performance*. Cambridge University Press. doi:10.1017/CBO9780511808678

Noseleit, F. (2013). Entrepreneurship, structural change, and economic growth. *Journal of Evolutionary Economics*, *23*(4), 735–766. doi:10.100700191-012-0291-3

Nothnagel, K. (2008). The Central Proposition of Resource-based Theory. In K. Nothnagel (Ed.), Empirical Research within Resource-Based Theory (pp. 11-49). Gabler.

Nugawela, S., & Sedera, D. (2020). *Analysis of Farm Management Information Systems: Opportunities and Pathways for Future Value*. PACIS.

Nwankwo, F. O., & Okeke, C. S. (2017). Rural Entrepreneurship and Rural Development in Nigeria. *Africa's Public Service Delivery and Performance Review, 5*(1).

Nwankwo, F. O., & Okeke, C. S. (2017). Rural Entrepreneurship and Rural Development in Nigeria. *Africa's Public Service Delivery and Performance Review*, *5*(1), 1–7.

Nylén, D., & Holmström, J. (2015). Digital Innovation Strategy: A Framework for Diagnosing and Improving Digital Product and Service Innovation. *Business Horizons*, *58*(1), 57-67.

Nylén, D., & Holmström, J. (2015). Digital Innovation Strategy: A Framework for Diagnosing and Improving Digital Product and Service Innovation. *Business Horizons*, *58*(1), 57–67. doi:10.1016/j.bushor.2014.09.001

O'Regan, G. (2010). *Introduction to software process improvement*. Springer Science & Business Media.

OECD. (2006). *The New Rural Paradigm: Policies and Governance*. OECD Report, Directorate for Public Governance and Territorial Development. Retrieved from https://www.oecd.org/cfe/regional-policy/thenewruralparadigmpoliciesand-governance.htm

OECD. (2011, January 25). *OECD Rural Policy Reviews: England, United Kingdom 2011*. Paris: OECD Publishing.

OECD/European Union. (2019). What Potential Does Digital Entrepreneurship have for Being Inclusive. In *The Missing Entrepreneurs 2019: Policies for Inclusive Entrepreneurship* (pp. 177–218). OECD Publishing.

Ohno, T. (1988). *Toyota production system: beyond large-scale production*. Productivity Press.

Okediran, O. O., & Ganiyu, R. A. (2019). E-Agriculture Reviewed: Theories, Concepts and Trends. *FUOYE Journal of Engineering and Technology*, *4*(1), 125–130. doi:10.46792/fuoyejet.v4i1.366

Okoli, C., Mbarika, V.W., & McCoy, S. (2010). The Effects of Infrastructure and Policy on E-Business in Latin America and Sub-Saharan Africa. *European Journal of Information Systems*, *19*(1), 5-20.

Okonkwo, C. W., Huisman, M., & Taylor, E. (2019). Socio-Economic Contributions of Mobile Applications in Africa: Impact of Local Mobile Applications. In *International Multidisciplinary Information Technology and Engineering Conference* (pp. 1-8). Vanderbijlpark, South Africa: IEEE. 10.1109/IMITEC45504.2019.9015912

Omar, F. I., Dimyati, H. A., Ahmad, N., & Khairuddin, S. M. H. S. (2018). Digital Inclusion Among Entrepreneurs of Small and Medium. *Journal of Education and Social Sciences*, *9*(2), 90–97.

Osarenkhoe, A. (2009). An integrated framework for understanding the driving forces behind non-sequential process of internationalization among firms. *Business Process Management Journal*, *15*(2), 286–316. doi:10.1108/14637150910949498

Othman, N., & Ishak, S. B. (2009). Attitude towards choosing a career in entrepreneurship amongst graduates. *European Journal of Soil Science*, *10*(3), 419–434.

Palacios-Lopez, A., Christiaensen, L., & Kilic, T. (2015). *How Much of the Labor in African Agriculture is Provided by Women?* World Bank Policy Research Paper 7282. World Bank.

Paraforos, D. S., Vassiliadis, V., Kortenbruck, D., Stamkopoulos, K., Ziogas, V., Sapounas, A. A., & Griepentrog, H. W. (2017). Multi-level automation of farm management information systems. *Computers and Electronics in Agriculture*, *142*, 504–514. doi:10.1016/j.compag.2017.11.022

Parikh, T. (2005). *'Rural Microfinance Service Delivery: Gaps, Inefficiencies and Emerging Solutions*. University of Washington.

Parrino, L. (2015). Coworking: Assessing the role of proximity in knowledge exchange. *Knowledge Management Research and Practice, 13*(3), 261–271. doi:10.1057/kmrp.2013.47

Patel, A. S. (1988). *Co-operative Dairying and Rural Development: A Case Study of AMUL.* In B. S. Baviskar & D. W. Attwood (Eds.), *Who Shares? Cooperatives and Rural Development* (pp. 362–377). Oxford University Press.

Pato, L., & Teixeira, A. A. C. (2018). Rural Entrepreneurship: the Tale of a Rare Event. *Journal os Place Management and Development, 11*(1), 46-59.

Pato, M.L., & Teixeira, A.A. (2016). Twenty Years of Rural Entrepreneurship: A Bibliometric Survey. *Sociologia Ruralis, 56*(1), 3-28.

Pato, L. (2015). Rural Entrepreneurship and Innovation: Some Successful Women's Initiatives. In *55th Congress of the European Regional Science Association.* Lisbon, Portugal: European Regional Science Association (ERSA).

Pato, L., & Teixeira, A. A. C. (2016). Twenty years of rural entrepreneurship: A bibliometric survey. *Sociologia Ruralis, 56*(1), 3–28. doi:10.1111oru.12058

Pato, L., & Teixeira, A. A. C. (2019a). Are New Rural Ventures Different from New Urban Ones? *Journal of Entrepreneurship and Public Policy.*

Pato, L., & Teixeira, A. A. C. (2019b). Determinants of performance of new ventures located in portuguese incubators and science parks with a focus on institutional factors. Do rural and urban new ventures differ? *European Planning Studies.*

Paulk, M. C., Curtis, B., Chrissis, M. B., & Weber, C. V. (1993a). *Capability Maturity Modelfor Software, Version 1.1.* Tech ReportCMUSEI-93TR-24, Software Engineering institute, Carnegie Mellon University, Pittsburgh, PA.

Paulk, M. C., Weber, C. V., Garcia, S. M., Chrissis, M. B., & Bush, M. (1993b). *Key practices of the capability maturity model, Version 1.1. Software Engineering institute.* Carnegie Mellon University.

Pavic, S., Koh, S. C. L., Simpson, M., & Padmore, J. (2007). Could e-business create a competitive advantage in UK SMEs? *Benchmarking: An International Journal, 14*(3), 320–351. doi:10.1108/14635770710753112

Pereiro, X. (2018). Abordagem exploratória do turismo rural de Trás-os-Montes e Alto Douro (Portugal). *Analise Social, 53*(226), 58–87. http://analisesocial.ics.ul.pt/documentos/n226a03.pdf

Pessôa, M., & Trabasso, L. G. (2017). *The Lean Product Design and Development Journey: A Practical View.* Springer International Publishing. doi:10.1007/978-3-319-46792-4

Pethig, F., & Kroenung, J. (2019). Specialized Information Systems for the Digitally Disadvantaged. *Journal of the Association for Information Systems, 20*(10), 1412-1446.

Pettigrew, A.M., Woodman, R.W., & Cameron, K.S. (2001). Studying Organizational Change and Development: Challenges for Future Research. *Academy of Management Journal, 44*(4), 697-713.

Pfeilstetter, R. (2013). Entrepreneurship and regional development in Europe: A comparative, socio-anthropological case study in Germany and Spain. *Anthropological Notebooks, 19*(1), 45–57.

Pham, H. C., Nguyen, T. T., McDonald, S., & Tran-Kieu, N. Q. (2019). Information sharing in Logistics Firms: An Exploratory Study of the Vietnamese Logistics Sector. *The Asian Journal of Shipping and Logistics, 35*(2), 87–95. doi:10.1016/j.ajsl.2019.06.001

Pham, L., & Massey, B. (2018). Effective Digital Participation: Differences in Rural and Urban Areas and Ways Forward. In M. Dezuanni, M. Foth, K. Mallan, & H. Hughes (Eds.), *Digital Participation through Social Living Labs* (pp. 315–332). Chandos Publishing. doi:10.1016/B978-0-08-102059-3.00017-4

Phan, P. H., Siegel, D. S., & Wright, M. (2005). Science parks and incubators: Observations, synthesis and future research. *Journal of Business Venturing*, *20*(2), 165–182. doi:10.1016/j.jbusvent.2003.12.001

Phelps, N. A., Fallon, R. J., & Williams, C. L. (2001). Small Firms, Borrowed Size and the Urban-Rural Shift. *Regional Studies*, *35*(7), 613–624. doi:10.1080/00343400120075885

Philpott, K., Dooley, L., O'Reilly, C., & Lupton, G. (2011). The entrepreneurial university: Examining the underlying academic tensions. *Technovation*, *31*(4), 161–170. doi:10.1016/j.technovation.2010.12.003

Pickernell, D., Senyard, J., Jones, P., Packham, G., & Ramsey, E. (2013). New and young firms: Entrepreneurship policy and the role of government–evidence from the Federation of Small Businesses survey. *Journal of Small Business and Enterprise Development*, *20*(2), 358–382. doi:10.1108/14626001311326770

Pina, P. (1988). *Portugal: o turismo no século XX*. Lucidus.

Pisching, M. A., Diolin, F. J., Filho, J. S., & Miyagi, P. E. (2015). Service composition in the cloud-based manufacturing focused on the Industry 4.0. *IFIP International Federation for Information Processing*, *2015*, 65–72.

Pitt, M., & Khandker, S. (1998). The Impact of Group-Based Credit Programs on Poor Households in Bangladesh: Does the Gender of Participants Matter? *Journal of Political Economy*, *106*(5), 958–996.

Planes, V., Miras, R., & Requena, A. (2006). *Teoría Fundamentada Grounded Theory: El desarrollo de teoría desde la generalización conceptual* (1st ed.). Centro de Investigaciones Sociológicas.

Plog, S. (1974). Why Destination Areas Rise and Fall in Popularity. *The Cornell Hotel and Restaurant Administration Quarterly*, *14*(4), 55–58. doi:10.1177/001088047401400409

Ply, J. K., Moore, J. E., Williams, C. K., & Thatcher, J. B. (2012). IS employee attitudes and perceptions at varying levels of software process maturity. *Management Information Systems Quarterly*, *36*(2), 601–624. doi:10.2307/41703469

Poeppelbuss, J., Niehaves, B., Simons, A., & Becker, J. (2011). Maturity models in information systems research: Literature search and analysis. *Communications of the Association for Information Systems*, *29*(1), 27.

Poirier, C. C. (2004). How are we doing? A survey of supply chain progress. *Supply Chain Management Review, 8*(8), 24-31.

Pollin, R., Feffer, J., & Daley-Harris, S. (2007). *Debate on microcredit.* Retrieved May 28, 2014, from http://fpif.org/debate_on_microcredit/

Powell, N., Swartling, Å. G., & Minh Ha, H. (2011). The national policy landscape: The legacy and the present situation. In N. Powell, Å. G. Swartling, & H. Minh Ha (Eds.), *Stakeholder Agency in Rural Development Policy: Articulating Cogovernance in Vietnam*. World Agroforestry Centre ICRAF.

Prahalad, C. K. (2005). Learning to Lead. *Vikalpa*, *30*(2), 1–10. doi:10.1177/0256090920050201

Prahalad, C. K. (2012). Bottom of the pyramid as a source of breakthrough innovations. *Journal of Product Innovation Management*, *29*(1), 6–12. doi:10.1111/j.1540-5885.2011.00874.x

Prasad, G. (2001). *Yes, you can do Business with Open Source*. Accessed August 9, 2006 at http://www.zdnetindia.com/techzone/linuxcentre/stories/32999.html

PRIVETUR – Associação Portuguesa de Turismo Rural. (2013). *Turismo Rural.pt. Quem somos*. Retrieved from: http://www.turismorural.pt/pt/quem-somos/

Proença, D., & Borbinha, J. (2016). Maturity models for information systems-a state of the art. *Procedia Computer Science, 100*, 1042–1049. doi:10.1016/j.procs.2016.09.279

ProRegio. (2015). Customer-driven design of product-services and production networks to adapt to regional market requirements: Deliverable D1.4: Market requirements regarding frugal innovation for products and product-services. Horizon2020 under GA-Nr. 636966. Patras, Greece: Laboratory for Manufacturing Systems and Automation (LMS).

Pugh, R., Lamine, W., Jack, S., & Hamilton, E. (2018). The entrepreneurial university and the region: What role for entrepreneurship departments? *European Planning Studies*, *26*(9), 1835–1855. doi:10.1080/09654313.2018.1447551

Pyzdek, T. (2003). *The Six Sigma Handbook: A Complete Guide for Green Belts, Black Belts and Managers at All Levels*. McGraw-Hill.

QS. (2020). *Universities in Portugal*. Retrieved from https://www.topuniversities.com/where-to-study/europe/portugal/guide

Qureshi, S., Kamal, M., & Good, T. (2008). *Adoption of Information by Micro-enterprises: Insights from a Rural Community*. AMCIS.

Radjou, N., & Prabhu, J. (2014). 4 CEOs Who Are Making Frugal Innovation Work. *Harvard Business Review*, *28*(4), 1–6.

Rahman, A. (1999). Microcredit initiative for equitable and sustainable development: Who pays? *World Development*, *27*(1), 67–82. doi:10.1016/S0305-750X(98)00105-3

Rahman, A. K. M. M. (2010). *NGO and development: Myth and reality*. AH Development Publishing House.

Raisanen, J., & Tuovinen, T. (2020). Digital Innovations in Rural Micro-Enterprises. *Journal of Rural Studies*, *73*, 56–67. doi:10.1016/j.jrurstud.2019.09.010

Raja, V. (2018, August 7). *12000 Households, 350+ Villages: How Crop Waste is Electrifying Rural India!* Retrieved from the better India: https://www.thebetterindia.com/155140/husk-power-system-renewable-energy-investment/

Randhawa, S. S. (2016). Technological innovations in dairy farming as a tool to boost rural income in Punjab, India. *Journal of Advances in Dairy Research*.

Rankin, K. (2002). Social capital, microfinance and the politics of development. *Feminist Economics*, *11*(8), 1–24. doi:10.1080/13545700210125167

Rantamaki-Lahtinen, L. (2002). Finnish pluriactive farms – the common but unknown rural enterprises. In H. W. Tanvig (Ed.), *Rurality, Rural Policy and Politics in a Nordic-Scottish Perspective. Working paper 1/02*. Danish Centre for Rural Research and Development.

Rao, K. M. (2004). *Microfinance Institutions in India*. Presented at the APRACA Seminar at Manila on Regulation of MFIs.

Rapoza, K. (2011). *What Makes Emerging Markets Great Investments?* http://www.forbes.com/pictures/eglg45gdjd/why-invest-in-emerging-markets-2/

Ratcliffe, M., Burd, C., Holder, K., & Fields, A. (2016, December 11). *Defining Rural at the US Census Bureau*. Retrieved July 12, 2020, from United States Census Bureau: https://www.census.gov/content/dam/Census/library/publications/2016/acs/acsgeo-1.pdf

Ratinho, T., & Henriques, E. (2010). The role of science parks and business incubators in converging countries: Evidence from Portugal. *Technovation*, *30*(4), 278–290. doi:10.1016/j.technovation.2009.09.002

Rauch, E., Dallasega, P., & Matt, D. T. (2016). The way from Lean Product Development (LPD) to Smart Product Development (SPD). *Procedia CIRP*, *50*, 26–31. doi:10.1016/j.procir.2016.05.081

Raymond, E. S. (2000). *The Cathedral and The Bazaar.* Available from http://www.catb.org/ esr/writings/cathedral-bazaar/cathedralbazaar/

Raymond, L. (2001). Determinants of web site implementation in small businesses. *Internet Research: Electronic Networking Applications and Policy*, *11*(5), 411–422. doi:10.1108/10662240110410363

Regy, P. V., & Mahajan, V. (2006). IT at BASIX: Successes and Failures, a Retrospective. *Information Development*, *IV*(5).

Rehm, S.-V., & Goel, L. (2017). Using information systems to achieve complementarity in SME innovation networks. *Information & Management*, *54*(4), 438–451. doi:10.1016/j.im.2016.10.003

Ring, J. K., Peredo, A. M., & Chrisman, J. J. (2010). Business Networks and Economic Development in Rural Communities in the United States. *Entrepreneurship Theory and Practice*, *34*(1), 171–195. doi:10.1111/j.1540-6520.2009.00307.x

Robinson, P. B., Stimpson, D. V., Huefner, J. C., & Hunt, H. K. (1991). An attitude approach to the prediction of entrepreneurship. *Entrepreneurship Theory and Practice*, *15*(4), 13–32. doi:10.1177/104225879101500405

Rodrigues, F. (2013). O Turismo de Habitação no Douro – para uma antropologia da hospitalidade nas casas de turismo. *Proceedings – Congresso Internacional da Casa Nobre – Um Património para o Futuro, Arcos de Valdevez, 3*, 1195-1209.

Roekel, J. V., Kopicki, R., Broekmans, C. J., & Boselie, D. M. (2002). Building agri supply chains: issues and guidelines. *A guide to developing agricultural markets and agroenterprises.*

Rogers, E. M. (1995). Diffusion of Innovations (4th ed.). New York: Free Press.

Roig-Tierno, N., Alcázar, J., & Ribeiro-Navarrete, S. (2016). Use of infrastructures to support innovative entrepreneurship and business growth. *Journal of Business Research*, *68*(11), 2290–2294. doi:10.1016/j.jbusres.2015.06.013

Röling, N. G. (1988). *Extension Science. Information System in Agricultural Development.* Cambridge University Press.

Rothaermel, F., Agung, S., & Jiang, L. (2007). University Entrepreneurship: A Taxonomy of the Literature. *Industrial and Corporate Change*, *16*(4), 691–791. doi:10.1093/icc/dtm023

Routroy, S., & Behera, A. (2017). Agriculture supply chain. *Journal of Agribusiness in Developing and Emerging Economies*, *7*(3), 275–302. doi:10.1108/JADEE-06-2016-0039

Rural, B. P. O. (2012). *DesiCrew raises Rs 7 cr in Series B funding from responsAbility Ventures and Ventureast Tenet Fund.* Retrieved from NextBigWhat: https://nextbigwhat.com/desicrew-funding/

Rutledge, K., Ramroop, T., Boudreau, D., McDaniel, M., Teng, S., Sprout, E., . . . Hunt, J. (2011, August 6). *Resource Library*. Retrieved July 12, 2020, from National Geographic: https://www.nationalgeographic.org/encyclopedia/rural-area/

Ruttan, V.W. (1959). Usher and Schumpeter on Invention, Innovation, and Technological Change. *The Quarterly Journal of Economics*, *73*(4), 596-606.

Ruzzier, M., Hisrich, R. D., & Antoncic, B. (2006). SME internationalization research: Past, present, and future. *Journal of Small Business and Enterprise Development*, *13*(4), 476–497. doi:10.1108/14626000610705705

Saeed, S., Yousafzai, S. Y., Yani-De-Soriano, M., & Muffatto, M. (2015). The Role of Perceived University Support in the Formation of Students' Entrepreneurial Intention. *Small Business Management*, *53*(4), 1127–1145. doi:10.1111/jsbm.12090

Sagie, A., & Elizur, D. (1999). Achievement motive and entrepreneurial orientation: a structural analysis. *Occupational and Organizational Psychology and Behavior*, *20*(3), 375–387. doi:10.1002/(SICI)1099-1379(199905)20:3<375::AID-JOB884>3.0.CO;2-Y

Salas, S., Chuenpagdee, R., Seijo, J. C., & Charles, A. (2007). Challenges in the Assessment and Management of Small-Scale Fisheries in Latin America and the Caribbean. *Fisheries Research*, *87*(1), 5–16. doi:10.1016/j.fishres.2007.06.015

Salemink, K., Strijker, D., & Bosworth, G. (2017). Rural development in the digital age: A systematic literature review on unequal ICT availability, adoption, and use in rural areas. *Journal of Rural Studies*, *54*, 360–371. doi:10.1016/j.jrurstud.2015.09.001

Salim, S. A., Sedera, D., Sawang, S., & Alarifi, A. (2014). Technology Adoption as a Multi-Stage Process. In *Australasian Conference on Information Systems (ACIS)*. Auckland, New Zealand: ACIS.

Sampaio, F. (2012). O turismo rural integrado e as rotas dos vinhos. In A. Cardoso, & S. Trilho (Eds.), *Proceedings – Congresso Internacional Vinhas e Vinhos, Arcos de Valdevez*. Porto: Câmara Municipal de Viana do Castelo.

Sanchez, E. C. (2003). *Microfinance and technology: the way to greater financial access*. Accessed 1 August 2006 at http://www.itmatters.com.ph/features.php?id=091503

Sandeep, M., & Ravishankar, M. (2015a). Impact Sourcing Ventures and Local Communities: A Frame Alignment Perspective. *Information Systems Journal*, *26*(2), 127-155.

Sandeep, M., & Ravishankar, M. (2015b). Social Innovations in Outsourcing: An Empirical Investigation of Impact Sourcing Companies in India. *The Journal of Strategic Information Systems*, *24*(4), 270-288.

Sanders, A., Elangeswaran, C., & Wulfsberg, J. (2016). Industry 4.0 implies lean manufacturing: Research activities in Industry 4.0 function as enablers for lean manufacturing. *Journal of Industrial Engineering Management*, *9*(3), 811–833. doi:10.3926/jiem.1940

Sanjay, Raghuram, & Vineet. (2015, Mar. 16). Winning the trust of rural consumers. *Business Standard, The Strategist*.

Sanner, T.A., Manda, T.D., & Nielsen, P. (2014). Grafting: Balancing Control and Cultivation in Information Infrastructure Innovation. *Journal of the Association for Information Systems*, *15*(4), 220-243.

Sanyal, P. (2009). From credit to collective action: The role of microfinance in promoting women's social capital and normative influence. *American Sociological Review*, *74*(4), 529–550. doi:10.1177/000312240907400402

Sarasvathy, S.D. (2001). Causation and Effectuation: Toward a Theoretical Shift from Economic Inevitability to Entrepreneurial Contingency. *Academy of Management Review*, *26*(2), 243–263.

Saraswathy, A. K. P., Panicker, K. S. M., & Sumi, M. (2008). Micro credit and women empowerment: A study in India. *International Journal of Global Business*, *1*(1), 184–213.

Sarkar, A. R. (2000). *Women in microcredit and their empowerment: Case study of BRAC societies under Sherpur Upazila of Bogra District. Bogra*. Tajma Art Press.

Sarumathi, S., & Mohan, K. (2011). Role of microfinance in women's empowerment; An empirical study in Pondicherry region rural SHGs. *Journal of Management and Science*, *1*(1), 1–10.

Satalkina, L., & Steiner, G. (2020). Digital Entrepreneurship and its Role in Innovation Systems: A Systematic Literature Review as a Basis for Future Research Avenues for Sustainable Transitions. *Sustainability*, *12*(7), 27–64. doi:10.3390u12072764

Sathya, I. (2019). Rural Entrepreneurship in India. *Research & Exploration*, *5*(22), 7–12.

Saxena, S. (2012). Problems Faced By Rural Entrepreneurs And Remedies To Solve It. *IOSR Journal of Business and Management*, *3*(1), 23–29. doi:10.9790/487X-0312329

Schmidt, J. P. (2006). *Free & Open Source Software for Microfinance: Increasing Efficiency and Extending Benefits to the Poor*. Academic Press.

Schumpeter, J. (1950). *Capitalism, Socialism and Democracy*. Harper and Row.

Schumpeter, J. A. (1934). *The Theory of Economic Development an Inquiry into Profits, Capital, Credit, Interest, and the Business cycle*. Transaction Publishers.

Schumpeter, J. A. (1934). *The Theory of Economic Development*. Harvard University.

Schumpeter, J. A. (1965). Economic Theory and Entrepreneurial History. In H. G. Aitken (Ed.), *Explorations in enterprise*. Harvard University Press.

Scott, H. (2007). *The Temporal Integration of Connected Study into a Structured Life: A Grounded Theory* (Unpublished Doctoral Dissertation). University of Portsmouth, Portsmouth.

Sears, G.J., & Baba, V.V. (2011). Toward a Multistage, Multilevel Theory of Innovation. *Canadian Journal of Administrative Sciences*, *28*(4), 357-372.

Sechele, L. (2016). Urban Bias, Economic Resource Allocation and National Development Planning in Botswana. *International Journal of Social Science Research*, 44-60.

Sedera, D., Lokuge, S., Grover, V., Sarker, S., & Sarker, S. (2016). Innovating with Enterprise Systems and Digital Platforms: A Contingent Resource-Based Theory View. *Information & Management, 53*(3), 366–379.

Sedera, D., Lokuge, S., Krcmar, H., Srivastava, S.C., & Ravishankar, M.N. (2014). The Future of Outsourcing in the Asia-Pacific Region: Implications for Research and Practice—Panel Report from Pacis 2014. *Communications of the Association for Information Systems*, *35*(1), 317-331.

Sedera, D., Rosemann, M., & Gable, G. (2001). Using Performance Measurement Models for Benefit Realization with Enterprise Systems - the Queensland Government Approach. In *European Conference on Information Systems*. Bled, Slovenia: AIS.

Sedera, D., Gable, G., & Chan, T. (2003). Survey Design: Insights from a Public Sector-ERP Impact Study. In *Proceedings of the 7th Pacific Asia Conference on Information Systems*. Adelaide, Australia: Association for Information Systems.

Sedera, D., & Lokuge, S. (2017). The Role of Enterprise Systems in Innovation in the Contemporary Organization. In R. G. Galliers & M.-K. Stein (Eds.), *The Routledge Companion to Management Information Systems* (p. 608). The Routledge. doi:10.4324/9781315619361-21

Sedera, D., Rosemann, M., & Gable, G. (2001). Using Performance Measurement Models for Benefit Realization with Enterprise Systems - the Queensland Government Approach. In *European Conference on Information Systems*. Bled, Slovenia: AIS.

SEI. (2010). *Process Maturity Profile: CMMI® for Development SCAMPISM Class A Appraisal Results 2010 Mid-Year Update. Software Engineering Institute*. Carnegie Mellon University.

Seripex. (2015). *Housing Tourism ID Plate*. Retrieved from: http://www.seripex.com/placas_classificativas/placas_classificativas.htm

Shah, R., & Ward, P. T. (2007). Defining and developing measures of lean production. *Journal of Operations Management*, *25*(4), 785–805. doi:10.1016/j.jom.2007.01.019

Shailo, I. (1994). Genesis and growth of NGOs: Their achievements and success in national development. *Alternative Development Journal*, *4*(13), 18–20.

Shane, S., & Venkataraman, S. (2000). The Promise of Entrepreneurship as A Field of Study. *Academy of Management Review, 25*(1), 217–226.

Sharma, A., & Iyer, G. R. (2012). Resource-constrained product development: Implications for green marketing and green supply chains. *Industrial Marketing Management, 41*(4), 599–608. doi:10.1016/j.indmarman.2012.04.007

Sharma, M., Chaudhary, V., Bala, R., & Chauhan, R. (2013). Rural entrepreneurship in developing countries: Challenges, problems and performance appraisal. *Global Journal of Management and Business Studies, 3*(9), 1035–1040.

Sheahan, M., & Barrett, C. B. (2017). Ten Striking Facts about Agricultural Input Use in Sub-Saharan Africa. *Food Policy, 67*, 12–25. doi:10.1016/j.foodpol.2016.09.010 PMID:28413243

Shehabuddin, R. (1992). *Empowering rural women: The impact of Grameen Bank in Bangladesh.* Grameen Bank.

Shepherd, J. (2004). *Social and Economic Transformation in the Digital Era.* IGI Global. doi:10.4018/978-1-59140-158-2.ch001

Shivani, S., Mukherjee, S. K., & Sharan, R. (2006). Socio-cultural influences on Indian entrepreneurs: The need for appropriate structural interventions. *Journal of Asian Economics, 17*(1), 5–13. doi:10.1016/j.asieco.2006.01.002

Shrimali, G., & Dhanaraj, C. (2014, July 18). *Case Summary: Husk Power Systems.* Retrieved from ISBINSIGHT: https://isbinsight.isb.edu/case-summary-husk-power-systems/

Shukla, M., & Jharkharia, S. (2013). Agri-fresh produce supply chain management: A state-of-the-art literature review. *International Journal of Operations & Production Management, 33*(2), 114–158. doi:10.1108/01443571311295608

Siddiquee, N., & Faroqi, M. (2009). Holding the giants to account? Constraints on NGO accountability in Bangladesh. *Asian Journal of Political Science, 17*(3), 243–264. doi:10.1080/02185370903403434

Sidhu, R.S., & Singh, S. (2004). Agricultural wages and employment in Punjab. *Econ & Pol Wkly, 39.*

Sidhu, R. S., & Bhullar, A. S. (2004). Changing structure of the farm economy in Punjab: Impact of livestock on income and employment. *Indian Journal of Agricultural Economics, 59*, 578–587.

Silerova, E., & Lang, K. (2006). Information systems - tool for changing our future. *Agricultural Economics –. Czech, 52*, 447–450.

Silva, L. (2010). Perspectiva antropológica do turismo de habitação. *Pasos: Revista de Turismo y Patrimonio Cultural, 8*(1), 31-46. Retrieved from: http://www.pasosonline.org/Publicados/8110/PS0110_3.pdf

Silva, S. (2012). *Ponte de Lima – Património histórico e turismo: As Casas Senhoriais ("Casas Antigas") como espaços de Turismo de Habitação* (Master's dissertation). Universidade do Porto, Porto. Retrieved from: https://sigarra.up.pt/flup/pt/pub_geral.show_file?pi_doc_id=13966

Silva, L. (2009). *Casas no Campo: Etnografia do Turismo Rural em Portugal.* ICS.

Simons, H. (2009). *Case Study Research in Practice.* Academic Press.

Simpeh, K. N. (2011). Entrepreneurship Theories and Empirical Research: A summary Review of the Literature. *European Journal of Business and Management, 3*(6), 1–8.

Singh, K., & Pundir, R. S. (2000). *Co-operatives and Rural Development in India.* Institute of Rural Management, Anand. https://www.irma.ac.in/pdf/randp/ 979_76324.pdf

Singh, R., Mathiassen, L., & Mishra, A. (2015). Organizational Path Constitution in Technological Innovation: Evidence from Rural Telehealth. *MIS Quarterly, 39*(3), 643-665.

Singh, A. P. (2013). Strategies for Developing Agripreneurship among Farming Community in Uttar Pradesh, India. *Academicia: An International Multidisciplinary Research Journal*, *3*(11), 1–12.

Singh, P., & Kumari, B. (2017). Importance of livestock sector in doubling farmers income by 2022. *International Journal of Economic Development*, *13*(2a), 136–140.

Singh, R. K. H., & Chandar, A. K. (2015). Impact of dairy cooperatives on income and employment in rural areas of Meghalaya. *Indian Journal of Dairy Science*, *68*, 173–179.

Sirmon, D.G., Hitt, M.A., Ireland, R.D., & Gilbert, B.A. (2011). Resource Orchestration to Create Competitive Advantage Breadth, Depth, and Life Cycle Effects. *Journal of Management*, *37*(5), 1390-1412.

Slavova, M., & Karanasios, S. (2018). When Institutional Logics Meet Information and Communication Technologies: Examining Hybrid Information Practices in Ghana's Agriculture. *Journal of the Association for Information Systems*, *19*(9), 775-812.

Sledzik, K. (2013). Schumpeter's View on Innovation and Entrepreneurship. In S. Hittmar (Ed.), Management Trends in Theory and Practice (pp. 89-95). Faculty of Management Science and Informatics, University of Zilina. doi:10.2139srn.2257783

Smallbone, D. (2009). Fostering entrepreneurship in rural areas. In J. Potter & A. Hofer (Eds.), *Strengthening entrepreneurship development in East Germany: lessons from local approaches* (pp. 161–187). OECD.

Smallbone, D. (2009). Fostering Entrepreneurship in Rural Areas. In J. Potter & A. R. Hofer (Eds.), *Strengthening entrepreneurship and economic development in East Germany: lessons from local approaches* (pp. 161–187). OECD.

Smallbone, D., & Welter, F. (2006). Conceptualising entrepreneurship in a transition context. *International Journal of Entrepreneurship and Small Business*, *3*(2), 190–206. doi:10.1504/IJESB.2006.008928

Sobhan, R. (1997). The political economy of micro credit. In G. D. Wood & I. Sharif (Eds.), *Who needs credit? Poverty and finance in Bangladesh* (pp. 131–144). Zed Books.

Sohns, F., & Diez, R. J. (2018). Explaining micro entrepreneurship in rural Vietnam—A multilevel analysis. *Small Business Economics*, *50*(1), 219–237. doi:10.100711187-017-9886-2

Sonka, S. (2015). Big data: From hype to agricultural tool. *Farm Policy Journal*, *12*(1), 1–9.

Sonne, L. (2010). Pro-Poor, Entrepreneur-Based Innovation and It's Role in Rural Development. In *UNU-MERIT Paper Series*. United Nations University.

Sørensen, C. A. G., Kateris, D., & Bochtis, D. (2019). ICT Innovations and Smart Farming. In M. Salampasis & T. Bournaris (Eds.), *Information and Communication Technologies in Modern Agricultural Development. HAICTA 2017. Communications in Computer and Information Science* (Vol. 953). Springer.

Sørensen, C. G., Fountas, S., Nash, E., Pesonen, L., Bochtis, D., Pedersen, S. M., Basso, B., & Blackmore, S. B. (2010a). Conceptual model of a future farm management information system. *Computers and Electronics in Agriculture*, *72*(1), 37–47. doi:10.1016/j.compag.2010.02.003

Sørensen, C. G., Pesonen, L., Fountas, S., Suomi, P., Bochtis, D., Bildsøe, P., & Pedersen, S. M. (2010b). A user-centric approach for information modelling in arable farming. *Computers and Electronics in Agriculture*, *73*(1), 44–55. doi:10.1016/j.compag.2010.04.003

Spear, S., & Bowen, H. K. (1999). Decoding the DNA of the Toyota production system. *Harvard Business Review*, *77*(5), 96–106.

Spigel, B. (2017). The Relational Organization of Entrepreneurial Ecosystems. *Entrepreneurship Theory and Practice, 41*(1), 49–72. doi:10.1111/etap.12167

Stam, E. (2015). Entrepreneurial Ecosystems and Regional Policy: A Sympathetic Critique. *European Planning Studies, 23*(9), 1759–1769. doi:10.1080/09654313.2015.1061484

Stansfield, M., & Grant, K. (2003). An investigation into issues influencing the use of internet and electronic commerce among small-medium sized enterprises. *Journal of Electronic Commerce Research, 4*(1), 15–33.

Stathopoulou, S., Psaltopoulos, D., & Skuras, D. (2004). Rural Entrepreneurship in Europe: A Research Framework and Agenda. *International Journal of Entrepreneurial Behavior & Research, 10*(6), 404-425.

Stathopoulou, S., Psaltopoulos, D., & Skuras, D. (2004). Rural entrepreneurship in Europe. A research framework and agenda. *International Journal of Entrepreneurial Behaviour & Research, 10*(6), 404–425. doi:10.1108/13552550410564725

Statista. (2020). Available at https://www.statista.com/topics/5653/agriculture-in-vietnam/

Steve, L. (2005). *Model Credit Buerau Open Source Solution Being tested in Morocco, submitted on July 3, 2005 9:00.* Accessed August 8, 2006 21:09 on http://www.nextbillion.net/newsroom/2005/07/03/model-creditbureau-open-source-solution-being-tested-in-morocco

Steyaert, C. (2007). 'Entrepreneuring' as a conceptual attractor? A review of process theories in 20 years of entrepreneurship studies. *Entrepreneurship and Regional Development, 19*(6), 453–477. doi:10.1080/08985620701671759

Stoop, A., & Sotto Mayor, J. (2015). *Arquitectura Senhorial do Minho*. Caminhos Romanos.

Storey, D. J., & Greene, F. J. (2010). *Small business and entrepreneurship*. Financial Times/Prentice Hall.

Storey, C., Cankurtaran, P., Papastathopoulou, P., & Hultink, E. J. (2016). Success factors for service innovation: A meta-analysis. *Journal of Product Innovation Management, 33*(5), 527–548. doi:10.1111/jpim.12307

Stough, R. R. (2016). Entrepreneurship and Regional Economic Development: Some reflections. *Investigaciones Regionales – Journal of Regional Research, 36*, 129-150.

Strano, A., Hudson, T., Redman, M., Hegarty, M., O'Hara, E., Buffet, C., ... Gardner, S. (2012). EU Rural Review Rural Entrepreneurship. *European Union.*

Strauss, A., & Corbin, J. (1994). Grounded Theory Methodology. In N. K. Denzin & Y. S. Lincoln (Eds.), *Handbook of Qualitative Research*. SAGE Publications.

Suan, C. T., Ai, Y. J., Raman, K., Loon, K. W., & Tanumihardja, J. (2011). Entrepreneurial intentions among university students. *Business & Management Quarterly Review, 2*(3), 33–38.

Sundar, K., & Srinivasan, T. (2009). Rural Industrialisation: Challenges and Proposition. *Journal of Social Science, 20*(1), 23–29.

Swati Bisht, N. P. (2019). Digital Entrepreneurship and The Bottom of The Pyramid- A Conceptual Framework. *International Journal on Recent Trends in Business and Tourism*, 33-42.

Sylvester, G. (2013). *Information and communication technologies for sustainable agriculture-indicators from Asia and the Pacific*. Rap Publication, (2013/14).

Szymczak, M. (Ed.). (2013). *Managing towards supply chain maturity: Business process outsourcing and offshoring*. Springer.

Tajfel, H. (1981). *Human Groups and Social Categories: Studies in Social Psychology*. Cambridge University Press.

Talug, C. (1990). *Agricultural research-development and the examination of extension services for agricultural productivity*. MPM Publishing.

Tamasy, C. (2007). Rethinking technology-oriented business incubators: Developing a robust policy instrument for entrepreneurship, innovation, and regional development? *Growth and Change*, *38*(3), 460–473. doi:10.1111/j.1468-2257.2007.00379.x

Tan, F.T.C., Tan, B., & Pan, S.L. (2016b). Developing a Leading Digital Multi-Sided Platform: Examining IT Affordances and Competitive Actions in Alibaba.Com. *Communications of the Association for Information Systems*, *38*(36), 738–760.

Tan, F. T. C., Ky, D., & Tan, B. (2016a). Toward a Process Theory of IT-Enabled Frugal Innovation: The Role of Organizational Bricolage in Koufu Singapore. In *Pacific Asian Conference on Information Systems*. AIS.

Tanriverdi, H., Rai, A., & Venkatraman, N. (2010). Research commentary—Reframing the dominant quests of information systems strategy research for complex adaptive business systems. *Information Systems Research*, *21*(4), 822–834. doi:10.1287/isre.1100.0317

Tan, S., Heerink, N., Kruseman, G., & Qu, F. (2008). Do Fragmented Landholdings Have Higher Production Costs? Evidence from Rice Farmers in Northeastern Jiangxi Province, P.R. China. *China Economic Review*, *19*(3), 347–358. doi:10.1016/j.chieco.2007.07.001

Taormina, R. J., & Lao, S. K. M. (2007). Measuring Classical Entrepreneurial Motivation, Personality and Environmental Influences. *International Journal of Entrepreneurial Behaviour & Research*, *13*(4), 200–221. doi:10.1108/13552550710759997

Tarafdar, M., Singh, R., & Anekal, P. (2013). Impact of Ict-Enabled Product and Process Innovations at the Bottom of the Pyramid: A Market Separations Perspective. *Journal of Information Technology*, *28*(4), 279-295.

Tate, M., Sedera, D., McLean, E., & Burton-Jones, A. (2013). Information Systems Success Research: The "Twenty Year Update?" Panel Report from Pacis, 2011. *Communications of the Association for Information Systems*, *34*, 1.

Teece, D., Peteraf, M., & Leih, S. (2016). Dynamic capabilities and organizational agility: Risk, uncertainty, and strategy in the innovation economy. *California Management Review*, *58*(4), 13–35. doi:10.1525/cmr.2016.58.4.13

Teirlinck, P. (2017). Configurations of strategic R&D decisions and financial performance in small-sized and medium-sized firms. *Journal of Business Research*, *74*, 55–65. doi:10.1016/j.jbusres.2017.01.008

Teixeira, A. A. C. (2017). The economic performance of Portuguese Academic Spin-offs: do Science & Technology infrastructures and support matter? In R. Fini & R. Grimaldi (Eds.), Process Approach to Academic Entrepreneurship: Evidence from the Globe (Vol. 11.1). World Scientific Reference on Entrepreneurship. doi:10.1142/9789813220621_0011

Thaker, J.K., Chakrawal, A., & Goyal, P. (2017). A Study of Innovative Attitude of Indian Entrepreneurs of Various Industries in the Context to Educational and Economic Background. *International Research Journal of Multidisciplinary Studies*, *3*(6), 1-10.

The Economic Times. (2014). *Mars Mission: India creates history as Mangalyaan successfully enters Mars orbit in first attempt*. http://economictimes.indiatimes.com/news/science/mars-mission-india-creates-history-as-mangalyaan-successfully-enters-mars-orbit-in-first-attempt/articleshow/43299562.cms

The Story Behind the Data. (2020). Retrieved from desicrew: https://desicrew.in/about/

Thomas, A. S., & Mueller, S. L. (2000). A case for comparative entrepreneurship: Assessing the relevance of culture. *Journal of International Business Studies*, *31*(2), 287–301. doi:10.1057/palgrave.jibs.8490906

Tiersky, H. (2018). *Navigating digital transformation.* Retrieved from https://www.cio.com/article/3179607/5-top-challenges-to-digital-transformation-in-the-enterprise.html

Tiwari, R., & Herstatt, C. (2012). Frugal Innovation: A Global Networks' Perspective. Die Unternehmung (Swiss Journal of Business Research and Practice), 66(3), 245-274.

Treasury, H. M. (2001). *Productivity in the United Kingdom: 3 – The Regional Dimension. Report.* HM Treasury.

Trettin, L., & Welter, F. (2011). Challenges for spatially oriented entrepreneurship research. *Entrepreneurship and Regional Development, 23*(7-8), 575–602. doi:10.1080/08985621003792988

Tsolakis, N. K., Keramydas, C. A., Toka, A. K., Aidonis, D. A., & Iakovou, E. T. (2014). Agrifood supply chain management: A comprehensive hierarchical decision-making framework and a critical taxonomy. *Biosystems Engineering, 120*, 47–64. doi:10.1016/j.biosystemseng.2013.10.014

Tumbas, S., Berente, N., & vom Brocke, J. (2017). Digital Capabilities for Buffering Tensions of Structure, Space, and Time During Entrepreneurial Growth. In *International Conference on Information Systems.* AIS.

Tummers, J., Kassahun, A., & Tekinerdogan, B. (2019). Obstacles and features of Farm Management Information Systems: A systematic literature review. *Computers and Electronics in Agriculture, 157*, 189–204. doi:10.1016/j.compag.2018.12.044

UNESCO. (2017). *Science Policy and Capacity-Building.* Retrieved from http://www.unesco.org/new/en/natural-sciences/science-technology/university-industry-partnerships/science-and-technology-park-governance/concept-and-definition/

United States Census Bureau. (2017, August 11). *What is Rural America?* Retrieved July 12, 2020, from United States Census Bureau: https://www.census.gov/library/stories/2017/08/rural-america.html

Upadhyaya, L. (2019). Digital Inclusion: Strategies to Bridge Digital Divide in Farming Community. *Journal of Agriculture Science and Technology*, 1079–1089.

Urbano, D., & Turró, A. (2013). Conditioning factors for corporate entrepreneurship: An in (ex) ternal approach. *The International Entrepreneurship and Management Journal, 9*(3), 379–396. doi:10.100711365-013-0261-8

Utsch, A., & Rauch, A. (2000). Innovativeness and initiative as mediators between achievement orientation and venture performance. *European Journal of Work and Organizational Psychology, 9*(1), 45–62. doi:10.1080/135943200398058

Utterback, J.M. (1971). The Process of Technological Innovation within the Firm. *The Academy of Management Journal, 14*(1), 75-88.

Utterback, J. M. (1994). *Mastering the Dynamics of Innovation.* Harvard Business School Press.

Van de Ven, A.H. (1986). Central Problems in the Management of Innovation. *Management Science, 32*(5), 590-607.

Van de Ven, A.H., & Poole, M.S. (1995). Explaining Development and Change in Organizations. *Academy of Management Review, 20*(3), 510-540.

Vanathi, R., & Swamynathan, R. (2013). A study on adoption of supply chain maturity model for enhancement of supply chain performance in industries. *Life Science Journal, 10*(2), 1921–1925.

Veit, D., Clemons, E., Benlian, A., Buxmann, P., Hess, T., Kundisch, D., & Spann, M. (2014). Business models. *Business & Information Systems Engineering, 6*(1), 45–53. doi:10.100712599-013-0308-y

Ven, A. H. V., & Johnson, P. E. (2006). Knowledge for theory and practise. *Academy of Management Review, 31*(4), 802–821. doi:10.5465/amr.2006.22527385

Venkatesh, V., & Sykes, T.A. (2013). Digital Divide Initiative Success in Developing Countries: A Longitudinal Field Study in a Village in India. *Information Systems Research*, *24*(2), 239-260.

Venkatesh, V., Bala, H., & Sambamurthy, V. (2016a). Implementation of an Information and Communication Technology in a Developing Country: A Multimethod Longitudinal Study in a Bank in India. *Information Systems Research*, *27*(3), 558-579.

Venkatesh, V., Morris, M.G., Davis, G.B., & Davis, F.D. (2003). User Acceptance of Information Technology: Toward a Unified View. *MIS Quarterly*, *27*(3), 425-478.

Venkatesh, V., Rai, A., Sykes, T.A., & Aljafari, R. (2016b). Combating Infant Mortality in Rural India: Evidence from a Field Study of Ehealth Kiosk Imlementations. *MIS Quarterly*, *40*(2), 353-380.

Venkatesh, V., Sykes, T.A., & Venkatraman, S. (2014). Understanding E-Government Portal Use in Rural India: Role of Demographic and Personality Characteristics. *Information Systems Journal*, *24*(3), 249-269.

Vidanapathirana, N. P. (2012). *Agricultural information systems and their applications for development of agriculture and rural community, a review study*. Paper presented at the 35th Information Systems Research Seminar in Scandinavia – IRIS 2012, Sigtuna, Sweden.

Vietnam Communist Party News. (2019). Retrieved from http://dangcongsan.vn/thoi-su/so-luong-doanh-nghiep-dau-tu-vao-nong-nghiep-tang-3-lan-541807.html

von Loeper, W. J., Drimie, S., & Blignaut, J. (2018). The Struggles of Smallholder Farmers: A Cause of Modern Agricultural Value Chains in South Africa. In *Agricultural Value Chain*. InTech. doi:10.5772/intechopen.75710

Vos, D. D., Lindgren, U., Ham, M. V., & Meijers, E. (2020). Does Broadband Internet Allows Cities to 'Borrow Size'? Evidence from the Swedish Labour Market. *Regional Studies*, *54*(9), 1175–1186. doi:10.1080/00343404.2019.1699238

Wasserman, S., & Faust, K. (1994). *Social Network Analysis: Methods and Applications*. Cambridge University Press. doi:10.1017/CBO9780511815478

Waterfield, C., & Ramsing, N. (1998). Handbook for Management Information Systems for Microfinance Institutions. CGAP Technical Tool Series No. 1, February 1998. Augsburg.

Weber, P. C., & Geneste, L. (2014). Exploring gender-related perceptions of SME success. *International Journal of Gender and Entrepreneurship*, *6*(1), 15–27. doi:10.1108/IJGE-04-2013-0038

Welter, F. (2011). Contextualizing Entrepreneurship—Conceptual Challenges and Ways Forward. *Entrepreneurship Theory and Practice*, *35*(1), 165–184. doi:10.1111/j.1540-6520.2010.00427.x

Welter, F., & Smallbone, D. (2011). Institutional Perspectives on Entrepreneurial Behavior in Challenging Environments. *Journal of Small Business Management*, *49*(1), 107–125. doi:10.1111/j.1540-627X.2010.00317.x

Weyrauch, T., & Herstatt, C. (2017). What is frugal innovation? Three defining criteria. *Journal of Frugal Innovation*, *2*(1), 1. doi:10.118640669-016-0005-y

Woller, G. (2002). Introduction to the second microfinance revolution: Creating customer centered microfinance institutions. *Journal of International Development*, *16*(2), 1–5.

Womack, J. P., & Jones, D. T. (2003). *Lean thinking*. Free Press.

Wood, S. L., & Swait, J. (2002). Psychological indicators of innovation adoption: Cross-classification based on need for cognition and need for change. *Journal of Consumer Psychology*, *12*(1), 1–13. doi:10.1207/S15327663JCP1201_01

Work Bank. (2018). *Trade Economics*. Retrieved from https://tradingeconomics.com/vietnam/rural-population-percent-of-total-population-wb-data.html

World Bank. (2017). ICT in agriculture: connecting smallholders to knowledge, networks, and institutions: e-sourcebook. International Bank for Reconstruction and Development, The World Bank.

Wortman, M.S. (1990). Rural Entrepreneurship Research: An Integration into the Entrepreneurship Field. *Agribusiness*, *6*(4), 329-344.

Wright, M., & Stigliani, I. (2013). Entrepreneurship and Growth. *International Small Business Journal*, *31*(1), 3–22.

Xiao, X., Califf, C.B., Sarker, S., & Sarker, S. (2013). Ict Innovation in Emerging Economies: A Review of the Existing Literature and a Framework for Future Research. *Journal of Information Technology*, *28*(4), 264-278.

Yang, K. C. (2005). Exploring factors affecting the adoption of mobile commerce in Singapore. *Telematics and Informatics*, *22*(3), 257–277. doi:10.1016/j.tele.2004.11.003

Ye, L., & Yang, H. (2020). From Digital Divide to Social Inclusion: A Tale of Mobile Platform Empowerment in Rural Areas. *Sustainability*, *12*(6), 2424. doi:10.3390u12062424

Yin, R. K. (2017). *Case study research and applications: Design and methods*. Sage publications.

Yin, R. K. (2017). *Case Study Research and Applications: Design and Methods*. SAGE Publications.

Yoo, Y., Boland Jr, R.J., Lyytinen, K., & Majchrzak, A. (2012). Organizing for Innovation in the Digitized World. *Organization Science*, *23*(5), 1398-1408.

Young, M., & Flores, I. (2011). Characteristics and Needed Assistance of Hispanic Women Business Owners: Emerging Entrepreneurs. *Small Business Institute Journal*, *7*, 80–105.

Young, N. (2010). Business networks, collaboration and embeddedness in local and extra-local spaces: The case of port Hardy, Canada. *Sociologia Ruralis*, *50*(4), 392–408. doi:10.1111/j.1467-9523.2010.00521.x

Zacharakis, A. L. (1997). Entrepreneurial entry into foreign markets: A transaction cost perspective. *Entrepreneurship Theory and Practice*, *21*(3), 23–40. doi:10.1177/104225879702100302

Zahra, S.A. (2007). Contextualizing Theory Building in Entrepreneurship Research. *Journal of Business Venturing*, *22*(3), 443-452.

Zahra, S. A., Wright, M., & Abdelgawad, S. G. (2014). Contextualization and the advancement of entrepreneurship research. *International Small Business Journal*, *32*(5), 479–500. doi:10.1177/0266242613519807

Zaman, M. A. 2002. *Present Status of Agricultural Information Technology Systems and Services in Bangladesh*. Retrieved from http//jsai.or.jp/afita/afita-conf/2002/part 1/p075.pdf

Zaremohzzabieh, Z., Samah, B., Muhammad, M., Omar, S., Bolong, J., Hassan, M., & Shaffril, H. (2015). A Test of the Technology Acceptance Model for Understanding the ICT Adoption Behavior of Rural Young Entrepreneurs. *International Journal of Business and Management*, *10*(2), 158–169. doi:10.5539/ijbm.v10n2p158

Zeschky, M. B., Winterhalter, S., & Gassmann, O. (2014). From cost to frugal and reverse innovation: Mapping the field and implications for global competitiveness. *Research Technology Management*, *57*(4), 20–27.

Zeschky, M., Widenmayer, B., & Gassmann, O. (2011). Frugal innovation in emerging markets. *Research Technology Management*, *54*(4), 38–45. doi:10.5437/08956308X5404007

Zimmerer, T.W. & Scarborough, N.M. (2005). *Essentials of Entrepreneurship and Small Business Management*. Pearson.

Zittrain, J.L. (2006). The Generative Internet. *Harvard Law Review*, *119*(7), 1974–2040.

Zolin, R., Stuetzer, M., & Watson, J. (2013). Challenging the female underperformance hypothesis. *International Journal of Gender and Entrepreneurship*, *5*(2), 116–129. doi:10.1108/17566261311328819

Zylbersztajn, D. (2017). Agribusiness Systems Analysis: Origin, Evolution and Research Perspectives. *Revista ADM*, *52*, 114–117.

About the Contributors

Sachithra Lokuge is a Lecturer in Information Systems at the College of Business and Law at the RMIT University, Australia. Her research mainly focuses on digital technologies, innovation, digital entrepreneurship and social media use. Her work has been published in journals such as the Information & Management, Information Technology and People, Communications of the Association for Information Systems, Journal of Information Technology Theory and Application (JITTA), and in the proceedings of conferences such as the International Conference on Information Systems and Academy of Management.

Darshana Sedera is a Professor of Information Systems and the Director of the Digital Enterprise Lab at the Southern Cross University in Australia. He is currently the Deputy Dean of the School of Business and Tourism. He has published over 200 publications in major refereed journals and conferences. His publications have appeared in Journal of the Association for Information Systems, Journal of the Strategic Information Systems, Information & Management, Information Technology & People, and Communications of the Association for Information Systems. For more details, please visit darshanasedera.com

***

Aurora A.C. Teixeira is a full professor at the University of Porto, Portugal, where she holds the Chairs of Macroeconomics and Innovation Management. She received her PhD from SPRU - Science Policy Research Unit (University of Sussex, UK), and she was a visiting scholar at the IC2, Texas Austin University (USA) and Bocconi University (Italy). She is member of the editorial board of Journal of Academic Ethics (Springer). Her current research interests include entrepreneurship, technology commercialization, U-I linkages, economic growth, structural change, scientometrics, and academic ethics. She (co)authored/ edited 15 books and published more than 100 articles in journals indexed in Scopus and/or Web of Science. Some main outlets include (alphabetic order): Applied Economics Letters; Cambridge Journal of Economics; European Planning Studies; Higher Education; Industrial and Corporate Change; Journal of Evolutionary Economics; Regional Studies; Research Policy; Review of Development Economics; Review of Managerial Science; Scientometrics; StructuralChange and Economic Dynamics; World Economy.

Branka Krivokapic-Skoko is an Associate Professor in the School of Management and Marketing at Charles Sturt University, Bathurst, NSW Australia. Branka's research interests are around the revitalization of regional and rural Australia. Her research has been funded by the Australian Research Council and Agrifutures Australia.

Caglar Ucler is an innovation strategist and a product development professional streamlining academic know-how with industrial expertise. Having worked over 20 years in R&D, innovation & management positions, he did contribute to the realization of many products in aerospace & defence, energy, automotive and cryogenics. He holds a PhD in engineering management and is a mechanical and aeronautical engineer. He is currently Associate Professor at the Faculty of Aviation and Aeronautical Sciences of Ozyegin University focusing on innovation systems, new product development and technology management.

Deepa Kapoor (Ph.D., University Business School (UBS), Panjab University at Chandigarh, India) is an Associate Professor in Amity School of Business, Amity University Uttar Pradesh, Noida, India. Her research interests are in the areas of Advertising, Services Marketing, Rural Marketing and Consumer Behavior. She has worked for more than 13 years in academics' field teaching Advertising and Marketing Management. She has got many research scholars pursuing Ph.D. under her supervision. Her papers have been published in reputed refereed International journals of Emerald, Inderscience, IGI and Sage in 'B' and 'C' category Scopus Indexed Journals.

Dinithi Abeysinghe is currently reading for her PhD at the Swinburne University of Technology and is currently researching on the topic of Digital Entrepreneurship and other aspects related on it. Her research interest dwells on the topic of supply chain management as well. Dinithi has worked as a Secondary School Teacher at Keble College; Sri Lanka for over 3 years (2015-2018). She then worked as a Business Development Intern (2018-2019) at Hayleys Advantis Limited which is a prestigious logistics company in Sri Lanka. Also, she worked in the capacity of a Tutor (2019-2020) at the National School Business Management (NSBM) Green University of Sri Lanka. She obtained her Higher National Diploma (2017) and the bachelor's degree (2018) from the Plymouth University UK, graduating with a First-Class Honours in the field of BSc (Hons) Operations and Logistics Management.

Faraha Nawaz is an Associate Professor of the Department of Public Administration, University of Rajshahi, Bangladesh. She has been awarded a prestigious Australian Government scholarship to complete her PhD degree from Flinders University of South Australia. Her research interests are on gender equality, poverty, human rights, social justice, gender-based violence, women's empowerment, women's in labor market and household economy, NGOs in development, public policy analysis, governance issues, environment protection and migration governance. She has published a number of refereed articles in national and international journals; book chapters in edited books and a sole authored book published from Palgrave MacMillan. An active member of a number of international professional groups and networks such as NAPSIPAG, ISTR, EROPA, NZSAC, Dev Net, IPPA and AWID, Dr Nawaz has participated and presented her research papers in various international conferences. She is a recipient of prestigious awards including gold medals, Charles Wallace award, Dev net Research award from New Zealand, Malaysian scholarly award, Australian Government scholarship etc. She is an international fellow of Watson Institute of International and Public Affairs, Brown University, USA and a Visiting Research Fellow of University of Oxford, UK.

Javad Shahreki is a Lecturer in the Faculty of Business at Multimedia University, Malaysia. He is also a member of the Faculty Research and Innovation Committee. He holds a PhD in Human Resource Management from University Technology Malaysia. His research interests are in human resource management and human resource information system.

José Luís Braga is currently an assistant professor at the Polytechnic Institute of Tomar and a guest lecturer at the *European Master on Wine Tourism Innovation - WINTOUR*. He has 10 years of experience as a lecturer at a higher education level. He obtained his PhD in *Tourism Planning and Management* from the University of Santiago de Compostela, in the scientific field of Rural Tourism, and received his MS in Tourism and Regional Development from the Catholic University of Portugal in 2007.

Khushboo Bhatt is a student at Indukaka Ipcowala Institute of Management, with a profound interest in research-based writing. She has been dedicated volunteer at faculty development programs and student welfare workshops. She aspires to become a research scholar as well as an academician. With her love for imparting knowledge, she currently helps in facilitating course-based studies for students pursuing secondary and higher- secondary education in Gujarat. Apart from this, she has also interned at Camp K12 Pvt. Ltd. as a Customer relationship and service optimization Intern. In her spare time, Khushboo, reads mythological readings and writes snippets on that too.

Lúcia Pato is an adjunct professor at the Polytechnic Institute of Viseu, Portugal, where she lectures subjects of Marketing, Management, Entrepreneurship and Tourism. She holds a PhD in Business and Management Studies from the University of Porto, a PhD in Tourism from the University of Aveiro, a MSc in Agronomic Engineering from the University of Trás-os-Montes and Alto Douro, a MSc in Management of Rural Development from the University of Trás-os- Montes and Alto Douro, and a degree in Agricultural Engineering from the University of Trás-os-Montes and Alto Douro. She integrates the Research Centre for Natural Resources, Environment and Society (CERNAS) of the Polytechnic Institute of Viseu. Lúcia Pato has participated in several national and international conferences on Tourism. She is author and co-author of several publications on tourism, entrepreneurship and rural development at the national and international level. Presently she coordinates in the Polytechnic Institute of Viseu the research project "TWINE – Co-creating sustainable Tourism & WINe Experiences in rural areas" (a project managed by the University of Aveiro). Her research interests include rural tourism, rural entrepreneurship, rural development and marketing in rural areas.

Manali Vin is a student at Symbiosis School of Media and Communication (Bangalore). Her interest lies in media planning, audio-visual production management and qualitative research. She has an experience of interning at various media houses and apart from that devotes her time in volunteering for events and heads the student welfare and discipline committee at her college. Her keen interest in reading fiction and autobiographies and writing on diverse subjects has also helped her in conducting workshops for the underprivileged children to make them understand the importance of literacy. Apart from this, she enjoys public speaking, team building assignments and moderating debates.

Marta Margarida Santos Dionísio is currently an Associate Professor from the Social Sciences Department at the Polytechnic Institute of Tomar. She has 20 years of experience as a lecturer at a higher education level. She obtained her Ph.D. in American Studies with the thesis entitled Oprah Winfrey –

the Art of Communicating from the University of Lisbon, Faculty of Letters, in 2015, in the scientific field of Studies of Literature and Culture; her Master in American Studies entitled Lucille Ball - an American Woman from the University of Lisbon, Faculty of Letters, in 2005; and her BA in English and German Teaching from the University of Aveiro, in 1997. She is also member of the Board of Directors of the Techn&Art Research Centre - Technology, Restoration and Arts Enhancement Centre as well as Integrated Researcher since 2018. She is Coordinator of the Languages Centre of IPT since 2010.

Michael Cook is a former honours student at Charles Sturt University where this research was conducted. He now works for the Australian Government Department of Industry, Science, Energy and Resources where he has worked across several policy areas including international tertiary and vocational education, international science and innovation, the service economy, entrepreneurship, and civil space.

Mohsin Malik has a diverse industry and academic work experience of over 19 years. Dr Malik has worked as a Professional Engineer for 7 years before earning a PhD in operations management from the University of Western Australia in 2012. Since then, Dr Malik has worked as an Assistant Professor at Abu Dhabi University (2013-2016) and as a Lecturer at the University of Melbourne (2016-2018). Dr Malik joined Swinburne in June 2018. Dr Malik researches sustainability in supply chains and the social and cultural aspects of project management. His research has featured in leading academic journals such as International Journal of Production Economics, Supply Chain Management: An International Journal, Annals of Operations Research, Renewable and Sustainable Reviews, Journal of Cleaner Production, Industrial Management and Data Systems, TQM Journal, Sustainability. Operations Research for Healthcare, IEEE Proceedings, Business Process Management Journal and International Journal of Managing Projects in Business.

Nguyen Van Tung is a PhD student at the Ho Chi Minh University of Transport, Vietnam. His research area is the logistics infrastructure system in the city. He has a master's degree in Economic Management and Traffic Engineering. He works as a manager of the Construction Investment Project Management Unit of Long Dien District in Ba Ria-Vung Tau Province, Vietnam.

Pham Van Hong is the Director of the National Institute for Science and Technology Policy and Strategy Studies, Vietnam and Adjunct Professor at Dai Nam University, Vietnam. His research interests are marketing, IT implementation and human resource management.

Pranav Desai is working as an Assistant Professor at Indukaka Ipcowala Institute of Management, Faculty of Management Studies, Charotar University of Science and Technology (CHARUSAT), Changa, Gujarat, India. He completed his PhD from Dharmsinh Desai University, Nadiad in 2016. He possesses more than 13 years of teaching experience in the areas of Entrepreneurship Development, Innovation Management, Marketing Management and Information Technology Management. He has authored a book titled "Multi-sector Product Recall Strategies" published from Germany. He is a highly motivated scholar working in the area of Marketing, Risk Management; IT Management and Entrepreneurship. He also has to his credit 28 research and concept papers published in national / International journals and chapters in books. Importantly, during his career as an Assistant Professor, he has guided 167 UG and 131 PG students for their research projects. Further, he has presented 28 academic and research papers at reputed institutes like IIM Bangalore, MICA and has undergone training during FDPs at premier institutes like IIM-Kozhikode and Entrepreneurship Development Institute of India (EDII), Gandhinagar.

R. Krishnadas is a Ph.D. Scholar in the field of Consumer Behaviour. He is a Teaching Assistant from the School of Management, SASTRA University, India. He has four years of corporate experience in the FMCG industry across leading MNC's in India. He has completed his Master of Business Administration (M.B.A.) from Thiagarajar School of Management, Madurai. His area of interest includes Consumer Behaviour, Brand Management, Marketing Research, and Entrepreneurship Development. He has published many articles in peer-reviewed journals. He has also presented several papers at national level and international level conferences.

R. Renganathan is a Professor from the School of Management, SASTRA Deemed University, India. In addition to the teaching experience of 21-years, he has 14 years of Corporate Experience. He has completed his FDP at the Indian Institute of Management, Ahemedabad (IIM-A). He is a recipient of the Best Professor in Marketing Management& award honoured by ET NOW (English-language business and finance news channel in India) in 2013. He has published 39 Scopus listed research papers and has presented 15 papers in National and International Seminars and Conferences. His area of interest includes Marketing, Services Marketing, Consumer Behavior, Tourism marketing.

Ravi Kumar Gupta, Associate Professor in the Department of Mechanical Engineering at Manipal University Jaipur; Dr. Gupta received PhD degree from Indian Institute of Science Bangalore and M.Tech. degree from Motilal Nehru National Institute of Technology Allahabad. He also pursued a postdoc program at Ecole Central de Nantes, France, being a partner of ProRegio project (EU funded project: Horizon 2020). He has 14 years Industry – Academia blended experience and has published more than 50 research papers. Research Interest includes Product Development; 3D Digital Modelling; CAD/CAM; Product Informatics; Reverse Engineering; Additive Manufacturing; Augmented and Virtual Reality.

Ruchi Jain is currently an Associate professor and Coordinator Ph.D. Program in Amity University Uttar Pradesh. She is having 16 years of research and academic experience with few years of enriched corporate stint. She has got many research scholars pursuing Ph. D. and M.Phil. under her supervision. Her research interests include emerging technological trends in marketing, customer relationship practices, experiential marketing and sustainable facets of marketing. She has been associated with many conferences and faculty development programs of premium institutes like IIMs, FICCI and GGSIP university. She is an integral part of review panel of many indexed journals and got published many research papers, articles, cases and book reviews. She currently teaches intricacies of Customer Relationship Management and enjoys consulting entrepreneurial start-ups on marketing strategies.

Ruchi Khandelwal, an academician in the field of Marketing and Strategy has a proven teaching career of 19 years. Her lucid teaching style infuses very well amongst the target audience. She is an alumnus the prestigious Delhi School of Economics, Delhi University where she pursued her postgraduate. Currently working as Deputy Director with Amity School of Business, AUUP, she balances her passion for teaching and her interest in research with her knack for administration very amicably. Ruchi's research interest lies in the Consumer Decision Making, Psychology of Marketing, Food Marketing and Nutrition, Entrepreneurship and Strategy and Emerging Market Economies. Her thesis is also in the area of consumer decision-making and baby food.

Saliya Nugawela is a PhD student in the Faculty of Business and Law at the Swinburne University of Technology, Australia. He received his Master by Research in Information Technology from the Queensland University of Technology, Australia. His research interests include farm management information systems, information systems usage and acceptance, and healthcare IT. He has previously served as a lecturer and a software developer. His work has been published in Pacific Asia Conference on Information Systems, International Conference on Innovation and Management and Statistical Concepts and Methods for the Modern World Conference.

Sophia Duan is a Lecturer in Information Systems at RMIT University, Melbourne, Australia. Her research interests include digital business, digital strategy, innovation adoption, multi-criteria decision analysis, and productivity analysis. Her research articles have been published in major information systems journals and conferences. She is an ad-hoc reviewer for top tier information systems journals including Information & Management, Decision Support Systems, Australasian Journal of Information Systems, among others.

Suchit Ahuja. Suchit Ahuja is Assistant Professor, Business Technology Management at the John Molson School of Business, Concordia University (Canada). Suchit holds a Ph.D. in Management Information Systems from the Stephen J.R. Smith School of Business at Queen's University and an MSc in Information Technology from Purdue University (USA). Suchit's research focuses on frugal innovation, digital strategy and transformation, digital entrepreneurship, and societal impacts of digital technology. His technical research includes topics such as health information systems, cloud computing, privacy, security, risk, and governance. Suchit's research has been published in academic and practitioner journals, international conferences, books, and news portals. He has been involved in research with and advising start-ups, SMEs, and corporations in India, USA, and Canada.

Thanh-Thuy Nguyen is a lecturer in the College of Business and Law at RMIT University, Australia and Adjunct Associate Professor at RMIT University Vietnam. She graduated her PhD Degree from Kobe University, Japan. Her researches focus mainly on maritime logistics, green logistics, collaboration, IT and human resource development in the supply chains.

Yolande Chan. Yolande is Associate Dean (Research and PhD-MSc Programs) and E. Marie Shantz Professor of IT Management at Queen's University in Canada. She holds a Ph.D. in Business Administration from Western University, an M.Phil. in Management Studies from Oxford University, and S.M. and S.B. degrees in Electrical Engineering and Computer Science from MIT. She is a Rhodes Scholar. Yolande studies IT strategy, knowledge strategy, digital innovation, and digital entrepreneurship, and publishes in leading journals such as *MIS Quarterly, Information Systems Research, Information Systems Journal, Journal of the AIS, Journal of Information Technology, Journal of Management Information Systems,* and *Journal of Strategic Information Systems.* Yolande has served on boards of journals such as *Information Systems Journal*, as an associate editor for journals such as *MIS Quarterly*, and as senior editor for *Journal of Strategic Information Systems* and *MISQ Executive*. Yolande is a Fellow of the Association for Information Systems.

Index

F

G

H

I

J

L

M

T

U

V

W

www.ingramcontent.com/pod-product-compliance
Lightning Source LLC
LaVergne TN
LVHW060417300926
849162LV00006B/1451